Edited by Deborah Green
and Deborah Price

# MAKING HUMANITIES AND SOCIAL SCIENCES COME ALIVE

## Early Years and Primary Education

CAMBRIDGE
UNIVERSITY PRESS

# CAMBRIDGE
## UNIVERSITY PRESS

University Printing House, Cambridge CB2 8BS, United Kingdom

One Liberty Plaza, 20th Floor, New York, NY 10006, USA

477 Williamstown Road, Port Melbourne, VIC 3207, Australia

314–321, 3rd Floor, Plot 3, Splendor Forum, Jasola District Centre, New Delhi – 110025, India

79 Anson Road, #06–04/06, Singapore 079906

Cambridge University Press is part of the University of Cambridge.

It furthers the University's mission by disseminating knowledge in the pursuit of
education, learning and research at the highest international levels of excellence.

www.cambridge.org
Information on this title: www.cambridge.org/9781108445436

© Cambridge University Press 2019

First published 2019

Cover designed by Marianna Berek-Lewis, 5678 Design
Typeset by SPi Global
Printed in China by C & C Offset Printing Co. Ltd, January 2019

*A catalogue record for this publication is available from the British Library*

*A catalogue record for this book is available from the National Library of Australia*

ISBN 978-1-108-44543-6 Paperback

Additional resources for this publication at www.cambridge.edu.au/academic/HASS

*Please be aware that this publication may contain several variations of Aboriginal and Torres
Strait Islander terms and spellings; no disrespect is intended. Please note that the terms
'Indigenous Australians' and 'Aboriginal and Torres Strait Islander peoples' may be used
interchangeably in this publication.*

# MAKING HUMANITIES AND SOCIAL SCIENCES COME ALIVE
## Early Years and Primary Education

Humanities and Social Sciences (HASS) education is integral to the development of active and informed citizens, and encourages learners to think critically, solve problems and adapt to change. *Making Humanities and Social Sciences Come Alive: Early Years and Primary Education* prepares pre-service educators to become high-quality HASS educators who can unlock the potential of all students.

Closely aligned with the Australian Curriculum and Early Years Learning Framework, this book is designed to enhance teaching practices in History, Geography, Economics and Business, and Civics and Citizenship. It provides readers with an in-depth understanding of the curriculum structure, individual disciplines, pedagogical approaches to teaching HASS, inclusivity, global connections and the transition to practice.

Examples are provided for early childhood and primary years education, making this an inclusive, versatile and comprehensive text. Each chapter is also supported by pedagogical features that showcase best practice, including learning objectives, educator tips, reflections, spotlights on HASS education, review questions and learning extensions.

Drawing on the expertise of a diverse team of academics and educators, *Making Humanities and Social Sciences Come Alive* is an invaluable resource that provides pre-service educators with the knowledge and skills to deliver this exciting curriculum.

**Deborah Green** is Program Director: Bachelor of Primary Education (Honours) and a Lecturer in the School of Education, University of South Australia.

**Deborah Price** is Associate Head of School Academic: Professional Engagement and Enterprise in the School of Education, University of South Australia.

This book is dedicated to our supportive families, friends and colleagues who have walked every step of the way with us in our quest to increase the passion for the Humanities and Social Sciences learning area.

# CONTENTS

LIST OF CONTRIBUTORS     xvii

PREFACE     xxi

ACKNOWLEDGEMENTS     xxiii

## PART I   HUMANITIES AND SOCIAL SCIENCES CURRICULUM     1

**CHAPTER 1**   **Making Humanities and Social Sciences come alive: The significance of curriculum in education**     3

*Deborah Green and Deborah Price*

Introduction     3

The development and history of the Early Years Learning Framework     4

The development and history of the Australian Curriculum     6

Introducing HASS in the Australian Curriculum     10

Key ideas and values underpinning the HASS learning area     11

Conclusion     15

Review questions     16

Learning extension     16

References     16

**CHAPTER 2**   **A guided tour of the HASS Australian Curriculum: Planning and integrating learning**     18

*Deborah Green and Deborah Price*

Introduction     18

Navigating the Australian Curriculum     19

The HASS curriculum     24

Teaching and planning approaches     31

What is an integrated curriculum?     36

Locating primary and secondary resources for future planning and teaching in HASS     38

Conclusion     39

Review questions     39

Learning extension     39

References     40

**CHAPTER 3**   **HASS in the early years: Connecting the Early Years Learning Framework and the Australian Curriculum**     42

*Helen Ovsienko*

Introduction     42

Foundations underpinning both the EYLF and the Australian Curriculum     43

Locating HASS education in the everyday     44

Differences between the EYLF and Australian Curriculum approaches                46

Similarities between the EYLF and Australian Curriculum approaches              48

Inquiry learning                                                                53

Emergent curriculum                                                             55

Conclusion                                                                      56

Review questions                                                                56

Learning extension                                                              56

References                                                                      57

CHAPTER 4   **Humanities and Social Sciences in the early childhood and
            primary years**                                                     **59**
            *Mallihai Tambyah, Deborah Green and Deborah Price*

Introduction                                                                    59

Nature and purpose of HASS learning in the early childhood and
primary years                                                                   60

Pedagogies for HASS learning in the early childhood and primary years           62

What is the role of disciplinary knowledge in HASS?                              67

Conclusion                                                                      72

Review questions                                                                73

Learning extension                                                              73

References                                                                      73

PART II **HASS CONCEPTS AND SUB-STRANDS**                                        **75**

CHAPTER 5   **Conceptual thinking in HASS**                                      **77**
            *Malcolm McInerney*

Introduction                                                                    77

The concept of concepts                                                         78

Developing the concepts in Geography                                            81

Conceptual thinking in History                                                  83

Conceptual thinking in Civics and Citizenship                                   92

Conceptual thinking in Economics and Business                                   93

Assessment and the concepts                                                     97

Conclusion                                                                      100

Review questions                                                                101

Learning extension                                                              101

References                                                                      101

CHAPTER 6   **The past in the present: Bringing History and Civics and
            Citizenship education to life in early years settings**             **103**
            *Peter Brett and Katia Duff*

Introduction                                                                    103

What are the links between History and Civics and Citizenship education
in early childhood settings?                                                    104

Integrating the curriculum to promote historical and citizenship conceptual understanding    107

Meaningful and memorable teaching and learning approaches    111

Planning and putting it into practice    112

Conclusion    116

Review questions    116

Learning extension    117

Further reading    117

References    117

CHAPTER 7   **History and historical inquiry**    **120**

*Deborah Henderson*

Introduction    120

What is distinctive about History as a discipline?    121

The structure of History in the Australian Curriculum    122

Conceptual understanding in History    126

Developing skills through historical inquiry    130

Conclusion    134

Review questions    134

Learning extension    134

References    134

CHAPTER 8   **Making Geography come alive by teaching geographical thinking**    **136**

*Malcolm McInerney*

Introduction    136

To think geographically    137

The geographical concepts and assessment    153

Teaching the concepts through an inquiry approach    153

Conclusion    155

Review questions    155

Learning extension    155

References    155

CHAPTER 9   **Civics and Citizenship in the 21st century**    **157**

*Andrew Peterson and Grace Emanuele*

Introduction    157

Understanding Civics and Citizenship    159

What is Civics and Citizenship?    160

Teaching/learning ethos and organising the Civics and Citizenship curriculum    164

Making connections: curriculum and communities    167

Conclusion    171

Review questions    171

Learning extension    172

References    172

CHAPTER 10 **Bringing Economics and Business into educational settings** 174
Anne Glamuzina

Introduction 174
Economics and Business in early years education 176
Economics and Business knowledge and understanding 176
Economics and Business inquiry and skills 185
Conclusion 193
Review questions 193
Learning extension 194
References 194

**PART III TEACHING AND LEARNING IN HASS** 197

CHAPTER 11 **Inquiry learning: The process is essential to the product** 199
Kim Porter and Madeline Fussell

Introduction 199
The intent of inquiry 199
Theory that underpins inquiry 205
What do effective educators of inquiry incorporate from constructivist theory? 207
Conclusion 211
Review questions 211
Learning extension 212
References 212

CHAPTER 12 **Engaging with ethical understanding in the early years and beyond: The community of inquiry approach** 213
Martyn Mills-Bayne

Introduction 213
Dialogic pedagogy and ethical understanding 214
The community of inquiry 215
Ethical understanding in the early years: Before school 219
Ethical understanding in the early years: Primary 221
Conclusion 225
Review questions 225
Learning extension 226
References 226

CHAPTER 13 **The power of play to engage and nurture creative, independent learners** 228
Jane Webb-Williams

Introduction 228
The value and role of play 229

The complexity of play                                               230

Defining play                                                        231

Characteristics of play                                              233

Playfulness and playful pedagogies                                   234

Types of play                                                        235

The role of the educator in playful pedagogies                       237

Conclusion                                                           242

Review questions                                                     243

Learning extension                                                   243

References                                                           244

CHAPTER 14 **Using picture books to develop language and literacies in HASS**                                          **247**

*Jann Carroll*

Introduction                                                         247

The integrated nature of literacy in HASS                            248

Why focus on language and literacy learning in HASS?                 249

Picture books: The power of story in teaching HASS                   250

Strategies to develop language and literacies in HASS                256

Conclusion                                                           260

Review questions                                                     260

Learning extension                                                   260

References                                                           261

CHAPTER 15 **Effective assessment practices**                        **263**

*Susanne Jones and Carmel Dineen*

Introduction                                                         263

Understanding the purpose of assessment                              263

Being assessment literate                                            267

Designing effective assessment                                       269

Collecting evidence and making judgements                            274

Conclusion                                                           276

Review questions                                                     276

Learning extension                                                   276

References                                                           277

PART IV **INTEGRATION ACROSS CROSS-CURRICULUM PRIORITIES**           **279**

CHAPTER 16 **The general capabilities' synergy with HASS**           **281**

*Malcolm McInerney, Deborah Green and Deborah Price*

Introduction                                                         281

Citizen capacity: What do learners think?                            283

The general capabilities                                             285

HASS and the general capabilities 294

The general capabilities in the achievement standards 302

Conclusion 304

Review questions 304

Learning extension 305

References 305

CHAPTER 17 **Authentic engagement with Aboriginal and Torres Strait Islander content in the P–6 Australian Curriculum** **307**

*Kevin Lowe and Janet Cairncross*

Introduction 307

The Australian Curriculum: Limitations and challenges 308

What pedagogy supports the aims of the Australian Curriculum? 311

Developing educators' understanding through authentic family and community engagement 315

Making curriculum work 319

Conclusion 320

Review questions 325

Learning extension 325

References 325

CHAPTER 18 **Studies of Asia and Australia's engagement with Asia** **327**

*Deborah Henderson*

Introduction 327

Why young Australians should study Asia and Australia's engagement with Asia 328

How the Asia priority is represented and structured in the HASS curriculum 330

Using the general capabilities to foster knowledge, understanding and skills about Asia and the development of Asia capability 334

Embedding studies in Asia via inquiry in HASS 338

Conclusion 339

Review questions 340

Learning extension 340

References 340

CHAPTER 19 **Educating for sustainability: Theoretical and practical insights for preservice educators** **343**

*Kathryn Paige, David Lloyd and Samuel Osborne*

Introduction 343

Engaging with ideas for living sustainably 343

The value of connecting learners to place 345

Planning learning experiences around the principles of EfS towards ecojustice 346

Incorporating EfS pedagogical practices into classroom experiences 348

| | |
|---|---|
| Conclusion | 357 |
| Review questions | 357 |
| Learning extension | 357 |
| References | 358 |

## PART V HASS FOR ALL LEARNERS 361

CHAPTER 20 **Values education and social justice** 363
Tace Vigilante

| | |
|---|---|
| Introduction | 363 |
| Values education | 364 |
| The community of inquiry approach | 369 |
| Community of ethical inquiry in HASS | 373 |
| Conclusion | 375 |
| Review questions | 376 |
| Learning extension | 376 |
| References | 376 |

CHAPTER 21 **Culturally responsive pedagogy: Respecting the diversity of learners studying HASS** 379
Dylan Chown

| | |
|---|---|
| Introduction | 379 |
| Advancing broad notions of citizenship characterised by equity and justice | 380 |
| Valuing the diversity of learners' cultural and religious knowledges | 386 |
| Culturally responsive pedagogical strategies to maximise learning outcomes within HASS | 387 |
| Strategies for supporting HASS learning for broad and inclusive notions of citizenship | 390 |
| Conclusion | 396 |
| Review questions | 396 |
| Learning extension | 397 |
| Acknowledgement | 397 |
| References | 397 |

CHAPTER 22 **HASS for everyone: Inclusive approaches respectful of learner diversity** 400
Deborah Price and Deborah Green

| | |
|---|---|
| Introduction | 400 |
| Inclusive principles | 401 |
| Responsibility in applying inclusive practices to the HASS learning experience | 403 |
| Universal design for learning in HASS | 409 |
| Differentiation in HASS | 411 |

Co-designing HASS learning experiences 412

Inclusive HASS learning experiences begin in the early years 414

Conclusion 414

Review questions 415

Learning extension 415

References 415

## PART VI **COMMUNITY AND GLOBAL CONNECTIONS** 419

CHAPTER 23 **Using community resources to develop active and informed citizens** 421

*Jann Carroll*

Introduction 421

Developing active and informed citizens through schooling 422

Community resources to support the teaching of HASS 424

Evaluating the use of community resources 426

Contribution of community resources to learning 428

Inquiry learning through community resources 431

Conclusion 433

Review questions 433

Learning extension 433

References 434

CHAPTER 24 **Uncovering hidden gems in the community** 437

*Mandi Dimitriadis*

Introduction 437

Community and learning 438

Resources in the local community 439

Using community resources to support HASS learning 443

Community resources in early childhood settings 444

Working with community members and organisations 445

Conclusion 449

Review questions 449

Learning extension 449

References 449

CHAPTER 25 **Enhancing HASS learning with technology** 451

*Mandi Dimitriadis*

Introduction 451

Embedding technology in learning tasks 451

Technology in the Early Years Learning Framework 454

Technology in the Australian Curriculum 455

Types of technology and their applications to HASS learning 458

Conclusion 463

Review questions 463

Learning extension 464

References 464

CHAPTER 26 **Libraries and librarians: At home with HASS** **465**

*Katie Silva*

Introduction 465

Libraries as rich sources for HASS learning and learners 466

Librarians at home with HASS 469

HASS with head, heart and hands 475

Conclusion 477

Review questions 477

Learning extension 477

References 478

CHAPTER 27 **Global education** **479**

*Andrew Peterson and Zea Perrotta*

Introduction 479

Understanding global education 481

What is global education? 483

The building blocks of global education 485

Organising the teaching and learning of global education within an
educational site 488

Conclusion 495

Review questions 495

Learning extension 495

References 495

**PART VII GETTING STARTED** **497**

CHAPTER 28 **Early career teaching in the early years** **499**

*Steven Cameron*

Introduction 499

Early childhood pedagogy: Your why and how 500

The cycle of planning 503

Learning for professional growth 508

Conclusion 511

Review questions 511

Learning extension 512

References 512

CHAPTER **29**  **Early career teaching in the primary years**  **513**
*Deana Cuconits*

Introduction                                                                    513
Step 1: Start with the curriculum                                              513
Step 2: Engage yourself – you need to love the content too!                    515
Step 3: Planning and programming – work backwards and start with the
end in mind                                                                     517
Step 4: Immersion and adventure                                                521
Step 5: Authentic assessment                                                   525
Conclusion                                                                      526
Review questions                                                                527
Learning extension                                                             527
Further reading                                                                 528
References                                                                      528

INDEX                                                                           529

# CONTRIBUTORS

DEBORAH GREEN is Program Director: Bachelor of Primary Education (Honours) and a Lecturer of Humanities and Social Sciences and Inclusive Education in the School of Education, University of South Australia. She is an active member of the University of South Australia Centre for Research in Education and Social Inclusion (CRESI), Inclusive Communities for Justice and Wellbeing Research group, Executive Secretary of the HASS SA committee, committee member of the Social and Citizenship Association of Australia (SCEAA) and co-editor of *The Social Educator*.

DEBORAH PRICE is Associate Head of School Academic: Professional Engagement and Enterprise and Lecturer Inclusive Education and Wellbeing in the School of Education, University of South Australia. She is the President of the Australian Curriculum Studies Association, and a member of the University of South Australia CRESI and the Inclusive Communities for Justice and Wellbeing Research group.

PETER BRETT is a Senior Lecturer in Education at the University of Tasmania, Burnie. He was a history and citizenship teacher educator at the University of Cumbria from 1993 to 2008.

JANET CAIRNCROSS is Assistant Principal at Our Lady of the Sacred Heart College, Kensington, New South Wales. She has worked in both government and Catholic schools throughout her 25-year teaching career.

STEVEN CAMERON is an Early Childhood Leader for the Department for Education (South Australia). He is President and co-founder of the Australian Association for Men in Early Childhood.

JANN CARROLL is a Senior Lecturer in Literacy and Education Studies at the Australian Catholic University, Canberra. In 2016 she won an Excellence in Teaching and Learning Innovation Award and in 2017 an Executive Dean's Commendation for Excellence in Teaching.

DYLAN CHOWN is a Research Fellow and Program Director for Islamic Education in the Centre for Islamic Thought and Education/School of Education, University of South Australia. He is a member of the University of South Australia in CRESI and the Inclusive Communities for Justice and Wellbeing Research group.

DEANA CUCONITS is a teacher of HASS in the primary years of schooling. She is a member of the executive committee of HASS SA.

MANDI DIMITRIADIS is Director of Learning at Makers Empire. She has managed museum education programs at a range of sites including the South Australian Maritime Museum. She played a key role in the implementation of the *Australian Curriculum: History F/6–7* in South Australia.

CARMEL DINEEN is a Primary Learners Project Officer in the Department for Education in South Australia. She has been a primary teacher for over 40 years, and in 2012 was awarded Primary Years Teacher of the Year by the Council of Education Associations of South Australia (CEASA).

KATIA DUFF is a practising classroom teacher who over the past 23 years has taught in the early childhood, secondary and tertiary sectors. She is also affiliated with the University of Tasmania, where she specialises in BEd early childhood course work and human development.

GRACE EMANUELE is a university tutor at the University of South Australia. She is an experienced primary school teacher and has taught for over 20 years in the classroom setting.

MADELINE FUSSELL is an independent educational consultant whose career has included roles in early childhood settings, primary schools, early intervention and as a university lecturer in education.

ANNE GLAMUZINA is a board member of the Business and Enterprise Teachers Association of South Australia and a member of the HASS SA Executive Committee.

DEBORAH HENDERSON is an Associate Professor in the Faculty of Education at Queensland University of Technology. She is a Past President of the Queensland History Teachers' Association (QHTA) and a Past President of the History Teachers' Association of Australia (HTAA).

SUSANNE JONES has been a primary and secondary teacher and leader in country and metropolitan schools. She has worked with teachers and leaders during the implementation of the Australian Curriculum. Susanne now works with leaders and teachers to support curriculum change and improve student learning, supporting their work in curriculum, pedagogy, assessment and moderation.

DAVID LLOYD is an adjunct research fellow in the School of Education, University of South Australia, where he was a Lecturer in Science, Mathematics and Environmental Education and coordinator of the general studies program until 2011.

KEVIN LOWE is a Gubbi Gubbi man from South-east Queensland. He is a Post-Doctoral Fellow at Macquarie University undertaking research on developing a model of sustainable improvement in Aboriginal education. He has been a high school teacher, TAFE administrator, university lecturer and NSW Board of Studies Inspector, Aboriginal Education.

MALCOLM McINERNEY is a teaching academic in HASS for the School of Education, University of South Australia. Malcolm was President of the Australian Geography Teachers' Association (2008–13), member of the Australian Curriculum, Assessment and Reporting Authority (ACARA) Australian Curriculum: Geography Writing Panel (2009–13), Executive Director of Education Services Australia's GeogSpace project and the Humanities

Curriculum Manager for the South Australian Department of Education and Child Development (2007–17).

MARTYN MILLS-BAYNE is a Lecturer in Early Childhood Education at the University of South Australia. He is a member of the South Australian Philosophy in Education Association (SAPEA).

SAMUEL OSBORNE is Associate Director for Regional Engagement (APY Lands) at the University of South Australia and also has roles teaching Pitjantjatjara language, Aboriginal Education and various research projects. He has worked in Aboriginal education since 1995 as a teacher, principal and Pitjantjatjara language teacher and interpreter. He is also Director (Education) of Nyangatjatjara College, an Independent Aboriginal School in the south of the Northern Territory.

HELEN OVSIENKO is a Lecturer in HASS Education, Education for Diversity and Critical Perspectives of Education at the University of South Australia. She is a member of the University of South Australia CRESI Pedagogies for Justice Research group.

KATHRYN PAIGE is a Senior Lecturer in Science and Mathematics Education at the University of South Australia. She taught for 17 years in primary classrooms in a range of schools, and has taught in science education for the last 20 years.

ZEA PERROTTA teaches HASS to preservice teachers in the Bachelor of Education programs at the University of South Australia. She has a background in teaching, youth engagement, family counselling, presenting and communication in the not-for-profit, government and private sectors.

ANDREW PETERSON is a Professor of Education at Canterbury Christ Church University and Adjunct Professor of Education at the University of South Australia.

KIM PORTER is a Lecturer and Unit Co-ordinator of HASS Education at the University of New England. Prior to this, she taught primary and secondary students in both the public and private sectors for over 20 years.

KATIE SILVA is Teacher Librarian at Wilderness School, an independent girls school in Adelaide, and the current President of HASS SA.

MALLIHAI TAMBYAH is a Senior Lecturer in Social Education in the Faculty of Education at Queensland University of Technology.

TACE VIGILANTE is a Teacher Education Lecturer at Charles Sturt University. She teaches in the HASS learning area as well as diversity and multiculturalism and Aboriginal and Torres Strait Islander studies in education.

JANE WEBB-WILLIAMS is a Lecturer at the University of South Australia. She is a leading early childhood expert and her career in education spans over 20 years in roles including deputy principal and primary school teacher.

# PREFACE

Humanities and Social Sciences (HASS) education is integral to the development of active and informed citizens, and scaffolds learners in developing skills to think critically, question, communicate effectively, make decisions, solve problems and adapt to change. Addressing the Australian Curriculum, HASS education embraces History, Geography, Civics and Citizenship, and Economics and Business. This unique learning area fosters empathy, social justice and equity through providing opportunities to critically analyse information from multiple perspectives. Therefore, being able to effectively teach and integrate this important learning area in the educational program is essential. Drawing on the expertise of national and international scholars, *Making Humanities and Social Sciences Come Alive: Early Years and Primary Education* prepares preservice and in-service educators to become high-quality HASS educators who can unlock the potential of all learners.

Strong HASS foundations in the early years nurture children's curiosity and inquiring minds to enrich their learning of HASS knowledge, understanding, skills and inquiry as they transition into the primary years of schooling. This comprehensive book aims to instil the importance of HASS education from early childhood to Year 6/7, with each chapter offering examples and resources for early and primary years education. Explicit chapters provide applications for integrating the general capabilities and cross-curriculum priorities of Asia and Australia's engagement with Asia, Sustainability, and Aboriginal and Torres Strait Islander histories and cultures.

The text is divided into six parts, providing readers with an in-depth understanding of the HASS curriculum structure, the individual disciplines, pedagogical approaches to teaching and learning, inclusive approaches to HASS education and global connections, and supporting the preservice educator's transition to practice. Chapters have been written by HASS early years educators, classroom educators, early career educators and research-informed academics, with examples provided across early childhood and primary education. Embedded throughout each chapter are pedagogical approaches to showcase best practice for preservice and in-service educators, including learning objectives, educator tips, reflections, spotlights on HASS education, review questions and learning extensions.

## OUTLINE

Part I: Humanities and Social Sciences Curriculum explores the significance of HASS in the Australian Curriculum and connections with the Early Years Learning Framework (EYLF). It provides a guided tour of the curriculum and framework before discussing the key concepts that underpin this learning area. The HASS disciplines are explored in Part II across early years and primary education through each of the Australian Curriculum sub-strands: History; Geography; Civics and Citizenship; and Economics and Business. Part III: Teaching and Learning in HASS draws Parts I and II together by providing pedagogical and assessment approaches, including inquiry, ethical understandings and the role of play in learning. Integration across cross-curriculum priorities is explored in Part IV, while Part V:

HASS for All Learners challenges educators to continue to integrate diverse perspectives for broad and inclusive notions of citizenship. This is addressed across areas that include promoting world views and philosophy, valuing and embracing learners' lifeworlds, employing culturally responsive pedagogy: e.g. engaging with technologies, universal design, co-design and differentiated approaches to learning experiences. Part VI: Community and Global Connections examines the use of community resources to develop active and informed citizens, uncovering hidden gems in the community, enhancing HASS learning with technology, effective use of libraries and librarians, and global education. The book concludes with Part VII: Getting Started, supporting in-service educators to begin teaching HASS across the early and primary years.

# ACKNOWLEDGEMENTS

Deborah Green wishes to thank her wonderful daughter, Nicole, who has supported her with love, encouragement and an endless belief in her abilities to make Humanities and Social Sciences come alive in classrooms. She would also like to thank her mother and her late father who have provided endless support and guidance. Deborah would like to dedicate this book in memory of her dear friend Mary Sneath who supported and motivated her to ensure that it became a reality.

Deborah Price wishes to thank her husband, Jamie, and daughters, Alexandra, Isabelle and Bridgette, whose inclusive and caring approach to life has been the driving motivation and inspiration for this book: ensuring all young people have access to and engage in Humanities and Social Sciences learning. A special dedication to Shannon Price, Barry Parbs, and Marlene and Allen Arthur for building the foundation for seeing people's capabilities, strengths and opportunities to grow.

We sincerely thank the authors of the book chapters for their dedication and insightful contributions. Without them this book would not be possible.

The authors and Cambridge University Press would like to thank the following for permission to reproduce material in this book.

**All ACARA material**: © Australian Curriculum, Assessment and Reporting Authority (ACARA) 2014 to present, unless otherwise indicated. This material was downloaded from the ACARA website (www.acara.edu.au) and was not modified. The material is licensed under CC BY 4.0 (https://creativecommons.org/licenses/by/4.0). ACARA does not endorse any product that uses ACARA material or make any representations as to the quality of such products. Any product that uses material published on this website should not be taken to be affiliated with ACARA or have the sponsorship or approval of ACARA. It is up to each person to make their own assessment of the product.

**Figure 4.1**: © Getty Images/Michael Gottschalk; **4.2**: © Getty Images/Bunlue Nantaprom/EyeEm; **4.3** and **24.1**: © Getty Images/Hero Images; **5.4**: (top) © Getty Images/ Bettmann, (bottom) © Getty Images/Robert Walker; **5.5**: © Getty Images/ullstein bild Dtl.; **5.6**: *The Queenslander*, 5 September 1925, p.21. Wikimedia Commons/State Library of Queensland; **5.7**: (top) Wikimedia Commons/Davis Sporting Collection, State Library of New South Wales, PXE 653 (v. 10), (bottom) © Getty Images/SAEED KHAN/AFP; **5.8**: © Getty Images/Keystone/Hulton Archive; **5.10**: © Getty Images/Heritage Images/Fine Art Images; **5.11**: Wikimedia Commons/State Library of Queensland; **5.13**: (top) © Getty Images/ Mlenny, (middle) © Getty Images/Chris Hepburn, (bottom) © Getty Images/Johannes Spahn/ EyeEm; **5.15**: (top) © Getty Images/chain45154, (middle) © Getty Images/Chuanchai Pundej/ EyeEm, (bottom) © Getty Images/Image Source; **6.1**: Wikimedia Commons/Damien Ramon Naidoo; **7.1**: Wellcome Library, London; **8.6**: © Getty Images/Nick Hawkins/SSPL; **8.7**: (top) © Getty Images/Jordan Lye, (middle) © Getty Images/Ilya Yakunin/EyeEm, (bottom) © Getty Images/Dorling Kindersley; **18.1**: Australia China Friendship Society Ltd/National Museum of Australia; **22.2**: © Getty Images/Scott T. Baxter; **24.2**: © Getty Images/Jutta Klee; **24.3**: © Getty Images/Hill Street Studios LLC; **25.2**: © Getty Images/valentinrussanov.

*Every effort has been made to trace and acknowledge copyright. The publisher apologises for any accidental infringement and welcomes information that would redress this situation.*

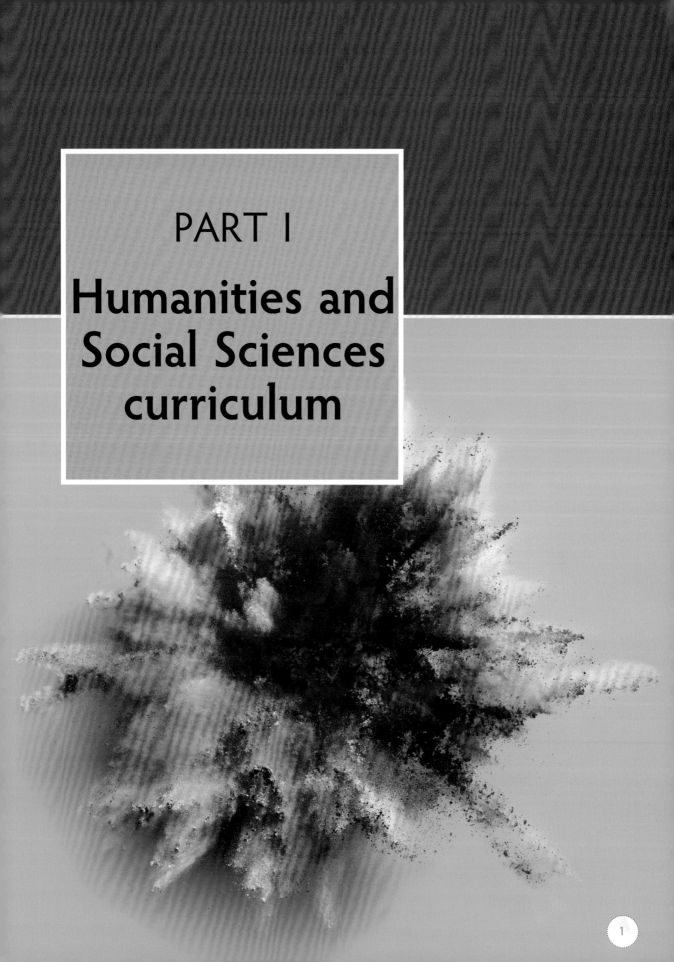

# PART I

# Humanities and Social Sciences curriculum

# MAKING HUMANITIES AND SOCIAL SCIENCES COME ALIVE: THE SIGNIFICANCE OF CURRICULUM IN EDUCATION

*Deborah Green and Deborah Price*

**1**

## Learning objectives

After reading this chapter, you should be able to:

- understand the development and history of the Australian Curriculum and the Early Years Learning Framework (EYLF), and the significance of Humanities and Social Sciences (HASS)
- understand the key ideas and values that underpin HASS
- identify each of the HASS sub-strands: History, Geography, Economics and Business, and Civics and Citizenship.

## INTRODUCTION

National educational goals describe the responsibility of governments, schools and **curriculum** to ensure learners develop into effective citizens who can participate in society and employment in a globalised economy. This is outlined in the vision of the *Melbourne Declaration on Educational Goals for Young Australians* (**Melbourne Declaration**) (MCEETYA 2008). In promoting values such as social justice, peace, sustainability and democracy, the **HASS** educational discipline provides the perfect vehicle to achieve this vision. While the rationale and aims are different for each sub-strand within the HASS **Australian Curriculum** learning area (History, Geography, Civics and Citizenship, and Economics and Business), the overarching theme involves stimulating curiosity, imagination and wonder about the world we live in. In reflecting on your own education, were you encouraged to have such curiosity and interest in the world around you?

By understanding how things were historically, and connecting with knowledge from other learning areas, HASS can help learners to develop a holistic understanding of the world. Tudball (2018) describes the Australian Curriculum HASS rationale as 'ensuring that young people develop purposeful learning about society, so they are empowered to be informed, active and participatory citizens in a changing world' (p. 79). Yet, despite this proposed significance, many preservice educators report focusing on one or maybe two of the HASS sub-strands within their schooling (i.e. History and/or Geography), experiencing mixed reactions, while others report no recollection of HASS at all (Green 2016). Unfortunately, these experiences typically impact on their motivation and engagement when they enter HASS

**curriculum**: outlines what learners should be taught in educational settings

**Melbourne Declaration**: outlines the future directions of and agreed educational goals for young Australians

**HASS** (Humanities and Social Sciences): is one of the core learning areas in the Australian Curriculum and is made up of four sub-strands (History, Geography, Civics and Citizenship, and Economics and Business)

**Australian Curriculum**: national curriculum that is employed from Foundation to Year 10 in most states/ territories across Australia

initial teacher education courses, while in-service educators also grapple with the complexity of the HASS curriculum, seeking additional professional support and development.

This chapter will briefly introduce the history of the Australian Curriculum and the EYLF with a particular focus on outlining the key ideas and values that underpin the HASS learning area. Through reflections and spotlights on HASS education, we will engage and ignite (or reignite) your interest in this fascinating and important learning area.

**Reflection**

Consider your time at school and particularly your learning of the subjects within HASS. You may have studied them as individual subjects (e.g. History, Geography), you may have studied them as an integrated approach (e.g. Studies of Society and the Environment [SOSE]), or you may not have studied them at all.

Take a moment to reflect on the following:

- What was the subject/s called? (e.g. History, Geography, Social Studies, SOSE, S&E)?
- How was the curriculum structured? Were you taught subjects separately, in an integrated format or in a combination of these?
- How much time was given to each subject? How often was it taught?
- What topics/themes do you remember studying and which of these did you enjoy or not enjoy? Why/why not?
- Were there any topics/themes that you did not, but would have liked to study?
- How well did your learning in HASS, or its equivalent, provide you with a depth and breadth of knowledge and understanding?
- Were you introduced to a range of perspectives in your learning of HASS, including those of Aboriginal and Torres Strait Islander peoples?
- How was your work assessed? How did you feel about this?
- How have you applied your HASS (or equivalent subject/s) learning as a citizen?

Now consider:

- If you were to capture in a few words your experiences in HASS, what would they be?
- How have these experiences influenced your confidence and self-efficacy in studying and teaching this learning area?
- What HASS learning experiences did you engage in in your early years prior to schooling?

# THE DEVELOPMENT AND HISTORY OF THE EARLY YEARS LEARNING FRAMEWORK

The Australian Government's productivity agenda in 2007 focused on strengthening the economy by increasing investment in social and human capital, to which education was central. A National Quality Framework was developed to ensure that high-quality, nationally consistent **early childhood education** and care occurred. To this end, *Becoming, Belonging and Being: The Early Years Learning Framework for Australia* (**Early Years Learning Framework (EYLF)**; DEEWR 2009) was developed as part of an extensive consultative process. This was the first time in Australia that young children's learning, particularly that of children aged from birth to five years of age, became a priority, with nationally agreed statements that guided teaching and learning across early childhood settings. The framework valued the work of early childhood educators and provided parents/carers with a coherent and agreed view on quality early childhood care and education (Connor 2011, p. 9).

As is evident from its title, *Belonging, Being and Becoming*, the EYLF embraces a strong connection between learners, family and community and the role these play in the development of children's security and identity. Within the framework, five principles underpin effective early childhood practice: secure, respectful and reciprocal relationships; partnerships; high expectations and equity; respect for diversity; and ongoing learning and reflective practice (DEEWR 2009).

Aligning with these principles are eight practices that have strong synergies with the teaching of HASS **concepts** and skills. These are:

1. adopting holistic approaches that recognise the connectedness of the mind, body and spirit while focusing on connections to the natural world

2. being responsive to children, which enables educators to embrace individual interests and strengths while stimulating thinking and learning

3. learning through play, which embraces inclusive practices and allows learners to extend their learning in an engaging way

4. intentional teaching that is deliberate, intentional and purposeful, which challenges thoughts and experiences that promote higher order cognition

5. learning environments that reflect and enrich lives and identities of children and their families while provoking complex and increasingly abstract thinking

6. developing cultural competence, whereby the culture of all learners and their families is respected

7. continuity of learning and transitions, which helps learners to transition from home to early childhood settings, between settings and to school

8. assessment for learning which enables educators to collect and analyse data that support learning and achievement of learning outcomes (DEEWR 2009).

Complementing the principles and practices are five broad and observable learning outcomes that provide a focal point for assessment of learning and development in the early years. These are:

1. children having a strong sense of identity

2. children being connected with and contributing to their world

3. children having a strong sense of wellbeing

---

**early childhood education**: refers to contexts that educate and care for children aged from birth to five years of age. These can include long day care, pre-schools and kindergarten.

**Early Years Learning Framework (EYLF)**: principles, practices and outcomes that support and enhance young children's learning from birth to five years of age, as well as their transition to school

**concept**: refers to an idea or abstract principle that can frame thinking

4. children being confident and involved learners
5. children being effective communicators (DEEWR 2009).

Through this approach, children's natural curiosity about their world and direct engagement with their local environment can set the foundation for building confidence in exploring HASS concepts such as place, environment and sustainability, and developing inquiry skills. Within these formative years, children can be encouraged to be active participants in their local community and be valued for their contribution to society.

The Melbourne Declaration (MCEETYA 2008) underpins both the EYLF and Australian Curriculum, with a commitment to equitable learning for all learners from birth to Year 10. Both are concerned primarily with quality of care, education and improved outcomes for learners in Australia. Thus, there are strong synergies between the two frameworks as they work to ensure that learners have the best opportunity to successfully transition from an early childhood setting to school (Connor 2011). The importance of children's early experiences and development from birth through to schooling has been well documented in recent years. How key HASS concepts and experiences can be shaped in these formative years will be integrated throughout the following chapters. In particular, Chapter 3 explores HASS in the early years, connecting the EYLF and the Australian Curriculum, while Chapter 16 outlines how the EYLF aligns with the general capabilities of the Australian Curriculum.

## EDUCATOR TIP

When planning HASS learning activities, an understanding of foundational learning and development in the early years supports your ability to build on children's prior knowledge, understandings and skills. The EYLF provides key considerations for educators across all ages of learners.

 Read the EYLF (available online). Where do you see HASS concepts and skills being promoted? How might you apply this framework to your current context?

## THE DEVELOPMENT AND HISTORY OF THE AUSTRALIAN CURRICULUM

As children's curiosity and interest in HASS concepts emerge in the early years and they transition into the schooling sector, it is important to understand the influences that led to the current shape of the Australian Curriculum, and in particular the HASS learning area. In 1976, the Fraser Government set up the Commonwealth Curriculum Development Centre to achieve its goal of a basic national educational framework. The Director of the

Centre, John Dawkins, together with Commonwealth Minister of Education, Training and Employment, lobbied for the states and territories to construct a common national curriculum (Yates & Collins 2008). There were many similar approaches to developing a national curriculum, yet the federal government was unable to enforce compliance, and the states and territories clung tightly to their nationally sanctioned autonomy (Piper 1997).

In 1993, a further attempt was made to develop a national curriculum with the formation of the Ministerial Council on Education, Employment, Training and Youth Affairs (MCEETYA), which included state, territory, Australian federal and New Zealand ministers. MCEETYA was responsible for improving the educational outcomes of all young Australians. At the 60th Australian Education Meeting, the Council met in Hobart (1989; see Education Council 2014), where it supported a national effort towards the education of young Australians in a statement that was updated in Adelaide as the *National Goals for Schooling in the Twenty-First Century* (DEST 1999), which guided the Melbourne Declaration in 2008.

The states and territories, through their representation on the Council of Australian Governments (COAG) and MCEETYA, developed a second shaping paper, the *Melbourne Declaration on Educational Goals for Young Australians* (MCEETYA 2008). This declaration clearly articulates 'nationally consistent future directions and aspirations for Australian schooling' (ACARA 2016) and was underpinned by two major goals:

1. Australian schooling promotes equity and excellence.
2. All young Australians become successful learners, confident and creative individuals, active and informed citizens.

The second of these goals has direct implications for HASS, as it is the foremost objective of this learning area.

Read the 2008 Melbourne Declaration (available online) and identify the direct implications for the HASS learning area.

Reflection

Although some argued that a national curriculum should reflect the values and beliefs of the country (Kennedy 2009), two rather contentious rationales were presented in the push for a national curriculum with the first focusing more on technical aspects. For instance, it was proposed that Australia needed a uniform curriculum that would enable learners to move between states with little disruption to their learning. The second rationale aimed to address variations in retention rates and academic achievement across the states and territories (Reid 2009). Debates about the validity of these arguments were raised, as neither had been tested (see Kennedy 2009; Reid 2009, 2018), with further questioning of how a national curriculum could address retention issues any better than a state or territory curriculum (Reid 2009). Such debates led to subsequent changes in curriculum design across Australia.

## Changes to curriculum construction and teaching over time

Until the implementation of Australia's first national curriculum (agreed in 2008 and implemented in 2011), the states and territories were responsible for their own curriculum design. In the 1980s and into the 1990s, curriculum in Australia was constructed in terms of 'statements and policies', whereas the turn of the millennium saw a shift in curriculum focus to one of 'essential learnings' and 'capabilities' based on the development of knowledge and understandings that were outside specific learning areas (Yates & Collins 2008, p. 8). This focus aimed to provide opportunities for learners to develop the skills necessary to find employment and manage the challenges of living in a globalised world. Such a shift has seen curriculum design that promotes learners developing skills and capabilities to become effective citizens, something that featured strongly in the Melbourne Declaration (MCEETYA 2008). Subsequently, the design of Australia's first national curriculum included learning areas, cross-curriculum priorities and general capabilities. As Reid (2018) outlines, Australia's first national curriculum was not developed without challenges; however, he identifies the importance of understanding that the **Australian Curriculum, Assessment and Reporting Authority (ACARA)** 'was charged with the task of developing an official curriculum text. It has no responsibility for, or role in, the implementation of the official curriculum, including approaches to teaching and assessment, the provision of curriculum materials and resources, and professional development' (p. 10). Subsequently, the Australian Curriculum began with the development of learning area curricula.

**Australian Curriculum and Assessment Authority (ACARA):** the body with the function to develop the national curriculum, and administer national assessments and associated reporting on schooling in Australia

**Reflection**

As an educator, what are your views on developing curriculum without designing approaches to teaching and assessment?

## Development of the Australian Curriculum learning areas

Learning area curriculum development occurred in stages, as outlined in Table 1.1.

History was one of the first learning areas to be written, along with Mathematics, English and Science, arguably emphasising its importance. After the initial release of these learning areas, others were developed and released. On 18 September 2015, the Education Council endorsed:

- the revised Foundation–Year 10 Australian Curriculum for English, Mathematics, Science, Humanities and Social Sciences, the Arts, Technologies, and Health and Physical Education

- Foundation–Year 10 Australian Curriculum: Languages for Arabic, Chinese, French, German, Indonesian, Italian, Japanese, Korean, Modern Greek, Spanish and Vietnamese
- Australian Curriculum: Work Studies Years 9–10 (an optional subject designed to ready young people for work) (ACARA 2016).

**TABLE 1.1   DEVELOPMENT OF THE LEARNING AREAS**

| Learning areas | Timeline |
|---|---|
| English | 2008–10 |
| Mathematics | 2008–10 |
| Science | 2008–10 |
| Humanities and Social Sciences:<br>• History<br>• Geography<br>• Economics, Business, Civics and Citizenship | 2008–10<br>2010–12<br>2011–13 |
| The Arts | 2010–12 |
| Languages | 2010–12 |
| Health and Physical Education | 2011–13 |
| Technologies | 2011–13 |

Source: ACARA 2010, 2016

In January 2014, the Australian Government conducted a Review of the Australian Curriculum, which aimed to determine whether the curriculum was meeting students' needs, parents' expectations and the nation's requirements. The *Review of the Australian Curriculum: Final report* was released in October 2014 (Donnelly & Wiltshire 2014). Feedback from school authorities and practising educators was sought and resulted in amendments to the curriculum. The impact of this on the HASS learning area will be discussed below.

## Do all states and territories follow the Australian Curriculum?

Education has always been a state/territory responsibility. Between 1975 and 2005, states and territories had charge of their own curriculum policies with research into these being conducted within the jurisdictions; thus, at this time, a national perspective was not considered. Prior to this, educators were free to choose what content they wanted to teach to ensure that learners achieved the prescribed performance outcomes for their key learning area (Yates & Collins 2008). It is important to note that even after the development of the national curriculum, 'constitutionally the power to decide on curriculum matters still resides with the states' (Reid 2009, p.4). Thus, without agreement from the states and territories, a national curriculum would not have occurred. Today, although all states and territories embrace the concepts of the Australian

Curriculum, Queensland and New South Wales have adapted these to form independent policies and Victoria has developed its own Progressive Curriculum. As of June 2017, Queensland schools were implementing the Australian Curriculum for English, Mathematics, Science and History in Prep to Year 10 and the Queensland Curriculum for the remaining areas of the curriculum in Prep to Year 10 (Department of Education and Training (Queensland) 2017).

In New South Wales, the Board of Studies, which reports to the NSW Minister of Education, decided to implement the Australian Curriculum through its own syllabi (NESA 2017).

From 2013–16, Victorian schools employed the AusVELS (2013–15/16) Curriculum, but as of 2017 they are required to follow the Victorian Curriculum from Foundation to Year 10. This Progressive Curriculum Framework was designed to enable educators, learners and stakeholders to identify the progression in expected skills and abilities (Reiter n.d.). In the Progressive Curriculum Frameworks:

1. Progression between the statements contained in each level descriptor and standard is clearly denoted by bold text. Each year level is assigned a specific colour.
2. The content descriptors and standards are clearly organised in tabular form to show:
   - Strands
   - Sub-strands, and
   - Elaborations.

The content descriptors contain the cross-curriculum priorities as denoted by the relevant icons. (Reiter n.d.)

**Reflection** Should the states and territories be allowed to develop their own curriculum or should there be a nationally consistent approach? What might the implications be of having different curricula in the various states and territories?

# INTRODUCING HASS IN THE AUSTRALIAN CURRICULUM

The HASS learning area has an important place in the curriculum as it works to prepare learners to be active, global citizens in the 21st century, a key goal of the Melbourne Declaration. Providing opportunities and teaching skills that enable learners to be workplace ready is important, and is often seen as the work of educators. Soft skills, such as those developed through the HASS curriculum, are among the most cited skills needed for employment and life in the 21st century (Klaus 2010; Maes, Weldy & Icenogel 1997; McInerney 2017; Mitchell, Skinner & White 2010; Nealy 2005; Smith 2007), with the following combination of skills being among the most sought after:

- interpersonal

- people skills

- social skills

- teamwork

- flexibility/adaptability

- communication skills

- character traits such as integrity and responsibility beyond the self

- attitudinal awareness

- emotional intelligence (McInerney 2017).

Prior to the Review of the Australian Curriculum in 2014, HASS in Foundation to Year 10 comprised four distinct sub-strands with each having time and space within the curriculum: History, Geography, Civics and Citizenship, and Economics and Business. However, after the review these subjects were collapsed into one for learners in Foundation–Year 6/7 (**primary education**), with fewer content descriptors and a single achievement standard for each substrand. The following illustrates how HASS is offered currently:

**primary education**: schooling contexts that typically educate learners from Foundation/Prep (five years of age) to Year 6/7 (11–13 years of age)

- Birth–five years – EYLF

- History: compulsory F–10

- Geography: compulsory F–8; available F–10

- Civics and Citizenship: compulsory 3–8; available 3–10

- Economics and Business: compulsory 5–8; available 5–10

- Years 7–10: depth studies are introduced

- Year 11–12: process of integration in senior secondary curriculum in each state/territory.

Consider what the above changes in curriculum might mean for the HASS learning area. What message does this send to parents/carers and colleagues about this learning area? What can we do to protect the integrity of HASS?

Reflection

# KEY IDEAS AND VALUES UNDERPINNING THE HASS LEARNING AREA

HASS involves the study of human behaviour and our interactions in social, cultural, environmental, economic and political contexts. Through the key ideas outlined below, learners develop an ability to question, think critically, solve problems, communicate effectively, make decisions and adapt to change (see also Figure 1.1).

As illustrated in Table 1.2 (page 13), these key ideas are developed across the sub-strands of HASS.

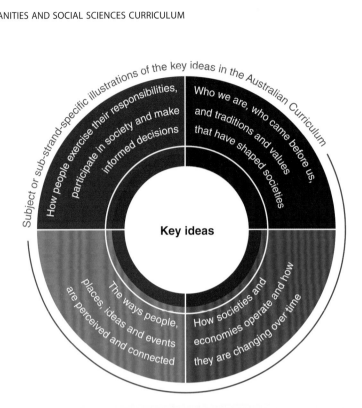

FIGURE 1.1   Subject or sub-strand-specific illustrations of the key ideas in the HASS curriculum
Source: ACARA 2018

Underpinning the key ideas are four clusters of values that also influence learning in the HASS area. These are:

1. Democratic processes: 'The key value of democratic process is based on a belief in the integrity and rights of all people, and promotes ideals of equal participation and access for individuals and groups' (QSCC 2000, p. 6).

2. Social justice: 'This includes concern for welfare, rights and dignity of all, empathy with people from different cultures, and fairness' (Marsh & Hart 2011, p. 164).

3. Ecological and economic sustainability: 'A sustainable environment is one in which the natural environment, economic development and social life are seen as mutually dependent – and the interaction between them contributes to the sustainability and natural environment' (Fien 1996, p. 21).

4. Peace: 'is based on the belief that to promote life is to promote positive relations with others and with the environment' (QSCC 2000, p. 6).

## EDUCATOR TIP

When planning activities, you will usually focus on at least one of the four values, as they represent the heart of all HASS learning. Such planning is not limited to primary school settings, as HASS values are also embedded in the EYLF.

| **TABLE 1.2**   SUBJECT OR SUB-STRAND-SPECIFIC ILLUSTRATIONS OF THE KEY IDEAS IN THE HASS CURRICULUM | | | | |
|---|---|---|---|---|
| Key idea | History | Geography | Civics and Citizenship | Economics and Business |
| • Who we are, who came before us, and traditions and values that have shaped societies | • Family, local and Australian history; and celebrations and commemoration<br>• The longevity of Aboriginal and Torres Strait Islander peoples' histories and cultures<br>• The legacy of Ancient Greece and Ancient Rome | • The influence of culture on the organisation of places, and their representations<br>• Aboriginal and Torres Strait Islander peoples' special connections to Country/Place<br>• The role of people's environmental world views in shaping societies | • The influence of social media in shaping identities and attitudes to diversity<br>• The shared values of Australian citizenship<br>• The values that underpin Australia's system of government (including British and American influences and a Christian heritage) | • The contribution of work to people's sense of identity<br>• The 'market system' as a defining feature of Australia's economy<br>• Influences on consumer and financial choices |
| • How societies and economies operate and how they are changing over time | • The social structure of ancient societies and their legacy<br>• The impact of the significant periods on societies (Industrial Revolution, Renaissance, Scientific Revolution, Enlightenment, British imperialism, nationalism and globalisation)<br>• The development of democracy in Australia | • The human alteration of environments<br>• The role of government and non-government organisations in improving human wellbeing and planning for sustainable futures<br>• Migration and the increasing concentration of people in urban areas | • The operation of the three levels of government and Australia's legal system in Australia<br>• The development of self-government in Australia<br>• How governments respond to social and economic change | • The influence of government on the ways markets operate in Australia<br>• The shifting importance of different sectors in the Australian economy<br>• How societies use limited resources for changing needs and wants now and in the future |
| • The ways people, places, ideas and events are perceived and connected | • Different perspectives on the arrival of the First Fleet and the colonial presence<br>• The causes of and relationship between events such as World War I, World War II and the Cold War<br>• Global influences on Australian culture | • People's perceptions of places and how these influence their connections to different places<br>• How human and natural systems are connected and interdependent<br>• How places in Australia are connected to other places across the world | • How groups within society perceive each other and relate to one another<br>• The influence of global connectedness and mobility on Australian identity Australians' rights and responsibilities towards each other and Australia's international obligations | • The performance of the Australian economy and how this is perceived by different groups<br>• How participants in the global economy are interdependent<br>• Different ways in which entrepreneurs and businesses succeed |

**TABLE 1.2** (CONT.)

| Key idea | History | Geography | Civics and Citizenship | Economics and Business |
|---|---|---|---|---|
| How people exercise their responsibilities, participate in society and make informed decisions | The development of rights in Australia for women, children, Aboriginal and Torres Strait Islander peoples and other groups<br><br>The participation of people in human rights and environmental campaigns in Australia<br><br>The contributions and achievements of individuals and groups to Australia's development | Strategies used to enhance the liveability of places<br><br>World views about sustainability and environments and how they are expressed<br><br>The management and planning of Australia's urban future | The role of the electoral and representative systems of government<br><br>The participation of groups in civic life, such as social, cultural, political and religious groups<br><br>The importance of active and informed citizenship in decision-making and the use of democratic processes | The responsibilities of employers and employees in the workplace<br><br>How individuals and businesses plan to achieve short- and long-term financial objectives<br><br>The concept of opportunity cost as a means of making informed decisions about alternative uses of resources |

Source: ACARA 2018

SPOTLIGHT ON HASS EDUCATION

# CONNECTING WITH PRIOR LEARNING

In planning for my Year 2 HASS class of 25 students at the beginning of the year in a metropolitan middle-class setting, my challenge was to explore and value the prior HASS knowledge, understandings and skills of each individual student. Such background information was central to tailoring planning for future learning experiences and identifying the key HASS sub-strands, ideas and values that can build upon learners' early years HASS conceptual understandings, through activities related to their interests and lifeworld. One of the concepts focused on in the early years is continuity and change. As it is important to connect to something with which learners are familiar, it was decided to use school holidays as a vehicle to explore their understanding of continuity and change. The following activity was used to determine each learner's prior knowledge.

Learners were initially asked to close their eyes and visualise/think about the school holidays. They were asked to describe:

- how they feel about the school holidays
- what they like to do on the school holidays.

They were then asked to think about their parents/carers and grandparent/s and whether they would have engaged in similar activities in the school holidays.

- Do they believe that school holiday activities have changed over time?

We next watched the ABC clip *Playgrounds and Billycarts*, which enabled learners to discover what school holidays were like for children in the past. In the clip, a reporter interviews children about how they feel about the school holidays, enabling learners to compare what school holidays were like in their parents/carers' and grandparent/s' times. While watching the clip learners were asked to note changes in the ways children spent their school holidays. Prompt questions were used to elicit understandings of continuity and change:

- Was this clip filmed in the past?
- How do you know that this clip was filmed in the past?
- Is playground equipment different today? If so, how is it different? Was there any equipment that was the same?
- What did children in the clip do for fun in the holidays?
- What are some common school holiday activities for children today?
- What things have changed and what have stayed the same?
- Why have things changed?

## EDUCATOR TIP

The following interactive resource enables learners to choose a room within the house by clicking on the house itself. They can then choose a year that they wish to explore. By doing this, learners can easily understand continuity and change. See: http://www.abc.net.au/abc3/myplace.

## CONCLUSION

This chapter has introduced the history and development of the EYLF and the Australian Curriculum, highlighting the importance of education and care. Consideration of the key ideas and values that underpin this important learning area provided opportunities to consider the importance of HASS before exploring the implications of the Review of the Australian Curriculum. Consequently, this chapter has provided an excellent platform from which understandings can be developed. As you embark on the following chapters, we challenge you to be bold as an educator, remembering that the curriculum presented are frameworks in which you can be innovative, responsive and enlightening. As the OECD 2030 position paper proposes:

> Children entering school in 2018 will need to abandon the notion that resources are limitless and are there to be exploited; they will need to value common prosperity, sustainability and well-being. They will need to be responsible and empowered, placing collaboration above division, and sustainability above short-term gain. In the face of an increasingly volatile, uncertain, complex and ambiguous world, education can make the difference as to whether people embrace the challenges they are confronted with or whether they are defeated by them. And in an era characterised by a new explosion of scientific knowledge and a growing array of complex societal problems, it is appropriate that curricula should continue to evolve, perhaps in radical ways. (OECD 2018, p. 3)

## REVIEW QUESTIONS

1. What are the goals of the Australian Curriculum?
2. What are the key ideas that guide learning in HASS?
3. What are the values underpinning learning in HASS?
4. What are the five principles of the EYLF?
5. What are the five learning outcomes identified in the EYLF?

## LEARNING EXTENSION

There are considerable synergies between the EYLF and the Australian Curriculum. What areas of HASS can you see within the five learning outcomes? How could you extend these so that learners entering the Foundation year of schooling are engaged with HASS learning experiences?

## REFERENCES

ACARA (Australian Curriculum, Assessment and Reporting Authority). (2010). *The Shape of the Australian Curriculum: Version 2.0.* Sydney: ACARA.

——(2016). Cross-curriculum priorities. Retrieved from: https://www.acara.edu.au/curriculum/cross-curriculum-priorities.

——(2018). *Australian Curriculum: Humanities and Social Sciences F-10, v8.3.* Key ideas. Retrieved from: http://australian-curriculum.org/humanities-and-social-sciences/key-ideas.

Connor, J. (2011). *Foundations for Learning: Relationships between the Early Years Learning Framework and the Australian Curriculum.* Retrieved from: http://foundationinquirylearning.global2.vic.edu.au/files/2013/06/ECA_ACARA_Foundations_Paper-2cq59mi.pdf.

DEEWR (Department of Education, Employment and Workplace Relations). (2009). *Belonging, Being and Becoming: The Early Years Learning Framework for Australia.* Canberra: DEEWR.

Department of Education and Training (Queensland). (2017). *Curriculum.* Retrieved from: http://education.qld.gov.au/curriculum.

DEST (Department of Education, Science and Training). (1999). *The Adelaide Declaration.* Retrieved from: http://www.scseec.edu.au/archive/Publications/Publications-archive/The-Adelaide-Declaration.aspx.

Donnelly, K. & Wiltshire, K. (2014). *Review of the Australian Curriculum: Final report.* Canberra: Department of Education.

Education Council. (2014). *The Hobart Declaration on Schooling (1989).* Retrieved from: http://www.educationcouncil.edu.au/EC-Publications/EC-Publications-archive/EC-The-Hobart-Declaration-on-Schooling-1989.aspx.

Fien, J. (1996). *Teaching for a Sustainable World.* Brisbane: Griffith University.

Green, D. (2016). Re-igniting the passion in HASS: An exploration of pre-service teachers' experiences. In *Refereed Proceedings of the 2016 ACSA Conference,* Adelaide, South Australia, 30 September–2 October.

Kennedy, K. (2009). The idea of a national curriculum in Australia: What do Susan Ryan, John Dawkins and Julia Gillard have in common? *Curriculum Perspectives, 29*(1), 1–9.

Klaus, P. (2010). Communication breakdown. *California Job Journal, 28,* 1–9.

Maes, J., Weldy, T. & Icenogel, M. (1997). A managerial perspective: Oral communication is most important for business students in the workplace. *Journal of Business Communication*, 34, 67–80.

Marsh, C. & Hart, C. (2011). *Teaching the Social Science and Humanities in an Australian Curriculum*, 6th edn. Sydney: Prentice-Hall.

MCEETYA (Ministerial Council on Education, Employment, Training and Youth Affairs). (2008). *Melbourne Declaration on Educational Goals for Young Australians*. Retrieved from: http://www.curriculum.edu.au/verve/_resources/National_Declaration_on_the_Educational_Goals_for_Young_Australians.pdf.

McInerney, M. (2017). The place of HASS in curriculum: Time to argue our case! Paper presented at HASS SA Conference, Adelaide, 25–26 February.

Mitchell, G.W., Skinner, L.B. & White, B.J. (2010). Essential soft skills for success in the twenty-first century workforce as perceived by business educators. *Delta Pi Epsilon Journal*, 52, 43–53.

Nealy, C. (2005). Integrating soft skills through active learning in the management classroom. *Journal of College Teaching & Learning*, 2(4), 1–6.

NESA (NSW Education Standards Authority). (2017). *The Australian Curriculum in New South Wales*. Retrieved from: http://www.boardofstudies.nsw.edu.au/australian-curriculum.

OECD (Organisation for Economic Co-operation and Development). (2018). *The Future of Education and Skills Education 2030: The future we want*. Paris: OECD.

Piper, K. (1997). *Riders in the Chariot: Curriculum reform and the national interest, 1965–1995*. Melbourne: ACER.

QSCC (Queensland School Curriculum Council). (2000). *Studies of Society and Environment, Years 1 to 10 Draft Syllabus*. Brisbane: Queensland School Curriculum Council.

Reid, A. (2009). Is this a revolution? A critical analysis of the Rudd government's national education agenda. Doctoral dissertation, Australian Curriculum Studies Association.

——(2018). The journey towards the first Australian Curriculum. In A. Reid & D. Price, eds, *The Australian Curriculum: Promises, problems and possibilities*. Canberra: Australian Curriculum Studies Association.

Reiter, A. (n.d.). *The Victorian Curriculum*. Retrieved from: http://effectivecurriculumideas.weebly.com/the-progressive-curriculum-frameworks-for-the-victorian-curriculum.html.

Smith, L. (2007). Teaching the intangibles. *T+ D*, 61(10), 23–5.

Tudball, L. (2018). The humanities and social sciences: Developing active and informed citizens for a changing world. In A. Reid & D. Price, eds, *The Australian Curriculum: Promises, problems and possibilities*. Canberra: Australian Curriculum Studies Association.

Yates, L. & Collins, C. (2008). Australian curriculum 1975–2005: What has been happening to knowledge. In *AARE Conference Paper Collection, AARE*, December. Retrieved from: http://www.aare.edu.au/08pap/abs08.htm.

# A GUIDED TOUR OF THE HASS AUSTRALIAN CURRICULUM: PLANNING AND INTEGRATING LEARNING

*Deborah Green and Deborah Price*

## Learning objectives

After reading this chapter, you should be able to:

- navigate the Australian Curriculum and understand the application of the general capabilities and cross-curriculum priorities within Humanities and Social Sciences (HASS) education
- navigate and understand the HASS curriculum (including knowledge and understanding; inquiry and skills; concepts; and achievement standards) and its relationship with the Early Years Learning Framework (EYLF)
- employ backward planning and emergent curriculum principles and explain constructivism
- understand the significance of integrated learning
- recognise and locate primary and secondary resources for future planning and teaching.

## INTRODUCTION

As discussed in Chapter 1, the Australian Curriculum and the EYLF guide learning experiences in Australian educational settings. Being able to navigate these documents and understand how to use them to support your teaching and learning is critical. Both the Australian Curriculum and EYLF are underpinned by constructivist principles, so understanding the importance of the constructivist approach and its place in teaching and learning is also important.

This chapter will initially help your familiarisation with the architecture of HASS in the Australian Curriculum and provide guidance for its implementation in the educational setting. Providing real-life experiences using interdisciplinary skills and knowledge is important; therefore, we will discuss different approaches to planning before highlighting the significance of employing an integrated approach. Discussions of planning and assessment will feature prominently, complemented with illustrations of curriculum resources. While the focus in this chapter is on the Australian Curriculum, the significance of planning HASS learning experiences that build on the EYLF are integrated throughout, drawing on the description of the EYLF that was presented in Chapter 1. It is important to recognise the central role of early years educators in promoting a passion for HASS and acquiring the skills and concepts.

## PARENT–TEACHER NIGHT

Imagine it is the beginning of the year. You have recently been appointed as the HASS educator and parent/carer information night is looming. The Australian Government's push towards promoting STEM (science, technology, engineering, mathematics) subjects has resulted in these learning areas stealing the limelight from HASS, so you need parents to understand and support you in teaching this learning area to their children. Here are some prompts to guide your thinking:

- What is HASS? Remember that for most parents, this topic may have aligned with learning areas such as Studies of Society and the Environment (SOSE), so you need to explain the similarities/differences in this learning area today.
- Why is it important to learn about HASS?
- Why should HASS have an equally important place in the curriculum as areas such as literacy and numeracy?
- What will their children be learning in HASS?
- What pedagogical approaches will you employ to ensure that learners gain the most out of their learning and become passionate about HASS?
- If you are an educator in a preschool, what does HASS look like for these learners?

## EDUCATOR TIP

While it is neither necessary nor expected that you are an expert in all areas of HASS, it is important to provide stimulating examples and learning experiences for learners to understand the concepts being taught and develop a passion for HASS. To achieve this, your planning needs to develop learners' interests through real-life experiences that explore the content and concepts of the HASS curriculum appropriate to their year level, ability and prior knowledge, skills and understandings.

## NAVIGATING THE AUSTRALIAN CURRICULUM

As highlighted in Chapter 1, the *Melbourne Declaration on Educational Goals for Young Australians* (Melbourne Declaration) (MCEETYA 2008) was the driving force behind the development of the first national curriculum. The Council of Australian Governments' (COAG) National Education Agreement (NEA) articulates that *all* Australian governments need to ensure learners have opportunities to acquire knowledge and skills that will enable them to participate effectively in society and employment in a globalised economy. Thus, the Australian Curriculum is based on the interrelationship between (a) knowledge and understanding and (b) inquiry and skills, which are summarised in the **year level descriptors**. Navigating the Australian Curriculum for the first time can be overwhelming. Therefore, a step-by-step guide will be presented in this chapter to help you understand the key components of the HASS learning area. Figure 2.1 illustrates the various components of the Australian Curriculum for each learning area.

**year level descriptors**: summarise the knowledge and understandings across learning areas for each year level

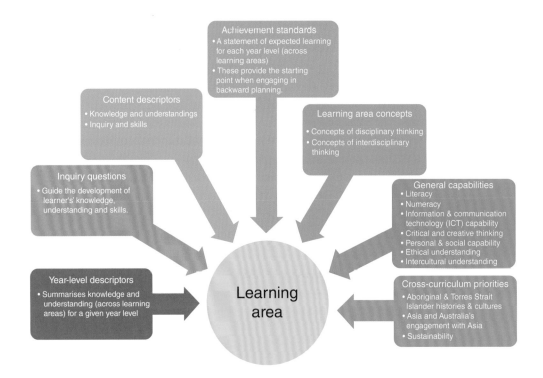

FIGURE 2.1   An overview of the Australian Curriculum

**inquiry questions**: guide the development of learners' knowledge, understanding and skills

**content descriptors**: highlight what learners are expected to learn in a particular year level and learning area

**achievement standards**: articulate what learners are expected to achieve at a particular year level and in a specific learning area

Directing the development of knowledge, understandings and skills for each year level and learning area are **inquiry questions** and relevant disciplinary and interdisciplinary concepts.

**Content descriptors** highlight what learners are expected to learn, while **achievement standards** articulate the expected outcomes for each year level. Overarching all learning areas and year levels are the cross-curriculum priorities and general capabilities, as discussed below and further detailed in Chapters 16–19. These provide opportunities for students to live and work successfully in the twenty-first century. They play a significant role in realising the goals set out in the *Melbourne Declaration on Educational Goals for Young Australians* (ACARA 2016). The cross-curriculum priorities are addressed, where appropriate, in all learning areas; however, they have a stronger presence in some areas, particularly HASS.

## EDUCATOR TIP

As an educator, it is important to understand that rich learning experiences occur when the learning area content draws on both the cross-curriculum priorities and the general capabilities.

# The cross-curriculum priorities

The Melbourne Declaration (MCEETYA 2008) identified key priority areas that needed to be addressed in the Australian Curriculum; these are the three **cross-curriculum priorities** of Sustainability, Aboriginal and Torres Strait Islander histories and cultures, and Asia and Australia's engagement with Asia. Providing opportunities to develop knowledge around national, regional and global dimensions, the cross-curriculum priorities are embedded in learning areas where they fit naturally (ACARA 2016). Each priority is supported by a rationale that is further developed by two or more 'organising ideas' that support the development of content knowledge, understandings and skills for both the priority and the learning area (ACARA 2016). In this way, they provide a framework that reflects the essential learning for the priority. To find out more about the organising ideas for each cross-curriculum priority, visit the Australian Curriculum website.

**cross-curriculum priorities**: the three priority areas identified as essential in the lives of Australian learners and the contemporary issues that they face moving into the 21st century. These areas are: Sustainability; Aboriginal and Torres Strait Islander histories and cultures; and Asia and Australia's engagement with Asia.

The cross-curriculum priorities do not exist as a curriculum on their own and require core learning areas to address them. It is, however, important that they are developed where they can be *appropriately* addressed and are therefore identified in only some of the learning area content descriptors. Values such as peace, democracy, social justice and sustainability are often cited as key to the HASS learning area and the cross-curriculum priorities feature prominently as there is a natural fit with these values. The content and learning related to each of the cross-curriculum priorities can be identified by distinct icons that are embedded throughout ACARA's curriculum documentation.

Each of the cross-curriculum priorities will be discussed in detail later in the book. Here we take a brief look at the focus of each.

## Sustainability

Sustainability has three main concepts: systems, world views and futures.

- *Systems* encourages an exploration of the interdependent and dynamic nature of systems that support life on earth and collective wellbeing.
- *World views* centres on the discussion and recognition of diverse world views on ecosystems, values and social justice when determining individual and community actions for sustainability.
- *Futures* aims at building capacities for thinking and acting so that a more sustainable future can be achieved. Reflective thinking is encouraged to empower learners to design actions for a more equitable and sustainable future (ACARA 2016).

## Aboriginal and Torres Strait Islander histories and cultures

Three organising ideas underpin this cross-curriculum priority: Country/Place, culture and people.

- *Country/Place* highlights the special connection that Aboriginal and Torres Strait Islander peoples have with their Country/Place and celebrates the unique belief that connects people physically and spiritually to Country/Place.
- *Culture* examines the diversity of Aboriginal and Torres Strait Islander peoples' cultures through language, ways of life and experiences as expressed through historical, social and

political lenses. This provides learners with opportunities to gain insight into Aboriginal and Torres Strait Islander peoples' ways of being, knowing, thinking and doing.

- *People* explores the diversity of Aboriginal and Torres Strait Islander societies by examining kinship structures and the significant contributions of Aboriginal and Torres Strait Islander peoples locally, nationally and globally (ACARA 2016).

## Asia and Australia's engagement with Asia

Asia in this context is defined by geographical terms, culture, religion, historical and language boundaries or commonalities. In Australian schools, studies of Asia focus on the following sub-regions:

- North-East Asia including China, Japan, Mongolia, North Korea, South Korea and Taiwan
- South-East Asia including Brunei, Cambodia, Indonesia, Laos, Malaysia, Myanmar (Burma), the Philippines, Singapore, Thailand, Timor-Leste and Vietnam
- South Asia including Bangladesh, Bhutan, India, the Maldives, Nepal, Pakistan and Sri Lanka (ACARA 2016).

This cross-curriculum priority has three organising ideas: Asia and its diversity; achievements and contributions of peoples of Asia; and Asia–Australia engagement.

- *Asia and its diversity* highlights the diversity in cultures, societies, traditions, environments and the effects on the lives of people in the Asia region.
- *Achievements and contributions of the peoples of Asia* examines the past and continuing achievements of peoples of Asia by identifying their contribution to world history and acknowledging the influences this region has on the world's aesthetic and creative pursuits.
- *Asia–Australia engagement* speaks to the nature of past and ongoing links between Australia and Asia. In line with the goals of the Melbourne Declaration (MCEETYA 2008), this concept develops the knowledge, understanding and skills that make it possible to engage actively and effectively with the peoples of the Asia region.

**Reflection**  The Melbourne Declaration was developed in 2008. These cross-curriculum priorities define what Australia believed to be crucial knowledge for learners to participate effectively in 21st-century society. As we look to draft new educational goals for the next decade, do you think these priorities remain relevant? Are there others that need to be included?

## Understanding the general capabilities

**general capabilities**: describe the capabilities that learners develop across all learning areas. They are: literacy; numeracy; information and communication technology (ICT); critical and creative thinking; personal and social; ethical understanding; and intercultural understanding.

A set of **general capabilities** promoting learners' development of knowledge, skills, behaviours and dispositions to effectively participate in the 21st century were included in the curriculum design. Applying knowledge and skills confidently, effectively and appropriately in complex and changing circumstances, both in their learning and in life generally, enables learners to develop these capabilities. Although state and territory education authorities determine how the general capabilities are assessed, the responsibility to teach and assess them rests with educators.

The general capabilities in relation to the HASS learning area will be explored further in Chapter 16, but being mindful of these capabilities from the outset will keep you thinking about their importance and how you might make them central to all learning and assessment experiences. There are seven general capabilities in the Australian Curriculum, with each being addressed through individual learning areas. Distinct icons appear alongside appropriate content descriptors and elaborations to illustrate where the general capabilities need to be addressed.

## EDUCATOR TIP

To further assist your planning, you can download a PDF from the Australian Curriculum, Assessment and Reporting Authority (ACARA) illustrating the development of each of the general capabilities over the years.

How are the general capabilities developed within the early years (i.e. children aged 0–5 years)? Refer to Chapter 16, and consider how the general capabilities extend the skills, behaviours and attitudes developed as part of the EYLF. Are there areas that are developed in early years learning settings that need to be fostered in a school context?

## UNITS ON SUSTAINABILITY, CARE AND THE ENVIRONMENT

Revisit your parent information evening scenario at the beginning of this chapter. When asked about how the cross-curriculum priorities and general capabilities are evident in your planning, teaching and assessment, you highlight the unit of work on sustainability, care and the environment. In this unit, you taught learners to care for the land and be empathetic, using the book or clip *You and Me, Murrawee* by Hashmi (1999). After hearing the story or watching the clip, you asked learners to close their eyes and visualise changes between the time illustrated in the story and now. They then drew an image of what the river looked like in the past, how it looks in the present and how they think it will look in the future.

   This was followed by viewing sections of *The Lorax* (Dr Seuss 1999) and engaging in a community of inquiry that enhanced the general capability of ethical understanding. The community of inquiry followed this discussion plan:

   - In *The Lorax*, how did the thneed industry affect the physical environment?
   - How did these environmental conditions affect local plants and animals?

**SPOTLIGHT ON HASS EDUCATION**

- How did thneed production affect Once-lers and people (employees, neighbours, etc.)?
- Based on your observations from this story, was this method of manufacturing thneeds sustainable?
- How would you define the phrase 'sustainable development'?
- How could the Once-lers have manufactured thneeds in a more sustainable manner?
- What federal, state and local agencies exist to protect the environment?
- Whose responsibility is it to protect the environment and ensure sustainable practices?

Source: adapted from Penguin Random House 2018

# THE HASS CURRICULUM

Knowledge and understanding, inquiry and skills, learning area concepts and year level achievement standards are defined for each learning area. They guide planning and learning by providing inquiry questions and learning outcomes.

## Knowledge and understanding

The knowledge and understanding strand of the HASS curriculum includes four sub-strands, depending on the year level:

- History
- Geography
- Civics and Citizenship
- Economics and Business.

In F-6/7 these strands are collapsed and presented as one learning area – HASS: F-6/7 – while in secondary school they are offered independently. History is compulsory from Foundation to Year 10; Geography is compulsory from Foundation to Year 8 but is available to Year 10; Civics and Citizenship is compulsory from Years 3–8 and is available from Years 3–10; and Economics and Business is compulsory from Years 5–8 and is available from Years 5–10. In the early years (0–5 years), the EYLF governs what needs to be taught in HASS, as outlined in Chapter 1. Table 2.1 shows the breakdown of HASS in the F-10 curriculum.

The knowledge and understandings provide an overarching theme that guides the learning experiences that educators plan. For example, Table 2.2 outlines the overarching themes and inquiry questions for History and Geography in each year level.

| TABLE 2.1 | HASS IN THE F–10 CURRICULUM | | | |
|---|---|---|---|---|
| | **F–Year 2** | **Years 3–4** | **Years 5–6/7** | **Years 7–10** |
| History | Humanities and Social Sciences | Humanities and Social Sciences | Humanities and Social Sciences | History |
| Geography | | | | Geography |
| Civics and Citizenship | N/A | | | Civics and Citizenship |
| Economics and Business | N/A | N/A | | Economics and Business |

Source: adapted from ACARA 2018a

| TABLE 2.2 | OVERARCHING THEMES FOR HISTORY AND GEOGRAPHY | |
|---|---|---|
| **Year level** | **Topic/theme** | **Inquiry questions** |
| Foundation | My personal world | • Who am I, where do I live and who came before me?<br>• Why are some places and events special and how do we know? |
| 1 | How my world is different from the past and can change in the future | • How has family life and the place we live in changed over time?<br>• What events, activities and places do I care about?<br>• Why? |
| 2 | Our past and present connections to people and places | • What does my place tell me about the past and present?<br>• How are people connected to their place and other places, past or present?<br>• How has technology affected daily life over time and the connections between people in different places? |
| 3 | Diverse communities and places and the contribution people make | • How do symbols, events, individuals and places in my community make it unique?<br>• How do people contribute to their communities, past and present?<br>• What events do different people and groups celebrate and commemorate and what does this tell us about our communities? |
| 4 | How people, places and environments interact, past and present | • How have laws affected the lives of people, past and present?<br>• What were the short- and long-term effects of European settlement on the local environment and Indigenous land and water management practices?<br>• What is the significance of the environment and what are different views on how it can be used and sustained, past and present? |

| TABLE 2.2 | (CONT.) | |
|---|---|---|
| **Year level** | **Topic/theme** | **Inquiry questions** |
| 5 | Australian communities – their past, present and possible futures | • How have individuals and groups in the past and present contributed to the development of Australia?<br>• What is the relationship between environments and my roles as a consumer and citizen?<br>• How have people enacted their values and perceptions about their community, other people and places, past and present? |
| 6 | Australia in the past and present and its connections with a diverse world | • How have key figures, events and values shaped Australian society, its system of government and citizenship?<br>• How have experiences of democracy and citizenship differed between groups over time and place, including those from and in Asia?<br>• How has Australia developed as a society with global connections, and what is my role as a global citizen? |
| 7 | Sustainable pasts, present, futures | • How is the ancient world investigated and why are investigations of ancient key people, events, ideas and developments significant in the modern world?<br>• How have the use, management and value of finite natural resources affected how people have lived and societies have evolved in the past and present, and what does this mean for future planning?<br>• What principles and processes underpin Australia's cohesive society and stable economy and what is the role of political, economic and social institutions in developing and maintaining these? |

Source: adapted from ACARA 2018d

 Table 2.2 outlines the overarching themes for History and Geography. Look at the Australian Curriculum and develop tables for the Civics and Citizenship, and Economics and Business sub-strands.

 You may feel more knowledgeable and confident about teaching certain concepts in History, for example; however, for learners to be successful you need to facilitate, motivate and direct learning across all areas of HASS. With this in mind, identify areas of HASS in which you feel less confident and consider ways that you will develop the necessary confidence and skills to ensure learners are engaged and motivated to learn this content.

## Inquiry and skills

Each year level and learning area has its own set of inquiry questions, which provide a framework for developing knowledge, understanding and skills. While the inquiry skills vary across learning areas, Figure 2.2 illustrates those in the HASS learning area.

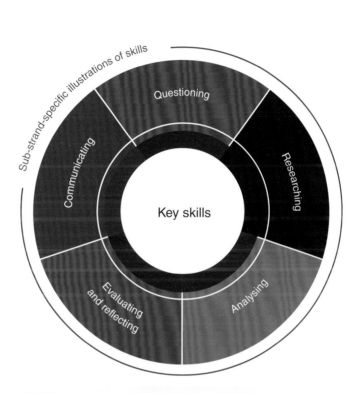

FIGURE 2.2    F-10 curriculum: HASS – structure
Source: ACARA 2018d

## EDUCATOR TIP

On the Australian Curriculum website, each of the skills in Figure 2.2 is hyperlinked to additional information. When planning, before you consider the questioning stage, develop a stimulus that grabs learners' interest and inspires them to learn more about the topic. This may be a poem, image, story or the way you set up your learning space. For example, when looking at 'Differences and similarities between learners' daily lives and life during their parents' and grandparents' childhoods, including family traditions, leisure time and communications' (ACHHK030) with Year 1 learners, you may make your learning environment look like it belongs to the 1950s. Once you have learners' interest and have sparked their curiosity, the journey begins.

## Stages of inquiry in the Australian Curriculum

The inquiry skills – questioning, researching, analysing, evaluating and reflecting, and communicating – are considered below.

### Questioning

During this stage of inquiry, it is important to provide learners with opportunities to develop questions about events, people, places, ideas, developments, issues and/or phenomena that can guide their explorations, satisfy their curiosity and revisit findings (ACARA 2016). Activities aimed at developing questioning skills should also help learners identify other areas to research before refining the questions on which they wish to focus.

Begin with activities that engage learners, spark their curiosity and motivate them to want to learn more about the topic. This is crucial to your planning, as it shapes learners' attitudes towards planned experiences. Spending time getting this right can make a significant difference to a learner's motivation and achievement in upcoming activities. Think back to the spotlight on sustainability, care and the environment, where the book *You & Me, Murrawee* (Hashmi 1999) was used to spark curiosity while inspiring learners to imagine what the river might look like in the past, present and future. Using learners' imagination, educators can encourage them to think of their own questions about the environment to which they would like to seek answers.

## EDUCATOR TIP

To ensure that learning is relevant and authentic, it is important to choose a stimulus that is relevant and connects with learners' lifeworlds – this will help them to develop questions about which they are interested and curious.

### Researching

As part of researching, learners identify and collect information, evidence and/or data from primary and secondary sources, including observations. They organise, sequence and categorise sources in various formats appropriate for HASS (ACARA 2016). To achieve this, learners need ideas and access to tools that help them to manage, sort and represent the collected information or data. In this stage, learners may refine their inquiry question to accommodate new information, thus informing the way the inquiry will be structured. Organising groups or teams, allocating roles, setting timelines and making decisions about where and how to locate information also occur at this time.

## EDUCATOR TIP

It is in the researching stage of inquiry that learners explore the questions they have developed in the questioning stage. Therefore, it is important that time is spent stimulating learners' curiosity and developing questions for exploration.

## Analysing

Analysing centres on providing concrete opportunities for learners to organise and represent the information and ideas they have gleaned from researching. Developing skills to critique data sources and determine their accuracy and reliability are critical in helping learners differentiate between what is an opinion and what is fact.

To be successful in analysing, learners need to:

- explore information, evidence and data
- identify and interpret features, distributions, patterns, trends and relationships, key points, facts and opinions, points of view, perceptions and interpretations
- identify the purpose and intent of sources and determine their accuracy and reliability (ACARA 2016).

Look at the questions in the discussion plan for *The Lorax* presented earlier in the chapter. How might you redesign these to ensure that learners acquire the analysing skills listed above?

## Evaluating and reflecting

In line with the goals of the Melbourne Declaration, this stage provides opportunities for learners to make choices that support their development towards becoming effective participants in society. Educators need to assist learners to make links between the knowledge they have acquired and how to apply their understanding to other situations and issues. Learners need to classify and modify ideas, compare and contrast findings, engage in discussions about the issue they are exploring and then interpret, synthesise, qualify and test the information they have gathered. The acquisition of new knowledge may challenge their current ideas, values and beliefs and cause a sense of disequilibrium, leading to potential change.

To help learners develop these skills, there need to be opportunities for them to propose explanations for events, developments and issues, draw evidence-based conclusions and then use a set of criteria and/or democratic processes to make informed decisions and judgements. This will help learners work with others respectfully and reflect on learning so they can suggest courses of action in response to issues or problems while predicting possible and preferred actions (ACARA 2016).

## Communicating

Communication provides learners with opportunities to process gathered information, reach a conclusion that they can defend and justify, and then communicate this in a range of ways. Learners need opportunities to present ideas using discipline-specific terminology that explains their findings, viewpoints, explanations, predictions, decisions, judgements and/or conclusions in appropriate digital and non-digital forms for different audiences and purposes (ACARA 2016). It is at this stage of an inquiry that summative assessment can take place.

## EDUCATOR TIP

Although the skills outlined above have a natural flow, they do not necessarily need to be taught sequentially. It is possible and even probable, for example, that you may work through researching and then go back to questioning before moving forward. It is important that learners experience and develop each of these skills in accordance with the achievement standards for their year level.

## Concepts

As articulated in Chapter 5, the Australian Curriculum outlines disciplinary and interdisciplinary concepts. For HASS, as illustrated below, each of the sub-strands has its own distinct disciplinary ways of thinking (see Figure 2.3).

- History concepts: sources, continuity and change, cause and effect, significance, perspectives, empathy and contestability

- Geography concepts: place, space, environment, interconnection, sustainability and change, applying this understanding to a wide range of places and environments at the full range of scales, from local to global, and in a range of locations

- Civics and Citizenship concepts: government and democracy, laws and citizens, citizenship, diversity and identity

- Economics and Business concepts: resource allocation and making choices, the business environment, and consumer and financial literacy (ACARA 2018c).

These concepts can form the focus of an inquiry or can be explored across all or some of the sub-strands involving interdisciplinary conceptual thinking. To encourage integration, the

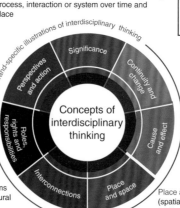

Drawing on the concepts of disciplinary thinking, the curriculum identifies seven concepts that underpin HASS understanding.

Significance: The importance of something such as an issue, current development, person, place, process, interaction or system over time and place

Students' understanding of these concepts can be strengthened as they are experienced in an integrated way across sub-strands and through different topics or contexts.

Perspectives and action: The ways in which different individuals and/or groups view something such as a plant or present issue, idea, event, development, person, place, process or interaction and how these views influence their actions

Continuity and change: Aspects of society, such as institutions, ideas, values and problems, that have stayed the same and changed over time (some point in the past and the present) or in the past (two points in the past)

Roles, rights and responsibilities: The roles, rights and responsibilities of social, economic, civic and environmental participation, including those of individuals, communities and institutions

Cause and effect: The long- and short-term causes and the intended and unintended consequences of an event, decision, process, interaction or development

Interconnections: The components of various systems such as social systems, resources systems and natural systems, and the connections within and between them, including how they impact on each other

Place and space: The characteristics of places (spatial, social, autonomic, physical, environmental) and how these characteristics are organised spatially (location, distribution, pattern)

FIGURE 2.3   Concepts of interdisciplinary thinking
Source: adapted from ACARA 2018c

Australian Curriculum identifies seven interdisciplinary concepts that underpin the HASS learning area: significance; continuity and change; cause and effect; place and space; interconnections; roles, rights and responsibilities; and perspectives and action (ACARA 2018b). Content descriptors for each year level are designed to provide opportunities for learners to be exposed to these concepts and develop conceptual thinking.

## Year level achievement standards

Assessment and achievement standards are discussed in detail in Chapter 15; however, we will explain them briefly here. Each learning area and year level has its own achievement standards, which outline learning outcomes. The first of two paragraphs for each achievement standard typically describes the learning outcomes in terms of expected understandings, while the second outlines what learners are expected to be able to do. Together with the content descriptors, the achievement standards determine what is taught and therefore provide a good starting point for planning learning experiences. They also provide a useful means of gauging a learner's progress while allowing for differentiation to occur. To help educators in their planning and assessment of the standards, annotated work samples are provided, which illustrate what a successful piece of work looks like for each year level and learning area.

# TEACHING AND PLANNING APPROACHES

Many preservice educators have little or no recollection of studying HASS or its equivalent during their education, and those who do often describe negative experiences (Green 2016). Primarily, this is due to the way the learning area was taught and the activities they engaged in (Green 2016). It is therefore essential for educators to plan learning activities that will enable learners to develop the necessary knowledge, understandings and skills in an engaging way so that learning is enjoyable and memorable. Enabling learners to construct their own knowledge is one way of achieving this.

## Constructing knowledge using constructivist approaches

Drawing on theories from Jean-Jacques Rousseau, John Dewey and Jean Piaget, constructivist approaches sit between educator-led and learner-centred learning. It is argued that these approaches maximise learner understanding and they feature prominently in the Australian Curriculum. Constructivism is underpinned by a belief that meaningful learning needs to be active, as opposed to educators merely transferring knowledge to learners, suggesting that educators and learners negotiate meaning jointly (Arends 2007). Constructivist approaches also centre on learners developing new understandings by building on what they already know, thus making learning authentic, relevant and engaging. In this way, learning embraces individual experiences and enables the learning experience to be different for all learners.

Constructivist activities, such as the community of inquiry discussed in Chapter 12, need to provide opportunities for learners to interpret their own experiences to match what they already know (i.e. assimilation) and then adjust their current understanding to align with their experience (i.e. accommodation). The Australian Curriculum embraces constructivism by including a set of inquiry skills that underpin inquiry-based learning, enabling learners to be active in their learning while developing a 'true' understanding of the content being taught. This approach encourages learners to develop their own questions while building on their prior knowledge. It is therefore important for educators to identify learners' understandings and how they construct the world in which they live (Reynolds 2012).

# EDUCATOR TIP

Embedding the inquiry skills from the Australian Curriculum in your lesson planning enables you to support constructivist approaches that link to learners' interests.

## Planning

Planning curriculum can be emergent or pre-planned, with the former evolving from the learners or participants and the latter taking a top-down approach that is controlled by the educator and is easy for others to follow (Stacey 2008). Backward planning is one form of a pre-planned curriculum.

### Backward planning

**backward planning:** involves identifying and working from learning outcomes to plan appropriate learning experiences

Wiggins and McTighe (2011) suggest that effective learning centres on **backward planning** as it ensures that goals are more clearly defined, assessments are more appropriate, lessons are aligned tightly to assessment and teaching is more purposeful. This form of planning embraces three stages: the desired results, the evidence and the learning plan, each of which is illustrated in Table 2.3.

Guskey (2002) cautions against planning that focuses on activities or methodology as opposed to learning outcomes, or what the educator wants learners to know and be able to do at the end of the lesson or unit of work. Backward planning starts with identifying desired results and then works backwards to develop appropriate and meaningful learning experiences and assessments (Wiggins & McTighe 1998). Once the learning outcome has been identified, the educator determines how they will know whether learners have met this and what the most appropriate and engaging pedagogical approach will be to help them achieve it.

Often the learning outcomes are governed by national and/or state/territory curriculum. For example, many of the learning outcomes that Australian educators will consider are set out in the achievement standards for each year in the Australian Curriculum or, in the case of early years learners, the learning outcomes articulated in the EYLF. In this instance, backward planning involves:

**TABLE 2.3** THE BIG PICTURE OF BACKWARD DESIGN

| Stage and description | Design question | Design considerations | Filters/design criteria | Results in |
|---|---|---|---|---|
| **Stage 1:** Commences with identifying the desired results for students by establishing the overall goal(s) of the lesson or unit of work using achievement standards. This stage focuses on what learners will understand, know and be able to do. | What should learners understand, know and be able to do at the conclusion of this lesson/unit of work? | National, state and local standards Educator's expertise and interest | Enduring ideas, opportunities for authentic, discipline-based work that is engaging | A lesson or unit of work that is framed around enduring understandings and essential questions |
| **Stage 2:** Focuses on evidence of learning by assessment. Educators plan performance tasks and evidence of understanding that is required. Performance tasks determine what the learners will demonstrate in the lesson or unit of work and what evidence will prove their understanding, including self-reflections and self-assessments of learning. | What is the evidence of learning or understanding? | Six facets of understanding | Valid, reliable, authentic and sufficient assessment | A lesson or unit of work that is credible and vital evidence of the desired learning |
| **Stage 3:** Outlines the learning activities that will lead learners to the desired outcomes. | What learning activities promote understanding, knowledge, skills and learner interest? | Research-based repertoire of learning and teaching strategies Essential and enabling knowledge and skills | W.H.E.R.E.T.O.: W – where and why H – hook and hold E – explore, experience, enable and equip R – reflect, rethink and revise E – evaluate, work and progress T – tailor and personalise the work O – organise for optimal effectiveness | Coherent learning experiences that evoke and develop the desired outcomes, promote interest and make excellent performance more likely |

Source: adapted from Department of Education and Communities, NSW 2014; Wiggins & McTighe 2001

- identifying the learning outcomes based on the achievement standards in the Australian Curriculum or the learning outcomes in the EYLF before distinguishing the key concepts within them

- determining forms of acceptable evidence – how will you know whether learners have accomplished the learning outcomes? McTighe and Thomas (2003) suggest an array of data is needed as opposed to focusing on a snapshot from a single test or piece of assessment (refer to Chapter 15 for a detailed discussion of assessment)

- planning learning experiences and instruction that will help learners achieve the desired outcomes in an engaging manner.

## Emergent planning and curriculum

While backward planning involves working from learning outcomes, an emergent curriculum evolves from and embraces the child's interests. Emergent planning is commonly employed in early years settings where planning of learning experiences is not based solely on curriculum but instead emerges from dialogue between educators, children and their families. In this way, children's interests are followed and explorations or inquiries are supported and facilitated by educators (Jones 2012; Pelo 2009; Sisson & Whitington 2017). Through the use of play, educators take note of learners' questions and use these to plan learning experiences, thus making emergent planning a constantly evolving process (refer to Chapter 13). The direction of planning evolves as children engage in learning activities and play, so relationships are pivotal – whether between children, or between educators, children and their families. As such, emergent planning centres on the belief that 'learning occurs in an existing relationship between two or more people, where both people are curious about something of mutual interest and can engage in extended conversation about this interest' (Sisson & Whitington 2017, p. 16). Knowing the learners will help you to recognise their interests, listen to their questions and plan engaging activities that allow them to explore these. According to Stacey (2008), the key characteristics of an **emergent curriculum** are that it:

**emergent curriculum:** transpires as a result of dialogue between educators, children and their families and often involves observing children engaging in learning experiences and play

- is designed by educators but child initiated, thus enhancing collaborations between children and educators

- is responsive to the child's needs while also being flexible to enable the ever-changing interests of the child to be met

- is facilitated by educators who rely on observations and discussions to help children construct their own knowledge

- is transparent in that a child's learning and educator's thinking and planning are visible to all stakeholders

- builds on theories of well-known educational theorists such as Dewey, Piaget and Vygotsky.

To aid understanding of this process, Sisson (2016) developed an inquiry planning cycle, as illustrated in Figure 2.4. The child is positioned at the centre of this model, alongside families and educators, highlighting the importance of engaging children in determining an issue or topic for inquiry. Such engagement aims to draw educators' and learners' intentions together in a democratic way by involving children in conversations and listening to them engage with peers, educators and families. Documentation enables learners' actions and conversations to be recorded, interpreted and shared. Reflection requires educators to think carefully about what they have observed and heard before considering how this may inform planning and practice. Questioning involves making decisions about whether the educator's and learners' intentions have been brought together. If this is not the case, a decision not to proceed to questioning can be made. While this model appears linear in nature, it is cyclic, as educators often come in and out of the cycle (Sisson & Whitington 2017; Stacey 2008).

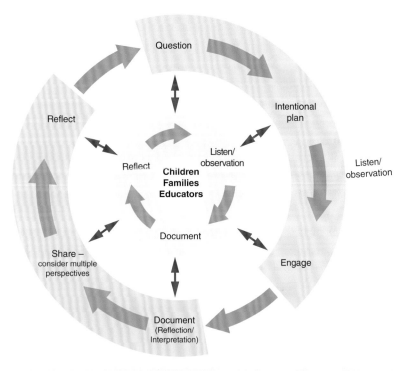

FIGURE 2.4   The inquiry planning cycle
Source: Sisson & Whitington 2017

The inquiry planning model is used extensively and effectively in early years settings. How effective do you think this approach would be in planning HASS in upper primary years? What are some of the strengths and limitations of the model? Would the model need any changes to be used in the upper primary years? If so, what might need to occur?

Reflection

Regardless of which model is employed, planning learning experiences often involves exploring emerging themes or topics of interest and integrating learning across different disciplines, learning areas, general capabilities and cross-curriculum priorities.

# WHAT IS AN INTEGRATED CURRICULUM?

**integrated curriculum:**
involves authentic learning experiences that go across more than one learning area, thus enabling learners to see connections between them

An **integrated curriculum** typically occurs in early and primary years, where learning areas are less discrete than in secondary settings. To support this style of curriculum, interdisciplinary concepts were developed for the learning areas in the Australian Curriculum. In HASS, these concepts enable learning to occur across all four sub-strands. It has long been recognised that organising 'common learnings' and skills are needed for people to function as effective citizens (Beane 1997; Parker 2008; Vars & Beane 2000), and it is argued that for true learning to occur, learners need to be able to apply new knowledge to a range of contexts. In this way, learners make sense of their own life experiences and learn how to participate in a democracy (Beane 1997), thus supporting the goals of the Melbourne Declaration (MCEETYA 2008). To explain this, Beane (1991) uses the analogy of a puzzle, describing how when we are working on a puzzle, we rely on the picture as it provides meaning. He proposes that without the picture, many of us would not bother to attempt the puzzle. Yet in educational settings, educators often do not provide opportunities for learners to put the pieces together to see the whole picture, leaving them feeling that learning is disjointed and disconnected. An integrated curriculum provides such opportunities – for example, when a real-life issue or problem arises we rarely think about which part of it is science, mathematics or HASS based, but instead we draw on our pool of knowledge to help us solve it. For true integration to occur, Beane (1991) suggests that learners need to be faced with questions that mean something to them personally and engage in learning experiences related to those questions. Learners can practise and recognise the relevance of their learning in developing as effective members of society.

Wraga (2009) suggests that an integrated curriculum:

- enables connections to be made across learning areas, thus providing a 'cumulative impact of all learning experiences' (p. 92)
- highlights the interconnectedness of learning experiences
- provides opportunities for learners to address social problems or issues using a range of interdisciplinary skills.

Of equal importance, research has found that the academic achievements of learners who engage in an integrated curriculum are equal to or greater than the achievements of those who do not. Learners also experience fewer attendance and behaviour problems and are more engaged in their learning – something that is paramount for all learners (Drake & Reid 2010). However, one of the challenges of the integrated curriculum rests with assessment, particularly if each learning area is assessed individually (Vars & Beane 2000). In the Australian Curriculum, this is less of a challenge as the year level achievement standards are designed with an integrated curriculum in mind. The EYLF takes a similar approach with its holistic assessment, which captures data from all stakeholders about a learner's progress and achievement. Challenges, however, do exist in the middle years where assessment is more discipline or learning area focused. Achieving integration at this level takes collaborative teamwork and careful planning.

# EDUCATOR TIP

How do we plan in an integrated curriculum? There are numerous models that have been proposed, but most adopt a backward planning approach as described above. You may find the template in Figure 2.5 useful when planning. Once these templates have been completed, you can choose an issue, theme or topic that will be the focus of your unit of work before brainstorming learning experiences to help learners achieve these. Involving learners in this planning is important as it increases their engagement by building on their interests, knowledge and skills.

## A planning triangle

The template in Figure 2.5 can be used to identify the learning requirements necessary for planning.

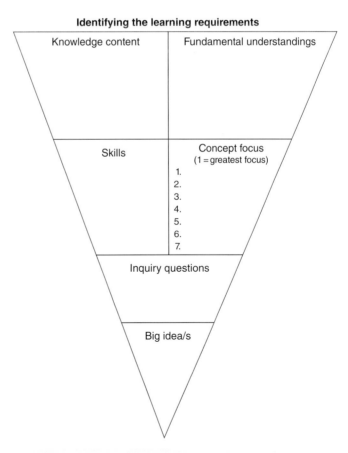

FIGURE 2.5   **Planning triangle**
Source: courtesy of Malcolm McInerney

When completing the template, think about the following:

- What is the HASS structure for the year level?
- What are the inquiry questions for the year level?
- What is the year level description?
- What are the concepts of disciplinary thinking?
- How do the key ideas link to the inquiry questions and concepts?
- Which content descriptors from the knowledge and understandings strand do you want to work with (remembering that sometimes, especially in the early years, they are closely linked)?
- Explain how you might be able to use the inquiry and skills strand to develop the knowledge and understandings descriptors you have chosen (you may want to focus on a small group of skills initially).
- Which parts of the achievement standards can you meet using the descriptors you have chosen?
- What is one cross-curriculum priority that links to your content descriptor?
- How could you link at least two of the general capabilities to the content descriptor you have chosen?

## LOCATING PRIMARY AND SECONDARY RESOURCES FOR FUTURE PLANNING AND TEACHING IN HASS

Having considered how to plan, we now need to briefly discuss resources and the role they play in planning, with more detailed discussions to follow later in the book. When talking about resources for HASS, we often refer to primary and secondary sources of information. Primary sources are factual, with no commentary, and can be found in many local communities (e.g. libraries, local councils and government offices). Secondary sources are written after the event or events and/or can form a commentary to explain the event. A textbook or book about World War II is a secondary source, as it has been compiled after the event and contains commentary and analysis. Sources can be both primary and secondary. For example, a photo taken during World War II is a primary source as it is a fact; however, commentary about or an interpretation of the photo written after the war would be classed as a secondary source. It is also possible for a secondary source to contain primary sources, such as photos or extracts of speeches.

One type of source is not necessarily better than the other. Instead, we suggest using them together as they can validate what has occurred (Barton 2005). An appropriate selection of primary and secondary sources is vital. Learners also need to be able to interrogate the sources of data they locate by questioning their authenticity and viewpoint, thus developing critical thinking skills. Learners need to recognise that an individual's viewpoint is shaped by their cultural and social experiences and these are reflected in texts, whether written, oral, visual or digital. These sources are powerful, and can inform and even persuade opinions and stances, so learners need to be able to recognise and acknowledge whose point of view is being portrayed; for example, do they reflect dominant viewpoints only? By challenging and interrogating sources, learners will 'compare objects from the past with those from the present and consider how places have changed over time' (ACHASSI006) (ACARA 2018c).

# CONCLUSION

HASS provides opportunities for dynamic and exciting learning that promotes the goals of the Melbourne Declaration (MCEETYA 2008). Having discussed the components of the Australian Curriculum, you have gained insight into this complex learning area. Understanding the interconnections between the sub-strands in the HASS learning area and their connections with the general capabilities and cross-curriculum priorities provides you with an excellent platform to plan integrated learning experiences that utilise primary and secondary sources of data for learners to explore and from which they can learn.

This chapter has also highlighted the importance of planning, regardless of your starting point. In some instances, it may be appropriate to start planning by exploring the achievement standards set out in the Australian Curriculum or the learning outcomes in the EYLF. At other times, listening to and observing children's dialogue and interactions may form the basis of your planning. Regardless, it is important that you provide stimulating examples and learning experiences to enable learners to understand the concepts being taught and thus develop a lifelong passion for HASS.

## REVIEW QUESTIONS

1.  What are the components/structure of the *Australian Curriculum: HASS*?
2.  What is meant by backward planning?
3.  What is an emergent curriculum?
4.  Why is integrated learning significant?
5.  What is the difference between primary and secondary data sources?

## LEARNING EXTENSION

As a passionate HASS educator, if you were assigned the job of rewriting the Australian Curriculum to further promote HASS inquiry, concepts and content, what changes would you make, and why? You may wish to draw on the Review of the Australian Curriculum (discussed in Chapter 1) and some of the references cited to develop your argument.

OR

It is critical that learners can evaluate whether data sources are authentic and reliable while also recognising their intent and viewpoint. With this in mind, choose an age group with which you would like to work and develop a checklist to support learners' critical analysis of data sources.

## REFERENCES

ACARA (Australian Curriculum, Assessment and Reporting Association). (2016). Cross-curriculum priorities. Retrieved from: https://www.acara.edu.au/curriculum/cross-curriculum-priorities.

——(2018a). *Australian Curriculum: F-10, v8.3*. Learning areas. https://www.australian curriculum.edu.au/f-10-curriculum/learning-areas.

——(2018b). *Australian Curriculum: F-10, v8.3*. Resources. Retrieved from: http://resources .australiancurriculum.edu.au/curriculum-connections/consumer-and-financial-literacy/ consumer-and-financial-literacy.

——(2018c). *Australian Curriculum: Humanities and Social Sciences F-10, v8.3*. Retrieved from: https://www.australiancurriculum.edu.au/f-10-curriculum/humanities-and-social-sciences/hass.

——(2018d). *AustralianCurriculum: Humanities and Social Sciences F-10, v8.3*. Structure. Retrieved from: https://www.australiancurriculum.edu.au/f-10-curriculum/humanities-and-social-sciences/hass/structure.

Arends, R.I. (2007). *Learning to Teach*, 6th edn. Boston: McGraw-Hill.

Barton, K. (2005). Primary sources in history: Breaking through the myths. *Phi Delta Kappan*, 89(10), 745–54.

Beane, J. (1991). The middle school: The natural home of integrated curriculum. *Educational Leadership*, 49(2), 9–13.

——(1997). *Curriculum Integration: Designing the core of democratic education*. New York: Teachers College Press.

Department of Education and Communities, NSW. (2014). The backward design model of curriculum planning. Retrieved from: http://www.ssgt.nsw.edu.au/documents/1_backward_design_model.pdf.

Dr Seuss (1999). *The Lorax*. New York: Random House.

Drake, S. & Reid, J. (2010). *Integrated Curriculum: Increasing Relevance While Maintaining Accountability*. Toronto: Ontario Ministry of Education. Retrieved from: http://www.edu.gov.on.ca/eng/literacynumeracy/inspire/research/WW_Integrated_Curriculum.pdf.

Green, D. (2016). Re-igniting the passion in HASS: An exploration of pre-service teachers' experiences. In *Refereed Proceedings of the 2016 ACSA Conference*, Adelaide, 30 September–2 October.

Guskey, T.R. (2002). Does it make a difference? Evaluating professional development. *Educational Leadership*, 59(6), 45–51.

Hashmi, K. (1999). *You and Me, Murrawee*. Hawthorn: Penguin.

Jones, E. (2012). The emergence of emergent curriculum. *YC Young Children*, 67(2), 66–8.

MCEETYA (Ministerial Council on Education, Employment, Training and Youth Affairs). (2008). *Melbourne Declaration on Educational Goals for Young Australians*. Retrieved from: http://www.curriculum.edu.au/verve/_resources/National_Declaration_on_the_Educational_Goals_for_Young_Australians.pdf.

McTighe, J. & Thomas, R. S. (2003). Backward design for forward action. *Educational Leadership*, 60(5), 52–5.

Parker, W. (2008). *Social Studies in Elementary Education*. New York: Allyn & Bacon.

Pelo, A. (2009). A pedagogy for ecology. *Rethinking Schools*, 23(4), 30–5.

Penguin Random House. (2018). The Lorax project in the classroom. Retrieved from: http://www.seussville.com/Educators/lorax_classroom/educatorlorax_discuss.php.

Reynolds, R. (2012). *Teaching History, Geography and SOSE in the Primary School*. Melbourne: Oxford University Press.

Sisson, J. (2016). Emergent curriculum in practice recorded. Retrieved from: https://vimeo.com/170729486.

Sisson, J. & Whitington, V. (2017). *Pedagogical Documentation: A South Australian perspective*. Thebarton, SA: Gowrie South Australia.

Stacey, S. (2008). *Emergent Curriculum in Early Childhood Settings: From theory to practice*. St Paul, MN: Redleaf Press.

Vars, G.F. & Beane, J.A. (2000). *Integrative Curriculum in a Standards-based World*. Champaign, IL: ERIC Clearinghouse on Elementary and Early Childhood Education.

Wiggins, G. & McTighe, J. (1998). *Understanding by Design*. Alexandria, VA: ASCD.

——(2001). What is backward design? In *Understanding by Design*. Upper Saddle River, NJ: Merrill Prentice Hall, pp. 7–19.

——(2011). *The Understanding by Design Guide to Creating High-Quality Units*. Alexandria, VA: ASCD.

Wraga, W.G. (2009). Toward a connected core curriculum. *Educational Horizons*, 87(2), 88–96.

# HASS IN THE EARLY YEARS: CONNECTING THE EARLY YEARS LEARNING FRAMEWORK AND THE AUSTRALIAN CURRICULUM

**3**

*Helen Ovsienko*

## Learning objectives

After reading this chapter, you should be able to:

- understand the place of Humanities and Social Sciences (HASS) learning in early years settings (0–5 years)
- articulate the differences between the Early Years Learning Framework (EYLF) and the Australian Curriculum
- identify the connections and continuities between the EYLF and the Australian Curriculum
- explain the potential of pedagogic approaches in the junior primary years that build on the foundations for learning developed in early years settings.

## INTRODUCTION

At graduation, early childhood teachers in Australia are qualified to teach children from birth through to eight years of age. This means they must be prepared to work across different settings: the early education and care setting (0–5 years); and the junior primary years of the formal school setting. A significant challenge is the need to be knowledgeable about, and comfortable working with, different curriculum framework documents. *Belonging, Being and Becoming: The Early Years Learning Framework for Australia* (EYLF) (DEEWR 2009) informs practice in early education and care settings, while the Australian Curriculum (ACARA 2018a) models the curriculum in the F–10 formal schooling years.

Educators have identified a lack of continuity between the two documents (Grieshaber & Shearer 2013; Hunkin 2014); for example, in the transition from play-based to more structured pedagogic approaches. It is not surprising that preservice teachers often struggle to consolidate their learning and practice when attempting to develop a cohesive pedagogical approach across the two sectors.

This chapter will provide a contextual foundation for teaching and learning in HASS, beginning with a broad discussion of the HASS curriculum in the early years of primary schooling, considered through the lens of the EYLF. Similarities and differences between the two curriculum documents will then be addressed. Finally, it will be argued that pedagogical practice, specifically inquiry-based learning rather than content-based learning, is the best vehicle for ensuring effective connections between the foundations for learning developed in the early years settings and transition to the first years of formal schooling.

# FOUNDATIONS UNDERPINNING BOTH THE EYLF AND THE AUSTRALIAN CURRICULUM

A complexity in comparing similarities and differences between these documents is that the key terms are contested, understood and used differently by various educators and researchers (for a detailed discussion on the contested meanings of curriculum, see Print 1993). When discussing the differences between the EYLF and Australian Curriculum, the term 'curriculum' is often used to describe what this chapter presents as a model (Children's Services Central 2010). For the purpose of clarification, this chapter will use the following terminology:

- curriculum: the subject matter to be taught (the most common understanding)

- **framework**: a set of guidelines or principles that support learning (think of a framework or scaffolding supporting building construction)

- **model**: a plan for learning, generally including the knowledge to be taught, learning activities and then evaluating or assessing the learning (think of a detailed house plan).

**framework**: a set of guidelines or principles that support learning

**model**: a plan for learning, generally including the knowledge to be taught, learning activities and then evaluating or assessing the learning

The EYLF is a framework for learning, while the Australian Curriculum is often seen as being a much more prescriptive model. Yet both documents are underpinned by the *Melbourne Declaration on Educational Goals for Young Australians* (Melbourne Declaration; MCEETYA 2008), in particular:

- Goal 1: Australian schooling promotes equity and excellence

- Goal 2: All young Australians become successful learners, confident and creative individuals, and active and informed citizens.

These goals are clearly **aspirational**, aiming to improve outcomes for both the individual learner and society more broadly. **Continuity** between the early learning and primary sectors does not mean that each must offer identical curriculum and pedagogy; however, it does imply consistency between early learning and formal schooling experiences (Petriwskyj 2014).

**aspirational**: desiring higher or better outcomes; in terms of education, this relates to better educational outcomes in order to improve self and society

**continuity**: a sense of similarity in practice, not necessarily identical but with enough links to ensure learners feel supported and scaffolded

A thoughtful consideration of the EYLF and Australian Curriculum makes clear the similarities, particularly between the EYLF and the cross-curriculum priorities and to a lesser extent the general capabilities of the curriculum. The potential for continuity also exists in terms of the pedagogic approaches of the educator.

## BLOCKED STORMWATER DRAIN

After a good deal of preparation, learners in the Butterfly Room at the Mountain View Play to Learn Centre headed off on their first excursion. They walked to the local greengrocer, where they bought fruit to be made into a fruit salad for their afternoon tea. Their preparation included learning about how to get to the shop and what they might see on the way, as well as discussing what fruit they preferred and, importantly, what was expected in terms of behaviour.

As they walked, the children pointed out different sights that caught their attention and discussion was lively. This was interrupted by a loud shout of 'Oh, no!' from four-year-old Lulu, who had come to an abrupt stop, pointing to a stormwater drain that was blocked by leaves and debris after recent rains. 'Look at all the rubbish!' she cried. 'Who is going to clean this up? What about all the little creatures? They will die and when you die you can't come back! This needs to be cleaned up! Who is going to clean it all up?' As one of the carers with the group put it, 'Lulu went full eco-warrior on us and we had to distract her to get the group focused and moving again.'

**Reflection**

How does this scenario connect to the HASS strands? What potential learning could come from this experience? While the educators had to ensure the excursion stayed on track, what could they have done differently, rather than 'distracting' Lulu?

Consider the prior understanding Lulu shows here. Where might this learning have come from, and are all learners of this age group likely to have similar levels of understanding?

# LOCATING HASS EDUCATION IN THE EVERYDAY

It is essential to recognise the importance of early childhood education as a time when children learn a great deal about the world around them through exploration and discovery. This can be understood as learning through play, which will be addressed in later chapters. This learning must be valued in its own right, rather than simply being seen as preparation for the 'serious' or 'real' learning in the primary years (VCAA 2008).

## Drawing on learners' natural curiosity

The *Australian Curriculum: HASS* learning area provides a structured way for learning about and understanding the world, including the social structures of which learners are a part. The HASS rationale stresses that:

> In a world that is increasingly culturally diverse and dynamically interconnected, it is important that students come to understand their world, past and present, and develop a capacity to respond to challenges, now and in the future, in innovative, informed, personal and collective ways. (ACARA 2018e)

Inquiry learning offers an opportunity to harness learners' curiosity and imagination by drawing on the foundation of their existing knowledge and experiences. Such learning is situated in the everyday and its value should not be underestimated.

In the early years learning context, while there is no formal HASS curriculum, much of the learning aligns with the HASS learning area; that is, learners' immediate environment and the people around them, as well as their varied interests, as demonstrated in the vignette above. Most importantly, it provides room for children's voices, by incorporating their interests, ideas and prior learning.

## Structure of the HASS curriculum

The focus in the HASS curriculum in the early years of primary schooling is on the learner's personal contexts, namely family (History) and place, or location (Geography) (ACARA 2018e). This builds on children's experiences within their preschool contexts, so the challenge is to ensure a greater depth of understanding in the Foundation to Year 2 curriculum. As learners progress through the years of formal schooling, the context broadens in depth, context and complexity, adding Civics and Citizenship from Year 3 and Economics and Business in Year 5, to eventually addressing global contexts and multiple perspectives.

## Past, present and a futures orientation

The past is studied from the earliest school years in order to help learners understand the present and develop a futures orientation. Human behaviour is investigated, as is human interaction in diverse social, cultural, environmental, economic and political contexts (ACARA 2018d). While the nature of learning in HASS is situated in the everyday context, when addressed properly it has the potential to incorporate a diverse range of experiences and possibilities, which ensures that all learners are included and develop the ability to recognise multiple perspectives and the way they interrelate.

A key focus of the HASS rationale is empowering learners to shape change by developing the skills and capabilities that will enable them to make informed decisions together with the capacity to face challenges and solve problems within the increasing diversity and complexity of the world as they grow to adulthood (ACARA 2018e).

Drawing on learners' own experiences and understandings, then acknowledging differences and similarities between them, creates the ideal opening for incorporating cross-curriculum priorities or general capabilities – for example, intercultural understanding or the foundations of Aboriginal and Torres Strait Islander histories and cultures – depending on the makeup of the class. In this manner, learners' experiences and understandings are drawn on to create the foundations for deep and authentic learning with a respect for social, cultural and religious diversity.

What possibilities for learning about HASS in learners' everyday experiences can you think of, particularly in early learning settings? What strategies can you think of to help ensure you (a) recognise and (b) document learning in both early educational and primary contexts?

Reflection

# DIFFERENCES BETWEEN THE EYLF AND AUSTRALIAN CURRICULUM APPROACHES

While their foundation on the goals of the Melbourne Declaration means that both the EYLF and Australian Curriculum agree at policy level, there are significant differences in their approaches to framing learning and the associated outcomes. This will potentially result in varied experiences of learning as well as differences in the way educators approach their practice.

## EYLF

As the title makes clear, the EYLF is a framework for learning that outlines principles, practices and outcomes to guide and support learning. It scaffolds, or frames, the way educators think about and interact with children and their families, understanding how children learn while recognising their capabilities. Educators are then free to make choices regarding the actual content, or curriculum, to be taught. Ideally, the learning will be based on, and informed by, the children's own interests. This creates the opportunity for dynamic, engaging and exciting learning.

The *Educators' Guide to the Early Years Learning Framework for Australia* (DEEWR 2010, p. 3) makes this clear distinction:

> When starting to use the Framework remember that it is just that – a framework. It is not a syllabus, not a program, not a curriculum, not a model, not an assessment tool, not a detailed description of everything children will learn. It is a framework of principles, practices and outcomes with which to build your curriculum.

The EYLF is structured around three interrelated elements: principles, practices and outcomes, as outlined in Table 3.1.

| TABLE 3.1 THE STRUCTURE OF THE EYLF: BELONGING, BEING AND BECOMING | | |
|---|---|---|
| **Principles** | **Practices** | **Learning outcomes** |
| • Secure, respectful and reciprocal relationships<br>• Partnerships<br>• High expectations and equity<br>• Respect for diversity<br>• Ongoing learning and reflective practices | • Holistic approaches<br>• Responsiveness to children<br>• Learning through play<br>• Intentional teaching<br>• Learning environments<br>• Cultural competence<br>• Continuity of learning and transitions<br>• Assessment for learning | • Children have a strong sense of identity<br>• Children are connected with and contribute to their world<br>• Children have a strong sense of wellbeing<br>• Children are confident and involved learners<br>• Children are effective communicators |

Source: DEEWR 2009

The learning outcomes include dispositions towards learning that underpin engagement, and the knowledge, skills and understandings that are essential foundations for future learning success.

## Australian Curriculum

The formalised structure of the Australian Curriculum can be seen as a model. It models learning by detailing content – that is, what will be learnt – presented as a continuum of learning across the school years. In HASS, inquiry-based learning is the expected teaching methodology. Learners are then formally assessed against expected outcomes via the achievement standards. However, futures-oriented 21st-century learning cannot fit neatly into a curriculum solely focused on and organised by learning areas or subject disciplines. To meet the needs of a transformative education, the Australian Curriculum has four major components (see also Chapter 2):

1. curriculum content – learning area knowledge, skills and understandings
2. general capabilities – sets of skills, behaviours and dispositions that apply across subject-based content
3. cross-curriculum priorities – selected because they represent key society issues and opportunities
4. achievement standards – the standards, or benchmarks, students are typically able to meet at each stage of learning.

Table 3.2 summarises key differences between the EYLF and the Australian Curriculum in terms of learning, content, pedagogy, assessment and reporting.

| TABLE 3.2 | COMPARING THE EYLF AND THE AUSTRALIAN CURRICULUM | |
|---|---|---|
| | **EYLF** | **Australian Curriculum** |
| Learning | Learning framework | Subject based, with cross-curriculum priorities and general capabilities interwoven to enrich and add depth. |
| Content | Educators have choice, informed by children's interests and input | Prescribed, although educators have some discretion |
| Pedagogy | Educators choose<br>Play based<br>Intentional teaching required | Educators choose but must focus on outcomes in terms of achievement standards |
| Assessment | Learning outcomes | Achievement standards |
| Reporting | Ongoing<br>Learning is documented against learning outcomes but not graded | Report twice yearly with an A–E grade against every subject<br>Certification on completion of schooling |

Source: adapted from Grieshaber & Shearer 2013

## Pedagogy

As outlined above, educators seemingly have more autonomy in developing their program or curriculum in early years settings. They can choose content, guided by learners' interests, to ensure it is appropriate and stimulates engagement and curiosity. A play-based pedagogy is stipulated, building on children's interests and play behaviours; however, educators must ensure that intentional teaching is implemented.

## Assessment

Assessment in the early years is informal and ongoing. While children's content learning is documented, there is an equal consideration given to the 'distance travelled', or the amount of learning taking place (DEEWR 2010, p. 17).

While ongoing formative and summative assessments take place within internal school contexts, in the primary years learning is formally assessed and reported on twice yearly. Student learning is rated using an A–E scale – a stark difference from that in early years settings.

**Reflection** A five-year-old child may be in an early childhood setting, which caters for developing dispositions for learning, but another may be in their first year of primary school, which has clearly defined expectations for learning outcomes in various learning areas.

- Will this mean entirely different learning experiences for each child?
- Do you think the learning experiences of one setting are richer than the other? Do you consider the learning in one setting to be more meaningful than the other?
- What strategies might educators implement to ensure continuity of practice and/or pedagogy?

# SIMILARITIES BETWEEN THE EYLF AND AUSTRALIAN CURRICULUM APPROACHES

## Underpinnings: goals of the Melbourne Declaration

Both the Australian Curriculum and the EYLF are underpinned by the Melbourne Declaration's commitment to quality in education and improved outcomes for all learners. As noted previously, these goals are clearly aspirational, aiming to improve outcomes for both the individual learner and society more broadly. Connor (2011, p. 4) echoes these aims:

> As a nation Australia values the central role of education in building a democratic, equitable and just society – a society that is prosperous, cohesive and culturally diverse, and that values Australia's Indigenous cultures as a key part of the nation's history, present and future.

## Building on the EYLF

The Australian Curriculum acknowledges that it builds on the foundations of the learning outcomes in the EYLF to establish effective learning strategies (ACARA 2018b). Connor (2011) found that the general capabilities most clearly link to the EYLF learning outcomes, but that there are also similar learning emphases between the two documents.

Table 3.3 provides an overview of similarities across the EYLF, the Melbourne Declaration and the Australian Curriculum. For greatest relevance for this chapter, the Australian Curriculum reference is limited to the Foundation year and Year 1, although links can be identified in other year levels.

Due to limitations of space, the descriptions are brief, but can be examined in more detail by reference to the original sources. Many more links could be made to the general capabilities, and those that have been included are examples demonstrating their relevance. The Australian Curriculum provides symbols under each content descriptor, both for knowledge and understanding, and inquiry and skills, which provide far more detail in a focused manner.

## EDUCATOR TIP

Ensuring the cross-curriculum priorities and general capabilities are included in your planning may seem complex. However, the Australian Curriculum provides considerable scaffolding for this. If you work closely with the document, you will cover the necessary elements.

Is it necessary to ensure you focus on all the cross-curriculum priorities and general capabilities for each content descriptor in your planning? If so, is there a danger that the content will become too complex? If not, how will you decide which to choose?

Reflection

### Assessment

Both the EYLF and Australian Curriculum confirm the importance of assessment for learning, and for diagnostic purposes in order to identify children who may need additional support to achieve expected or desired outcomes (refer also to Chapter 22).

Connor (2011) found both documents agree that the key purposes for assessment are to:

- plan for learning
- communicate about progress
- determine what might be impeding progress
- identify children who might need additional support
- evaluate the effectiveness of teaching programs
- reflect on pedagogy that will suit the context and students.

**TABLE 3.3** RELATIONSHIP BETWEEN THE MELBOURNE DECLARATION, EYLF AND AUSTRALIAN CURRICULUM

| Melbourne Declaration | EYLF | HASS Curriculum (ACARA) | General capabilities (ACARA) | Cross-curriculum priorities (ACARA) |
|---|---|---|---|---|
| **Goal 1: Promoting equity and excellence:** Ensure that schooling contributes to a socially cohesive society that respects and appreciates cultural, social and religious diversity.<br><br>**Goal 2: Confident individuals:** [Children] have a sense of self-worth, self-awareness and personal identity that enables them to manage their emotional, mental, spiritual and physical wellbeing. | **Learning outcome 1:** Children have a strong sense of identity<br><br>**Learning outcome 2:** Children are connected with and contribute to their world<br><br>**Learning outcome 3:** Children have a strong sense of wellbeing<br><br>**Learning outcome 4:** Children are confident and involved learners<br><br>**Learning outcome 5:** Children are effective communicators | **HASS Foundation year: 'My personal world'**<br>Inquiry questions:<br>• Why are some places and events special and how do we know?<br>• Who am I, where do I live and who came before me?<br><br>Children develop understanding of their personal worlds, including:<br>• their personal and family histories<br>• the places they and their families live in and belong to<br>• representation of places<br>• sources of information including stories from family members and different cultures. | **Critical and creative thinking:** Students are encouraged to be curious and imaginative and to consider multiple perspectives about issues and events. Students learn to pose questions and think logically and deeply.<br><br>**Personal and social capability:** Students' personal and social capability is enhanced as they learn to understand themselves and others more fully, and to manage their relationships, lives, learning and work effectively.<br><br>**Ethical understanding:** Students develop ethical understanding as they learn to recognise and understand matters of ethical concerns, make reasoned judgements and, in so doing, develop a personal ethical framework. Students become aware of their own roles, rights and responsibilities as participants in their social, economic and natural world. | **Sustainability:** Futures key concept … aimed at building the capacities for thinking and acting in ways that are necessary to create a more sustainable future.<br><br>**Aboriginal and Torres Strait Islander histories and cultures:** To ensure that all young Australians … gain a deeper understanding and appreciation of Aboriginal and Torres Strait Islander histories and cultures.<br><br>**Asia and Australia's engagement with Asia:** To reflect on the importance of young people knowing about Asia and Australia's engagement with Asia. |

**Goal 2: Successful learners:**
- develop their capacity to learn and play an active role in their own learning
- are able to think deeply and logically, and obtain and evaluate evidence in a disciplined way.

**Goal 2: Confident and creative individuals:**
- develop personal values and attributes such as honesty, resilience, empathy and respect for others
- have a sense of self-worth, self-awareness and personal identity that enables them to manage their emotional, mental, spiritual and physical wellbeing
- are well prepared for their potential life roles as family, community and workforce members.

**Goal 2: Active and informed citizens:**
- appreciate Australia's social, cultural, linguistic and religious diversity, and have an understanding of Australia's system of government, history and culture

**Learning outcome 1:** Children have a strong sense of identity

**Learning outcome 2:** Children are connected with and contribute to their world

**Learning outcome 3:** Children have a strong sense of wellbeing

**Learning outcome 4:** Children are confident and involved learners

**Learning outcome 5:** Children are effective communicators

**HASS Year 1: 'How my world is different from the past and can change in the future'**
Inquiry questions:
- How has family life and the place we live in changed over time?
- What events, activities and places do I care about? Why?

Students examine and investigate:
- how changes occur over time in relation to themselves, their families and the places they and others belong to
- daily family life; how it is similar and different to previous generations
- their place (location) and other places, their natural, managed and constructed features and the activities located in them
- future events and personal milestones
- seasons and weather, and how different groups describe them
- citizenship, through family roles and the ways people care for places.

**Critical and creative thinking:** Developed as students investigate historical and geographical concepts and ideas, clarifying questions and interpreting the past. They are encouraged to be curious and imaginative and to think deeply.

**Personal and social capability:** Students develop an appreciation of the insights and perspectives of others, past and present; and an understanding of what informs their personal identity and sense of belonging, including place and their cultural and national heritage. They are encouraged to develop personal and interpersonal skills, behaviours and dispositions that enable communication, empathy, teamwork, negotiation and conflict resolution.

**Ethical understanding:** Students investigate the ways that diverse values and principles have influenced human activity.

**Sustainability:** Futures key concept … aimed at building the capacities for thinking and acting in ways that are necessary to create a more sustainable future.

**Aboriginal and Torres Strait Islander histories and cultures:** To ensure that all young Australians … gain a deeper understanding and appreciation of Aboriginal and Torres Strait Islander histories and cultures.

**Asia and Australia's engagement with Asia:** To reflect the importance of young people knowing about Asia and Australia's engagement with Asia.

*Each of the cross-curriculum priorities is relevant across both years. How the educator incorporates these in response to the local context may vary.

**TABLE 3.3** (CONT.)

| Melbourne Declaration | EYLF | HASS Curriculum (ACARA) | General capabilities (ACARA) | Cross-curriculum priorities (ACARA) |
|---|---|---|---|---|
| • understand and acknowledge the value of Indigenous cultures<br>• are committed to national values of democracy, equity and justice<br>• are responsible global and local citizens. | | | Students develop informed, ethical values and attitudes as they explore different perspectives, ambiguities and ethical considerations related to social and environmental issues. Students become aware of their own roles, rights and responsibilities as participants in their social, economic and natural world. | |

Source: adapted from Connor 2011

## Connecting pedagogies

While the goal of teaching is always to progressively deepen learners' understanding, the Australian Curriculum does not mandate pedagogy. This means that primary school educators can use their professional judgement and discretion in how to best deliver the curriculum in ways that are appropriate to the age of their learners and likely to pique their interest and generate engagement. This is of prime importance for educators in the early years of primary school, as it provides the opportunity to ensure continuity of practice and teaching methodologies.

The Australian Curriculum is organised by discipline, although *The Shape of the Curriculum: Version 4.0* (ACARA 2012, p. 22) stresses that 'disciplines are interconnected, dynamic and growing' and ideally 'should allow for **cross-disciplinary learning** to broaden and enrich each student's learning'. The general capabilities and cross-curriculum priorities also reflect the interconnected nature of learning through the Australian Curriculum.

**cross-disciplinary learning:** also referred to as thematic learning, this is an approach that includes multiple learning areas in curriculum design centred around a particular theme or topic

A cross-disciplinary approach bears a stronger resemblance to the holistic approach of the EYLF and opportunities for continuity; it also offers the potential to maximise the engagement of all learners through the incorporation of wider ranges of potential interests.

The flexibility of the Australian Curriculum provides the opportunity to apply key principles and practices as articulated in the EYLF, including:

- holistic approaches (through cross-disciplinary learning and incorporating the cross-curriculum priorities and general capabilities)
- ongoing learning and reflective practices (assessment and data collection)
- responsiveness to learners and contexts
- play-based learning
- intentional teaching to deepen knowledge, skills and understanding (Connor 2011).

Play-based learning is not necessarily limited to early years settings and, increasingly, research is evidencing the benefits of this pedagogy in the primary school years (Hunkin 2014), creating a potential continuity (refer to Chapter 13). Although there is often a perception that the more formal setting may challenge opportunities for play-based learning, this type of learning offers many potential benefits and it is important for educators to keep abreast of research findings in this area.

# INQUIRY LEARNING

What it means to learn has changed over recent decades and it is often maintained that the needs of the 21st-century learner are distinctly different from those of earlier generations. While somewhat dated, the quote from Simon (1996, cited in National Research Council 2000, p. 5) that 'the meaning of "knowing" has shifted from being able to remember and repeat information to being able to find and use it' summarises this shift.

As Touhill (2012) asserts, anyone who comes into contact with young children knows that they love to ask questions as a way of learning about the world around them, and this tendency is harnessed in powerful ways through inquiry learning. A large body of research has identified many benefits of inquiry learning, and this approach has been implemented in both the EYLF and the Australian Curriculum. The EYLF highlights the importance of inquiry learning in Outcome 4, 'children are confident and involved learners', through developing 'a range of skills and processes such as problem solving, inquiry, experimentation, hypothesising, researching and investigating' (DEEWR 2009, p. 35), while the HASS curriculum incorporates inquiry learning as a tool to build the knowledge and understanding strand (ACARA 2018c).

## Curriculum strands: HASS

As discussed in Chapter 2, the HASS curriculum is explicitly structured into two strands: knowledge and understanding, which refers to content knowledge, and inquiry and skills, which refers to processes of learning. Research demonstrates that inquiry learning has become a standard approach in educational policy, curriculum and practice (Kidman & Casinader 2017, p. vii), yet the application of inquiry learning is not always well understood or well practised.

### Process and content

Inquiry learning places as much emphasis on the process of inquiry as it does on the content, and therefore both strands should be intertwined throughout the learning process. Figure 2.2 provides an overview of the inquiry and skills strand in HASS education.

**Reflection**

At this stage of your understanding, how do you envision inquiry learning in both the early years and early primary learning settings? How does your experience of schooling inform your ideas about how you should teach HASS? What, if any, is your experience of inquiry learning? For example, do you remember being asked to create 'projects' in SOSE (or whichever version of HASS you were taught at school)? Does this, in your opinion, constitute inquiry learning?

Hoepper (2017) posits that all inquiry learning revolves around three key stages:

1. what we want to find out
2. finding out
3. what to do with what we have found.

The skills in the HASS curriculum can be matched with these stages, and educators may find it useful to keep these three broad stages in mind when planning for inquiry learning. As discussed in Chapter 11, there are many different models of inquiry learning available to educators, highlighting its flexibility. Ultimately, however, the models work around the three key stages identified above. They do not need to be followed in a lock-step process and while inquiry learning would generally go through the entire cycle, at times the learning may only draw on two or three skills of the Australian Curriculum.

## EDUCATOR TIP

Remember, it is often hard to let go of the idea of teaching being about transmitting sanctioned knowledge, which inevitably raises questions of 'what knowledge?' and 'whose knowledge?' Always consider who has sanctioned the knowledge and what that means for diverse groups of learners.

# EMERGENT CURRICULUM

Emergent curriculum is a form of inquiry learning and is used extensively in early learning settings (ACECQA 2016). Educators using an emergent curriculum for planning listen to children and observe their activities and ideas, and respond in ways that offer developmentally appropriate opportunities to further learning. It is an ideal way to introduce both information and communication technology (ICT) and print materials as part of the inquiry.

The following vignette describes a sensitive and meaningful learning opportunity using emergent curriculum planning.

## THE BUTTERFLY ROOM

Educators from the Butterfly Room at the Mountain View Play to Learn Centre heard several discussions among the children concerning death. Amelia had come to class one day upset about the death of her pet rabbit. Lulu contributed a story about her pet goldfish dying, and stated, 'It's OK, you can just get another one.' Over the next weeks, the topic came up several times. Oliver then shared that his grandfather was very ill and might die. The children were overheard discussing what happens when someone dies, with contributions ranging from 'you go to Heaven to be with Jesus' through to 'you get put in a hole in the ground and that's it'.

Using emergent curriculum planning, the educators developed an inquiry learning program that lasted a month. During this period, Oliver's grandfather passed away. Although his family provided strong support, Oliver missed his grandfather dreadfully.

As part of this program, the class read *Lifetimes: The beautiful way to explain death to children* (Mellonie & Ingpen 1983), which introduced the idea of a lifetime, explaining beginnings and endings, several times over the course of the inquiry. The children's ideas and questions were investigated using developmentally appropriate internet sites previously sourced by the educators and shared on the smartboard. These provided an opportunity for deep discussion and questioning. Using the idea of lifetimes for all living creatures enabled them to talk openly about death as a part of the cycle of life, from leaves to animals to humans.

The unit culminated with the story *Rabbityness* (Empson 2012), which explains loss as a big 'hole' in the other rabbits' lives. The children shared their thoughts, feelings and experiences with loss. Oliver related very strongly to this book and talked about the things he loved doing with his grandfather, including feeding birds and gardening. Together, educators and children decided to do what the rabbits in the book did: celebrate memories of loved ones. To this end, they completed the inquiry learning by planting flowering shrubs in the garden, in memory of both Oliver's grandfather and others they had lost.

SPOTLIGHT ON HASS EDUCATION

## Educator role in inquiry learning

As the above vignette demonstrates, inquiry learning provides room for learners' 'voice'. The children were actively involved in constructing new understandings through hands-on experiences, research, processing and communicating their understandings in various ways. The educators were positioned as 'coaches' or 'facilitators' in a **learner-centred learning** (or **learner-centred pedagogy**) process. However, it is important to note that inquiry learning cannot be a haphazard process. In the vignette described above, careful planning was based on strong theoretical knowledge of the children's development as well as a pedagogic understanding. It was inquiry based, with the children's experiences being part of the information or 'data' gathered and intentional teaching was applied.

**learner-centred learning (learner-centred pedagogy):** the understanding that students' own interests should drive inquiry, although guided by the educator

The educators' content knowledge and expertise in effective inquiry-based teaching is as important as the focus on learner-driven inquiry (Kidman & Casinader 2017).

Grief is a very hard experience, and could have been seen as too difficult or too controversial to address. However, this experience had the happy outcome of introducing the learners to death and loss in a very gentle manner, which is likely to be an important life skill.

# CONCLUSION

While many early childhood preservice teachers initially struggle to see where the HASS curriculum fits within early learning contexts, this chapter has made clear that HASS is a very natural fit with the EYLF. While the perception of lack of continuity between the EYLF and Australian Curriculum is justified in some aspects, there are also clear alignments and avenues for overcoming discontinuity through pedagogy and thoughtful planning that are learner-centred and co-constructed.

The HASS curriculum is a structured way of learning about the world, and it is precisely this learning that is the focus within early years settings, with the Australian Curriculum building on the foundations of learning in the EYLF.

## REVIEW QUESTIONS

1. What are some key similarities between the EYLF and the Australian Curriculum?
2. What are some key differences between the EYLF and the Australian Curriculum?
3. How does the Melbourne Declaration position learning in the current social context?
4. Name at least four key characteristics of inquiry learning.
5. What does the EYLF have in common with the Foundation and Year 1 content of the Australian Curriculum?

## LEARNING EXTENSION

Reread the excursion scenario recounted earlier in this chapter, and think about how you could use Lulu's knowledge and interest in order to develop an inquiry-based learning plan for use in an early learning centre.

Ensure that you consider the following questions:

- How will you ensure that the learners are on a relatively equal footing in terms of existing knowledge?

- What will you do to generate and maintain student interest in the topic?

- While questions will ideally be developed by the learners themselves, how will you stimulate discussion and questioning? How will you ensure that the class has enough collective knowledge in order to be able to ask further questions? What are some activities, prompting questions or standby questions you could have on hand?

- What are some potential social actions learners could carry out, whereby students are taking meaningful action in order for the learning to have a purpose? How will you guide them to actions that are practical and doable for their age group?

## REFERENCES

ACARA (Australian Curriculum, Assessment and Reporting Authority). (2012). *The Shape of the Australian Curriculum: Version 4.0*. Retrieved from: https://acaraweb.blob.core.windows.net/resources/The_Shape_of_the_Australian_Curriculum_v4.pdf.

——(2018a). *Australian Curriculum: F-10, v8.3*. Retrieved from: https://www.australiancurriculum.edu.au.

——(2018b). *Australian Curriculum: F-10, v8.3*. Learning F-2. Retrieved from: https://www.australiancurriculum.edu.au/f-10-curriculum/learning-f-2.

——(2018c). *Australian Curriculum: Humanities and Social Sciences F-10, v8.3*. Retrieved from: https://www.australiancurriculum.edu.au/f-10-curriculum/humanities-and-social-sciences/hass.

——(2018d). *Australian Curriculum: Humanities and Social Sciences F-10, v8.3*. Introduction. Retrieved from: https://www.australiancurriculum.edu.au/f-10-curriculum/humanities-and-social-sciences/introduction.

——(2018e). *Australian Curriculum: Humanities and Social Sciences F-10, v8.3*. Rationale. Retrieved from: https://www.australiancurriculum.edu.au/f-10-curriculum/humanities-and-social-sciences/hass/rationale.

ASECQA (Australian Children's Education & Care Quality Authority). (2016). Emergent curriculum . . . doesn't mean no need to plan. Retrieved from: https://wehearyou.acecqa.gov.au/2016/09/07/emergent-curriculum-doesnt-mean-no-need-to-plan.

Children's Services Central (CSCentral). (2010). Belonging, Being and Becoming: What is the difference between a 'framework' and a 'curriculum'? Retrieved from: https://www.youtube.com/watch?v=yPvAv3FQ8cM.

Connor, J. (2011). *Foundations for Learning: Relationships between the Early Years Learning Framework and the Australian Curriculum*. Retrieved from: http://foundationinquirylearning.global2.vic.edu.au/files/2013/06/ECA_ACARA_Foundations_Paper-2cq59mi.pdf.

DEEWR (Department of Education, Employment and Workplace Relations). (2009). *Belonging, Being and Becoming: The Early Years Learning Framework for Australia*. Canberra: DEEWR.

——(2010). *Educators Belonging, Being, Becoming: Educators' Guide to the Early Years Learning Framework for Australia*. Canberra: DEEWR.

Empson, J. (2012). *Rabbityness*. Swindon: Children's Play International.

Grieshaber, S. & Shearer, A. (2013). Continuity? The early years learning framework and the Australian curriculum. *Every Child*, 19(4), 16–17.

Hoepper, B. (2017). Planning for critical inquiry. In R. Gilbert & B. Hoepper, eds, *Teaching Humanities and Social Sciences*, 6th edn. Melbourne: Cengage Learning, pp. 50–72.

Hunkin, E. (2014). 'We're offering true play-based learning': Teacher perspectives on educational dis/continuity in the early years. *Australasian Journal of Early Childhood*, 39(2), 30–5.

Kidman, G. & Casinader, N. (2017). *Inquiry-Based Teaching and Learning Across Disciplines: Comparative theory and practice in schools*. London: Palgrave Macmillan.

MCEETYA (Ministerial Council on Education, Employment, Training and Youth Affairs). (2008). *Melbourne Declaration on Educational Goals for Young Australians*. Retrieved from: http://www.curriculum.edu.au/verve/_resources/National_Declaration_on_the_Educational_Goals_for_Young_Australians.pdf.

Mellonie, B. & Ingpen, R. (1983). *Lifetimes: The beautiful way to explain death to children*. New York: Bantam Doubleday.

National Research Council. (2000). *How People Learn: Brain, mind, experience and school*. Washington, DC: National Academy Press.

Petriwskyj, A. (2014). Early years national curriculum documents: Revisiting inclusive education. *Curriculum Perspectives*, 34(1), 22–8.

Print, M. (1993). Introducing curriculum. In *Curriculum Development and Design*. Sydney: Allen & Unwin, pp. 1–24.

Touhill, L. (2012). Inquiry Based Learning, National Quality Standard Professional Learning Program. *e-Newsletter*, no. 45. Retrieved from: http://www.earlychildhoodaustralia.org.au/nqsplp/wp-content/uploads/2012/10/NQS_PLP_E-Newsletter_No45.pdf.

VCAA (Victorian Curriculum and Assessment Authority). (2008). *Analysis of Curriculum/Learning Frameworks for the Early Years (Birth to Age 8)*. Melbourne: VCAA.

# HUMANITIES AND SOCIAL SCIENCES IN THE EARLY CHILDHOOD AND PRIMARY YEARS

**4**

*Mallihai Tambyah, Deborah Green and Deborah Price*

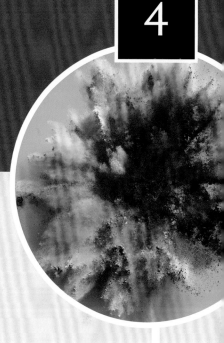

## Learning objectives

After reading this chapter, you should be able to:

- describe the nature and purpose of Humanities and Social Sciences (HASS) education in the early childhood and primary years
- understand and apply play-based and inquiry-based pedagogical approaches within HASS early childhood and primary years learning experiences
- demonstrate understanding of the role of disciplinary knowledge and skills in HASS
- justify the need to invite debate and multiple perspectives of HASS concepts.

## INTRODUCTION

Considering the significance of the HASS learning area, it is important that learners are engaged as early as possible. Children explore historical and geographical **concepts** of place, care/sustainability, significance, change and continuity before they even reach school. Upon entering school, as discussed in Chapter 3, further intradisciplinary and interdisciplinary concepts are developed and refined. Thus, early in young people's lives, educators aspire to introduce children to the humanities; that is, the study of what in essence makes us human. The question arises, what does make us human?

> **concepts:** the key ideas that collectively underpin the substantive and procedural knowledge in a discipline such as Geography, Business and Economics, or Civics and Citizenship

This is a philosophical question that can provide direction and purpose for studying and teaching HASS. At his trial for alleged corruption of young people by philosophising, the Greek philosopher Socrates argued that, 'an unexamined life is not worth living' (Guthrie 1975). According to the Australian philosopher Raimon Gaita, Socrates actually meant that 'our humanity … is not given to us by virtue of belonging to a biological species; it is something we must rise to' (Gaita 2014). HASS educators play an important role in nurturing this aspiration by engaging learners in HASS throughout their educational journey. Pedagogies that are play-based and/or inquiry-based are central to achieving this as they support learning experiences that engage early and primary years learners with the core content and skills in HASS.

This chapter explores the nature of HASS learning and pedagogy in the early childhood and primary years; considers the role of the social science disciplines of knowledge and skills; and presents the importance of engaging learners in debates to develop respect for multiple perspectives. The significance of maintaining the integrity of discipline-based ways of 'knowing' and 'doing' to deliver a deeper understanding of key HASS topics and issues are also discussed.

# NATURE AND PURPOSE OF HASS LEARNING IN THE EARLY CHILDHOOD AND PRIMARY YEARS

HASS educators have the opportunity to harness children's natural curiosity and wonder about the wider world and to give context and meaning to learning in an educational setting. Children live in a globalised world that is increasingly more complex, mobile and interconnected. Therefore, from the outset of their educational journey in the early years, children need learning experiences that develop their HASS knowledge and skills to support them in making meaning of the world around them in ways that are appropriate to their cognitive and social development. In the early years, learners focus on themselves, their place in the world and how to care for their local environment, while developing general capabilities such as critical and creative thinking, personal and social competence, and ethical and intercultural understanding (see Chapter 16 for a more detailed discussion). Developing knowledge of identity and connection to others and the world enables a natural progression for learners to explore how to care for others and the environment. Subsequently, this provides a strong foundation for future learning in HASS and 'empowers students to shape change by developing a range of skills to enable them to make informed decisions and solve problems' (ACARA 2018, p. 10). This is facilitated through learners understanding their own history while becoming critically aware of the world in which they live. Young people's inquisitive and curious nature makes the early childhood and primary years the optimal age to introduce and develop social science skills. This can be achieved through investigation and exploration of historical, social and environmental matters at age-appropriate levels, with a specific focus on their local area.

As learners move through the primary years of schooling as represented in the *Australian Curriculum: HASS F-6/7*, the rationale for their learning acknowledges the impact of global integration on education. This asserts that 'in a world that is increasingly culturally diverse and dynamically interconnected, it is important that students come to understand their world, past and present, and develop a capacity to respond to challenges, now and in the future, in innovative, informed, personal and collective ways' (ACARA 2018, p. 10). In aligning learners' educational outcomes with national and global imperatives, the HASS curriculum empowers them to make a positive contribution, 'locally, nationally, regionally and globally' (ACARA 2018, p. 10).

As highlighted in earlier chapters, it is important that educators engage learners by sparking their interest and enthusiasm for HASS. By employing inquiry-based and play-based pedagogies through real-life learning experiences connected to learners' lifeworlds, educators can bring the realities of history and the world into their learning contexts. During learners' formative years, developing learning experiences with a specific focus on their local environment supports them in making meaning of personal, social, cultural, economic and environmental issues that directly impact their personal lives. For example, learners might re-enact the First Fleet, as outlined in Chapter 13, before exploring the significance of Australia Day. Learners might explore the purpose and origin of Australia Day, why it is celebrated on 26 January and whether this has always been the case. They can then explore whose perspectives are/are not represented by celebrating Australia Day, which could lead to discussions about whether the date should be changed.

Significantly, HASS supports education to realise key features of Goal 2 of the *Melbourne Declaration on Educational Goals for Young Australians* (Melbourne Declaration): 'all young Australians become successful learners, confident and creative individuals, and active and informed citizens' (MCEETYA 2008). In particular, this goal highlights that successful learners 'are able to think deeply and logically, and obtain and evaluate evidence in a disciplined way as the result of studying fundamental disciplines' and 'are able to make sense of their world and think about how things have become the way they are' (MCEETYA 2008, p. 8). Through activities similar to the one above, HASS encourages learners to develop such citizenship qualities as outlined in these national educational goals.

---

**Reflection**

The nature and purpose of HASS learning in the early and primary years involves learners in making meaning of their world, their history, place and contribution to society, while developing citizenship and general capabilities including critical and creative thinking, personal and social competence, and ethical and intercultural understanding. Within these formative years, learning experiences need to focus specifically on the local contexts of the children. As an educator, take time to reflect on your own local area and identify an issue or event, such as fundraising for a charity, or a local cause, such as rehabilitating a local waterway through an initiative like Clean Up Australia. Given your understanding of the nature and purpose of HASS, challenge yourself in responding to the following questions:

- How might you spark learners' natural curiosity to explore this issue?
- How might you facilitate exploration of this issue with early years learners from birth to five years of age?
- How might you facilitate exploration of this issue with primary years learners across F-6/7?
- Make a list of three to five points that have brought the issue to local attention and design an age-appropriate 15-minute learning experience/activity. How does this learning experience promote being an active citizen in the local area?

The above reflection aims to challenge your thinking in applying your understanding about the nature and purpose of HASS learning within educational contexts and across early childhood and primary year age ranges. It is natural to feel that you have many unanswered questions in attempting to respond to this task, so be reassured that the remainder of this chapter and book will scaffold deeper knowledge, skills and understandings to support you in developing as a quality HASS educator. Being self-reflexive regarding your current approaches to HASS education is important for ensuring that your design of future learning experiences reflects contemporary curriculum and evidenced-based pedagogies that are responsive to the learners in your care. In reflecting on your responses above, consider what pedagogies were evident in the learning experience that you designed. The following section will explore play-based and inquiry-based pedagogies that are highly valued in supporting HASS learning.

# PEDAGOGIES FOR HASS LEARNING IN THE EARLY CHILDHOOD AND PRIMARY YEARS

Although the HASS curriculum does not identify a preferred teaching approach, play-based and inquiry-based pedagogical approaches foster a learner-centred philosophy that values an individual's prior knowledge, emergent understandings, interests, skills and abilities, and natural curiosity about the world.

Play-based pedagogy is the foundation of early years learning experiences as promoted in the Early Years Learning Framework (EYLF) (DEEWR 2009) with evidenced cognitive, social, emotional and physical benefits for learners. Chapter 13 will critically analyse the role of play, particularly in its application to the HASS learning area. However, in beginning to explore the nature and purpose of HASS learning and the role of the dimensions of knowledge and skills within the early childhood and primary years, it is important that play, which is a child-centred pedagogy (Hewett 2001), is central in your initial design of learning experiences. It is also important to understand that curriculum, pedagogy and assessment are inextricably linked and should not be viewed as separate entities (Boomer 1999; Price 2015). For example, in the early years, applying a play-based approach will see children's emerging interests and understandings arise from interactions with others and their environment. These will influence the curriculum focus and how young children's development and learning can be observed, documented and shared with parents/carers. As Chapter 13 will explore, play experiences can be different for each child, but common characteristics include children being intrinsically motivated, having agency in what and how they play, and can be co-constructed between the child, peers and adults. Play is educational, not something that is used to fill in time. As this book will demonstrate, play can have significant personal, cognitive, physical, social and emotional outcomes across the early childhood and primary years.

## A PLAY-BASED APPROACH

Ellen is an early years educator, working with learners aged three to five years. The following is an example of her play-based approach to learning.

Early one morning, the children in the early years centre were actively playing in the outdoor environment. A small part of the outdoor area had been left bare and Ellen noticed a small group of children were using the soil in their sociodramatic play. As Ellen observed the group, she was approached by four-year-old Sarah, who was keen to talk about what she and her friends were doing. Ellen noticed Sarah had something in her hand, so she smiled and asked, 'What are these?' Sarah replied, 'They are seeds, we're growing them.' Sarah returned to her friends and the children busily prepared the 'garden bed'; ploughing, planting and watering, while excitedly talking and planning. Ellen took photographs and recorded the children's dialogue, documenting their connection with the land and environment. She interpreted the play as significant, enabling her to make connections with Aboriginal culture, creating a learning story and linking the children's learning to the EYLF Outcome 2: Children are connected with and contribute to their world, sub-heading 4, Children become socially responsible and show respect for the environment; and Outcome 4: Children are confident and involved learners, sub-heading 4, Children resource their own learning through connecting with people, place, technologies and natural and processed materials (adapted from Raymond 2018).

**SPOTLIGHT ON HASS EDUCATION**

Complementing play-based pedagogies, **inquiry-based learning** (Hamston & Murdoch 1996; Hoepper 2016; Nayler 2000), which is discussed in detail in Chapter 11, provides a valuable learner-centred pedagogical framework to structure teaching and learning HASS experiences. An essential part of designing inquiry experiences and unit plans is to determine a central issue or 'key question' that will guide the investigation and teaching and learning activities in the unit. To this end, the HASS curriculum provides two sets of inquiry questions for each year level:

**inquiry-based learning**: a form of active, student-centred learning encouraging learners to ask questions and seek answers on issues or topics of interest to them

1. 'subject inquiry questions', to guide learning in two or more sub-strands
2. 'sub-strand inquiry questions', which frame the teaching of specific topics in each sub-strand.

These inquiry questions may be used or adapted to suit the circumstances of the unit of work or context. By introducing the HASS skills in the early years, learners have the opportunity 'to question, think critically, solve problems, communicate effectively, make decisions and adapt to change' (ACARA 2018, p. 10), skills they have already begun to develop in their preschool years.

The use of inquiry-based learning promotes a critical outlook on any of the HASS topics because it encourages learners to investigate a topic/issue deeply, question the underlying assumptions and consider it from multiple perspectives. For example, in Year 1 History, the question 'How has family life changed or remained the same over time?' encourages learners to explore the idea of 'continuity and change' in relation to family and not just 'describe' family life in the past and the present. HASS encourages critical thinking

(Habermas 1971; Hoepper 2016) by introducing topics in history such as the historical marginalisation of Aboriginal and Torres Strait Islander peoples and migrant groups, and social justice issues such as human rights. The Year 4 subject inquiry question, 'What is the significance of the environment and what are different views on how it can be used and sustained, past and present?' encourages learners to study a range of historical and geographical perspectives on environmental sustainability. A Year 6 Economics and Business sub-strand inquiry question, such as 'Why do businesses exist and what are the different ways they provide goods and services?', would lead to a straightforward inquiry. However, by reframing the question as, 'How does the production of goods and services in businesses in our town support the sustainability of our community?', learners can go beyond the original question to learn about the broader contribution of the business to society. In undertaking these inquiries, learners develop and refine their HASS inquiry skills.

# EDUCATOR TIP

The **disciplinary knowledge** of History, Geography, Civics and Citizenship, and Economics and Business are revealed daily in current events and examples from local, national and international contexts. As a HASS educator, it is important to make time to regularly check links to the 'real world' so that you remain abreast of what is happening around you and your learners. This will also help you to provide a strong rationale for the value of HASS in a crowded school curriculum. This can be facilitated through play-based and inquiry-based pedagogies.

**disciplinary knowledge:** knowledge of the content and ways of working associated with a discipline such as History or Geography

The following spotlight provides an example from early childhood and primary years settings of how inquiry-based pedagogies using tangible objects can develop a deeper understanding of people and places, past and present.

## THE POTENTIAL OF THE FOUNDATION YEARS

Sarah is an early childhood educator teaching Foundation at a large metropolitan primary school. As a recent graduate, she feels a strong sense of responsibility for her young charges – she knows that in the Foundation year her learners need a quality foundation in literacy and numeracy so that they will go on to be successful learners. Equally, Sarah wants them to 'love' being at school and shares their excitement about forming new friendships and discovering the world around them. She quickly realises that her job is to create real opportunities for her learners to discover more about themselves and their families, their neighbourhood and the local environment.

Therefore, in term 2 Sarah and her teaching partner selected the area of History using the concept of 'Me and My World'. Using an inquiry-based approach to learning, they began the unit with an old suitcase that was locked and displayed thoughtfully in the classroom. Sarah explains that an old suitcase like this was found at their local train station some 30 years ago, yet no one came forward to claim it. A question simply asking the children what they thought might be in the suitcase was used as a provocation to 'spark' their curiosity and interest about the unit ahead. The children were asked to think carefully about the age of the suitcase, its size and what things they might pack in a suitcase. Eventually, the suitcase was opened, which led to an inquiry into the objects that were inside, who the items may have belonged to and where the owner was going. They were encouraged to speculate about the owner of the suitcase, what the contents revealed about their interests and where they may have lived. Play centres were set up around the room to encourage dramatic play and opportunities for children to wonder and develop their own theories about their world. A process of forward planning and back-mapping was used to document the children's learning as they participated in the co-construction of the learning experiences. The unit inevitably went off on different tangents, depending on the children's interests, which required skilful intervention by Sarah and her colleague to guide the children towards the intended learning outcomes (adapted from Raymond 2018).

## HUMAN RIGHTS AND GLOBAL CITIZENSHIP IN PRIMARY LEARNING

The Year 6 HASS class is reading an article headlined 'Malala Yousafzai: the power of one' (Wheatley 2015). They learn that Malala Yousafzai is the youngest Nobel Prize laureate, who has campaigned for the rights of girls to have an education since she was an 11-year-old girl living in Pakistan. When she was 15, Malala was shot in the face by a Taliban terrorist. The learners also listen to a video clip of Malala addressing the United Nations on her 16th birthday when she proclaimed her message of achieving peace through education: 'One child, one teacher, one book and one pen can change the world' (Yousafzai 2013). The learners develop an inquiry to explore her leadership as a young person in their study of the 'obligations citizens may consider they have beyond their own national borders as active and informed citizens' (ACHASSK148). They further explore human rights through Malala's questioning of 'why there are 130 million girls out of school'. By doing this, they begin to realise that young people can exert enormous influence as informed local and **global citizens**.

FIGURE 4.1 Malala Yousafzai, activist for children's rights

**global citizen**: a person who understands their rights and responsibilities at a global level, based on their experience of local citizenship

In applying play-based and inquiry-based pedagogical approaches to HASS learning experiences, the aim in each of the above vignettes was to help young people make sense of their world.

## How can we help young people 'make sense' of their world?

Educators play an important role in introducing learners to local, national and global issues, while developing their capacity for critical thinking as they engage with the world around them. In Foundation, Sarah wanted to harness her young learners' interest in the world by studying local, social and community issues. In the second vignette, the Year 6 learners are keenly aware of their own potential as citizens of the future. Their study of Civics and Citizenship has extended internationally to a famous, young human rights activist from Pakistan, who at their age was fighting for children's, and particularly girls', rights to an education. Each vignette illustrates the significant role of the educator to dedicate time to HASS, interpret the curriculum and bring the content alive so that it engages learners while they develop the skills outlined in the curriculum.

### Working for the 'common good'

The Melbourne Declaration's second national educational goal for young Australians promotes *active and informed citizens*, who can 'act with moral and ethical integrity', 'are committed to national goals of democracy, equity and justice, and participate in Australia's civic life' and 'work for the **common good**, in particular sustaining and improving natural and social environments' by being 'responsible global and local citizens' (MCEETYA 2008, p. 9). A key aspect of working for the common good is through participatory citizenship skills and taking action.

**common good**: in the best interests of all people in society

HASS provides rich material to contextualise the teaching of literacy and numeracy in the early childhood and primary years, and takes on 'greater scope and increasing specialisation as students move through the years of schooling' (MCEETYA 2008, p. 14). HASS lays the foundation for active citizenship through knowledge and skills to enhance learners' understanding of the 'common good'.

## EDUCATOR TIP

You come to teaching HASS in early childhood and primary learning with your own disciplinary knowledge and passion that has developed over years of study and life experiences, which is a great foundation for teaching social science. Yet, given the significance of science, technology, engineering and mathematics (STEM), literacy and numeracy in an educational climate of school performativity and high-stakes testing, you may need to defend your discipline to colleagues and educators. A good starting point is to outline the philosophy of equity and excellence that underpins the national goals of education and highlight how they are a powerful driver for the work of HASS educators. It is also important to explain how equity and social justice – core values of HASS – form a crucial element of quality education. HASS provides an important counterpoint and promotes a balanced curriculum, especially in the early and primary years, by providing learners with the crucial soft skills necessary to develop into successful citizens in the 21st century.

# WHAT IS THE ROLE OF DISCIPLINARY KNOWLEDGE IN HASS?

In understanding the importance of person-centred pedagogical approaches in supporting young people to make sense of their world and work for the common good, it is also important to understand the role of disciplinary knowledge in HASS education.

Learners bring a range of knowledge and experiences related to the social science disciplines to their study of HASS. They already have an understanding of the past and present (their personal history), about the local area and places that are significant to them (their personal geography) and notions of what is fair or unfair (making rules and collective decision-making). In supporting young learners to acquire HASS knowledge, understandings and skills, educators will further develop these emergent understandings by introducing disciplinary thinking based on each of the four sub-strands.

As noted in this and earlier chapters, the HASS F-6/7 curriculum promotes concepts of interdisciplinary thinking such as cause and effect, place and space, interconnections and roles, and rights and responsibilities, which draw on the disciplinary concepts that underpin HASS. Some of these concepts align more obviously to a particular sub-strand; for example, place and space are clearly linked to Geography and cause and effect to History. However, the concepts are interrelated. For instance, 'the concept of interconnections is drawn from geography but also relates to social systems and structures in civics and citizenship and resources systems in economics and business' (ACARA 2018, p. 13). Harnessing integrated frameworks to the study of the disciplines will achieve meaningful interdisciplinary learning (Tambyah 2011). Each sub-strand teaches concepts from the relevant discipline, laying the foundation for disciplinary thinking in HASS. We turn now to see how young people's personal histories and geographies can be integrated effectively into HASS teaching and learning.

## Teaching 'personal' history and geography

What can educators expect of young learners when introducing disciplinary thinking in the early childhood and primary years of education? Hilary Cooper's (2004) research into children's understanding of history has noted that the capacity to enter into imaginative understandings of the past through stories and play requires knowledge and skills. Regardless of whether the stories are accurate or even possible, Cooper maintains that the process is important because it helps children make sense of the world around them. 'This, in an embryonic way, is how all accounts of the past are constructed: by imagining, from what is known, how people in the past may have thought and felt and why they acted as they did' (Cooper 2004, p. 7).

Learners also come to educational settings with a wide variety of experiences and places that attest to a strong sense of place and space through their personal geography (Catling 2003). But can young learners engage with disciplinary thinking? The view that young learners can 'situate' themselves in history by exploring their family history and can develop 'everyday geography' (Martin 2006) is fundamental to commencing the study of history and geography in the early years of schooling and for this reason is embedded in the EYLF (DEEWR 2009). As noted above, a key feature of the HASS curriculum is to engage with the concepts of disciplinary thinking as each sub-strand has 'its own way of thinking' (ACARA 2018, p. 11). However, HASS educators also need to support learners in identifying their own personal histories and geographies.

## Identifying our 'personal history' and 'everyday geographies'

**historical thinking**: draws on history concepts and processes of historical inquiry to understand the past

The topics of family history in Foundation and Year 1 provide an early opportunity for young children to develop **historical thinking** and recognise that there are multiple perspectives on the past, depending on who is telling the story. History involves exploring questions about continuity and change over time in topics such as 'Me and My Family' in the early years, providing learners with opportunities to learn about themselves and their family through the concepts of contestability, evidence, chronology, interpretation and significance. The foundations of historical reasoning – especially cause and effect, motives, empathy and perspectives – can also be laid at this stage. The use of tangible evidence is one of the first historical concepts that young learners are introduced to, as it provides a means of identifying elements of the past, investigating the difference between past and present while introducing 'historical thinking'.

Cooper (2002) indicates that young children already have existing ideas about the past through artefacts, stories and pictures, which are used for speculating about what life may have been like in the past. Although some young learners come to school with a sense of past and present, others have difficulty entering the experience or perspectives and motives of those who lived in the past (Cooper 2004). Determining what is 'significant', and explaining why it is of importance in relation to the event, situation or person, is key to developing historical thinking at an early age. For learners in Year 1 or Year 2, investigating how family life has changed or remained the same over time (Year 1) or what remains of the past are important to the local community (Year 2) offers opportunities for historical inquiry (questioning, researching, analysing) and interpretation (evaluating, reflecting, communication).

Figure 4.2 shows members of a family looking at photographs together. It is in such moments that young learners can develop the idea of generations and see how family photographs are a form of 'evidence' that capture memories from the past.

Geography is defined as 'the study of places – their biophysical and human characteristics, their interconnectedness and interdependencies and their variation across space' (McInerney et al. 2009, p. 7). In studying places, learners will explore and ask questions about the characteristics of places and the relationship between them, sustainability, spatial

FIGURE 4.2 Three generations in a family sharing memories

patterns, the possible, probable and preferred futures in places and interpreting the nature of place. The conceptualisation of learners' 'everyday geographies' (Martin 2006) comes from their early understandings of place and space in relation to their environment, an understanding of why places are special, and how these locations can be conserved and managed; these are concepts that are developed through the EYLF. Learners develop an understanding of the geographical meaning of 'place' through a variety of approaches, including location, spatial interaction and analysis, sustainable use of environments and the interrelationships between people and their environment, and human agency, which explores how the characteristics of places are shaped by individuals or groups (McInerney et al. 2009, p. 7).

Catling and Willy (2009, p. 9) assert that 'everyday geographical encounters' are so commonplace in daily life that we overlook 'our use of the environment, our connections with people and places, the goods that we consume, and the decisions we make about how we go about our daily business'. Learners come to educational settings with an awareness of their local and wider environment; they are able to describe their journey from home to the local shops or to school, provide basic directions and create drawings that represent the features of the local natural and built environment. Learners' experiences of the local environment and places such as their home and garden, the local shops, parks, beaches and other recreational areas, roads and traffic, school grounds and local institutions such as the library and health facilities are held to be very important to their appreciation of place and spatial skills: 'through their experience in places children develop their sense of place' (Catling & Willy 2009, p. 24).

In Figure 4.3 learners are immersed in their task of reading a map while experiencing the environment of their local park. This activity helps learners to develop geographical inquiry skills, including practical fieldwork, observation, data collection, identifying distributions and patterns, interpreting data and cartography.

FIGURE 4.3　**Learners at a park studying their maps**

## Skills in History and Geography

The concept of time and chronology are core skills in History as they provide a fundamental foundation for understanding continuity and change (Cooper 2002). By working with sources of the past, learners pose their own questions and make inferences about what they were used for and how they were used. Sources may include family photographs; items of clothing that were special to past events; stories of family traditions and rituals; investigating artefacts from home, such as old toys and books; writing implements like fountain pens; and kitchen items such as an old whisk or wooden spoon. Through the tangible use of evidence, children may display early understandings of continuity and change, cause and effect, motives, interpretation (seen through imaginative role play), while recognising different perspectives.

The core skills in Geography in the early childhood and primary years of education include observation, location, data collection and observing patterns in the use of space and place, such as the popularity of playground equipment and different areas of the school. Learners also encounter different environments and places to develop an understanding of the nature of 'place' and learn to interpret relationships with special places based on culture and ethnicity. Early skills in map reading and developing an orientation to place can be nurtured through drawing a map of the classroom or the learner's bedroom, or a simple map of their street that gives directions to nearby places such as a friend's house or the local park. Learning from these local experiences provides a basis for broadening the context to other places and people. Learners identify special places in their local area and region to identify the ways in which people maintain interconnection with these places. Learning about the relationship between places and spaces and Aboriginal and Torres Strait Islander peoples' connections to Country/Place is an important dimension of primary Geography and supports one of the cross-curriculum priorities.

Identifying and interpreting our experience of the nature of 'place' is a feature of historical and **geographical thinking**. Undertake the following think/pair/share reflection:

Reflection

- Take a few minutes to think of a place that is special to you and identify its 'significance' to you and your past connections with it (History). Then make a few notes about how you have interpreted your experience to describe the nature of this 'place' (Geography). Share your 'perspectives' on this place. What are some other ways in which this 'place' can be interpreted? Which HASS skills did you draw on in this reflection?

## Inviting debate and voicing different views

HASS addresses issues in topics relating to society, culture, human experience and sustainability, many of which invite debate and controversy. From the early childhood units that explore personal and family history and the roles of family members in the past and present (History), to Year 3 where learners explore the perceptions of sacred places and the need to protect those that have special significance (Geography), to Year 5 when the meaning and importance of key values in Australian democracy are explored (Civics and Citizenship), there are few areas of HASS that escape discussion and debate. These will be explored in the following sections.

> **geographical thinking**: draws on geography concepts and processes of geographical inquiry to investigate geographical issues, processes or phenomena

## Promoting respect for different views

Many topics in HASS are values laden, and to teach them well educators must promote an open, caring and thoughtful educational environment where different perspectives and points of view can be voiced and explored respectfully. This promotes the personal and social capability as well as critical thinking. For example, the topic of family history can be controversial even during a short period of time in a child's life. Examining family history (Foundation), the effects of contact between Aboriginal and Torres Strait Islander peoples and Europeans (Year 4 History), custodial responsibilities for land (Year 4 Geography), and opportunity costs in relation to sustainability of natural environments (Year 6 Economics and Business) can generate tension and deep personal feelings, depending on learners' individual circumstances.

## Role of the educator

Educators attuned to the needs of their learners acknowledge that different cultural and socio-economic backgrounds may result in different viewpoints and encourage learners to view all topics from multiple perspectives and recognise potential biases in these viewpoints. Acknowledging personal sensitivities surrounding the topics of family life and daily life enables learners in the early childhood and primary years to explore key historical and geographical concepts such as continuity and change, perspectives of different members of the family, place and space in relation to where family members live and work, and change in relation to the changing characteristics of the places familiar to them. Engaging in controversial topics provides educators with ways to explore different perspectives on sensitive topics in HASS, thus harnessing general capabilities such as critical and creative thinking and the personal and social capability.

**Reflection**
The general capabilities refer to knowledge, skills, behaviours and dispositions. When teaching topics such as care in the early years, sustainability of resources such as water and forestry and migration in the primary years, what behaviours and dispositions are you aiming to promote? Why are these important for young learners to develop? How do you invite debate and promote respect for multiple perspectives?

# CONCLUSION

The nature and purpose of HASS education are to promote children's natural curiosity and wonder about the wider world, and enable them to make meaning of and contribute to their local and global environment. Through your efforts as an effective HASS educator, learners will develop identity and connection to others and the world, which enables a natural progression to exploring how to care for others and the environment. The disciplinary knowledge promoted in the HASS curriculum provides the structure and substance for a multifaceted curriculum that explores a range of topics involving social, cultural, economic and political phenomena. This is founded on employing play-based pedagogies in early childhood (birth to five years), where children's natural inquiry and curiosity is encouraged and supported through learning activities exploring their history, sense of identity, space and place. This is built upon through inquiry-based learning with key inquiry questions providing a powerful way to ensure that HASS in early and primary years is taught through a learner-centred approach. Starting with the learner in their family and community, the *Australian Curriculum: HASS F-6/7* expands learners' horizons from local to national, regional and international perspectives. Central to this is that learners are encouraged to engage in considerate debate, respectful of multiple viewpoints.

## REVIEW QUESTIONS

1. How can educators spark their learners' curiosity?

2. How can you, as a HASS educator, promote respect for different viewpoints?

3. What is the HASS focus for learners in the early childhood years and why is it important?

4. Why is play-based pedagogy important for HASS education in both the early childhood and primary years?

5. What are the two inquiry questions that are presented for each year level?

6. How can you, as a HASS educator, help learners to develop 'working for the common good'?

## LEARNING EXTENSION

Choose either an early childhood or primary years focus to create a play-based and/or inquiry unit of work that aligns with the relevant curriculum. Consider the following:

- What age group will your inquiry focus on?

- What resources will you need to spark learners' curiosity?

- How will you ensure that learners develop their own questions that will drive the inquiry?

- What type of prompt questions might you employ?

- How will you ensure that every learner's questions are heard and considered?

## REFERENCES

ACARA (Australian Curriculum, Assessment and Reporting Authority). (2018). *Australian Curriculum: Humanities and Social Sciences F-10, v8.3*. Retrieved from: http://australian-curriculum.org/download/f10.

Boomer, G. (1999). Curriculum and teaching in Australian schools, 1960–1990: A tale of two epistemologies. In B. Green, ed., *Designs on Learning: Articles on curriculum and teaching*. Canberra: Australian Curriculum Studies Association, pp. 127–46.

Catling, S. (2003). Curriculum contested: Primary geography and social justice. *Geography*, 88(3), 164–210.

Catling, S. & Willy, T. (2009). *Teaching Primary Geography*. Exeter: Learning Matters.

Cooper, H. (2002). *History in the Early Years*, 2nd edn. London: Routledge/Falmer.

——(2004). *Exploring Time and Place Through Play. Foundation stage – key stage one*. Abingdon: David Fulton.

DEEWR (Department of Education Employment and Workplace Relations). (2009). *Belonging, Being and Becoming: The Early Years Learning Framework for Australia*. Canberra: Commonwealth Government.

Gaita, R. (2014). Why study humanities? *The Conversation*, 21 March. Retrieved from: https://theconversation.com/why-study-humanities-24569.

Guthrie, W.K.C. (1975). *A History of Greek Philosophy*, vol. 4. Cambridge: Cambridge University Press.

Habermas, J. (1971). *Knowledge and Human Interests*. London: Heinemann.

Hamston, J. & Murdoch, K. (1996). *Integrating Socially: Planning integrated units of work for social education*. Armadale, Vic.: Eleanor Curtin.

Hewett, V.M. (2001). Examining the Reggio Emilia approach to early childhood education. *Early Childhood Education Journal*, 29(2), 95–100.

Hoepper, B. (2016). Planning for critical inquiry. In R. Gilbert & B. Hoepper, eds, *Teaching Humanities and Social Sciences: History, Geography, Economics and Citizenship in the Australian Curriculum*. 6th edn, Melbourne: Cengage Learning, pp. 50–72.

Martin, F. (2006). *Teaching Geography in Primary Schools: Learning how to live in the world*. Cambridge: Chris Kington.

MCEETYA (Ministerial Council on Education, Employment, Training and Youth Affairs). (2008). *Melbourne Declaration on Educational Goals for Young Australians*. Retrieved from: http://www.curriculum.edu.au/verve/_resources/National_Declaration_on_the_Educational_Goals_for_Young_Australians.pdf.

McInerney, M., Berg, K., Hutchinson, N., Maude, A. & Sorensen, L. (2009). *Towards a National Geography Curriculum for Australia*. Brisbane: Australian Geography Teachers Association, Institute of Australian Geographers and The Royal Geographical Society of Queensland. Retrieved from: http://www.agta.asn.au/files/Resources/2009/Towards_a_nat_geog_curric_Final.pdf.

Nayler, J. (2000). Inquiry approaches in secondary Studies of Society and Environment key learning area. Retrieved from: https://www.qcaa.qld.edu.au/downloads/. . ./research_qscc_sose_secondary_00.docx.

Price, D. (2015). Pedagogies for inclusion of students with disabilities in a national curriculum: A human capabilities approach. *Journal of Educational Enquiry*, 14(2), 18–32, special edn, *Social Justice and Pedagogies*.

Raymond, S.K. (2018). Teacher self-efficacy and pedagogy: A case study of eight South Australian Reception teachers. Unpublished thesis, University of South Australia.

Tambyah, M. (2011). 'More tick-the-box': The challenge of promoting interdisciplinary learning in the middle years through the Australian history curriculum, *Curriculum Perspectives*, 31(3), 72–7.

Wheatley, J. (2015). Malala Yousafzai: The power of one. *Sydney Morning Herald*, 4 November. Retrieved from: https://www.smh.com.au/lifestyle/malala-yousafzai-the-power-of-one-20151020-gkdmca.html.

Yousafzai, M. (2013). Malala Yousafzai inspirational speech at United Nations. YouTube. Retrieved from https://www.youtube.com/watch?v=plPggZPmcel.

# PART II

# HASS concepts and sub-strands

# CONCEPTUAL THINKING IN HASS

*Malcolm McInerney*

## Learning objectives

At the end of this chapter, you should be able to:

- understand the nature of concepts
- consider the nature of the Geography concepts
- illustrate the importance of the History concepts for historical thinking
- introduce the Civics and Citizenship concepts
- introduce the Economics and Business concepts
- explore the relationship between assessment and the Humanities and Social Sciences (HASS) concepts.

## INTRODUCTION

> Concepts are to us like the air we breathe. They are everywhere. They are essential to our lives, but we rarely notice them. Yet only when we have conceptualized a thing in some way, only then, can we think about it. (Paul & Elder 2012)

When discussing curriculum, there is often a focus on content as a thing to learn and sometimes disparaging remarks are made that educators just want to fill heads with facts and figures when studying the *Australian Curriculum: HASS*. However, these comments view content in a very limited way. When writing of the *Australian Curriculum: HASS* commenced in 2008, there were frequent conversations about what the content of the curriculum actually was:

- Was it the factual knowledge?
- Were skills part of the content?
- Were concepts content?

It was decided that the content of the curriculum is all of these: the knowledge, skills and concepts. Moreover, it can be strongly argued that the concepts are fundamental to the successful application of the knowledge and skills. This chapter explores the concepts within the HASS learning area and why they are so important for quality learning; that is, what is the role of the concepts in developing learners' critical and creative thinking

**History**: a disciplined process of inquiry into the past that develops learners' curiosity and imagination (ACARA 2018b)

in the subjects of **History**, **Geography**, **Civics and Citizenship** and **Economics and Business**? If we intend to develop higher-order critical and creative thinking in the HASS learning environment, it is fundamental that learners understand HASS concepts.

> Create a definition that reflects what *you* consider a concept to be, and surmise how concepts guide your thinking in everyday life.

**Geography**: a structured way of exploring, analysing and understanding the characteristics of the places that make up our world (ACARA 2018b)

**Civics and Citizenship**: learning that investigates political and legal systems, and explores the nature of citizenship, diversity and identity in contemporary society (ACARA 2018b)

**Economics and Business**: learning that develops the capacity of learners to secure their financial futures and participate in and contribute to the wellbeing and sustainability of the economy, environment and society (ACARA 2018b)

# THE CONCEPT OF CONCEPTS

Without the concepts, HASS learning assumes only an informative role. Investigating and evaluating the key concepts gives learning in HASS a formative character.

## What is a concept?

When is a concept a concept? This is a question that is frequently asked by educators when writing curriculum for any learning area. The term is used loosely, probably because it is difficult to articulate. A concept has been defined as something conceived in the mind (Merriam-Webster 2018), and as an abstract or general idea inferred or derived from specific instances (Vocabulary.com 2018). In its discussion of critical and creative thinking, the Australian Curriculum, Assessment and Reporting Authority (ACARA) describes concepts as 'mental activity that helps us compare, contrast and classify ideas, objects, and events. Concept learning can be concrete or abstract and is closely allied with metacognition. What has been learnt can be applied to future examples. It underpins the organising element' (ACARA 2018a).

It is an important and influential professional learning activity for a group of educators to contemplate the nature and purpose of concepts in their subject and to develop a contextualised definition of the term. The use of concepts is very much about meaning-making, because everything we do and consider is given meaning by the power of our thinking to create a conceptualisation and make inferences from it.

As educators, we cannot critique learners' acquisition of the concepts in HASS unless we have an agreed definition of the term itself and the ability to develop an age-appropriate 'sound bite' for learners and parents on what constitutes a concept.

# What makes a HASS subject a HASS subject?

The conceptualisation aspect of a subject is closely tied to the idea of **Pedagogical Content Knowledge (PCK)**. Conceptual understanding by an educator in a subject is what provides the 'expert' knowledge of an educator when approaching the teaching of a particular subject. The question must be asked whether the facts/knowledge and, to a lesser extent, the skills employed can be learnt 'on the job' if one has never taught the subject before. What is harder to learn 'on the job' is the deep understanding of the thinking in a subject that is provided by the concepts. Such deep conceptual understanding is often acquired only by some type of immersion and discourse with expert educators of the subject involved. Even for the expert educators involved in the *Australian Curriculum: HASS* development process, the articulation of what was unique about their subject/s was a surprisingly difficult task, involving much discussion and debate.

> **Pedagogical Content Knowledge (PCK):** the knowledge an educator knows about teaching related specifically to the learning in their subject

Consider the following questions related to one of the HASS subjects:

- What makes history history?
- What makes history teaching history teaching?

Implicit in these questions is the realisation that the PCK for every subject is different; that is, the underpinnings of every subject are fundamentally different in terms of conceptualisation, subject knowledge and skills, educational contexts, cultural contexts, and general pedagogical knowledge and teaching approaches.

Associated with the discussion of the unique PCK of HASS subject areas is the idea of **powerful knowledge**. Despite frequent references to the development of 'soft skills' in HASS, the HASS learning area has powerful knowledge involving the academic rigour associated with critical and creative thinking. The concept of 'powerful knowledge' was first introduced into the education debate in 2009 by Professor Michael Young, a British sociologist of education. The term relates to a discussion of the importance of subject knowledge in the school curriculum, as opposed to a focus on generic skills and learning outcomes. Young (2013) suggests that an emphasis on generic skills and learning outcomes does not build the capacity of learners to gain the knowledge to understand and think beyond the limits of their own experience. Young argues that we need to develop and clearly articulate the kind of knowledge that he describes as 'powerful'. He also argues that entitlement to this knowledge is a matter of social justice, in that all learners should have access to it, not just those fortunate enough to be taught particular subjects at the whim of a jurisdiction, school or even an educator (Young 2013). In relation to HASS, we need to ask: what is the powerful knowledge that HASS provides for learners that they cannot gain by the osmotic process of living? Focusing on the concepts of HASS, it can be argued that it is the **conceptual thinking** and way of looking at the world through the HASS concepts that is the powerful learning gained in HASS classes and learning activities, which may not be available or accessible to learners in their everyday life and experiences.

> **powerful knowledge:** the knowledge (understandings and skills) that a subject provides, which learners cannot gain by the osmotic process of living

> **conceptual thinking:** when an idea or abstract thinking involved in a concept is applied to a particular area of learning or situation; that is, historical thinking

# EDUCATOR TIP

Talk to your fellow HASS educators and try to develop a sound bite that explains what makes HASS teaching HASS teaching.

## The grammar of a subject

If we were to imagine learning to think in a subject to be a bit like learning a language, then we need both vocabulary and grammar in order to do it (Figure 5.1). In 2012, the geographer Professor David Lambert argued that geography's 'core knowledge' can be thought of as vocabulary of geography – the extensive, factual basis of the "world subject"' (Lambert et al. 2012, p. 1). Lambert says that if 'core knowledge is geography's vocabulary, geography's conceptual framework forms its grammar'. This is a useful way of looking at the content of HASS in general and seeing that the fundamental purpose of learning in HASS relates to learners developing conceptual thinking as they view the world, to make sense of their place and the society in which they live. This 'meaning making' for learners through the concepts provides the lenses that HASS educators use as the basis for learner understanding in History, Geography, Civics and Citizenship, and Economics and Business. If learners are not looking through the conceptual lenses (the grammar of HASS), they may just be learning the facts and information (the vocabulary of HASS) for the sake of it. This will result in limited understanding of the complexity of the world in which they live and greatly reduce their capacity to think critically about the present and the future. Knowing the factual knowledge and skills in HASS does not mean that learners have the HASS way of thinking as embodied in the concepts. Vocabulary without the grammar is not the powerful knowledge we want learners to acquire in HASS (Lambert & Young 2014). For example, knowing the date when Australia was settled with no conceptual understanding related to cause and effect, perspectives, empathy, change and continuity, and contestability would provide little powerful knowledge for a learner to participate in a discussion about whether we should change the date of Australia Day. It is the historical concepts involved that provide the meaning to this discussion for learners, not the date!

**A WAY OF THINKING ABOUT HASS LEARNING**

**The vocabulary of HASS subjects**
The knowledge and skills of the subject

**The vocabulary is a means to an end and not an end in itself!**

**The grammar of HASS subjects**
The conceptual understandings involved in thinking in HASS subjects

FIGURE 5.1   **The vocabulary and grammar analogy**
Source: Lambert & Young 2014

What, then, are the HASS concepts in the study of History, Geography, Civics and Citizenship, and Economics and Business?

Before reading the rest of this chapter, use your knowledge of the HASS subjects to develop a list of the key concepts you think were identified by the writers of the *Australian Curriculum: HASS* as the key concepts of the curriculum.

Reflection

# DEVELOPING THE CONCEPTS IN GEOGRAPHY

To illustrate the complexity of defining the term 'concept', it is interesting to consider how the notion of concept has been applied to geographical thinking. A geographical concept is often described as an abstract idea that is usually emphasised in instruction (e.g. mobility, variation, distribution, energy flow). As a result of such a broad interpretation, a huge number of 'things' in geography have been described as concepts. In addition to the four listed above, the list can grow to include hundreds or almost anything we observe and imagine in geography. In the early stages of curriculum development for the *Australian Curriculum: Geography*, a long (but not finite) list of geographical concepts were identified. They were *change, distance, diversity, interaction, interdependence, landscape, pattern, perception location, place, process, proximity, relationship, risk, scale, space, spatial distribution, sustainability* and *system*.

The writers soon realised that this expansive list needed to be reduced to a manageable and valid number, with validity being based on whether the concepts were fundamental to an understanding of the discipline of Geography and the development of learners' geographical thinking. For many years, Geography curriculum writers around the world have been trying to develop a concise, coherent, workable and relevant list of concepts. It seems that a list of five to seven concepts is appropriate when looking at some of their results:

- cause and effect, classification, decision-making, development, inequality, location, planning and systems (Leat 1998)
- space, time, place, scale, social formations, physical systems, landscape and environment (Holloway, Rice & Valentine 2003)
- space and place, scale and connection, proximity and distance, relational thinking (Jackson 2006)
- location, place, human environment interaction, movement and region (World Atlas 2017)
- place, space, time, change, diversity, perception and representation and interaction (Taylor 2008).

The identification of the key concepts in the HASS learning area was an informative professional learning activity for educators to contemplate what the fundamental concepts were for thinking in their subject. Concepts are really very much about the thinking in a subject, and without them the focus of learning is just about learning the information and facts. Concepts in a subject can be said to be about the big picture of what we really want learners to understand. To gain understanding and in turn contemplate wise decisions, educators and learners need to be conversant with the concepts in any subject and able to contextualise the factual knowledge they study.

Reflection

With the nature of learning in HASS in mind, what do you think astronomer Clifford Stoll meant when he was quoted as saying, 'Data is not information, Information is not knowledge, Knowledge is not understanding, Understanding is not wisdom' (http://brainyquote.com)?

After much debate and consultation, it was agreed that in the *Australian Curriculum: Geography* seven key concepts could be identified as fundamental to geographical thinking and learning. However, the number of geographical concepts identified in curriculum documents varies from country to country. For example, over the years the English geography curriculum refers to the three concepts of place, space and environment (Department for Education 2013) and the Irish Department of Education and Science identifies only two key concepts of sense of place and sense of space (Government of Ireland 1999).

The seven concepts in the *Australian Curriculum: Geography* are space, change, scale, environment, sustainability, interconnection and place.

It is important to note that the concepts for Geography were agreed to before the writing of the curriculum knowledge commenced, and as a result the concepts are woven through the curriculum content descriptors and achievement standards. They were the foundation for the building of the curriculum and, as a result, educator understanding of and familiarity with the seven concepts are imperatives for quality teaching of the subject. Without them, there are only data, information and knowledge with limited understanding and wisdom. An interesting discussion is whether educators should teach the concepts overtly or allow learners to gain an understanding of the concepts by osmosis through the knowledge and teaching approaches employed. However, learners cannot learn a concept without learning how to use it. Hence, to learn the concept of sustainability is to learn how to figure out whether or not some group is functioning sustainably.

As shown in Figure 5.2, the key concepts have related concepts nestled within them. The concept wheels for all the HASS subjects will be discussed in this chapter. It is important to note that they have been visualised as wheels because the key concepts are interrelated and make up a whole, rather than being separate non-connected entities. For example, we cannot teach about the environment in Geography without considering change, sustainability and interconnection.

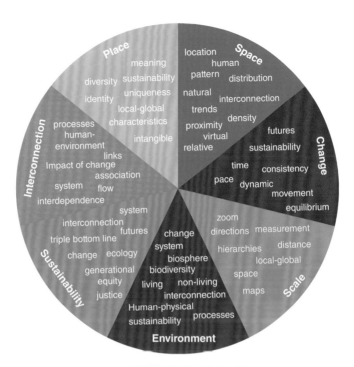

FIGURE 5.2   **The Geography concept wheel (based on *Australian Curriculum: Geography* concepts)**
Source: McInerney 2015

The Geography concepts will be discussed in greater detail in Chapter 8, and their ability to enhance geographical thinking and enliven geography will be explored.

## CONCEPTUAL THINKING IN HISTORY

As was the case with Geography, the History curriculum writers identified seven concepts that they considered fundamental to historical thinking. Interestingly, at times these concepts are referred to as skills in the curriculum documents. For the purpose of this discussion, we will refer to them as historical concepts, and provide a context for each concept through case studies. These illustrations for understanding elaborate on the concepts to develop understanding of what they bring to historical thinking.

The seven historical concepts are perspective, significance, continuity and change, contestability, evidence, cause and effect, and empathy.

As with the Geography concept wheel, the key History concepts have related concepts nestled within them (Figure 5.3). For example, to explore the concept of significance, a learner needs to consider the ideas/concepts of bias, place and time, effect and reliability, to name just a few. When reading the brief clarification statements for the concepts below, consider the nestled concepts and think about what other concepts may be relevant to the effective exploration of each of the key historical concepts.

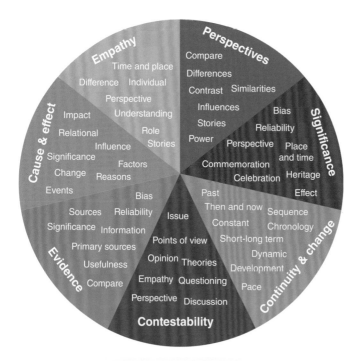

FIGURE 5.3   The History concept wheel (based on *Australian Curriculum: History* concepts)
Source: McInerney 2015

## EDUCATOR TIP

Choose a year level and, for each of the concepts in Figure 5.3, write a 'learner-friendly' statement that you could use in your classroom to describe and discuss the History concepts.

## Illustration to understand perspective

*Perspective* as a concept relates to a recognition of social and cultural differences across time. When studying the past, learners begin to realise that what people did in the past made sense in terms of their ideas about the world. Such realisation involves an appreciation that people in the past perceived and understood the happenings and issues of their day quite differently from the people studying these events today. This difference of perception may be a result of differences in values and beliefs, access to information, morals, social settings, changing cultural norms and experiences over time. An historical figure, for example, could have been seen as a freedom fighter by some and a freedom 'frighter' (terrorist) by others. As L.P. Hartley wrote in the opening lines of *The Go-Between*, a novel set in Victorian England: 'The past is a foreign country: *they do things differently there*' (Hartley 1952, p. 1).

To think historically is to explore the perspective of those living in the past, to be aware of and not to take as a given that what we think today about events, people and issues is the same as those who lived in the past. For example, how can we interpret the perspective on the events surrounding the Vietnam War in 1971 when we try to understand the thinking of an American soldier on one side and an anti-Vietnam War protester on the other (Figure 5.4)? Unravelling these perspectives from the past, without the overlay of our contemporary values and knowledge, is what makes History so challenging in terms of thinking.

FIGURE 5.4   **A US soldier in the Vietnam War (top) and anti-war protesters (bottom)**

## Illustration to understand empathy

*Empathy* as a concept focuses on human emotions, motives and actions. It involves learners trying to place themselves in the situation of a person living in the past to understand how and why individuals acted the way they did and why events played out in the way they did. This concept is intrinsically linked to the concept of perspective: it is difficult to develop empathy for a person without an understanding of the perspective of the individuals or groups involved. To be truly empathetic, learners must gain a sound historical knowledge of the time and events (context) and make a conscious effort to 'make sense' of human motives and actions within that context. It is important when teaching empathy to go beyond the idea of creative writing through imagination and to engage learners in 'real-life' decision-making situations and structured debate, always cognisant of the historical knowledge and context in which the persons were living.

To think about what is happening in the photograph in Figure 5.5 is to explore the concept of empathy to understand what this woman is thinking in taking such a huge personal risk to avoid being forced to stay in East Berlin. Perhaps she had family and friends in West Berlin, or perhaps she worked in West Berlin. Within the context of stories about the inhumanity involved in the erection of the Berlin Wall, viewing this image through the lens of empathy provides the history learner with the opportunity to ask many questions and enter into a rich discussion about this period of European history.

FIGURE 5.5 A woman living in a building situated right on the borderline between West and East Berlin waits on the ledge in West Berlin for the fire brigade to rescue her.

**Reflection** What are the fundamental differences between the concepts of perspective and empathy?

## Illustration to understand significance

*Significance* as a concept relates to the importance that is given to particular aspects of the past. The discourse regarding historical importance can relate to the work of an individual, an event, a particular issue or the contribution of a group. The discussion of significance is complex and one of the most difficult tasks for the history learner because it requires an understanding of perspective and a response to the question: significant for what and whom? This concept requires considerable clarity of purpose and discussion to determine what may be significant and what may not. Inevitably, this often comes down to a point of view in relation to values, extent of outcomes, who it impacted upon and, most importantly, the parameters of the questions asked. A relatively small event could be considered to have a great impact on a limited group of people in history and as a result be considered significant for that particular time and place in the past. Significance varies over time and from people to people.

FIGURE 5.6    A Chinese immigrant, Queensland 1925

Chinese immigrants worked in all Australian colonies as station hands, plantation workers, miners, on public works, as cabinetmakers, as personal servants and in laundries (Figure 5.6). Are their stories told and, most importantly, are their stories important? These questions could be the basis of a discussion of significance when studying 19th-century Australia.

## Illustration to understand continuity and change

*Continuity and change* as a concept requires learners to investigate aspects of life that have remained the same and those that show signs of change over time. The application of chronological skills and representations is often an important aspect when exploring this concept. The nested concepts of place, similarity, differences, dynamic, short and long impact, progress and development provide some guidance when exploring the complexity of continuity and change.

For both of the teams shown in Figure 5.7, what things have changed and what things continue to be the same? While relating to sport, this image is a valid example of change and continuity over time. This is as much a conceptualisation of an aspect of history as the study of political events when trying to develop learner understanding of the concept of change and continuity.

FIGURE 5.7 The Australian Test Cricket teams in the 1930s (top) and in 2015 (bottom)

## Illustration to understand contestability

*Contestability* as a concept is an important ingredient of historical learning in developing the skills of interpretation to the study of the past. The interpretation of a person, event or phenomenon from the past is subject to factors such as the values of the historian, the reliability and availability of the evidence, the purpose of the study, events since the time of study and other characteristics of the historian (gender, ethnicity, education, etc.). Effective history teaching should challenge learners to consider alternative interpretations of the past and provide evidence to support these interpretations. A premise when considering the contestability concept is that almost every person, event or phenomenon from the past involves a multiplicity of views and interpretations that may tell conflicting stories. Controversy often results if there is a collision of values and perspectives when interpreting the past. An example of contestability in Australian history is the debate over whether the arrival of Europeans in 1788 was an invasion or settlement. History in the classroom should challenge learners to think critically, not be blinkered in their thinking and not necessarily think there is a 'correct answer'.

Former Australian prime minister Gough Whitlam is a source of controversy between those who consider he was Australia's greatest visionary and those who see him as a free-spending egotist (Figure 5.8). The contestability topic encourages the questioning of the interpretations of the past and invites learners to consider their opinions after examining and discussing the evidence.

FIGURE 5.8   Gough Whitlam

## Illustration to understand evidence

*Evidence* as a concept requires learners to be aware that to undertake valid historical interpretation and discussion, they need to seek and apply relevant information obtained from sources. Learners find evidence by analysing sources and asking a series of questions about the sources. Evidence can be used to develop an explanation or to support or challenge an argument or interpretation. There are many historical sources that can be used for evidence. They include objects (artefacts) from the past such as household items, letters, photographs and paintings, through to written or visual items such as newspapers, journals, letters or films. Sources from the time are called primary sources and sources produced after the time being studied are called secondary sources.

The primary source in Figure 5.9 provides evidence that this soldier, when facing combat, was so scared he could 'hardly hold the pen'.

6 / 16 / 69

Just got word that we are supposed to leave or at least be on the plane back to the states July 5th. I will let you know for sure when I find out for sure.

I will have to go back into the field. I'm so shaking that I feel like I'm going to crack. Our last operation is supposed to be the 26th of this month. I'll have to get used to it all over again. I cant [sic] write that, I'm so tense. I can hardly hold the pen.

I hope God's still with me. I cant [sic] make it alone.

FIGURE 5.9   A journal entry from an American soldier in Vietnam

## Illustration to understand cause and effect

*Cause and effect* as a concept is frequently considered by historians. The concept requires an understanding of why events and phenomena occur and the subsequent outcomes and impact. Engaging with the concept of cause and effect involves considerable complexity and critical thinking. There is rarely just one cause identified and learners need to consider myriad causes of varying importance when studying an event. The discussion of causes and apportioning importance is at the heart of much historical debate and interpretation. To address the concept of cause and effect in the classroom, learners need to use their understanding of the significance, perspective and contestability concepts before they embark on any discussion or debate on the topic. Usually causes are related and even interdependent. The process of determining effect is also complex, with learners being encouraged to consider alternative interpretations of the impact of the events, people and phenomena in question. During their engagement with this concept, learners will encounter ideas such as long- and short-term causes, social reasons, economic factors and political settings.

The Russian Revolution is an excellent example of an event that continues to fascinate historians, who argue about whether it was the strength of the revolutionaries, the impact of World War I or the weakness of the old regime that caused the revolution (see Figure 5.10). In terms of effect, we are

FIGURE 5.10   Revolutionary leader Vladimir Lenin talks to a crowd in 1920

still finding out the impact of this 'significant' event for the modern world as we consider the actions of communist totalitarian regimes in places such as North Korea today.

## A case study using the History concepts

It is important to note that the History concepts are not stand-alone in nature, but inform each other in many ways – hence the wheel visualisation of the concepts. For example, how could one talk about the impact of European settlement in Australia without considering all of the historical concepts? To further illustrate this point, the following case study of Eddie Gilbert shows how when studying any topic the concepts provide a conceptual framework for thinking about a person, event or phenomenon.

The story of Aboriginal cricketer Eddie Gilbert (Figure 5.11) is more than just a review of his bowling statistics and a chronology of his career.

FIGURE 5.11    Eddie Gilbert, first-class cricketer in Australia in the 1930s

## EDUCATOR TIP

Find out as much as you can about the story of Eddie Gilbert, who played cricket for Queensland in the 1930s. We can refer to such research as 'harvesting' information prior to engaging in the historical thinking on a topic.

Learners need to develop an understanding of the context of Australian society at the time Gilbert was playing cricket before they can 'make sense' of his story. To do so using the concepts, we can frame the following questions for an inquiry to develop conceptual understanding of his story:

- Why is the story of Eddie Gilbert a *significant* story to explore?
- What would be the *perspective* of the Queensland Government, cricket administrators, fellow players and cricket fans at the time when selecting and reviewing Gilbert's career.

- How can we have any *empathy* and understanding for the actions and perspective of those mentioned above?
- What was the *cause* of Gilbert's treatment as a cricketer and what was the *effect* of this treatment on him and other Aboriginal cricketers who came after him?
- Is it *contestable* that Gilbert was treated badly by the cricket authorities?
- Has the treatment of Aboriginal cricketers in Australia *continued* to reflect Gilbert's story or has it *changed* in recent years?
- What *evidence* is available to support or refute the statement that Gilbert should have played test cricket for Australia?

After discussing these questions relating to the seven history concepts, learners will have developed a deep conceptual understanding of the story of Eddie Gilbert. They will have studied his life through the lens of historical thinking and will not simply view it as just another story about an individual.

# CONCEPTUAL THINKING IN CIVICS AND CITIZENSHIP

The Civics and Citizenship curriculum was conceptualised under the broad themes of government and democracy, laws and citizens, and citizenship, diversity and identity. While these are useful categories for knowledge and understanding in Civics and Citizenship, as in History it is useful to consider the key concepts for thinking embedded in the content of the curriculum. The concepts suggested in this chapter are the result of studying the Civics and Citizenships curriculum and looking for common conceptual threads in the content. As a result of this process, seven concepts have been identified to be used to develop learning in Civics and Citizenship. Although it is not ACARA's work, the concept wheel has proven to be a valuable tool for educators to develop learner conceptual thinking in this area of HASS. It is used in this chapter as a possible approach aligned to our desire for HASS to have a 'grammar' and rigour to develop deep learner understanding.

The Civics and Citizenship concepts embedded in the curriculum can be discussed as governance, citizenry, diversity, contention, justice, social order and equity (Figure 5.12).

- *Governance* as a concept is about developing learner understanding of the structures and laws for a functioning society.
- *Citizenry* as a concept is about the responsibilities, rights and actions of being a citizen.
- *Diversity* as a concept involves having an understanding of the variety of people, institutions, beliefs and views that make up society.
- *Contention* as a concept is the realisation that all issues have two or more sides.
- *Justice* as a concept involves balancing views to reach a just outcome.
- *Social order* as a concept is an appreciation of the maintenance of law and order to create a functioning society.
- *Equity* as a concept is about equal access, opportunity and treatment for all in society.

FIGURE 5.12    The Civics and Citizenship concept wheel (based on *Australian Curriculum: Civics and Citizenship*)
Source: McInerney 2015

As was the case with the History and Geography concept wheels, a range of concepts is nestled within each of the key concepts, and the key concepts themselves are interrelated to varying extents.

## Illustration to understand the concepts for Civics and Citizenship

In Figure 5.13 (page 94), for each of the concepts an image is shown that provides a discussion point and potential elaboration of the concepts. Interestingly, in workshops educators immediately identified the concept when it was shown in association with the concept wheel.

Match the images in Figure 5.13 with the seven Civics and Citizenship concepts in Figure 5.12.

# CONCEPTUAL THINKING IN ECONOMICS AND BUSINESS

As discussed in relation to the *Australian Curriculum: Civics and Citizenship*, the *Australian Curriculum: Economics and Business* did not develop the concepts beyond references

FIGURE 5.13   A series of images, each associated with one of the Civics and Citizenship concepts

to resources, market consumers, opportunity, etc. The concept wheel in Figure 5.14 builds on these references and provides a conceptual framework for the study of the curriculum. Again, it is not the work of ACARA, but you will see in the next section of this chapter that all the Economics and Business concepts proposed below are evident. As was the case with the other concept wheels, a range of concepts is nestled within each of the key concepts, and the key concepts themselves are interrelated to varying extents.

The Economics and Business concepts embedded in the curriculum can be discussed as consumerism, market, globalisation, choice, work, opportunity and resources.

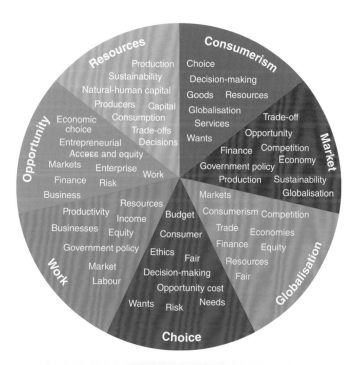

FIGURE 5.14   The Economics and Business concept wheel (based on *Australian Curriculum: Economics and Business*).
Source: McInerney 2015

## Identifying the concepts for Economics and Business

In Figure 5.15, for each of the concepts an image is shown that provides a discussion point and a potential elaboration of the concepts.

- *Globalisation* as a concept explores an economically globally connected world.
- *Choice* as a concept is to inform decision-making as a consumer.
- *Work* as a concept is understanding the nature and role of paid and unpaid labour in society.
- *Opportunity* as a concept is to create and make the most of economic situations.

FIGURE 5.15    A series of images, each associated with one of the
Economics and Business concepts

- *Resources* as a concept is to be informed about production, allocation and the use of natural and human resources for economic development.
- *Consumerism* as a concept is to be aware of the need to purchase and accumulate belongings.
- *Market* as a concept is to learn about the places of purchase, work and finance, involving the organised exchange of goods, services or resources between buyers and sellers.

## Illustration to understand the concepts for Economics and Business

Match the images in Figure 5.15 with the seven Economics and Business concepts in Figure 5.14.

## ASSESSMENT AND THE CONCEPTS

If we agree that the concepts and associated conceptualisation of thinking are important aspects of HASS learning, the next step is for educators to be able to identify the concepts in the assessment processes in HASS. It can be argued that in the *Australian Curriculum: HASS*, it is the concepts and skills we assess; that is, we essentially assess the grammar and skills of HASS. The factual content (vocabulary) in the knowledge and understanding strand of the curriculum is really the vehicle for the development of learners' conceptual thinking and skill development. We do not see in the achievement standards the need for learners to recall dates and facts, but rather to show evidence of understanding the concepts (know and understand) and an ability to execute skills (inquire and do). It is acknowledged that there are differences in assessment from state to state, but the essence of the conceptual thinking in HASS is alive and well in the assessment component of the *Australian Curriculum: HASS* across Australia.

It is suggested that for learners to meet the conceptual level required in HASS learning, educators of HASS are required to be proficient in:

- their understanding of the conceptual thinking (the grammar) of the subject (the purpose of this chapter)
- locating the concepts in the assessment component of the year level they teach
- developing assessment tasks that provide learners with the opportunity to show their conceptual thinking and skills (discussed in Chapter 15).

In relation to the second point, we will use the Australian Curriculum achievement standard for Year 7 HASS to map the concepts to provide clarity of what conceptual thinking is required from learners in Year 7 HASS.

## MAPPING THE CONCEPTS USING THE YEAR 7 *AUSTRALIAN CURRICULUM: HASS* ACHIEVEMENT STANDARD

The HASS concepts in the achievement standard are indicated in italics. If the actual term for the concept is not used, the concept term has been inserted in brackets.

By the end of Year 7, students explain the role of groups and the *significance* of particular individuals in past societies. They suggest reasons for *continuity and change* over time. They describe the *effects of change* on societies, individuals and groups and describe events and developments from the *perspective* of people who lived at the time. They identify past events and developments that have been interpreted in different ways *(cause and effect)*. Students describe *geographical processes (environment)* that influence the characteristics of *places*. They explain *interconnections* between people and places and people and *environments*, describing how these interconnections *change* places and environments. Students identify the ideas, values and principles that underpin the institutions and processes in Australia's *political and legal systems (governance, social order and justice)*. They explain the *diverse (diversity)* nature of Australian society, and identify the importance of *shared values (citizenry)* in contemporary Australian society. Students describe the interdependence of *consumers (consumerism)* and producers in the *market* and identify factors and *strategies that contribute to the financial success (opportunity)* of businesses and individuals. They identify why individuals choose to *work* and the various sources of income that exist. Students recognise that people have different perceptions of places, events and issues *(empathy and perspective)* and explain how this and other factors influence views on *how to respond to an issue or challenge (sustainability, contention)*.

Students formulate significant questions and propositions to guide investigations. They locate and collect useful data, information and *evidence* from a range of primary and secondary sources. They examine sources to determine their origin, purpose and reliability and to identify past and present values and perspectives. They interpret and analyse data to propose simple *explanations for distributions, patterns, trends and relationships (space)*, and evaluate and synthesise evidence to draw conclusions.

Source: ACARA 2018a

## EDUCATOR TIP

Before designing assessment tasks for a HASS unit, review the achievement standards and identify the key concepts for that year level. Highlight the concepts in red/bold for future reference.

## Locating the HASS concepts across Year 7

Table 5.1 maps the location of the HASS concepts from the Year 7 HASS achievement standard to identify the conceptual thinking in HASS required at that year level. The achievement standard also includes a range of skills on which learners are to be assessed. Overall, these skills are not mapped because, although involving a range of general conceptual thinking to execute the skills, they are not considered as part of specific conceptualisation for HASS as identified in this chapter.

**TABLE 5.1**  THE CONCEPTS ARE MAPPED ACROSS HASS IN YEAR 7 USING THE ACHIEVEMENT STANDARDS

| History | Achievement standards |
| --- | --- |
| **Perspectives** | Describe events and developments from the *perspective* of people who lived at the time. Identify past events and developments that have been interpreted in different ways. |
| **Significance** | Explain the role of groups and the *significance* of particular individuals in past societies. |
| **Continuity and change** | Suggest reasons for *continuity and change* over time. |
| **Contestability** | Explain different perceptions of places, events and issues and other factors that influence views on *how to respond to an issue or challenge*. |
| **Evidence** | Locate and collect useful data, information and *evidence* from a range of primary and secondary sources. Examine sources to determine their origin, purpose and reliability, and to identify past and present values and perspectives. |
| **Cause and effect** | Identify past events and developments that have been interpreted in different ways. |
| **Empathy** | Recognise that people have different perceptions of places, events and issues. |
| Geography | Achievement standards |
| **Space** | Interpret and analyse data to propose simple explanations for *distributions, patterns, trends and relationships*, and evaluate and synthesise evidence to draw conclusions. |
| **Change** | Suggest reasons for *continuity and change* over time. |
| **Environment** | Describe *geographical processes* that influence the characteristics of *places*. |
| **Sustainability** | Explain different perceptions of places, events and issues and other factors that influence views on *how to respond to an issue or challenge*. |
| **Interconnection** | Explain *interconnections* between people and places and people and *environments*. |
| **Place** | Describe characteristics of *places.* |

| TABLE 5.1 (CONT.) | | |
|---|---|---|
| **Civics and Citizenship** | **Achievement standards** | |
| **Governance** | Identify the ideas, values and principles that underpin the institutions and processes in Australia's *political and legal systems*. | |
| **Citizenry** | Identify the importance of *shared values (citizenry)*. | |
| **Diversity** | Explain the *diverse (diversity)* nature of Australian society. | |
| **Contention** | Explain different perceptions of places, events and issues and other factors that influence views on *how to respond to an issue or challenge*. | |
| **Justice** | Identify the ideas, values and principles that underpin the institutions and processes in Australia's *political and legal systems*. | |
| **Social order** | Identify the ideas, values and principles that underpin the institutions and processes in Australia's *political and legal systems*. | |
| **Economics and Business** | **Achievement standards** | |
| **Consumerism** | Describe the interdependence of *consumers (consumerism)* and producers. | |
| **Market** | Describe the interdependence of *consumers (consumerism)* and producers in the *market*. | |
| **Work** | Identify why individuals choose to *work* and the various sources of income that exist. | |
| **Opportunity** | Identify factors and *strategies that contribute to the financial success* of businesses and individuals. | |

Note that not all concepts are part of the Year 7 achievement standards – they will appear in different year levels for teaching and assessment purposes.

Source: ACARA 2018a.

# CONCLUSION

There is a literacy to learning in HASS that involves understanding what the key concepts are for each of the HASS subjects. This literacy involves educators and learners engaging with the conceptual thinking of the learning area and providing learners with activities, experiences and resources that enable them to develop their conceptual thinking skills. For learners, HASS should not just be about learning dates, drawing maps, structures of institutions or merely looking at the world in which they live without thinking conceptually, creatively and critically through the concepts. By studying History, Geography, Civics and Citizenship, and Economics and Business through the lens of the concepts, learners develop a particular way of thinking that helps them to make sense of the world in which they live. It is this way of thinking that is embodied in the 'grammar' of the subject; this is what makes HASS learning HASS learning and in turn HASS teaching HASS teaching. HASS is a unique and distinct learning area with a level of rigour and richness that provides 'powerful knowledge' for learners that they may not acquire in their everyday lives.

## REVIEW QUESTIONS

1.  What is a concept considered to be?

2.  What is meant when we refer to conceptual thinking in a subject?

3.  For one of the HASS subjects, articulate what conceptual thinking is involved.

4.  For one of the HASS subjects, consider what makes the subject unique; for example, what makes history history.

5.  Choose one of the concepts and develop an 'Illustration to understand' example.

## LEARNING EXTENSION

Consider what 'powerful knowledge' is acquired when learners study HASS. To do so, review the knowledge, understandings and skills that are taught in the *Australian Curriculum: HASS* and suggest what the HASS learning area provides that learners cannot gain specifically from other learning areas or through the 'osmotic process of living'.

## REFERENCES

ACARA (Australian Curriculum, Assessment and Reporting Authority). (2018a). *Australian Curriculum: Humanities and Social Sciences F-10, v8.3*. Retrieved from: https://www.australian curriculum.edu.au/f-10-curriculum/humanities-and-social-sciences.

——(2018b). *Australian Curriculum: Humanities and Social Sciences F-10, v8.3*. Year 7 level description. Retrieved from: https://www.australiancurriculum.edu.au/f-10-curriculum/ humanities-and-social-sciences.

Department for Education. (2013). *Geography Programmes of Study: Key stage 3*. National curriculum in England. Retrieved from: https://assets.publishing.service.gov.uk/government/ uploads/system/uploads/attachment_data/file/239087/SECONDARY_national_curriculum_-_ Geography.pdf.

Government of Ireland (1999). *Primary School Curriculum: Geography*. Retrieved from: https://www.curriculumonline.ie/getmedia/6e999e7b-556a-4266-9e30-76d98c277436/ PSEC03b_Geography_Curriculum.pdf.

Hartley, L.P. (1952). *The Go-Between*. London: Hamish Hamilton.

Holloway, S.L., Rice, S.P. & Valentine, G. (2003). *Key Concepts in Geography*. Thousand Oaks, CA: Sage.

Jackson, P. (2006). Thinking geographically. Retrieved from: http://citeseerx.ist.psu.edu/ viewdoc/download?doi=10.1.1.466.2210&rep=rep1&type=pdf.

Lambert, D., Rawling, E., Hopkin, J. & Kinder, A. (2012). *Thinking Geographically*. Retrieved from: https://www.geography.org.uk/write/MediaUploads/Support%20and%20guidance/GA_ GINCConsultation_ThinkingGeographically_NC_2012.pdf.

Lambert, D. & Young, M. (2014). *Knowledge and the Future School: Curriculum and social justice*. New York: Bloomsbury Academic.

Leat, D. (1998). *Thinking Through Geography*. London: Chris Kington.

McInerney, M. (2015). *Conceptual Thinking in HASS*. Retrieved from: http://humsteach.blogspot .com.au/2015/11/hass-back-at-para-hills-p-7.html.

Merriam-Webster.com. (2018). *Merriam-Webster.* Retrieved from: https://www.merriam-webster .com/dictionary/concept.

Paul, R. & Elder, L. (2012). *Critical Thinking: Tools for taking charge of your learning and your life*, 3rd edn. Upper Saddle River, NJ: Prentice Hall

Taylor, L. (2008). GTIP think piece – concepts in geography. Retrieved from: https://www.geography.org.uk/write/mediauploads/research%20library/ga_tp_s_ concepts.pdf.

Vocabulary.com. (2018). Retrieved from: https://www.vocabulary.com.

World Atlas. (2017). The five themes in Geography. Retrieved from: https://www.worldatlas .com/the-five-themes-in-geography.html.

Young, M. (2013). On the powers of powerful knowledge. *Knowledge and the Future of the Curriculum*, 1(3), 229–50.

# THE PAST IN THE PRESENT: BRINGING HISTORY AND CIVICS AND CITIZENSHIP EDUCATION TO LIFE IN EARLY YEARS SETTINGS

*Peter Brett and Katia Duff*

**6**

## Learning objectives

After reading this chapter, you should be able to:

- explain the links that can be made between History and Civics and Citizenship education in early years settings
- identify ways in which the curriculum can be integrated to promote conceptual understanding linked to the goals of History and Civics and Citizenship education
- apply your knowledge and understanding to create engaging learning activities that promote historical thinking and active citizenship
- plan learning experiences that promote both historical and citizenship learning consistent with the interests and capabilities of early years learners.

## INTRODUCTION

A sense of curiosity and active citizenship can be nurtured in children from a young age. Through a range of immersive and place-based experiences (Power & Green 2014; Somerville 2007), children can start to make sense of the world around them and demonstrate their social agency. The early years History curriculum focuses on developing an awareness of key features of family and local history and community heritage from the Foundation year through to Year 2. Its key purpose is to make early historical inquiry meaningful, memorable, creative and exploratory. Civics and Citizenship education can help to provide opportunities for children to express their ideas and understand their communities. A dynamic, multiperspectival and affective understanding of the past, and its relationship with the present, is essential in a democracy.

In this chapter we explore the planning challenges for early childhood educators in seeking to interpret the Humanities and Social Sciences (HASS) curriculum in the context of the Early Years Learning Framework (EYLF) (DEEWR 2009).

## FIREFIGHTING PAST AND PRESENT

This unit will enable learners to discover more about the community in which they live and to explore the memory of past events, particularly in relation to the Country Fire Authority (CFA). This will be achieved through an excursion to the Fire Services Museum of Victoria.

Learning about the origins of the CFA will provide learners with a platform to inquire about what it is like to be a firefighter, find out more about community life over the past 150 years and think about how things have changed, consistent with the Year 2 History curriculum (ACARA 2018). Sources such as photographs, local records and residents' recollections will engage learners' interest in their local history.

Learners' inquiry skills can be developed and their ability to empathise with people from the past enhanced. Asking questions such as 'Why did firefighters wear these clothes?', 'What did people do when they heard the bell ring?' and 'What dangers did people face with fire?' will develop empathetic understanding as learner curiosity directs them to further levels of inquiry. There may be opportunities for the learners to reflect upon the devastating consequences of recent bushfires in Victoria.

While at the museum, learners will collaborate in pairs, using digital cameras to record images of artefacts relevant to their inquiry. They will have the opportunity to dress in firefighter attire, experiencing firsthand the weight and texture of the clothing. The excursion will be enhanced by a visit to the contemporary working fire station adjacent to the museum where learners will participate in an equipment demonstration with questioning opportunities. On their return to the school, learners will use these experiences to create a record of their visit, and be given a creative choice about how they contribute to a class exhibition explaining the importance of the fire service as a community resource, past and present.

Source: reproduced with permission from Stephanie Cummings

**Reflection**    What features of effective early years pedagogy and HASS practice can you detect in this Spotlight on HASS education?

# WHAT ARE THE LINKS BETWEEN HISTORY AND CIVICS AND CITIZENSHIP EDUCATION IN EARLY CHILDHOOD SETTINGS?

When teaching History and Civics and Citizenship education, the most accessible content matter for younger children relates to material culture and patterns of everyday life around themes such as transport, communication, food, clothing, healthcare, education, safety and shelter (Brophy & Alleman 2002). Educators need to place greater teaching and learning emphasis upon history that can be seen and that connects with children's direct experience. This involves working with a rich variety of images and artefacts related to what things looked like, what people did and how they did it.

Helping children to think and reason historically (Levesque 2008; Seixas & Morton 2013; van Drie & van Boxtel 2008) can contribute to fostering a range of civic virtues in learners, including critical thinking, a concern for the common good (Barton & Levstik 2004), tolerance and understanding (Noddings 2005), appreciation of their own and others' identities (Ahonen 2001) and civic responsibility (Friedrich 2010). Exploring the degree of individual and collective agency in historical events can enable young learners to see how 'the decisions made in history affected later events, just as the decisions people make now will affect the future' (Barton 2012, p. 133). In doing so, learners can become conscious of their own agency and perhaps motivated to critically engage in collective action to effect change in their own right.

## Can learners engage with the demands of History and Civics and Citizenship education in the early years?

Research that has analysed children's responses to historical photographs, artefacts, museum displays and historical fiction over the past 30 years has clarified the ways in which young learners are able to engage with history (Cooper 2000; De Groot-Reuvekamp et al. 2014; Levstik & Barton 2011). Findings from these studies indicate that young children can possess substantial knowledge of social history and employ a variety of conceptual strategies to organise their thinking.

Leading 20th-century learning theorists Jean Piaget, Lev Vygotsky and Jerome Bruner all offered support for the idea that young children can put past events into some kind of reasoned order and explore historical sources. Bruner (1963) argued that the concepts and inquiry processes central to a discipline like History could be understood by learners at any level. This was particularly the case if emphasis was placed on experiential learning and educators deployed appropriate imagery and stimuli to connect to learners' imaginations. Piaget (1926) had earlier recognised that children could start to reason – using the language of 'because', 'although' and 'therefore'. With this understanding, early childhood educators can play an important role in helping children to observe sources and artefacts more closely and make sense of their observations. This role is consistent with contemporary constructivist views on children's learning, with the educator providing scaffolding for a deeper articulation of children's learning across the 'zone of proximal development' (Vygotsky 1978).

Similarly, in relation to the demands of Civics and Citizenship education, children's awareness is not restricted to their immediate surroundings. Young learners are starting to develop views about a range of regional, national and global issues. They can often articulate a sense of what is fair or unfair about the world in which they live (Holden 2003). Overall, young children are capable of deductive reasoning about both the past and the social world around them if the context is meaningful and of interest to them.

Are four- to eight-year-old children too young to learn about History and Civics and Citizenship education? How can History and Civics and Citizenship topics be introduced in age-appropriate ways?

## Making sense of the curriculum guidance

The Foundation year level description for History in the Australian Curriculum notes that 'learning about their own heritage and their own place contributes to learners' sense of **identity** and belonging, beginning the idea of **active citizenship**' (ACARA 2018). The Year 1 History level description advises that learners should have opportunities 'to explore how changes occur over time in relation to themselves and the places they and others belong to' (ACARA 2018). In Year 2, 'Students examine remains of the past in their local area, coming to understand how connections have changed the lives of people over time and space and how their community values and preserves connections to the past' (ACARA 2018). It is also important for young learners to know how their place is also special to Aboriginal or Torres Strait Islander peoples. The emphasis across these attainment statements is on exploring the importance of the past in the present through participating in different historical experiences.

**identity:** young people develop a complex, multidimensional understanding of who they are related to place, nationality, history, gender, ethnicity, religion, lived experience and other factors

**active citizenship:** participation in activities that contribute to sustaining and improving communities and the quality of daily life, often incorporating problem-solving, working with others and reflection

While not a statutory Australian Curriculum requirement before Year 3, Civics and Citizenship learning is an important part of the curriculum in the early years. There is an official recognition that children are citizens now, not citizens in waiting (ACARA 2012, p. 12). The EYLF is rich with active citizenship learning possibilities. The potentially wide-ranging implications of children realising their rights to participate and having a voice in early years settings have only been recognised relatively recently, as identified and discussed by a number of early childhood researchers (Ailwood et al. 2011; Moss 2007; Phillips 2010). Bae (2009, p. 395) wrote insightfully about the importance of early years educators identifying 'democratic moments' that 'allow space for small children's participation and freedom of expression'.

## How does the EYLF link to History and Civics and Citizenship education?

Strong links can be made between the goals of History education and the EYLF through Outcome 1: 'Children develop knowledgeable and confident self-identities'; Outcome 2: 'Children develop a sense of belonging to groups and communities'; and Outcome 5: 'Children engage with a range of texts and gain meaning from these texts'.

The EYLF also supports fundamental citizenship education learning – notably, but not limited to, Outcome 1: 'Children learn to interact in relation to others with care, empathy and respect' and Outcome 2: 'Children are connected to and contribute to their world' (DEEWR 2009, pp. 3–4). The EYLF 'recognizes the importance of children connecting with people and place, being effective social communicators and using skills to access information, investigate ideas and represent their thinking' (ACARA 2012, p. 12).

## EDUCATOR TIP

Identify some learning outcomes in the EYLF specific to Civics and Citizenship education, to augment and build upon historical content or investigations in the following areas:

1. a project on changing types of technology
2. an experience where the children have started to construct a family tree
3. a circle time discussion of Aboriginal artefacts.

# INTEGRATING THE CURRICULUM TO PROMOTE HISTORICAL AND CITIZENSHIP CONCEPTUAL UNDERSTANDING

There are several ways in which early years History can help learners see how the past has relevance in the present and can support active citizenship; for example, through:

- analysis of **heritage** constructions of the past in the present, linking to community involvement

- a focus upon historical **significance**

- exploration of issues around identity

- emotive history that considers the feelings and motives of people in the past via historical **empathy**.

## Museums, heritage and neighbourhood learning opportunities

Opportunities to access museums can enrich learners' understanding around the importance of history and heritage. One unifying question to ask that links past and present is, 'What remains of the past are important to the local community, and why?'

**heritage**: incorporates a wide range of inherited traditions, monuments, objects and cultures; how the past is displayed, debated and represented in the present; active public history.

**significance**: in History education, an assessment of importance, relevance and resonance of an individual, building or other aspect of the past that has been remembered long after the event

**empathy**: the capacity to put oneself in someone else's shoes and view the world as it was seen by people in the past with an informed imagination, without imposing contemporary values

## EXPLORING A SIGNIFICANT LOCAL SITE

A Year 2 educator in Tasmania planned for her class to visit an old shot tower, close to the school (Figure 6.1). The Taroona Shot Tower was built in 1870 for the production of gun ammunition; molten lead was dropped from the top to the bottom of the 58-metre hollow sandstone tower and its rapid descent and cooling roughly shaped it into pellets.

Prior to a site visit, learners looked at old photographs of the shot tower and participated in a 'think, puzzle and explore' exercise to access prior knowledge. They addressed and thought about a few questions: What do you know about this site? What questions do you have? How might we find out more about this building? A word-wall was developed to note any new or important history-specific vocabulary. The educator was keen for the children to explore concepts such as significance, empathy and perspectives. She then presented a (fictional) scenario that the local council had decided to demolish the shot tower in favour of a modern housing development. The children had to think about and respond to

FIGURE 6.1   Taroona Shot Tower, Tasmania

the key questions: Should the tower be preserved? Why, or why not? Who cares about it? What was the shot tower used for in the past? How is it different today?

On visiting the tower, the children viewed artefacts in the attached museum, took photographs, drew pictures and asked questions of the staff. They gathered information about the shot tower and its relevance to the community (both past and present). They asked their parents, grandparents, other relatives and family friends about their views on the tower. Learners created a class display of their work and some of them presented their finished arguments to parents and local community members, including invited local councillors.

Source: reproduced with permission from Liz Parry

In developing a Civics and Citizenship education dimension around a local history visit, educators might ask the learners to be involved in the organisation of the event. The children could also create a class newspaper to bring together examples of their follow-up work. They could send examples of their work to a museum for display, thereby embedding an even stronger community involvement dimension within their history project. Encouraging greater participation in civic activities among young people is one of the goals of the Civics and Citizenship curriculum. There is a particular need for schools to provide tailored support that is inclusive of learners who may otherwise be least likely to be afforded the opportunity to participate in community activities (Hampden-Thompson et al. 2015). The educator in this case study helped young learners to appreciate that people can have a voice in decisions that affect the built environment.

Why is this example both good early years History pedagogy *and* good Civics and Citizenship education? What do you see as the main challenges in organising a heritage visit learning experience like this one?

Reflection

## Thinking about historical significance

'Significance' features quite heavily as a curriculum driver in the Year 2 History curriculum as learners study 'The history of a significant person, building, site or part of the natural environment in the local community and what it reveals about the past' and 'The importance today of an historical site of cultural or spiritual significance' (ACARA 2018). History can be immediate and visible to children across Australian towns and communities: Who or what is memorialised in local statues, monuments, street and park names, sports stadia and cultural buildings? Who remains 'hidden from history' (possibly women, Aboriginal representatives and ordinary working people)?

The consideration of significance encourages learners to explain where they stand on some of the enduring issues that arise from the study of people or buildings in the past (Phillips 2002). Phenomena are assessed as significant when one or more of the following five Rs (Counsell 2004) are present. An event is:

- revealing – of some aspect of the past
- remarked upon – noted as significant by people at the time or since
- remembered – important at some stage of history within the collective memory of groups
- resonant – affected people long after the event
- resulting in change – had consequences for the future.

The five Rs constitute a useful thinking frame for both educators and young learners looking to bring together their History and Civics and Citizenship education understanding.

## Exploring identity

There are many issues related to identity and diversity that learners can investigate historically. Naturally, the starting point when working with younger children is their own identity. In order for learners to develop a sense of who they are, they need a notion of how they, their family and community have become as they are. Children can be asked to create a mini-biography outlining their roots and the connections they have with the wider world. Have they moved from another country or part of Australia? What helps them to feel that they belong – or indeed not belong? What has happened in the past when people have felt that they don't belong?

Young people can be helped to understand how history and heritage affect their identity. Story is integral to history, which is recognised in the Foundation stage focus of the History curriculum for five year olds ('What stories do other people tell about the past?') (ACARA 2018; Brett 2013). Moss (2011) recommends teaching approaches around identity in the early years that encourage respect for diversity by explicitly educating for democratic citizenship. This means accepting and embracing difference rather than attempting to make the 'Other' the same (Dahlberg & Moss 2005).

## Emotive history

One of the most important skills promoted by historical inquiry is that of empathy; that is, a capacity to mentally walk in the shoes of other people from different time periods and cultures. Empathy is a powerful emotion that helps children to recognise and understand diversity. It is an important prerequisite for achieving reconciliation across society in many countries (Barton & Levstik 2004; Yilmaz 2007). Australian history throws up plenty of examples of sections of society or individuals being treated badly; for example, the experiences of the Stolen Generations. Asking children to think about how they might have felt in particular historical circumstances can result in thoughtful empathetic responses. There is a close relationship between Civics and Citizenship education and human rights education.

## EDUCATOR TIP

Identify a local or state museum that you might visit with young children.

- How would you organise a one-hour museum visit to maximise learners' historical and citizenship learning?
- How would you follow up the visit back in the classroom?

# MEANINGFUL AND MEMORABLE TEACHING AND LEARNING APPROACHES

The most effective forms of learning in both History and Civics and Citizenship education with young learners are: *active* (emphasise learning by doing); *interactive* (contain plenty of purposeful talk and discussion); *relevant* (focus on real-life issues facing young people and society); *critical* (encourage children to think for themselves); *collaborative* (incorporate opportunities for cooperative learning); and *participative* (build from the children's interests and give them a say in their own learning).

## How is this achieved?

Learning of this nature requires a learning climate that is enjoyable, encouraging and non-threatening. Educators should try to create opportunities for learners to engage in hands-on experiences and talk about issues that have mattered in the past and continue to matter in the present. In discussing artefacts, images, fictional stories with historical or citizenship themes, or age-appropriate accounts of the past, children learn to develop arguments, listen to others' views and perhaps change their own ideas as a result (Cooper 2015). Learners' discussions should be structured around key procedural History and Civics and Citizenship concepts such as change over time, perspectives, significance, or rights and responsibilities.

## Teaching strategies for History and Civics and Citizenship

Curriculum activities to support both History and Civics and Citizenship learning can include:

- fictional stories – for example, about fair and unfair situations in the past and present, memories or change in different contexts. Picture books can be effective resources for promoting learning (see Chapter 14).
- puppets – for example, exploring issues related to safety and children 'playing out' (past and present) through characters
- role play – activities like kitchens and cooking technology, past and present
- chronological sequencing of themed images and artefacts; for example, around communication technologies
- photographs, paintings or video clips on topical issues affecting children that have a historical or citizenship dimension; for example, transport or education, past and present
- artwork and modelling – for example, children create dot paintings to represent their families and cultures and make 'feeling envelopes' to describe how they felt as Indigenous Australians when strangers came and took away things that were special to them and changed their homes
- visits – for example, to significant neighbourhood places and museums
- visitors to school – for example, parents and grandparents to assist with oral history projects (e.g. using toys and games, past and present)

- play and simulation activities – for example, mystery/detective activities and inquiries, purposeful dressing-up opportunities
- thinking circles – for example, discussing real issues prompted by historical events that have resonated into the present (e.g. vandalism of a local memorial).

Activities emphasising use of imagination and play can help learners to engage with historical and citizenship issues that they may be unable to experience firsthand.

**Reflection** What sorts of real-life citizenship issues do you think most concern early years learners? Which of these do you think can be addressed directly? Which might be better addressed indirectly through techniques such as storytelling or role play?

# PLANNING AND PUTTING IT INTO PRACTICE

A difference in planning when using the EYLF compared with the Australian Curriculum is that, generally, the latter encourages a backward-design planning method, whereas the EYLF can support and promote forward planning (DEEWR 2009; Wiggins & McTighe 2005). Forward planning implies that educators tie daily informal learning to the EYLF's learning outcomes and learning intentions. This enables educators to plan child-centred learning experiences for children while also capturing opportunistic teaching moments.

The EYLF advocates that educators use both play-based learning and intentional teaching with young students. The emphasis of the EYLF on intentional teaching is relatively new. This requires educators to make informed, thoughtful decisions regarding the facilitation, scaffolding, supporting and co-constructing of purposefully framed learning opportunities for children (Edwards 2017). The relationship between the young learner with agency over their play and 'the teacher as pedagogic driver is a very delicate one' (Leggett & Ford 2013, p. 44). The goal of an intentional educator in the context of exploring History and Civics and Citizenship education themes is to create experiences that develop intentional learning skills within children.

## EDUCATOR TIP

Reflect upon and list the differences between using the EYLF and the Australian Curriculum to support your planning. What good practice have you observed in preschool settings that links to implementing and documenting forward planning as opposed to backward planning?

## Where does the educator begin?

Children are exposed to HASS-related issues from birth. At each stage of their development – infant, toddler, kindergarten and early primary school – they are continually exploring and trying to make sense of their social and physical environment (Mindes 2005). For this reason, History and Civics and Citizenship sequences of learning often begin with activities designed to establish prior learning, such as having circle news time and seeing what topics children contribute to the circle; recording questions asked as a story is read; providing opportunities to draw a spontaneous response to a stimulus or question; or instigating 'rounds', where every child in turn contributes something that they know about a topic.

## HOSPITALS PAST AND PRESENT

Recently, I was teaching a Kindergarten group in a regional Australian community, and when the year began two of the children's mothers were in the nearest city hospital, which was more than an hour's drive away. The children were a little unsettled and when Dad was visiting Mum, they would be unsure about who was collecting them at the end of the day. Looking to reassure the children, and seeking to apply the principles of the Reggio Emilia approach (Edwards, Gandini & Forman 2012), which strongly influenced the pedagogical guidance of the EYLF, I decided to create learning experiences that would incorporate past and present perspectives on hospitals and medical care. I began by creating a vintage hospital corner for children's dramatic play. This included dress-up opportunities, medical toys and suitable real-life instruments. There was also a bed, dolls and teddies for patients, and items for creating medicine/potions such as test tubes, beakers, a mortar and pestle, and bowls. The children had a creative time in the corner and contributed a stretcher that they made during outside playtime from bamboo sticks and material. A doctor's desk, small filing cabinet and chairs for visiting patients were set up. Clipboards and paper and pencils were provided for doctors' notes, which provided opportunities for children to practise their emerging writing skills. Past and present medical artefacts, a range of picture books and images of early 20th-century medical scenes were arrayed around the class. As children explored and played in the classroom, and when they were listening to stories being read about past and present hospitals, I was able to scaffold their thinking and document their new learning in relation to key EYLF outcomes.

**Reggio Emilia approach:** an educational philosophy focused on preschool and primary education. It is a pedagogy described as learner-centred and constructivist, which utilises self-directed, experiential learning in relationship-driven environments.

**SPOTLIGHT ON HASS EDUCATION**

How would you document and assess the learning taking place in the vignette?

Reflection

## Exploring a History and Civics and Citizenship learning sequence in an early learning setting

When designing History and Civics and Citizenship learning experiences for young learners, educators should remember to delve into their knowledge bank of effective evidence-based early childhood education pedagogy (DEEWR 2009). For example, when beginning a new topic, educators can let families/carers know about the new learning their children will be undertaking to build collaborative relationships and a sense of learning together (Thornton & Brunton 2014). This will also enable the educator to become aware of any family cultural sensitivities.

In the vignette above, medical artefacts for hands-on exploration were sourced from children's families, colleagues, friends, a local hospital and personal resources. The school librarian helped with the collation of numerous picture books related to medicine and health, which were spread around the classroom. The artefacts, picture books and images enabled the children to ask questions, test assumptions, ponder and discover more. Many stories based on past and present medical situations were read to the children and they created craft and artwork to demonstrate their new understandings. The rich learning environment that was created enabled plenty of unscripted play opportunities and talk.

In terms of intentional teaching, the focus was on seeking to foster a sense of the language of historical time in the context of medicine and change. This was scaffolded through questions posed during play and general classroom interaction. A timeline of artefacts ranging from the early 20th century through to the present was created. This timeline had an explicit focus on using simple historical terms and language related to the past, such as 'a long time ago', 'before', 'when my grandparents were little', 'old' and 'past and present'.

To incorporate community involvement as part of the learning, excursions were organised to the local hospital medical centre and local paramedics and family members were invited to talk to the children in the classroom. The children were involved in the decision-making and invitation processes around these visits. Moreover, it was discovered that the nearby university's visual art school had an exhibition of past artefacts used by an apothecary and this provided a wonderful opportunity for community interaction to be extended with a visit to the university. Through these experiences the children became familiar with community health services and aspects of medical care in both present and past times. There was an advocacy campaign at the time to keep a small local cottage hospital open and the children became involved with this. A local nurse (a parent at the school) came to explain what the services were at this site.

## Linking to eight ways pedagogy to develop Indigenous cultural competence

When designing meaningful History and Civics and Citizenship learning experiences for young learners, it is beneficial to consider ways to incorporate the eight ways framework of Aboriginal pedagogy. This framework (see Figure 6.2) allows teachers to include Aboriginal and Torres Strait Islander perspectives by using Aboriginal and Torres Strait Islander learning techniques. The framework provides positive methods to incorporate Indigenous children's preferred ways of learning. The framework draws upon the work of Australian Indigenous researchers Martin Nakata and Tyson Yunkaporta (see Nakata 2007; Yunkaporta 2009; Yunkaporta & Kirby 2011).

There is much common ground between the EYLF's recommended principles and practices, mainstream good practice primary education pedagogy and Aboriginal and Torres Strait Islander pedagogies, including:

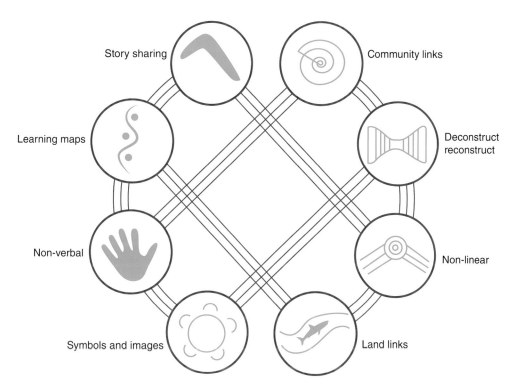

FIGURE 6.2 **The eight ways framework to develop Indigenous cultural competence**
Source: Yunkaporta 2009

- learning through narrative
- planning and visualising explicit processes
- working non-verbally with self-reflective, hands-on methods
- learning through images, symbols and metaphors
- learning through place-responsive, environmental practice
- using indirect, innovative and interdisciplinary approaches
- modelling and scaffolding by working from wholes to parts
- connecting learning to local values, needs and knowledge.

Advocates of eight ways pedagogy also point to some of the elements that distinguish it from Western pedagogies. Both the story-sharing and non-verbal pedagogies are notably introspective and reflective. Indigenous teaching is also non-linear and highly contextualised with a strong sense of country and place.

What strands of eight ways pedagogy can you see reflected in the hospital learning unit scenario? Where might the opportunities lie to further embed eight ways pedagogy in this context?

Reflection

## Assessing and documenting the learning

During the hospital learning unit, there was a significant amount of rich learning to assess and document. This was achieved through photographing children's learning, such as when they placed artefacts in chronological order, video-recording children's conversations, making anecdotal and opportunistic notes, and keeping copies of any craft or artwork related to the theme.

There was evidence of children attaining Outcome 3 of the EYLF: 'Children have a strong sense of wellbeing', and Outcome 4: 'Children are confident and involved learners' (DEEWR 2009), as they participated and contributed to their learning by posing questions, making decisions and offering opinions on ways of doing things. Moments of the children demonstrating new knowledge were captured as they played with others, explored the classroom or processed their understanding on the topic by thinking out loud.

In line with recommended early childhood education pedagogical strategies, the children's learning was celebrated and made visible (Kline 2008; Reynolds & Duff 2016). Their learning was shared with families and the school community by way of classroom and gallery displays and work shown at a school assembly. The wider community also shared in the children's learning through a display in the town's library and thank you letters were sent to the people who assisted the children on their learning journey.

# CONCLUSION

History 'introduces us to a variety of human experience, enables us to see the world through the eyes of others, and enriches our appreciation of the nature of change' (ACARA 2009, p. 4). Martha Nussbaum (2010), echoing John Dewey, is a powerful advocate that the humanities make a vital contribution to the maintenance and health of democracy. This is based on the belief that they help to develop attitudes and skills – such as empathy, questioning and critical thinking – essential to active citizenship in a democratic society.

These claims might seem somewhat broad when we are talking about young children, but it is precisely in the early years that community understanding, identity, an innate sense of belonging and of what things matter, and a growing curiosity about the world are being powerfully moulded. Bringing together the goals of History and Civics and Citizenship education in some of the ways suggested in this chapter can help to create a space in the early childhood curriculum for the development of the dispositions necessary for active and humane citizenship in a complex and rapidly changing information age.

## REVIEW QUESTIONS

1. Imagine you are explaining the purpose of Civics and Citizenship education to (a) six year olds and (b) their families/carers. What would you say to promote it?

2. What are the main ways in which History and Civics and Citizenship education are linked and can be integrated?

3. List eight to ten important factors to consider in planning high-quality History and Civics and Citizenship education learning experiences for young learners.

4. When and why would you employ 'forward planning' strategies and 'backward planning' strategies when teaching early years History and Civics and Citizenship?

5. What are the main features of History and Civics and Citizenship attainment that you are seeking to capture when you assess children's thinking and work? How will you do this?

## LEARNING EXTENSION

The principal at your school wants to send a positive message to parents/carers about the place of HASS in early years education by showcasing what children will be learning in and beyond the classroom. This is to happen via a series of 500-word blog posts. One of these posts will focus on Civics and Citizenship education learning in the context of the History curriculum. Create a post that informs parents about:

- what children will be learning (knowledge, skills and values)
- why they are learning it (purpose)
- how they will be learning it (pedagogy)
- how parents can play a part in supporting their child's learning in this area.

Choose a specific age/year group upon which to focus your curriculum and pedagogical thinking and parental communication. Think about the professional, but approachable, tone that you will use.

## FURTHER READING

Reynolds R. (2011). Teaching history in primary school: Interrogating the Australian Curriculum. *Curriculum Perspectives*, 31, 78–83.

Tudball, L. & Forsyth, A. (2009). *Effective practice in Civics and Citizenship Education: A Guide for Pre-Service Teachers*. Canberra: Commonwealth of Australia. Retrieved from: http://www.civicsandcitizenship.edu.au/verve/_resources/Effective_practice_in_Civics_and_Citizenship_Education_-_A_guide_for_pre-service_teachers_(2).pdf.

## REFERENCES

ACARA (Australian Curriculum Assessment Reporting Authority). (2009). *The Shape of the Australian Curriculum: History*. Sydney: ACARA.

——(2012). *The Shape of the Australian Curriculum: Civics and Citizenship*. Sydney: ACARA.

——(2018). *Australian Curriculum: Humanities and Social Sciences F-10, v8.3*. Retrieved from: https://www.australiancurriculum.edu.au/f-10-curriculum/humanities-and-social-sciences/hass.

Ahonen, S. (2001). Politics of identity through history curriculum: Narratives of the past for social exclusion – or inclusion? *Journal of Curriculum Studies*, 33(2), 179–94.

Ailwood, J., Brownlee, J., Johansson, E., Cobb-Moore, C., Walker, S. & Boulton-Lewis, G. (2011). Educational policy for citizenship in the early years in Australia. *Journal of Education Policy*, 26(5), 641–53.

Bae, B. (2009). Children's right to participate – challenges in everyday interactions. *European Early Childhood Education Research Journal*, 17(3), 391–406.

Barton, K.C. (2012). Agency, choice and historical action: How history teaching can help students think about democratic decision making. *Citizenship Teaching & Learning*, 7(2), 131–42.

Barton, K. & Levstik, L. (2004). *Teaching History for the Common Good*. Mahwah, NJ: Lawrence Erlbaum.

Brett, P. (2013). Beyond 'navel-gazing' and 'mush': Learning about identity in Australian classrooms. *Citizenship, Social and Economics Education*, 12(1), 3–17.

Brophy, J. & Alleman, J. (2002). Learning and teaching about cultural universals in primary-grade social studies. *The Elementary School Journal*, 103(2), 99–114.

Bruner, J. (1963). *The Process of Education*. Cambridge, MA: Harvard University Press.

Cooper, H. (2000). *The Teaching of History in Primary Schools*, 3rd edn. London: David Fulton.

——(2015). How can we plan for progression in primary school history? *Revista de Estudios Sociales*, 52, 16–31.

Counsell, C. (2004). Looking through a Josephine Butler-shaped window: Focussing pupils' thinking on historical significance. *Teaching History*, 114, 30–6.

Dahlberg, G. & Moss, P. (2005). *Ethics and Politics in Early Childhood Education*. London: Routledge.

De Groot-Reuvekamp, M.J., Van Boxtel, C., Ros, A. & Harnett, P. (2014). The understanding of historical time in the primary history curriculum in England and the Netherlands. *Journal of Curriculum Studies*, 46(4), 487–514.

DEEWR (Department of Education, Employment and Workplace Relations). (2009). *Belonging, Being and Becoming: The Early Years Learning Framework for Australia*. Canberra: DEEWR.

Edwards, C., Gandini, L. & Forman, G. (2012). *The Hundred Languages of Children*, 3rd edn. Santa Barbara, CA: Praeger.

Edwards, S. (2017). Play-based learning and intentional teaching: Forever different? *Australasian Journal of Early Childhood*, 42(2), 4–11.

Friedrich, D. (2010). Historical consciousness as a pedagogical device in the production of the responsible citizen. *Discourse: Studies in the Cultural Politics of Education*, 31(5), 649–63.

Hampden-Thompson, G., Jeffes, J., Lord, P., Brampley, G., Davies, I., Tsouroufli, M. & Sundaram, V. (2015). Teachers' views on students' experiences of community involvement and citizenship education. *Education, Citizenship and Social Justice*, 10(1), 67–78.

Holden, C. (2003). Citizenship in the primary school: Going beyond circle time. *Pastoral Care in Education*, 21(3), 24–9.

Kline, L. (2008). Documentation panel: The making learning visible project. *Journal of Early Childhood Teacher Education*, 29(1), 70–80.

Leggett, N. & Ford, M. (2013). A fine balance: Understanding the roles educators and children play as intentional teachers and intentional learners within the Early Years Learning Framework. *Australasian Journal of Early Childhood*, 38(4), 42–50.

Levesque, S. (2008). *Thinking Historically: Educating students for the twenty-first century*. Toronto: University of Toronto Press.

Levstik, L. & Barton, K. (2011). *Doing History: Investigating with children in elementary and middle schools*, 4th edn. New York: Routledge.

Mindes, G. (2005). Social studies in today's early childhood curricula. *Beyond the Journal: Young Children on the Web*, September, 1–8.

Moss, P. (2007). *Bringing Politics into the Nursery: Early childhood education as a democratic practice*. The Hague: Bernard Van Leer Foundation.

——(2011). Democracy as first practice in early childhood education and care. In J. Bennett, ed., *Encyclopedia on Early Childhood Development*. Montreal: Centre of Excellence for Early Childhood Development, pp. 1–7.

Nakata, M. (2007). The cultural interface. *The Australian Journal of Indigenous Education*, 36, 7–14.

Noddings, N. (2005). Global citizenship: Promises and problems. In N. Noddings, ed., *Educating Citizens for Global Awareness*. New York: Teachers College Press, pp. 1–22.

Nussbaum, M. (2010). *Not for Profit: Why democracy needs the humanities*. Princeton, NJ: Princeton University Press.

Phillips, L. (2010). Social justice storytelling and young children's active citizenship. *Discourse: Studies in the Cultural Politics of Education*, 31(3), 363–76.

Phillips, R. (2002). Historical significance – the forgotten key element? *Teaching History*, 106, 14–19.

Piaget, J. (1926). *The Language and Thought of the Child*. New York: Harcourt Brace & Company.

Power, K. & Green, M. (2014). Re-framing primary curriculum through concepts of place. *Asia-Pacific Journal of Teacher Education*, 42(2), 105–18.

Reynolds, B. & Duff, K. (2016). Families' perceptions of early childhood educators' fostering conversations and connections by sharing children's learning through pedagogical documentation. *Education 3–13*, 44(1), 93–100.

Seixas, P. & Morton, T. (2013). *The Big Six Historical Thinking Concepts*. Ontario: Nelson Education.

Somerville, M. (2007). Place pedagogies. *Australian Journal of Language & Literacy*, 30(2), 149–64.

Thornton, L. & Brunton, P. (2014). *Bringing the Reggio Approach to Your Early Years Practice*, 3rd edn. London: Routledge.

van Drie, J. & van Boxtel, C. (2008). Historical reasoning: Towards a framework for analyzing students' reasoning about the past. *Educational Psychology Review*, 20(2), 87–110.

Vygotsky, L. (1978). Interaction between learning and development. In M. Gauvain & M. Cole, eds, *Readings on the Development of Children*. New York: Scientific American Books, pp. 34–40.

Wiggins, G. & McTighe, J. (2005). *Understanding by Design*, 2nd edn. Alexandria, VA: ASCD.

Yilmaz, K. (2007). Historical empathy and its implications for classroom practices in schools. *The History Teacher*, 40(3), 331–7.

Yunkaporta, T. (2009). Aboriginal pedagogies at the cultural interface. PhD thesis, James Cook University, Queensland. Retrieved from https://researchonline.jcu.edu.au/10974/4/04Bookchapter.pdf.

Yunkaporta, T. & Kirby, M. (2011). Yarning up Indigenous pedagogies: A dialogue about eight Aboriginal ways of learning. In R. Bell, G. Milgate & N. Purdie, eds, *Two Way Teaching and Learning: Toward culturally reflective and relevant education*. Melbourne: ACER Press, pp. 205–13.

# 7

# HISTORY AND HISTORICAL INQUIRY

*Deborah Henderson*

## Learning objectives

After reading this chapter, you should be able to:

- understand what is distinctive about History as a discipline
- understand how History is structured in the *Australian Curriculum: HASS*
- appreciate how historical knowledge and understanding can be developed through inquiry
- appreciate why conceptual knowledge is significant for the development of historical thinking in the Humanities and Social Sciences (HASS)
- learn how skills can be developed through historical understanding
- plan an historical inquiry process for a HASS unit.

## INTRODUCTION

History is challenging for learners as it concerns something that no longer exists – the past. Yet, as Christopher Portal (1987, p. 13) reminds us, 'in another sense, of course, the past is not dead at all; it exists through the ways in which we understand the past, and in the personal, cultural and intellectual inheritance we each have'. Herein lies our fascination with history and desire to learn about the past. Our connections with the past can vary, from engaging with family members' or friends' recollections, photographs and memorabilia to viewing historical dramas on television and mobile devices. Reading historical fiction, visiting museums or observing a public commemoration such as an Anzac Day march or a National Sorry Day event can also prompt interest in finding out more about the past.

We need to be mindful that young learners will already have some firm ideas and assumptions about what history is and what it entails. Research from the US National Research Council of the National Academies (NRCNA) found that learners enter educational settings with preconceptions about the ways in which the world works and that if their initial understandings are not engaged, they may not understand the new concepts and information being taught, or learners might only engage in learning new material for the purposes of an assessment task but then 'revert to their preconceptions outside the classroom' (NRCNA 2005, p. 1). This chapter draws from this research and other research findings to consider how teaching and learning in History in the *Australian Curriculum: HASS F-6/7* can enable young people to investigate the traces of the past in authentic and meaningful ways. Making sense of the past and learning how to think critically about it empowers young people to relate history to their lives in the 21st century and better prepares them to be informed, confident and active citizens.

## WHAT IS DISTINCTIVE ABOUT HISTORY AS A DISCIPLINE?

Can we ever really know about something that happened in the past when, at best, all that remains are some traces of it? What are the key ideas that make knowledge of the past possible? In this part of the chapter, we will explore some of the characteristics of History as a discipline by focusing on the work of historians.

Historians aim to interrogate the remaining relics and fragments, or **sources**, that survive the past, in order to understand what might have transpired. This work is complex. As Husbands (1996, p. 13) observes, working with sources is tricky 'because of the ambiguous relationship between our interests, the relics we might have or find, elisions and distortions which the relics contain, and of course the past which generated the relics'. Historians and philosophers have grappled with the challenges of reconstructing what might have happened in the past and the nature of such work. The historian Jack Hexter (1971, p. 228) theorised the problematic nature of the historian's work by referring to two different, but intersecting, records. According to Hexter, the first record consists of the relics or fragments of the past that survive. The knowledge, expertise, values, beliefs and imagination that historians bring to their work shape the second record. It is when historians apply the second record to the first that 'history' is produced. It is worth noting, however, that the quality of such history depends on the nature of the sources and each historian's characteristics.

Hexter's (1971) notion of the historian's work as the interconnection of two records provides some insights into why historians working with the same set of sources can interpret them differently and write conflicting narrative accounts of an event or process. This raises another fascinating yet problematic aspect of the historian's work with which learners often struggle: it is tentative and can be contested as new sources are discovered.

Such brief insights into the complex work of historians indicate that history has distinctive features and processes that allow for debate about the uncertain nature of the past in a **disciplinary framework**. This sets history apart from other forms of inquiry, such as those used in physics or sociology. Some of the distinctive disciplinary features of history that are important for our work with learners include the formulation of questions to guide an inquiry into past events, processes and human behaviour; locating, interpreting and analysing sources; determining which sources can be considered as items of **evidence**; using discipline-specific concepts to guide making judgements about claims; and communicating such decision making in rigorous and engaging ways.

*The Shape of the Australian Curriculum: History* (National Curriculum Board 2009), which established the parameters for drafting the *Australian Curriculum: History*, endorsed this

**source**: written or non-written material used to investigate the past, such as coins, photographs, gravestones, buildings and transcripts. Sources are examined critically to determine whether they can provide insights or 'evidence'.

**disciplinary framework**: the distinctive concepts and inquiry processes that collectively shape the nature of history as a distinct form of knowledge and way of making sense of the past

**evidence**: what can be learnt from a primary or secondary source to help construct an historical narrative

view of history. In doing so, it reflected the widely held view that history should be taught in Australian schools in ways that link it to the academic discipline (Henderson 2012, 2017). This is explained further with reference to how history is described and structured in the Australian Curriculum with a particular emphasis on conceptual understanding and the skills of historical inquiry. Research from the United Kingdom has indicated that learning history in a discipline-specific way matters to young people:

> In discussing sources or accounts of the past, children need to learn to develop arguments, defend them, listen to the views of others and perhaps change their own ideas as a result. This process, as it becomes more complex with maturation and increased knowledge, is fundamental to social development, emotional development, cognitive development, and participation in a democratic society. (Cooper 2015, p. 17)

# THE STRUCTURE OF HISTORY IN THE AUSTRALIAN CURRICULUM

History is described as a disciplined process of inquiry in the Australian Curriculum and it can be studied across all year levels from Foundation to Year 10. Learners can encounter history in the early and primary years as a sub-strand of F-6/7 HASS via an integrated curriculum or as a separate subject. Regardless of how history is positioned in a specific educational setting, it is important to note that all learners can engage meaningfully in historical inquiry if educators shape and structure activities appropriately. Drawing from her engagement with the research literature and her work with young learners, the British history curriculum specialist Hilary Cooper (2015), whose work was referred to above, contends that primary school children can learn history through processes of historical inquiry in increasingly complex ways and that this approach enriches children's cognitive, social and emotional development as well as their sense of identity. Cooper refers to some common pedagogical factors that have implications for teaching history in the early and primary years. These include:

> the importance of engaging with sources, working with others, discussion, working with a variety of types of resources, questioning, teacher interventions and relating an enquiry to pupils' interests and previous knowledge. (Cooper 2015, p. 61)

It is important to consider these insights and how educators might draw from and apply them with young learners. Prior to exploring this, it is important to be cognisant that history is structured with five distinctive components in the Australian Curriculum. Two of these components are critical to the discipline and interconnect: historical knowledge and understanding, and historical inquiry and skills. We will explore these two components in depth.

The three other components were designed by the Australian Curriculum, Assessment and Reporting Authority (ACARA 2018) to shape all learning areas in the curriculum and these are referred to briefly. Where appropriate, ACARA advises that to enrich learning, links should be made to the cross-curriculum priorities and the general capabilities (see Part IV). Furthermore, links to other learning areas are also encouraged. For instance, History can be linked to learning areas such as English and the Arts.

In summary, the five components of History in the Australian Curriculum are:

1. historical knowledge and understanding
2. historical inquiry and skills
3. general capabilities
4. cross-curriculum priorities
5. links to other learning areas.

The next section explores the nature of historical knowledge and understanding and historical inquiry and skills.

## Developing historical knowledge and understanding through inquiry

The writers of the Australian Curriculum drew on international research on young people's historical thinking to frame history as a process of inquiry that aims to foster learners' curiosity and imagination about the past. Understanding the connection between past and present, and changes and continuities across time, were also positioned as essential components of historical study. This focus on encouraging learners to become curious about the past, so that they can develop their own opinions and values based on a respect for evidence, and to build a deeper understanding of the present by engaging with and questioning the past, can be traced back to the innovative work of the Schools Council History 13–16 Project (SCHP) in the United Kingdom in 1972. This chapter briefly refers to the findings of the evaluation of the project, and more recent research on historical thinking and reasoning, to show why conceptual understanding and skills are prioritised in the *Australian Curriculum: History*.

In stark contrast to the traditional practice of teaching history through textbooks and teacher-directed note-taking during the 1970s in the United Kingdom and other nations, the SCHP aimed to rethink the purpose and nature of school history by engaging learners in the process of **historical inquiry**. Influenced by Jerome Bruner's (1960) view that any learning area can be taught to any child during their development, provided the structures of the subject or discipline are made explicit, the SCHP took as its starting point the distinctive character of history. The SCHP's 'New History' emphasised that the study of history 'involves some attempt to rethink the past, to re-enact it and to empathise with the people concerned in any past situation' (Schools Council History 13–16 Project 1976, p. 17). It also advocated that historical knowledge was contested and that young people needed opportunities in the history educational setting to learn to think like historians.

> **historical inquiry**: the processes used to investigate the past; historical inquiry is structured and shaped by questions

Interrogating sources as potential items of evidence, and using historical concepts, were core components of the SCHP's alternate curriculum. The SCHP underwent a formal evaluation and some notable findings of the History 13–16 Evaluation Study (Shemilt 1980) were that evidence constitutes the building blocks of historical explanation and narrative; that inquiry approaches assist learners' thinking about historical evidence; and that educators' grasp of the principles and processes of history teaching and learning affects the growth and quality of young people's historical reasoning, among others. Researchers in other nations, including

Australia, have continued to probe the nature of young people's thinking and understanding in History. The following Spotlight on HASS education indicates the ways in which learners can engage with sources from the past as they pursue an inquiry.

## LIVING CONDITIONS IN LONDON: AN ACTIVITY WITH YEAR 5 LEARNERS

In a Year 5 history classroom, learners are investigating the reasons for the establishment of British colonies in Australia after 1800 (see the *Australian Curriculum: History*, ACHASSK106). So that they understand why the First Fleet was formed, in the first part of the inquiry learners investigate what life was like in England in the 1700s and research the events that led to the transportation of convicts to Australia. In small groups, they inquire into the harsh living conditions faced by many people in London during the 1750s. Through reading extracts from the Old Bailey's Court Proceedings; interpreting a range of primary sources about the experiences of individuals and groups; and accessing and responding to a series of questions about images and line drawings of London slums, such as Gustav Dore's (1872) wood-engraving *Wentworth Street, Whitechapel* (Figure 7.1), learners prepare a summary of such conditions to share with their peers.

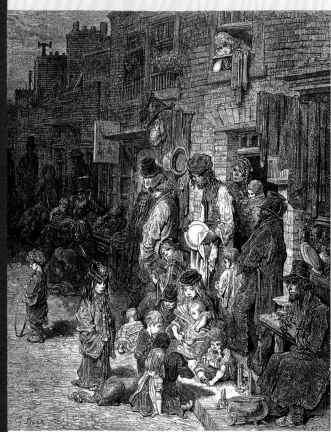

FIGURE 7.1    Gustave Dore, *Wentworth Street, Whitechapel* (1872), from *London: A Pilgrimage*

Once learners have shared their findings, educators can lead a discussion that focuses on understanding what caused so many people to live and work in such poor conditions, why it was difficult for them to escape their harsh environment and, if they were unemployed, why they often resorted to crime to survive. In pairs, learners investigate sections from trial reports and Old Bailey sentences of transportation, and individual testimonies to engage with a range of perspectives. Their inquiry culminates when they research a prisoner on the First Fleet by accessing other sources and websites such as Convict Records (https://convictrecords.com.au/timeline/1787).

This type of inquiry-based work provides rich opportunities for young people to learn about a range of concepts such as justice and injustice, evidence, cause and effect, and perspective, as they reflect on how challenging life was for some people at this time.

How might you adapt this approach for Year 5 learners who have English as an additional language/dialect (EAL/D)?

Reflection

## What topics can be selected for inquiry?

Preservice educators will need to know how other topics can be selected for inquiry from those included in the curriculum. The historical knowledge and understandings strand provides subject content descriptions that are sequenced in scale from Foundation to Year 10 in terms of 'personal, family, local, state or territory, national, regional' and 'world history' (ACARA 2018). It also includes a study of 'societies, events, movements and developments that have shaped world history from the time of the earliest human communities to the present day' (ACARA 2018).

Educators also need to spend time reading the content descriptions in the online curriculum in order to appreciate the scope and sequence of the History content descriptions. Also helpful are the resources and support materials that are available as PDF documents on the Australian Curriculum website, including:

- Sequence of achievement F-6/7, which provides the achievement standard at each year level for the history sub-strand of the F-6/7 Humanities and Social Sciences subject: http://docs.acara.edu.au/resources/F-67_History_Sequence_of_Achievement.pdf
- Year F-6/7 Humanities and Social Sciences: Sequence of content: http://docs.acara.edu.au/resources/F-67_HASS_-_Sequence_of_Content.pdf
- Humanities and Social Sciences: Sequence of achievement F-6/7: http://docs.acara.edu.au/resources/F-67_HASS_Combined_Sequence_of_Achievement.pdf.

As discussed previously, younger learners can engage in historical inquiry and develop historical knowledge, understanding and skills at age-appropriate stages (Cooper 2015). The curriculum provides useful year level descriptions, aims, inquiry questions, knowledge, understanding and historical skills to help structure meaningful work with sources in the classroom. Similarly, by engaging with historical concepts, younger and older students can learn how to think historically, and this is explored in the next part of the chapter.

## EDUCATOR TIP

See 'Planning an historical inquiry process' later in the chapter for more guidance on the 'what' and 'how' of planning a unit of work in History.

# CONCEPTUAL UNDERSTANDING IN HISTORY

**substantive knowledge:** specific and broad knowledge about the topic undergoing inquiry; also known as content knowledge

**first-order concepts:** historical phenomena that result from engaging with historical content. In an inquiry on World War I, examples could include conscription, militarism, nationalism, and alliances, among others.

**second-order concepts:** the 'big ideas' that distinguish how historians work and think. Seven second-order concepts are identified in the Australian Curriculum. Also known as procedural concepts or metaconcepts.

International research on learners' conceptual understanding and the skills of historical inquiry influenced the writers of the Australian Curriculum. UK-based history educator Peter Lee's (2006, 2017) research on how young people orient themselves in time by making sense of historical content and facts (**substantive knowledge**), as well as the 'big ideas' of history, was significant. Lee uses the terms '**first order**' and '**second order**' with reference to a framework for organising historical concepts. Second-order concepts encompass key ideas about the discipline of history and how it works. As Lee (2006, p. 131) puts it, these 'organising ideas... give meaning and structure to our ideas of the discipline of history'. Lee's terminology is not used in the Australian Curriculum; however, the historical knowledge and understandings section consists of an infinite number of first-order, and seven second-order, concepts together with historical content (substantive knowledge). Table 7.1 provides an example of a Year 5 HASS educator's planning for these three different forms of knowledge in a History unit that inquires into what life in colonial Australia during the 1800s was like for different groups of people.

**Reflection** How might you plan to engage learners with these different components in a unit of work in an accessible and age-appropriate way?

Research conducted by Lee, Ashby and Shemilt (2005) into seven- to 14-year-old learners' ideas about evidence and explanation in history under the Concepts of History and Teaching

| TABLE 7.1 | AN EXAMPLE OF PLANNING FOR CONCEPTUAL UNDERSTANDING IN HISTORY |
|-----------|----------------------------------------------------------------|

**Year 5 History focus:** Australian communities – their past, present and possible futures
**Topic:** The nature of convict or colonial presence, including the factors that influenced patterns of development, aspects of the daily life of the inhabitants (including Aboriginal Peoples and Torres Strait Islander Peoples) and how the environment changed (ACHASSK107).
**Inquiry question:** What do we know about the lives of people in Australia's colonial past and how do we know?

| Historical topic knowledge content (or substantive knowledge) examples | Historical concepts: first-order examples | Historical concepts: second-order examples (meta-concepts or procedural concepts) |
|---|---|---|
| *Knowledge and information about an historical development, event or individual being studied as prompted by inquiry questions* | *Concepts about historical phenomena that are relevant to, or emerge from, the knowledge and information (content) being studied* | *Concepts from history's disciplinary framework, i.e. what constitutes history and how history is studied* |
| *Learners find out:* What was life in colonial Australia during the 1800s like for different groups of people (sources)? How did different groups and individuals respond to each other and to the environment? Why was there conflict between some groups and some Aboriginal peoples? What were the reasons for their actions (cause and effect, perspectives, empathy)? | *Learners understand and use:* Penal settlement Colonial Racism Resistance Frontier Wars | *Learners understand and use:* Evidence Continuity and change Significance Perspective Empathy |

Approaches (CHATA) project demonstrated that the development of second-order concepts was critical to their capacity to reflect on and control their own learning. The authors note that 'students can acquire and refine the conceptual tools necessary to organize and manipulate information only to a limited extent until they are explicitly aware of what they are doing' (Lee, Ashby & Shemilt 2005, p. 80). Findings from the CHATA project serve to remind us that history educators need to use **metacognitive strategies** and explicit questions to prompt deeper levels of thinking in history. Similarly, Peter Seixas (1997) argues that historical thinking is essential to history teaching, for it is only when learners start to develop the skills to 'think historically' that they are engaged in deeper levels of historical understanding.

> **metacognitive strategies:** prompt learners to reflect on the nature of their thinking. In history, these strategies relate to how to interpret and use sources as items of evidence.

The seven second-order concepts in the Australian Curriculum are evidence, continuity and change, cause and effect, significance, perspective, empathy and contestability. As we explore these concepts below, note that all learners from Foundation to Year 6/7 are expected to engage with them in an accessible and relevant way.

## Evidence

Dealing with the nature of *evidence* involves how to find, select and interpret historical sources. Few learners come to educational settings cognisant of the complexity of this process. Young learners need assistance in differentiating between **primary sources** and **secondary sources**. They need specific learning experiences that enable them to understand that reading, interpreting and analysing both primary and secondary sources for evidence involve different skills from reading a source for information. Primary sources, for example, need to be read in their historical context so that learners can develop inferences from them to understand more about the period of time in which these sources were created.

**primary source**: an item or object created or written during the time being investigated, such as laws, treaties, inscriptions, pottery, statues, diaries, letters, photographs and artworks

**secondary source**: an item produced after the period of investigation, such as writings of historians and other historical narratives, textbooks, websites, documentaries, encyclopedias, film and media articles

## Continuity and change

Many young learners come to the study of history assuming it consists of a series of sequential events that unfold in a linear way. The concept of *continuity and change* is essential for any historical investigation as it presents insights into dealing with the complexity and messiness of the past and making sense of what changes and what remains the same. The notion of time is critical in history: learners need to engage with mechanisms such as chronological dating systems and other strategies to consider what might constitute a period of time in history; for example, the French Revolution. Questions prompting engagement with continuity and change often commence with 'what', 'where' and 'when'. Levstik and Barton (2005, p. 21) argue that learners need to develop chronological outlines as 'intellectual map[s] of the past'. Accordingly, learners need to situate specific periods for investigation within broader histories and connect the links between events to gain a fuller grasp of why things occurred.

## Cause and effect

Causes are the necessary conditions that are present for an event to occur. Although some *causes* and *effects* can be relatively straightforward, others are much more complex and multilayered. They can be intended or unintended, small or large scale, and short or long term. Long-term factors such as the development of ideologies, conditions and institutions, as well as short-term factors including actions, events and motivation, indicate their complexity, and historians can interpret them differently. The concept of *cause and effect* is closely linked to continuity and change, and history educators frequently frame questions to extend that focus by addressing the 'how', 'why' and 'with what consequences' in the search for cause and effect. These questions also raise the notion of human agency, as individuals and groups take part in responding to and shaping change.

## Significance

*Significance* in the study of history encompasses the principles behind the selection of what should be remembered, investigated, taught and learnt in educational settings. Carla Peck and Peter Seixas (2008) draw from their work on the Benchmarks of Historical Thinking project in Canada to propose some useful criteria for considering significance with learners.

These include, first, considering whether the event, person or development resulted in change and had 'deep consequences for many people, over a long period of time' (p. 1019). The second criterion is 'revealing'; that is, whether the event, person or development 'sheds light on enduring or emerging issues in history and contemporary life or was important at some stage in history within the collective memory of a group or groups' (p. 1019).

## Perspective

Learners need to understand that two forms of *perspective* are critical in history: the range of different perspectives of people *in* the past and the range of different perspectives *on* the past. Understanding the perspectives of people in the past can be challenging for learners as the views of individuals in other times, cultures and places can differ significantly from those in the present. Young learners require opportunities to inquire into how the views of individuals from past times were shaped by the social, cultural, intellectual and physical contexts that influenced their lives and actions. They also need to engage with multiple perspectives, and appreciate that events in the past need to be considered from the point of view of a range of participants in, and observers of, the event or process. As well as comprehending the differences between how we think in the present compared with people in the past, learners need to understand that historians adopt different perspectives when they research and write about the past, and that these perspectives influence their interpretations.

## Empathy

Learners often assume that *empathy* in history equates with feeling sorry for someone in the past. Rather, the capacity to gain a perspective on the past that is empathetic involves the ability to see and understand the world from a perspective that is not our own. It requires us to imagine ourselves in the position of another in the past so we can make sense of their practices and contextualise their actions. However, such imagining must be informed by, and based on, historical evidence if it is to have any meaning. Also, as noted above, it is important that learners do not perceive and judge people in the past by present values and standards (Wineburg 2001). Hence, as a historical thinking skill, empathy is dependent upon the methodological skills involved in 'doing history', such as understanding contextual knowledge, analysing sources and critiquing prior interpretations. Empathy can be thought of as a cognitive process that requires 'perspective recognition' (Barton & Levstik 2004, p. 207) and as an affective process that involves caring about people's lives and choices.

## Contestability

Given the provisional nature of historical explanations, history is subject to debate and contention in the public and political spheres. The Australian Curriculum refers to *contestability* as occurring when particular interpretations about the past are open to debate in response to insufficient evidence or contrasting perspectives. Learners need to understand that debates are an important part of historical thinking. Moreover, historians hold strong views about particular issues, such as the debates about whether Australia was 'invaded' or 'settled'. Debates among professional historians are also open to interpretation and need to be investigated in the same ways that other sources of evidence are interrogated. Accordingly, young learners need to interpret, analyse and interrogate items of evidence about contesting viewpoints, before synthesising their findings and arriving at a tentative judgement. Lee (1984) contends that learners should not shy away from the politicised nature of contention in history. He argues that teaching history is concerned with providing opportunities to do more than learn about some aspects of the past; it is also about acquiring historical ways of making sense of what is learnt. Such decision making links to the second interconnecting strand in the history curriculum: historical inquiry and skills.

# DEVELOPING SKILLS THROUGH HISTORICAL INQUIRY

In F-6/7 HASS, History shares the inquiry and skills component with Geography, Civics and Citizenship, and Economics and Business. These skills are questioning, researching, analysing, evaluating and reflecting, and communicating. In relation to young learners cooperating and working together, Cooper (2015, p. 22) notes that:

> Group discussion also accelerated children's thinking. Analysis of pupils' talk showed that they were not only sharing the materials, they were also sharing ideas. They were using their peers' talk to support their own thinking; in other words, they were using each other as a learning resource. Research into peer collaboration supports this conclusion.

In addition to the benefits of constructing historical inquiry in ways that incorporate independent and collaborative group work, Cooper (2014) argues in another paper that children's learning in history may be progressed by using teaching methods that engage learners' skills in creative thinking and writing activities, based on their engagement with sources. When such activities are carefully scaffolded to structure a range of levels of thinking tasks, educators can provide opportunities for learners to write accounts of their findings in genres that interest them, such as a letter, a diary extract, a proclamation, a poem or a newspaper report.

As noted earlier, History is also linked to the other HASS subjects via the common set of achievement standards, and opportunities for integrating units of work in knowledge and understandings. The curriculum is structured so that the sub-strands of History and Geography are positioned in Foundation to Year 2 and continue to Years 6/7. The F-6/7 HASS: Sequence of content shows how the inquiry and skills in F-6/7 HASS are presented in an increasing level of sophistication. Although our focus is on the early and primary years, understanding the developmental nature of such skill development as it progresses to the lower secondary school is critical to the work as educators. The example in Table 7.2 illustrates this point.

Reflection

How will you work with learners in your classroom to ensure that you are fostering the inquiry skills at an appropriate level?

| **TABLE 7.2**  THE DEVELOPMENTAL ASPECTS OF SKILLS IN HASS | |
| --- | --- |
| **Years F–2 HASS inquiry and skills** | **Years 9–10 History historical skills** |
| *Evaluating and reflecting* | *Perspectives and interpretations* |
| Draw simple conclusions based on discussions, observations and information displayed in pictures and texts and on maps (ACHASS1008) | Identify and analyse the perspectives of people from the past (ACHHS172)<br>Identify and analyse different historical interpretations (including their own) (ACHHS173) |

# EDUCATOR TIP

Choose two different year levels and access the relevant achievement standards for F–6/7. You will find descriptions of the depth of conceptual understanding and the sophistication of skills expected of learners. Note that the second paragraph focuses on skills. Planning for skill development is critical for a unit of work or depth study and this is explored below.

## Planning an historical inquiry process

First, we will consider some general principles that are important for planning a sequence of history lessons prior to planning a unit of work. These include knowing what learners have done previously, and how well they remember and understand this, and explicitly planning what new knowledge, understanding and skills you want learners to achieve in terms of what they will know and be able to do. You need to consider how to plan for **differentiation** and know what resources are available for learners to engage with; plan and manage the length of each stage of a lesson; and have arranged what you and any other colleagues or community members you have invited into the classroom will be doing at each stage of an individual lesson.

**differentiation**: in broad terms, means tailoring teaching and learning to meet the needs of individual learners in educational settings. This can involve HASS educators designing different content or specific learning tasks, or setting different learning outcomes for their learners.

A second consideration relates to formative or diagnostic assessment, often referred to as assessment for learning (AfL). In educational settings, formative assessment is employed to ascertain what learners have or have not learnt, and for children to know what they have already learnt and what the next step may be. This requires learning environments that support dialogue and trusting relationships so children can learn from their mistakes and their successes. In such contexts, children can be supported to take ownership of their progress by learning to self-assess and to make suggestions about activities for doing so. The following insights of Chrystal, an experienced Year 3 teacher, are worth noting.

> I think it is so important to plan to gather examples of children's work at key stages in a series of lessons, and of course, when I teach a unit of work. I collect examples from a range of writing genres that are objective and creative, as well as drawings, diagrams, charts, and simple timelines the children have created as evidence of their learning. I use checklists and criteria sheets to record my observations of the children and how they respond to my questions individually, in pairs and groups as they participate in set tasks. I use this data to inform my judgements about how my students are progressing and

make sure my feedback is proactive. I always provide words and symbols of encouragement. My students love brightly coloured stickers, such as smiley faces and stars, on their work. I also make dedicated time to conference with my students. By this I mean making a quiet time to talk individually with each child about their work. This creates a supportive and safe environment for feedback. And I encourage my students to take risks by thinking critically and creatively about their work.

**Reflection** To what degree are you confident you can plan for some of the processes Chrystal has outlined above? What do you think you can do well? What do you think you need to fine-tune? Why? Share your reflections with a supportive colleague.

A third planning consideration involves selecting an inquiry question from the F-6/7 HASS Curriculum to frame the development of a unit of work. With reference to the Year 4 level descriptor, 'How people, places and environments interact, past and present', the curriculum provides four inquiry questions for planning History units of work across the year. For example, the fourth question: 'What was the nature and consequence of contact between Aboriginal and Torres Strait Islander Peoples and early traders, explorers and settlers?', can serve as the focus for planning and is often referred to as the 'big' question for the unit. The next step involves considering how to embed one of the cross-curriculum priorities and a relevant general capability. Given the focus of this question, the educator could embed the cross-curriculum priority of Aboriginal and Torres Strait Islander histories and cultures, and the general capability of intercultural understanding, so that learners are able to explore and develop respect for cultural knowledge, beliefs and practices. Accordingly, the next step involves breaking the 'big' inquiry question down into chronologically sequential smaller questions. These 'small' questions will assist in planning a series of individual lessons. A useful reflective strategy to adopt at this stage of planning is to consider whether, when learners have worked through the 'small' questions, they will be able to answer the 'big' question for the unit.

These steps and some other general stages to think through when planning a unit of work in History for F-6/7 HASS are considered in Table 7.3.

## EDUCATOR TIP

The Dutch history educators Jannet van Drie and Carla van Boxtel (2008) focus on historical thinking by emphasising the development of 'historical reasoning' through disciplined inquiry in the classroom. Access their framework, which identifies six interactive components.

Consider the similarities and differences between this emphasis on reasoning with the positioning of conceptual learning and skills in the *Australian Curriculum: History*. Make a list of these similarities and differences.

**TABLE 7.3** PHASES OF PLANNING AN INQUIRY-BASED UNIT OF WORK

| Phase | Characteristics |
|---|---|
| Framing inquiry questions to investigate the topic | How will you structure 'big' and 'small' inquiry questions that provide a focus for investigation and encompass an aspect of time, location and either change/and or continuity or cause and effect? |
| Backward mapping assessment with reference to the achievement standard and assessment for learning (AfL) | How will you check to see what your learners are expected to *know* (knowledge and understanding) and *do* (skills) by the end of the year? How does learning in this unit contribute towards such knowledge and skills? How will you assess this formatively (AfL) and summatively in this unit? |
| Identifying the historical topic knowledge content | Check the content descriptor and read the elaborations in the Australian Curriculum Where appropriate, how will you make links to the cross-curriculum priorities and general capabilities? How will you employ timelines and maps to locate content in time and place? |
| First-order concepts | Which concepts are important for illustrating an aspect of the content in this topic? |
| Second-order concepts | Which of the seven concepts are important for the development of historical thinking in this unit? |
| Selection of sources | What primary and secondary sources do you want your students to engage with and interrogate? |
| Selection of other resources | What documentaries, films, YouTube clips, websites, guest speakers and/or excursions will you provide for your learners to engage with? |
| Planning for a range of teaching strategies and learning activities | How will you plan for: <br> • individual, pair, small group learning <br> • a mixture of expository teacher, teacher as guide, as critical respondent <br> • audio, visual and kinaesthetic learning activities differentiation? |
| Working out a teaching and learning sequence | How will you plan a series of sequential lessons that explore the 'big' and 'smaller' inquiry questions? |
| Making decisions | What sort of reflective activities will you devise to prompt learners to arrive at a conclusion or judgement based on evidence? |
| Communicating knowledge | What genre/format will learners use; for example, paragraphs, essays, ICT-format in multimedia presentation, creative presentation in art or drama, poster, video, other formats? |

# CONCLUSION

This chapter has provided insights into what distinguishes history as a way of making sense of the past and how it is positioned in the HASS learning area in the *Australian Curriculum: F-6/7*. It has drawn from international research on the ways in which children and young people develop historical knowledge, understanding and skills and how they learn to think historically. Emphasis was placed on the critical role of conceptual understanding in this process. You are encouraged to draw from these ideas as you design and plan a unit of work for the learners in your History classroom in a rigorous and reflective way. Making sense of the past and learning how to think critically about it empowers young people to relate history to their lives in the present and the challenges of the 21st century.

## REVIEW QUESTIONS

1. Why should History educators engage with the ideas and assumptions that learners bring to the classroom?
2. What does historical inquiry involve?
3. What are the differences between first-order and second-order concepts in History?
4. What are the differences between primary and secondary sources?
5. How do sources become evidence in History?

## LEARNING EXTENSION

Select the research task most relevant to your interests and access the specific PDFs from the Australian Curriculum website.

### Foundation to Primary

Hilary Cooper (2015) emphasises that primary school learners need to encounter history progressively as appropriate to their different stages of development. When history is taught in this context, Cooper suggests young learners can encounter historical concepts and develop historical skills in meaningful ways. Access these PDFs:

- F-6/7 HASS: Sequence of content, which includes inquiry and skills and also the knowledge and understanding: History sub-strand. Note how the history skills are embedded with the other HASS skills
- F-6/7 History: Sequence of achievement.

Imagine you have to provide a short presentation to your school's Parents and Friends Committee on the value of history for learners and their conceptual development across the F–6/7 years. Prepare your presentation as a PowerPoint and include references to the information in the PDFs.

## REFERENCES

ACARA (Australian Curriculum, Assessment and Reporting Authority). (2018). *Australian Curriculum: Humanities and Social Sciences F-10, v8.3*. History. Structure. Retrieved from https://www.australiancurriculum.edu.au/f-10-curriculum/humanities-and-social-sciences/history/structure.

Barton, K. & Levstik, L. (2004). *Teaching History for the Common Good*. Mahwah, NJ: Lawrence Erlbaum.

Bruner, J. (1960). *The Process of Education*. Cambridge, MA: Harvard University Press.

Cooper, H. (2014). *Professional Studies in Primary Education*. London: Sage.

——(2015). How can we plan for progression in primary school history? *Revista de Estudios Sociales*, 52, 16–31.

Henderson, D. (2012). A situated approach to historical thinking in the Australian Curriculum: History. *Agora*, 47(3), 4–11.

——(2017). 'It's more complex than I assumed': Examining pre-service teacher reflections on preparing to teach history in the Australian Curriculum in Years 7–10. *International Journal of Historical Learning, Teaching and Research*, 15(1), 118–36.

Hexter, J.H. (1971). *The History Primer*. New York: Basic Books.

Husbands, C. (1996). *What is History Teaching? Language, ideas and meaning in learning about the past*. Maiderhead: Open University Press.

Lee, P. (1984). Why learn history? In A.K. Dickinson, P.J. Lee & P.J. Rogers, eds, *Learning History*. London: Heinemann, pp. 1–18.

——(2006). Understanding history. In P. Seixas, ed., *Theorizing Historical Consciousness*. Toronto: University of Toronto Press, pp. 129–64.

——(2017). History education and historical literacy. In I. Davies, ed., *Debates in History Teaching*, 2nd edn. London: Routledge, pp. 55–65.

Lee, P., Ashby, R. & Shemilt, D. (2005). Putting principles into practice: Teaching and planning. In S. Donovan & J. Bransford, eds, *How Students Learn: History, mathematics and science in the classroom*. Washington, DC: National Academies Press, pp. 79–178.

Levstik, L. & Barton, K. (2005). *Doing History: Investigating with children in elementary and middle school*. Mahwah, NJ: Lawrence Erlbaum.

National Curriculum Board. (2009). *The Shape of the Australian Curriculum: History*. Melbourne: NCB.

NRCNA (National Research Council of the National Academies). (2005). *How People Learn: Brain, mind, experience and school*. Washington, DC: The National Academies Press.

Peck, C. & Seixas, P. (2008). Benchmarks of historical thinking: First steps. *Canadian Journal of Education*, 31(4), 1015–38.

Portal, C. (ed.) (1987). *The History Curriculum for Teachers*. Lewes: Falmer Press.

Schools Council History 13–16 Project. (1976). *A New Look at History*. Edinburgh: Holmes McDougall.

Seixas, P. (1997). Mapping the terrain of historical significance. *Social Education*, 61(1), 22–7.

Shemilt, D. (1980). *History 13–16 Evaluation Study*. Edinburgh: Holmes McDougall.

van Drie, J. & van Boxtel, C. (2008). Historical reasoning: Towards a framework for analyzing students' reasoning about the past. *Educational Psychology Review*, 20, 73–87.

Wineburg, S. (2001). *Historical Thinking and Other Unnatural Acts: Charting the future of teaching the past*. Philadelphia, PA: Temple University Press.

# MAKING GEOGRAPHY COME ALIVE BY TEACHING GEOGRAPHICAL THINKING

*Malcolm McInerney*

## Learning objectives

After reading this chapter, you should be able to:

- consider the nature of the Geography concepts in Humanities and Social Sciences (HASS)
- understand the place of conceptual thinking in Geography for the early and primary years of schooling
- illustrate the Geography concepts through case studies
- explore the relationship between assessment and the Geography concepts
- provide a critical and creative way to explore the Geography concepts with learners.

## INTRODUCTION

It is not an uncommon view that geography is only learning about places and maps with the academic rigour being focused primarily on learning the names of geographical features such as oceans, cities and rivers. For years, geographers have been challenging this view of their discipline and articulating the complexity of the thinking involved in the study of geography.

This chapter will argue that much of the complexity and rigour of the subject of Geography revolves around the sophisticated conceptualisation that is involved in thinking geographically, something that begins to develop in preschool. It is not so much what the geographer studies but the way they look at the human or physical phenomena they are exploring that makes the study of Geography what it is. This leads some to say that everything can be studied geographically or everything is geography! Going back to the discussion on the 'grammar' of a subject as discussed in Chapter 5, we can again highlight that what many people perceive as geography is purely the vocabulary of the subject and what makes geography is the grammar of the subject; that is, it is the implicit conceptual thinking involved when exploring and trying to make sense of the world in which we live.

## EDUCATOR TIP

As a professional learning activity, work with a group of educators to develop a two-sentence age-appropriate, learner-relevant and engaging sound bite in response to the question: What is this thing called geography?

What do you think the top 10 responses would be if you asked 100 people the question: What first comes to mind when you hear the word 'geography'? What comes to your mind when you think about geography?

Reflection

# TO THINK GEOGRAPHICALLY

In the early years, learners begin to 'think' geography as they develop their identity within families and communities, including their relationships with place and space. They further develop geographical concepts when exploring how they are connected to the world around them and how they care for their local environment (DEEWR 2009). Building on these early understandings, the *Australian Curriculum: Geography* aims 'to ensure that students develop the ability to think geographically, using geographical concepts' (ACARA 2018). To this end, the curriculum identifies seven key concepts as fundamental to the development of geographical thinking. These concepts are place, space, environment, interconnection, change, sustainability and scale. See Chapter 5 for a general discussion of concepts.

The key concepts have related concepts nestled within them and have been visualised as a wheel because they are all interrelated and make a whole, rather than being separate, non-connected entities. For example, how can we teach about sustainability in geography without considering the environment and interconnection and change in places over time? This chapter delineates the nature of each of the concepts through the use of case studies and then provides a method for applying the concepts in the educational setting to illustrate how they are all interrelated as a way of thinking geographically.

## Place: a sense of place

The concept of **place** is developed very early in a child's life and is of prime importance in both the Early Years Learning Framework (EYLF) and the Australian Curriculum. In the EYLF, young learners start to explore their place in the world: in Outcome 1, where children start to learn about their identity including relationships between people and places, and in Outcome 4, which focuses on children resourcing their own learning by connecting with people, place, technologies and materials (DEEWR 2009). Building from this foundation, the rationale for the *Australian Curriculum: Geography* states that 'geography is a structured way of exploring, analysing and understanding the characteristics of the places that make up

**place**: the significance of places, what they are like and what they mean to people

our world' (ACARA 2018). It is hard to argue that knowledge of where things are is not important in modern geography – such knowledge helps us to perceive spatial relationships and interconnections, and spatial variation and distribution, and to analyse associations, impacts and consequences.

The concept of place is not just the traditional view of geography about where places are, but is about the diverse nature and importance of places to the humans that inhabit and visit them. More specifically, place relates to the significance of places and how their uniqueness is closely linked to culture, providing meaning and identity for people. Places describe specific areas of the earth's surface, ranging from small places such as educational settings or local areas, to countries and through to major world regions. Some characteristics of places, such as those of rivers or buildings, are tangible, while others, such as those of wilderness, aesthetics or socioeconomic status, are intangible. Places also provide the services and facilities needed to support and enhance life and influence wellbeing and opportunities for people. No two places on the earth's surface are the same, and geographers study the environmental and cultural characteristics (climate, economy, landscape, vegetation, water resources, built environment, population and culture) of a place to determine geographical factors such as liveability, sustainability and connectivity and the impact of change.

An interesting consideration examined by geographers in this concept is 'sense of place' and the varying perceptions people have of place. Contentiously, it can be argued that the concept of place is a human construct and that some locations on the earth's surface are certainly geographical locations, but not places because they do not have meaning to humans. In regard to perception of place, there is usually no one view, with disparity in opinions constantly occurring between people in regard to the beauty and aesthetics of places as diverse as cities, forests or streets.

The groundbreaking 'place geography' work of Professor Yi-Fu Tuan (1990, 2013) is particularly pertinent to this discussion: he states, 'People think that geography is about capitals, land forms, and so on. But it is also about place – its emotional tone, social meaning, and generative potential' (Tuan 2013). Such humanistic geography emphasises people's perceptions, creativity, personal beliefs and experiences in developing attitudes to their environments.

Reflection Is a location on the earth's surface a place if it does not have a name and/or is uninhabited or rarely visited?

## An illustration for understanding

There are many wonderful case studies that illustrate the love of a place felt by those living there. An interesting phenomenon is when tourists visit a location and consider that place to be undesirable and not where they would wish to live or even visit again, while those living there consider the location to be their special place, providing them with meaning and identity. Such conflicting perceptions of place are often demonstrated by tourists, who compare the visited place to their own place and make disparaging comments about a place that local residents love.

We also see the importance of the place concept for humans when places are changed due to 'progress' or the impact of economics. Such changes provide useful case studies to illustrate the concept of place in terms of meaning and identity.

McDowell County, situated in the coalfields of West Virginia in the United States, is one such case study. McDowell County has experienced a great boom-and-bust since 1950 as a result of the downturn in coal production (Vimeo 2018). Despite the economic decline and population loss, many still call it home and feel a great sense of purpose among the mountains. Although not seen as an attractive or desirable place to live by those visiting, residents speak about their connection to this place and the meaning of 'home'.

## EDUCATOR TIP

It is important to find resources that are authentic and link to learners' lifeworlds. A useful activity for understanding the concept of place is for learners to find a case study at the local, state or national level that illustrates variance in perceptions of place such as described for McDowell County. The case study should be an example of a place that has economically and/or aesthetically declined in recent years but where the people continue to live because of their love for it.

## Space: everything is somewhere

As opposed to the concept of place, **space** is not a human construct but rather the definitive location of the features across the surface of the earth. It is the component of geography that is often seen as what geography is only about – where places are! Naturally, in order for a place to exist, it needs a space and for that reason the concepts of place and space are dependent upon one another.

**space**: knowing where places and landscapes are located, why they are there and the patterns and distributions they create

The *Australian Curriculum: Geography* describes the concept of space as being about location and spatial distribution, and the ways people organise and manage the spaces in which they live (ACARA 2018). All human and natural features of the earth have locations within space, and within such spaces we can locate human features such as cities, towns, specific sites (cemeteries, mines) and natural features such as forests, lakes and oceans, to name just a few. What is important to our understanding of the space concept is that the features of the world are organised spatially, and geographers map and analyse those features in terms of *location*, *distribution* and *pattern*. When undertaking analysis of the locations, distributions and patterns shown by features on a map, the geographer considers the impact of environmental, economic, social and political factors, and explores the reasons why places are located where they are. In relation to the space concept, it is often said that geography is about the 'why of the where'. The spaces of the earth are structured, organised and increasingly managed by people. With the advancement of technology, many spaces (cities, rivers, forests, lakes, coastlines) are increasingly being designed and redesigned to achieve particular purposes and, as a result, locations, distributions and patterns are subject to change over time.

## An illustration for understanding

Mapping is the tool geographers use to represent space and in turn undertake analysis of spatial arrangements and change. It is important for learners to realise that geography is not just putting features on a map, but also explaining why they are where they are and whether any trend and patterns can be observed. Modern geography has access to amazing mapping software packages called Geographical Information Systems (GIS) that are supported by accessible and comprehensive spatial data.

Although the production of a GIS map such as that illustrated in Figure 8.1 is impressive, it does no more than provide learners with a map that could be in a book. What is important is to introduce higher-order problem solving into the educational setting through the development of specific inquiry questions that can be answered by map production. In the early years, learners could draw a map of their local environment and direct people to different locations within this environment. Geography educational settings can now use mapping technology and resources to bring to life map-making in Geography, with the capacity for learners to be geographical detectives exploring analytical possibilities way beyond the dreams of Geography educators only a few years ago. The following example of a geographical detective exercise on world earthquakes shows the potential for Geography educators to develop high-level problem-solving exercises in the educational setting.

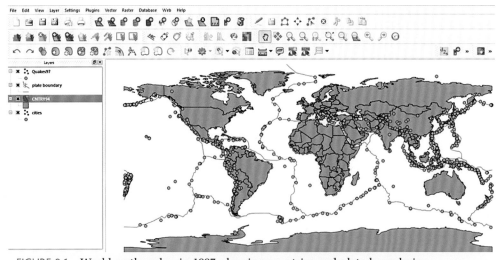

FIGURE 8.1   World earthquakes in 1997, showing countries and plate boundaries

# A SPATIAL CASE STUDY FOR THE EDUCATIONAL SETTING

*The spatial question to answer:* What world cities with a population greater than three million people would you avoid visiting in 1997 if you were worried about the occurrence of a damaging earthquake greater than magnitude 7?

*Software to use:* Any GIS software available is suitable for the exercise but free Open Source software such as QGIS (http://www.qgis.org/en/site) is excellent for the primary classroom and is compatible with the most commonly used spatial data files in the form of Shapefiles.

*Data to use:* Readily available spatial data from US Geological Survey (https://freegisdata .rtwilson.com) contains the magnitude and location of all earthquakes in 1997 and ESRI data (https://www.arcgis.com/home/item.html?id=dfab3b294ab24961899b2a98e9e8cd3d) provides the files for world cities and countries.

*The process:* Using GIS, learners create maps of the countries of the world, showing the location of world earthquakes greater than magnitude 7. Once that is done, learners then draw a buffer of 500 kilometres around each of the world cities with a population greater than three million.

*The answer:* Upon analysis (a spatial query) of the map (see Figure 8.2) it was found that there were two world cities with a population greater than three million and the travel advice in 1997 would be to not visit these places because of their proximity to a major earthquake. They were Mexico City, Mexico, and Santiago, Chile.

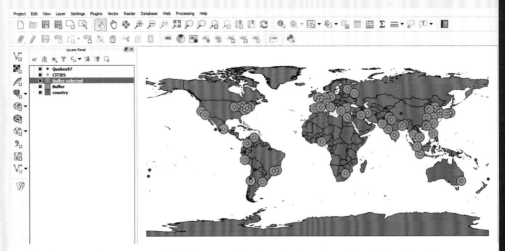

FIGURE 8.2   GIS map created by learners showing the location of world earthquakes greater than magnitude 7 (red points), a 500-kilometre buffer zone (green circle) around each world city with a population greater than three million (yellow points)

This is an example of an exercise focused on mapping space using GIS technology and doing spatial analysis based on comprehensive and expansive spatial data. Such inquiry processes using modern technology are essential to explore the location, distribution and patterns aspects of the space concept in the 21st-century Geography educational setting. The power of such spatial work is that learners can create unique questions to create unique maps, which is way beyond the regurgitation of facts and copy-and-paste exercises.

## EDUCATOR TIP

It is important for learners to go beyond published maps and create their own original maps. To enable original map-making, provide learners with data attached to a location (spatial data) to develop an original inquiry question. Ask learners to be creative in their thinking to construct a question that requires a number of maps to be developed, using a range of GIS skills to answer a question that is unique and challenging.

## Clarifying the difference between space and place

FIGURE 8.3   A shop window of a new store in Adelaide that recognised the distinction between place and space in a novel way

The place and space concepts are certainly different, but also interrelated in many ways. Space is about being able to map and analyse locations, distributions and patterns at a range of scales, while place is very much about human perception and sense of place with the implicit meaning and identity for people relating to a particular location or area. To put this another way, every place comprises space that can be represented and mapped and most spaces are places with which humans can identify and that provide meaning and identity, and a range of perceptions for individuals and communities.

Reflection   If you are in a boat in the middle of the Indian Ocean, are you in a space or place? Is the difference between a house and a home a useful analogy for understanding the difference between space and place?

# Environment: the human–environment link

The approach to this concept in modern geography challenges many of the topics taught in physical geography over the years. It can be argued that much of traditional physical geography was more the teaching of earth science than geography. The key point to make here is that for a subject to be Geography, we must consider the significance of the **environment** to human life, and the important interrelationships between humans and the environment. If a physical phenomenon is studied in isolation and does not consider the impact of humans on the landscape and vice versa, it is not geography. This is a contentious view among physical geographers, but when we look at the *Australian Curriculum: Geography*, it is clear that such a link is fundamental in all of the content descriptions related to the physical world. For example, if studying volcanoes, for it to be geography we must consider the reasons why people live near volcanoes and the impact of volcanoes on the people and communities in proximity to volcanoes – not just study the shape of the volcano as a geological structure. However, as discussed earlier in this chapter, it is quite legitimate when considering the space concept to study and analyse the locations, distributions and spatial patterns of volcanoes around the world. But when we study the environment as the product of geological, atmospheric, hydrological, geomorphic, edaphic (soil) and biotic factors, we must consider human processes as well.

**environment**: the significance of the environment in human life and the important interrelationships between humans and the environment

The environment has intrinsic value and is essential for ongoing human wellbeing in terms of providing raw materials and food, absorbing and recycling wastes, maintaining safe habitats and being a source of enjoyment and inspiration. The environment also determines the limits of human settlement and economic development that are increasingly being reduced, but not eliminated, by technology and human organisation. For example, no matter how hard humans try, we are limited in reducing the impact of earthquakes and volcanoes as hazards. The geographer is also cognisant that culture, population density, type of economy, level of technology, values and environmental world views influence the ways people perceive, adapt to and use similar environments.

If it is agreed that environment refers to the biosphere, including living and non-living elements, an interesting conversation to have with geographers is whether we can broaden the application of the environment concept to include the study of social, cultural, economic and political environments. Such a broadened interpretation of the environment concept enriches the study of human geography. For example, the hectic cultural environment someone experiences when they travel to Calcutta in India is vastly different from that of a small, orderly city like Adelaide, and the economic environment of a mining town such as Roxby Downs in South Australia is very different from the fishing economy of Eden in New South Wales. Such differentiation of environments is congruent when considering environmental, social, economic and political sustainability, as will be discussed later in this chapter.

Another important aspect of the human–environment link is the associated phenomenon of interdependency, as the link is often two-way and creates degrees of interdependencies between humans and the environment. Hence there is a close connection between Geography and the interconnection concept, which is the focus of the next section.

## Illustration for understanding

Children start to learn about the importance of caring for their environment even before they enter school when they explore how they are connected with and contribute to their world (DEEWR 2009). It is here that learners begin to become socially responsible and develop respect for their environment. There are many geogstories from environments around the world to stimulate learners' thinking about the complex interdependencies between humans and the environment. Here are just two amazing geogstories that can be used in the educational setting to illustrate this concept.

### Case study: Mussel gathering under sea ice

The people of Kangiqsujuaq in Canada go to great lengths to add variety to their diet of seal meat by venturing 40 metres under the sea ice during the extreme low tides of the spring equinox to gather mussels. The gatherers only have 30 minutes to make their way under the ice to gather the mussels before the tide reclaims the sea bed. This hazardous practice by humans to find a very inaccessible food source is a wonderful example of how humans used their close relationship with the environment to supplement their diet by taking enormous risks in their harsh environment.

### Case study: Walking on the sea bed

This geogstory is of the Bajau fisherman who freedive to walk on the ocean floor to catch their food. The Bajau live off the coast of Malaysia and have forged an intimate relationship with the water, which they rarely leave. After being banned from living on Malaysian soil because of their refugee status, the Bajau people have severed ties with the mainland, and instead choose to live a nomadic lifestyle on the open ocean. Out of necessity, they have adapted to their environment to survive, and have built an offshore community that relies solely on the ocean. The Bajau fisherman can survive below the surface for up to five minutes at a depth of 20–30 metres on one breath as they walk across the seafloor searching for fish. By doing so, they break all the rules of buoyancy as a result of a lifetime of training and discipline, a process that has been handed down the generations. This is a geogstory that shows how, if required, humans have an amazing ability to adapt to challenging environments to survive on meagre resources.

**Reflection**

Who were the first people in these locations to go under the sea ice to the find mussels and to learn to dive and walk on the seafloor? Was it really necessary to develop such a treacherous relationship with the environment to survive? How many died in the process of human adaptation and risk-taking?

# Interconnection: all things are connected

Geographers understand that everything has a consequence, whether positive, slightly left or right of neutral, or negative. Nothing in the human and physical environment can be introduced, removed or changed without some type of impact. Hence the concept of **interconnection** has a close relationship with those of change and sustainability. When studying interconnection, the debates between conservation and economic progress and between remediation and mitigation processes are often 'front and centre'. In essence, the concept of interconnection emphasises that no aspect of geographical study can be viewed in isolation.

**interconnection**: emphasises that no object of geographical study can be viewed in isolation

Places and people are interconnected with other places and people in a variety of ways. These interconnections have a significant influence on the nature of places and how people and communities change over time. Environmental and human processes, such as the water cycle and urbanisation, involve a multiplicity of cause-and-effect interconnections that can operate between and within places. These interconnections are often organised as systems involving interdependencies, shown through flows of material, energy, information and ideas.

These interconnections and possible interdependencies can be through tangible links such as roads or railways or via intangible links such as political, economic or electronic systems. In the study of geography, interconnections are important in understanding why things are changing or need to be changed in different places or environments. To see the complexity of interconnections, learners begin to view their own locality in a wider national and global context, and gain an understanding of the external factors that influence the locality's present and future. The concept of interconnection has become critical for geographical understanding as a result of the increasing number and complexity of human links across the globe due to technology. Modern technologies such as the Internet and cheap air travel enable people and communities to connect anywhere, at any time and have changed the way the world works. In fact, technology is making space diminish, leading to increased global interconnection. Real-time internet sites that plot, track and provide information on all flights (e.g. Plane Finder) and boats (e.g. Marine Traffic) across the world are just two resources that can be used in an educational setting to demonstrate the magnitude and complexity of global and regional interconnections in the 21st century (Figure 8.4). With such powerful modes of interconnection across the planet, it is no mystery why the topic of globalisation – economic, cultural and political – is central to much geographical discussion.

While discussing global interconnection, it is worth referring to the new age of the Anthropocene: the age of humans and interconnection. The Anthropocene is best defined as the current human-dominated period of the earth's history, an age of interconnection around the globe. The Anthropocene is the most recent period of the Quaternary, succeeding the Holocene. The Quaternary is a period of the earth's history characterised by numerous and cyclical glaciations, starting 2 588 000 years ago. The Quaternary is divided into three epochs: the Pleistocene, the Holocene and now the Anthropocene. The term and the concept of the Anthropocene – that is, the idea that human activity affects

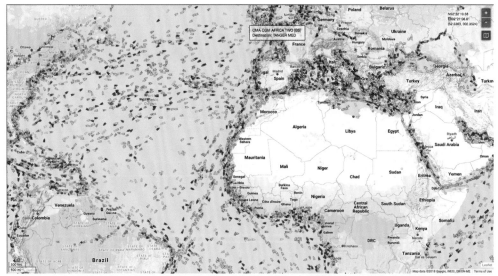

FIGURE 8.4  Screen captures from Plane Finder (2018) and Marine Traffic (2018)

the earth to the point where it can be classified as a new age – dates to the late 19th century. However, today such thinking is at the centre of issues such as climate change and global warming.

# EDUCATOR TIP

It is important for learners to realise that the nature of human–environment interconnections and spatial relationships has changed over time. To illustrate this point, ask learners to consider what interconnections a person living in 1900 would have had with the rest of the world compared with people today. Ask them to consider availability and access to travel, food, clothing, entertainment, sport and other areas of human activity in their discussion.

## Illustrations for understanding

### Case study 1: The unexpected consequences of the reintroduction of wolves into Yellowstone National Park

This is an excellent biogeographical example of the complexity of the interconnections within the physical world. The reintroduction of grey wolves into Yellowstone National Park in 1995 not only had massive positive impacts on habitats and animal life but also affected the nature of the rivers in the park due to changes in patterns of erosion caused by the demise of some of the animals upon which the wolves have impacted. Generally, this is considered to be a positive biogeography story based on interconnection and interdependency. Although positive in a biogeographical sense, it is interesting to consider the views of the farmers surrounding the park who are disturbed by the increase in the numbers of wolves and the impact on their livestock. This case study highlights that nothing is simple when looking at geographical issues and that no object or change can be viewed in isolation.

### Case study 2: The simple pencil as a human and environmental interconnection story

Geography educators using spatial technology are constantly deconstructing features of the world so that learners can see that nothing is simple and everything is interconnected, often interdependent and extremely complex. The essay 'I, Pencil' by Leonard Read (1958) highlights the interconnections between the physical and human world. Written in the first person from the point of view of a pencil, the pencil details the complexity of its own creation, listing its components (cedar, lacquer, graphite, ferrule, factice, pumice, wax, glue) and the numerous people involved, down to the sweeper in the factory and the lighthouse keeper guiding the shipment into port – and highlighting how a world of order can be created from the complexities of interconnection. The video *I, Pencil* is an exposé on these issues, using the simple pencil (not so simple!) to show the role geography plays in explaining the complexities of our world. It also opens the door to some great conversations about the economics of capitalism and globalisation, and the concept of spontaneous order.

Modern technology has had a significant impact on the interconnectedness between humans and places across the earth. To enable learners to see the interconnection impact of items they use on an everyday basis, ask them to consider a modern technology they use that is an enabler for increasing regional and global interconnections.

## Change: the geographical past and future

**change**: explains geographical phenomena by investigating how they have developed over time

The discussion on interconnection leads naturally to the concept of **change**. As discussed, change is often inevitable if interconnections are modified due to the removal, interruption or introduction of a feature or process. The concept of change in geography relates to the study of geographical phenomena and explaining how the human and physical features of the earth have developed over time and are likely to change in the future. The geographical phenomena studied through this conceptual lens could involve environmental (short- and long-term), economic, social and technological change. Such change is spatially uneven, affects places differently and alters over time with regard to degree, speed and duration.

Change is about the future as well as the past. By understanding the processes of change, geographers can predict and even model change and consider possible, probable and preferred futures. Such a focus on the future makes the change concept of fundamental importance to the study of the sustainability of the human and physical environments.

Change as a concept when studying world environments is dynamic. Places, environments and spatial patterns may be in a state of equilibrium for extended periods until an event such as a flood, cyclone or political decision occurs and alters them.

### Illustration for understanding

A demographic visualisation that has been used extensively in schools to show change over time is the website Gapminder (2018). Developed by Hans Rosling, this powerful learning tool is a multidimensional graph that shows the progress of countries over time in relation to human and environmental data (see Figure 8.5). Whether using data on births and deaths, energy use, pollution levels, literacy, health or education, Gapminder aims to increase the use and understanding of statistics and other information about social, economic and environmental development at the local, national and global levels. Gapminder challenges world views and presumptions, and promotes the questioning of data to develop an understanding of change over time and predictions for the future. GeogSpace, the resource to support the teaching of the *Australian Curriculum: Geography*, has an exemplar available that uses Gapminder to explore issues of world development and change over time (http://www.geogspace.edu.au/core-units/years-5-6/exemplars/year-6/y5-exemplars-y6-illus2.html). The Gapminder site also has extensive support materials for the educational setting.

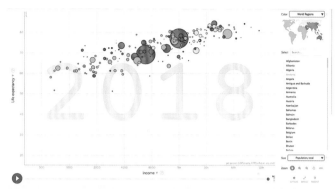

FIGURE 8.5 The Gapminder tool showing income and life expectancy years for countries between 1800 and 2018

# EDUCATOR TIP

After viewing the data available on Gapminder, ask learners to pose a geographical question related to either human or environmental change over time. Learners are to pose the question, select the data available on either of the Gapminder axes, then use the Gapminder tool to answer the question.

## Sustainability: sustaining life on earth

**Sustainability** addresses the ongoing capacity of the earth to maintain all life by meeting the needs of the present and not compromising the survival of future generations. To develop a world view on sustainability, the learner of geography needs to draw on all that they have learnt about the concepts of change, interconnection and environment. Environmental sustainability requires deep understanding of the processes, human uses and interventions that impact on the environmental functions that sustain all life and human wellbeing (economic and social). The concept of sustainability involves developing an understanding of sustainability as a broad social goal, linking the wellbeing of the natural environment (ecological) with the social and economic wellbeing of humans. To achieve this, geographers often use the systemic way of thinking that identifies inputs, processes, interconnections of component parts and outputs when studying geographical features or phenomena. This systems way of thinking can apply just as well to rainforests as to cities, to deconstruct and analyse the sustainability of a place. To provide a comprehensive view of earth systems, geographers often refer to the quadruple bottom line of sustainability: environmental, social, economic and political (governance) sustainability. The area of sustainability is one with many contested views on how economic progress and sustainability should be achieved, and these are often informed by world views such as stewardship and economic growth.

**sustainability**: the capacity of the environment to continue to support life into the future

As well as being a cross-curriculum priority of the Australian Curriculum, sustainability has been a long-term and fundamental focus for the teaching of Geography in schools. In the *Australian Curriculum: Geography*, the importance of the concept of sustainability is affirmed as one of the specific aims of the curriculum, to ensure that students develop 'as informed, responsible and active citizens who can contribute to the development of an environmentally and economically sustainable, and socially just world' (ACARA 2018).

## Illustration for understanding

### Case study: Fishing frenzy for sustainability

This is a geogstory about the thousands of men who gather for an annual fishing competition at Lake Antobo in Mali. This case study provides a stunning example of sustainable practice intermixed with traditional cultural norms. As was the case with the mussel hunters from Canada, this story shows the complex and interconnected relationship humans have with nature so as to maintain a sustainable existence. The lake remains untouched by humans for all of the year with the exception of one day when the local elders supervise a fishing competition (Figure 8.6). The ensuing frenzy sees the lake emptied of fish in minutes, an event not repeated until the same time the following year. The timing of the fishing frenzy is critical because it is at the end of the dry season and food is in short supply. However, one of the cultural norms of the Dogon people is that they are strictly forbidden to fish the lake at other times. This cultural practice ensures the sustainability of this precious resource and survival for the Dogon. It is an excellent example of environmental, social, economic and governance factors all working together to ensure a sustainable future for humans and the lake as a resource.

FIGURE 8.6   A fishing frenzy occurs just once a year at Lake Antobo, Mali

# EDUCATOR TIP

To help learners see that what they do and use has a direct impact on the resource depletion of the earth, ask them to use a relevant internet site to calculate their ecological footprint. These sites invite learners to input data that determines the number of planets that would be required if everyone on the planet continued to consume resources at their current level. After finding out their ecological footprint, ask learners to review their questionnaire responses to see how they could reduce their footprint.

## Scale: the zoom tool

'The concept of scale is about the way that geographical phenomena and problems can be examined at different spatial levels' (ACARA 2018). Having provided this definition from the *Australian Curriculum: Geography*, an interesting way to look at the concept of **scale** is to consider it as being analogous to a mental zoom tool. Such an approach is supported by the fact that, as 21st-century citizens, we zoom in and out of spatial levels as we think about geographical events, phenomena and processes. One minute we may be thinking at the spatial level of the global, then regional, then national and then local (not necessarily in that order). We repeatedly zoom in and out as we try to make sense of our world in geographical terms. This has not always been the case, with citizens of the past being much more locally focused, without the access to travel, education and media that allow a broader perception of scale. It can be argued that there is a difference in scale perception between rural and city dwellers; between less developed and more developed countries; and between isolated and less isolated places. Continuing along this line of thinking, the creation of a map at a particular scale is simply a snapshot of where we are thinking at the time – if thinking globally, we create a map of the world at the appropriate scale.

> **scale**: the way that geographical phenomena and problems can be examined at different spatial levels

It is important that learners develop their mental zoom tool so that they have a broader world view than just the local, and to realise that relationships found at one level of scale may be different at a higher or lower level and there are cause-and-effect relationships across scales from the local to the global and from the global to the local. For example, local events can have global outcomes, such as the effects of local vegetation removal on global climate.

### Illustration for understanding

The following are some ideas to demystify scale (refer to Figure 8.7):

1. The use of different size Tupperware containers can demonstrate how one spatial level fits into another.

2. The use of babushka dolls (Russian dolls of diminishing size that fit within each other) can demonstrate the spatial levels of scale.

3. A learner-friendly way to engage the concept of map scale and ratio is through the study of model trains/planes/boats. The model-to-real-life ratio is a good way for learners to relate to the concept of scale before trying to understand a map ratio (also referred to as a representative fraction – RF) such as 1:100 000.

FIGURE 8.7  Some learner-friendly visual representations of scale

## EDUCATOR TIP

The above examples show the concept of scale at a practical level. To further learners' understanding, ask them to think of other practical examples that could be used to demonstrate the concept of scale and the idea of hierarchy of scale.

# THE GEOGRAPHICAL CONCEPTS AND ASSESSMENT

As mentioned in Chapter 5, the concepts are overt in the achievement standards and cannot be ignored as a key component of assessment and task design. For example, the achievement standards for Year 2 and Year 6 Geography below show that the concepts (highlighted in italics) are clearly evident and should be the focus of learning and program design in Geography at those year levels.

> By the end of Year 2, students identify the features that define *places* and recognise that places can be described at different *scales*. Students recognise that the world can be divided into major geographical divisions (*Space*). They describe how people in different places are *connected* to each other and identify factors that influence these connections. They explain why *places* are important to people, recognising that places have meaning. (ACARA 2018)

> By the end of Year 6, students describe the location of places in selected countries in absolute and relative terms (*Space*). They describe and explain the diverse characteristics of *places* in different locations from local to global *scales*. They describe the *interconnections* between people in different places, identify factors that influence these interconnections and describe how interconnections *change* places and affect people. They identify and compare different possible responses to a geographical challenge (*Sustainability*). (ACARA 2018)

In addition to the inquiry and skills of Geography, understanding of the concepts regardless of the subject content is paramount in the teaching of Geography. Put another way, the grammar of Geography through the concepts is primarily what we are assessing, rather than just content knowledge of the subject matter.

# TEACHING THE CONCEPTS THROUGH AN INQUIRY APPROACH

A key aspect of teaching the *Australian Curriculum: Geography* is the idea of developing learner curiosity through the use of inquiry methodology. The inquiry process delineated in the inquiry and skills strand of the HASS curriculum is discussed in Chapter 11. The years F–6/7 of the HASS curriculum have a general inquiry process. The suggested approach discussed below is not to replace the stages of inquiry as outlined in the curriculum, but rather provides a way of inquiring through the concepts as described in this chapter. Educators have found that the use of such a conceptual approach when studying virtually any physical or human topic, feature or phenomenon enlivens the thinking involved and helps learners to identify with and understand the geographical concepts; that is, to be able to think geographically.

*Stage 1: Harvesting stage:* This stage involves learners gathering as much data, information and knowledge from primary and secondary sources as they can in relation to the topic or question posed. This process of harvesting is often framed by the foundation questions, such as what? where? when? how much and how?

*Stage 2: Deconstruction:* Learners are asked to work in groups of seven. Each learner selects one of the Geography concepts and then applies/discusses the topic posed through that concept. Some educators provide learners with the concept slice from the concept wheel shown in Figure 8.8 and ask them to try to only talk about that concept in the group. Naturally, it is extremely difficult to talk about a concept in isolation, and eventually the learners start to also talk about the other concepts; this naturally leads to the stage of construction.

*Stage 3: Construction:* As the learners find it harder and harder to discuss the concepts in any other way than interrelated, they enter the construction stage and start seeing the interconnectedness and complexity of the topic/issue discussed. It is interesting to hear learners at this stage discuss a topic in conceptual terms, looking at the topic not just as knowledge or facts but thinking geographically by using the geographical language of the concepts.

*Stage 4: Questioning stage:* After gaining knowledge and developing understanding through the conceptual discussions in the previous stages, the learners are at the important stage of questioning. In the harvesting stage, the learners asked the knowledge acquisition questions, but in this stage they ask the 'rich' critical and creative thinking questions, such as can? should? what if? why not? This is in-depth geographical thinking, based in conceptual understanding that provides the rigour to the study of Geography.

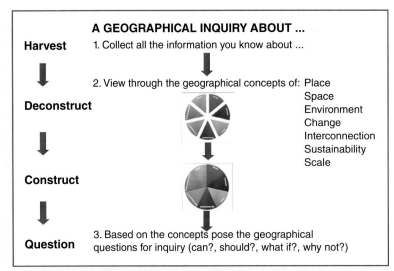

FIGURE 8.8 **Inquiring through the concepts to develop geographical thinking**

## EDUCATOR TIP

Ask learners to select any topic of their choice and apply the process of geographical inquiry and thinking as outlined above. The emphasis is on *any* topic, because it can be argued that everything can be studied geographically if viewed through the geographical concepts. Challenge learners to think of a topic that cannot be studied geographically!

# CONCLUSION

As is the case with all the HASS subjects, there is a grammar to learning in Geography that involves understanding what the key concepts are and how they can be applied to the subject matter studied. This literacy involves educators and learners engaging with the conceptual thinking involved in Geography through an overt understanding of the seven concepts of the *Australian Curriculum: Geography*. The geographical thinking that is developed enriches Geography beyond just knowing about places and where they are. The thinking is high order and involves a deep understanding of the intricacies, complexities and importance of human–environment relationships. Without such understandings, learners will not be equipped to address the decisions of the future, as an interconnected and exploited world challenges individuals, communities and governments on all scales.

## REVIEW QUESTIONS

1.  What make Geography Geography?
2.  Why is place such an important concept for learners to understand?
3.  Is it accurate to say that Geography is about the 'why of the where'?
4.  Compared to other disciplines, what is distinctive about the geographical concept of change?
5.  How does the creative inquiry process use the geographical concepts?

## LEARNING EXTENSION

Think of a topic that is not normally viewed as something that is studied in the Geography educational setting and use the geographical concepts in a critical and creative way to develop a unit of work that clearly requires geographical thinking.

## REFERENCES

ACARA (Australian Curriculum, Assessment and Reporting Authority). (2018). *Australian Curriculum: Humanities and Social Sciences F-10, v8.3*. Geography. Retrieved from: https://www.australiancurriculum.edu.au/f-10-curriculum/humanities-and-social-sciences/geography.

DEEWR (Department of Education, Employment and Workplace Relations). (2009). *Belonging, Being & Becoming: The Early Years Learning Framework for Australia*. Canberra: DEEWR.

Gapminder.org. (2018). Gapminder. Retrieved from: https://www.gapminder.org.

Marinetraffic.com. (2018). Global Ship Tracking Intelligence. Retrieved from: https://www.marinetraffic.com.

Planefinder.net (2018). Flight Tracker. Retrieved from: https://planefinder.net.

Read, L. (1958). I, pencil. Foundation for Economic Education. Retrieved from: https://fee.org/resources/i-pencil.

Tuan, Y.-F. (1990). *Topophilia: A study of environmental perceptions, attitudes, and values*. New York: Columbia University Press.

——(2013). The fascination of topophilia and place. *Spatialworlds*, 16 May. Retrieved from: spatialworlds.blogspot.com/2013/05/the-fascination-of-topophila-and-place.html.

Vimeo. (2018). West Virginia, still home. Retrieved from https://vimeo.com/71032050.

# CIVICS AND CITIZENSHIP IN THE 21ST CENTURY

*Andrew Peterson and Grace Emanuele*

## Learning objectives

After reading this chapter, you should be able to:

- understand what citizenship and education for citizenship are
- know the Australian Curriculum requirements for Civics and Citizenship education, with a particular focus on the primary school years
- understand and analyse the importance of the learning environment for Civics and Citizenship education, as well as different ways in which the subject might be taught
- analyse the importance of making connections within Civics and Citizenship education
- apply your developing understanding of Civics and Citizenship education to educational settings with which you are familiar.

## INTRODUCTION

This chapter introduces you to **Civics** and **Citizenship**, one of the four subjects that comprise the Humanities and Social Sciences (HASS) learning area. It presents Civics and Citizenship as an active, participatory subject area that requires educators to promote an open and supportive educational environment through which learners can be engaged in discussing issues that affect them and their communities, and enables them to engage in democratic decision-making processes. The chapter covers the main elements of the *Australian Curriculum: Civics and Citizenship*, as it appears both within the combined HASS curriculum for the primary years and as a stand-alone subject for Year 7. It also introduces methods and approaches through which Civics and Citizenship can be taught effectively. Throughout the chapter, key points are supported by research evidence, and supporting

**civics:** usually refers to education about formal political and legal institutions, processes and systems

**citizenship:** can refer to the legal status of being a citizen within a given nation. Commonly, citizenship also refers to being a participating member of various communities, and relates to notions of identity and belonging.

tasks and reflections will help you to develop your understanding of Civics and Citizenship. The chapter has three main sections. In the first you will be introduced to Civics and Citizenship. In the second, we consider and explore teaching and learning approaches, as well as how the Civics and Citizenship curriculum might be structured in schools. The third section focuses on connections – those with other elements of the Australian Curriculum and those with communities.

The following vignette illustrates one way that Civics and Citizenship teaching and learning can happen in a school. Year 3 learners were developing their understanding of the idea of rules, including why rules are important for participating in communities as active citizens. The school is committed to all learners having an active voice in decision-making in the school. The content of the lesson on rules connected to the curriculum through:

## KNOWLEDGE AND UNDERSTANDING

- How and why decisions are made democratically in communities (ACHCK001)
- How and why people make rules (ACHCK002)

## INQUIRY AND SKILLS

- Pose questions
- Distinguish between facts and opinions
- Develop a point of view
- Interact with others in a group

## INQUIRY FOCUS

- How are decisions made democratically?
- Why do we make rules?
- How can I participate in my community as an active citizen?

The lesson started with a 'graffiti wall' where the word 'rules' was written on paper. Learners worked in their table groups and wrote down their thoughts and feelings about the word 'rules'. This then led to a whole-class discussion on what rules are, including the sharing of different points of view.

In small groups, learners discussed:

- What are some rules for games with which you are familiar?
- Why do sports have rules?
- What are some of the school's rules?
- Which of the school rules do you like?
- If you could choose one rule to change at school, which would it be and why?

The answers to these questions were gathered and discussed as a whole class.

Learners then played 'Guess My Rule', a simulation game where the learners have to work out the rules of the game. The premise of this game is that the educator is the only one who knows the rule; for example, a rule could be that every time a ball is thrown to a boy, they need to sit out (this rule is not shared with the class). As the game progresses, there is discussion on how the learners are feeling about what they are experiencing. The game can be extended; for example, with the educator telling some learners the rules but not the rest of the class.

The purpose of the game is to instigate discussion about fairness, equality and participation. Asking learners to discuss their feelings on the above issues can open up dialogue about fair play, safety, respecting the rights of others and responsibilities. This can provide a valuable lead-in for learners to formulate classroom rules and to look at the rights and responsibilities of themselves and of others.

# UNDERSTANDING CIVICS AND CITIZENSHIP

Citizenship is a contested term, which can mean different things to different people in different contexts. Yet, while it may be difficult to define precisely, citizenship is a concept that fundamentally shapes the relationships we have in and through our public lives. It is therefore important that before we start to think about how we might teach about and for citizenship, we spend some time thinking about what citizenship means.

> What does citizenship mean to, and for, you? Do you hold multiple forms of citizenship? What rights and responsibilities do citizens possess?
>
> **Reflection**

Often, citizenship is approached through considering the relationship between the citizen and the state, which immediately brings into focus the connection between rights and responsibilities. On a broadly liberal view, citizenship is a legal status that involves some sort of reciprocal relationship between rights and responsibilities. Here, for example, the liberal state protects the rights of individual citizens to follow their own lives; in return, citizens have the responsibility to obey the law, pay their taxes and exercise their democratic voice on certain occasions (such as when electing people to public office). On another view – and here civic republican traditions provide an illustrative example – citizenship is more than a legal status; it is also a practice, through which we engage in responsible and active ways within our political communities. This richer notion of citizenship recognises that active forms of citizenship involve ongoing relationships between not only the citizen and the state, but between citizens themselves.

Central to understanding citizenship as a practice is the idea that each citizen brings particular identities to their political relationships. As Peterson and Brock (2017, p. 84) suggest:

> Citizenship is a legal status, but it is also much more than this. To assert that 'I am a citizen' of a given jurisdiction (of this or that town or city, of this or that nation-state, of this or that community) is generally to claim membership in that entity, and all that it entails. It is also often to proclaim a particular identity, providing citizenship with an accompanying emotional bond or tie (usually in a way that is proud, though sometimes in a way that includes shame or regret). For these reasons, citizenship can be an inclusionary force – as, for example, when citizenship of a nation-state is granted to those seeking a new home – or it can serve to exclude – as for example when full citizenship rights are denied to particular individuals or groups.

However, identities come in many forms, which may be 'citizenship' identities (national, regional or local, for example) or other forms of identity that intersect with citizenship in various ways (gender, sexuality, class or ethnicity, for example). The intersectionality brought about by multiple identities means that citizenship is constructed and experienced in various ways, and often shaped by particular contextual factors.

# WHAT IS CIVICS AND CITIZENSHIP?

Although there is not sufficient space within this chapter to provide a full historical account of the development of Civics and Citizenship as a subject (see Print 2016 for a detailed history), it is worth noting briefly that while Civics and Citizenship is a relatively new subject in Australian schools, most schools have long sought to develop active and informed citizens. Three elements of such practices are relevant here. First, for some time education for citizenship in Australian schools has formed a general aim of schooling. Most recently, the *Melbourne Declaration on Educational Goals for Young Australians* (Melbourne Declaration) included as one of the main goals of education and schooling the idea that all young Australians become 'active and informed citizens' (MCEETYA 2008, p. 9). As such, while learning to be and become a citizen might be taught through a timetabled school subject, this general goal appreciates that education for citizenship also results from a range of other school practices, including school ethos, school values and extracurricular activities.

**democracy**: a system of government in which eligible people participate in the decision-making process, either directly or, more commonly, through the election of representatives

Second, previous attempts have been made at a federal level to develop materials through which schools could educate students about **democracy**, government and the political system, most notably through the *Discovering Democracy* initiative (http://www1.curriculum.edu.au/ddunits/units/units.htm). Third, prior to the development of the Australian Curriculum, elements of what now appear in the Civics and Citizenship curriculum were taught through other subjects within state and territory curricula, most prominently through combined humanities and social sciences courses such as Studies of Society and Environment (SOSE).

These brief historical reflections highlight that education for citizenship can be included within a given school's curriculum through a variety of means, something to which we return later in this chapter. In addition, they remind us that while the goal of educating for citizenship may be long-standing in Australia, the teaching of the discrete and dedicated subject Civics and Citizenship within secondary schools is a relatively new endeavour.

**Reflection**  Thinking about a school you know, which elements of its practice combine to educate learners for citizenship? Are these various elements disparate or connected? If the latter, what practices are in place to ensure that connections are made?

As noted, in the Australian Curriculum, Civics and Citizenship comprises one of the four subjects within the HASS learning area. Currently integrated within a combined HASS curriculum in the primary years and as a separate subject in the secondary years, the aims of the subject as set out in the Australian Curriculum are expansive and bold. The first aim of the curriculum is to develop 'a lifelong sense of belonging to and engagement with civic life as an active and informed citizen in the context of Australia as a secular democratic nation with a dynamic, multicultural, multi-faith society and a Christian heritage' (ACARA 2018e).

Mirroring practices in other nations, Civics and Citizenship within the Australian Curriculum seeks to bring together learning about formal elements of relevant political, economic and social systems with the development of the skills and attributes necessary for being an active and informed citizen. The second and third aims of the subject indicate this coming together of the two strands – knowledge and understanding with inquiry and skills – and understanding this relationship is crucial to the effective teaching and learning of Civics and Citizenship education. The content of the two strands, as well as their interconnectedness, is clearest in the Civics and Citizenship curriculum for Years 7–10 and although not all preservice educators will be working specifically with this age range, understanding the nature of the subject discipline acts as a crucial prerequisite for its integration within the primary HASS curriculum.

In setting out the rationale for Civics and Citizenship, the Australian Curriculum (ACARA 2018e) makes the following statement:

> The Civics and Citizenship curriculum aims to reinforce students' appreciation and understanding of what it means to be a citizen. It explores ways in which students can actively shape their lives, value their belonging in a diverse and dynamic society, and positively contribute locally, nationally, regionally and globally. As reflective, active and informed decision-makers, students will be well placed to contribute to an evolving and healthy democracy that fosters the wellbeing of Australia as a democratic nation.

What is your opinion about these aims? If you were asked, how would you justify the inclusion of Civics and Citizenship in the Australian Curriculum?

**SPOTLIGHT ON HASS EDUCATION**

## Civics and Citizenship knowledge and understanding

Central to understanding Civics and Citizenship education are a set of concepts through which learners can understand and make sense of the subject and its connections with other areas of the curriculum within and beyond HASS. Knowledge and understanding of central democratic processes and institutions is fundamental to Civics and Citizenship education. In order to be and act as citizens, learners need to develop a sound and coherent understanding of the core elements, institutions and processes involved in political life.

The Australian Curriculum for Civics and Citizenship for both Years 3–6/7 and Years 7–10 (ACARA 2018e) breaks the knowledge and understanding strand into three elements:

1. *Government and democracy:* This includes key features of the Australian constitution; the federal system of government; citizen rights and participation; political parties; the role of the media; other systems of government; and Australia's role internationally.

2. *Law and citizens:* This includes how laws are made; different types of law, including the place of Aboriginal and Torres Strait Islander customary law; key principles underpinning the Australian court and justice systems; the role of the High Court of Australia; and how international legal obligations affect Australian law and policies, including those relating to Aboriginal and Torres Strait Islander peoples.

3. *Citizenship, diversity and identity:* This includes Australia as a secular nation, with a diverse and multi-faith society; how values can promote cohesion; the expression of identities; the values and beliefs of religions practised in Australia; ways of understanding Australian identity, including Aboriginal and Torres Strait Islander perspectives; the role of national identity in shaping belonging; how and why diverse groups contribute to civic life; the role of the media in shaping identities and attitudes to diversity; the influence of global connections and mobility on Australian identity; and sustaining democracy and social cohesion.

Of course, such learning need not be based on dry rote-learning of the minutiae of the Australian Curriculum. Rather, learning should engage learners with political issues, ideas, concepts and practices in ways that help them to make connections to their own lives and communities. A useful way of framing this way of approaching political knowledge is through the concept of political literacy, which can be defined as not just possessing political knowledge, but knowing when, why and how to apply such knowledge in active ways within real communities.

The mention here of public issues is important; it asks educators to consider the ways in which learners already are, and can be, engaged in issues within their communities. These issues may occur in learners' school, local, regional, national or global communities, but what is important is that they are real-life issues of relevance and concern to the young people themselves. Focusing on political literacy in this way also helps to bring alive the concepts central to Civics and Citizenship education – such as democracy, justice, power, legitimacy and representation – in ways that are meaningful to learners, extending them beyond the classroom.

## Civics and Citizenship inquiry and skills

If Civics and Citizenship education is to have meaning in the lives of learners, and if the subject is to be more than a classroom-based activity, the development of requisite skills is crucial. Central to effective Civics and Citizenship education is the idea that a learner must be able to 'use his or her knowledge, or at least see how it could be used and have a proclivity for using it' (Crick & Porter 1978, p. 37). This means that while knowing is one thing, using that knowledge appropriately requires critical capacities.

The Australian Curriculum for Civics and Citizenship for both Years 3–6/7 and Years 7–10 (ACARA 2018e) breaks the inquiry and skills strand into four elements:

1. *Questioning and research:* This includes developing questions, researching and collating information from a range of sources, and analysing sources.

2. *Analysis, synthesis and interpretation:* This includes engaging critically with a range of sources, including those with different perspectives.

3. *Problem-solving and decision-making:* This includes employing strategies for balancing different viewpoints and planning action through democratic processes.

4. *Communication and reflection:* This includes presenting arguments and positions using Civics and Citizenship-related knowledge and ideas, and reflecting on the role of the citizen.

## Bringing the two strands together

According to Andrew Lockyer (2010, p. 164), 'politics is a branch of ethics. It requires practical wisdom (phronesis) and right judgement. It is not required by book learning or doctrinal instruction, but through experience'. As this statement suggests, effective citizenship requires us to *use* and *apply* our knowledge and understanding to real-life events. In turn, effective Civics and Citizenship education requires educators to provide learning experiences through which learners engage as active participants in issues and decisions that affect their lives. This necessarily involves learners in critical thinking, researching information, exploring and interpreting information, communicating ideas and making decisions.

The crucial interconnection and interdependency between the Civics and Citizenship knowledge and understanding strand and the Civics and Citizenship inquiry and skills strand is clear within the achievement standards of the Years 7–10 curriculum. For example, the Year 7 curriculum requires that:

> When researching, students develop a range of questions and gather and analyse information from different sources to investigate Australia's political and legal systems. They consider different points of view on civics and citizenship issues. When planning for action, students take into account multiple perspectives to develop solutions to an issue. Students develop and present arguments on civics and citizenship issues using appropriate texts, terms and concepts. They identify ways they can be active and informed citizens. (ACARA 2018e)

Through combining knowledge and understanding with inquiry and skills, Civics and Citizenship provides an education about citizenship, through citizenship and for citizenship. The Civics and Citizenship concept wheel from Chapter 5 is shown again in Figure 9.1.

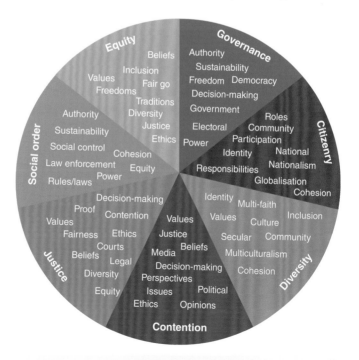

FIGURE 9.1 **Civics and Citizenship concept wheel**
Source: *McInerney 2015*

Reflection Look at Figure 9.1, and think about each of the seven concepts depicted. Consider the ways in which each concept relates to the *Australian Curriculum: Civics and Citizenship.*

## EDUCATOR TIP

Visit the Australian Curriculum website to make sure you are familiar with the content of the Civics and Citizenship curriculum. Are there any gaps in your subject knowledge? If there are, make a list of these with a plan for how you will address them.

## TEACHING/LEARNING ETHOS AND ORGANISING THE CIVICS AND CITIZENSHIP CURRICULUM

In this section we will consider the various processes through which schools teach the Civics and Citizenship curriculum. Given that Civics and Citizenship education is a relatively new subject, one that resides within the HASS learning area, and also connects with the wider aims of education and schooling, these processes are varied, and individual sites are likely to combine more than one approach. However, before we outline these approaches it is important to recognise that no matter which of the approaches are employed, their effectiveness is likely to be affected by the teaching and learning ethos that informs them. In other words, effective Civics and Citizenship education is not simply about what we teach and how we structure the curriculum, but also about the environment in which it is taught. Picture a school without a student representative committee, which requires learners to sit passively in lessons learning through memorising information dictated by the teacher. While this is a rather stark example (no school we know of operates in such a fashion!), it illustrates that if we want learners to be critical and active participants within their communities, it is important that we give serious thought to how their environments, including schools and classrooms, support or constrain such participation.

### Creating a conducive environment for Civics and Citizenship

Researchers of education for citizenship in different contexts typically point to a range of environmental factors that underpin effective practice. When they do so, they often remind us that to be meaningful for learners, Civics and Citizenship education requires learning climates that are supportive of open dialogue and positive relationships. While it is difficult to distil the nature of these learning environments into words on a page, they include:

- strong and committed leadership, which places education for citizenship as core to the school's mission and ethos

- educators with specialist subject knowledge, who are committed to the subject and convey their expertise and enthusiasm to learners through varied teaching activities
- open school and classroom environments, which encourage and support learners to discuss ideas and share opinions and to learn through a range of teaching and learning strategies, including those that require active and experiential learning
- clear democratic processes for the representation of student views, through which learners are able to inform and take part in decision-making processes appropriate to their ages and through which learners develop a strong sense of efficacy

- strong, sustainable and reciprocal connections with the local community, providing opportunities for experiential learning and active citizenship
- clear and appropriate assessment procedures that take account of the Australian Curriculum achievement standards, and that also appreciate that assessment of Civics and Citizenship must involve a range of strategies and methods.

**formative assessment**: assessment that aims to support and inform further learning, commonly referred to as assessment *for* learning

**summative assessment**: assessment that seeks to make a judgement about learning outcomes achieved, often against a particular benchmark or rubric

## EDUCATOR TIP

Looking at the Civics and Citizenship achievement standards within HASS (Years 3–6/7), devise an assessment task for a unit of work on the theme of 'Living together in a diverse Australia'. How can you structure the assessment task to include both **formative** and **summative assessment**? How do the formative and summative assessment tasks connect to the achievement standards?

Return to the earlier Reflection in this chapter where you were asked to think about an educational setting you know and which elements of its practice combine to educate students for citizenship. For that educational setting, which elements of the learning environment that are necessary for education for citizenship, as outlined above, are in place?

## Integrating Civics and Citizenship education: a combined approach

A key question facing all those committed to the teaching of Civics and Citizenship education in schools is how best to integrate the subject into the curriculum and life of the school. To answer this question abstracted from the actual educational setting is not necessarily possible, given that the best way to integrate citizenship must be shaped by the context of the school – including its communities, educators and learners. In other words, what might be best for one school may not be fully appropriate for another, and what might be appropriate for younger learners may not be appropriate for older learners. However, there are eight common ways in which educational settings might look to 'deliver' Civics and Citizenship education. These are through:

1. discrete, timetabled Civics and Citizenship lessons in which key concepts and skills are the central, explicit focus and in which active, participatory pedagogies are used

2. a combined HASS subject, in which key concepts and skills are related to the concepts, ideas and topics found within History, Geography and Economics and Business

3. forging links with other aspects of the Australian Curriculum, including other subjects, the three cross-curriculum priorities, and the seven general capabilities (we will return to these connections in the next section)

4. the educational setting's ethos, mission and values

5. positive relationships within the setting's culture, including those between educators, between educators and learners, and between educators, parents and the communities with which the setting connects

6. carefully planned extracurricular activities that engage learners in active, experiential learning via which they can engage in democratic, reciprocal learning with their peers and other members of their communities

7. democratic processes and structures within the educational setting, including through school representative councils

8. visits to educational sites connected to the Civics and Citizenship curriculum.

## EDUCATOR TIP

### MISSIONS, AIMS AND VALUES

Visit the websites of 10 schools. Try to choose a mixture of sites, including urban/rural, independent/state, single-sex/co-educational and primary/high school. Look at the key information about each setting, including its mission, aims and values. Now make sure you are familiar with the rationale (http://australiancurriculum.edu.au/f-10-curriculum/humanities-and-social-sciences/civics-and-citizenship/rationale) and aims (http://australiancurriculum.edu.au/f-10-curriculum/humanities-and-social-sciences/civics-and-citizenship/aims) of Civics and Citizenship. How closely do each setting's mission, aims and values align with the aims and rationale for Civics and Citizenship? Is this alignment explicit or implicit?

While identifying these eight ways of delivering Civics and Citizenship within educational settings, it is helpful to understand that there are many aspects of education that can contribute to education for citizenship, and no educational setting relies on just one way alone. Rather, settings are likely to integrate the subject through more than one of these eight methods, seeking to develop a combined approach to the teaching of Civics and Citizenship. When we consider individual settings, it should also be noted that it may not be the case that each of these ways is visible and valued to the same extent. In other words, some settings may place more emphasis on some ways of integrating Civics and Citizenship education than on others.

In their extensive research on citizenship education in England, Kerr et al. (2007, p. iv) identified four school types based on their approach to the subject:

- *School type 1 – curriculum driven citizenship:* provides a firm grounding of citizenship education in the curriculum but is less strong in the areas of participation and has inconsistent levels of student **efficacy**.

  **efficacy**: the belief and ability that one can influence events, decisions and processes

- *School type 2 – student efficacy-driven citizenship:* has a sound or high level of student efficacy in the school, but is weak on student take-up in extracurricular activities and its delivery of citizenship through the curriculum.

- *School type 3 – participation-driven citizenship:* has higher than average levels of student participation but its students feel low levels of efficacy and the importance placed on citizenship as a curriculum subject is average.

- *School type 4 – citizenship-rich driven citizenship:* in which students not only express high levels of efficacy and show high levels of participation, but citizenship education is also viewed as a strong and central subject within the curriculum.

To conclude this section, and as we have suggested throughout this chapter, while Civics and Citizenship is a subject, its boundaries extend beyond the classroom, permeating various aspects of the school. This means that Civics and Citizenship education is experienced by learners as more than a subject, and is learnt through a variety of methods and approaches. This is both a strength of the subject (it can literally be experienced everywhere within the life of the educational setting) and a potential challenge. It is a challenge because it requires educators – and indeed learners – to make connections between these potentially diffuse teaching and learning activities. Indeed, making connections can help to broaden Civics and Citizenship, supporting learners to relate their learning to other aspects of the curriculum and their lives.

# MAKING CONNECTIONS: CURRICULUM AND COMMUNITIES

Effective planning for Civics and Citizenship is all about making connections. In this section, we explore two crucial connections that should underpin all Civics and Citizenship education – those with other aspects of the curriculum and those with the settings' communities. When thinking through these connections, it is important to keep in mind the ways in which the whole curriculum, including Civics and Citizenship, does/should prepare young people for their role as active citizens in the 21st century.

# Curriculum

There are myriad ways in which Civics and Citizenship education might be connected to other aspects of the curriculum. Before we look at such connections, it is worth starting with the question of why we might want to make such connections in the first place. In broad terms, there are a number of positive reasons for doing so, including the following:

- Such connections help us to shed light on, or think in particular ways, about core concepts, such as power, democracy and freedom (think, for example, about the ways in which these concepts are portrayed in various works of literature).
- Different subjects seek to develop similar skills, such as inquiry and communication.
- Through learning in other subjects, learners are able to make sense of the present-day institutions and practices central to citizenship.
- Civics and Citizenship requires learners to consider the local, regional, national and global communities to which they belong. This can only be achieved through an understanding of the richness and diversity of such communities, which means engaging with English, science, modern languages, the arts and other curriculum dimensions.
- The inclusion of Civics and Citizenship learning within or combined with other curriculum subjects affords Civics and Citizenship essential time within an over-crowded/pressured curriculum.

## The cross-curriculum priorities and general capabilities

As discussed in earlier chapters, the Australian Curriculum has three cross-curriculum priorities: Aboriginal and Torres Strait Islander histories and cultures; Asia and Australia's engagement with Asia; and Sustainability. Central to each of the cross-curriculum priorities are notions of belonging and our place in the world, and it is important as educators of Civics and Citizenship that we give some serious consideration to the connections involved. This means there are many varied ways that Civics and Citizenship can connect with each of the three cross-curriculum priorities. Brett (2016, p. 10) highlights, for example, that Civics and Citizenship and education for sustainability have 'the potential to be natural partners in their promotion of global awareness, a more socially just future and informed citizen action; and there are strong reasons why there is a need for this partnership'. Consider, for example, the following extract from the Australian Curriculum (ACARA 2018d):

> Education for sustainability develops the knowledge, skills, values and world views necessary for people to act in ways that contribute to more sustainable patterns of living. It enables individuals and communities to reflect on ways of interpreting and engaging with the world. Sustainability education is futures-oriented, focusing on protecting environments and creating a more ecologically and socially just world through informed action. Actions that support more sustainable patterns of living require consideration of environmental, social, cultural and economic systems and their interdependence.

Similar to Civics and Citizenship, the focus of sustainability is on responsible and informed action within communities. In addition, this cross-curriculum priority requires us to think beyond the here and now, and to consider how our actions can and do shape the future.

The Australian Curriculum's seven general capabilities (see Chapter 16), like the cross-curriculum priorities, allow notable and positive possibilities for connecting with Civics and Citizenship. Some examples are:

- *intercultural understanding*, and its focus on learners valuing 'their own cultures, languages and beliefs, and those of others', as well as becoming 'responsible local and global citizens, equipped through their education for living and working together in an interconnected world'. Through learning intercultural understanding, young people are supported to 'make connections between their own worlds and the worlds of others, to build on shared interests and commonalities, and to negotiate or mediate difference' (ACARA 2018b).

- *ethical understanding*, and its focus on learners understanding 'the nature of ethical concepts, values and character traits, and … how reasoning can assist ethical judgement', and discussing 'complex issues' which 'require responses that take account of ethical considerations such as human rights and responsibilities, animal rights, environmental issues and global justice' (ACARA 2018a)

- *personal and social capability*, and its focus on learners understanding 'themselves and others' and 'establishing and building positive relationships, making responsible decisions, working effectively in teams, handling challenging situations construct-ively and developing leadership skills' (ACARA 2018c). The Australian Curriculum also states that this general capability 'is a foundation for learning and for citizen-ship' (ACARA 2018c).

## EDUCATOR TIP

Look at the Australian Curriculum website (http://australiancurriculum.edu.au) and explore the cross-curriculum priorities and the general capabilities sections. What connections can you identify between these and Civics and Citizenship?

### Other subjects

There are many potential and important connections that can be made between Civics and Citizenship education and other subjects within the Australian Curriculum. Clearly, the closest connections are with the other HASS subjects of History, Geography and Economics and Business. Through your engagement with this chapter and other chapters in this book, you will have already started conceptualising the links within HASS. It is also important, however, to look beyond HASS and think about the ways that meaningful links can be developed with other curriculum subjects, such as English, science and the arts. The following example and task should help to further your thinking and understanding of what effective cross-curricular links require.

# EDUCATOR TIP

Using the Australian Curriculum website (http://australiancurriculum.edu.au), look through the curriculum of:

1. at least two other subjects (it might be a good idea to look at one from within HASS and one from outside of HASS)
2. one of the cross-curriculum priorities
3. one of the general capabilities.

What potential links can you draw between the content of these subjects, priorities and capabilities? Make sure you focus on both knowledge and understanding and inquiry and skills.

## Communities

If Civics and Citizenship education is to be the active, participatory and experiential subject it should be, then connections with the various communities learners inhabit (whether local, regional, national or global) are vital. One way in which young people can be supported to engage with their communities (remembering that young people may already be engaged outside of their formal education and schooling) is through **service-learning**.

**service-learning**: an active, participatory educational approach that involves learners undertaking and critically reflecting on their involvement in community-based projects

Service-learning is an experiential learning process through which learners work with others to engage critically with issues, debates and processes within a given community or communities. Based on active forms of learning, service-learning draws on a range of pedagogical theories, particularly those of John Dewey and David Kolb (see Chapter 23). For example, many service-learning programs are based on Kolb's (1998) experiential learning cycle, which involves four stages in a cyclical pattern: concrete experience, reflective observation, abstract conceptualisation and active experimentation.

Research evidence suggests that effective service-learning can bring personal, educational and societal benefits (Speck & Hoppe 2004). Hecht (2003, p. 28), for example, illustrates the potential benefits of service-learning in the following way:

> Service-learning enriches a student's world, providing new experiences and challenges. Through planning, service and reflection, students are encouraged to examine the tasks at hand, to develop plans for dealing with the obvious and unexpected, to take action, and to consider how these actions are understandable given other academic and life knowledge. Service-learning is neither passive nor solitary. Rather, students deal with real-life activities in naturalistic settings. It is these features that make service-learning unique from most other types of learning.

While these benefits are important, we should note also that effective and meaningful service-learning requires conscious planning. Not least, as Peterson and Warwick (2014, p. 39) point out, the 'challenges for educators integrating this particular pedagogical approach within the schooling system include the complexity of teachers needing to move their learning spaces beyond the classroom and school, and out into community, including perhaps engagement with international settings'. In addition, when participating within communities (for adults as well as young people) the process is often dynamic and at times complex. The best forms of service-learning support 'young people by providing a mediating space that facilitates deliberative processes and reflective learning for those who might initially lack the confidence and interpersonal attributes to participate without structured support' (Peterson & Warwick 2014, pp. 39–40). Leighton (2012) raises a further criticism from his own research on education for citizenship, citing incidents of students being *compelled* to volunteer in the community rather than participating in discussing, planning and evaluating community action of their own volition.

A fruitful way to mitigate these challenges is to develop sustainable, reciprocal relationships with partners outside of the school, including with youth and community organisations, which often have rich experiences engaging young people in participatory activities. Through working in partnership in this way, Civics and Citizenship educators can ensure that learners have the opportunity to engage in service within their communities, and that such service has an explicit pedagogical underpinning.

Should service-learning be compulsory or voluntary? Would making service-learning compulsory compromise the endeavour?

Reflection

# CONCLUSION

In this chapter we have suggested that, while a relatively new subject in the Australian Curriculum, Civics and Citizenship connects in important ways with wider educational aims and goals. In addition, we have suggested that Civics and Citizenship education goes beyond narrower forms of learning about key political/legal systems and processes to embrace an active, participatory notion of citizenship. By viewing Civics and Citizenship through this active, participatory lens, educators are able to connect learners' experiences beyond the subject's curriculum to other curriculum areas, to the whole life of the school and to the communities within which young people live. For this to happen, educators need to pay attention to the school and classroom environments, ensuring that they are receptive to the involvement of learners in appropriate ways. In doing so, Civics and Citizenship can be brought to life in ways that connect to and enrich the lives of young people.

## REVIEW QUESTIONS

1. What is citizenship?
2. What concepts are central to Civics and Citizenship?
3. How might Civics and Citizenship be organised within educational sites?

4.  What teaching and learning strategies are particularly suited to Civics and Citizenship education?

5.  How can Civics and Citizenship make connections beyond the school gates?

## LEARNING EXTENSION

Visits to educational sites outside of the school provide important learning opportunities connected to Civics and Citizenship education. Research three educational sites that you could visit with learners and/or that provide educational resources for use in schools. What resources are available? How do these connect to the Civics and Citizenship curriculum? What might learners gain from engaging with the educational site? What amendments might you need to make to the resources to make them relevant and appropriate for your learners?

## REFERENCES

ACARA (Australian Curriculum, Assessment and Reporting Authority) (2018a). *Australian Curriculum: F-10, v8.3.* Ethical understanding. Retrieved from: http://australiancurriculum.edu.au/f-10-curriculum/general-capabilities/ethical-understanding.

——(2018b). *Australian Curriculum: F-10, v8.3.* Intercultural understanding. Retrieved from: http://australiancurriculum.edu.au/f-10-curriculum/general-capabilities/intercultural-understanding.

——(2018c). *Australian Curriculum: F-10, v8.3.* Personal and social capability. Retrieved from: http://australiancurriculum.edu.au/f-10-curriculum/general-capabilities/personal-and-social-capability.

——(2018d) *Australian Curriculum: F-10, v8.3.* Sustainability. Retrieved from: http://australiancurriculum.edu.au/f-10-curriculum/cross-curriculum-priorities/sustainability.

——(2018e). *Australian Curriculum: Humanities and Social Sciences F-10, v8.3.* Civics and Citizenship. Retrieved from: http://australiancurriculum.edu.au/f-10-curriculum/humanities-and-social-sciences/civics-and-citizenship.

Brett, P. (2016). Making connections between civics and citizenship education and education for sustainability. In A. Peterson & L. Tudball, eds, *Civics and Citizenship Education in Australia: Challenges, practices and international perspectives.* London: Bloomsbury, pp. 165–87.

Crick, B. & Porter, A. (1978). *Political Education and Political Literacy.* London: Longman.

Hecht, D. (2003). The missing link: Exploring the context of learning in service-learning. In S. Billig & J. Eyler, eds, *Deconstructing Service-learning: Research exploring context, participation, and impacts.* Greenwich, CT: Information Age, pp. 25–49.

Kerr, D., Lopas, J., Nelson, J., White, K., Cleaver, E. & Benton, T. (2007). *Vision Versus Pragmatism: Citizenship in the secondary school curriculum in England.* London: Department for Education and Skills.

Kolb, D. (1998). *Experiential Learning.* Eaglewood Cliffs, NJ: Prentice Hall.

Leighton, R. (2012). *Teaching Citizenship: A radical approach.* London: Continuum.

Lockyer, A. (2010). Young people as active political citizens. In B. Crick & A. Lockyer, eds, *Active Citizenship: What could it achieve and how?* Edinburgh: Edinburgh University Press, pp. 154–70.

MCEETYA (Ministerial Council on Education, Employment, Training and Youth Affairs). (2008). *Melbourne Declaration on Educational Goals for Young Australians.* Retrieved from:

http://www.curriculum.edu.au/verve/_resources/National_Declaration_on_the_Educational_
Goals_for_Young_Australians.pdf.

McInerney, M. (2015). *Conceptual Thinking in HASS*. Retrieved from:
http://humsteach.blogspot.com.au/2015/11/hass-back-at-para-hills-p-7.html.

Peterson, A. & Brock, C. (2017). Citizenship. In F. Moghaddam, ed., *The Sage Encyclopedia of
Political Behavior*. Thousand Oaks, CA: Sage.

Peterson, A. & Warwick, P. (2014). *Global Learning and Education: Key concepts and effective
practice*. Abingdon: Routledge.

Print, M. (2016). The recent history of teaching Civics and Citizenship education in Australia,
1989–2015. In A. Peterson & L. Tudball, eds, *Civics and Citizenship Education in Australia:
Challenges, practices and international perspectives*. London: Bloomsbury, pp. 7–22.

Speck, B. & Hoppe, S. (2004). Introduction. In B. Speck & S. Hoppe, eds, *Service-learning: History,
theory and issues*. Westport, CT: Praeger, pp. vii–x.

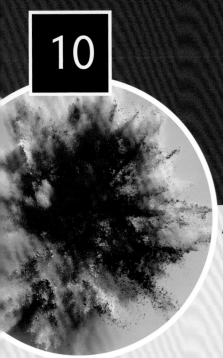

# BRINGING ECONOMICS AND BUSINESS INTO EDUCATIONAL SETTINGS

*Anne Glamuzina*

## Learning objectives

After reading this chapter, you should be able to:

- understand and creatively teach Economics and Business knowledge and understanding to Years 5, 6 and 7
- integrate Economics and Business knowledge and understanding with other learning areas in the early and primary years
- understand and creatively teach Economics and Business inquiry and skills to Years 5, 6 and 7
- integrate Economics and Business inquiry and skills with other learning areas in the early and primary years.

# INTRODUCTION

**resources**: a means to produce goods and services that satisfy needs and wants. The four economic resources (factors of production) are land, labour, capital and enterprise. Production usually requires a combination of resources.

**needs**: in economics and business, goods and services that consumers consider necessary to maintain a standard of living

**wants**: goods or services that are desired in order to satisfy a consumer but which are not necessary for survival or to meet the basic standard of living in a community

> Australia needs enterprising individuals who can make informed decisions and actively participate in society and the economy as individuals and more broadly as global citizens. (ACARA 2018c)

Economics is the study of decisions made when allocating scarce **resources** to satisfy **needs** and unlimited **wants**, and business is the enterprise engaged in the production of goods and services, usually for a profit (ACARA 2018c). Australia needs innovative individuals (National Innovation and Science Agenda 2015) with a knowledge and understanding of economics and business who question, process and analyse information, make informed decisions and reflect upon outcomes. Reductions in manufacturing due to offshoring of labour, the depletion of Tier-1 mines (Barnes 2014) and the end of the mining boom mean that innovation and entrepreneurship are necessary for a prosperous Australian economy in the future.

**Economics** and **Business** is an Australian Curriculum subject from Year 7 to 10 in the Humanities and Social Sciences (HASS) learning area and a HASS sub-strand from Years 5 to 7. The Year 7 HASS sub-strand and Year 7 Economics and Business subject are identical. Economics and Business contains two strands: knowledge and understanding, and inquiry and skills. Concepts contained in the strands and sub-strands have potential for integration across learning areas in the early and primary years. Educators must have an insightful understanding of Economics and Business to contextualise the cross-curriculum priorities of Sustainability, Aboriginal and Torres Strait Islander histories and cultures, and Asia and Australia's engagement with Asia using real-world examples (ACARA 2018a).

**economics**: a social science, study of human behaviour, that studies decisions made by individuals, households, businesses/firms, governments and other groups about how scarce resources are allocated in attempting to satisfy needs and unlimited wants

**business**: an organisation or enterprise engaged in production and trade of goods and services, usually for profit

Curriculum delivery in Economics and Business is underpinned by the general capabilities with an emphasis on ethics, and critical and creative thinking. Ethics becomes a focus as learners create sustainable production solutions, feed healthy food to young people in schools and learn about slave-free supply chains. In order to create solutions, numeracy and **consumer** and financial literacy are applied to critically analyse quantitative data, processed using information and communication technology (ICT). Qualitative data are critically analysed using intercultural understanding and personal and social capabilities as part of the problem-solving process.

**consumer**: a person or group that is the final user of goods and services

This chapter introduces Economics and Business knowledge and understanding and illustrates integration with other learning areas from the early years to Year 7. Economics and Business inquiry and skills can be delivered through the creation and implementation of a business plan and similarities with inquiry skills in other learning areas will be described for the purposes of integration from Foundation to Year 7. Useful resources that have been tested in educational settings are listed at the end of the chapter.

## ESTEAM: ENTREPRENEURSHIP, SCIENCE, TECHNOLOGY, ENGINEERING, ARTS AND MATHEMATICS

ESTEAM highlights entrepreneurship so that all learners, inventors, creators and innovators can transform ideas into products to deliver to **market**. Successful **entrepreneurs** organise resources to produce valuable goods and services for market and to benefit society. Unification of concepts from Economics and Business, together with science, technology, engineering, arts and mathematics, will provide learners with the relevant insights, knowledge, understanding and skills to lead and transform society.

**market**: an exchange of goods, services or resources between buyers and sellers

**entrepreneur**: a person who sets out to build a successful business in a new field. An entrepreneur's methods are sometimes regarded as groundbreaking or innovative.

**SPOTLIGHT ON HASS EDUCATION**

# ECONOMICS AND BUSINESS IN EARLY YEARS EDUCATION

Curriculum for the early years extends from birth to age eight with the Early Years Learning Framework (EYLF) covering birth to five years. The framework is underpinned by the essential understandings of belonging, being and becoming (DEEWR 2009). Play-based programs enable learners to develop communication skills and connections with the world through creativity, discovery, communication and imagination (Department of Education and Training 2014). Although Economics and Business is not described in the early years curriculum, many connections can be drawn between this field of study and other learning areas.

> When students understand that each discipline's particular methods can contribute to decision making in all contexts – academic or not – they have made the transition to the highest stage of cognitive development, making contextually appropriate decisions. Students come to realise that they can make choices on the basis of different discipline specific methods and criteria in the context of their own values. (Borg & Borg 2001)

From birth, learners use deductive reasoning to make sense of their world, assimilate knowledge and develop intelligence (Piaget 1955). Play in the early years of education can be directly linked to future understanding of economic thinking, behaviour and game theory. Vygotsky (1997) described games as 'the first medium to teach the child rational and conscious behaviour ... thinking arises as a response to a particular difficulty'. In an Economics and Business classroom, rollback equilibrium can be used to analyse sequential moves after a game has finished (Dixit 2006). This process can be transferred to analysis of the share market and other markets, and therefore problem-solving from Foundation to Year 7 provides a basis for Economics and Business thinking and analysis. This illustrates the importance of integrating multidisciplinary knowledge with Economics and Business in real-life contexts to develop critical and creative thinking in learners (Bangs 2012; Borg & Borg 2001). Early years HASS, Science, Mathematics, Digital Technologies, Design and Technologies, English, the Arts, Health and Physical Education provide a foundation for Economics and Business.

# ECONOMICS AND BUSINESS KNOWLEDGE AND UNDERSTANDING

Students will be introduced to a wide range of concepts and subject-specific terminology in Economics and Business knowledge and understanding (ACARA 2018c). Definitions are available on the Australian Curriculum website. The content descriptions for Economics and Business knowledge and understanding begin in the Year 5 and 6 HASS sub-strands, followed by Economics and Business in Year 7. These can be integrated with content from other learning areas during the early and primary years, and expanded using the inquiry questions and four key organising ideas:

- resource allocation and making economic choices
- the business environment
- consumer and financial literacy
- work and work futures.

FIGURE 10.1   Learners have an understanding of
Economics and Business prior to formal education.
Source: Helen Nicholaou

## EDUCATOR TIP

Dr Sandra Kaplan (2010) developed prompts and icons for depth and complexity for gifted learners to encourage creativity and critical thinking. These assist all learners in processing, understanding and retaining new language and concepts 'because the rising tide lifts all ships' (Renzulli 1998). The prompts are: language of the discipline, details, patterns, unanswered questions, rules, trends, ethics, big ideas, points of view, over time, across disciplines and multiple perspectives. The icons are available online at http://envisiongifted.com, and can be used as visual cues to assist with the introduction and retention of content.

## Resource allocation and making choices

The economic problem of scarcity states that limited resources are available to produce goods and services to satisfy unlimited wants. This key idea is investigated in Years 5, 6 and 7 with the inquiry questions set out in Table 10.1.

| TABLE 10.1 | INQUIRY QUESTIONS FOR SCARCITY | |
|---|---|---|
| Year level | Content description | Inquiry questions |
| 5 | The difference between needs and wants and why choices need to be made about how limited resources are used (ACHASSK119) Types of resources (natural, human, capital) and the ways societies use them to satisfy the needs and wants of present and future generations (ACHASSK120) | Why do I have to make choices as a consumer? What influences the decisions I make? |
| 6 | The reasons businesses exist and the different ways they provide goods and services (ACHASSK151) How the concept of opportunity cost involves choices about the alternative use of resources and the need to consider trade-offs (ACHASSK149) | Why do businesses exist and what are the different ways they provide goods and services? Why are there trade-offs associated with making decisions? |
| 7 | The ways consumers and producers interact and respond to each other in the market (ACHEK017) | Why is there a relationship between consumers and producers in the market? |

Source: adapted from ACARA 2018c

A study of the limited resources of land, labour and capital begins in Year 5 Economics and Business. Land includes all natural resources, labour is the human effort involved in production and capital is all human-made resources. Activities asking students to classify resources according to economic definitions can be integrated with Years 4 to 7 Geography when studying sustainable management of natural resources, water scarcity and the economic value of water. Integration is possible with Foundation Science when studying basic needs of living things, and from Years 2 to 7 when studying resource use and the water cycle. Foundation to Year 2 Design and Technologies studies how plants and animals are grown for food, clothing and shelter.

Consumers and producers meet in markets to exchange goods and services, and Foundation learners of French, German, Hindi, Italian and Vietnamese participate in transactions. Modern Greek and Turkish learners begin transactions in Years 3 and 4; Korean and Spanish learners begin transactions in Year 5. Consumers have unlimited wants and the factors affecting wants include biological needs, gender, income, social status, climate and weather. Goods are material items used to satisfy wants, such as basketballs for recreation, and services are non-material items used to satisfy wants, such as legal advice. Learners can collect images of examples to clarify understanding.

The two-sector circular flow model in Figure 10.2 shows that households own the resources – land, labour and capital – that are sold to firms in exchange for income in a resource market. Firms use the resources to produce goods and services, which households can purchase with consumption expenditure.

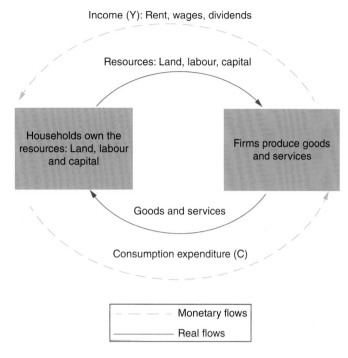

FIGURE 10.2   Two-sector circular flow model

## Economic decisions

Economic decisions are made to allocate limited resources to satisfy unlimited wants. Planned, traditional and market economies make the three economic decisions of 'what', 'how' and 'for whom' production occurs, as described in Table 10.2.

| **TABLE 10.2**   ECONOMIC DECISIONS: WHAT, HOW AND FOR WHOM? | | | |
|---|---|---|---|
| | **Planned or command economy** | **Traditional economy** | **Market economy** |
| Economic decisions | *Decisions are determined by* | | |
| **What will be produced?** | Government or Central planning authority | Tradition or Custom | What consumers demand will be produced. |
| **How will it be produced?** | Government or Central planning authority | Tradition or Custom | Producers will generally use the least cost method of production. |
| **For whom production occurs?** | Government or Central planning authority | Tradition or Custom | Production is usually consumed by those with the largest incomes. |

Production involves an **opportunity cost** as limited resources are directed towards one form of production rather than another. Opportunity cost is what is given up in order to gain something else. For example, the cost of using land for gas fracking is loss of agricultural production.

**opportunity cost:** what is given up in order to gain something else; the value of a next-best alternative when a choice is made

Production integrates with Foundation to Year 2 Design and Technologies when identifying product and environment design to suit personal and community needs. Year 5 and 6 Design and Technologies learners evaluate community priorities with competing social, ethical and sustainability considerations when combining materials and equipment to create products and environments. Understanding can be integrated with Year 5 Geography studies of Aboriginal and Torres Strait Islander influences on the environment and Year 2 and 5 History care for significant sites and studies of environmental changes after colonisation and significant development (ACARA 2018a).

Learners in Year 2 to 7 Science study materials and sustainable production, understand the effects of actions, and solve personal and community problems with new evidence and innovative technologies involving ethical considerations. Science from Years 1 to 7 provides an understanding of agriculture when studying the environment, living organisms and effects of human activities.

Traditional economies integrate with Year 7 History studies of ancient societies, Year 4 Geography Aboriginal and Torres Strait Islander peoples' custodial responsibility and sustainability, and Year 5 to 7 Design and Technologies investigations of food and fibre production technologies in modern and traditional societies.

Planned economies integrate with Civics and Citizenship from Years 3 to 6 when learners study regulations, shared beliefs and values, and the effects of business laws.

## Consumer and financial literacy

'Financial literacy is a combination of financial knowledge, skills, attitudes and behaviours necessary to make sound financial decisions, based on personal circumstances, to improve financial wellbeing' (ASIC 2017; OECD 2011). Consumer literacy involves managing money and assets, and making responsible decisions relating to consumer issues such as sustainability, animal testing or slave-free supply chains; it affects the quality of life of the community and individuals (ACARA 2018b). Learners examine issues associated with sustainable and ethical consumption. When purchasing sports equipment, tea, coffee or chocolate that is Fairtrade, UTZ or Rainforest Alliance certified, consumers are assured that slavery has not been part of the supply chain.

Consumer and financial literacy is an Australian Curriculum connection, and is investigated in Years 5 to 7 Economics and Business with the content descriptions and inquiry questions outlined in Table 10.3.

From Years 1 to 7, Mathematics provides fundamental understandings for consumer and financial literacy when studying money, decimals, percentages, calculating change, discount and best buys. Contextual connections with Economics and Business can be used in worded problems in Years 4, 5 and 7. Through game playing, educators can distinguish Economics and Business from Mathematics and encourage confidence, creativity, enthusiasm, optimism and resilience to achieve the consumer and financial capability dispositions shown in Figure 10.3.

| **TABLE 10.3** | CONSUMER AND FINANCIAL LITERACY INQUIRY QUESTIONS | |
| --- | --- | --- |
| Year level | Content descriptions | Inquiry questions |
| 5 | Influences on consumer choices and methods that can be used to help make informed personal consumer and financial choices (ACHASSK121) | Why do I have to make choices as a consumer? What influences the decisions I make? What can I do to make informed decisions? |
| 6 | How the concept of opportunity cost involves choices about the alternative use of resources and the need to consider trade-offs (ACHASSK149) The effect that consumer and financial decisions can have on the individual, the broader community and the environment (ACHASSK150) | Why are there trade-offs associated with making decisions? What are the possible effects of my consumer and financial choices? |
| 7 | Why and how individuals and businesses plan to achieve short-term and long-term personal, organisational and financial objectives (ACHASSK200) | Why is personal, organisational and financial planning for the future important for consumers and businesses? |

Source: adapted from ACARA 2018a

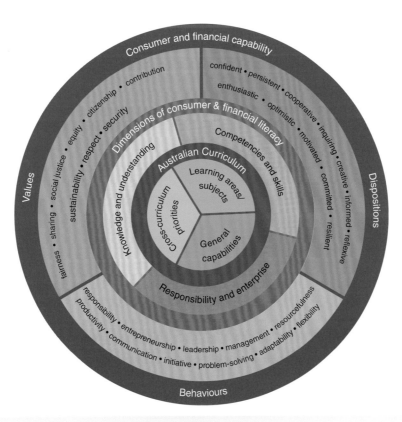

FIGURE 10.3 Consumer and financial capability
Source: ACARA 2018b

Activities asking learners to imagine personal, career and financial goals at particular milestones provide an introduction to plan financial objectives, including budgets. Simple financial plans in Year 5 Mathematics can involve budgeting for an excursion. If there are 30 students in the class and the bus costs $150, learners can calculate a charge of $5 each and present the information as shown in Figure 10.4. Budgeting is also part of Year 5 and 6 French, German, Japanese and Turkish.

| **Budget for bus to the beach**<br>**10 May 2020** | |
|---|---|
| **Estimated receipts** | $ |
| Sales 30 × $5 | 150 |
| **Less estimated payments** | |
| Bus hire | 150 |
| **Estimated excess receipts / Payments** | $0 |

FIGURE 10.4   **An excursion budget**

## The business environment

Businesses exist to produce goods and services to satisfy consumers' unlimited wants. The business environment's, key idea is investigated with the content descriptions and inquiry questions from Years 6 and 7 in Table 10.4.

**TABLE 10.4**   THE BUSINESS ENVIRONMENT INQUIRY QUESTIONS

| Year level | Content description | Inquiry questions |
|---|---|---|
| 6 | The reasons businesses exist and the different ways they provide goods and services (ACHASSK151) | Why do businesses exist and what are the different ways they provide goods and services? |
| 7 | Characteristics of entrepreneurs and successful businesses (ACHASSK201) | How does entrepreneurial behaviour contribute to a successful business? |

Source: adapted from ACARA 2018a

'Entrepreneurship is the pursuit of opportunity beyond the resources you currently control' (Stevenson 2000). Opportunity involves pioneering a truly innovative product, devising a new business model, creating a better or cheaper version of an existing product, or targeting an existing product to new customers (Eisenmann 2013). An introduction to this topic begins by showing photographs of entrepreneurs to learners to identify. Students research and print an A4 photograph of an entrepreneur to place on the wall. Successful Australian entrepreneurs such as Andrew Forrest and Gina Rinehart can be included. Life events are recorded and read aloud as the class identifies patterns in the lives of entrepreneurs. Learners write a summary of similarities, including initiative, overcoming adversity, excellent business idea or innovation, problem solving, managing change, adaptability and leadership. Learning from others is also a common experience in the lives of entrepreneurs: Bill Gates worked for Steve Jobs; Henry Ford worked for Thomas Edison; and Estée Lauder worked for her uncle, John Schotz, to gain skills and insights into operating a successful business.

From Foundation, visual arts, media arts, music, drama and dance involve communicating with an audience. This provides a basis for investigations into the entrepreneurship of visual artists such as Pablo Picasso, Salvador Dalí and Sidney Nolan, and actors such as Toni Colette and Rachel Griffiths, who have experienced success during their lifetimes. Each art form mentions responding to art and identifying intended purpose, assisting future artists in preparing a viable product for the arts market.

A similar process occurs from Foundation English as learners identify favourite stories, developing knowledge and skills for professional writing which, when linked to entrepreneurial skills, provide learners with an understanding of how to become a published and successful author, playwright or lyricist with investigations of J.K. Rowling, Charles Dickens, Roald Dahl, Tennessee Williams or Tim Minchin, for example. Preparatory English knowledge begins in Years 1 and 2 when learners understand texts, purpose, audience and vocabulary choices to entertain.

## EDUCATOR TIP

To reinvigorate interest in Economics theory lessons, remind learners of the major reasons for business failure: failure to manage money, failure to manage people, failure to plan and failure to execute. A good source of motivation at the beginning of this topic, or when interest is waning, might be to pose a challenging question such as: What businesses does Australia need now that the car industry and other manufacturing industries have moved offshore?

### Aboriginal and Torres Strait Islander histories and cultures, and Asia and Australia's engagement with Asia

Year 4 History integrates with Economics and Business in the study of Asia and Australia's engagement with Asia. Since at least 1700, the Yolngu people in Arnhem Land have traded with the Makassar people of Sulawesi in Indonesia. The Makassar would collect Trepang sea cucumbers and trade calico and metal blades with the Yolngu people. Trepang were processed by the Makassar, then traded with China. Primary source evidence exists in cave paintings in Kakadu National Park and in Matthew Flinders' diary entries from 1803, which have been reproduced on the National Museum of Australia website (National Museum of Australia 2018). This trade was banned by the Australian Government in 1901 and links with Civics and Citizenship and regulation (ACARA 2018a).

Economics and Business integrates with Geography from Years 2 to 7 with the use of maps to determine location, characteristics, climate and connections of people and countries with Australia and the influence of purpose, distance and accessibility on trade, migration and tourism. Geography covers contacts and conflicts resulting in trade expansion, peace treaties and economic, demographic and social differences. Learners can select a country and investigate its location on a map, and its government and trade links with Australia, to produce posters.

## Work and work futures

The Australian Bureau of Statistics (ABS) defines employed persons as people aged over 15 years who: worked one hour or more for pay, profit, commission or payment in kind, at a job, business or farm; one hour or more without pay on a family business or farm; have a job but were not at work; or employers, own-account workers who had a job, business or farm but were not at work (ABS 2018). The work and work futures key idea is investigated in Year 7 with the content description and inquiry question outlined in Table 10.5.

**TABLE 10.5** WORK AND WORK FUTURES INQUIRY QUESTIONS

| Year level | Content description | Inquiry question |
| --- | --- | --- |
| 7 | Why individuals work, types of work and how people derive an income (ACHEK020) | What types of work exist and in what other ways can people derive income? |

Source: adapted from ACARA 2018c

People work to earn income, to improve living standards, for a sense of self-worth and enjoyment, or to contribute to the community. Work definitions, available on the Fair Work Commission website (https://www.fwc.gov.au), include full-time, part-time, casual, at home, paid, unpaid, unrecognised, volunteer, permanent and casual. Learners can discuss how much work they do at home, research child labour during the Industrial Revolution and investigate child labour laws in Australia.

Income from work in the form of salary, wages or commission can be saved or spent. Income also occurs in the form of transfer payments such as pensions. Currently, by law, an amount equalling 9.5 per cent of workers' income must be paid by employers into superannuation funds for workers' retirement. Educators can introduce this idea for analysis: 'You work hard for your money, so your money should work hard for you.'

Savings can be used to earn interest, purchase collectables for resale, purchase property to earn rent or purchase businesses to earn profit. The profits of public and private companies are distributed as dividends, and the Sharemarket Game on the ASX (Australian Securities Exchange) website will assist with understanding and engagement (see https://www.asx.com.au/education/sharemarket-game.htm).

From Foundation, History can provide an understanding of investing when exploring historical stories through photographs, artefacts, books and digital media (ACARA 2018a), and some items can become worthy investments as collectables for the future. If learners introduce the term 'gambling' when studying probabilities during Year 5 or 6 Mathematics, it is important for educators to explain that gambling is not an investment. Economic models classify gambling as consumption, and investment as increased production. In business, investment occurs after fundamental analysis of accounting and qualitative information such as mining reports and market announcements to determine profitability before purchasing shares. Investing in gold can be linked to the gold rushes when studying economic reasons for British colonies in Australia during the 1800s in Year 5 History. Both History and Science provide an understanding of investing in technological advances.

# ECONOMICS AND BUSINESS INQUIRY AND SKILLS

Inquiry is described as posing questions, identifying and clarifying information and ideas, then organising and processing information (ACARA 2018a). Economics and Business inquiry and skills can be delivered through planning and operating a business, and this is an effective way of motivating learners. This is a synthesis task involving production of a unique communication, a plan and a proposed set of operations, based on inferred relationships between consumers, producers, suppliers and competitors (Bloom 1956). In Years 5, 6 and 7, the business plan can be scaffolded under the headings: questioning and research; interpreting and analysing; economic reasoning and decision making; and communication and reflection. This process can be enriched with the eight ways Aboriginal pedagogy: tell a story, make a plan, think and do, draw it, take it outside, try a new way, watch first then do, share it with others (Yunkaporta 2009; Yunkaporta & Kirby 2011; see also Chapter 6).

Businesses profit by producing goods and services for consumers, and planning is required for entrepreneurs to organise resources to meet consumer demand, make a profit and collect cash. Opportunities for business planning arise in most educational settings where learners are involved in fundraising, such as school fetes or fundraising days. A business template is shown in Table 10.6.

| TABLE 10.6  BUSINESS PLAN TEMPLATE | |
|---|---|
| **Business description** | Business name, activities, location and description of premises |
| **Product or service description** | Details of what will be sold |
| **Goals** | Personal and business goals |
| **Supply** | Identifies suppliers |
| **Manufacturing process** | Lists steps in making the product |
| **Materials and equipment** | Lists equipment used to make the product |
| **Market description** | Lists the potential customers; e.g. age, gender and location |
| **Promotion** | How will the product be advertised? Newsletters, school notices, posters, flyers, social media or email? |
| **Budget and income statement** | Prepare a budget to determine the viability of the product, ensuring enough cash to cover costs before trading. An income statement indicates financial performance after trading. |

# EDUCATOR TIP

The Walt Disney Company (Disney) organisation flow chart is available online and illustrates relationships between different ventures: theatrical films, music, comics, television, business films, merchandise and Disneyland. The flow chart is an effective way of introducing business to young learners, many of whom are consumers of Disney products. Learners can analyse the features of the flow chart using a graphic organiser.

Synthesis of Economics and Business inquiry and skills with other HASS learning areas, Science, Mathematics, Digital Technologies, Design and Technologies and English is possible due to similarities in the inquiry process. Reproductive assimilation occurs through repetition as learners rediscover fortuitous results (Piaget 1955). It involves the association of similar elements, rejection of random elements and synthesis of remaining elements into an integral concept (Vygotsky 1997; see Table 10.7). Subject-specific terminology can be introduced by educators as learners assimilate business concepts with existing understanding.

**TABLE 10.7**   SYNTHESIS OF ECONOMICS AND BUSINESS WITH OTHER LEARNING AREAS

| Learning area | Economics and Business inquiry and skills connections |
|---|---|
| **Humanities and Social Sciences** | |
| ACHASSI123, ACHASSI126, ACHASSI156, ACHASSI157, ACHASSI127 ACHASSI036, ACHASSI041 ACHASSI124, ACHASSI154, ACHASSI130, ACHASSI081, ACHASSI104, ACHASSI132, ACHASSI162 | Economics and Business inquiry and skills are enhanced by other HASS sub-strands when analysing primary and secondary sources to determine origin, purpose, reliability, viewpoints, values and perspectives. From Year 2, HASS learners sort and record information and data to draw simple conclusions based on observations and displayed information. Learners transfer skills across disciplines, organise data in discipline-appropriate formats, understand how to propose personal or collective action in response to a challenge, and predict effects, while understanding different perspectives and expected outcomes. |
| **Digital Technologies** | |
| ACTDIK002, ACTDIP003, ACTDIP005, ACTDIP006, ACTDIK008, ACTDIP009, ACTDIP016, ACTDIP022, ACTDIP025, ACTDIP027, ACTDIP031, ACTDIP032 | Foundation to Year 7, learners of Digital Technologies recognise patterns and present, interpret and validate data to create information and solve problems. |
| **Design and Technologies** | |
| All content descriptions | From Foundation to Year 7, learners of Design Technologies study how things are designed and produced, then generate and communicate design ideas. Eventually learners critique and justify design choices, referring to health and sustainability. |
| **English** | |
| ACELT165 | Foundation learners of English record and report ideas and events. |

| TABLE 10.7 (CONT.) | |
|---|---|
| **Learning area** | **Economics and Business inquiry and skills connections** |
| | **Mathematics** |
| ACMSP011 ACMSP262, ACMSP048, ACMSP068, ACMSP095, ACMSP118, ACMSP263, ACMSP050, ACMSP069, ACMSP096, ACMSP119, ACMSP070, ADMSP148, ACMSP172, ACMAN180 | Foundation learners of Mathematics answer yes/no questions to collect information and make simple inferences. From Year 1 to 7, learners choose questions, gather responses, make inferences then represent, describe and interpret data. |
| | **Science** |
| ACSIS012, ACSIS233, ACSHE050, ACSHE061, ACSIS218, ACSIS221, ACSHE098, ACSHE021, ACSHE100 | From Foundation to Year 7, learners of Science share observations, represent data, ask questions, describe changes in objects and events, make predictions, describe patterns and relationships, compare data with predictions as evidence to develop explanations, reflecting historical and cultural contributions, and solve problems. |

Source: adapted from ACARA 2018a

## Questioning and research

Questioning and research involves asking questions about an event and then planning and conducting an investigation (ACARA 2018c). Research is important in Economics and Business because gathering reliable data and conducting market research for analysis results in decisions based on information, rather than on personal beliefs, and increases the likelihood of business profitability.

At this stage of the inquiry process, learning is guided by the content descriptions outlined in Table 10.8.

| TABLE 10.8 | QUESTIONING AND RESEARCH CONTENT DESCRIPTIONS |
|---|---|
| **Year level** | **Content descriptions** |
| 5 and 6 | Locate and collect relevant information and data from primary sources and secondary sources. To organise and represent data in a range of formats including tables, graphs and large- and small-scale maps, using discipline-appropriate conventions. |
| 7 | Gather relevant data and information from a range of digital, online and print sources. |

Source: adapted from ACARA 2018a

Generation of business ideas for quality products can be stimulated when learning social connectedness and strategies to improve liveability for young people in Year 7 Geography. Learners who elect to operate food businesses will follow government healthy eating guidelines (SA Health 2018) for food sold in educational contexts. These guidelines stimulate thinking about product quality and the ethics of selling unhealthy foods and drinks in schools. Learners can question and research foods provided in educational settings and fundraising activities.

# EDUCATOR TIP

Online audiovisual resources engage students when introducing or reinforcing concepts. For example, Jamie Oliver showing children how chicken nuggets are made and films showing hot dog and sausage production provide catalysts for discussion about competition with quality products. The Australian Cancer Council publishes material about potentially carcinogenic foods such as sausages and preserved meats, which contain nitrites that convert to nitrosamine, a known carcinogen, during digestion (World Health Organization 2015).

By the end of this process, learners have selected a product and begin gathering data by conducting market research to determine demand for products by preparing questionnaires that ask potential customers:

- Are consumers interested in purchasing products?
- What are consumers prepared to pay?
- What are the demographic indicators, such as age and gender?

Learners can use online survey methods to generate graphical information or create and rehearse a script before visiting classes and recording data. At the end of this process, data have been gathered and collated.

## Interpretation and analysis

Interpretation and analysis involve critical examination of data, information and accounting from different perspectives. Bloom (1956, p. 144) provides a useful description of analysis:

> Analysis emphasises the breakdown of the material into its constituent parts and detection of the relationships of the parts and of the way they are organised. It may also be directed at the techniques and devices used to convey the meaning or establish the conclusion of communication . . . Analysis of elements, relationships and organizational principles is a prelude to evaluation.

Analysis is an important business planning skill as, to avoid business failure, decisions are made after interpretation of credible evidence. It is introduced into educational settings using the content description outlined in Table 10.9.

| **TABLE 10.9** | INTERPRETATION AND ANALYSIS CONTENT DESCRIPTION |
|---|---|
| **Year level** | **Content description** |
| 5, 6 and 7 | Interpret data and information displayed in a range of formats to identify, describe and compare distributions, patterns and trends, and infer relationships and trends. |

Source: adapted from ACARA 2018a

Learners can now use their collated data for market research analysis to determine whether there is enough demand for the product. Qualitative analysis involves processing data and information that cannot be represented numerically. Investigations into sustainable packaging, food additives, nutrition, slave-free supply chains, safety and ethical business practices contribute to product quality decisions.

Quantitative analysis involves processing data and information that can be represented numerically. Business viability is determined by assessing whether enough sales will occur to cover costs and generate profit. The example of the language class that purchased pizzas from a local business for $10 and sold each slice for $1, each pizza having eight slices, reinforces the idea that businesses must sell products to cover costs before making a final decision to trade. Learners can prepare a budget where the business decides to trade after market research with consumers indicates an intention to purchase 48 slices of pizza. This will generate $16 profit.

At the end of this process, learners have collected and analysed their own data and information. These skills can be used for analysis and interpretation of data from the ABS and other sources in future Economics and Business investigations.

## EDUCATOR TIP

To introduce the concept of interpretation and analysis, discuss the election of Donald Trump, whose market research resulted in more effective branding and promotion than Hillary Clinton's campaign (Danieli 2016). Trump's brand, 'Make America Great Again', motivated people to vote for him. People were largely unaware of Clinton's brand, which was 'I'm With Her'. Republican Trump visited previously safe Democratic states in the northeast amid media speculation. His unexpected victories in these states suggest that market research and analysis were key to his success.

## Economic reasoning, decision-making and application

Economic reasoning, decision-making and application involve making informed decisions by applying economic and business knowledge, skills and concepts (ACARA 2018c). Bloom (1956, p. 185) provides this description:

> Evaluation is defined as the making of judgments about the value, for some purpose, of ideas, works, solutions, methods, materials, etc. It involves the use of criteria as well as standards for appraising the extent to which particulars are accurate, effective, economical, or satisfying. The judgments may be either quantitative or qualitative, and the criteria may be either those determined by the student or those which are given.

Comprehension is the demonstration of specific knowledge, skills and concepts, whereas application involves the correct use of knowledge, skills and concepts in contexts where no solution is specified (Bloom 1956). Educators can encourage learners to use deductive reasoning and draw conclusions based on experience (Piaget 1955), and share information based on knowledge and experience, while encouraging Economics and Business reasoning through open questioning.

Learners are now ready to execute the business plan and to trade, so will need to understand how to develop a brand, advertise, purchase from suppliers, manufacture and operate a business. Application of the business plan is now possible with guidance from the content descriptions outlined in Table 10.10.

| TABLE 10.10   ECONOMIC REASONING, DECISION-MAKING AND APPLICATION CONTENT DESCRIPTIONS | |
| --- | --- |
| **Year level** | **Content descriptions** |
| 5 and 6 | Evaluate evidence to draw conclusions, work in groups to generate responses to issues and challenges, use criteria to make decisions and judgements and consider advantages and disadvantages of preferring one decision over others. |
| 7 | Generate a range of alternatives in response to an observed economic or business issue or event, and evaluate the potential costs and benefits of each alternative. Apply Economics and Business knowledge, skills and concepts in familiar, new and hypothetical situations. |

Source: adapted from ACARA 2018c

## Logistics

Decisions about costs and benefits can be made using budgets to generate and justify alternatives in manufacturing, branding, advertising and business location, timing and execution. Each option is evaluated before one is selected.

### Location

Demographics can be used to predict preferred locations for the business. For example, if more Year 7s express intentions to purchase, then locating the business near the Year 7 classrooms can be considered. This relates to Year 5 and 7 Geography when considering location, livability of places and accessibility to services and facilities. Selecting the location also relates to Year 1 Science when studying how living things live in different places where their needs are met.

### Timing

Business planning integrates with Year 3 History when selecting an Australian or international day for fundraising. In Years 1, 3 and 4, Mathematics provides fundamental knowledge about time, months, seasons, maps and planning using a calendar and informs future decisions such as higher staffing during harvesting periods.

Learners will have experienced cancellation of school events due to storms or heat, and the application of geographic and scientific knowledge to inform personal and community decisions. Business operations alter according to observable changes in sky and landscape, and weather events.

## Execution

Year 6 and 7 Health and Physical Education investigates planning, promoting and using correct health and safety practices for individuals and communities. Year 5, 6 and 7 Design and Technologies analyses sustainability in food preparation, maintaining good health and the importance of food safety and hygiene. Year 7 Digital Technologies evaluates how information systems solutions meet needs. All of these learning areas inform production processes.

A competitive advantage with consumers is created by using ethical supply chains, providing free-range eggs or slave-free chocolate. These decisions may be more expensive but relate to competing on quality and brand rather than price. Design and Technologies from Foundation to Year 7 identifies and records sustainable product design, ensuring equipment is used safely, collaboratively and sustainably.

## Advertising

Economics and Business integrates with English and drama in developing critical and consumer literacy, and crafting persuasive advertising texts. The purpose of advertising is not to inform, but to create sales and profits, and success is determined by increased sales and brand recognition. Year 1 and 2 English describes differences between imaginative, informative and persuasive texts and identifies audience. Learners can view a movie or television show while recording product placement to analyse how they are being targeted by marketers. This will assist learners in understanding more subtle forms of advertising and brand imprinting.

English prepares learners for producing advertising from Foundation to Year 2, when innovating familiar texts through play, responding to texts, stories, authors and illustrators; discussing and analysing images in narratives to create meaning; and recreating, innovating and presenting texts using images, characters, repetitive patterns and vocabulary. Drama includes how to establish roles, which assists in creating successful advertising texts.

If constraints prevent business operation, learners can present reasoned arguments with evidence in a pitch. A pitch is a persuasive text to encourage investment in a business and should include a unique product; a well-constructed business plan with a clear understanding of finances and budget projections; distribution channels, people skills; and coachability. Pitching and public speaking are important forms of business literacy and examples from television shows such as *Dragon's Den* and *Shark Tank* are available online. These skills integrate with Year 2 to 7 English, when learners begin oral presentations with multimodal elements (ACARA 2018a).

## Communication and reflection

Communication and reflection involve presenting findings, arguments and evidence-based conclusions using Economics and Business concepts, conventions and language to reflect on intended and unintended consequences of decisions (ACARA 2018c). Communication and reflection are important in Economics and Business to assure the ongoing prosperity of a business or economy. To conduct an authentic communication and reflection process, learners are guided by the content descriptions outlined in Table 10.11.

| **TABLE 10.11** COMMUNICATION AND REFLECTION CONTENT DESCRIPTIONS | |
| --- | --- |
| **Year level** | **Content descriptions** |
| 5 and 6 | Present ideas, findings, viewpoints and conclusions in a range of texts and modes that incorporate source materials, digital and non-digital representations and discipline-specific terms and conventions. Reflect on learning to propose personal and or collective action in response to an issue or challenge, and predict the probable effects. |
| 7 | Present evidence-based conclusions using Economics and Business language and concepts in a range of appropriate formats, and reflect on the consequences of alternative actions. |

Source: adapted from ACARA 2018a

Production of a unique communication is a synthesis task of 'getting ideas, feelings, and experiences across to others' (Bloom 1956, p. 168). Effective business communication between entrepreneurs, investors, customers, suppliers and employees requires correct spelling, punctuation and grammar. These skills develop in Foundation English when creating short texts and continue through the primary years as learners refine ideas and use words for impact. Correctly structured business communications, using subject-specific language, can form English activities and the Economics and Business glossary is available on the Australian Curriculum website to assist in this process.

## EDUCATOR TIP

Communication with technology involves managing risk when publishing online. To prevent identity theft, learners should not publish any information identifying them (ASIC 2018): a name and date of birth are enough to steal an identity, and images should not be on the Internet. Year 7 Digital Technologies also takes social contexts into account when communicating online (ACARA 2018a).

Reflection is the analysis and evaluation of quantitative and qualitative information to determine the success of Economics and Business decisions. Quantitative information in the form of a simple income statement outlines revenue minus expenses and communicates financial information in the business plan and the achievement of intended consequences (see Figure 10.5).

Intended consequences includes meeting budgeted objectives and the surplus of $42 has achieved more than budget projections. Unintended consequences of decisions might include financial losses or externalities such as pollution, environmental destruction, health problems, animal cruelty or slavery. Opportunities for integration with other HASS subjects include: ancient studies in Year 7 History, where slaves were part of ancient societies; and Year 7 Civics and Citizenship issues concerning freedom and a 'fair

```
┌─────────────────────────────────────────────────────────┐
│                      Fiona's Pizzas                       │
│                    Income statement                       │
│                       May 2020                            │
│         Revenue                                    $      │
│         Sales 56 × $2                             112     │
│                                                           │
│         Less expenses                                     │
│         Pizzas 7 × $10                            70      │
│                                                           │
│         Net Profit                              $42       │
└─────────────────────────────────────────────────────────┘
```

FIGURE 10.5   An income statement

go', where learners become aware of consumers' obligations as global citizens (ACARA 2018a). Learning activities can include purchasing slave-free chocolate before Easter or products free of palm oil. In these ways, ethics and sustainability become part of economic thinking.

# CONCLUSION

This chapter has provided a brief introduction to Economics and Business, but it is essential for educators to undertake further reading and monitor current events, statistics and government policies to competently deliver the necessary knowledge and skills. Newspapers and periodicals such as the *Australian Financial Review*, *Business Review Weekly* and *Forbes*, television programs such as *Gruen*, *The Checkout* and *Insiders*, and peak bodies such as the Australian Council of Trade Unions and Business Council of Australia, are invaluable resources that provide a deeper understanding of the complex thinking that underpins Economics and Business.

As future leaders, learners must have a knowledge of Economics and Business to become effective participants in a prosperous economy and a society free of exploitation. Learners can appraise government policy, set goals for themselves and their community, and work towards a more sustainable and equitable planet.

## REVIEW QUESTIONS

1. Explain the four main reasons for business failure.
2. What is 'the economic problem'?
3. Explain opportunity cost.
4. Explain how the cross-curriculum priority Aboriginal and Torres Strait Islander histories and cultures is linked to Economics and Business.
5. Analyse why the ethics capability is an important focus in Economics and Business education.

## LEARNING EXTENSION

### Game Theory – Beauty Contest

A group of learners is invited to stand at the front of the class, choose a number between 0 and 100 and write it on a piece of paper (Dixit 2006). They show the number to the class, but not to each other. The educator and observers calculate the mean of the numbers and the learner who selected the number closest to the mean is the winner. Explain this process before beginning the task.

The same group of learners repeats this process several times. Patterns in behaviour will begin to emerge and learners will alter their selections to choose numbers closer to a predicted mean based on past experience.

Through two-way sharing, observers discuss patterns, then the educator leads a discussion of behaviour with the entire class. Learners observe the patterns in the choices of other learners and explain the metacognitive processes used in making and changing decisions.

This learning experience can then be compared with participation in the share market or operation of a business in a market. Individuals have no control over other participants, but can succeed by exhibiting conscious behaviours (Vygotsky 1997) after the assimilation of experiences and observations (Piaget 1955).

Research other game theory.

## REFERENCES

ABS (Australian Bureau of Statistics). (2018). *Labour Statistics: Concepts, sources and methods, February 2018*. Cat. no. 6102.0.55.001. Retrieved from: http://www.abs.gov.au/ausstats/ abs@.nsf/Lookup/by%20Subject/6102.0.55.001~Feb%202018~Main% 20Features~Unemployment~6.

ACARA (Australian Curriculum, Assessment and Reporting Authority). (2018a). *Australian Curriculum: F-10, V8.3*. Retrieved from: https://www.australiancurriculum.edu.au/f-10-curriculum.

——(2018b). *AustralianCurriculum: F-10, v8.3*. Curriculum connections. Consumer and financial literacy. Retrieved from: https://australiancurriculum.edu.au/resources/curriculum-connections/portfolios/consumer-and-financial-literacy.

——(2018c). *AustralianCurriculum: Humanities and Social Sciences F-10, v8.3*: Economics and Business. Retrieved from: https://www.australiancurriculum.edu.au/f-10-curriculum/ humanities-and-social-sciences/economics-and-business.

ASIC (Australian Securities and Investments Commission). (2014). *National Financial Literacy Strategy 2014–2017*. Retrieved from: http://www.financialliteracy.gov.au/media/546585/ report-403_national-financial-literacy-strategy-2014-17.pdf.

——(2018). Identity fraud. Retrieved from: https://www.moneysmart.gov.au/scams/other-scams/identity-fraud.

Bangs, J. (2012). Teaching with context rich problems. In G.M. Hoyt & K.M. Goldrick, eds, *International Handbook on Teaching and Learning Economics*. Northampton, MA: Edward Elgar, pp. 48–57.

Barnes, B. (2014). The future of the mining industry and opportunities for Australian students: Navigating across horizons. Paper presented at the Business Educators Australasia biennial conference, October. Fremantle, Western Australia.

Bloom, B.S. (1956). *Taxonomy of Educational Objectives: Book 1: Cognitive domain*. New York: Longman.

Borg, J.R. & Borg, M.O. (2001). Teaching critical thinking in interdisciplinary economics courses. *College Teaching*, 49(1), 20.

Danieli, K. (2016). Hillary Clinton might be winning the war but Donald Trump is winning the battle of the brands. *heatst.com*, 12 October. Retrieved from: https://heatst.com/politics/hillary-clinton-might-be-winning-the-war-but-donald-trump-is-winning-the-battle-of-the-brands.

DEEWR (Department of Education, Employment and Workplace Relations). (2009). *Belonging, Being and Becoming: The Early Years Learning Framework for Australia*. Canberra: DEEWR.

Department of Education and Training. (2014). *National Quality Framework for Early Childhood Education and Care, Early Years Learning Framework*. Retrieved from: https://www.education.gov.au/national-quality-framework-early-childhood-education-and-care-1.

Dixit, A. (2006). Restoring fun to game theory. In W.E. Becker, M. Watts & S.R. Becker, eds, *Teaching Economics: More Alternatives to Chalk and Talk*. Northampton, MA: Edward Elgar, pp. 2–11.

Eisenmann, T.R. (2013). Entrepreneurship: A working definition. *Harvard Business Review*, January, Retrieved from: https://hbr.org/2013/01/what-is-entrepreneurship.

Kaplan, S. (2010). Introduction to prompts of depth and complexity – project linking learning. USC Rossier. Retrieved from: https://www.youtube.com/watch/?v=McEldMETSnw.

National Innovation and Science Agenda. (2015). *The Agenda*. Retrieved from: https://www.innovation.gov.au/page/national-innovation-and-science-agenda-report.

National Museum of Australia. (2018). Defining moments in Australian history: Trade with the Makasar. Retrieved from: http://www.nma.gov.au/online_features/defining_moments/featured/trade_with_makasar.

OECD (Organisation for Economic Cooperation and Development). (2011). Measuring financial literacy: Questionnaire and guidance notes for conducting an internationally comparable survey of financial literacy. Retrieved from: https://www.oecd.org/finance/financial-education/49319977.pdf.

Piaget, J. (1955). *The Construction of Reality in the Child*. London: Routledge & Kegan Paul.

Renzulli, J. (1998). A rising tide lifts all ships: Developing the gifts and talents of all students. *The Phi Delta Kappan*, 80(2), 104–11.

SA Health. (2018). Healthy eating guidelines for schools. Retrieved from: http://www.sahealth.sa.gov.au/wps/wcm/connect/public+content/sa+health+internet/healthy+living/healthy+communities/schools/healthy+eating+guidelines+for+schools.

Stevenson, H.H. (2000). Why entrepreneurship has won. Coleman white paper plenary address at United States Association for Small Business and Entrepreneurship, 17 February. Retrieved from: http://www.unm.edu/~asalazar/Kauffman/Entrep_research/e_won.pdf.

Vygotsky, L.S. (1997). *Education Psychology* (R. Silverman, trans.). Boca Raton, FL: St Lucie Press.

World Health Organization. (2015). Links between processed meat and colorectal cancer. Retrieved from: http://www.who.int/mediacentre/news/statements/2015/processed-meat-cancer/en.

Yunkaporta, T. (2009). Aboriginal pedagogies at the cultural interface. PhD thesis, James Cook University. Retrieved from https://researchonline.jcu.edu.au/10974/4/04Bookchapter.pdf.

Yunkaporta, T. & Kirby, M. (2011). Yarning up Indigenous pedagogies: A dialogue about eight Aboriginal ways of learning. In R. Bell, G. Milgate & N. Purdie, eds, *Two Way Teaching and Learning: Toward culturally reflective and relevant education*. Melbourne: ACER Press, pp. 205–13.

# PART III

# Teaching and learning in HASS

# INQUIRY LEARNING: THE PROCESS IS ESSENTIAL TO THE PRODUCT

*Kim Porter and Madeline Fussell*

**11**

## Learning objectives

After reading this chapter, you should be able to:

- define the intent of inquiry learning in Humanities and Social Sciences (HASS) education
- understand the theories that underpin inquiry learning
- identify the role of the educator in the inquiry process in HASS learning.

## INTRODUCTION

HASS teaching is aimed at developing **lifelong learning** skills that will enable learners today to be active citizens of their communities, their nation and the world. It is hoped that the knowledge and skills learnt in educational settings will be utilised and built on over the course of learners' lives. Inquiry learning provides an excellent vehicle to achieve these goals because it allows learners to go further than assimilating knowledge. The inquiry process in HASS places great emphasis on learners viewing different perspectives and values and using critical thinking skills to evaluate and make decisions. The result of this approach is that learners themselves develop opinions, form values and acquire skills that will underpin their behaviour, both now and in the future.

**lifelong learning:** through exposure to authentic situations, problem-solving tasks and explicit teaching about citizenship issues, allows learners to develop knowledge and skills that will enable them to participate constructively in their community on a local, national and global level. Skills learnt through inquiry will assist learners in their adult lives.

## THE INTENT OF INQUIRY

Inquiry is a teaching approach that is not new and has been advocated in HASS syllabus and curriculum documents for some time. An **inquiry learning** approach is implicit in the current Australian Curriculum: HASS, with key inquiry questions set 'as a framework for developing students' knowledge, understanding and skills' (ACARA 2018, p. 23). Inquiry does not so much change *what* is taught but *how* it is taught. When learners 'discover' information for themselves rather than being told, it creates opportunities for learners to evaluate and decide whether to act on the learning. Learners need to experience the relevance of the information to their own community and how this impacts on their lives and those of others. In this way, social knowledge and understanding are developed that are applied to broader contexts as learners mature. Reynolds (2014, p. 50) maintains that it

**inquiry learning:** a form of active learning that is guided by questioning and investigating scenarios to develop understanding

is 'the interrogation of ideas and perspectives that requires time and which makes inquiry learning useful as a way of developing deep understanding of complex issues of importance to all citizens'. Educators need to be mindful of time constraints and the interests and abilities of learners. This means the inquiry process needs to be flexible so that educators can impart quick facts (transmission), give clear explanations (explicit teaching) and allow students to build their own knowledge and understanding through a range of carefully balanced activities (inquiry learning). The overall intent of inquiry in HASS is long-term learning that will enable learners to understand how to take an active role in their communities (local, national, global), and possess the skills with which to do so and the understanding that individuals can make a difference.

However, there are many interpretations (and, we would maintain, many misinterpretations) of the intent and process of inquiry. This chapter will demonstrate how the inquiry process in HASS facilitates deeper learning and that the skill sets developed create the ability for lifelong learning and the capacity for learners to be active citizens.

## How do we learn?

Imagine you are a passenger in a car going to a function at a destination that is new to you. The driver is engaging you in conversation for some of the trip, but you are taking in some of the scenery along the way. At times you are lost in your own thoughts about something that happened earlier in the day. The following day, you need to return to the function venue to retrieve a personal item you left behind. Can you remember how to get there?

It's likely that most of us would struggle with the above scenario unless we had driven the route ourselves. As a passenger, the route had little significance for you, there was no need to give it your full concentration or to remember landmarks or directions. However, if you had been the driver and had to ensure you knew how to get there by actively navigating the route, it is more likely that you would make the second trip easily.

For most people, learning is much the same. We need to know the purpose if we are to become fully engaged and remember and learn from what we do. In this chapter, we will refer to this as *active learning*.

## MAKING LEARNING RELEVANT

Consider the reaction learners would have to information on the impacts of water shortages in Australia when this information is gained through fieldwork, video clips, surveys, guest speakers or other relevant community information sources. Once learners see the relevance of this issue to their own community, they can relate to it, and motivation to actively resolve the issue is greatly enhanced. Learners explore the barriers to full resolution; the reasons why people may/may not conserve water; and the awareness of what individuals, groups and governments can achieve. Learners are then motivated and encouraged to form their own values that will underpin their current and future behaviours regarding this issue.

This scenario illustrates that it is the focus inquiry places on making learning relevant, and identifying conflicting perspectives and values, that allows learners to clarify their own values and perspectives on issues to which they can contribute now and in the future.

## Active learning

Active learning means learners are involved and not passively following instructions such as copying notes from a board. **Transmission teaching** is when educators literally try to transpose their own knowledge to learners. The theoretical view of transmission teaching is that rote learning results in only superficial learning. However, there is still a need for transmission teaching within HASS inquiry. Educators need to keep the focus on the inquiry question, so quick facts that learners need can be supplied by the teacher; for example, when learners are investigating school life in the past in Australia, the subject of the small bottles of milk provided in schools after World War II often arises. The educator can quickly explain why these were distributed rather than divert from the original inquiry purpose.

> **transmission teaching**: utilises mainly rote learning with no option for learner questioning

Active learning always has a clear purpose, and is presented so that learners can process and personalise the new information. Learners learn by adding new knowledge to what they already know, even if this means changing their original views. An example of this is a young child learning about the concept of home and the huge number of variations this concept encapsulates. Homes can be temporary or permanent; a caravan or an apartment; a brick house or a tent; a game board destination or a winning circuit run in softball or baseball.

Rather than telling learners the answer, the educator wants them to discover it so that they will internalise it. The teaching outcome remains constant, but the activities (or process) change so the learner has first-hand experiences; their **prior knowledge** is built upon; they can question, analyse and evaluate the information to which they are exposed and they then reach the planned conclusion through their own (guided) discovery. Piaget's (1955) research demonstrates how we all have ideas and conceptions and then we adjust these as new knowledge is presented. Through learning this way, know-ledge is internalised and used more effectively. Educators need to build on what learners already know from both home and educational settings. The images in Figure 11.1 show a child in an early learning setting investigating how babies grow and change. This has been personalised for her by investigating how she has grown and changed as well as by other information sources such as a mother with a new baby visiting and demonstrating care, and discussing the development of young babies.

> **prior knowledge**: learners best acquire knowledge when they build on what they already know and have encountered

## Skill sets

Active learning allows learners to explore; experiment; research; share, debate and brain-storm ideas; and communicate and use findings. However, for learners to be actively involved, skill sets are required. These skill sets are diverse, ranging from conflict resolution to being able to download a photo from a camera or phone to insert in a document. **Explicit teaching**, which allows for learner questioning, practice and constructive feedback, and then implementation within authentic contexts, is required to ensure skill proficiency is developed throughout educational settings to facilitate transferable skills that will be used in the long term.

> **explicit teaching**: an educator-centred approach, but the role the educator plays is to clearly show (demonstrate and/or model step by step) *how*, *why* and *when* the information or skills will be used

FIGURE 11.1 Active learning: a four-year-old investigating how she has grown and changed by filling and holding a sand bag equivalent to her birth weight
Source: Private collection of M. Fussell, 2017

Child-centred learning, where learners explore questions and issues that are meaningful and relevant to their lives, often generates a picture of learners working constructively in groups to find information from books, journals, newspaper articles, artefacts and the Internet and then being guided by the educator to sort and classify their information using strategies such as visual organisers. The educator's dream classroom is also one where learners are moving from lower-order to higher-order thinking, and discussions, questions and ideas are continually becoming more involved and interesting. In this educational setting, learners are making links to their learning in other key learning areas and this is providing a cohesive framework within which to teach. Easy to establish? Not exactly!

Classrooms that resemble the description above are very dependent on learners having the skills that each task requires. This skill base must cover:

- cognitive skills (thinking)
- research skills (locate, organise, analyse, evaluate data)
- social skills (group work, team building, interpersonal)
- communication skills (reading, writing, listening, speaking, computing, visual)
- affective skills (values analysis, clarification, critique)
- manipulative skills (dexterity).

In addition to these generic skills, there are also the discipline-specific skills needed for teaching the different strands within the HASS curriculum. For example, in History learners need the skills to be able to interrogate information sources for evidence; in Geography, mapping skills are crucial; Civics and Citizenship requires critical thinking skills that inform decision-making and predict action; and in Economics and Business skills in collecting and analysing data are fundamental. Research indicates that educators who lack discipline-specific skills such as mapping usually only focus on knowledge content, and skills are often avoided or taught superficially, resulting in learning deficiencies. When learners are deprived of skill learning, they miss out on learning how to learn. For example, consider the many uses of maps in finding absolute positions, navigating, communicating about locations, identifying safety issues and showing environmental changes. Everyday life can include the use of satellite maps (Google Earth; weather maps), road maps and venue maps. Learners who have had little or no experience with mapping skills are hampered in their ability to use or communicate mapping directions.

## What are skills?

Skills are procedures or ways of doing things that can be learnt and practised. Skills are learnt because they can be used purposefully. They enable other tasks to be performed and social action to be taken, and are best learnt when they are needed – having a purpose makes the effort of learning worthwhile (Noble 2010). A common challenge for educators is providing interesting and worthwhile learning activities. Lessons can be deemed a failure due to no prior checking of learners' skill levels and/or educators presuming learners already understand and/or are competent in a skill required for the lesson to function successfully. The educator may assume that an inquiry approach is not a successful teaching approach, when in fact it was the poor skill level that resulted in the lesson not achieving its intended outcomes.

Figure 11.2 demonstrates steps that support educators in adapting skill teaching for all ages. Identifying skills involved in HASS learning experiences ensures that lessons are

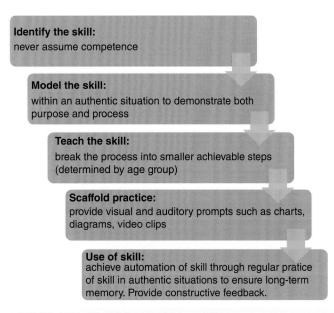

FIGURE 11.2   Model for teaching a skill

meaningful and productive, and learners can fully participate in them. Once the educator has identified the skill (the steps involved in mastering it) and the current proficiency of learners, it is crucial to make the teaching explicit. The educator models the skill using self-talk so that learners gain a clear understanding of each step. Where possible (e.g. a graph), the educator can ask learners to complete the skill alongside them, making a clear chart of the steps that can be displayed in the classroom for learners' reference. The educator then reinforces the skill by having learners explain each step back to them, and ensures that new skills are taught with known content so that learners are not overwhelmed by the task. For example, when teaching how to use a Venn diagram for the first time, the educator can compare and contrast familiar concepts (e.g. dogs and cats), which makes it easier to learn the skills required to construct this type of graphic organiser. This skill can then be used more proficiently to complete a Venn diagram that compares and contrasts how toys have changed or remained the same over time. It is crucial that learners are given the opportunity to use and practise a particular skill for a real purpose as soon as possible after instruction. It is important also to give learners feedback, and to again make this explicit and constructive. Competency is only achieved when a skill can be used automatically, so it is vital to ensure learners are provided with plenty of opportunities to practise skills taught in the classroom.

An inquiry approach, therefore, is skill intensive as learners are learning *how* to learn and not just assimilating educator-chosen content. Clearly, the teaching of skills takes extra teaching time but those in favour of this approach argue that the end result – learners who can learn from each other, work collaboratively, independently research and use analytical and critical thinking skills – gain deeper and more effective learning of both knowledge content and transferable skills. Future employers are also supporting this approach, stating that the qualities fostered in the inquiry approach, such as teamwork, communication skills, critical and analytical thinking, initiative, IT skills and social responsibility, are attributes that are now essential in the workplace (Dixson 2017; Hodge & Lear 2011).

## EDUCATOR TIP

Ensure when you plan activities to explore HASS content that you identify the skills needed so you can incorporate instruction if necessary. Remember, explicit teaching is needed for skill acquisition.

Reflection How do you best learn? What assists you to acquire and use new skills? What hinders your learning?

# THEORY THAT UNDERPINS INQUIRY

Imagine you tried to teach a two-year-old child the differences between a dog, horse, alpaca and donkey by showing four photos and telling the child the appropriate names. The child might parrot the names after you and even point to the right photo; however, the learning would rarely go beyond this surface level because it does not allow for analysis of the characteristics that define the differences between each animal. However, if the child has experience with dogs, sees them in the neighbourhood and then encounters a horse, the child may say 'dog', but will more easily accept the correction to horse when hearing the different sounds and be encouraged to observe the difference in height, feet, mane, tail and so on. When the child then sees a donkey or alpaca, the first reaction will be to label it 'horse', but the same process needs to be established so the child can absorb and use the new information. This constant revision of information (fitting new with old), and thus building on prior learning through one's own experiences, is the basis of the constructivist approach that underpins the inquiry process in HASS education. It is based on the premise that 'each individual's learning comprises their own cumulative experiences, so each learner will view the world differently and adjust their constructions appropriately' (Kriewaldt 2012a, p. 96).

## Constructivist theorists

In the past, educators believed learners were a blank slate that needed writing on and it was the educator's role to transmit the perceived knowledge, values and beliefs of the time. As a result, rote learning of facts was the most dominant perspective in education. Being able to regurgitate knowledge through tests and exams was prioritised. Current HASS education aims to develop and equip learners with skills that will result in lifelong learning, which in turn will allow for active citizenship. In the past there was little room for analysis, questioning, problem-solving or creative and critical thinking. Today these skills are considered essential for learners to be able to investigate different perspectives and values, and ensure a holistic picture of events and issues is achieved in HASS.

The method by which we learn will usually dictate the quantity and quality of what we learn and how we use that learning. Many people have probably had one or more of the following experiences:

- doing a project and finding lots of different information on the topic, but remembering little without a specific focus
- copying and pasting large slabs of information from an encyclopedia or the Internet about a topic but not clearly understanding all the vocabulary used, let alone all the concepts
- listening to an educator's explanation and copying notes from the board
- wondering how what is being taught fits in with other events before and after, and thus feeling only one piece of the jigsaw has been given
- memorising dates and places but not understanding their significance to people today or why they are being learnt

• struggling to learn something in which they have no interest and having no expectation that the knowledge will ever be useful.

It is presumed that we do not want to replicate such teaching and learning experiences as those above, so *how* we teach is as crucial as *what* we teach.

The constructivists, as they came to be known, were a group of educational researchers who explored how children learn and retain knowledge. Their research demonstrated that for information to be retained for longer than needed for test results, it needs to be more than surface learning. Additionally, learners need to be aware of the purpose of the learning – that is, there needs to be a clear learning objective – and be able to apply the learning to life outside the classroom (i.e. authentic learning). **Authentic learning** puts classroom content into real-world contexts. For example, children hypothetically write a letter or tweet to the editor of a newspaper about a local issue rather than summarise notes in an exercise book. This type of deep learning results from the use of a range of perspectives and sources and from incorporating **critical thinking**.

**authentic learning**: the use of real-life situations (hypothetical or actual) to engage learners and ensure they make the connection between the learning and life outside the classroom

**critical thinking**: the ability to analyse, evaluate, explain and question rather than accept facts blindly; the skill to evaluate an information source and realise that further evidence is needed for a complete understanding

## Research that underpins inquiry methodology

There are many constructivist theorists; however, Piaget, Vygotsky, Bruner and Dewey have especially informed the inquiry approach used in HASS education.

**conceptual development**: the analysis and grouping of factual information into the big ideas or concepts; for example, social justice, freedom, discrimination.

The importance of building on prior learning (like the example given earlier of the two-year-old differentiating between animals) and progressing from concrete to abstract thinking (**conceptual development**) arose from research by Piaget (Cornish & Garner 2009). In this thinking, concepts are abstract, so a shared knowledge base built up through concrete examples is essential when discussing concepts (the big ideas). Thus learners move from facts to concepts to generalisation. Piaget's findings are incorporated into HASS inquiry as educators focus in the initial stages of an investigation on ascertaining and building on learners' prior knowledge; ensuring that when finding information, concepts are made visual; and planning hands-on activities that allow learners to explore and build their own understandings of concepts through experience (McInerney & McInerney 2006, p. 38).

Social language is used throughout the HASS inquiry process in whole-class, small-group and partnered discussions. Vygotsky identified social language and interaction as crucial to cognitive development (Cornish & Garner 2009). This research is validated in HASS inquiry when learners are working in cooperative groups, sharing information and problem-solving together, brainstorming a topic as a class, or communicating results and ideas. When the learning is collaborative and ideas are shared, this enables scaffolding and extension of learners to use the input of ideas to challenge and extend their own thinking and experiences.

The Australian Curriculum requires young learners to be exposed to some complicated issues such as immigration, Aboriginal and Torres Strait Islander issues, and government structures and policies. Bruner's research focused on how even very young children could assimilate complicated ideas – it all depends on how the teaching is presented (Cornish & Garner 2009). This is a crucial factor for HASS when a learning base for active citizenship is being developed prior to adulthood. Bruner was an advocate of the spiral curriculum approach, where learners commence learning about themselves and their family, then broaden to their community, state, nation and finally a global outlook, and this is evident in the *Australian Curriculum: HASS* (Kriewaldt 2012b). Bruner's work reminds us of the importance of making learning relevant to learners' lives and ensuring that they see the learning as purposeful and not just as a school activity.

HASS inquiry emphasises '**hands-on learning**' so learners learn from experience rather than being 'told' information. Dewey saw constructivist teaching, with its emphasis on hands-on learning, language, **social interaction** and discovery, as a way to bring about social change and improvements in society (Cornish & Garner 2009). Dewey's research reinforces the importance of educators taking child development into account and the need to build on prior learning and experiences. This is an integral part of inquiry in HASS learning, where activities are carefully and logically sequenced to ensure knowledge and understanding is built up systematically. HASS inquiry also ensures there are adequate activities that encourage learners to reflect on what they have learnt, how it was learnt and how this learning will change

> **hands-on learning**: involves learners building on their own understanding, which requires a range of visual and tactile learning experiences
>
> **social interaction**: discussion, brainstorming and group problem solving which encourages extension of conceptual understanding and ideas

their thinking and/or behaviour in the future. In this way, learners are encouraged to transfer skills and knowledge to other contexts, evaluate their learning and be conscious of the significance of what they have learnt, both to themselves and others (Cornish & Garner 2009). Piaget's research addressing how young children struggle with abstract concepts also underpins the emphasis in inquiry for the use of concrete (actual) materials with young learners. A deeper knowledge, understanding and longer memory retention are achieved when learners are actively involved. In relation to social interaction, researchers such as Vygotsky have shown that when learning is collaborative and ideas are shared, this allows scaffolding for those who need it and extension for others who will use the input of ideas to challenge and extend their own thinking and experiences (Cornish & Garner 2009).

In the hands-on learning activity demonstrated in Figure 11.3, learners inquired into what life was like for the ANZACs. This activity investigated a typical day's ration for a soldier at Gallipoli. Learners were able to view, feel and sort items into those that added flavouring and those that provided actual energy. In this illustration, the educator is facilitating a small-group discussion aimed at analysing the limited amount and monotony of these rations and the subsequent effects on health and morale. Can you identify how the theories of the constructivists (outlined above) are being incorporated into this lesson?

## WHAT DO EFFECTIVE EDUCATORS OF INQUIRY INCORPORATE FROM CONSTRUCTIVIST THEORY?

Varied pedagogical approaches have sprung from constructivist theories and it is important to recognise where they are embedded in an inquiry approach. The list below outlines where constructivist theories are upheld within an inquiry methodology:

- Fundamental to inquiry methodology is the belief that learners need to build their own understandings. We need to do things ourselves to remember.

FIGURE 11.3 **Hands-on learning**
Source: Private collection of M. Fussell and K. Porter, 2014

- We need to question, experience, experiment and use trial and error to fully understand.
- We benefit from listening to the experiences of others and sharing our own.
- Educators help us learn when they build on what we already know and scaffold new learning so our learning is dynamic.
- When we listen to the ideas of others, we can often adapt or build on these. When we hear new vocabulary and concepts discussed in familiar contexts, we gain understanding, so group work can be of great assistance.
- Younger learners need concrete resources to handle.
- All learners benefit through 'hands-on' learning and authentic contexts. We need a context we can relate to and are interested in, and to see why and how this learning relates to the world outside the classroom.
- We need to know how the learning can be used.

# Identifying the role of the educator within an inquiry approach

True constructivist learning is completely child centred, whereas inquiry, in the HASS context described in this chapter, is a collaboration between educator and learner with both playing an active role. Educators often underestimate their role in providing learners with rich, reliable and relevant information sources and the skills to retrieve and analyse information. 'This approach to learning is not just about sending students to the library to "research", asking them to do a "Google" or getting them to cut and paste a Wikipedia entry' (Taylor 2012, p. 124). The educator needs to facilitate the learning in such a way that learners have the opportunity to explore, question, analyse, communicate and determine the answer rather than just being fed information. Effective inquiry will only be established when both learners and educators are aware of, and take responsibility for, their roles and share the same clear learning purpose.

## Educator role

Vygotsky, Piaget, Bruner and Dewey believed that we could understand the world only through actively making sense of it for ourselves; knowledge cannot be transmitted to us ready made. This does not mean that a young person is alone in the world 'discovering' meaning or developing conceptual understanding. This discovery is assisted or mediated by family members, educators and peers, a process that is often referred to as *scaffolding*. Scaffolding requires the educator to play an active role within the inquiry approach if it is to be effective. The types of scaffolding that an educator might provide during any given inquiry investigation will include questioning, prompting, probing, provision of adequate and reliable information sources, skill mentoring, constructive feedback and the planning and implementation of activities that supports learners in developing conceptual understanding.

Educators are thus guiding learners to identify the big ideas or concepts relevant to the inquiry. Thus inquiry is sometimes referred to as **guided discovery**, and can be likened to a treasure hunt. Many constructivist theories, such as hands-on learning, use of authentic experiences and social learning, are utilised in guided discovery, but it is the educator who plans and facilitates the inquiry process. The educator plans the objective (inquiry question that addresses a syllabus/curriculum outcome) and plants clues along the way (activities) that allow learners to find the treasure (answer to the question). The learners are involved in active learning that allows them to personalise and process the information being learnt. It is important to note that the educator (and the curriculum) determines the destination – it is the journey to that destination that may vary, depending on the skill level, interests and cultural backgrounds of the learners.

> **guided discovery**: inquiry methodology is not completely learner-centred as the educator is required to implement the syllabus/curriculum

Table 11.1 outlines the roles of the educator and learners within an inquiry model. The model used is an adaptation of the inquiry model that was published in *Human Society and Its Environments K-6* (Board of Studies, NSW 1998, p. 12). This is just one example of an inquiry model; the choice of what inquiry model to use will be often determined by the purpose and topic. Note how the levels within the model are clearly linked and designed to sequentially build up knowledge and understanding.

**TABLE 11.1** EDUCATOR–LEARNER ROLES WITHIN INQUIRY

| Level in model | Educator role | Learner role |
| --- | --- | --- |
| **1. Activate** | • Establish the context using an information source.<br>• Arouse curiosity and engagement with the topic through questioning.<br>• Check for and use learners' prior knowledge.<br>• Introduce inquiry question that will be explored. | • Reflect on prior knowledge and share.<br>• Consider how they might find information to fully answer the question. |
| **2. Check it out** | • Ensure learners have access to information sources that provide a balanced view of the topic/issue/event.<br>• Use questioning to assist learners to analyse and evaluate the reliability and balance of their information.<br>• Guide learners to record information in an easily retrievable format.<br>• Ensure learners understand new vocabulary and subject-specific terms. | • Evaluate data for richness, reliability and relevance.<br>• Select appropriate evidence to the enable an answer to the question.<br>• Record information. |
| **3. Educator guides** | • Assist learners to analyse and link information collected to the answer being sought.<br>• Plan an activity that sorts information to see the emergence of key concepts.<br>• Use questioning that assists learners to move from lower-order thinking (facts) to higher-order thinking (concepts). | • Sort information to see patterns, connections and relevance to the question.<br>• Identify key concepts from information.<br>• Analyse results to propose an answer to the question. |
| **4. Information learnt** | • Build whole-class understanding of the answer to the question through group discussion.<br>• Provide opportunities for all learners to demonstrate an answer to the inquiry question through an authentic task. | • Justify answers and share with the group.<br>• Complete a task that demonstrates their knowledge, understanding and skills developed during the inquiry. |
| **5. Venture further (when appropriate)** | • Provide a new information source to further investigate the purpose and relevance of the learning in this topic. | • Explore a wider perspective of the issue<br><br>OR<br><br>• Consider whether they need to act on this new knowledge. |
| **6. Evaluate** | • Assist learners to reflect on *what* has been learnt and *how*.<br>• Connect to learning that may follow. | • Evaluate how their new learning can or will be used.<br>• Identify and evaluate new knowledge and skills gained and where these are transferable. |

## EDUCATOR TIP

Inquiry learning is not about the educator having less to do and the learner more, but rather a different focus: guided discovery. Tap into the knowledge of families and community to enrich learning in the classroom and provide authentic learning experiences.

What do you remember from your own humanities and social sciences learning at school, and why? What inquiry learning processes were evident?

Reflection

# CONCLUSION

HASS teaching is aimed at developing lifelong learning skills that will enable learners to participate effectively as active citizens of their local, national and global community. As a result, a teaching methodology that encourages learners to form opinions, develop values and understand the perspectives and values of others is a crucial part of HASS teaching. We want learners to be able to see how their learning in HASS assists them to understand their world – how it has been, how it is and how it could change – and, most importantly, how they can be part of, and influence, that change. This approach to learning means we want active learners who are excited about new knowledge, understanding and skills because they see how they can be used outside of the classroom.

A full understanding of an issue or event can only be achieved when multiple perspectives are investigated using rich, reliable and relevant information sources. Critical thinking skills are developed through the interrogation of such sources. When learning goes beyond the what, where and when to the *why* and *how*, learners are better placed to understand the ramifications of their actions and behaviour in local, national and global communities. Inquiry takes time to plan and teach, but this is true of any quality teaching, and many of the skills developed through inquiry are used across the curriculum and all are needed for adult life. Thus the process of inquiry is as important as the product, and we would strongly argue that the product will not be achieved without this process.

## REVIEW QUESTIONS

1. Why is the inquiry approach advocated for HASS teaching?
2. What are the important components of active learning?
3. What planning and preparation does the educator need to do when using an inquiry approach?
4. How might the skills used for inquiry benefit learning in other curriculum areas?

## LEARNING EXTENSION

At the beginning of each school year, educators usually meet with the parents/guardians/carers of learners to discuss the learning content and class routines. Many parents/guardians/carers have only experienced a transmission style of teaching. How would you explain to this audience the purpose and implementation of the inquiry approach in HASS teaching?

## REFERENCES

ACARA (Australian Curriculum, Assessment and Reporting Authority). (2018). *Australian Curriculum: Humanities and Social Sciences F-10, v8.3*. Retrieved from: https://www.australian curriculum.edu.au/f-10-curriculum/humanities-and-social-sciences/hass.

Board of Studies, NSW. (1998). *Human Society and Its Environments K-6*. Sydney: Board of Studies, NSW.

Cornish, L. & Garner, J. (2009). *Promoting Student Learning*, 2nd edn. Sydney: Pearson Education.

Dixson, L. (2017). How K–12 teachers prepare students for skills of the future. *Talent Economy*. Retrieved from: http://www.talenteconomy.io/2017/12/01/k-12-teachers-prepare-students-skills-future.

Fussell, M. (2017). How we grow and change [jpeg]. Project approach: Private collection M. Fussell.

Fussell, M. & Porter, K. (2014). Hands on learning [jpeg]. Inquiry investigation ANZACs: Private collection M. Fussell and K. Porter.

Hodge, K. & Lear, J. (2011). Employment skills for 21st century workplace: The gap between faculty and student perceptions. *Journal of Career and Technical Education*, 26(2). Retrieved from: https://ejournals.lib.vt.edu/JCTE/article/view/523/721.

Kriewaldt, J. (2012a). Developing thinking and understanding in secondary geography. In T. Taylor, C. Fahey, J. Kriewaldt & D. Boon, eds, *Place and Time. Explorations in teaching geography and history*. Sydney: Pearson Education, pp. 90–101.

——(2012b). Progression in understanding in geography. In T. Taylor, C. Fahey, J. Kriewaldt & D. Boon, eds, *Place and Time. Explorations in teaching geography and history*. Sydney: Pearson Education, pp. 177–90.

McInerney, D. & McInerney, V. (2006). *Educational Psychology: Constructing learning*. Sydney: Pearson Education.

Noble, K. (2010). Teaching for Skills Development in HSIE/SOSE [Topic notes]. Armidale, NSW: University of New England.

Piaget, J. (1955). *The Construction of Reality in the Child*. London: Routledge & Kegan Paul.

Reynolds, R. (2014). *Teaching Humanities and Social Sciences in the Primary Classroom*, 3rd edn. Melbourne: Oxford University Press.

Taylor, T. (2012). Introduction to inquiry-based learning. In T. Taylor, C. Fahey, J. Kriewaldt & D. Boon, eds, *Place and Time. Explorations in teaching geography and history*. Sydney: Pearson Education, pp. 123–8.

# ENGAGING WITH ETHICAL UNDERSTANDING IN THE EARLY YEARS AND BEYOND: THE COMMUNITY OF INQUIRY APPROACH

**12**

*Martyn Mills-Bayne*

## Learning objectives

After reading this chapter, you should be able to:

- explain the need to support children's ethical understanding in early childhood and primary education
- describe the benefits of employing the community of inquiry approach for supporting children's ethical understanding
- understand the complex challenges facing young children when engaging in ethical understanding across the three organising elements of this general capability
- use relevant activities to foster young children's ethical understanding, such as building their conceptual vocabulary, exploring continuums of ethical decisions and discussing hypothetical scenarios.

## INTRODUCTION

Young children are developing and learning within an increasingly complex world where competing ideas are being contested and enacted in ways that impact on their daily experiences. The ethical nature of many of the decisions and beliefs that children encounter in their lives often requires complex reasoning and decision-making in which many children may not be supported. The development of ethically reasonable citizens within a society concerned for the emotional wellbeing of its members needs to begin early in life. Parents and families are primary socialisers for young children's moral and ethical development; however, early learning centres and schools have a responsibility for providing children with opportunities for social emotional learning (SEL) intended to foster ethical reasoning and empathic concern for others. The *Melbourne Declaration on Educational Goals for Young Australians* (Melbourne Declaration) supported this educational imperative by highlighting the need to support young children to act with ethical integrity as part of its educational goals for young Australians (MCEETYA 2008).

The early years of children's educational experiences can involve a range of contexts including long day care settings, kindergartens and junior primary schools. There is a requirement for children to be supported in their ethical understanding across each of these settings, despite the contextual, developmental and pedagogical differences in each. In long day care and kindergarten settings, the Early Years Learning Framework (EYLF) requires educators to support young children's ethical understanding of the reciprocal rights and responsibilities of individuals within communities through the notion of 'belonging', and suggests that educators should 'provide opportunities for children to investigate ideas, complex concepts and ethical issues that are relevant to their lives and local communities' (DEEWR 2009, p. 26). In primary school settings, the Australian Curriculum sets out ethical understanding as one of the seven general capabilities that are addressed through the content of each learning area (ACARA 2018). The learning area where children engage most with ethical understanding is Humanities and Social Sciences (HASS).

This chapter introduces early years and primary educators to some of the key aspects of dialogic pedagogies (namely an empathic pedagogy that incorporates community of inquiry approaches), and sets out an argument for its use within the HASS learning area to support children's ethical understanding. The ways in which ethical understanding are described in early years and primary curricula are explored, and suggestions provided for activities that can foster learners' ethical understanding.

# DIALOGIC PEDAGOGY AND ETHICAL UNDERSTANDING

Research has demonstrated that dialogic pedagogies such as the community of inquiry can be used in schools to develop learners' critical, creative and caring thinking (Fair et al. 2015; Trickey & Topping 2007). There is growing support from research (Daniel & Delsol 2004; Daniel, Pettier & Auriac-Slusarczyk 2011) suggesting that engagement with dialogue supports young children's emotional development, their thinking about ethical concerns and their growing empathy for others (Mills-Bayne 2016; 2017). The community of inquiry provides learners with opportunities to engage with their peers in discussion about ethical concerns that have an impact on their daily lives in educational settings and beyond. A community of inquiry approach has proven successful in fostering ethical practice with learners as part of some SEL programs that have also supported young children's holistic social and emotional development (Australian Primary Schools Mental Health Initiative 2014).

While the addition of dialogic pedagogical approaches such as the community of inquiry does take time to develop, it can efficiently complement existing pedagogies by providing a safe space to explore any number of issues across curriculum areas. In this way, the community of inquiry does not add to a crowded curriculum, but instead gives educators an additional method with which to explore concepts and foster young children's dispositions for learning. Furthermore, despite competing and dominating messages about the importance of some curriculum areas over others – such as a federal government focus on literacy, numeracy and STEM subjects – both the EYLF (DEEWR 2009) and the Australian Curriculum (ACARA 2013, 2018) position children's ethical understanding as an important educational goal in describing the pedagogical practices and general capabilities, respectively, that inform educators' practice in early years and schooling settings. The community of inquiry provides educators with a vehicle for exploring ethical concerns in meaningful ways through specific curriculum areas such as HASS, or as part of a broader cross-curricular approach that can foster learners' critical, creative and caring thinking in a range of contexts and curriculum areas.

# THE COMMUNITY OF INQUIRY

The **community of inquiry** is a pedagogical approach to exploring ethical and philosophical concerns with children through guided dialogue in a shared **inquiry** (Fisher 2013; Lipman 2003). The term *enquiry* is often used interchangeably with the term *inquiry* in literature and educational communities, particularly in the United Kingdom. We will use the term *inquiry* throughout this chapter as this aligns with the origins of its application in education, and reflects the common terminology within the Australian context. The use of the community of inquiry in schools first appeared in the philosophy for children approach devised by Matthew Lipman (Lipman & Sharp 1978), and was strongly influenced by the work of Pierce, Dewey and Vygotsky. The community of inquiry approach explicitly aims for children to engage in shared inquiry about a stimulus idea(s) and to move towards a deeper understanding of the truth of the idea(s) being explored. The community of inquiry acts as a forum and testing ground for ideas where young learners can put forward their claims about the ideas being explored. In this forum, these claims are justified, contested, contrasted and shaped through dialogic exchange by all participants. As such, it is an ideal pedagogical approach for young children to explore ethical concerns, improve their own thinking and develop sound reasoning with others (Fisher 2013; McGuinness 2005; Millett & Tapper 2012; Schleifer et al. 2003; Wegerif 2007).

**community of inquiry**: a pedagogical approach that involves dialogue across an inward-facing circle of participants where philosophical ideas are posed, justified, challenged and discussed with the aim of gaining a deeper shared understanding of the question or ideas presented by a stimulus

**inquiry**: a collaborative exploration involving dialogic interaction, asking questions and giving reasons that leads to a shared understanding of a topic or question

> The term 'inquiry' is often used to describe a range of processes in which children engage to gain deeper knowledge or answer a question. What do you already know about inquiry and its use in education?
>
> Reflection

As with many pedagogical approaches, there are various forms that the community of inquiry may take. The general structure and key elements that comprise a community of inquiry session commonly include the following process:

- *Children are seated in a circle* (on the floor or on chairs). The circular structure provides children with clear access to the voices, bodies and faces of others in an equal manner.

- *A stimulus is provided.* **Stimulus material** can be in the form of stories, pictures, videos or artefacts.

- *Questions are asked and constructed.* Children spend time thinking about the stimulus and ask questions. These are recorded by the

**stimulus material**: the focal point for inquiry within the community of inquiry. This could be a story, picture or other form of media that raises questions of a philosophical nature.

**big questions**: questions posed by learners that are aimed at gaining deeper understanding of the nature of the stimulus material

educator and clarified, categorised and refined to elicit '**big questions**' that are both open-ended and philosophical or ethical in nature.

- *Dialogue is facilitated*. Children's big questions are discussed and the educator acts as a facilitator who supports the children to work together to build on each other's ideas, seek clarification, provide examples and counter-examples, and develop deeper thinking about the topic/idea being discussed.

- *Discussion plans are used*. Discussion plans act as a framework or map to support the educator in their facilitation towards deeper understanding of the topic. These discussion plans set out a continuum of questions that move from simple to complex, and concrete to abstract. Each stimulus may allow a range of topics to be explored, and the educator needs to have some ideas about where the inquiry might lead.

A plethora of books, websites and resources are available that provide educators with a wealth of stimulus material, discussion plans and support activities that can help build learners' developing inquiry skills. The work of Philip Cam and others in Australia provides an accessible and contextually relevant range of resources upon which to draw (Cam et al. 2007).

## EDUCATOR TIP

Educators do not need to reinvent the wheel; use the materials that are already available, and with time and experience the creation and development of stimuli, discussion plans and support materials can be added.

**SPOTLIGHT ON HASS EDUCATION**

## COMMUNITY OF INQUIRY

HASS and ethical understanding truly go hand in hand, and there are many texts and images that can be used as stimulus for discussion in a community of inquiry. Engaging young learners in dialogue around ethical ideas does not need to start with complex ideas to foster deep inquiry. The simple image of a bird in a cage, for example, can stimulate young learners to ask quite complex ethical questions such as: *Is it fair to keep pets? Should we cage animals? Why do some birds stay in one place?* Using engaging and thought-provoking stimuli allows educators to develop a range of likely questions as a discussion plan that acts as a template and guide for a community of inquiry. Discussion plans should set out questions and ideas that build from simple to complex, and from concrete to abstract concepts (see Figure 12.1). The links that can be made to HASS subject matter related to time and place through ethical dialogue within the community of inquiry approach can enrich children's learning in all areas of their lives.

There are some important distinctions between the discussions in a community of inquiry session and any other circle work or discussion with children. These are:

1. The educator acts as a facilitator who does not impose their own views on the group, but listens carefully, asks relevant questions, highlights poor reasoning and models the inquiry skills needed to delve deeper.

2. The community of inquiry provides children with a safe space where ideas can be offered, contested and built upon with peers in a way that focuses on the central ideas, not the children holding them.

3. The community drives the inquiry to gain a deeper understanding of the topic.

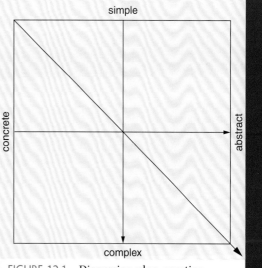

FIGURE 12.1  Discussion plan question quadrant

There is, however, no prescribed route, consensus does not have to be reached, and an ultimate answer to each question does not have to be found. Educators can struggle with all of these notions, and it can take time and practice to allow learners to drive the inquiry, and to avoid tying things up neatly at the end of each community of inquiry session.

## EDUCATOR TIP

Knowing how to pull all the threads of a community of inquiry together (or leave big questions hanging) takes experience and an understanding of the needs of the children in each class/group. Use a phrase such as 'I think our inquiry has led to some interesting ideas and bigger questions. Let's keep thinking about these, and see whether we can add to our discussion next time', to let children see that some thinking develops over time and continues to puzzle both educators and learners beyond discrete blocks of lesson time.

## Educator as facilitator

The community of inquiry requires the educator to act as a facilitator who artfully uses questions and prompts to guide learners' responses, draw out any **justifications** for their claims, and help learners to respectfully seek justification for their peers' claims (Fisher 2013; Lipman 2003). The educator's role changes as learners develop increased autonomy and come to understand and care about the processes and goals of the community of inquiry (Davey 2004). As learners take increasing responsibility for the process of inquiry and justification of claims, the teacher's facilitation shifts from more explicit skill building

**justification:** the inquiry skill of giving reasons to support statements

of processes and practice towards a lighter touch in guiding and supporting learners' ideas (Fisher 2013; Gillies 2016; Teo 2013). This shift can be a challenge for young learners new to egalitarian and democratic educational approaches because they are likely to initially be deferential towards the educator when sharing their thoughts and ideas. Thus, the facilitation role of the educator is a challenge in developing effective community of inquiry processes (Gillies 2016; Lushyn & Kennedy 2003). Ideally, the educator performs the dual role of facilitator and equal and active contributor to the discussion, and is able to respond to the dynamic nature of learners' **exploratory talk** (Barrow 2015).

**exploratory talk**: discussion that involves a range of viewpoints where justification for opinions is sought and learners speak and listen critically to each other's ideas

## Creating a safe dialogic space

The community of inquiry allows educators to support young learners' expression of their thoughts and feelings in a safe dialogic space. The creation of this safe space for children to express their emotions and thoughts within a supportive community of peers allows for the development of cooperative learning and **empathic concern** for others (Kristjansson 2004; Schertz 2006; Verducci 1999). This is one of the true strengths of the community of inquiry, particularly where ethical concerns, dilemmas and ideas are being discussed as part of classroom or centre practice. The nature of the community of critical learners that evolves when an atmosphere of trust and support is fostered through the use of the community of inquiry is one where learners feel safe to express and negotiate ideas (Aslanimehr 2015; Davey 2004; Fisher 2013; Sprod 2001). This can be a challenge for young learners, as there is often judgement from peers about the expression of ethical reasoning and the often emotive responses to differing opinions. In this sense, showing frustration, disapproval or anger towards a peer's ideas during dialogic encounters can be a high-risk reaction for social relations within the classroom community (Hubbard & Coie 1994). While the community of inquiry provides a safe space where ideas can be discussed and sometimes fiercely contested by peers, educators need to provide complementary spaces for the multimodal expression of these thoughts and feelings. This can be achieved through individual thinking journals, shared spaces for written ideas, small-group work, **floor books**, or opportunities for children to illustrate their ideas.

**empathic concern**: involves empathy for the emotional states of others through verbal and non-verbal interactions or actions that demonstrate an ability to see another's perspective

**floor books**: a learner-led approach for observation and documentation of the learner's voice through collaborative engagement with a shared exploration of ideas through talking, thinking, drawing and creating on large books or sheets of paper

 **Reflection** What other strategies can you use to help create a safe space for children to express their thoughts and feelings in your early learning centre/classroom? How can we document children's ideas when expressed verbally through dialogic encounter?

## Driving the inquiry

The community of inquiry is a vehicle for learners' expression of views and ideas because it provides social learning conditions where learners can engage collaboratively and intersubjectively with peers. In the community of inquiry, educators provide structure and focused guidance as facilitators of the dialogic process rather than acting as authority figures whose power influences learners' responses (Fisher 2013). These components provide spaces for learners to develop autonomy and agency in their discussions about ethical concerns. Schertz (2006) claims that through interaction with peers, alongside guidance from educators who are cognisant of their inherent power, the community of inquiry can provide learners with rich philosophically grounded learning about ethical concerns.

The inherent power differential between educator and learner can impact on learners' responses during the community of inquiry. Learners may initially direct their opinions towards the educator, and educator requests for clarification can disqualify some learners' thinking and limit their subsequent involvement in discussion. It is vital for educators facilitating community of inquiry sessions to make clear to young learners from the start that the process allows for all ideas to be put forward, regardless of their alignment with the educator's own thoughts. This can be a challenge for young learners, and can impact on their responses and justifications as the socio-moral values and views of educators are often imitated and reflected in classroom discussions (Darling-Hammond 1998; Maslovaty 2000; Tirri 1999).

# ETHICAL UNDERSTANDING IN THE EARLY YEARS: BEFORE SCHOOL

In prior-to-school settings such as long day care and kindergarten, children engage in rich social experiences that help frame their sense of belonging and lay the foundations for positive interactions with others in the future. Notions of young learners' developing ethical understanding are woven throughout the principles, practices and learning outcomes articulated in the EYLF. Primarily, the elements that describe ethical understanding are carried in the EYLF principles of secure, respectful and reciprocal relationships, and respect for diversity (DEEWR 2009).

## Secure, respectful and reciprocal relationships

Young children need to be able to recognise their own emotional states and to engage in complex considerations of the feelings of others with positivity and respect. Educators provide sensitive and responsive modelling and guidance to support young learners in developing the skills and understandings that foster their growing empathic concern for others. Learners are also encouraged to develop a sense of personal and communal responsibility for supporting their peers.

### Secure, respectful and reciprocal relationships in practice

Recognising the thoughts and feelings of others can be tricky for young children, whose view of the world can sometimes be quite egocentric in nature. Supporting young learners to expand their understanding of their own emotions and the emotions of others plays a pivotal role in fostering their ability to step outside their own perspective and see the world through the eyes and mind of another. Building an emotional vocabulary that can be used by young learners to better describe their own thoughts and feelings is a critical first step towards building empathy for others.

## ACTIVITY: FACES AND FEELINGS

1. Collect pictures of children showing a range of emotions.
2. Show learners the pictures and discuss what they think the child is feeling.
3. Place each picture on a board/poster and add learners' ideas about the feelings for each one.
4. Display the 'face and feeling' boards and use them to help learners describe their thoughts and feelings when required.

## Respect for diversity

Families and communities play an important role in shaping young children's ways of being in society. Early childhood educators are required to sensitively and critically help young learners to recognise and celebrate the sociocultural practices and ideas they bring to their learning and relationships, as well as valuing and better understanding the diversity of other families and children. Through an increased awareness and understanding of the rich and diverse nature of families and communities, young children are better able to consider the ethical understandings required for lifelong learning in our diverse Australian society.

### Respect for diversity in practice

For young learners, our diverse society can be paradoxical, as often children accept a wide range of difference across peer groups, and at the same time categorise and structure their social understandings of the world around explicit and often arbitrary differences between their peers. Early childhood educators can support young learners' capacity for accepting

## ACTIVITY: SIMILARITIES AND DIFFERENCES

1. Sit children in pairs facing each other.
2. Ask each child to look carefully at their partner and describe the things they see that are the same as themselves.
3. Ask each child to look carefully at their partner and describe the things that are different.
4. In a group, children share what they noticed about the similarities and differences between each other.
5. Discuss how there are often many more similarities than differences between people, and that often the differences are superficial (eye, hair, skin colour), while the similarities tend to be important (eyes, ears, body, etc.).

difference and diversity by raising their understanding of the similarities across diverse groups of children and families.

## Laying the foundations for the community of inquiry before school

The traditional community of inquiry approach needs to be considered flexibly in before-school settings due to the developmental needs and capacities of young children. Sitting in a circle for a 40-minute inquiry lesson is unlikely to capture and maintain the interest of very young children. Therefore, the community of inquiry needs to be thought about very differently from what might be considered and implemented within a junior primary classroom. In early childhood settings, there should be more of a focus on building young children's foundational skills of listening, talking, turn-taking and reason-giving. Other ideas that can be used in childcare and preschool settings include:

- using circle-based games to practise looking at/listening to others
- activities that involve learners giving reasons (using *because*)
- short inquiry sessions that connect to centre/room themes
- providing stimulus in group time, then discussion at the end of the day/session.

For young children in before-school settings, the most important aspect about which educators need to be mindful is that dialogue and discussion of each other's thoughts and ideas about the world are separated from the individual child offering them up for discussion. This is paradoxical in a sense, as we want to encourage children's agency and ownership of their ideas at the same time. However, young children's confidence and willingness to share their thoughts and feelings with others are all too often stifled when they feel attacked by others who disagree with their ideas. It is the educator's ability to carefully support children's dialogue, and foster a willingness to share while helping children to contest ideas (not people), that is critical for supporting children's ethical understanding.

# ETHICAL UNDERSTANDING IN THE EARLY YEARS: PRIMARY

In primary school settings (5–12 years of age), ethical understanding is positioned as one of the seven general capabilities (see Chapter 16) that need to be taught across and within the learning areas in the Australian Curriculum. As with the other general capabilities, ethical understanding is needed for children's lifelong learning and engagement as active and informed citizens (MCEETYA 2008). The three elements that comprise ethical understanding are discussed in more detail below.

## Understanding ethical concepts

The first element of the ethical understanding learning continuum is 'Understanding ethical concepts and issues' (ACARA 2018). This element requires young children to be able to recognise ethical concepts and explore these within a range of familiar contexts.

Young children need to be able to identify actions and behaviours that may be considered good or bad in familiar contexts, such as the classroom, playground, home and community settings. Furthermore, young children are expected to be able to describe and discuss quite complex and nuanced ethical concepts such as honesty, fairness and tolerance, which can occur in these same familiar contexts.

## Understanding ethical concepts in practice

**conceptual exploration:** activities that provide learners with opportunities to gain deeper and possibly share understandings of concepts, and to realise that others may have different perceptions of concepts that may be taken for granted or misunderstood

Supporting young learners' understanding of ethical concepts and ideas helps them to better understand the shades of grey that occur in a concept, such as fairness. This deeper knowledge of concepts also allows young learners to engage in richer dialogue when discussing these same concepts within the community of inquiry. An activity that can support understanding of ethical concepts is **conceptual exploration**. In this activity, learners' vocabulary is extended through an exercise in exploring words with similar and opposite meanings, and building their lexicon of words and ideas around a concept such as fairness (see Figure 12.2).

**SPOTLIGHT ON HASS EDUCATION**

## ACTIVITY: CONCEPTUAL EXPLORATION – FAIRNESS

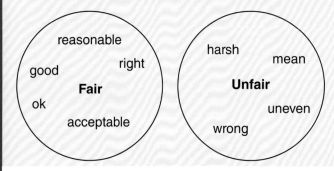

FIGURE 12.2   Conceptual exploration of ethical concepts: fairness

1. Draw two large circles and write the words describing an ethical concept and its opposite in each.

2. Encourage learners to think about  words they know that are similar in meaning to one of the words. Add each word into each circle as learners offer their ideas.

3. If learners are stuck (or as part of the above process), ask them whether they can think of a word that is the opposite of one already noted and write it in the opposing circle.

4. Keep prompting learners until all ideas are noted. Some finessing may be required to move children away from simply adding a prefix such as 'un' or putting 'not' in front of words.

# Reasoning in decision-making

The second element of the ethical understanding learning continuum is 'Reasoning in decision-making and actions' (ACARA 2018). This element requires young children to be able to develop the ability to reason and make ethical decisions, to consider the consequences of actions and to reflect on the ethical actions of people. This means young children need to be able to engage in some quite complex processes that many adults may find difficult to apply consistently in their lives. Being able to identify and explain how people make decisions, and why the reasoning underlying these choices differs, requires complex inference and perspective taking from young children. Young children are encouraged to identify and describe the links between emotions and behaviours, and how personal feelings and situational factors may impact on the ethical actions of others.

## Reasoning in decision-making in practice

Fostering young learners' increasing ability to reason soundly when considering and making decisions is at the heart of the creation of classrooms, and in the community and society where critical, creative and caring thinking are applied to the ethical considerations that learners will face throughout their lives. Educators often assume that children will develop sound reasoning skills through their everyday exposure to social and ethical dilemmas in schools, centres and beyond. However, explicit teaching of foundational skills such as listening, asking questions and providing reasons is required to ensure that children have the tools required to engage in sound reasoning that supports their ethical understanding of the world. An exercise that can support young children's reasoning skills is the *decision-making continuum*. In this activity, hypothetical scenarios are provided that describe ethical decision-making, and children are asked to make choices and justify their placement of each scenario on a continuum.

## ACTIVITY: ETHICAL ACTION AND DECISION-MAKING CONTINUUM

1. Draw or create a straight line on the floor and write 'Good' at one end and 'Bad' at the other. This represents a continuum of decision-making.
2. Give learners short descriptions of situations that involve decision-making and describe actions and emotions involved (see Figure 12.3).
3. Ask learners to place each description somewhere along the continuum.
4. Investigate the placement of each description and encourage learners to discuss their reasoning about each, focusing on the elements of ethical action and possible emotional impacts.
5. This activity should be complemented with an individual task where learners are able to place each description where they think it belongs and consider their own thinking about these decisions.

**SPOTLIGHT ON HASS EDUCATION**

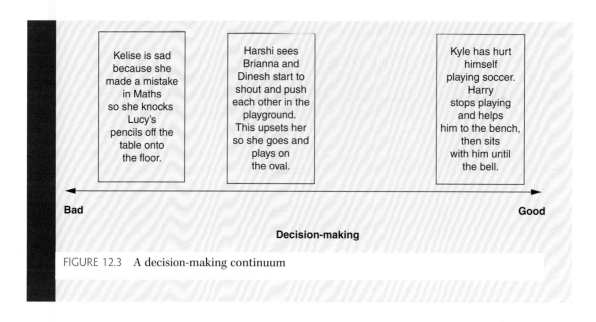

FIGURE 12.3 A decision-making continuum

## Exploring values, rights and responsibilities

The third element of the ethical understanding learning continuum is 'Exploring values, rights and responsibilities' (ACARA 2018). This element requires young children to examine and identify values, explore ideas around rights and responsibilities, and begin to consider a range of points of view. Young children need to be able to understand that people's behaviour is guided by a set of values that in turn informs their own rights and responsibilities as well as those of their classmates and local communities. Furthermore, by engaging in discussions about values, rights and responsibilities relevant to ever-expanding social systems, children develop their ability to express their own ideas and consider the points of view of others. Through the community of inquiry, learners have the opportunity to share their own ideas, hear the ideas of others, and engage in critical, creative and caring thinking about values with their peers within a collaborative and **intersubjective space**.

**intersubjective space**: the safe space created in the community of inquiry where children feel confident to express their opinions, justify their thinking and seek clarification from their peers to further a shared and collaborative inquiry as part of a community of critical learners

### Exploring values, rights and responsibilities in practice

Children are raised within an invisible sea of sociocultural meaning that is bi-directional in nature, with children affecting, and being affected by, the values of their family, peers, communities and societies. An exploration of values, rights and responsibilities can help to support children's ethical understanding and empathic concern for others through an increasing awareness of the similarities and differences between their own views and those of others. An activity that can help educators to facilitate children's exploration of values, rights and responsibilities is the use of an **emotive stimulus** to spark ethical inquiry within the community of inquiry. In this activity, a series of images from a

**emotive stimulus**: a stimulus for inquiry that either aims to provoke emotional responses or provides opportunities for inquiry about the emotional states of the self and others

page of Shaun Tan's (2006) illustrated book *The Arrival* is used to stimulate inquiry questions to guide discussion.

## ACTIVITY: EMOTIVE STIMULUS (*THE ARRIVAL*)

1. Share the image on page 10 of *The Arrival* (Tan 2006) with learners.
2. Ask learners to think about the images and the story being told on this page, and create a question they might ask. Provide a few minutes of thinking time.
3. Arrange learners in small groups (two to four) to share their questions, discuss any similarities and decide on a shared question for group discussion.
4. Collate shared questions on a whiteboard or paper for all learners to see.
5. Democratically choose a question to explore within the community of inquiry.

# CONCLUSION

Engaging with ethical understanding in early years and primary education settings is not something that educators need to add to their already busy programs. Young learners are swimming in a sea of ethical dilemmas as they engage with their families, communities, educational settings and societies. They already have opportunities to develop the skills and attributes needed to effectively navigate their way in the world. What educators must do is capitalise on those opportunities and ensure that children practise their ethical reasoning in a safe space with care and support. The community of inquiry approach, and connected activities that work alongside large-group dialogue to support concept and skill development, are powerful tools to encourage young learners' critical, creative and caring thinking about the social and emotional concerns of others.

## REVIEW QUESTIONS

1. Why do educators have a responsibility for providing learners with opportunities for ethical reasoning?
2. How does the community of inquiry differ from other types of discussion carried out in early years and primary educational settings?
3. What are the challenges facing learners' ethical understanding in the early years?
4. In what way do you already foster young children's ethical understanding and empathic concern for others? How does your existing practice fit with the use of the community of inquiry pedagogical approach?
5. How do other general capabilities within the Australian Curriculum, or practices within the EYLF, connect to the notion of ethical understanding?

## LEARNING EXTENSION

Consider some of your favourite stories to share with young children. Create a list of questions you might ask about the storyline, characters, setting or illustrations. Be creative! Highlight those questions that you think are ethical in nature. Start to keep a sheet of these inquiry questions for each book you use in your teaching practice. Be brave and try to implement a community of inquiry approach as part of your literacy program.

## REFERENCES

ACARA (Australian Curriculum, Assessment and Reporting Authority). (2013). *General Capabilities in the Australian Curriculum*. Sydney: ACARA.

——(2018). *Australian Curriculum: F-10, v8.3*. Retrieved from: https://www.australiancurriculum .edu.au/f-10-curriculum.

Aslanimehr, P. (2015). Uncovering the efficacy of philosophical inquiry with children. *Childhood & Philosophy*, 11(22), 329–48.

Australian Primary Schools Mental Health Initiative. (2014). KidsMatter. Retrieved from: http://www.Kidsmatter.edu.au.

Barrow, W. (2015). 'I think she's learnt how to sort of let the class speak': Children's perspectives on philosophy for children as participatory pedagogy. *Thinking Skills and Creativity*, 17, 76–87.

Cam, P., Fynes-Clinton, L., Harrison, K., Hinton, L., Scholl, R. & Vaseo, S. (2007). *Philosophy with Children: A classroom handbook*. Canberra: Australian Curriculum Studies Association.

Daniel, M. & Delsol, A. (2004). Learning to dialogue in kindergarten: A case study. *Analytic Teaching*, 25(3), 23–52.

Daniel, M., Pettier, J. & Auriac-Slusarczyk, E. (2011). The incidence of philosophy on discursive and language competence in four-year-old pupils. *Creative Education*, 2(3), 296–304.

Darling-Hammond, L. (1998). Teachers and teaching: Testing policy hypotheses from a national commission report. *Educational Researcher*, 27, 5–14.

Davey, S. (2004). Consensus, caring and community: An inquiry into dialogue. *Analytic Teaching*, 25(1), 18–51.

DEEWR (Department of Education, Employment and Workplace Relations). (2009). *Belonging, Being and Becoming: The Early Years Learning Framework*. Canberra: DEEWR.

Fair, F., Haas, L.E., Gardosik, C., Johnson, D.D., Price, D.P. & Leipnik, O. (2015). Socrates in the schools from Scotland to Texas: Replicating a study on the effects of a philosophy for children program. *Journal of Philosophy in Schools*, 2(1), 18–37.

Fisher, R. (2013). *Teaching Thinking: Philosophical enquiry in the classroom*, 4th edn. London: Bloomsbury.

Gillies, R.M. (2016). Dialogic interactions in the cooperative classroom. *International Journal of Educational Research*, 76, 178–89.

Hubbard, J.A. & Coie, J.D. (1994). Emotional correlates of social competence in children's peer relationships. *Merrill-Palmer Quarterly*, 40(1), 1–20.

Kristjansson, K. (2004). Empathy, sympathy, justice and the child. *Journal of Moral Education*, 33(3), 291–305.

Lipman, M. (2003). *Thinking in Education*, 2nd edn. New York: Cambridge University Press.

Lipman, M. & Sharp, A.M. (1978). *Growing Up with Philosophy*. Philadelphia, PA: Temple University Press.

Lushyn, P. & Kennedy, D. (2003). Power, manipulation and control in a community of inquiry. *Analytic Teaching*, 23(2), 103–10.

Maslovaty, N. (2000). Teachers' choice of teaching strategies for dealing with socio-moral dilemmas in the elementary school. *Journal of Moral Education*, 29(4), 429–44.

MCEETYA (Ministerial Council on Education, Employment, Training and Youth Affairs). (2008). *Melbourne Declaration on Educational Goals for Young Australians*. Retrieved from: http://www.curriculum.edu.au/verve/_resources/National_Declaration_on_the_Educational_ Goals_for_Young_Australians.pdf.

McGuinness, C. (2005). Teaching thinking: Theory and practice. *BJEP Monograph Series II, Number 3 – Pedagogy – Teaching for Learning*, 1(1), 107–26.

Millett, S. & Tapper, A. (2012). Benefits of collaborative philosophical inquiry in schools. *Educational Philosophy and Theory*, 44(5), 546–67.

Mills-Bayne, M. (2016). Building an empathic pedagogy. *The Space*, 44, 18–19.

——(2017). Fostering children's capacity for empathic reasoning: The role of community of inquiry in an empathic pedagogy. Unpublished thesis, University of South Australia.

Schertz, M. (2006). Empathic pedagogy: Community of inquiry and the development of empathy. *Analytic Teaching*, 26(1), 8–14.

Schleifer, M., Daniel, M., Peyronnet, E. & Lecomte, S. (2003). The impact of philosophical discussions on moral autonomy, judgement, empathy and the recognition of emotion in five year olds. *Thinking: The Journal of Philosophy for Children*, 16(4), 4–12.

Sprod, T. (2001). *Philosophical Discussion in Moral Education: The community of ethical inquiry*. Abingdon: Routledge.

Tan, S. (2006). *The Arrival*. Melbourne: Lothian Books.

Teo, P. (2013). 'Stretch your answers': Opening the dialogic space in teaching and learning. *Learning, Culture and Social Interaction*, 2, 91–101.

Tirri, K. (1999). Teachers' perceptions of moral dilemmas at school. *Journal of Moral Education*, 28, 31–47.

Trickey, S. & Topping, K.J. (2007). Collaborative philosophical enquiry for school children: Cognitive effects at 10–12 years. *British Journal of Educational Psychology*, 77(2), 271–88.

Verducci, S. (1999). Empathy, morality and moral education. Unpublished PhD thesis, Stanford University.

Wegerif, R. (2007). *Dialogic Education and Technology: Expanding the space of learning*. New York: Springer.

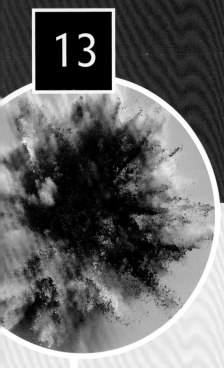

# THE POWER OF PLAY TO ENGAGE AND NURTURE CREATIVE, INDEPENDENT LEARNERS

*Jane Webb-Williams*

## Learning objectives

After reading this chapter, you should be able to:

- understand the value of play
- understand the different definitions of play
- identify the characteristics and types of play to support learning about Humanities and Social Sciences (HASS)
- understand playfulness and playful pedagogies
- analyse the educator's role in supporting children's play and the importance of planning, observation and co-construction in creating effective playful experiences.

## INTRODUCTION

Educators have long searched for the best way to support learners to reach their full potential. Technological advancements provide educators with easy access to numerous modern teaching and curriculum resources on the Internet. While these are useful for supporting educators, they can fail to motivate learners. **Intrinsic motivation** is a vital aspect of learning; without it, children can lack enthusiasm and willingness to engage, lack effort and persistence in tasks, give up easily and fail to develop independence in their learning. So how can we motivate and inspire learners so they become passionate advocates of their own development through self-driven exploration, questioning, problem-solving and discovery? Play is the key.

**intrinsic motivation:** any behaviour that is driven by internal rewards where the motivation stems from within the person because they experience natural satisfaction. It is the opposite of extrinsic motivation, where rewards are external.

Throughout history, and in all cultures, children have played. It is a natural instinct; you do not have to encourage children to play – they want to! If educators can harness this natural motivation and use the power of play in educational settings, they can plan engaging lessons with learners at the centre, supporting their freedom to develop their interests, co-construct their understandings and try out new experiences without fear of failure. Educators who can do this successfully can capture the minds of learners so that they build on their natural creativity, challenge themselves and take risks in their learning journey. Play provides an excellent vehicle to achieve these aims.

The cognitive, social, emotional and physical benefits of play in early childhood are widely recognised (Fleer 2017; Hughes 2010). Despite this, few educators fully understand what play is, and thus are not fully equipped to effectively support children's play. In contexts such as preschool and childcare centres, play is the accepted **pedagogy**, supported through the Early Years Learning Framework (EYLF; DEEWR 2009). However, in the primary classroom, views appear to be mixed about the role of play, with many educators being unsure about how to include play in their practice, and tending to rely on narrow **transmission learning** approaches. This chapter discusses the benefits of play and explores how a 'playful' pedagogical approach enhances creativity, problem-solving and critical thinking, and can be used to effectively engage, motivate and stimulate learners from early childhood to adolescence in the HASS learning area.

**pedagogy:** the art, science or profession of teaching

**transmission learning:** inactive learning experience consisting of didactic teaching where information is presented to learners and they are expected to remember it

## THE VALUE AND ROLE OF PLAY

Think back to when you played as a child. Where were you? What were you doing? Who was with you? How do think this differed from how your parents or grandparents played? As you recall and reflect on these play experiences, consider what the word 'play' means to you.

Reflection

Research involving play suggests that play contributes to:

- emotional development: self-esteem, resilience
- physical development: coordination, motor skills
- social development: identity and relationships
- cognitive development: thinking, concentration, language.

Educators have long maintained that play is crucial for child development (Fleer 2017). Moreover, neuroscience and animal play research attests to the value of play for brain development (Hughes 2010), showing the importance of providing a variety of rich experiences in the early years to lay the foundation for future health, development and wellbeing. Play can increase community connectedness (Webb-Williams 2017b) and helps children to explore their world, feel safe to express their emotions and reveal their inner feelings, thereby gaining emotional balance and achieving mental wellbeing (Brooker & Edwards 2010). Play ensures that children develop a sense of who they are and understand those around them by learning to empathise, share and negotiate. Through play, children are imaginative and innovative problem-solvers who move from requiring support to independence, developing communication and language skills, self-regulation (Whitebread et al. 2012) and belief in their capabilities (self-efficacy), which leads to effort and persistence (Webb-Williams 2017a).

Children's play reflects their prevailing interests as they practise, develop and master skills, progressing from learning through their senses to using symbols as a form of representation (symbolic function) to finally developing abstract thought. Play has a central role in learning and, together with first-hand experiences, enables young learners to

**metacognition:** thinking about one's thinking; higher-order thinking that enables understanding, analysis, and self-control

**co-construction:** when more than one individual is involved in the learning process

immerse themselves in **metacognitive** thinking. Play at the centre of a play-based curriculum ensures that learners lead the learning, make decisions, pose questions and are actively engaged in the process of **co-constructing** meaning with other learners in their environment; that is, they are not passive recipients of knowledge – rather, they interact with others and the culture in which they live, which shapes the development of cognition (for more on sociocultural theory, see Vygotsky 1978). Play therefore provides an engaging and creative means for learners to construct, test and apply their developing knowledge in HASS as they learn about themselves, their environment, the history of those around them, places and how to care for them. There also are theoretical arguments that posit play as intrinsic to a child's development and that play is a fundamental right of the child. Within the United Nations Convention of the Rights of the Child (http://www.unicef.org), to which Australia is a signatory and a ratifying country, Article 31 states that every child has 'the right to engage in play'. So play is inscribed into the early childhood curriculum both theoretically and as a right – it is one of the most basic human rights of all children, thus giving serious recognition to the role of play in children's lives.

## EDUCATOR TIP

Being able to clearly articulate the benefits of play ensures that you not only are able to advocate for play but also justify a playful pedagogical approach to parents, colleagues and school leaders (see Gleave and Cole-Hamilton 2012).

## THE COMPLEXITY OF PLAY

Current views of teaching and learning in many contexts convey that play is the accepted pedagogy. However, it is often associated with the young developing child and thus can also be viewed as something that children do when they are not 'working'. This suggests play is trivial or lacking importance. We can observe this view of play in schools across Australia, where learners are permitted to engage in play only during recess and lunch-time or as a reward for finishing their 'work'. Classroom teaching can often be devoid of play, instead focusing on the seemingly 'serious' business of learning through formal instruction.

Given the misconceptions and trivialisation of the concept of play, it is easy to see why educators fail to embrace play. Thus educators need to be able to clearly rationalise and justify their use of play in their teaching if they are to be supported by school leadership and parents. Unfortunately, although many educators are aware of the benefits of play, they are unable to clearly articulate and defend the place it has in the site or classroom. With the pressure to ensure educators are covering the curriculum because of increased accountability measures, transmission learning practices continue despite their inability to engage, motivate and inspire many learners. Indeed, as we will see later in this chapter, research has attested to the enriched development and robust achievement outcomes of children learning through play. So why don't all educators use play as a vehicle for learning?

Often the issue is not that educators don't want to use play in their teaching, but they don't know how to, or they may be overwhelmed by the idea of it. Play means different things to different people in different contexts, which makes it a difficult thing to pin down. For example, just think about the following uses of the word 'play'. The babies *play* with their toes, the adults *play* chess, the children are *playing* with blocks, and the educator calls out 'stop *playing* around and get on with your work'. We can see from these examples that the word 'play' refers to different types of play. Furthermore, we can think about play in a natural environment with sand, water, mud, secret dens hidden in bushes, and so on. We can imagine children playing in this environment, and compare this with the sorts of play we can imagine in a typical urban school playground with a barren, concrete landscape. The play will be very different – which environment would children prefer?

Think about a HASS activity where learners complete a worksheet about an event in history. Compare this with a learning experience where learners have the freedom to select from a wide range of materials, including dress-up clothes, boxes, wooden blocks and puppets, to explore a historical event. Which context do you think will encourage engagement together with greater imagination and creativity?

## DEFINING PLAY

Understanding what play means is the key to being able to embrace the complexity of play and plan effective learning environments. The best way to do this is for educators to be exposed to a range of different definitions of play and engage in conversations to develop shared understandings with colleagues within their workplace. In educational settings, it is often assumed that there is a shared understanding of the word 'play' between educators, management, learners, parents, the community and policymakers. However, in practice, often there is not a shared understanding and educational settings vary widely in how they incorporate play and the amount and types of play they support. Many activities that preschools and schools call play would not be called play by others, such as academics, theorists, policymakers or other educators. Likewise, play can be found in all cultures, but what is considered play is not the same in all cultures (Fasoli et al. 2010, p. 218). This may create misunderstanding and tension, which can be difficult for educators to navigate, so it is vital that educators can clearly articulate their under-standing of what play is.

Below are three different definitions of play. These definitions have been chosen because they present different viewpoints and lend themselves well to comparison. The difficulty is that in order to create a definition, we need to use other terms that are already understood, yet some words have different meanings in different contexts. This adds to the complexity and in some cases, one simply comes to understand the *use* of the term. Play is an example of this. We all *use* the term play in everyday language but what does it really mean? As you read the definitions, compare and contrast them so you become fluent in the key points. It is important that you reflect on the information in relation to your own experiences of play so you are able to analyse and further develop your understanding.

## Definition 1

Listed here are the main points of Garvey's (1991) definition of play.

- Play is pleasurable.
- Play is intrinsically motivated.
- Play is unproductive: there is no end product to play.
- Play is spontaneous: it is not structured or planned.
  - Play is freely chosen: it is not forced upon the player or controlled by others.
  - Play is actively engaging.

**learner-initiated**: learners engage in self-chosen pursuits, developing their knowledge and skills through play without educator direction

This definition asserts that play is an experience that is **learner-initiated**, enjoyable and captivates the minds and imaginations of learners so that their attention is fully immersed.

## Definition 2

According to Tina Bruce's definition of play (adapted from Bruce 1991, 2011), play:

1. is an active process without a product
2. is intrinsically motivated
3. has no pressure
4. is imaginative, creative, supposing
5. means wallowing in ideas and metacognition
6. uses previous first-hand experience
7. is sustained
8. uses previously developed skills
9. can be initiated by learner or educator
10. can be solitary
11. can be in partnerships
12. brings together learning, feeling and understanding.

In this definition of play, Bruce talks about self-chosen 'free flow' play as being an integrated mechanism where learners bring together many aspects of their learning, which they coordinate to bring about and reinforce new learning. For example, prior learning and new experiences, such as a new skill, will be incorporated into play in a way that allows learners to rehearse and cement their development and learning.

## Definition 3

A more recent definition is offered by Smidt (2010, p. 2):

> Play can be defined as the way in which children in a context, a culture, a family and a community set about doing any or all of the following: 1) Trying to solve a problem they have set themselves, 2) Exploring and experiencing something that interests or concerns or scares or excites them, 3) Expressing and communicating their feelings related to their experiences.

In this definition of play, there is a sense of agency as the learner needs to solve the problem, or experience, express or explore something. The learner is in control of *what* to do and *how* to do it. No one directs the learner to play and from this it follows that all play is purposeful because the learner is using it for a reason. The learner owns the reason and therefore owns the play. It is important to note here that Smidt says play is always purposeful for the learner, but she does not mean that it needs to be consciously purposeful. It may have a purpose that is unconscious and cannot be stated explicitly by the player and may not always be understood by the observer or other participants in play.

You may not agree with all aspects of these three definitions, but it is important to consider why you agree or disagree with each part as you reflect on what play means to you. For example, do you think play should only be learner initiated or do you think educators can initiate play too? Do you think play should always be fun or can it also be frightening?

**Reflection**

# CHARACTERISTICS OF PLAY

Play differs according to context, culture, gender, development, socio-economic status and age. As discussed earlier in this chapter, this makes it impossible to create one single definition of play. We have seen that researchers have differing perspectives of play; however, the concept tends to share some general characteristics, which include:

1. The process is vital; the end product, if there is one, may not be relevant to the learning that actually takes place.
2. It is self-chosen, either at the initiation stage or through active sustained engagement and self-direction. This notion of freedom within play is a vital one, to which we will return later in this chapter when we consider the educator's role in learners' play.
3. It involves imagination and creativity.
4. It is governed by rules that emanate from the minds of the players (see Vygotsky 1978 for further discussion).
5. It is active and stress-free.

If we consider the characteristics of play in light of the aims of the *Australian Curriculum: HASS F-6/7*, we can see that much of it resonates with the philosophy of a play-based approach. For example, the aims make reference to ensuring 'a sense of wonder, curiosity and respect', 'interest in and enjoyment', 'inquiry skills' including questioning and communicating, and 'critical and creative problem-solving' (ACARA 2018).

When considering the definitions and characteristics of play, it is important to understand three points. First, there isn't one single characteristic that denotes an activity as play, rather it needs to involve a number of characteristics – the more characteristics observed, the more likely that it is play. Second, play involves motivation and cognition so educators have to decide whether it is play from their inference of learners' actions, attitudes and experiences; for example, two children may be doing the same thing yet one will be playing while the other is not. Third, some researchers make the distinction between work and play; however, it is possible to be doing both – we can talk about the 'degree of playfulness' of an activity.

## EDUCATOR TIP

Engage in additional reading and aim to reflect on how your understanding of play impacts your practice. There is a vast array of information on the Internet, but you need to consider credible sources such as Play Australia (https://www.playaustralia.org.au/library) and Play England (http://www.playengland.org.uk/resources-list).

## PLAYFULNESS AND PLAYFUL PEDAGOGIES

Although educators can state the value of play, in practice very few actually adopt play all day in their settings (Moyles 2010). There are multiple reasons for this paradox, including top-down pressure, fear of not being seen to teach and a lack of appreciation/understanding of play from parents, policymakers and educators. For these reasons, putting theory into practice is extremely challenging particularly within the school setting. Furthermore, technological advancements of the 21st century have transformed childhood (OECD 2016) and influenced how children understand, interpret and engage in play (Jarvis, Brock & Brown 2014). Findings from a recent study (Webb-Williams, Mills-Bayne & Raymond 2015) provide insight into children's perceptions of play that challenge traditional definitions and support a 'playfulness' conception of play. We will return to this point later in the chapter when we discuss co-construction. The important point here is that the notion of 'playfulness' as a way to view play enables educators to overcome issues of theoretical complexity, misunderstanding and difficulty in embedding play into the curriculum (Howard & McInnes 2010) and empowers them to embrace play in their daily teaching practice. Moreover, the term 'playful pedagogies' (Moyles 2010) can be used to incorporate play, playful learning and playful teaching.

1. *Play*: play in its 'pure' form (as posited in the definitions earlier in this chapter) is learner-initiated and requires extremely open-ended planning and an emergent curriculum (as discussed in Chapter 2).
2. *Playful learning*: learning experiences where children are engaged in playful ways but that are not necessarily viewed as play by children – can be learner or educator initiated. Educators observe, assess, reflect and link to the curriculum.

3. *Playful teaching*: teaching that is based on presenting tasks that appeal to children's natural enjoyment in what they perceive to be 'playful' – tasks aim to incorporate aspects of play; they are open-ended and imaginative yet are planned according to curriculum learning outcomes.

Of course, just making an activity 'fun' to get learners to comply does not ensure active engagement. Nor does it necessarily promote self-driven exploration or testing of ideas – basic tenets of playful pedagogy. One could argue that having an agenda or outcome and requiring learners to participate in an activity mean that the activity cannot be called play regardless of how 'playful' we make it. That said, with careful, insightful planning, educators can authentically harness the power of play in the classroom. It comes down to their understanding of play, their relationships with learners and, in particular, the role they choose as an educator in learners' play (see later in this chapter for discussion of the educator's role).

## TYPES OF PLAY

In order to plan effective learning experiences, it is important to consider how play will be incorporated into the curriculum. It can be challenging for educators to think about tailoring content to individual learners in their particular context. It is thus helpful to consider the different forms and types of play when planning for playful engagement in HASS. Despite there being different perspectives offered in the literature, many ideas overlap. Below we consider four different perspectives.

The early work of Parten (1932) focused on children's social interactions and she proposed five categories of play:

1. onlooker: observing others engaged in play

2. solitary: playing alone

3. parallel: playing alongside others with similar objects without interaction

4. associative: playing with others without shared goals or coordination

5. cooperative: playing within a group with coordination and cooperation among players (e.g. players organise themselves into roles with specific goals in mind).

Together, the above categories can be seen as being different aspects of 'social play' according to Smith and Pellegrini's (2008) classification of play, in which they describe the following play types: locomotor play, social play, object play, language play, pretend play, war play and rough-tumble play. An alternative classification of five- to 11-year-old children's play is offered by Briggs and Hansen (2012), who suggest that play in the primary classroom falls into the following types: artistic or design play, controlled imaginary/sociodramatic play, exploratory play, games play, integrated play, play with whole school environment, replication play, small world play, role play and virtual play. These 10 categories are similar to the five forms of play offered by Smilansky (1990):

1. functional and exploratory play

2. constructive play

3. games with rules

4. dramatic play

5. sociodramatic play, which is considered to be the most complex and combines elements of the other forms of play.

Family roles, character roles and functional roles are most commonly featured in sociodramatic play (Hughes 2010) and thus can be utilised for any part of the HASS curriculum where learners need to understand about people, places and community. Indeed, by taking on the roles of people in the past, learners can deepen their understanding and empathy for life at that time. For example, educators could look at children's family life in the past (Year 1), life at school in the 1940s (Year 2), those who experienced the First Fleet (Year 4), life during the gold rush in the 1850s goldfields (Year 5) and the roles/responsibilities of different people within government (Year 6). Through imagination within sociodramatic play, learners create the characters, develop the plot, and are the scriptwriters and the directors. Learners assign themselves roles, and create the rules of the play, the dialogue and storyline. If set up correctly, learners will naturally engage in cooperative play (Parten 1932) and in doing so will work together on a shared goal.

## SPOTLIGHT ON HASS EDUCATION

### SOCIODRAMATIC PLAY AND THE FIRST FLEET

A series of sociodramatic play activities were linked to the Year 4 history sub-strand in the Australian Curriculum for HASS. Focusing on stories of the First Fleet (ACHASSK085). Different roles, such as captain, convicts, guards, sailors, surgeon, superintendent and convict overseer, were researched. Many of the children were interested in the rats on board the ships. They had the freedom to develop this role and other ideas themselves. Using costumes and materials, learners engaged in role play, experiencing the lives of people on the First Fleet. In doing so, they developed an understanding of social conditions in the past. As they became more familiar with their roles, learners started to develop narratives in their sociodramatic play. Together with the educator, learners identified possible challenges that people of that time would have encountered, such as building the ships, selecting provisions, loading the ships, dealing with rats on board, life at sea, rationing, sickness, arrival and settlement. These events featured in the learners' sociodramatic stories and they were observed exploring being at sea, what people ate and where they slept. Over time, the narratives developed and the learners could be seen empathising with the fear and anxiousness of the settlers, thinking about having never been to sea before, grieving at leaving home, and battling with seasickness, cramped quarters and illness. Sociodramatic play was the ideal vehicle to explore history by creating narrative recounts using their imagination and creativity, taking on the perspectives of those in the past, describing the experiences of different people and empathising with the lives of others in the past. The learners developed their knowledge and understanding in History (ACHASSK083 to ACHASSK086) as well as inquiry skills such as posing questions, sequencing information about events, locating information, sharing points of view, and reflecting on learning and communicating (ACHASSI073 to ACHASSI082).

# THE ROLE OF THE EDUCATOR IN PLAYFUL PEDAGOGIES

One of the most important roles of the educator is to give learners the power to engage with their own learning. Yet, as we saw earlier in this chapter, learner initiation is a key feature of play. So how do educators have a role if play comes from the learner? In order to answer this, we need to view the educator's role along a continuum (see Figure 13.1).

FIGURE 13.1   **Continuum of educator roles**

## Educator role: facilitator

Along the continuum are a number of different educator roles that facilitate learners' play, such as:

- onlooker/spectator – the educator serves as an appreciative audience but does not join in
- stage manager – the educator sets up the environment and organises the placement of props/resources
- co-player – the educator is an active participant in learners' play
- play leader – the educator exerts influence when co-playing and takes deliberate steps to enrich and extend learners' play.

These are not the only roles found in literature (e.g. Dockett 2008; Jones & Reynolds 1992; Van Hoorn et al. 2015). They are provided here as a starting point to encourage educators to examine different roles within their own context (see also the Learning extension activity at the end of this chapter). Some roles will be appropriate and others not – it will depend on the setting, the educator's pedagogy and the intention of the learning. However, there are two key points that apply to all settings. First, at the very heart of play is freedom, yet educators invariably try to take over (in the misguided belief that this is their role), thereby interrupting the play and disrupting the learning. It is important for the educator to consider their place on the continuum while still ensuring that they allow time to stand back, observe and listen to learners. There is no set pattern to the educator's involvement. At times they may constantly be moving along the continuum during a learning experience, while at other times they remain at the same point. Second, in thinking about the environment being constructed and co-constructed with learners, the educator can draw on the Reggio Emilia approach (Malaguzzi 1993) and the notion of the environment/ context as the 'third teacher' (the educator and other learners being the first and second teachers). Children learn through different forms of expression or 'hundred languages' (Edwards, Gandini & Forman 1993) and thus it is vital to carefully consider the materials and resources being purposely offered to learners so that they are stimulating, thought-provoking, rich and varied, and develop wonderings and deep conversations among children.

## EXPLORATION OF MATERIALS

In HASS, 'hands-on' exploration of materials can benefit learners at all year levels. The stage manager role is one that requires minimal involvement in learners' play and supports self-driven creativity and independence. By setting out the materials within the environment, the educator is able to provide provocations for learning. For example, in relation to the Year 4 First Fleet example given earlier in this chapter, different materials can be used to promote exploration of concepts, including:

- large cardboard boxes – ideal for constructing the First Fleet ships
- water table – to construct boats to represent the different First Fleet ships
- puppet theatre/shadow theatre – to create and present stories of the First Fleet
- wooden blocks or 'loose parts' – to construct the convicts' quarters, for example
- a variety of materials and small world/Lego figures – to create a story table/ storytelling
- clay – to explore making props for dramatic play.

The educator will have a reason for setting out the materials and an idea about how they will be used by learners. However, the freedom for learners to explore materials often provides wonderings and new directions that the educator hasn't anticipated. Educators can 'go with' the learners' interests while supporting them to achieve the curriculum outcomes.

## Educator role: planner

Planning is collaborative and responsive to learners' needs and requires observation, documentation, relationship building, creative brainstorming and flexibility. An emergent curriculum is one that starts with the observation of learners for insight into their interests and ideas (see the role of the observer later in this chapter). While emergent curriculum is most commonly seen in early childhood settings, it can be adopted at all year levels. Indeed, many primary schools adhere to the philosophy that 'knowing' learners is the key, and inquiry and play-based learning is prioritised. Kath Murdoch's (2018) cycle of inquiry can be used to inform planning, but it is important that it is used *with* learners in a way that is emergent and flexible (see http://kathmurdoch.com.au and Chapter 14).

A play-based curriculum 'uses the power of play to foster children's development. It is an emergent curriculum in which teachers take an active role in balancing spontaneous play, guided play, directed play and teacher-directed activities' (Van Hoorn et al. 2015).

A play-based curriculum uses learners' interests as a foundation for planning meaningful learning experiences where learners explore, create, solve problems and experiment in the process of learning curriculum content (Saracho 2012). In order for play to be utilised successfully at the centre of the curriculum, the play needs to be carefully planned and co-constructed with both the learners and educators (Howard & McInnes 2010). Thus, in a similar way to the Reggio Emilia approach, play-based curriculum is a child-centred pedagogy (Hewett 2001), drawing on social constructivist theorists such as Vygotsky (1978) and Bruner (1996), that utilises self-directed, experiential (hands-on) learning in relationship-driven environments.

With the above points in mind, below are several aspects that should be at forefront of educator planning:

- Start with the learner (child-centred): **observation** is crucial.
- Document, analyse and reflect on learners' play.
- Co-construct and brainstorm with learners.
- Base play on learners' ideas and interests; that is, make it authentic and meaningful.
- Include learner-initiated/learner-led experiences.
- Balance spontaneous, guided and educator-directed play.
- Build on previous knowledge and first-hand experiences.
- Allow learners to drive the play, own the play, be in control: freedom is vital.
- Include time for exploration, wallowing and creativity.

**observation**: acquiring and recording firsthand information captured by viewing something or someone

There is no magic rule about the type or quantity of play that is offered or what play should look like at each year level – it will alter for each context because it is tailored to the learners in each unique setting. In thinking about the definitions of play provided earlier in this chapter, the aspect of freedom is one that needs to be considered when planning. In a primary school classroom, there will always be a need for direct instruction at times, but when setting up an activity and calling it play, educators need to recognise the value of unstructured, learner-initiated, self-driven experiences where learners have the freedom to play, use and explore however they like. Similarly, adopting the notion of 'playfulness' does not mean that educators should not embrace a degree of freedom and choice for learners – the most engaged creative experiences tend to give rise to the nurturing of innovative thinking and learning.

## Educator role: observer, listener, reflector

The educator's role of observing play is crucial. Observation is the key to understanding learners' ideas, interests, motives, views, attitudes and learning needs. From this, educators can plan appropriate curriculum that provides for the full range of needs within the setting. Figure 13.2 shows the integral role of observation in all aspects of the planning process (see also the EYLF planning cycle). The important point is that educators cannot plan effectively without observation. By starting with the learner, they can develop an emergent curriculum where their plans can build on what learners already know and draw on their interests, reflecting the Reggio Emilia view of the child as competent and capable.

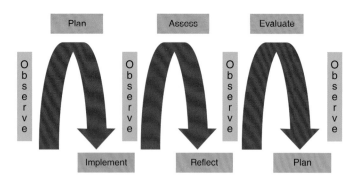

FIGURE 13.2    Rolling planning process

Observation can be pre-planned or incidental, recorded and shared. Different observational methods such as narrative, structured, checklist and time/event sampling not only allow educators to identify learners' interests and what motivates them, but have multiple purposes such as tracking a learner over time, focusing on specific areas of development, evaluating and improving provision as well as assessment (it is important to note that observations offer a snapshot in time and thus assessments need to be based on a number of observations). Observation on its own is not the hallmark of successful planning: educators need to analyse, reflect, listen and talk *with* (not *to*) learners. By using different ways of capturing learners' views and opinions ('voices'), including video, photographs, learning stories, photo elicitation, puppetry and drawings (Byrnes & Wasik 2009; Epstein et al. 2007; Leitch 2008), educators are able to make learners' thinking visible. In a learner-centred play-based approach, children's 'voices' are instrumental in the collaborative learning between learner and educator. This resonates with the Australian Curriculum for HASS rationale, which discusses the empowering of learners 'to actively shape their lives' and 'make reflective, informed decisions' (ACARA 2018).

## SPOTLIGHT ON HASS EDUCATION

### USING PUPPETS TO EXPLORE PERSONAL WORLDS

Mrs Williams is working with her Foundation class. It is the first term and she wants to capture learners' views about themselves, linking to the Foundation year Australian Curriculum for HASS, which focuses on children's personal worlds. Mrs Williams uses puppets to provide learners with the opportunity to talk about their thoughts and feelings from a 'safe place'. She carefully introduces the puppets (Rosie and Bob) to the class. 'Hello everyone, this is Rosie and Bob and it is their first day at school. Will you all help me look after them?' she asks. Sitting in a circle, the learners pass around the puppets and are given time to hold them. Mrs Williams observes the learners carefully and once they appear at ease with the puppets she starts to uses the puppets to communicate with them. She uses the puppets in four different ways:

1. The puppets ask the learners questions: 'What is school like?'

2. Mrs Williams describes how the puppets feel: 'Rosie feels a bit scared about the playground – what should she do?'

3. The learners use the puppets to communicate with Mrs Williams.

4. The learners use the puppets together.

Mrs Williams fluently moves in and out of different roles, sometimes playing alongside the learners with her puppet and at times stepping back and observing what learners are doing, documenting their dialogue, taking photographs and capturing their experiences.

# EDUCATOR TIP

Learners' interests are an avenue to look into their world and are not in themselves the key to effective planning. Educators need to look deeply into learners' interests and reflect on the theories, wonderings, understandings and misunderstandings that create and motivate them. Listening deeply to what learners are telling us and thinking about 'what' the learner is doing helps us to uncover the 'why' and the 'how'.

## Educator role: co-constructor and creator of a thinking environment

In a play-based curriculum, the educator works with learners in a process of co-constructing meaning and knowledge of the world. Educators co-construct knowledge with learners when they emphasise the study of meaning rather than transmission learning and the acquisition of facts. Meaning is how we make sense of and understand or interpret or give significance to our experiences. Of course, acquisition of information and data about the world is important, but in a play-based curriculum the community of learners is created through inquiry, discussion, analysis, interpretation and co-construction of the meaning of this information. Thus learners are 'authors of their own learning' (Malaguzzi 1994, p. 55) and educators take on the role of co-learner. Howard and McInnes (2010) offer a framework for co-constructing a play-based curriculum that includes collecting and reflect- ing on learners' views of practice, reflecting on the educator's role in practice and informed classroom practice. Reflection (Dewey 1938), a culture of talk (Alexander 2008) and **sustained shared thinking** (Siraj-Blatchford et al. 2002) are necessary to acquire deep understandings. In this way, learners not only collaborate with educators but also other learners, so it is essential to consider peer interaction and peer influence (Webb-Williams 2018). One of the most valuable things that educators can do is create a thinking environment in which a culture of trust, respect, innovation and creativity is inspired and nurtured so that learners are able to think for themselves. Educators can create an environment that:

> **sustained shared thinking:** two or more individuals 'work together' in an intellectual way to solve a problem, clarify a concept, evaluate activities, extend a narrative, etc. Both parties must contribute to the thinking and it must develop and extend.

- promotes equality so that all learners' voices are heard

- ensures attentive listening

- gives learners time to think and respond

- encourages learners to treat others with respect
- appreciates cultural diversity and diversity of thinking
- adopts questioning practices that enhance creative, independent thinking.

To stretch, develop and encourage deep thinking, questions need to be posed so they provoke learners to search for new insights, directions or answers. How the question is asked, when it is asked and the type of question all influence the way the question is assimilated and whether it can be transformative in providing an 'aha moment'.

**SPOTLIGHT ON HASS EDUCATION**

## UNDERSTANDING PLACE, SPACE AND ENVIRONMENTAL CHANGE

Through observation, listening and reflection, Mrs Williams documented learners' ideas and became cognisant of their interest in a local building site. She linked this natural curiosity into her planning for the Year 1 HASS Geography sub-strand in which learners develop understandings of place, space, environment and change. Learners brainstormed their ideas while Mrs Williams supported their thinking through open-ended questions such as: What do you think? That's an interesting idea, why do you think that? Can you tell me more about that? How could you find out more about that? What do we need to know? How could we test that idea? What are the other possibilities? Listening to the class as a whole and in separate groups, to ensure all 'voices' were heard, Mrs Williams documented the experiences. Together they co-constructed the 'class inquiry'. Multiple methods of capturing the experiences were suggested by the learners, with many interested in using technology such as cameras, handheld video cameras and iPads. Mrs Williams 'went with' this interest and gave learners the opportunity to record the construction and identify changes. In this way she was able to build on learners' interests and develop a number of playful activities with curriculum links to activities in the local place and reasons for their location (ACHASSK033), and the natural, managed and constructed features of places, their location, how they change and how they can be cared for (ACHASSK031).

## CONCLUSION

This chapter has shown that play/playfulness is vital in enabling and empowering educators to nurture independent and autonomous learners, encouraging them to be creative, self-directed and confident in making choices. Understanding what play is and why it is important helps educators to critically reflect on their practice, ensuring that they support learning and provide a balance of spontaneous, guided and directed play opportunities. Play is a powerful pedagogy for the HASS learning area as it supports learners to 'see' things from different perspectives, harnessing their imagination and motivation to explore the world. Learners are encouraged to voice their opinions, ideas and input into *what* they are learning and *how* they are learning. Educators encourage co-construction of meaning and individual growth as well as promoting the importance of belonging. This enables learners to build the skills and attitudes necessary for positive engagement in diverse globalised communities, reflecting on their place in the world and actively shaping their lives – key elements of the Australian Curriculum for HASS.

## REVIEW QUESTIONS

1. Name five characteristics of play.
2. Why is play an ideal vehicle for exploring the HASS learning area?
3. What is meant by 'playful pedagogies'?
4. Describe the continuum of educators' roles.
5. What is the role of observation in the planning process?

## LEARNING EXTENSION

Discuss the importance of educators adopting differing roles in learners' play and the benefits and limitations of these roles. You need to demonstrate sensitivity in responding to the needs of diverse learners (see Casey 2010) through your understanding of appropriate and inappropriate roles. Aim to research at least five different educators' roles, listing the disadvantages, advantages and examples of how you would use them in a HASS learning experience. A good place to start is the nine orchestration roles suggested by Van Hoorn et al. (2015) (see Figure 13.3).

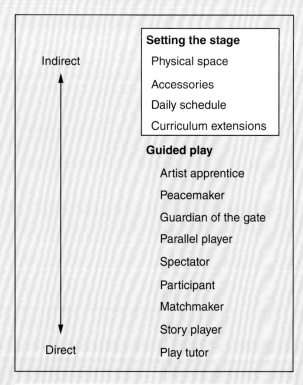

FIGURE 13.3   Continuum of play orchestration strategies
Source: Van Hoorn et al. 2015, p. 83

## REFERENCES

ACARA (Australian Curriculum, Assessment and Reporting Authority). (2018). *Australian Curriculum: Humanities and Social Sciences, v8.3*. Key ideas. Retrieved from: http://australian-curriculum.org/humanities-and-social-sciences/key-ideas.

Alexander, R.J. (2008). Culture, dialogue and learning: Notes on an emerging pedagogy. In N. Mercer & S. Hodgkinson, eds, *Exploring Talk in School*. Thousand Oaks, CA: Sage, pp. 93–114.

Briggs, M. & Hansen, A. (2012). *Play-based Learning in the Primary School*. Thousand Oaks, CA: Sage.

Brooker, L. & Edwards, S. (eds). (2010). *Engaging Play*. Maidenhead: McGraw-Hill.

Bruce, T. (1991). *Time to Play in Early Childhood Education*. London: Hodder Education.

——(2011). *Learning through Play: For babies, toddlers and young children*. London: Hodder Education.

Bruner, J. (1996). *The Culture of Education*. Cambridge, MA: Harvard University Press.

Byrnes, J. & Wasik, B. (2009). Picture this: Using photography as a learning tool in early childhood classrooms. *Childhood Education*, 85(4), 243–8.

Casey T. (2010). Enabling inclusive play opportunities: The role of adults. In *Inclusive Play: Practical strategies for children from birth to eight*. London: Sage, pp. 41–55.

DEEWR (Department of Education Employment and Workplace Relations). (2009). *Belonging, Being and Becoming: The Early Years Learning Framework for Australia*. Canberra: DEEWR.

Dewey, J. (1938). *Logic: Theory of inquiry*. New York: Holt and Co.

Dockett, S. (2008). Adult roles in children's play. In S. Dockett & M. Fleer, eds, *Play in Early Childhood Education: Learning in diverse contexts*. Melbourne: Cengage Learning, pp. 169–200.

Edwards, C., Gandini, L. & Forman, G. (eds). (1993). *The Hundred Languages of Children*. Norwood, NJ: Ablex.

Epstein, I., Stevens, B., McKeever, P., Baruchel, S. & Jones, H. (2007). Using puppetry to elicit children's talk for research. *Nursing Inquiry*, 15(1), 49–56.

Fasoli, L., Wunungurra, A., Ecenarro, V. & Fleet, A. (2010). Play as becoming: Sharing Aboriginal Australian voices on play. In M. Ebbeck & M. Waniganayake, eds, *Play in Early Childhood Education: Learning in diverse contexts*. Melbourne: Oxford University Press, pp. 213–32.

Fleer, M. (2017). *Play in the Early Years*. Melbourne: Cambridge University Press.

Garvey, C. (1991). *Play*, 2nd edn. London: Fontana.

Gleave, J. & Cole-Hamilton, I. (2012). A world without play: A literature review. British Toy & Hobby Association; Play England. Retrieved from: http://www.playengland.org.uk/media/371031/a-world-without-play-literature-review-2012.pdf.

Hewett, V.M. (2001). Examining the Reggio Emilia approach to early childhood education. *Early Childhood Education Journal*, 29(2), 95–100.

Howard, J. & McInnes, K. (2010). Thinking through the challenge of a play based curriculum: Increasing playfulness via co-construction. In J. Moyles, *Thinking About Play: Developing a reflective approach*. Maidenhead: Open University Press, pp. 30–44.

Hughes, F.P. (2010). *Children, Play, and Development*. London: Sage.

Jarvis, P., Brock, A. & Brown, F. (2014). Three perspectives on play. In A. Brock, P. Jarvis & Y. Olusoga, eds, *Perspectives on Play: Learning for life*. London: Routledge, pp. 2–28.

Jones, E. & Reynolds, G. (1992). Understanding and supporting children's play. In E. Jones, G. Reynolds & S. Ryan, eds, *The Play's the Thing: Teachers' roles in children's play*. New York: Teachers College Press, pp. 7–21.

Leitch, R. (2008). Creatively researching children' s narratives through images and drawings. In P. Thomson, ed., *Doing Visual Research with Children and Young People*. London: Routledge.

Malaguzzi, L. (1993). History, ideas and basic philosophy. In C. Edwards, L. Gandini & G. Forman, eds, *The Hundred Languages of Children*. Norwood, NJ: Ablex.

——(1994). Your image of the child: Where teaching begins. *Child Care Information Exchange*, 3, 52–61.

Moyles, J. (2010). *Thinking About Play: Developing a reflective approach*. Maidenhead: Open University Press.

Murdoch, K. (2018). Kath Murdoch Education Consultant. Retrieved from: https://www.kathmurdoch.com.au.

OECD (Organisation for Economic Cooperation and Development). (2016). *Education at a Glance 2016: OECD indicators*. Paris: OECD Publishing.

Parten, M.B. (1932). Social participation among preschool children. *Journal of Abnormal and Social Psychology*, 27(3), 243–69.

Saracho, O.N. (2012). *An Integrated Play-based Curriculum for Young Children*. New York: Taylor and Francis.

Siraj-Blatchford, I., Silva, K., Muttock, S., Gilden, R. & Bell, D. (2002). *Researching Effective Pedagogy in the Early Years*. Oxford: University of Oxford, Department of Educational Studies.

Smidt, S. (2010). *Playing to Learn: The role of play in the early years*. Abingdon: Routledge.

Smilansky, S. (1990). Sociodramatic play: Its relevance to behaviour and achievement in school. In E. Klugman & S. Smilansky, eds, *Children's Play and Learning: Perspectives and policy implications*. New York: Teachers College Press, pp. 18–42.

Smith, P.K. & Pellegrini, A. (2008). Learning through play. In R.E. Tremblay, M. Boivin & R. DeV. Peters, eds, *Encyclopedia on Early Childhood Development*. Retrieved from: http://www.child-encyclopedia.com/play/according-experts/learning-through-play.

Van Hoorn, J., Nourot, P.M., Scales, B. & Alward, K. (2015). *Play at the Center of the Curriculum*, 6th edn. Boston: Pearson.

Vygotsky, L. (1978). *Mind in Society: The development of higher psychological processes*. Cambridge, MA: Harvard University Press.

Webb-Williams, J. (2017a). Science self-efficacy in the primary classroom: using mixed methods to investigate sources of self-efficacy. *Research in Science Education*, pp. 1–23. Retrieved from: https://www.researchgate.net.

——(2017b). *Connecting Community Through Children's Play: A collective impact research project*. Adelaide: University of South Australia. Retrieved from: http://researchoutputs.unisa.edu.au/11541.2/126701.

——(2018, in press). How others shape the development of children's self-perceptions: Implications for early childhood education. In D. Whitebread & D. Pino-Pasternack, eds, *SAGE Handbook of Developmental Psychology and Early Childhood Education*. Thousand Oaks, CA: Sage.

Webb-Williams, J., Mills-Bayne, M. & Raymond, S. (2015). *Children's Voices in Play: Research report prepared for City of Salisbury Council 2015*. Adelaide: University of South Australia.

Whitebread, D., Basilio, M., Kuvalja, M. & Verma, M. (2012). *The Importance of Play: A report on the value of children's play with a series of policy recommendations*. Brussels: Toys Industries for Europe.

# USING PICTURE BOOKS TO DEVELOP LANGUAGE AND LITERACIES IN HASS

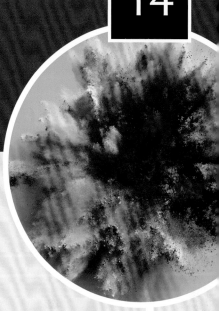

**14**

*Jann Carroll*

## Learning objectives

After reading this chapter, you should be able to:

- understand the integrated nature of language and literacy in Humanities and Social Sciences (HASS)
- understand key skills and difficulties in relation to language and literacy in HASS
- plan effective learning experiences/lessons using picture books to develop literacy and disciplinary knowledge
- apply strategies to expand learners' understanding of key HASS concepts and literacy skills using picture books
- choose good-quality picture books to use across the HASS curriculum.

## INTRODUCTION

It is difficult to think of anything more widespread and enduring than the lure of a good story. It is the warp and weft that weaves old, young, rich and poor of different cultures together and enables the opening of new worlds, concepts and understandings of past, present and future. We can empathise, imagine and live vicariously through stories that are an inseparable part of who we are as human beings. History documents these stories based on evidence interpreted through different lenses over time; Geography lends its knowledge to significance of place, space, time and perspective, providing context and reason; and Civics and Citizenship stories help us to understand our roles and responsibilities, as we seek models of the heroes and heroines found in a good story.

For this chapter, a broad view of literacy has been adopted, one that defines it as a social practice that involves teaching learners how to participate in, understand and gain control of the literacy practices embedded within society (Winch et al. 2004). Inherent within this definition, Luke and Freebody (1995, in Winch et al. 2004, p. xxxii) also suggest that education is ultimately about building identities, cultures, communities, institutions and the types of citizens needed for an effective society. Therefore, a **literate person** has the tools to live and work for the common good of society and understand the implications of their actions. This chapter examines the integrated nature of literacy in HASS through the inclusion of picture books to open and explore issues relating to HASS.

> **literate person:** one who can use language and literacy to interact with and contribute to society

# THE INTEGRATED NATURE OF LITERACY IN HASS

HASS is the study of humans and their society, and the network in which society operates, so it follows that literacy is the connector. Literacy is an essential 21st-century skill (MCEETYA 2008) that is the foundation of learning across all curriculum areas and central to full participation in society. The Australian Curriculum includes literacy as one of the key general capabilities that supports learners to be creators and consumers of texts relevant to every learning area. The advantage of the HASS curriculum in building literacy capacity is that it delivers opportunities for literacy to be taught at the point of need within authentic learning situations. When reading or searching for information, readers draw upon their prior knowledge to make inferences, and through discussion, critical thinking and writing they make connections, and build content knowledge and vocabulary skills.

**literacy**: is far broader than 'English' and, as a general capability, is part of every curriculum area, acquired through school and home reading and viewing practices by every child every day. Literacy learning is continuous through life.

**English**: the official language of Australia, is timetabled in schools, has distinct assessment, and is sequenced in year levels and measured in achievement standards

There is often confusion between the terms 'literacy' and 'English', and it is important to understand the difference. The Australian Curriculum distinguishes between these terms by making English a learning (content) area and literacy a general capability. English is timetabled in schools, has distinct assessment, is sequenced in year levels and measured in achievement standards. On the other hand, literacy is far broader and, as a general capability, it is part of every key learning area, acquired through preschool, school and home reading and viewing practices by every child every day. Every educator is an educator of literacy because when they teach specific geographical vocabulary – for example, abrasion, erosion and meridian, how to read a financial graph or how to create a timeline of events gleaned from source documentation – they are teaching literacy (Donnelly 2016). Fisher, Frey and Hattie (2015) talk about literacy being the 'currency of other learning' (p. 3) and this is no more so than in HASS.

The *Australian Curriculum: HASS* (ACARA 2018a) relies heavily on learners being able to read, write, listen, view, speak and create to demonstrate their understanding as well as to learn. In the Foundation year in both History and Geography, students are required to 'present narratives, information and findings in oral, graphic and written forms using simple terms to denote the passing of time and to describe direction and location' (ACHASS1010; ACARA 2018a).

By the time learners embark on Year 10 History,

> students sequence events and developments within a chronological framework, and identify relationships between events across different places and periods of time. When researching, students develop, evaluate and modify questions to frame a historical inquiry. They process, analyse and synthesise information from a range of primary and secondary sources and use it as evidence to answer inquiry questions. Students develop texts, particularly explanations and discussions, incorporating historical argument. (ACARA 2018c)

Learning rests on using language to understand and communicate ideas.

# WHY FOCUS ON LANGUAGE AND LITERACY LEARNING IN HASS?

HASS has a valuable pedagogical and literacy-based foundation that can motivate and engage all learners. The essence of HASS is that it teaches about almost every aspect of living a good life and the **interactions** therein. For example, through reading and researching about the lives of others, learners gain insight into the personal, social, professional, civic and cultural lives of historical figures and can transfer, with effective teaching, the lessons learnt to critique current events. Mendelson (2010, p. 185) points out that 'the connection to literacy requires a capacity for critical judgement about complex, even contradictory issues that is crucial to academic success'. Therefore, learners require strong literate abilities, strategies and tools within a **connected education**.

**interactions**: relate to how the world works through both natural and human systems. Every decision affects these systems and has effects on them.

**connected education**: learners read about their own culture and educators learn more about the cultures, experiences and values of the learners in their setting to enable deeper understanding

## Key literacy skills

The following list is adapted from Mendelson (2010), who provides a comprehensive list of literate activities required to be successful in HASS. Learners of all ages need to be able to:

- conduct critical inquiry by examining text through analytical reading
- engage in critical analysis of informed and appropriate resources
- engage in debates and complex discussions
- understand others' points of view through critical reasoning
- wrestle with complexity and difference
- write, speak, view and listen through critical and empathetic lenses
- improve intellectual capacity and make connections
- articulate their own position on complex problems
- develop critical questions and engage in deep reflection
- comprehend, critique and put new ideas to work in productive ways.

The world is complex and pluralistic. Learners require the tools to reconcile opposing views and values, and to avoid 'either/or' solutions on their way to independent, deep thought – a key requirement of developing into an active and informed citizen. However, there are difficulties in achieving all the skills listed above, despite their obvious benefits.

## Challenges to achieving key literacy skills

Educators and learners face several challenges in achieving key literacy skills:

- Learners may not have the basic skills to read critically for understanding and application.
- Educators may not have the skills or the time and inclination to develop learners' critical reading.
- The crowded curriculum may result in surface rather than deep learning.

- Curriculum reform may not deliver the emphasis on HASS that is required.
- Learners may not have the cultural capital on which to build understanding through reading.
- Educational settings may not have access to quality resources to support critical reading in HASS.
- The digital revolution demands new literacies and pedagogies to which some educational settings may not have access.
- The quality of some online resources remains questionable, which underlines the importance of teaching critical reading.

## EDUCATOR TIP

Depending on the age of the learners you are teaching, choose one or two critical literacy skills to work on each term. Model them often and provide plenty of authentic opportunities for practice. Provide targeted feedback to assist your learners to improve.

Reflection  Why is critical reading and rereading a vital skill for interpreting texts used in HASS?

## PICTURE BOOKS: THE POWER OF STORY IN TEACHING HASS

Picture books support children's language development as well as providing a bridge to greater understanding in HASS. Children love a good story, and regularly reading to and with young children provides a solid foundation for early literacy development. Children's literature is more than a good story; it enables the reader and listener to know what it is to be human and provides access to the most fundamental experiences of life – love, loss, joy, loneliness, empathy, adventure, fear, belonging and hope. According to Short, Lynch-Brown and Tomlinson (2014, p. 4), 'literature is the imaginative shaping of experience and thought into the forms and structures of language ... to challenge them to think in new ways about their lives and the world'.

**children's literature:** includes picture books, chapter books, poetry, fiction and non-fiction – good-quality books that cover topics of interest and relevance to children, which reflect their own life experiences or those of others

A commonly accepted definition of **children's literature**, which includes picture books, chapter books, poetry, fiction and non-fiction, refers to good-quality books that cover topics of interest and relevance to children, which reflect their own life experiences or those of others (Short, Lynch-Brown & Tomlinson 2014; Winch et al. 2014). Additionally, picture books are viewed as sophisticated aesthetic objects and literary texts with the potential to provoke inquiry, as words and pictures work together to produce meaning and convey cultural messages (Purcell 2016, p. 2). Stephens (1992) identifies that picture books enable critical evaluation of how values and ideology are transmitted to children, often through emotional and cognitive engagement. Chomsky (2000) writes that good-quality literature provides deeper insights into the full human person than any model of scientific inquiry is able to convey. It is through the telling of stories, which address our deepest insights and concerns, engaging both senses and intellect, that meaning is made and appropriated. A good story invites the reader to share in the experience and appropriate meaning for their own lives.

Good-quality picture books also reflect diverse cultural identities and experiences rather than stereotypical, monocultural options. Ross Johnston (2014, in Winch et al. 2014, p. 656) refers to the *ethics of hope* being present in children's literature that addresses complexities of the unknown, as well as the known; this provides options, possibilities and agency in personal response. Having an element of hope in realistic fiction is especially important. For example, a book such as *My Two Blankets* by Kobald and Blackwood (2014), which addresses a child's experience of being a refugee in a new country, provides hope alongside the challenges of relocating. However, children's life experiences do not always end like 'happily ever after' movies, so when choosing books to support topics in HASS it is important to provide a balanced view. See the checklist in Table 14.1 for some key questions to consider when choosing an effective picture book for learning.

| TABLE 14.1 GUIDING QUESTIONS FOR CHOOSING RELEVANT PICTURE BOOKS |
| --- |
| ☐ Is the story interesting and relevant to the topic and the age of the students? |
| ☐ Does the story contain interesting language? |
| ☐ Are factual and historical details accurate? |
| ☐ Is this an award-winning or short-listed picture book? |
| ☐ Are universal human emotions, attitudes, needs and experiences reflected? |
| ☐ Are a variety of cultural groups, genders and perspectives represented? |
| ☐ Is the book free from bias and stereotyping? |
| ☐ Are historical facts and settings, and geographical features, represented accurately? |
| ☐ Does the story offer a variety of situations, concepts and new ideas on which to critically reflect, question and build knowledge? |
| ☐ Do the illustrations represent diversity, authenticity and respect? |

## The value of using picture books to teach HASS

According to the Australian Bureau of Statistics 2016 Census data, of the 23 million people living in Australia, one in four was born overseas, 49 per cent had at least one parent born overseas and 21 per cent spoke a language other than English at home (ABS 2016). The Australian Curriculum addresses cultural diversity, which is represented in every classroom through the general capability of intercultural understanding and through two of the three cross-curriculum priorities, namely Aboriginal and Torres Strait Islander histories and cultures, and Asia and Australia's engagement with Asia (ACARA 2018a). It is important to realise as educators that there is no single story that reflects the culture in an educational setting/classroom; rather, it is through a collection of stories that intercultural understanding is gained. Through picture books, educators can assist learners to explore and question stated and unstated cultural beliefs and assumptions, and appreciate intercultural meaning and sensitivities. Using picture books as a model, learners are given opportunities to comprehend and create a range of texts to demonstrate their understanding of diverse cultural perspectives and develop empathy and respect.

> Students learn to question stated and unstated cultural beliefs and assumptions, and appreciate issues of intercultural meaning and sensitivity. In this way, students use intercultural understanding to comprehend and create a range of texts that present diverse cultural perspectives, and to empathise with a variety of people and characters in various cultural settings. (ACARA 2018a)

The integrated nature of literacy is demonstrated in the sharing of ideas through literature and is a powerful opportunity for widening learners' perspectives. Collecting good-quality picture books to share with learners of all ages has many benefits. Research by Nelson, Palonsky and McCarthy (2004) found that every learner benefits from stories about their family, pastimes, community and country. Learners from refugee and immigrant backgrounds need opportunities to listen to and reflect on tales that resonate with their lived experiences so they can gain understanding about their place and part in Australian culture. Singh (2005) refers to this as 'connected education'. The connection is powerful when learners read about their own culture and educators learn more about the cultures, experiences and values of the learners in their setting. In this way, picture books provide both a mirror and a window to enable participants to reveal their own cultural beliefs and understandings to develop acceptance of difference and geographical, historical and intercultural understanding.

## Benefits of including children's literature in HASS educational settings

There are many benefits of including a good-quality, extensive variety of children's literature in educational settings from preschool onwards, with reference to HASS content. Picture books provide:

- models of writing styles, expression, vocabulary, punctuation and the connections between text and image
- both a mirror and a window to learners' own and other's perspectives, cultures and circumstances (Bishop 1997)
- a vicarious experience that is less expensive and more accessible than excursions
- role models for children through the exploration of the qualities of characters (Adam 2015)
- opportunities to deal with controversial issues
- a broadening of minds through presenting differing perspectives, intercultural awareness and unpacking stereotypes (Adam & Harper 2016)

- access to other world views that invite readers to think or see things differently (Phillips 2016)
- opportunities to create authentic forums for discussion
- alternative sources and formats for new information
- opportunities to establish conditions that arouse curiosity and wonder (Nottingham 2016)
- tools to build critical literacy skills, questioning, listening, analysis and appreciation (Sipe & Panteleo 2008)
- culturally diverse literature to address the principles of diversity while meeting curriculum requirements (Adam & Harper 2016)
- opportunities to inspire action to create change in their community.

## How to choose good-quality children's literature

We all have our favourite books from childhood that made an impact at a significant time. Perhaps we fell in love with the characters or we were inspired to go on a grand adventure because of what we read. Perhaps it was the beauty of the prose or images that inspired us to write and illustrate our own texts. The Australian Curriculum is predicated on the foundational concept that every child has the right to an education that prepares them to be participating citizens in society, maximises their ability and respects family, cultural and other identities and languages. Additionally, Australian schools are to promote *equity* and *excellence* for all young Australians (DEEWR 2009; MCEETYA 2008). The values espoused in these key documents are reflected in the Australian Curriculum as the cross-curriculum priorities and the personal and social and intercultural understanding general capabilities, with the overarching goal that all children in Australia achieve equitable educational outcomes. In all disciplines, it is important for educators to provide access to a selection of texts that reflect the diversity of society. Learners who can see themselves or their situations in a picture book are more likely to grasp abstract ideas and develop a positive sense of identity and belonging (Morgan 2009). Additionally, the use of quality picture books serves to support and enhance the learning of English grammar, expression, punctuation, spelling, vocabulary and comprehension – skills central to being literate.

How have you seen educators integrate literacy and picture books into their HASS units of work? Provide four examples.

In choosing good-quality books for the educational setting/classroom (see also Table 14.1 above), the following points need to be kept in mind. Good-quality books:

- promote quality writing, increase vocabulary and understanding of how texts work
- have original and important ideas

- are written with imaginative language supported by interesting, thought-provoking illustrations
- have longevity and can be repeatedly read for layers of meaning
- reflect a society's cultural capital and provide insight into other's cultures, history and societies
- contain memorable characters and situations that provide insights into what it is to be human
- can be enjoyed by young and old alike
- are enjoyable when read aloud or silently
- challenge the reader/listener to see the world from another's perspective and to consider other possibilities
- provide non-threatening, authentic forums to contemplate a range of ideas
- carry educational, social and emotional benefits and can be a bridge between educational settings and home reading
- are often short-listed and/or recognised with awards (Adam & Harper 2016; Short, Lynch-Brown & Tomlinson 2014; Winch et al. 2014).

A list of good-quality picture books can be found in Table 14.2.

**TABLE 14.2    PICTURE BOOKS TO DEVELOP LANGUAGE AND LITERACY IN HASS**

| Title | Author and illustrator | Publication date |
| --- | --- | --- |
| *A Forest* | Marc Martin | 2012 |
| *A True Person* | Gabiann Marin and Jacqui Grantford | 2007 |
| *Benno and the Night of Broken Glass* | Meg Wiviott and Josee Bisaillon | 2010 |
| *Big Mama Makes the World* | Phyllis Root and Helen Oxenbury | 2004 |
| *Circle* | Jeannie Baker | 2016 |
| *Dear Greenpeace* | Simon James | 2005 |
| *Dust* | Save the Children | 2007 |
| *Faithful Elephants* | Yukio Tsuchiya (translated by Tomoko Tsuchiya Dykes) and Ted Lewin | 1951 |
| *Flood* | Jackie French and Bruce Whatley | 2012 |
| *Here We Are: Notes for living on planet earth* | Oliver Jeffers | 2017 |
| *Kaito's Cloth* | Glenda Millard and Gaye Chapman | 2006 |
| *Lest We Forget* | Kerry Brown with Isobel Knowles and Benjamin Portas | 2015 |
| *Letters from Felix* | Annette Langen and Constanza Droop | 1994 |
| *Limpopo Lullaby* | Jane Jolly and Dee Huxley | 2004 |

**TABLE 14.2**  (CONT.)

| Title | Author and illustrator | Publication date |
| --- | --- | --- |
| *Lin Yi's Lantern* | Brenda Williams and Benjamin Lacombe | 2009 |
| *Listen to Our world* | Bill Martin Jr and Michael Sampson | 2016 |
| *Maralinga, the Anangu Story* | Christobel Mattingley | 2009 |
| *Memorial* | Gary Crew and Shaun Tan | 2012 |
| *Mirror* | Jeannie Baker | 2010 |
| *My Mother's Eyes: The story of an Australian boy soldier* | Mark Wilson | 2009 |
| *My Name is Lizzie Flynn* | Claire Saxby and Lizzy Newcomb | 2015 |
| *My Two Blankets* | Irena Kobald and Freya Blackwood | 2014 |
| *New Year Surprise!* | Christopher Cheng and Di Wu | 2016 |
| *Of Thee I Sing: A letter to my daughters* | Barack Obama and Loren Long | 2010 |
| *Our World: Baardi Jaawi: Life at Ardiyooloon* | One Arm Point Remote Community School | 2010 |
| *Radio Rescue!* | Jane Jolly and Robert Ingpen (National Library of Australia) | 2016 |
| *Stepping Stones: A refugee family's journey* | Margaret Ruurs and Nizar Ali Badr | 2016 |
| *Stolen Girl* | Trina Saffrotti and Norman McDonald | 2012 |
| *Terrible Things: An allegory of the Holocaust* | Eve Bunting | 1980 |
| *The Arrival* | Sean Tan | 2008 |
| *The Beach They Called Gallipoli* | Jackie French and Bruce Whatley | 2014 |
| *The Colour of Home* | Mary Hoffman and Karin Littlewood | 1993 |
| *The Harmonica* | Tony Johnson and Ron Mazellan | 2008 |
| *The Most Magnificent Mosque* | Ann Jungman and Shelley Fowles | 2004 |
| *The Number on My Grandfather's Arm* | David A Adler. Photographs by Rose Eichenbaum | 1987 |
| *The Peace Tree from Hiroshima: The little bonsai with a big story* | Sandra Moore and Kazumi Wilds | 2015 |
| *The Roses in My Carpets* | Rukhsana Khan and Ronald Himler | 1988 |
| *The Shack that Dad Built* | Elaine Russell | 2005 |
| *The Whispering Town* | Jennifer Elvgren and Fabio Santomauro | 2014 |
| *Wandihnu and the Old Dugong* | Elizabeth Wymarra and Wandihnu Wymarra | 2007 |

## EDUCATOR TIP

Start your collection of good-quality picture books today! Visit the Children's Book Council of Australia website (https://cbca.org.au) for award-winners; scrounge at garage sales and book fairs; look for specials in bookstores, supermarkets and online; ask other educators for their recommendations and read, read, read! See Table 14.2 for examples to get you started.

# STRATEGIES TO DEVELOP LANGUAGE AND LITERACIES IN HASS

**receptive language skills**: include reading, viewing and listening using books, film, image and audio books

**expressive language skills**: include speaking, writing and creating through discussion, essays, art pieces, infographics or videos

One of the key objectives in effective teaching of HASS is for learners to develop understandings, inquiry processes and reasoning with a real-world, hands-on approach. This is often referred to as 'authentic learning', described by Reynolds (2014, p. 218) as 'learning in the classroom which is closely related to and relevant for the world outside the classroom'. The following strategies are designed to assist learners to engage with complex ideas, collaborate to make decisions and develop both **receptive** and **expressive language skills**.

## Strategies for building language, literacy and critical thinking in HASS

### Create a headline

**geo-literacy**: a term adopted by National Geographic to provide information and understanding to assist people all around the world to make decisions that have as little negative impact on the environment, society and their health as possible

Learners form small groups and read a short article or paragraph or study an image on a topic being studied. Drawing on background knowledge and information presented in the source material, learners are asked to create a headline that conveys the implications and inter-actions succinctly. Learners present their headlines, with justification, to the class either orally or digitally. Instead of text, photographs or images can also be used.

## EDUCATOR TIP

Choose a range of sources and provide different source material to each group on the same topic. This promotes rich discussion and enables all ability levels to participate. Teach your learners about geo-literacy.

## Two questions and one statement (2Q1S)

To build inquiry skills, learners need to be able to ask and respond to open questions that lead to deep, critical thinking. Inquiry thinking demands that educators and learners do not take a surface, either/or stance when answering questions that are complex and intriguing. A strategy that assists learners to probe below the surface is 2Q1S (Murdoch 1998). Two questions and one statement require learners to create two questions from the upper levels of Bloom's taxonomy (apply, analyse, evaluate, synthesise) that will engage their partner in higher-order thinking skills based on the topic being studied. Once each person in the pair has answered the two questions, they each write a statement synthesising what they have understood about the topic, which is shared on the class wiki or Google Docs. Repeating 2Q1S with different partners enables learners to understand different facets of the topic being studied as well as learning collaboration, listening and synthesising skills.

## THE 2Q1S STRATEGY

**Topic:** Year 6 Democracy: Learners explain the importance of people, institutions and processes to Australia's democracy (Year 6 achievement standard)

**Read:** *Who Really Created Democracy?* by Amie Jane Levitt (2011) and/or *The Class Vote: Roshan learns democracy* by Deborah Chancellor (2017)

**Activity:** Learners pair up and create two questions and one statement. For example:

- **Question 1:** Why do we have different political parties in Australia?
- **Question 2:** Why is it important to have different political parties for democracy to function effectively?

**Statement:** There are two major political parties in Australia: the Liberal–National Coalition and the Australian Labor Party. Traditionally, one of these two parties has gained the most seats to form government. However, the Australian Parliament also has representatives from the Greens, independents and smaller parties, which ensures that many views are represented in both the lower and upper houses. As a result of many views being represented, the people of Australia are secure in the knowledge that democracy is at work when parliament makes laws. The opposite of a democracy is a dictatorship, where the people do not have any representation in government and their views are not heard.

**SPOTLIGHT ON HASS EDUCATION**

## Inside-outside circle

The inside-outside circle can be used in small groups of learners or with an entire class. The strategy works well when learners have been asked to read or view, for example, a range of short vignettes, websites or case studies on one topic. The aim is to provide opportunities for learners to hear others' points of view and discuss more deeply what they have read in preparation for writing. 'Writing floats on a sea of talk' is a phrase coined by Britton (1970). Research suggests that when learners are given the opportunity to discuss their ideas first, their writing is clearer and they are more focused (Carroll 2011).

To set up the inside-outside circle:

- Provide a range of sources for learners to use. These may include images, websites, picture books or excerpts from texts. Provide time for learners to read or view and understand the texts. Clearly state the focus question.

- Direct each learner to find a partner. Ask learners to stand in a circle facing their partner with one partner on the inside of the circle and the other forming the outside circle.

- To begin, learners in the outer circle have one minute to talk while their partner listens, then the learner in the inner circle has one minute to speak uninterrupted to discuss the focus question before the educator calls: 'Change'.

- At the end of the two minutes, the outside circle takes one or two steps clockwise while the inner circle remains in place and the process of dialogue and listening is repeated. Learners gain and express differing points of view on the topic.

- The educator's role is to time-keep and record key points so learners can refer to these in the follow-up writing activity. The number of rotations is discretionary; however, three rotations works well (Murdoch 1998).

## SPOTLIGHT ON HASS EDUCATION

## STRATEGY IN ACTION

Practise the inside-outside circle strategy, using the following task. Once you have practised, create a lesson for a primary or lower primary or preschool class using this strategy and the following achievement standard:

**Topic:** Social Justice Initiatives: Year 8 Civics and Citizenship key question:

> The aim of the Civics and Citizenship curriculum is to foster students' commitment and understanding of the national values of democracy, equity and justice. Through highlighting Australia's diversity and what it means to be a citizen, the curriculum explores ways in which students participate in Australia's civic life and make a positive contribution as local and global citizens. (ACARA 2018b)

**Topic:** Social justice initiatives: Year 8 Civics and Citizenship key question.

**Key question:** What are the freedoms and responsibilities of citizens in Australia's democracy?

**Civics and Citizenship knowledge and understanding (ACHCK062):** How citizens can participate in Australia's democracy, including use of the electoral system, contact with their elected representatives, use of lobby groups and *direct action*.

**Civics and Citizenship curriculum links:**

- Critically analyse information and ideas from a range of sources in relation to civics and citizenship topics and issues (ACHCS070).
- Appreciate multiple perspectives and use strategies to mediate differences (ACHCS071).
- Present evidence-based civics and citizenship arguments using subject-specific language (ACHCS073).
- Reflect on their role as a citizen in Australia's democracy (ACHCS074).

**Activity:** Learners read a range of case studies explaining how individuals and community groups have sought to assist marginalised and vulnerable people in the community to fulfil the responsibilities of citizenship through direct action. Examples include:

- *Orange Sky Laundry* – a free, mobile laundry service for homeless people: http://www.orangeskylaundry.com.au
- *OzHarvest* – a perishable food rescue organisation in Australia that collects quality excess food from commercial outlets and delivers it, direct and free of charge, to charities that feed people in need: http://www.ozharvest.org
- *Global School Partners* – seeks to partner schools in Australia with schools in Africa to support African girls' education and to empower Australian school students to think globally and act locally: http://www.globalschoolpartners.org.au
- *Indigenous Literacy Foundation* – aims to deliver free books and literacy resources to Aboriginal and Torres Strait Islander children and their families in remote communities to build a lifelong love of reading: http://www.indigenousliteracyfoundation.org.au
- *Refugee Action Coalition* – a community activist organisation campaigning for the rights of refugees: http://www.refugeeaction.org.au.

**Assessment:** Write a persuasive piece to raise awareness for the plight of a marginalised group and to highlight the community organisation that you believe to be best at taking direct action to meet the needs of the people concerned.

The inside-outside circle provides opportunities to talk through your understanding of what you have read as well as to help you to begin to formulate opinions that may be congruent (the same) with or contrary (different) to your initial knowledge and understanding of the group of marginalised people. Refer to the list below of other complex, controversial or sensitive issues to plan your activity for a grade of your choice.

## EDUCATOR TIP

Choose a familiar topic and practise the inside-outside circle strategy with your learners before you launch into a more complex topic.

## Complex, controversial or sensitive issues in HASS

Due to the nature of HASS, there are topics that require sensitivity. It is important for educators to present a balanced view and set ground rules in the educational setting around respect, listening and cultural awareness when addressing issues such as:

- the Stolen Generations
- Aboriginal and Torres Strait Islander rights and sacred sites
- treatment of refugees
- black armband view of history

- the White Australia policy
- war and conflict
- climate change
- religion and the role of the church
- capital punishment
- homelessness
- geopolitical conflict.

# CONCLUSION

This chapter has provided knowledge, skills and understandings about the integrated nature of language and literacy in HASS using quality picture books and effective strategies. The disciplinary area of HASS coupled with impactful picture books, web resources and non-fiction resources provides rich material for learners to expand their understanding and engage in deep, critical thinking. Insight gained from HASS develops learners into active and informed citizens who will contribute to a just and empathetic society. Educators' knowledge and passion for picture books will form a strong basis on which to teach learners the HASS curriculum.

## REVIEW QUESTIONS

1. Explain, using examples, the statement 'Picture books provide both a mirror and a window.'

2. Choose two award-winning picture books you may like to use in the HASS educational setting. Evaluate each book using the questions in Table 14.1, and write a rationale for how you would use each one in either a History or Geography learning experience.

3. What are the benefits of using picture books to teach HASS? Support each benefit with an example of a good-quality picture book.

4. Why are stories so powerful in assisting learners to develop intercultural understanding and identity?

5. What do educators need to bear in mind when choosing good-quality picture books to support learning in HASS educational settings?

## LEARNING EXTENSION

1. Select one quality picture book from Table 14.2 or select your own book using the questions in Table 14.1. Read the book thoroughly and create a lesson, including effective pedagogy and assessment, to demonstrate one of the cross-curriculum priorities as it relates to a topic in History, Geography, Civics and Citizenship, or Economics and Business. Find a companion picture book, poem or ebook and create two extension activities.

2. Evaluate and justify the following statement: 'There is a connection between using good-quality picture books and improving literacy skills required to be successful in HASS.'

# REFERENCES

ABS (Australian Bureau of Statistics). (2016). *Census Stories: Australia revealed, 2016*. Retrieved from: http://www.abs.gov.au/census.

ACARA (Australian Curriculum, Assessment and Reporting Authority). (2018a). *Australian Curriculum: Humanities and Social Sciences F-10, v8.3*. Retrieved from: https://www .australiancurriculum.edu.au/f-10-curriculum/humanities-and-social-sciences/hass.

——(2018b). *Australian Curriculum: Humanities and Social Sciences F-10, v8.3*. Civics and Citizenship. Retrieved from: https://www.australiancurriculum.edu.au/f-10-curriculum/ humanities-and-social-sciences/civics-and-citizenship.

——(2018c). *Australian Curriculum: Humanities and Social Sciences F-10, v8.3*. History. Year 10 achievement standards. Retrieved from: https://www.australiancurriculum.edu.au/ f-10-curriculum/humanities-and-social-sciences/history/?strand=Historical+Knowledge+and +Understanding&strand=Historical+Skills&capability=ignore&priority=ignore&year=12321& elaborations=true.

Adam, H. (2015). Picture books: A key to the Australian Curriculum. A summary of the plenary session. PETAA conference, Perth.

Adam, H. & Harper, L. (2016). Assessing and selecting culturally diverse literature for the classroom. *Practical Literacy: The Early and Primary Years*, 21(2) June, 10–13.

Bishop, R. (1997). Selecting literature for a multicultural curriculum. In V. Harris, ed., *Using Multiethnic Literature in the K–8 Classroom*. Norwood, MA: Christopher-Gordon, pp. 1–20.

Britton, J. (1970). *Language and Learning*. London: Allen Lane.

Carroll, J. (2011). Boys' writing experiences in a Year 6 classroom: Supportive strategies. *Australian Journal of Middle Schooling*, 11(2), 20–7.

Chomsky, N. (2000). *New Horizons in the Study of Language and Mind*. Cambridge: Cambridge University Press.

DEEWR (Department of Education, Employment and Workplace Relations). (2009). *Belonging, Being and Becoming: The Early Years Learning Framework for Australia*. Canberra: DEEWR.

Donnelly, P. (2016). It's about time: The role of literacy across the curriculum and why everyone misses out when it is left to English. *Practical Literacy: The Early and Primary Years*, 21(3), 4–5.

Fisher, D., Frey, N. & Hattie, J. (2016). *Visible Learning for Literacy: Implementing the practices that work best to accelerate student learning*. Thousand Oaks, CA: Corwin Sage.

Kobald, I. & Blackwood, F. (2014). *My Two Blankets*. Richmond, Vic.: Little Hare Books.

MCEETYA (Ministerial Council on Education, Employment, Training and Youth Affairs). (2008). *Melbourne Declaration on Educational Goals for Young Australians*. Retrieved from: http://www.curriculum.edu.au/verve/_resources/National_Declaration_on_the_Educational_ Goals_for_Young_Australians.pdf.

Mendelson, M. (2010). Teaching the humanities. *The International Journal of the Humanities*, 8(8), 183–97.

Morgan, H. (2009). Gender, racial and ethnic misrepresentation in children's books: A comparative look. *Childhood Education*, 85(3), 187–90.

Murdoch, K. (1998). *Classroom Connections: Strategies for integrated learning*. Melbourne.: Eleanor Curtain Publishing.

Nelson, J., Palonsky, S. & McCarthy, M. (2004). *Critical Issues in Education*, 5th edn. Boston, MA: McGraw-Hill.

Nottingham, J. (2016). *Challenging Learning: Theory, effective practice and lesson ideas to create optimal learning in the classroom*, 2nd edn. London: Routledge.

Phillips, L. (2016). Learning and teaching with cultural stories. *Practical Literacy: The Early and Primary Years*, 21(2), 20–2.

Purcell, J. (2016). 'Seeing the light': A cognitive approach to the metaphorical in picture books. *Children's Literature in Education*, 1–20, doi: 10.1007/s10583-016-9309-z.

Reynolds, R. (2014). *Teaching Humanities and Social Sciences in the Primary School*, 3rd edn. Melbourne: Oxford University Press.

Short, K., Lynch-Brown, C. & Tomlinson, C. (2014). *The Essentials of Children's Literature*, 8th edn. New York: Pearson Education.

Singh, M. (2005). Education, socio-economic change and globalisation: Learning, creativity and the knowledge-based innovation economy. Paper presented to the Annual Conference of the Pacific Circle Consortium, Sydney.

Sipe, L.R. & Panteleo, S. (2008). *Postmodern Picturebooks: Play, parody and self-referentiality*. London: Routledge.

Stephens, J. (1992). *Language and Ideology in Children's Fiction*. London: Longman.

Winch, G., Ross Johnston, R., Holliday, M., Ljungdahl, L. & March, P. (2004). *Literacy: Reading, writing and children's literature*, 2nd edn. Melbourne: Oxford University Press.

Winch, G., Ross Johnston, R., March, P., Ljungdahl, L. & Holliday, M. (2014). *Literacy: Reading, writing and children's literature*, 5th edn. Melbourne: Oxford University Press.

# EFFECTIVE ASSESSMENT PRACTICES

## 15

*Susanne Jones and Carmel Dineen*

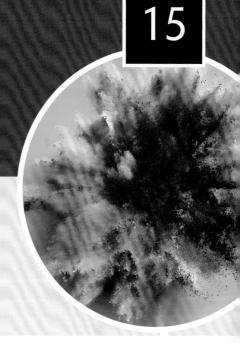

### Learning objectives

After reading this chapter, you should be able to:
- understand the purpose of assessment
- consider assessment literacy and identity
- recognise quality assessment tasks
- collect evidence of student learning for validation through moderation.

## INTRODUCTION

> The fundamental purpose of assessment in education is to establish and understand where students are in an aspect of their learning at the time of the assessment. (Masters 2014, pp. 1–2)

Assessment is a fundamental part of the design process of teaching and learning. Educators knowing and understanding their own beliefs and values about the professional work they do in assessment is crucial to learner success and progress. Being able and willing to write quality assessment tasks, to collect the evidence of student learning and to moderate this evidence with colleagues are all part of the science and art of being a professional in education. Assessment enables the educator to understand what students have learnt and determine what they will learn next. It allows educators to set goals for improvement, design the learning program in collaboration with learners beginning with the end in mind, and monitor progress. Educators are continually assessing and this chapter endeavours to make sense of this important professional skill, which impacts on teaching and learning. To illustrate these ideas and skills in relation to Humanities and Social Sciences (HASS), examples from the *Australian Curriculum: HASS* will be used.

## UNDERSTANDING THE PURPOSE OF ASSESSMENT

Assessment is the process of collecting and interpreting evidence to make judgements about student learning, with the link between standards, content and learning activities providing opportunities for rich assessment. Assessment is used by educators and learners to decide where learners are in their learning, where they need to go and how best to get there. Assessment is linked in the Australian Curriculum to the achievement standards:

> The Australian Curriculum achievement standards are an important focus for teachers in initial planning and programming of teaching and learning activities. They provide teachers with a statement of learning expected of students at the end of a year or band of years, and assist in developing teaching and learning programs. (ACARA 2018b)

Many educators consider the marking of learners' work to be a challenging task. Educators talk about how they 'just know' where a learner is in their learning, and assessment is not necessarily planned for. This idea was challenged when a group of South Australian Department for Education HASS educators from Foundation to Year 10 came together in 2014 to focus on designing quality teaching in HASS, including designing the assessment **tasks** from the beginning of the planning – in other words, to begin with the end in mind; that is, backward planning (see Chapter 2). Their challenge was to design learning and assessment that would maximise student engagement and achievement. Before beginning, the educators found that a thorough understanding of the HASS curriculum was essential, including knowledge, skills and concepts (the content) and the achievement standards. They also determined that deep educator consideration of how learners' knowledge, conceptual understandings and skills change with increasing proficiency is crucial in assessing and measuring progress and achievement. The third key message that came from this planning was the importance and desirability of educators planning collaboratively, especially on designing effective assessment.

> **tasks**: refer to assessment tasks designed to assess learning; different from classroom activities that are sometimes called tasks, particularly in primary settings

There is only one fundamental purpose of assessment in education, and that is to establish 'where students are in their learning', which 'means establishing what they know, understand and can do . . . to establish and understand where students (either as individuals or groups) are in an aspect of their learning at the time of assessment' (Masters 2014, pp. 1–2).

> **feedback**: targeted information provided to learners during the assessment process which is clear, meaningful and leads to further learning

To help learners make progress, **feedback** must be precise, diagnostic, based on success criteria and task specific. To provide this feedback, educators must have an understanding of misconceptions as well as substantial knowledge of what learners are expected to know, understand and be able to do. The focus on assessment helps learners know exactly what to do to improve their knowledge and understanding, and inquiry and skills, in HASS – not just their grade for reporting. Assessment is far more positive and useful to learners when they are given opportunities to respond to feedback and improve their work.

When sharing a learner's progress and achievement in HASS with parents/carers, educators should focus on the evidence of their learning, rather than on **grades** alone. This includes whether they know, understand and have skills in History, Geography, Civics and Citizenship and/or Economics and Business, and how to support a learner's particular learning needs in HASS. When reporting to parents/carers, the information must be easy to understand and be as consistent as possible across the school.

> **grades**: student achievement reported as A, B, C, D or E (or word equivalent) for each subject/learning area studied

# Assessment principles

The research-based principles of assessment shown in Figure 15.1 guide teachers in effective classroom practice. They:

1. are part of planning for effective teaching and learning

2. focus on how and what students learn

3. involve educators and learners in reflection, conversation and decision-making about how learning can be improved

4. are a key professional skill (AITSL 2015) for educators in observing learning, providing feedback and supporting learners in peer and self-assessment

5. provide sensitive and constructive comments that focus on the learning

6. focus on encouraging learners by emphasising progress and achievement

7. link to clear **assessment criteria** from the achievement standard using exemplars of quality learning

8. provide learners with guidance about how to improve

9. teach learners how to self-assess to become reflective and self-managing students

10. recognise all learners and their learning and are fair, valid and reliable.

**assessment criteria**: assessment designed to enable learners to show their learning against predetermined criteria, including achievement standards

If assessment is reliable, the results from that assessment will be consistent, dependable and able to be replicated. In other words, educators and learners are confident that the assessment will truly reflect what they know, understand and can do. Having clear success criteria to measure against the achievement standard, and collaboratively moderating learning, also increase reliability. This leads to consistency and confidence in the judgements educators make about where learners are in their learning and quality assures grades for reporting. The validity of assessment will be compromised if it does not reflect the content, knowledge, skills and understandings that learners have been taught.

# Effective assessment

How do educators and learners make sense of assessment? How does the educator know students have learnt what was taught? A further question is: what decisions will the educator make with the assessment information?

*Formative assessment* is also known as reflective teaching or assessment *for* learning, depending on when the research was written or who has written it. All of these terms generally agree that this assessment term refers to providing ongoing evidence of individual learner progress towards understanding concepts, gaining knowledge and using skills. This assessment can be formal products in the form of written short answers or extended writing, oral responses, tests or models; or it can be informal in the form of questioning, checklists and observations. One of the great joys of teaching HASS is in the discussion, questioning and debate that happen every day in the classroom. To assess this, educators could include a short quiz or informal debate to

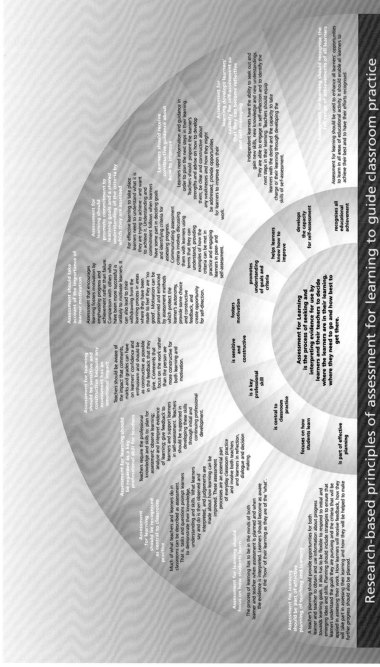

FIGURE 15.1  Assessment for learning

Source: Assessment Reform Group 2002, p. 2

check for learner knowledge and understanding of events, developments, challenges or decision-making.

*Summative assessment* is generally defined as assessing at a point in time and is also referred to as assessment *of* learning. This type of assessment is usually at the end of a unit of work or teaching period.

Educators will use a range of methods of assessment, such as standardised tests, classroom observations, performance assessments, written exams and authentic tasks. Often these distinctions are presented as either/or options and may result in unhelpful divisions in the understanding of assessment. No one assessment purpose or method is better or worse than another. What is useful is to determine the way the assessment information is used. Supporting this in his article 'Assessment: Getting to the essence', Geoff Masters (2014, pp. 1–2) writes about assessment becoming over-conceptualised and over-complicated. He determines that it is more important to determine how assessment is used, and so he uses the phrase 'assessment and learning' to cover all assessment.

Educators should think about using assessment as a means of diagnosing where learners are in their learning and what to do with that information. **Diagnostic assessment** refers to the level of detail the educator is seeking and how they will use that information; for example:

**diagnostic assessment**: designed to identify specific areas of understanding and learning needs

- at a general level where a learner is in their proficiency of a HASS subject in relation to broader enduring ideas that underpin HASS, such as the key ideas
- in more detail within one of the four sub-strands
- at a more detailed level of their progress within each strand of HASS; that is, knowledge and understanding or inquiry and skills.

This means that assessment is about the degree of information collected rather than how it is collected.

At a national level, the Australian Professional Standards for Teachers (APST) Standard 5, in the professional practice domain, articulates what educators are expected to know and be able to do regarding assessment. This makes clear that knowing and understanding assessment do matter. This standard has focus areas and descriptors that provide characteristics within the complex process of teaching (AITSL 2015).

How would you answer this question for learners and parents/carers: 'Why does assessment matter?' If you are at Graduate level in the five focus areas for APST Standard 5, consider the gaps for you in the assessment focus areas.

# BEING ASSESSMENT LITERATE

Educators' capabilities to conduct classroom assessment and use assessment evidence are central to quality assessment practice; this is traditionally conceptualised as assessment literacy (Looney et al. 2016, p. 1). Assessment literacy is the ability to apply assessment knowledge and an understanding of the assessment principles to school and classroom situations and challenges (Ridden & Heldsinger 2015, p. 5).

The language of the assessment must be accessible so that each learner can access every task. Increasing verbosity makes any task less accessible for some learners. For example, 'Determine the means of survival of homo sapiens in an arid environment' can be made more accessible if worded: 'How do people live in the desert?'

Changing language from passive to active can also make it easier for learners to understand what is being asked of them. For example, 'Why was the Antarctic desert crossed by Mawson?' can become 'Why did Mawson cross the Antarctic desert?' Using dot points or a table may be a more accessible way for educators to present information in a task; or differentiating can accommodate the 'readability' or reading age of any selected text.

The way educators see themselves as professionals, their attitudes and beliefs around assessment and how they perceive their role in the assessment process will all be significant and impact on their classroom assessment. It is therefore important for educators to understand the literacy associated with assessment.

## Assessment literacy for educators

Assessment measures progress and achievement, so how educators think about assessment influences how they think about learning and learners. To become assessment literate:

- Know what effective questions to pose to the class to determine how well they have understood a concept or the depth of their knowledge.
- Use assessment to collect information data that can be understood, about whole classes and individual learners, to judge progress and further inform future planning and teaching.
- Build assessment into all lessons and be able to redirect the teaching based on the information collected.
- Provide feedback that is clear, meaningful and useful to the individual learner.
- Create tasks that provide learners with meaningful information about where they are in their learning in relation to knowledge, skills and conceptual understandings.
- Recognise which mode of assessment is most appropriate given the context and purpose of the assessment task.
- Communicate accurate achievement and progress information effectively to learners and parents.
- Understand how to use assessment to maximise learner engagement and learning by involving learners in assessment recording and communication.

Reflection

Write and share some effective questions to ask Year 2 learners to find out their understanding of the significance of a local event in their community.

Design a way to record assessment information for a class of learners that will inform the next steps in learning and reporting, and involve learners.

What is an appropriate mode of assessment to assess Year 4 learners' ability to record and represent data about early Australian exploration? Now think of another mode to assess the same skills.

# DESIGNING EFFECTIVE ASSESSMENT

Leaders and educators in schools develop systems and structures to ensure effective teaching and monitoring of learning progress. Within these structures, educators design assessment tasks that have increasing complexity and differentiated success criteria.

As educators design learning programs, they clearly identify the **learning intentions**, strategies, resources and assessment modes, use **data** and evidence to identify learner needs and tailor differentiated programs to meet the needs of all learners.

When educators talk about **authentic** tasks, they are asking students to consider their response to a real and relevant challenge, event or situation. HASS has many opportunities for designing tasks that are authentic. For example, to provide learners with opportunities to show they understand empathy, educators might set tasks that include personal aspects of real people in real places in real time. In Year 3 this may mean learners researching an ANZAC service person who lived in the local district and is remembered through a commemoration place in the community. The naming of places within the town may also be explored both historically and geographically. Educators may provide opportunities for learners to explore connections between people and places. Again, in Year 3 this may be through considering the perspective of a family in Australia and a family in Indonesia, which might involve a deeper look at the significance and differences of social and cultural celebrations in these communities, including artworks, music, dance and food.

Authentic tasks give learners opportunities to use a range of skills, which are evident in the second paragraph of the relevant achievement standard in the Australian Curriculum. When used together, they make tasks richer and more meaningful. When asking learners to show understanding of chronology, educators can consider asking them to produce a timeline that shows more than the events being studied, and includes developments both nationally and globally. This provides an opportunity for learners to meet the achievement standard at Year 4, where learners sequence information about events and the lives of

**learning intentions**: the educator shares the learning intention with learners to direct their attention to the learning and emphasise what they will *learn*, rather than what they will *do*

**data**: assessment information collected, documented and used by educators at the system, school and individual level to provide information about learning achievement and progress

**authentic assessment**: related to real-world people, issues and solutions, as well as creating worthwhile products

individuals in chronological order with reference to key dates; and at Year 5, where learners sequence information about events, the lives of individuals and selected phenomena in chronological order using timelines.

## FAMILY STORIES AND AUTHENTIC TASKS

Involve learners in creating engaging, worthwhile artefacts that show their learning. This could include Year 1 learners producing a display for the community library that depicts their family stories now, from the past and in different places. For example, this could be a great-grandparent's recorded story of their past life in China and in Australia, including places on maps. The Year 1 achievement standard includes 'sharing stories about the past, and presenting observations and findings using everyday terms to denote the passing of time and to describe direction and location' (ACARA 2018c).

Above all, authentic tasks allow seamlessness between the sequence of classroom learning and assessment tasks.

## Characteristics of quality assessment activities

It is important to develop and use quality assessment, which should:

- be underpinned by agreed assessment principles
- have clear assessment criteria from the achievement standard that have been made known to the learners in advance
- provide a range of opportunities for learners to demonstrate what they know, understand and can do
- align directly with the Australian Curriculum content and achievement standard
- inform the educator and learner about what needs to be learnt next
- address the diverse needs and abilities of learners, and differentiates the assessment to be inclusive of all learners. While teaching the knowledge and understanding for the age-appropriate year level, educators may consider using an achievement standard from a year level other than that in which the learner is placed to assess the learning. For example, in Year 5 learners learn about Australian settlement. At the Year 5 level, the achievement standard asks learners to *describe* the *significance of people in bringing about change*. It may be appropriate to assess some learners against the Year 3 achievement standard to *identify individuals that have significance in the present*.

The *Australian Curriculum: HASS* outlines specific content in the two interrelated strands of knowledge and understanding and inquiry and skills for each of the four sub-strands. These govern what is taught and assessed. In HASS, students develop key historical, geographical, civics and economic knowledge of people, places, values and systems, past and present, in local to global contexts (ACARA 2018d).

Specific assessment activities are designed to collect evidence of where learners are in their learning. When designing assessment in HASS educators should consider the following:

- Tasks should enable the collection of evidence of learners' conceptual understanding using evidence from the knowledge strand of each sub-strand.

- The last sentence of each achievement standard emphasises communication and is where literacy demands can be met. For example, in Year 4 learners present their conclusions about an environmental issue using HASS-specific language, such as significance of place, change, climate, community responsibility and economic viability in a digital or oral presentation or a poster or debate.

- Short tasks should be provided that require learners to apply their knowledge, skills and conceptual understandings in new contexts. In Year 6, after an actual or virtual experience with a state or territory parliament, learners can show their understanding of democratic law by debating a new bill that enforces strict curfews on young people under the age of 13, for example.

- Specific skills – for example, primary *or* secondary sources – are focused on to give learners opportunities to show holistic understanding rather than trying to cover too much, which may lead to fragmented responses.

- Inquiry questions can be used to allow learners to sharpen their focus and foster deep thinking. Using the inquiry questions in the year level description for Year 6 – *How have key figures, events and values shaped Australian society, its system of government and citizenship* – can become: *What did Henry Parkes do to shape the federation of the Australian colonies?*

- Learning should be assessed from beyond the classroom; for example, via fieldwork excursions, guest speakers and visitors from business and the community, museums and institutions.

- Tasks must be supported with clear success criteria that can be developed with learners using previous excellent exemplars.

- Think of the highest responses likely from the task, and then what would be considered satisfactory to ensure all learners can engage with it.

- Collaborate with other educators when designing effective assessment tasks that align with the achievement standard.

- Propose actions for a geographical issue or challenge. This should provide a positive focus and not just be about 'problems'. An example might be to propose an improved urban public transport system rather than the generalised 'problem' of urban pollution.

- The application of spatial technology – for example, Google Earth – should be evident in the assessment.

- Learners should be provided opportunities to be involved in fieldwork and demonstrate fieldwork skills, such as observing and recording information in the field.
- Oral presentations, historical accounts, journals and empathy writing should be included.

**Reflection**

How well do you know the achievement standards? What steps will you take to familiarise yourself with them?

If sharing assessment tasks with colleagues, is the assessment valid in terms of content, literacy and numeracy skills, and the culture or background of learners?

## Collaborative problem-solving

Collaborative problem-solving is a 21st-century skill and a highly desirable capability. In the HASS classroom there could be a risk of overusing this pedagogy because stories, discussion and communicating are essential to humanities education. Educators need to use collaborative work wisely, with learners prepared with the skills to be able to do this well. This involves educators carefully planning how to assess when learners work together on inquiry and how to determine how they will present and communicate their action response to a challenge.

In collaborative problem-solving, resources are divided between learners, rather than focusing on roles or tasks. Learners will then be dependent on each other to answer the inquiry or solve the problem; for example, the primary and secondary sources are used for different purposes in the inquiry. What is important is being able to see the thinking in which learners have engaged, not simply the product at the end. Learners can be asked about their participation in the task. This is valid data on how well they may have cooperated and demonstrated the skills of collaborative problem-solving, and links to the personal and social capability (ACARA 2018a), where the social management element is clear, specific to the task and connected to the HASS curriculum.

## Quality evidence

When assessing learners, educators need to be able to collect and report on evidence of learning. They can do this in a number of ways, one of which is rubrics. These are teaching tools that make explicit to learners what they need to show they understand, know and can do. Rubrics should be task-specific and qualitatively, not quantitatively, defined. The descriptors in a rubric should describe the quality of the learning – for example, in-depth understanding, thorough knowledge, high-level competence – rather than the quantity – for example, some, few or many. In other words, the benefit to educators is the clarity about the quality expected before giving the task to learners. Rubrics also communicate expectations to learners about the anticipated responses and quality of work associated with the task.

Rubrics should use the language, particularly the verbs, of the achievement standard. This assists with educator judgement when allocating a grade because it specifies benchmarks for success.

In order to use rubrics to provide evidence of progress, they need to be designed using a clear sense of the specific knowledge, concepts and skills across the year levels of HASS. This requires expert knowledge of the learning area of HASS and each sub-strand within the learning area. When connecting sub-strands – for example, History and Civics and Citizenship – aspects of both achievement standards should be evident in the rubric.

All rubrics, if provided to learners with the assessment task, will require significant explanation to clarify distinctions between the levels. The same is true if a rubric is shared between educators.

As learning progresses, it becomes more complex. The structure of the observed learning outcome, **SOLO**, is a means of classifying learning outcomes in terms of their complexity, enabling educators to assess learners' work in terms of its quality, not how many parts of it they have 'got right' (Biggs & Collis 1982).

> **SOLO**: structure of the observed learning outcome – a taxonomy, which is a model of learning that describes student responses at five different levels of complexity

SOLO was developed by two Australian researchers (Biggs & Collis 1982) who studied the learning outcomes of a range of learners from preschool to adulthood in a wide range of intellectual and physical skills and understanding. In its simplest form, SOLO describes five levels towards the understanding of any concept; for example, for Year 5 HASS characteristics of places:

- *Prestructural* – does not/unable to engage with the concept at any level other than basic vocabulary; for example, describes basic or irrelevant features of places or environment; for example, the sea is blue, the hills are big.
- *Unistructural* – knows one thing/idea related to the concept; for example, the river ends at the sea.
- *Multistructural* – knows more than one thing about the concept, but sees only the obvious connections between them; for example, describes weather conditions, describes physical and human features of places, describes conditions humans need to survive in this place.
- *Relational* – understands how the ideas fit together to form the big picture of the concept; for example, explains how the physical features of a place influence human use of that place.
- *Extended abstract* – can identify the key aspects of the concept and apply them to other contexts; for example, describes and explains a range of human adaptations to different places.

To apply the SOLO taxonomy, educators start by thinking about learners' understanding of a History or Geography concept. Educators look at examples of learning for evidence of students avoiding or not engaging with the concept (prestructural), reproducing facts and processes as they were learnt (unistructural/multistructural), then using the concept as a whole in the context the educator provided and taking this to a context where they have not worked with it before (extended abstract). To ensure learners have opportunities to provide evidence of relational or extended abstract thinking, educators should ask whether the task allowed them to do this. Using learner work samples of a high level is helpful for illustrating expected performance and clarifying what described levels mean (Goss & Hunter 2015, pp. 41–2).

For example, in a Year 6 class, learners were having difficulty interpreting a primary source to answer an inquiry question. To clarify expectations, the educator took an example of an 'A' piece of work from a previous class and asked learners, in pairs, to define and describe what they believed made this achieve an 'A' level against the achievement standard. This was followed by a whole-class discussion where all ideas were shared. This strategy proved so successful that every learner in the class achieved satisfactory or above on this activity. The educator in this example has continued to use this strategy of collecting learner work samples as models that illustrate the expectations described in the rubric or success criteria.

## EDUCATOR TIP

Assessment tasks are never important in themselves. They are transient and changeable. Tasks are a convenient way of collecting evidence of where a learner is in their learning. They provide evidence of what is unobservable. They show progress. No one assessment method is better than any other.

Reflection How would you work with students using rubrics and examples of work to help them improve their learning? What are some of the benefits of collecting and keeping evidence of learning?

# COLLECTING EVIDENCE AND MAKING JUDGEMENTS

## Portfolios

**portfolio**: a collection of evidence, over time, which aligns with the Australian Curriculum achievement standard for one particular learner and is used for collaborative moderation purposes

A **portfolio** comprises a set of a learner's work samples that, when considered in an on-balance way, will provide an accurate picture of the learning across the year in relation to the relevant achievement standard in the Australian Curriculum. A portfolio should comprise as many work samples as necessary from one learner to demonstrate learning against the achievement standard.

## Collecting evidence of learning in a portfolio

A student's evidence of learning is collected in a portfolio to provide a true picture of learning across the year against the HASS achievement standard and to be used in the **collaborative moderation**: process. Schools will make decisions about how many students in each year level will have their evidence of learning collected in a portfolio to be used in the moderation process.

**collaborative moderation** process of educators working together to make consistent professional judgements about the evidence of learning in a portfolio for reporting purposes

The usefulness of portfolios in assisting educators in the moderation process to make on-balance judgements about learner progress and achievement depends on how well the portfolio contents provide evidence that address the achievement standard over the year. The evidence in a learner portfolio should contain:

- high-quality assessment activities
- sufficient work samples against the aspects of the achievement standard taught to this point in time – this could include anecdotal records, checklists, photos, videos
- a cover sheet that shows links to the Australian Curriculum achievement standard (what is being assessed) and content description (what has been taught).

The development of portfolios should start early in the year to ensure educators have adequate evidence against the achievement standard prior to moderation and reporting.

## Collaborative moderation

When educators gather information to provide valid information on learner progress and achievement, they recognise that A–E grades for reporting require professional judgements that are informed and consistent. They must be quality assured. These professional judgements are an integral part of the picture of student learning, along with the National Assessment Program – Literacy and Numeracy (NAPLAN), progressive achievement tests (PAT) and other data sets.

Educators make professional judgements about student achievement on a daily basis – it is a key professional skill. When they assign A–E grades and report these to parents or carers, they want to be confident that the grades are fair and consistent. Educators recognise that to be highly regarded, their professional judgements need to be consistent, informed, reliable and of high quality. This is vital in valuing the daily work of educators and in ensuring public confidence in the education system. Educators need to be able to demonstrate with certainty that learning is at the expected standard and that schools are meeting the goals of education.

Collaborative moderation is one of the most effective methods of assuring quality judgements, as it strengthens the consistency of educators' judgements. Quality assured through moderation processes assures that a 'C' is a 'C' no matter where or when it was assigned. Working with colleagues across schools to consider students' evidence of learning through collaborative moderation ensures that educator judgements are adjusted or validated, quality is assured and assessment practices are deprivatised; that is, sharing their practice openly and honestly.

One of the most powerful value-added aspects of collaborative moderation is the professional learning that occurs. Educators reflect on their own practice, share strategies with others, enhance their understanding of the achievement standards and content descriptors, confirm their judgements and adjust their teaching and assessment for improved learning.

It is important for educators to have confidence in their assessment practices, in the feedback that they give to learners and in the information they provide for parents/carers about their child's progress, including grades in a report. Quality assuring educators' judgements through the collaborative moderation process can provide that confidence (Department for Education and Child Development South Australia 2016).

# CONCLUSION

The subjects of History, Geography, Civics and Citizenship, and Economics and Business give learners a broad understanding of what it is to participate in the political, social, economic, cultural and physical world. Through the learning of HASS, they develop skills in questioning, critical thinking, problem-solving, communicating, decision-making and adapting to change. Knowing whether learners have learnt what was taught is the heart of educators' work. Designing quality assessment is hard. Educators need to be prepared to work with colleagues to design, reflect and redesign assessment tasks, and share practice through the learning activities and evidence of learning. This can be achieved by educators giving professional considered feedback to other educators and being open to receiving feedback. It is educators' professional responsibility to develop and improve their assessment capability so that students have every opportunity to demonstrate their learning and can progress and achieve to their highest capacity.

## REVIEW QUESTIONS

1. What is the purpose of assessment?

2. What is the relationship between teaching and assessment?

3. How will you check for learner understanding during teaching activities?

4. When will learners have opportunities to self- and peer-assess and provide feedback to each other? How will you provide the skills and opportunities for this to happen?

5. When collecting portfolios, what will you need to consider to ensure they are useful in the collaborative moderation process?

6. How will you provide timely, meaningful and useful feedback that directly relates to your learning intentions? How will you make sure learners read or hear the feedback and not just the grade?

## LEARNING EXTENSION

1. Research principles of assessment and determine your top five and how you will use them in your practice.

2. Dylan Wiliam has written extensively about reflective teaching and formative assessment. What strategies and techniques does he recommend to improve student learning outcomes?

3. How will you provide multiple opportunities for learners to provide evidence of what they have learnt?

4. What is meant by *differentiation in learning*? Describe some ways of differentiating the learning and assessment activities in the classroom.

5. Describe ways to use assessment to achieve maximum learner engagement and learning through involving them in the assessment.

## REFERENCES

ACARA (Australian Curriculum, Assessment and Reporting Authority). (2018a). *Australian Curriculum: F-10, v8.3*. General capabilities. Retrieved from: https://www.australiancurriculum .edu.au/f-10-curriculum/general-capabilities/personal-and-social-capability.

——(2018b). *Australian Curriculum: F-10, v8.3*. Implications for teaching, assessing and reporting. Retrieved from: https://www.australiancurriculum.edu.au/f-10-curriculum/ implications-for-teaching-assessing-and-reporting.

——(2018c). *Australian Curriculum: F-10, v8.3*. Year 1 achievement standard. Retrieved from: https://www.australiancurriculum.edu.au/f-10-curriculum.

——(2018d). *AustralianCurriculum: Humanities and Social Sciences F-10, v8.3*. Aims. Retrieved from: https://www.australiancurriculum.edu.au/f-10-curriculum/humanities-and-social-sciences/hass/aims.

AITSL (Australian Institute for Teaching and School Leadership). (2015). Australian Professional Standards for Teachers, Standard 5. Retrieved from: https://www.aitsl.edu.au/docs/default-source/general/australian-professional-standands-for-teachers-20171006.pdf?sfvrsn= 399ae83c_12.

Assessment Reform Group (2002). Assessment for Learning: 10 principles. Retrieved from: http://www.hkeaa.edu.hk/DocLibrary/SBA/HKDSE/Eng_DVD/doc/Afl_principles.pdf.

Biggs, J. & Collis, K. (1982). Evaluating the quality of learning: The SOLO taxonomy. Retrieved from: http://www.johnbiggs.com.au/academic/solo-taxonomy.

Department for Education and Child Development South Australia. (2016). Moderation matters: A guide to leading collaborative moderation in schools. Retrieved from: http://dlb.sa.edu.au/ ctmoodle/pluginfile.php/3316/mod_resource/content/1/moderationmatters.pdf.

Goss P. & Hunter J. (2015). *Targeted Teaching: How better use of data can improve student learning*. Melbourne: Grattan Institute.

Looney, A., Cumming, J., van Der Kleij, F. & Harris, K. (2017). Reconceptualising the role of teachers as assessors: Teacher assessment identity. *Assessment in Education: Principles, Policy and Practice*, doi: 10.1080/0969594X.2016.1268090.

Masters, G. (2014). Assessment: Getting to the essence. *Designing the Future*, 1. Centre for Assessment Reform and Innovation. Melbourne: ACER Press. Retrieved from: https://www.acer.org/files/uploads/Assessment_Getting_to_the_essence.pdf.

Ridden, P. & Heldsinger, S. (2015). *What Teachers Need to Know About Assessment and Reporting*. Melbourne: ACER Press.

# PART IV
# Integration across cross-curriculum priorities

# THE GENERAL CAPABILITIES' SYNERGY WITH HASS

16

**Malcolm McInerney, Deborah Green and Deborah Price**

## Learning objectives

After reading this chapter, you should be able to:

- understand learners' perspectives of their capability as citizens
- understand the nature, place and purpose of the general capabilities in the Australian Curriculum
- illustrate the relevance of each of the general capabilities to Humanities and Social Sciences (HASS) through the aims, content, understandings and skills of History, Geography, Civics and Citizenship, and Economics and Business
- explore the idea that the general capabilities can be identified assessments of HASS.

## INTRODUCTION

> Schools play a vital role in promoting the intellectual, physical, social, emotional, moral, spiritual and aesthetic development and wellbeing of young Australians, and in ensuring the nation's ongoing economic prosperity and social cohesion. (MCEETYA 2008)

In aspiring for world-class education, the *Melbourne Declaration on Educational Goals for Young Australians* (Melbourne Declaration; MCEETYA 2008) provided the blueprint for the subsequent development of the Australian Curriculum. Preparing learners for the 21st century meant encouraging Australian schools to address not only academic achievement but also their holistic development and wellbeing. Subsequently, during the Australian Curriculum design process, some of the approaches to achieving these goals were identified as not solely fitting into the traditional content learning areas. Rather, it was argued by some that such approaches needed to be immersed across learning areas. This was to ensure that intellectual, physical, social, emotional, moral, spiritual and aesthetic development and wellbeing of young Australians were respected and treated as part of the teaching and learning requirements and as a student entitlement. Hence, the general capabilities and cross-curriculum priorities were created as additional dimensions to be embedded across learning areas and purported to be of equal importance. The seven capabilities aim to develop the knowledge, skills, behaviours and dispositions that, together with curriculum content in each learning area and the cross-curriculum priorities, will assist learners to live and work successfully in the 21st century as confident and creative individuals, and active and informed citizens (ACARA 2018b).

The Melbourne Declaration considered that schooling required 'a broader frame', and therefore the following elements were proposed as essential when designing learning in Australian schools:

- a respect for cultural and religious diversity and the sense of global citizenship
- literacy and numeracy skills
- the promotion of an active and informed citizenship with moral and ethical integrity
- creative problem-solving approaches
- information and communication skills and awareness
- social interaction capacity of individuals and awareness of personal values and attributes
- development of confident and creative individuals
- outcomes for Indigenous Australians
- an ability to relate to and communicate across cultures, especially the cultures and countries of Asia
- sustaining and improving natural and social environment pressures (MCEETYA 2008, pp. 5–10).

The resulting curriculum with learning areas, general capabilities and cross-curriculum priorities has been referred to as a three-dimensional curriculum that sets out to meet the broader curriculum frame in terms of intent and aims of the goals of Australian schooling as delineated in the Melbourne Declaration (see Figure 16.1).

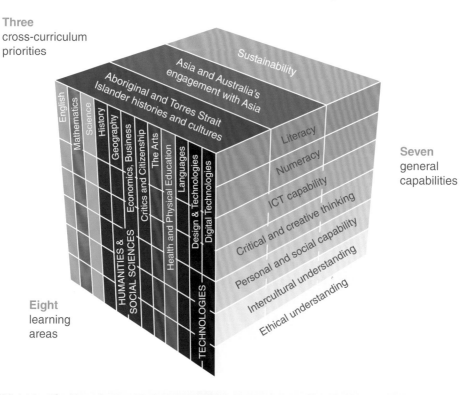

FIGURE 16.1 The Foundation–Year 10 Australian Curriculum is described as a three-dimensional curriculum that recognises: the central importance of disciplinary knowledge, skills and understanding; general capabilities; and cross-curriculum priorities.
Source: ACARA 2018a

From your educator perspective, be creative and develop another three-dimensional visual representation that reflects how you perceive the interrelationship between the Australian Curriculum learning areas, general capabilities and cross-curriculum priorities that would be a useful tool to describe the curriculum to other educators.

While there has been uncertainty around the nature, role and implementation of the general capabilities, this chapter presents opportunities to explore the place and nature of the general capabilities in young people's learning and, in particular, their relevance and very real synergy with the HASS learning area.

## CITIZEN CAPACITY: WHAT DO LEARNERS THINK?

While not specifically addressing the general capabilities, it is a useful starting point to consider what learners think about their capacity as citizens in society, as this has the potential to inform the range of humanities-based capabilities that are implicit in the general capabilities. The 2016 National Assessment Program sample testing of Civics and Citizenship (NAP-CC) unearthed interesting data in relation to learners' attitudes and perceptions of living in and being a citizen in Australia (ACARA 2017).

The attitudinal survey component of the NAP-CC found that 74 per cent of learners in both Year 6 and Year 10 (ACARA 2017) considered it to be important to:

- learn about political issues
- participate in activities that benefit the local community
- promote human rights and protect the environment.

Another interesting finding revealed that Year 6 learners had very high levels of trust (complete trust of quite a lot of civic institutions), including in national (76%), state (79%) and local government (79%), the law courts (80%) and the police (90%). Interestingly, they demonstrated significantly less trust in the media (56%) and social media (37%).

In relation to attitudes towards Indigenous cultures, Year 6 students showed very strong agreement (more than 89%) to the following statements:

- Australia should support the cultural traditions and languages of Indigenous Australians.
- Australia has a responsibility to improve the quality of life of Indigenous Australians.
- It is important to recognise the traditional ownership of the land by Indigenous Australians.
- All Australians have much to learn from Indigenous Australian cultures and traditions and people.
- All Australians should be given the chance to learn about reconciliation between Indigenous and other Australians.

(ACARA 2017, p. 68)

In terms of cultural diversity, these Year 6 learners strongly endorsed the idea that Australia benefited greatly from having people from many cultures and backgrounds (84% agreement), and that immigrants should be encouraged to keep their cultural traditions and languages (84% agreement), and this highlights the development of the general capability of intercultural understanding. Other insightful questions from the NAP-CC related to students' civic-related participation at school, as these questions can be interpreted as relating to a learner's personal and social capacity. The results in this area are less positive than those related to institutional trust and cultural understanding as described above. Of Year 6 students, only 62 per cent (66% female and 57% male) identified that they had participated in activities in the community. While it is understandable that not all Year 6 learners, being relatively young, would be involved in community activities, the results for the Year 10 NAP-CC learners showed that by Year 10, these learners had generally disengaged with the community. Despite the majority of Year 6–10 students agreeing that it is important to engage in activities that benefit the local community, the overall results for Year 10 learners evidenced that during the last few years:

- 30 per cent collected money for a charity or social cause
- 34 per cent had been involved with a voluntary group helping the community
- 15 per cent participated in a youth organisation (scouts, cadets, youth clubs, etc.) (ACARA 2017).

Similarly, Year 6 females demonstrated a higher rate of community participation than males. Associated with this low participation was both Year 6 and 10 learners' relatively low interest in civics issues, with:

- 64 per cent reporting they were quite or very interested in what was happening in their local community
- 38 per cent were quite or very interested in Australian politics
- 60 per cent were quite or very interested in social issues in Australia (ACARA 2017).

Curiously, learners in both Year 6 and Year 10 were more interested in what was happening in other countries (75%) and global issues (74%).

Beyond just perception, the questions relating to engaging in civic action also provided insights into learners' social and personal capabilities as citizens. At Year 6 level, the results pertaining to confidence to actively engage in civics action were:

- 54 per cent were fairly or very confident to argue their opinion about a political or social issue
- 40 per cent were fairly or very confident to write an email to a newspaper to express their views on a current issue
- 45 per cent were fairly or very confident to give a speech to the class on a social or political issue
- 40 per cent were fairly or very confident to present information about a political or social issue on social media (ACARA 2017).

Although only a snapshot of the 2016 NAP-CC report, these responses provide insight into learners' thinking on and perceived capabilities in being active and informed citizens as we begin to discuss the nature and purpose of the general capabilities as a dimension of the curriculum. In many cases, we suggest that the general capabilities have a significant synergy with HASS and relevance to the citizenship attitudes and capacities that are developed in the HASS classroom.

## EDUCATOR TIP

Ask learners to design the attitudinal questions for the next NAP-CC testing. Ask them to think of some questions that they would like to include in the Year 6 test to inform them about the perceptions, attitudes and capacities of other learners in Australia, particularly in relation to being confident, creative and active and informed citizens.

## THE GENERAL CAPABILITIES

In addition to the three cross-curriculum priorities of Aboriginal and Torres Strait Islander histories and cultures, Asia and Australia's engagement with Asia, and Sustainability, the designers of the Australian Curriculum identified seven general capabilities. They are: literacy; numeracy; information and communication technology (ICT); critical and creative thinking; personal and social; intercultural understanding; and ethical understanding (ACARA 2018a). According to Reid (2009), the general capabilities are not new, as they appear to be an extension of the key competencies found in previous curriculum documents. It is important to acknowledge the considerable debate surrounding which capabilities and 21st-century skills young people need for optimal participation in society in the coming years. For example, a recent report by the Foundation for Young Australians (2017) states that today's 15-year-olds are likely to make 17 changes in employers across five different careers, and young people need to be prepared to learn on the job. The report identifies skills of problem-solving, critical thinking and judgement, entrepreneurial skills, interpersonal skills and creativity, among others, as essential to being work smart. Many of these skills are facilitated through the general capabilities of the Australian Curriculum and, given that it is Australia's first national curriculum, this chapter specifically addresses the documented general capabilities. Although the general capabilities are to be addressed in each learning area, Reid (2009) cautions against merely identifying them as opposed to embedding them in a meaningful way. Gilbert (2018) further challenges educators by advocating a developmental approach that connects the general capabilities deeply with content knowledge, concepts and inquiry skills rather than what Biesta and Priestley (2013) describe as a 'tick-box curriculum'. This section describes the general capabilities in general terms, before applying them specifically to the HASS learning area.

According to the Australian Curriculum, Assessment and Reporting Authority (ACARA 2018a), the general capabilities encompass knowledge, skills, behaviours and dispositions that, together with curriculum content in each learning area and the cross-curriculum priorities, will assist students to live and work successfully in the twenty-first century ... as confident and creative individuals, and active and informed citizens.

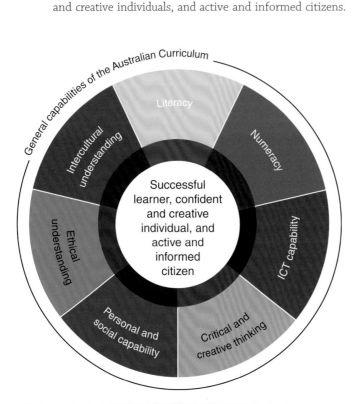

FIGURE 16.2 **The seven general capabilities of the Australian Curriculum**
Source: ACARA 2018b

## Summary of the general capabilities

### General capability 1: Literacy

**literacy**: the capability that develops the knowledge, skills and dispositions of learners to interpret and use language to participate effectively in society (ACARA 2018b)

This general capability aims to help learners become literate by developing the knowledge, skills and dispositions to interpret and use language to participate effectively in society. **Literacy** efficacy involves the confidence and ability to listen, read, view, speak, write and create oral, print, visual and digital texts. It enables learners to use and modify language for different purposes in a range of contexts and involves an ability to access, understand, analyse and evaluate information, make meaning, express thoughts and emotions, present ideas and opinions, interact with others and participate in activities at school and in their lives beyond school. Yet Hammond (2012) questions where learners with English as an additional language are placed within the Australian Curriculum and what guidance and support are provided for educators to ensure that these learners are supported in their literacy development.

## General capability 2: Numeracy

Learners become numerate by developing the knowledge and skills to use mathematics confidently in their studies and everyday life. **Numeracy** efficacy helps learners to develop the capacity to use mathematics in a wide range of situations, understanding the role of mathematics in the world and having the capacity to use mathematical knowledge and skills effectively. To be numerate involves the skills to measure, estimate and calculate with whole numbers; recognising and using patterns and relationships; using fractions, decimals, percentages, rations and rates; having spatial reasoning; and interpreting statistics. For this reason, there are a multitude of opportunities across learning areas for these skills to be developed (see Geiger et al. 2013; Goos, Dole & Geiger 2012).

**numeracy**: the capability that develops the knowledge and skills of students to use mathematics confidently in their studies and in their everyday life (ACARA 2018b)

## General capability 3: Information and communication technology (ICT) capability

Learners develop the **ICT capability** by learning to use ICT effectively and appropriately to access, create and communicate information and ideas, solve problems and work collaboratively in all learning areas and in their lives beyond an educational setting. This capability works towards learners making the most of the digital technologies available to them in a knowledge-based economy, and adapting to changes in technologies while limiting the risks to themselves and others. The use of digital environments transforms how learners think and learn, and gives them greater control over how, where and when they learn. As well as developing knowledge and skills related to information access, management and presentation, this capability focuses on learner research, analytical problem-solving/decision-making, communication, creative expression and empirical reasoning skills. Most importantly, learners develop critical literacy skills in relation to the use of ICT and its potential impact on individuals, groups and communities. The importance of this general capability is highlighted by the inclusion of multimodal texts in each of the achievement standards in the English learning area (Leu et al. 2011). Similarly, informational inquiry practices feature strongly in the Science learning area, while the use of ICT generally is a prominent feature in HASS.

**ICT capability**: develops the ability of learners to use ICT effectively and appropriately to access, create and communicate information and ideas, solve problems and work collaboratively (ACARA 2018b)

## General capability 4: Critical and creative thinking

> Thinking that is productive, purposeful and intentional is at the centre of effective learning. Responding to the challenges of the twenty-first century – with its complex environmental, social and economic pressures – requires young people to be creative, innovative, enterprising and adaptable, with the motivation, confidence and skills to use critical and creative thinking purposefully. (ACARA 2018b)

This general capability enables learners to develop the two strongly linked skills of critical and creative thinking as they learn to create and evaluate knowledge, clarify concepts and ideas, investigate possibilities, consider alternatives and solve problems. To do so, learners are encouraged to think widely and in depth by employing skills such as reasoning, logic, resourcefulness, imagination and innovation in their studies and everyday life.

With critical thinking, learners begin to develop an argument or point of view by using evidence and information to draw reasoned conclusions to solve problems. To think critically involves skills such as interpreting, analysing, evaluating, explaining, sequencing, reasoning, comparing, questioning, inferring, hypothesising, appraising, testing and generalising, all of which are crucial in everyday life.

Learners create and apply new ideas in different settings and view things in new ways while seeing and contemplating alternative explanations. To be creative in thinking may involve developing something original, analysing ideas to discover possibilities and constructing theories and objects. There are a range of outcomes of creative thinking, which may include representations and images, investigations, performance, and digital and computer-generated displays.

**critical and creative thinking**: the capability that develops critical and creative thinking as students learn to create and evaluate knowledge, clarify concepts and ideas, investigate possibilities, consider alternatives and solve problems (ACARA 2018b)

The importance of **critical and creative thinking** is not new – Vygotsky's (1978, 1987) theory, unlike many others of his time, included creativity as a central focus. Using Vygotsky's thinking around the transformative nature of emotions, Cross (2012) suggests that creativity is at the core of teaching and learning, as it engages learners and provides opportunities across all learning areas to develop critical and creative thinking. The *21st Century Readiness Act (Partnership for 21st Century Learning) 2011* identifies four core capabilities: critical thinking and problem-solving; communication; collaboration; and creativity and innovation. It suggests that for learners to be creative they need to have the knowledge of a wide range of techniques, and the ability to develop innovative and creative ideas, and be open with a responsive attitude towards new ideas. To be critical thinkers, the Act suggests that learners need to analyse how parts of a whole interact with each other to produce certain outcomes, which means they need to be trustful of reason, inquisitive, open and fair-minded (Partnership for 21st Century Learning 2011).

Figure 16.3 provides a diagrammatic representation of the critical and creative thinking general capability.

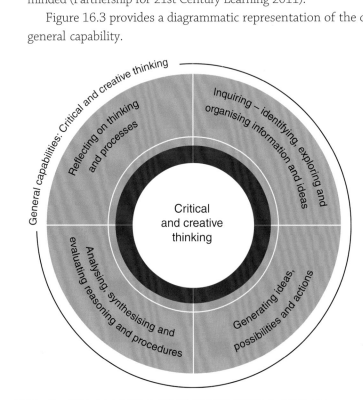

FIGURE 16.3 **The critical and creative thinking general capability**
Source: ACARA 2018b

Within this capability, the area of conceptualisation by the identification, understanding and application of concepts is fundamental to the development and application of critical and creative thinking. To be critical and creative thinkers, learners are encouraged to be inquisitive, fair and objective in thinking, intellectually flexible, and willing to do things, think differently and resolve to work through an issue or problem to seek a solution.

## PEOPLE AND THE ENVIRONMENT

Year 5 students are exploring how people and environments influence one another. To begin, they watch the video *MIDWAY: A message from the gyre: a short film by Chris Jordan from Midway* (3.54 minutes; see https://www.youtube.com/watch?v=hDiA5HgBl1M). This film was made in one of the most remote islands on the planet, where tens of thousands of baby albatrosses lie dead on the ground, their bodies filled with plastic from the Pacific Garbage Patch. Having viewed the video, learners are asked to research the issue of pollution and its impact on wildlife. As part of their research, they engage in developing their critical and creative capabilities through critical analysis and subsequent development of a creative plan to address the issue.

To stimulate thinking, learners will also watch *How the oceans can clean themselves: by Boyan Slat at TEDxDelft* (11.21 minutes; see https://www.youtube.com/watch?v=ROW9F-c0kIQ). Slat decided to dedicate half a year of research to understand plastic pollution and the problems associated with cleaning it up. His work ultimately led to his passive clean-up concept, which he presented at TEDxDelft 2012.

Learners present their solutions to the school assembly and local government representatives.

**SPOTLIGHT ON HASS EDUCATION**

## General capability 5: Personal and social capability

> The development of personal and social capability is a foundation for learning and for citizenship. (ACARA 2018b)

Learners often see the purpose of school as relating directly to employment whether this be via university, a trade or direct entry into the workforce. This means that supporting personal and social capabilities provides the basis for developing those soft skills that enable learners to be workplace ready (see also Chapter 1) (Klaus 2010; Maes, Weldy & Icenogel 1997; McInerney 2017; Mitchell, Skinner & White 2010; Nealy 2005; Smith 2007; Yates & Collins 2010). The **personal and social capability** aims for learners to understand themselves and others, manage their relationships, lives and work, and learn more effectively. To do so, the capability focuses on learners 'recognising and regulating emotions, developing empathy for others and understanding relationships, establishing and building positive relationships, making responsible decisions, working effectively in teams, handling challenging situations constructively and developing leadership skills' (ACARA 2018b), all of which are highly desirable skills in the workplace (see Figure 16.4).

**personal and social capability**: the capability that develops learners' understanding of themselves and others, to manage their relationships, lives and work, and to learn more effectively (ACARA 2018b)

An implication of this capability is for educational settings to provide opportunities for learners to manage themselves, relate to others, develop resilience and a sense of self-worth, resolve conflict and engage in teamwork in order to develop a degree of positivity about themselves and the world around them. The personal and social capability encompasses learners' personal/emotional and social/relational dispositions, intelligences, sensibilities and learning. It develops effective life skills for learners, including understanding themselves, their relationships, learning and work.

Reflection | What is the difference between a conversation and discussion? Which of the two do you think is most important in a classroom, and why?

Figure 16.4 provides a diagrammatic representation of the personal and social capability.

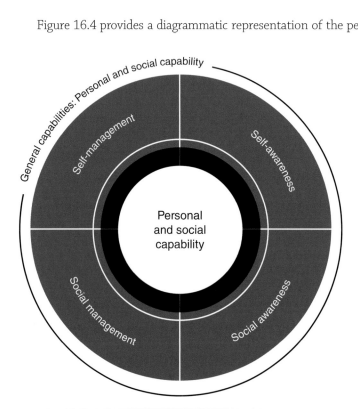

FIGURE 16.4   The personal and social capability
Source: ACARA 2018b

Reflection | Think of ways that you could redesign your classroom and teaching processes to encourage greater interaction between learners and improve opportunities for discussion and conversations.

## General capability 6: Intercultural understanding

> Three dispositions – expressing empathy, demonstrating respect and taking responsibility – have been identified as critical to the development of Intercultural Understanding in the Australian Curriculum. (ACARA 2018b)

As the world becomes more interconnected and societies grow increasingly multicultural, the need for intercultural understanding and sensitivity is crucial (Perry & Southwell 2011). There are two domains of **intercultural understanding**: cognitive and affective. The cognitive aspect enables us to have knowledge of our own and others' culture while the affective domain allows intercultural sensitivity (Hill 2006; Straffon 2003), which ultimately leads to increased intercultural understanding and competence (Perry & Southwell 2011).

**intercultural understanding:** the capability that aims for learners to learn about and value their own cultures, languages and beliefs, and those of others (ACARA 2018b)

The intercultural understanding capability enables learners to value their own cultures, languages and beliefs, as well as those of others. The capability focuses on learners understanding how personal, group and national identities are shaped, and the variable and changing nature of culture. Learners learn about how and where to engage with other cultures to recognise commonalities and differences, create connections and cultivate mutual respect, which helps them to develop as responsible local and global citizens, preparing them to live and work together in an interconnected world.

Intercultural understanding challenges ethno-centric attitudes and develops an understanding of the diversity of culture and enables learners to view the cultures of others in an objective and global manner. The capability requires schools to provide opportunities for learners to communicate and empathise with others from different cultural backgrounds and to analyse intercultural experiences critically. Figure 16.5 provides a diagrammatic representation of the intercultural understanding general capability.

The Australian Curriculum clearly recognises the importance of intercultural understanding; however, little is known about the myriad ways in which this can be developed (Perry & Southwell 2011), highlighting a potential challenge for educators.

## EDUCATOR TIP

In addressing the challenge of developing the intercultural understanding, research and present a case study aligned to the curriculum at a year level that could be used in the HASS classroom to develop this capability.

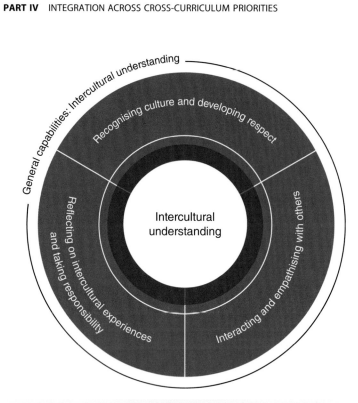

FIGURE 16.5   **The intercultural understanding general capability**
Source: ACARA 2018b

## General capability 7: Ethical understanding

**ethical understanding** the
capability that develops
learners' ethical
understanding, so that they
can identify and investigate
the nature of ethical
concepts, values and
character traits. They
develop an understanding of
how reasoning can assist
ethical judgement and
awareness of the influence
that their values and
behaviour have on others
(ACARA 2018b).

For learners to develop **ethical understanding** they identify and investigate the nature of ethical concepts, values and character traits while
understanding how reasoning can assist ethical judgement and developing an awareness of the influence their values and behaviour have on
others. An implication of this capability is the need to focus on and
provide opportunities for learners to develop 'personal values and attributes such as honesty, resilience, empathy and respect for others', and
the capacity to 'act with ethical integrity' (MCEETYA 2008, p. 9).

With the increasing complexity, changes and interconnections of societies around the world, this capability requires learners to study and
consider complex issues requiring responses that take into account ethical
considerations such as human rights and responsibilities, animal rights,
environmental issues and global justice. To develop ethical understanding
when considering ethical issues, learners need opportunities in the curriculum, classroom
and school setting to interact with others, have conversations and learn to be responsible
members of a democratic community. It can be argued that to develop the efficacy to make
reasoned ethical judgements through inquiry, learners need to develop the capabilities of
social and personal competency, critical and creative thinking and intercultural understanding. Engaging in a community of inquiry as discussed in Chapter 12 is an ideal platform
from which to develop learners' ethical understanding. Figure 16.6 provides a diagrammatic representation of the ethical understanding general capability.

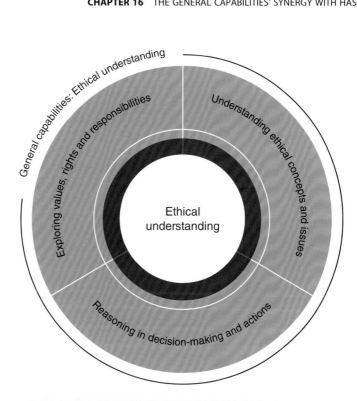

FIGURE 16.6   The ethical understanding general capability
Source: ACARA 2018b

## EDUCATOR TIP

Think of a contemporary issue aligned with the curriculum and appropriate for a particular year level that could be used in the HASS classroom to develop learners' ethical thinking. Also engage learners in brainstorming ethical issues that they see as important to them.

Reid (2009) suggests that other capabilities are needed in the Australian Curriculum. Imagine you have been asked to redesign the general capabilities dimension. Suggest a capability that would be worthy of inclusion and describe your rationale.

## Aligning the general capabilities with the Early Years Learning Framework

Having gained an understanding of the general capabilities, it is important to assess what learners have experienced in early years settings and realise the opportunities for promoting a continuum of capabilities development from birth through to senior secondary education, and potentially lifelong learning. Providing educators with insights into the similarities between the Early Years Learning Framework (EYLF; DEEWR 2009) and the Australian Curriculum, Connor (2011, p. 18) conducted an in-depth research and reported the following overlaps between the general capabilities and the learning outcomes in EYLF:

- Children have a strong sense of identity (Outcome 1), children are connected with and contribute to their world (Outcome 2) and children have a strong sense of wellbeing (Outcome 3) provide essential foundations for a developmental continuum in promoting the personal and social capability.
- Children are connected with and contribute to their world (Outcome 2) underpins the capacity for developing the ethical behaviour and intercultural understanding general capabilities. In particular, developing fairness, social responsibility, and understanding reciprocal rights and responsibilities are necessary for active community participation.
- Children are confident and involved learners applying creativity, problem solving, inquiry, experimentation, hypothesising, researching and investigating (Outcome 4) is integral to developing the general capabilities disposition for critical and creative thinking.
- Children are effective communicators, interacting with others verbally, non-verbally, via media, ICT, texts, for a range of purposes (Outcome 5), which provides fundamental concepts and skills required for the Australian Curriculum general capabilities of literacy, numeracy and ICT competence.

Given the commitment within the Australian Curriculum to promoting general capabilities from the foundational years of a learner's education, we now turn to explore how learners can be encouraged to connect deeply with HASS knowledge and the general capabilities (Gilbert 2018; Yates 2017) for quality learning of matters of real importance (VCAA 2015).

## HASS AND THE GENERAL CAPABILITIES

ACARA (2018b) advises 'that teachers are expected to teach and assess general capabilities to the extent that they are incorporated within learning area content. However, state and territory education authorities have determined to differing degrees whether student learning of the general capabilities is to be assessed or reported'.

You would have noted that in the summaries of the general capabilities in this chapter, detailed diagrams were not displayed for the general capabilities of literacy, numeracy and ICT (general capabilities 1–3), but were shown for critical and creative thinking (Figure 16.3), social and personal capability (Figure 16.4), intercultural understanding (Figure 16.5) and ethical understanding (Figure 16.6) (general capabilities 4–7). This is in recognition that the first three general capabilities apply to HASS as well as all other learning areas in a variety of legitimate and comprehensive ways. However, it is considered that general capabilities 4–7 have a special place in HASS education and require greater consideration as critical capabilities that should be developed to a high degree in HASS learning. As Gilbert (2018, p. xx) suggests, 'ethical understanding, intercultural understanding and personal and social capabilities are distinct areas of knowledge, skills and dispositions', whereas literacy, numeracy and ICT are arguably skills and tools that support learning. That is not to say that other learning areas do not address these capabilities, but it can be argued that the general capabilities of critical and creative thinking, social and personal capability, intercultural understanding and ethical understanding have a significant synergy with the aims, content and skills developed in HASS.

In the Australian Curriculum learning areas, the general capabilities are identified wherever they are developed or applied in the content descriptions, as indicated by the presence of icons throughout the online presentation of the curriculum. The general capabilities are also identified where they offer opportunities to add depth and richness to learning in the content elaborations. Gilbert (2018) challenges educators to not just link these general capabilities to the content descriptors as an opportunity to acquire capabilities, but also to link to developing deep knowledge, conceptual understandings and inquiry skills in a developmental approach.

## Literacy in HASS

The HASS learning area is language rich; consequently, learners are required to engage with written, graphed and drawn materials as they use a wide range of informational, persuasive and imaginative texts in multiple modes. These texts include stories, narrative accounts, reports, explanations, arguments, debates, timelines, maps, tables, graphs and images that are often supported by references from primary and secondary sources. These sources of information include topic-specific vocabulary; appropriate-tense verbs; and complex sentences that enable learners to 'make meaning' of and evaluate texts to formulate an opinion. Supporting the development of literacy in the HASS classroom is the expectation that learners will participate in debates and discussions to develop considered points of view when communicating conclusions to a range of audiences.

The importance of literacy skills is particularly evident in the inquiry and skills sub-strand of the HASS curriculum. For example, at Year 4 level, as part of the inquiry process, learners need to be involved in the literacy-based challenges of:

- posing questions
- locating and collecting information from different sources
- examining information to identify different points of view
- interpreting information
- drawing simple conclusions based on analysis of information
- interacting with others with respect to shared points of view
- presenting ideas, findings and conclusions in texts (ACARA 2018b).

## Numeracy in HASS

In HASS, learners develop the 'numeracy capability as they apply numeracy skills in relation to historical, geographical, civic and economic inquiries' (ACARA 2018b). When researching using data and statistics, learners are required to count, measure, calculate, interpret statistics, and construct and interpret tables and graphs. In History, learners are taught to use scaled timelines, calendars and dates for sequencing and patterning purposes. However, it is also important to recognise that Goos, Dole and Gieger (2012, p. 320), in their audit of numeracy in the History curriculum, found that although there are many opportunities to provide an engaging and meaningful context to explore numeracy, there is a 'lack of alignment between claims about numeracy development in the different sections of the history curriculum'. They argue that 'creating timelines to make meaning of the past is meant to help learners develop an understanding of scale and proportion, and yet the content descriptions focus exclusively on sequencing of people and events as the only skill involved in chronology' (p. 320). Geography, on the other hand, is particularly rich in numeracy through mapping and fieldwork requiring data collection, the construction and interpretation of maps, models, diagrams and satellite images, working with the numerical concepts of grids, scale, distance, area and projections, locational specification and analysis, and the measurement of distance.

All the HASS subjects require varying degrees of analysing numerical data to:

- make meaning of the past by viewing statistics over time in History
- identify patterns, such as the effects of location and distance on physical and human features of the landscape in Geography
- examine voting patterns over time to determine possible election outcomes in Civics and Citizenship
- use data over time to make predictions, forecast outcomes and manage funds in Economics and Business.

Regardless of the content to which numeracy skills are applied, it is important in HASS that learners appreciate how numeracy knowledge and skills are used in society while having opportunities to apply these to hypothetical and/or real-life experiences.

Like literacy, numeracy skills are particularly evident in the inquiry and skills strand of the HASS curriculum. For example, at Year 5, as part of the inquiry process, learners are to be involved in the numeracy based challenges of:

- locating and collecting relevant data from primary and secondary sources
- organising and representing data in a range of formats including tables and graphs
- sequencing information about people's lives, events, development and phenomena using timelines
- interpreting data displayed in a range of formats to identify, describe and compare distributions, patterns and trends and infer relationships
- presenting ideas, findings, viewpoints and conclusions in a range of modes (ACARA 2018b).

## Information and communication technology (ICT) capability in HASS

In HASS, learners develop the ICT capability when they locate, process, analyse, evaluate and communicate historical, geographic, civic and economic information using digital technologies. Learners are encouraged to use digital technologies in a meaningful way for the purpose of critical inquiry and creative thinking. This is particularly true with the use of spatial technologies such as Geographic Information Systems (GIS) and remote sensed visualisations such as Google Earth. If these powerful and accessible technologies are used purposefully and critically, they have the potential to provide a large amount of quality locational data to resolve complex inquiry questions or challenges of historical, geographic, civic and economic relevance. Digital technologies are also an important enabler for learners to represent and present their learning using multimodal elements to a range of audiences.

The ICT capability is also important in the HASS classroom for learners to source, represent, share and analyse information to develop conclusions and possible futures, while always being cognisant of the impact of technologies, both negative and positive, on people, places and civic and economic activity.

The importance of the ICT capability is particularly evident in the inquiry and skills strand of the HASS curriculum. For example, at Year 6, as part of the inquiry process, learners are to be involved in the use of ICT by:

- locating and collecting relevant information and data from primary and secondary sources
- organising and representing data in a range of formats including tables, graphs and large- and small-scale maps, using discipline-appropriate conventions
- evaluating evidence to draw conclusions
- presenting ideas, findings, viewpoints and conclusions in a range of modes that incorporate digital representations (ACARA 2018b).

## Critical and creative thinking in HASS

An important and overt aim of HASS is for learners to develop critical and creative thinking as they inquire using the concepts, discussed in Chapter 5, within History, Geography, Civics and Citizenship, and Economics and Business. As investigators, inquirers, problem-solvers and conversationalists, learners in HASS are encouraged to develop a conceptual-ised approach to their learning while becoming critical and creative thinkers. Such thinking involves framing 'rich' inquiry questions, conducting critical analysis of sources, developing an argument based on logic when using evidence, interpreting and analysing data and/or information, and systems thinking to propose solutions and consider possible, probable and preferred futures. The HASS learner thinks conceptually and deeply about questions posed and develops the realisation that no question is simple as a multiplicity of points of view and possible solutions usually exist for any one issue. Such an approach in HASS requires learners to be inquisitive and creative as they analyse, speculate and develop interpretations to explain features, events and phenomena.

For example, critical and creative thinking could be applied to:

- interpret and analyse the causes of World War I in History
- find solutions to traffic congestion in the CBD of a large city in Geography
- develop a strategy to involve young people in the community to be more interested and involved in political discussions in Civics and Citizenship

    • develop a product that is an opportunity in the market to create a business in Economics and Business.

Again, the importance of critical and creative thinking is particularly evident in the inquiry and skills strand of the HASS curriculum. For example, at Year 5, as part of the inquiry process, learners are to:

    • develop appropriate questions to guide an inquiry

    • examine primary and secondary sources to determine purpose

    • examine different viewpoints on actions, issues and phenomena

    • evaluate evidence to draw conclusions

    • work in groups to generate responses to issues and challenges

    • use criteria to make decisions and judgements and consider the advantages and disadvantages of preferring one decision over others

    • reflect on learning to propose personal and/or collective action in response to an issue or challenge and predict the probable effects (ACARA 2018b).

## EDUCATOR TIP

For one of the proposed content descriptions listed above for the critical and creative thinking capability, develop an original elaboration that could be taught in the HASS classroom to promote quality learning of matters of real importance to the learner and that embeds the development of the capability.

## Personal and social capability in HASS

> Inquiry-based learning assists students to develop their capacity for self-management, directing their own learning and providing opportunities to express and reflect on their opinions, beliefs, values and questions appropriately. (ACARA 2018b)

HASS is a learning area that focuses on the question of 'being human'. Hence, the personal and social capability, and understanding about people, places, processes and phenomena, is a capability with which educators are very comfortable when designing and teaching HASS programs. Implicit in the HASS learning area are the practices of collaboration, reflection, communication, appreciation of the insights and perspectives of others and exploration of personal identity and a sense of belonging.

Reflecting the goal of developing active and informed citizens, the HASS curriculum and HASS classrooms aim at providing opportunities for students to make a contribution to their communities and society more broadly. Such capacity building involves the development of leadership, resilience, goal-setting, advocacy skills, and informed and responsible decision-making by individuals.

For example, the personal and social capability can be applied:

- when learners investigate the motivation and achievements of individuals through biographical studies in History
- when learners are working in teams conducting fieldwork on excursions in Geography
- with the participation of learners in debates and discussions on social issues in Civics and Citizenship
- by learners working in teams to develop a business enterprise in Economics and Business.

The importance of the personal and social capability is particularly evident in both the knowledge and understanding, and inquiry and skills strands of the HASS curriculum. For example, in Year 5:

- In the knowledge and understanding strand, learners learn about:
  - the reasons people migrated to Australia and the experiences and contributions of a particular migrant group within a colony in the History sub-strand
  - the environmental and human influences on the location and characteristics of a place in the Geography sub-strand
  - the key values that underpin Australia's democracy and how people with shared beliefs and values work together to achieve a civic goal in the Civics and Citizenship sub-strand (ACARA 2018b).
- In the inquiry and skills strand, learners are challenged to:
  - examine different points of view on actions, issues and phenomena
  - work in groups to generate responses to issues and challenges
  - reflect on learning to propose personal and/or collective action in response to an issue or challenge, and predict the probable effects
  - present ideas, findings, viewpoints and conclusions in a range of texts and modes (ACARA 2018b).

## EDUCATOR TIP

For one of the proposed content descriptions listed above for the personal and social capability, develop an original elaboration that could be taught in the HASS classroom to promote quality learning of matters of real importance to the learner and that embeds the development of the capability.

## Intercultural understanding in HASS

students . . . demonstrate respect for cultural diversity and the human rights of all people and learn to facilitate dialogue to understand different perspectives. (ACARA 2018b)

In HASS, learners develop intercultural understanding by learning about the diversity of the world's places, peoples and their lives, cultural practices, values, beliefs, ways of knowing and world views. By studying their own and other's histories and cultures and the contribution of migrants to present-day Australia, learners gain an understanding of the complexity of cultures, and the interactions and interdependencies within and between cultures and countries. Studying the significance of place to cultural identity enables learners to gain an understanding of cultural values and experiences of groups and the nature of interaction across cultural boundaries. Such studies involve the exploration of how phenomena such as group membership, traditions, values, customs, and religious and cultural practices impact on civic life. The HASS classroom encourages learners to reflect on their own intercultural experiences, 'exploring similarities as well as differences within and across cultural groups, recognising the importance of practising empathy and learning to challenge stereotypical or prejudiced representations of social and cultural groups where they exist' (ACARA 2018b).

For example, in Year 4:

- In the knowledge and understanding strand, learners learn about:
  - the nature of contact between Aboriginal and Torres Strait Islander peoples and others, such as the Macassans and the Europeans, and the effects of these interactions on, for example, people and environments in the History sub-strand
  - the importance of environments to people and the custodial responsibility Aboriginal and Torres Strait Islander peoples have for Country/Place, and how this influences views about sustainability in the Geography sub-strand
  - the different cultural, religious and/or social groups to which they and others in the community belong in the Civics and Citizenship sub-strand (ACARA 2018b).

## EDUCATOR TIP

For one of the proposed content descriptions listed above for the intercultural understanding capability, develop an original elaboration that could be taught in the HASS classroom to promote quality learning of matters of real importance to the learner and that embeds development of the capability.

## Ethical understanding in HASS

> Students learn about ethical procedures for investigating and working with people and places. (ACARA 2018b)

Through historical, geographical, civics and citizenship, and economics and business inquiries, learners develop an understanding of the ways in which diverse values and principles influence human activity and the views of individuals and groups. By embedding this capability in HASS, learners develop informed, ethical values and attitudes through the study of social, economic, political and environmental issues, while also becoming aware of their own roles, rights and responsibilities as informed citizens.

For example, the ethical understanding capability could be applied in:

- History when examining the ethics involved in the removal of Aboriginal children during the period of the Stolen Generations
- Geography when considering the ethics of developed countries advocating that less-developed countries should limit car ownership due to ever-increasing global pollution levels
- Economics and Business by challenging learners to consider the ways by which they can reduce their level of consumerism
- Civics and Citizenship when discussing contestable social issues relating to equality, justice and human rights; for example, the same-sex marriage plebiscite.

## EDUCATOR TIP

For each of the HASS subjects, suggest other possible issues that could be developed in the classroom to develop ethical understanding.

In the knowledge and understanding strand, learners learn about:

- experiences of Australian democracy and citizenship, including the status and rights of Aboriginal and Torres Strait Islander peoples, migrants, women and children in the History sub-strand
- the world's cultural diversity, including that of its Indigenous peoples, in the Geography sub-strand
- the responsibilities of electors and representatives in Australia's democracy, the shared values of Australian citizenship, the formal rights and responsibilities of Australian citizens, and the obligations citizens may consider they have beyond their own national borders as active and informed global citizens in the Civics and Citizenship sub-strand
- how the concept of opportunity cost involves choices about the alternative use of resources and the need to consider trade-offs, and the effects that consumer and financial decisions can have on the individual, the broader community and the environment in the Economics and Business sub-strand (ACARA 2018b).

In the inquiry and skills strand, learners are challenged to:

- examine different viewpoints on actions, events, issues and phenomena in the past and present, and draw simple conclusions based on analysis of information and data
- evaluate evidence to draw conclusions
- reflect on learning to propose personal and/or collective action in response to an issue or challenge, and predict the probable effects
- reflect on learning to propose actions in response to an issue or challenge and consider the possible effects of proposed actions (ACARA 2018b).

The content descriptions used in this section to show the synergy of the general capabilities to HASS have been focused on Years 4, 5 and 6. Review the F–3 HASS year levels and identify the application of the general capabilities in the content descriptions for those years.

# THE GENERAL CAPABILITIES IN THE ACHIEVEMENT STANDARDS

Since the implementation of the Australian Curriculum, there have been frequent discussions among educators relating to the need and potential of assessing the general capabilities. Just as the general capabilities can be identified in the content descriptions in the HASS knowledge and understanding, and inquiry and skills strands, they can also be identified in each HASS achievement standard.

Reid (2009) suggests that the general capabilities should be assessed using a set of achievement standards. How practical would this approach be? What are some of its strengths and limitations?

Table 16.1 identifies the general capabilities as assessable components of HASS, as articulated in the achievement standard for Year 6. Note that not all the achievement standard aspects are listed, just those where there is sound evidence of a degree of synergy with the general capabilities – which is the case for most of the aspects.

| **TABLE 16.1** THE GENERAL CAPABILITIES MAPPED TO THE ACHIEVEMENT STANDARD ASPECTS FOR YEAR 6 HASS | |
| --- | --- |
| **Achievement standard aspects for Year 6.**<br>**By the end of Year 6, learners:** | **General capability synergy** |
| Explain the significance of an event/development, an individual and/or group. | Critical and creative<br>Personal and social |
| They describe the causes and effects of change on society. | Critical and creative |
| They compare the experiences of different people in the past. | Critical and creative<br>Intercultural understanding |
| Learners describe, compare and explain the diverse characteristics of different places. | Critical and creative<br>Intercultural understanding |
| They describe how people, places, communities and environments are diverse and globally interconnected, and identify the effects of these interconnections over time. | Intercultural understanding<br>Critical and creative |
| They describe the rights and responsibilities of Australian citizens and the obligations they may have as global citizens. | Ethical understanding<br>Personal and social |

| TABLE 16.1   (CONT.) | |
| --- | --- |
| **Achievement standard aspects for Year 6. By the end of Year 6, learners:** | **General capability synergy** |
| They explain why it is important to be informed when making consumer and financial decisions. | Ethical understanding |
| They explain different views on how to respond to an issue or challenge. | Critical and creative<br>Personal and social |
| Learners develop appropriate questions to frame an investigation. | Numeracy<br>Critical and creative |
| They locate and collect useful data and information from primary and secondary sources. | Literacy<br>Numeracy<br>ICT |
| They examine sources to determine their origin and purpose. | Literacy<br>Numeracy<br>Critical and creative |
| They interpret data to identify, describe and compare, and to infer relationships, and evaluate evidence to draw conclusions. | Literacy<br>Numeracy<br>ICT<br>Critical and creative |
| Learners sequence information about events, the lives of individuals and selected phenomena in chronological order and represent time by creating timelines. | Numeracy<br>ICT |
| They organise and represent data in a range of formats. | Numeracy<br>Literacy<br>ICT |
| They collaboratively generate alternative responses to an issue, use criteria to make decisions and identify the advantages and disadvantages of preferring one decision over others. | Critical and creative<br>Personal and social<br>Ethical understanding<br>Intercultural understanding |
| They reflect on their learning to propose action in response to an issue or challenge and describe the probable effects of their proposal. | Critical and creative<br>Personal and social<br>Ethical understanding<br>Intercultural understanding |
| They present ideas, findings, viewpoints and conclusions in a range of communication forms. | Literacy<br>ICT |

Source: adapted from ACARA 2018a

As educators, we are challenged to consider Biesta and Priestley's (2013) concerns in both planning and assessing general capabilities, particularly the possibility of a focus on concrete functional skills whereby the deeper understanding and judgement needed to apply the skills in real and diverse situations may be omitted. Further to this, Gilbert (2018) challenges educators to be mindful of the 'matrix approach' to general capabilities, advocating that they should not be seen as secondary to the learning areas. Price (2015) encourages educators to broaden their understandings to include human capabilities (aligned with Sen 1985 and Nussbaum 2003) that inclusively build on learners' diverse capabilities rather than narrow educational capabilities, which commonly have been characterised as predetermined skills, competencies, outcomes and processes focused primarily on an individual's functioning.

# CONCLUSION

One of the primary goals of the Melbourne Declaration was for schooling to develop informed and responsible citizens, a goal supported by the development of capabilities with which HASS educators strongly identify. Despite the findings by Goos, Dole and Geiger (2012), most HASS educators are comfortable with the opportunities the HASS learning area provides for sound embedding of the general capabilities within learning activities and assessment. However, as Reid (2009) cautions, it is important that the general capabilities are embedded in a meaningful way. In endeavouring to achieve this goal, this chapter has described the nature of the general capabilities, articulated their place in the HASS curriculum and classroom, and identified their relevance to the HASS achievement standards. The presence of all the general capabilities is visible in HASS in a meaningful and extensive way and HASS educators do not have to 'fit a square peg in a round hole' to address the general capabilities or create tokenistic connections to the curriculum to justify a discussion of their place in HASS. There is a strong synergy between the aims of the HASS learning area and the intent of the general capabilities to develop young people with the capabilities to be informed, responsible and active Australian citizens. HASS will continue to play an important role in a balanced school curriculum to deliver in a meaningful and contextually relevant manner these important environmental, social, economic and political capabilities for young people to develop.

## REVIEW QUESTIONS

1. What are the goals of the *Melbourne Declaration on Educational Goals for Young Australians*?

2. Why is the Australian Curriculum referred to as a three-dimensional curriculum?

3. What are the general capabilities of the Australian Curriculum?

4. What do you consider is the relationship between the EYLF and the general capabilities identified in the Australian Curriculum?

5. Taking into account the result of the NAP-CC report (ACARA 2017), why do you think it is important to profile the general capabilities to a greater extent as part of the Australian Curriculum?

6. Choose two of the general capabilities and discuss how they can be said to reflect the core purposes of HASS learning.

7. For a particular HASS year level, identify the content descriptors of the knowledge and understanding, or inquiry and skills strands that can be seen as relating to the general capabilities in a meaningful way. Explain the reasons for your choices.

## LEARNING EXTENSION

There is considerable debate among educators regarding whether the general capabilities should be overtly taught and possibly even be part of the formal assessment of the Australian Curriculum. What is your view on this question? How do you think the general capabilities could comprise part of the assessment of student performance when studying the Australian Curriculum?

## REFERENCES

ACARA (Australian Curriculum, Assessment and Reporting Authority). (2017). *NAP Sample Assessment. Civics and Citizenship Report. Years 6 and 10. 2016*. Sydney: ACARA. Retrieved from: http://nap.edu.au/docs/default-source/default-document-library/nap-cc-report-2016-final-081217.pdf?sfvrsn=0.

——(2018a). *Australian Curriculum: F-10, v8.3*. Curriculum structure. Retrieved from: https://www.australiancurriculum.edu.au/f-10-curriculum/structure.

——(2018b). *Australian Curriculum: F-10, v8.3*. General capabilities. Retrieved from: http://www.acara.edu.au/curriculum/general-capabilities.

Biesta, G. & Priestley, M. (2013). Capacities and the curriculum. In M. Priestley & G. Biesta, eds, *Reinventing the Curriculum: New trends in curriculum policy and practice*. London: Bloomsbury, pp. 35–50.

Connor, J. (2011). *Foundations for Learning: Relationships between the Early Years Learning Framework and the Australian Curriculum*. An Early Childhood Australia and ACARA paper. Retrieved from: http://foundationinquirylearning.global2.vic.edu.au/files/2013/06/ECA_ACARA_Foundations_Paper-2cq59mi.pdf.

Cross, R. (2012). Creative in finding creativity in the curriculum: The CLIL second language classroom. *The Australian Educational Researcher*, 39(4), 431–45.

DEEWR (Department of Education, Employment and Workplace Relations). (2009). *Belonging, Being and Becoming: The Early Years Learning Framework for Australia*. Canberra: DEEWR.

Foundation for Young Australians. (2017). *The New Work Smarts: Thriving in the new work order*. Retrieved from: https://www.fya.org.au/wp-content/uploads/2017/07/FYA_TheNewWorkSmarts_July2017.pdf.

Geiger, V., Goos, M., Dole, S., Forgasz, H. & Bennison, A. (2013). Exploring the demands and opportunities for numeracy in the Australian Curriculum: English. In V. Steinle, L. Ball & C. Bardini, eds, *Mathematics Education: Yesterday, today and tomorrow (Proceedings of 36th Annual Conference of the Mathematics Education Research Group of Australasia)*. Melbourne: Mathematics Education Research Group of Australasia.

Gilbert, R. (2018, in press). General capabilities in the Australian Curriculum: Promise, problems and prospects. In A. Reid & D. Price, eds, *The Australian Curriculum: Promises, problems and possibilities*. Canberra: Australian Curriculum Studies Association.

Goos, M., Dole, S. & Geiger, V. (2012). Auditing the numeracy demands of the Australian Curriculum. In J. Dindyal, L.P. Cheng & F. Ng, eds, *Mathematics Educations: Expanding horizons (Proceedings of 35th Annual Conference of the Mathematics Education Research Group of Australasia)*. Singapore: Mathematics Education Research Group of Australasia.

Hammond, J. (2012). Hope and challenge in the Australian curriculum: Implications for EAL students and their teachers. *The Australian Journal of Language and Literacy*, 35(2), 223–40.

Hill, I. (2006). Student types, school types and their combined influence on the development of intercultural understanding. *Journal of Research in International Education*, 5(1), 5–33.

Klaus, P. (2010). Communication breakdown. *California Job Journal*, 28, 1–9.

Leu, D.J., McVerry, J.G., O'Byrne, W.I., Kiili, C., Zawilinski, L., Everett-Cacopardo, H., Kennedy, C. & Forzani, E. (2011). The new literacies of online reading comprehension: Expanding the literacy and learning curriculum. *Journal of Adolescent & Adult Literacy*, 55(1), 5–14.

Maes, J., Weldy, T. & Icenogel, M. (1997). A managerial perspective: Oral communication is most important for business students in the workplace. *Journal of Business Communication*, 34, 67–80.

MCEETYA (Ministerial Council on Education, Employment, Training and Youth Affairs). (2008). *Melbourne Declaration on Educational Goals for Young Australians*. Melbourne: Curriculum Corporation. Retrieved from: http://www.curriculum.edu.au/verve/_resources/National_Declaration_on_the_Educational_Goals_for_Young_Australians.pdf.

McInerney, M. (2017). Keynote presentation. HASS SA Conference, Adelaide, 25–26 February.

Mitchell, G.W., Skinner, L.B. & White, B.J. (2010). Essential soft skills for success in the twenty-first century workforce as perceived by business educators. *Delta Pi Epsilon Journal*, 52, 43–53.

Nealy, C. (2005). Integrating soft skills through active learning in the management classroom. *Journal of College Teaching & Learning*, 2(4), 1–6.

Nussbaum, M. (2003). Capabilities as fundamental entitlements: Sen and social justice. *Feminist Economics*, 9(2–3), 33–59.

Partnership for 21st Century Learning (2011). *21st Century Readiness Act* introduced. Retrieved from: http://www.p21.org/news-events/press-releases/993-21st-century-readiness-act.

Perry, L.B. & Southwell, L. (2011). Developing intercultural understanding and skills: Models and approaches. *Intercultural Education*, 22(6), 453–66.

Price, D. (2015). Pedagogies for inclusion of students with disabilities in a national curriculum: A human capabilities approach. *Journal of Educational Enquiry*, 14(2), 18–32.

Reid, A. (2009). Is this a revolution? A critical analysis of the Rudd government's national education agenda. PhD thesis, Australian Curriculum Studies Association.

Sen, A. (1985). *Commodities and Capabilities*. Amsterdam: North-Holland.

Smith, L. (2007). Teaching the intangibles. *T+D*, 61(10), 23–5.

Straffon, D.A. (2003). Assessing the intercultural sensitivity of high school students attending an international school. *International Journal of Intercultural Relations*, 27(4), 487–501.

VCAA (Victorian Curriculum and Assessment Authority). (2015). *Victorian Curriculum F-10: Revised curriculum planning and reporting guidelines*. Melbourne: VCAA. Retrieved from: http://www.vcaa.vic.edu.au/Documents/viccurric/RevisedF-10CurriculumPlanningReporting Guidelines.pdf.

Vygotsky, L.S. (1978). *Mind in Society*. Cambridge, MA: Harvard University Press.

——(1987). Thinking and speech (trans. N. Minick). In R.W. Rieber & A.S. Carton, eds, *Problems of General Psychology. Vol. 1 of The Collected works of L.S. Vygotsky*. New York: Plenum Press, pp. 39–285.

Yates, L. (2017). Curriculum: The challenges and the devil in the details. In T. Bentley & G. Savage, eds, *Educating Australia: Challenges for the decade ahead*. Melbourne: Melbourne University Publishing, pp. 85–99.

Yates, L. & Collins, C. (2010). The absence of knowledge in Australian curriculum reforms. *European Journal of Education*, 45(1), 89–102.

# AUTHENTIC ENGAGEMENT WITH ABORIGINAL AND TORRES STRAIT ISLANDER CONTENT IN THE P–6 AUSTRALIAN CURRICULUM

**17**

*Kevin Lowe and Janet Cairncross*

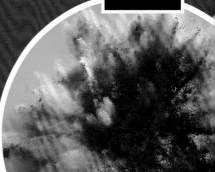

## Learning outcomes

After reading this chapter, you should be able to:

- understand why the Aboriginal and Torres Strait Islander histories and cultures cross-curriculum priority was included in the Australian Curriculum and explain the challenges facing educators as they integrate this content meaningfully into their teaching programs
- define what is meant by culturally responsive pedagogy and identify the key features that underpin successful practice
- understand the importance of community engagement to Aboriginal and Torres Strait Islander peoples, to learners and educators
- describe the importance of a thematic, or backward mapping, approach to the development of rigorous and engaging lessons that will meet the aims of the cross-curriculum priority
- understand the need for educators to take responsibility to affect the development of a culturally responsive curriculum and to work in collaboration with colleagues and Aboriginal and Torres Strait Islander peoples in establishing a school-wide framework for effective teaching and learning of the cross-curriculum priorities.

## INTRODUCTION

While the Australian Curriculum, Assessment and Reporting Authority (ACARA) prioritises the history and culture of Aboriginal and Torres Strait Islander peoples, it does not make explicit how to give effect to their aspirations for a national curriculum that provides learners with the knowledge and understanding of the complex history and culture of these peoples. This chapter provides educators with a new way of looking at how Aboriginal and Torres Strait Islander peoples have been represented within the Australian Curriculum.

We commence with an open discussion about the structure and potential shortcomings of the cross-curriculum priorities as evident in content descriptions across the Australian Curriculum. A systematic method will be presented to help educators develop quality learning programs. This method aims to engage learners in moral, historical and epistemic

**custodianship** refers to Aboriginal and Torres Strait Islander peoples' responsibility for Country/ Place. Everything was formed of the same substance by the Ancestors. The importance of this notion of Country is that it expresses interdependence of relationships between the people of that Place, with the ever-present physical and metaphysical worlds that reside within it. This includes the speaking of language and the following of lore to sustain it.

**Indigenous agency** refers to the capacity of individuals to act independently and make their own free choices, based on their responsibilities to kin and Country

questions of Indigenous connectedness to Country/Place and their **custodianship** of it; and the nature of **Indigenous agency**, resistance and national reconciliation between Indigenous and non-Indigenous Australians.

This chapter is divided into four sections. We look at cross-curriculum content structure; provide a pedagogic model for culturally responsive teaching; advise on establishing authentic school and community engagement; and suggest a framework for the development of rich, contextually situated and holistic programs for teaching the Aboriginal and Torres Strait Islander cross-curriculum content across the primary years of schooling.

# THE AUSTRALIAN CURRICULUM: LIMITATIONS AND CHALLENGES

This section outlines why the Aboriginal and Torres Strait Islander histories and cultures cross-curriculum priority was included in the Australian Curriculum as a mechanism for addressing national reconciliation. The cross-curriculum priority aims to provide national, regional and global dimensions that will enrich the curriculum through development of considered and focused content that fits naturally within learning areas, while the curriculum itself is a statement outlining what students should learn about and what they should learn (knowledge) and do (skills); it outlines the learning standards and a process of interacting between learners, educators and knowledge. We will trace how the Aboriginal and Torres Strait Islander histories and cultures content came to take its current form within the national curriculum and look at some of the key challenges faced by educators when developing learning that meets the aims of this priority.

## SPOTLIGHT ON HASS EDUCATION

### CULTURALLY RESPONSIVE EDUCATION

The Year 2 Humanities and Social Sciences (HASS) curriculum requires learners to see how places have meaning to people and the connection Aboriginal and Torres Strait Islander peoples have with Country/Place (place, environment, interconnection). The following example shows how the culturally responsive educator may address this content.

The educator begins the lesson by asking all learners to talk about a family heirloom that is important to them. By discussing learners' heirlooms, the educator can help learners to understand that heirlooms are significant as they capture the memories and traditions of families. Prompt questions such as 'Do you own an heirloom?' and 'How would you feel if the heirloom were lost or broken?' help learners to develop an understanding of custodianship; that is, custodians care for and protect something of great importance. They do not own it, but care for it so that it can be passed on to future generations. This simple lesson provides a context for learners to develop a deeper appreciation of Aboriginal and Torres Strait Islander peoples' custodial connections to Country/Place.

What will you need to do through your teaching to ensure learners are knowledgeable and well equipped to contribute to genuine local and national reconciliation?

## Where is Aboriginal and Torres Strait Islander content in the Australian Curriculum?

In 1989, the Commonwealth, state and territory governments signed off on the educational undertakings within the Hobart Declaration (AEC 1989). This document was largely developed out of a growing concern that Australian learners needed to be explicitly prepared to meet the social, technological and economic changes that loomed at the end of the 20th century. One of those concerns was the alarming rates of Aboriginal and Torres Strait Islander educational underachievement and disengagement with education. Later that year, the Australian governments signed the first Aboriginal Education Policy, which in part committed all governments to both enable Aboriginal[1] [sic] learners to have an appreciation of their history, cultures and identity, to enable 'all learners to deepen their knowledge of Australia by engaging with the world's oldest continuous living cultures'. This commitment has remained largely unchanged in the three following decennial Declarations; namely, Hobart (AEC 1989), Adelaide (DEST 1999; MCEEDYA 1999) and Melbourne (MCEETYA 2008), as well as Aboriginal and education policies over this period. The states and territories agreed to give effect to these 'requirements' largely in the form of curriculum perspectives. Unsurprisingly, the interim National Curriculum Board (2009) took the same path and committed to addressing this content through the development of Aboriginal and Torres Strait Islander cross-curriculum priorities, which are to be embedded in learning across the curriculum.

## Challenges and shortcomings

State, territory and national reviews of Aboriginal education have identified that while many schools had made significant efforts to develop teaching and learning programs that addressed the intentions of the cross-curriculum content, others had enacted teaching programs that failed to meet Aboriginal and Torres Strait Islander peoples' expectations that learners would develop an informed appreciation of their history, cultures and identities (NSW AECG & NSW DET 2004; Santoro et al. 2011). In part, these problems

---

[1] References within these documents have vacillated between using terminology such as 'Aboriginal', 'Indigenous' and 'Torres Strait Islanders' to collectively identify the first peoples of Australia. The use of these homogenised terminologies has been contentious, as it has stripped these communities of their individual Place-based affinities to their language nations. There are 500 sovereign language nations within the Australian state. Each iteration of terminology has the effect of aggregating the diverse peoples of the mainland and Torres Strait Islands under dehumanising terms such that governments can refer to the First Peoples in ways that deny their particular connections to Country and Dreaming. It is strongly suggested that educators and schools know the name of the language group who have claim to that Country on which the school, town and community reside.

emanated from the inherent tensions between the requirements to both establish content that supported all learners to 'respect and recognise' Aboriginal cultures, while supporting Aboriginal and Torres Strait Islander learners' identities and culture in the curriculum. Inherent within this epistemic binary is that Indigenous people's experiences of colonisation, settlement and dispossession are not represented from their experiences of invasion, dispersal, dispossession and marginalisation. The curriculum hardly represents the Indigenous experience of these encounters, but instead renders them largely invisible, overwhelmed within a discourse of nation making and Australian statehood. Critiques of the Aboriginal and Torres Strait Islander cross-curriculum priorities have identified that Aboriginal and Torres Strait Islander people's experiences are tokenised, ignored or rendered to the margins of curriculum. It is therefore little wonder that many Aboriginal learners express feeling marginalised by schooling and see educators as being at the frontline of states' and territories' efforts to assimilate them (Yunkaporta 2009b).

## Looking to develop a moral imperative

One of central tenets of a critical approach to teaching the cross-curriculum content is that educators need to establish site-wide historical, social and moral narratives that will inform the development of curriculum and build on the authentic experiences of Aboriginal and Torres Strait Islander peoples, providing opportunities for an informed basis for learners to engage in the necessary debates needed to underpin genuine **reconciliation**.

**reconciliation**: a process between Aboriginal and Torres Strait Islander people and the wider community to address the practices, processes and policies that underpin Aboriginal and Torres Strait Islander disadvantage

Developing this narrative has two primary functions. The first provides educators with the necessary pedagogic tools to develop coherent narratives about issues such as reconciliation, Aboriginal knowledge and the ongoing experiences of colonisation. The second is more practical, and aims to help educators to manage the learning even though it unfolds through discrete or detached content throughout the primary years (see Table 17.3, page 321). Educators need to have an overarching understanding of what this discrete content will have taught the typical Year 6 learner as they transition to their secondary education.

ACARA (2012, p. 9) states that a national curriculum would produce learners who are active and informed citizens who 'understand and acknowledge the value of Indigenous cultures, and possess the knowledge, skills and understandings to contribute to, and benefit from, reconciliation between Indigenous and non-Indigenous Australians'. Educators are responsible for ensuring that all learners are informed and understand the national significance of genuine reconciliation, and are enabled to actively contribute to it. These are as much moral questions as pedagogic ones. Educators need to think reflexively about issues that have disabled Australia's efforts to achieve consensus and work towards meaningful reconciliation.

## Building a reflexive pedagogy

It is essential to think about the big picture. If research on educator effectiveness tells us one thing, it is that educators have the single biggest impact on learner success (Hattie

2012). This is not surprising, as 'good' educators have constantly sought ways to go beyond the minimalist construct of Aboriginal and Torres Strait Islander content through their inclusion of learning that is powerful in its rendering of local, contextual narratives that are inclusive of Aboriginal communities' languages, knowledge, cultures and experiences. The next section provides a guide to what these educators have learnt about a pedagogy that is culturally situated and consequently responsive to the learning needs of not just Aboriginal and Torres Strait Islander learners, but all learners. As educators develop teaching programs, they will need to have an eye for the specifics of these small-atomised elements and the bigger picture, and consider what they want learners to really understand about the key concepts across their education.

## EDUCATOR TIP

Educators should recognise the dual purpose of the cross-curriculum priority to inform all learners about the histories and cultures of Aboriginal and Torres Strait Islander peoples and provide learning that supports Aboriginal and Torres Strait Islander learners' cultural and learner identities.

What are the benefits and challenges for inclusion of the Aboriginal and Torres Strait Islander histories and cultures cross-curriculum priority within the Australian Curriculum?

Reflection

## WHAT PEDAGOGY SUPPORTS THE AIMS OF THE AUSTRALIAN CURRICULUM?

The Australian Curriculum is much more than a syllabus document or a statement outlining what learners should learn about and what they should learn to do. It is also a process of interactions between learners, educators and knowledge. This is evidenced by a cycle of teaching and learning, assessment and reporting. So, while ACARA has the responsibility of defining the scope of cross-curriculum priorities within the Australian Curriculum, it is the task of educators to put this into practice. Thus educators operationalise the curriculum through the construct of pedagogy and the design of quality assessment. For the Aboriginal and Torres Strait Islander cross-curriculum priority to be addressed meaningfully, educators need to be prepared to design and implement lessons and assessment that are inclusive and respectful of both the HASS curriculum and the aims and purpose of the cross-curriculum priority.

## EDUCATOR TIP

No matter what value education authorities place on cultural inclusivity, this will not be a reality until it is supported by effective pedagogy. Educators have a moral imperative to address the inequity between Indigenous and non-Indigenous communities in Australia by constructing lessons that allow all learners to access learning and achieve success.

## Australia's culturally diverse classrooms

Since 1945, approximately seven million people have immigrated to Australia from over 200 countries. Consequently, Australia has a culturally dynamic population, in which over 28 per cent of Australians were born overseas (ABS 2017). The cultural diversity of Australia's population is reflected in its educational settings. Comparatively, the proportion of Aboriginal and Torres Strait Islander learners is quite small with only 2.8 per cent of the population identified as Indigenous. ACARA has highlighted the need for cultural inclusivity in its paper on curriculum design, which underpins the development of the national curriculum that 'reflects the diversity of knowledge, experience and cultural values of students' (National Curriculum Board 2009, p. 10).

## Learning through culture: culturally responsive pedagogy

Lessons that regularly incorporate the cultural knowledge of diverse social groupings (such as economic class, gender, ethnicity, race, sexuality, disability, language and religion) are seen as an essential indicator of quality teaching (Ladwig, King & NSW Department of Education and Training 2003, p. 21). This is based on the assertion that when learners are encouraged to draw on their own cultural knowledge, prior experiences and frames of reference, learning becomes more relevant and effective, in turn leading to higher levels of learner engagement and achievement. Of particular interest are those practices defined as culturally responsive. There is growing international evidence that **culturally responsive pedagogy** – a term first coined by Ladson-Billings (1995) when describing the characteristics of successful pedagogy for African American learners – improves outcomes for all learners, but especially among students from non-dominant cultures. The application of this pedagogy has, by its very nature, contextualised teaching to the localities, languages, histories and cultures of Aboriginal and Torres Strait Islander students.

**culturally responsive pedagogy**: a student-centred approach to teaching in which the students' unique cultural strengths are identified and nurtured to promote student achievement and a sense of wellbeing

One such approach that clearly demonstrates a culturally responsive pedagogy is Yunkaporta's relational eight ways pedagogy (Yunkaporta 2009a) and his research on classroom practice. The discussion in Table 17.1 comes from a systematic analysis of the literature on culturally responsive pedagogies that also underpins the foundational principles of Yunkaporta's framework and other work in this area (Perso, Kenyon & Darrough 2012).

**TABLE 17.1  THE REFLECT FRAMEWORK**

Culturally responsive educators:

**R  Reject deficit thinking**

- A central tenet of culturally responsive pedagogy is the belief in the intellectual potential of all learners, and the educator's role in ensuring that all learners meet their potential.
- Culturally responsive educators do not blame the learner for failure but instead reflect on what they themselves can do better. In other words, if an educator believes that problems are entirely of the learner's own creation, the result is a breakdown in the relationship and a lowering of expectations.
- The culturally responsive educator needs to engage in critical reflection on their own practice and reject deficit thinking, replacing it with the belief that all learners can do well.

**E  Expect high academic achievement**

- 'Teachers have to care so much about ethnically diverse students and their achievement that they accept nothing less than high level success from them and work diligently to accomplish it' (Gay 2002, p. 109).
- Educators in culturally diverse classrooms must demonstrate high academic expectations for learners. This can be achieved by selecting challenging academic curricula or by promoting the use of higher-order thinking skills.
- High academic expectations are accompanied by high behavioural expectations – in culturally responsive settings, educators will not permit learners to choose failure.

**F  Foster positive relationships**

- Learners who do not feel valued in educational settings are likely to develop lower self-esteem, alienating them further from learning. Thus safe, inclusive and respectful learning environments are vital to the academic success of all learners.
- Educators who demonstrate that they value the cultural experiences of learners will have greater success in building meaningful relationships. In the context of classroom management, educators should develop a positive relationship with learners.
- Storytelling and sharing are seen to be effective when encouraging learners to persist with tasks. As a result, relationships based on respect, rather than power, can be established.

**L  Learn through culture**

- The culturally responsive educator will connect cultural experiences to the content and practices of the educational setting by finding opportunities to use the strengths and experiences of learners. This is consistent with a constructivist view of instruction where new learning requires the activation of prior knowledge.
- Some examples of ways to learn through culture include allowing the learners to use home language and actively engaging parents and community members in the educational setting to share their experiences and knowledge.
- Culturally responsive educators must respect and acknowledge who owns the knowledge. This emphasises the importance of developing a detailed understanding of the culture through research and personal relationships.
- Without an authentic understanding and positive relationship with the learners, attempts at incorporating cultural knowledge may at best seem tokenistic, and at worst seem alienating to learners.

**E  Explicitly support learners**

- While an educator may have high academic expectations for learners, this is not enough to ensure success. For learners to meet educators' expectations, they must be supported. That is, the educator is both personally warm towards and respectful of learners, and is academically demanding.

| **TABLE 17.1** (CONT.) |
| --- |
| **Culturally responsive educators:** |
| • Supportive educators use explicit quality criteria, modelling and scaffolding to ensure that the learner understands what they are expected to do, and then remove scaffolding when the learner achieves proficiency. They will provide examples, scenarios and vignettes to build bridges to connect prior knowledge with new knowledge and connect similar knowledge content between subject disciplines. |

**C   Create a learning community**

- In preference to competitive individual achievement, culturally responsive educators encourage learners to learn collaboratively. By establishing a community of learners, all learners become responsible for the academic success of others.
- Strategies such as group work and peer teaching assist learners to share their experience and prior knowledge. Strategies to support learners' self-regulation include setting clear goals, provision of adequate resources and the negotiation of a code of conduct.
- In collaborative learning environments, the educator needs to share power with the learners; that is, acknowledge that they are not the only one who possesses knowledge. When learners share power with the educator, they have some say over what happens with their learning and their unique cultural knowledge is valued.

**T   Transform curriculum and assessment**

- Culturally responsive educators take a critical stance towards curriculum and are prepared to make changes to improve overall quality.
- They will plan when and how cultural knowledge will be used, rather than adding it in an unconnected way. They will ensure local knowledge, language and culture are fully integrated into learning programs.
- When different cultural perspectives are validated, learners from these cultures are affirmed.

Source: Cairncross 2009

In culturally responsive settings, educators use the characteristics, experiences and perspectives of culturally diverse learners as conduits for teaching them more effectively and improving academic outcomes. Further, this pedagogy helps learners to affirm their own cultural identity and challenge inequities that educational settings and other institutions often perpetuate.

Culturally responsive pedagogies can be categorised according to common features of effective practice. Table 17.1 outlines the REFLECT framework – a summary of the key features of culturally responsive practice, elements of which will be explored later in the chapter.

For the Aboriginal and Torres Strait Islander histories and cultures cross-curriculum priority to be addressed meaningfully, educators must be prepared to design and implement lessons that are inclusive and respectful. The REFLECT framework outlines the key features of a pedagogy that uses the characteristics, experiences and perspectives of culturally diverse learners as conduits for learning. Culturally responsive educators need to respect and acknowledge who owns the knowledge. This emphasises the importance of developing a detailed understanding of culture through research and personal relationships. The next section will address how educators can engage authentically with Aboriginal and Torres Strait Islander communities to acquire this knowledge and understanding.

## EDUCATOR TIP

A culturally responsive educator is open to having their view of knowledge and understanding of the world challenged and changed.

Which element of the REFLECT framework aligns most closely to your belief about what good educators do? Why?

Reflection

# DEVELOPING EDUCATORS' UNDERSTANDING THROUGH AUTHENTIC FAMILY AND COMMUNITY ENGAGEMENT

As previously stated, culturally responsive educators will spend time developing an understanding of culture through research and establishing personal relationships with Aboriginal and Torres Strait Islander peoples. It is also critical to acknowledge that this takes time, and there are, like in all communities, different voices and experiences. We will discuss how educators can meaningfully connect cultural knowledge and experiences to the learning practices in their educational setting.

## The significance of community engagement

Engagement between educational sites and the community can best be defined as the interconnections between educational sites and individuals, businesses, and formal and informal organisations and institutions in a community. In the formal sense, these interactions should be based on relationships, purposeful, focus on learners, and authentic and genuine in intent. As such, these relationships will develop as trust and two-way respect are established and nurtured.

There are many reasons for the chronic underachievement of Aboriginal and Torres Strait Islander learners. While many educators and also parents may claim to know the primary reasons for this, there is no one cause or event that can be singly identified, and this is common in most cases of complex intergenerational disadvantage. However, what has been established is that educators who have being able to collaborate with Elders and/

or community members have spoken of being professionally liberated, through being challenged to interrogate their 'knowledge' of these communities and attitudes towards them and the consequent pedagogic practices that guide their everyday understanding about the education of the Aboriginal and Torres Strait Islander child, and the place and role of their family.

## Challenging educator preconceptions and beliefs about Aboriginal learners, communities and Country

Educators' foundational beliefs about learners, their families and communities are critically linked with their 'professional knowledge' of these often-alien environments (Lowe 2017). It is argued that it is this limited knowledge that impacts on educators' deeply held views, attitudes and beliefs about the teaching of Aboriginal learners, their capacity and aspirations, as well as their understanding of the histories, cultures and epistemologies of the communities in which they reside (Ladwig 2010).

Research from both New Zealand (Berryman, SooHoo & Nevin 2013; Glynn et al. 2010) and North America (Gay 2002; Genao 2016) demonstrates the need for educational settings and educators to reflexively understand how practices and policies that relate specifically, or are applied, to their children are characterised. In part, these practices and policies are underpinned by deficit views that have a collective role in pursuing and maintaining assimilatory school policies and community interactions.

## Benefits of educational settings and community engagement

There are several key assumptions that sit behind the calls for educational settings to actively seek to partner with families and/or communities. Typically, the research has pointed to positive effects that accrue to both learners and educators when parents and the wider community are able to forge productive collaborative relationships (Muller 2012). Some of these benefits include:

- challenging underpinning cultural discontinuities between Western and Indigenous knowledge systems
- identifying, challenging and reconceptualising those educational discourses where deficit theorising directly impacts on educators' everyday interactions with learners in such a way that it affects their decisions about learners' educative capacities, aspirations and interests, the implementation of school policies and quality curriculum development, and pedagogic practices and assessment
- developing cultural programs through direct collaboration with the community
- working collaboratively in identifying where and how educational settings are enabled to share Aboriginal and Torres Strait Islander people's knowledge and skills to initiate new curriculum, teaching and/or programs that directly support learners
- understanding how power, responsibility and ownership are exercised and how these can be shared between parents and the educational setting

· developing an understanding of the sensitivities surrounding teaching about a local community's cultural business (inclusive of sacred Dreaming places and narratives) and appreciating the need to work with and seek advice from the local community. Many school systems and curriculum authorities have provided general and syllabus-specific advice on these matters (QCAA n.d.)

## Defining community engagement and understanding protocols for engagement

**Community consultation** is an ongoing process that benefits all participants in helping to ensure that Aboriginal and Torres Strait Islander voices are effectively incorporated into the curriculum. It involves establishing a respectful relationship with Aboriginal communities and demonstrating a willingness to share, learn and negotiate (Board of Studies NSW 2009). At their heart, **Indigenous cultural protocols** are a way of acting that is respectful and emanates from an understanding that there is an appropriate way to engage. They are about showing respect for the diversity of Aboriginal and Torres Strait Islander peoples, their lived experiences and histories. The best advice will come through engaging with local people and, where possible, having them support educators to segue into the community. At all times, educators need to be mindful that there will be many issues that will require considerable sensitivity.

**community consultation**: a process that enables educators to become aware of community views and sensitivities and involves getting to know members of the local community and making people aware of what is happening in the school

**Indigenous cultural protocols**: the customs, lores and codes of behaviour of a particular group; they exist to ensure people behave and interact in an appropriate manner

While many government agencies and Indigenous organisations provide advice to educators on protocols for engaging with community, educators should seek advice to ensure protocols are applied appropriately to the local context. Some useful examples include *Working with Aboriginal Communities* (https://ab-ed.nesa.nsw.edu.au/go/partnerships; Board of Studies, NSW 2008) and resources from the Queensland Curriculum and Assessment Authority (https://goo.gl/JbweFj).

## Planning for meaningful discussion: key questions to consider

The following questions and strategies will help educators to commence developing a collaborative and productive relationship with the Aboriginal and/or Torres Strait Islander support staff who may be in their setting, the regional/diocesan/Aboriginal Interpreter Service (AIS) office or another agency in the community. Alternative strategies are to seek advice from Aboriginal or Torres Strait Islander parents, who may be identified by colleagues; or seek advice directly from the state or territory Aboriginal Education Consultative Group (AECG) or another community agency such as the local Aboriginal medical, health or legal service.

It is important for educators to remember that they are looking to connect, get advice and begin a dialogue with Aboriginal and Torres Strait Islander parents, workers or agencies for the purpose of helping them to engage with and know their local community. The greater the levels of trust and respect people have for the educator, the more insights about cultural knowledge, events and learners will be made known to them. Table 17.2 outlines some key questions and considerations for educators attempting to establish partnerships with the community.

| TABLE 17.2 ESTABLISHING EDUCATIONAL COMMUNITY PARTNERSHIPS | |
|---|---|
| **Key questions** | **Things to think about** |
| Determine your real need. What issue/s do you need to address and whose problem is it? | • One of the key questions is to think through what you really need to know. While an immediate need might be to locate and incorporate local examples in a teaching program, the deeper issue is how to understand Indigenous knowledge and its legitimacy, and how to incorporate it into classroom practice.<br>• An example of this is how you teach Aboriginal spirituality, Dreaming narratives and people's connection to Country/Place.<br>• What is your cultural positioning and how does it affect your views about Aboriginal and Torres Strait Islander religious beliefs? |
| What does the educational setting and community need you to achieve? | • Think through what the educational setting and parents/community want to effect in this engagement. You may want to ask someone to talk to learners. Parents, on the other hand, might be more interested in legitimating their community's claims to Country and in questioning their dispossession. |
| Who are the key players and what role do they play? | • It is important to ensure that you talk to several different people to make sure you have the right people at the table. It's not necessary that all will want/need to participate, but it is necessary that everyone is invited. |
| What issues will affect success? | • Think about what would motivate you to be involved in an educational program. Issues such as time, location and expectations are going to be important.<br>• Are your intentions clear? Are you expecting too much?<br>• Are you wanting someone to legitimate what you do or are you wanting to have others do parts of the teaching? |

Other questions to work through with colleagues, the site's leadership team and community include:

• What if any compensatory consideration will be made to parent/community participation?

- How are you imagining that participation will affect both learner understanding and outcomes, and educator understanding?
- How might you sustain these relationships in this and other projects?
- What are your role and responsibility to aid this?

This section has explored the importance of educators establishing authentic links with communities. This is critical for educators wanting to develop high-quality teaching and learning programs about Aboriginal and Torres Strait Islander peoples. In summary, we argue that, first, educational setting and community engagement is about trust, respect and two-way interactions that value the knowledge of educators and Aboriginal and Torres Strait Islander peoples. Second, these interactions must be reciprocal as it is the relationship that provides the conduit into the worlds of educational settings and communities. Third, an authentic engagement facilitates educational settings developing insight into the lived experiences, histories, attitudes and beliefs about the schooling of Aboriginal and Torres Strait Islander learners. Lastly, in the process of establishing and maintaining these two-way learning relationships, educational settings begin to understand and become responsive to the aspirations of communities about what school success could be for Aboriginal and Torres Strait Islander learners.

## EDUCATOR TIP

Educational settings and community engagement are about trust, respect and two-way interactions.

Outline the importance of community engagement to Aboriginal and Torres Strait Islander people, learners and educators.

Reflection

# MAKING CURRICULUM WORK

To this point, we have argued that educators need to think deeply about what it is they want their learners to know and understand about the histories, cultures, languages and knowledge of Aboriginal and Torres Strait Islander peoples. We have spoken of some of the inherent problems in whether the cross-curriculum content enables Aboriginal and Torres Strait Islander learners to see themselves as represented coherently within these documents, and whether all learners are armed with the necessary knowledge and understanding to partake in the national discussions about the place, rights and acknowledgement of Aboriginal and Torres Strait Islander peoples within contemporary Australia.

## EDUCATOR TIP

To avoid addressing this cross-curriculum priority as a tokenistic, tick-the-box process, educators should look to identify the deep knowledge that learners will need to possess if they are to be best equipped for working towards genuine local and national reconciliation post school. In doing so, the priority will be addressed in a way that genuinely honours the culture and histories of Aboriginal and Torres Strait Islander peoples.

What follows is an approach to curriculum development that provides a framework through which educators are able to identify a holistic understanding of the curriculum's key concepts of Country/Place, culture and people, and develop a clear picture of how to identify the 'big idea' that will sustain teaching of these themes across the learning continuum. The thematic mapping table (Table 17.3) frames the mandatory content descriptions across the stages of learning and the cross-curriculum priorities' three key themes. At this point, we have identified a range of explicit or inferred concepts that need to be taught in the content within each key theme. Finally, we have looked back to the Shaping Papers for the Australian Curriculum and identified overarching ideas, such as *reconciliation*, *custodianship* (connectedness to knowledge and Country/Place) and Aboriginal and Torres Strait Islander *agency and resistance*. We have mapped the complex big idea of *custodianship* and provided a backward map to show how this critical notion of Indigenous people's deep and enduring spiritual relationship to Country/Place can be taught authentically. This mapping will make explicit links to the culturally responsive pedagogy engagement with Aboriginal and Torres Strait Islander community members discussed in earlier sections of the chapter.

The diagram in Figure 17.1 (page 324) takes one 'big idea' – custodianship and connectedness – from the thematic mapping table, and shows what the learning could look like from Foundation to Year 5. The strategies within the diagram explicitly address the content descriptors within the HASS curriculum. The theme of connection and custodianship is present throughout each learning stage, providing a continuum of learning that progressively builds a deep and enduring understanding. Also evident within the mapping are strategies identified within the REFLECT framework. In particular, culturally responsive educators will build bridges between different belief and knowledge systems, provide authentic and contextual learning opportunities, have high expectations and explicitly support learners to achieve.

## CONCLUSION

This chapter has shown that educators hold the key to help address the alarming rates of Aboriginal and Torres Strait Islander people's underachievement in educational settings. Educators have always had the capacity to cut through injustice and talk directly to all learners about what they know to be good and moral. We have put forward this challenge, and have shown how, with forethought, planning, engagement and collaboration, educators are able to take up this challenge and work on being educators who help Aboriginal and Torres Strait Islander learners to engage with and achieve success in their learning.

**TABLE 17.3:** THEMATIC MAPPING

| Aboriginal and Torres Strait Islander cross-curriculum key concepts | Target content descriptors | The big idea<br>By the end of Year 6, learners will have engaged with the following big ideas. |
|---|---|---|
| **Country and Place** | **Foundation**<br>ACHASSK016<br>**Year 1 & Year 2**<br>ACHASSK032<br>ACHASSK049<br>**Year 3**<br>ACHASSK062<br>ACHASSK064<br>**Year 4**<br>ACHASSK083<br>ACHASSK089<br>**Year 5**<br>ACHASSK112 | Key concepts from: **content descriptions**<br> • Concept of Place and Country contextual and local<br> • Indigenous knowledge of weather and seasons based on a unique belief system<br> • Custodial responsibility<br> • Continuous connection to land and place<br> • The importance to Aboriginal and/or Torres Strait Islander people and how this influences sustainability<br><br>**By the end of Year 6, learners will understand the big idea of CUSTODIANSHIP and CONNECTEDNESS. They will:**<br> • develop a clear and positive understanding of the theme 'custodianship'. In particular appreciate its complex, all-encompassing and relational meaning, and how it connects Aboriginal and Torres Strait Islander Peoples to Place and Space<br> • understand concepts including: |

active caring:
 • connectedness
 • spiritual wellbeing

belonging:
 • being – Totems
 • responsibility
 • lore

sustaining Country:
 • honouring knowledge and culture responsibility

**TABLE 17.3** (CONT.)

**Question:**

How does this concept link to or challenge Western concepts of ownership, and of privately owned and used cultural capital?

**Teaching ideas:**

Learning through culture, making links in learning, Dreaming, custodial responsibilities for Dreaming, kin, family traditions and knowledge

**Links to culturally responsive pedagogy:**

Teaching through culture and building bridges between different belief and knowledge systems

---

**Culture**

**Year 3**
AHASSK064
**Year 4**
ACHASSK092
**Year 7**
ACHASSK186
ACHASSK171

Key concepts from: **content descriptions**

- Rules and laws – governing through cultural norms and beliefs
- Moral questions of settlement
- Aboriginal and Torres Strait Islander identity – and the impact of removal and dispossession
- Impact – social and physical trauma
- Deeper understanding of reconciliation

**By the end of Year 6, learners will understand the big idea of RECONCILIATION. They will:**

- develop a deeper understanding of the difference between reconciliation and 'Reconciliation' and what is to be reconciled between the coloniser and colonised
- recognise the complexity of Indigenous knowledge systems and their legitimacy as systems of knowing the world
- articulate the social, cultural and political life in Australia and how it would be represented if reconciliation were achieved
- understand the history of their local community, highlighting the history of colonisation, interactions and reconciliation

**Links to culturally responsive pedagogy:**

Authentic and contextual teaching that addresses deeper understanding of contentious historic, social and cultural issues

**People**

**Year 4**
(ACHASSK086)
**Year 5**
ACHASSK107
ACHASSI099
**Year 6**
ACHASSK135

Key concepts from: **content descriptions**
- Invasion or peaceful contact and colonisation
- The impact of colonisation on Aboriginal and Torres Strait Islander peoples
- Indigenous agency

**By the end of Year 6, learners will understand the big idea of AGENCY AND RESISTANCE. They will:**
- Focus on the concepts of truth and reconciliation, understanding the impact and ongoing effects
- Understand contentious topics including invasion, colonisation, dispersal and dispossession
- Cite local and national examples of Aboriginal and Torres Strait Islander people's resistance and their ongoing acts of agency in adapting and being active participants in the making of modern Australia
- Describe the rights of Aboriginal and Torres Strait Islander peoples as First Peoples, and the value of reconciliation and treaties in protecting these rights
- Value the importance of reconciliation for all people at a local and national level, and how this can and is achieved

**Links to culturally responsive pedagogy:**
High expectations and explicit support, and the need to unpack difficult concepts to support learners to understand

**Teacher planning starts here**

**The 'Big' idea**
CONNECTION &
CUSTODIANSHIP
For tens of thousands of years, Aboriginal and Torres Strait Islander peoples have had a profound connection to the land. It sustains language, Law and art. Aboriginal and Torres Strait Islander peoples belong to the land, rather than taking ownership of it.

**Why does the learning matter?**
Country is a source of strength and resilience for Aboriginal and Torres Strait Islander peoples against the historic and contemporary impacts of colonisation. Understanding this is essential when exploring issues such as displacement in Year 6 and beyond. Contemporary Australians can also learn much about conservation and care for the environment

**Target content descriptions**

| | |
|---|---|
| ACHASSK016 | ACHASSK049 |
| ACHASSK062 | ACHASSK064 |
| ACHASSK083 | ACHASSK089 |
| ACHASSK112 | |

**Year 5**
Students can describe the influence of Aboriginal and Torres Strait Islander peoples on the environmental characteristics of Australian places. They identify evidence within their local area of middens, scar trees and grinding grooves, to show how the local people used the resources of the area in a sustainable way. Students evaluate Indigenous environmental land management practices, such as fire stick farming, to show how the environment was cared for and maintained, while at the same time meeting people's needs for survival.

**Year 3**
Students recognise that Australia can be divided into language groups and can identify the language group where the school is located. They can name important local sites using the common name and the Aboriginal name. By talking to local Elders or community members they recognise a connection between language, country and spirituality. Students recall how they welcome people into their home and investigate how other cultures, such as Maori will welcome visitors. Further, students will unpack 'Welcome to Country' and 'Acknowledgement of Country' statements and discuss the role of Aboriginal people as custodians of land.

**Year 4**
Students recognise that Australia has two Indigenous cultural groups: Aboriginal peoples and Torres Strait Islander peoples. By studying an archaeological site (such as Lake Mungo) students can draw conclusions about the long and continuous connection of Aboriginal people to Country. Students can provide examples of totems that are given to many Aboriginal or Torres Strait Islander people at birth that provide them with a spiritual connection to Place. Students can explain that they are responsible for the care and preservation of the totem, Dreaming and Country.

**Year 2**
Students can explain that Aboriginal or Torres Strait Islander peoples have special connections to particular Country/Place through marriage, birth or residence. Students explore the concept of custodianship through a comparison with an heirloom – something that is significant and needs to be cared for, to be passed on to the next generation. Students can discuss family heirlooms, why they are important to their family and how they would feel if the heirloom were lost. Through this learning, students begin to understand the deeper meaning of connection to Country and Place.

**Foundation and Year 1**
Students can name the Aboriginal or Torres Strait Islander Country/Place on which the school is located, thus establishing evidence of prior occupation. After listening to a local Elder or a local Dreaming story, students can identify why Country/Place is important to Aboriginal and Torres Strait Islander people.

**Student learning starts here**

FIGURE 17.1   Backward mapping

## REVIEW QUESTIONS

1.  Outline why the Aboriginal and Torres Strait Islander histories and cultures cross-curriculum priority was included in the Australian Curriculum.

2.  Articulate one challenge facing educators as they integrate this content meaningfully into their teaching programs.

3.  Identify five key features of culturally responsive pedagogy.

4.  Outline the benefits of community engagement to Aboriginal and Torres Strait Islander people, to learners and to educators.

5.  Describe the importance of a thematic or backward mapping approach to the development of rigorous and engaging lessons.

## LEARNING EXTENSION

Explore Yunkaporta's relational eight ways pedagogy (Yunkaporta 2009a) and explain how this pedagogy informs successful classroom practice for all students (see https://www.aitsl .edu.au/tools-resources/resource/eight-ways-of-learning-illustration-of-practice).

## REFERENCES

ABS (Australian Bureau of Statistics). (2017). *Migration, Australia 2015–16*. Retrieved from: http://www.abs.gov.au/ausstats/abs@.nsf/mf/3412.0.

ACARA (Australian Curriculum, Assessment and Reporting Authority). (2012). *The Shape of the Australian Curriculum: Version 04*. Sydney: ACARA.

AEC (Australian Education Council). (1989). *Common and Agreed National Goals for Schooling in Australia*. Hobart: AEC.

Berryman, M., SooHoo, S. & Nevin, A.I. (2013). Culturally responsive research from the margins. In M. Berryman, S. SooHoo & A.I. Nevin, eds, *Culturally Responsive Methodologies*. Bingley: Emerald Group, pp. 1–12.

Board of Studies, NSW. (2008). *Working with Aboriginal Communities: A guide to community consultation and protocols*. Sydney: Board of Studies, NSW.

——(2009). Aboriginal education timelines in NSW. Retrieved from: http://ab-ed.boardofstudies.nsw.edu.au/go/aboriginal-studies/timeline.

Cairncross, J. (2009). To what extent does culturally relevant pedagogy engage students from ethnically diverse backgrounds? Unpublished MEd thesis, University of Sydney.

DEST (Department of Education, Science and Training). (1999). *The Adelaide Declaration*. Retrieved from: http://www.dest.gov.au/sectors/school_education/policy_initiatives_reviews/ national_ goals_for_schooling_in_the_twenty_first_century.htm.

Gay, G. (2002). Preparing for culturally responsive teaching. *Journal of Teacher Education*, 53, 106–16.

Genao, S. (2016). Culturally responsive pedagogy: Reflections on mentoring by educational leadership candidates. *Issues in Educational Research*, 26(3), 431–45.

Glynn, T., Cowie, B., Otrel-Cass, K. & Macfarlane, A. (2010). Culturally responsive pedagogy: Connecting New Zealand teachers of science with their Māori students. *The Australian Journal of Indigenous Education*, 39, 118–27.

Hattie, J. (2012). *Know Thy Impact: Visible learning in theory and practice*. Routledge Free Book. Retrieved from: https://s3-us-west-2.amazonaws.com/tandfbis/rt-files/docs/FreeBooks +Opened+Up/Know_Thy_Impact_Visible_Learning_in_Theory_and_Practice.pdf.

Ladson-Billings, G. (1995). Towards a theory of culturally relevant pedagogy. *American Educational Research Journal*, 32(3), 465–91.

Ladwig, J. (2010). Curriculum and teacher change. In P. Peterson, E. Baker & B. McGaw, eds, *International Encyclopedia of Education*. Oxford: Elsevier.

Ladwig, J., King, B. & NSW Department of Education and Training. (2003). *Quality Teaching in NSW Public Schools: An annotated bibliography*. Sydney: NSW DET.

Lowe, K. (2017). *Walanbaa warramildanha*: The impact of authentic Aboriginal community and school engagement on teachers' professional knowledge. *The Australian Educational Researcher*, 44(1), 35–54. DOI: 10.1007/s13384-017-0229-8.

MCEECDYA (Ministerial Council for Education, Early Childhood Development and Youth Affairs). (1999). *The Adelaide Declaration on National Goals for Schooling in the Twenty-First Century*. Retrieved from: http://www.scseec.edu.au/archive/Publications/Publications-archive/The-Adelaide-Declaration.aspx.

MCEETYA (Ministerial Council on Education, Employment, Training and Youth Affairs). (2008). *Melbourne Declaration on Educational Goals for Young Australians*. Retrieved from: http://www.curriculum.edu.au/verve/_resources/National_Declaration_on_the_Educational_ Goals_for_Young_Australians.pdf.

Muller, D. (2012). *Parents as Partners in Indigenous Children's Learning*. Canberra: Family–School and Community Partnerships Bureau. Retrieved from: https://goo.gl/CF4mEy.

National Curriculum Board. (2009). *The Shape of the Australian Curriculum*. Melbourne: National Curriculum Board.

NSW AECG & NSW DET. (2004). *The Report of the Review of Aboriginal Education: Yanigurra Muya: Ganggurrinyma Yarri Guurulaw Yirringin.gurray: Freeing the spirit: Dreaming an equal future*. Sydney: NSW Department of Education and Training.

Perso, T., Kenyon, P. & Darrough, N. (2012). Transitioning Indigenous students to Western schooling: A culturally responsive program. Paper presented at the 17th Annual Values and Leadership Conference: Ethical Leadership: Building Capacity for those Moments of Challenging Choices, Brisbane. Retrieved from: https://goo.gl/VDaRhA.

QCAA (Queensland Curriculum and Assessment Authority). (n.d.). Aboriginal and Torres Strait Islander perspectives. Retrieved from: https://goo.gl/SwcsMd.

Santoro, N., Reid, J.-A., Crawford, L. & Simpson, L. (2011). Teaching Indigenous children: Listening to and learning from Indigenous teachers. *Australian Journal of Teacher Education*, 36(10), doi: 10.14221/ajte.2011v36n10.2.

Yunkaporta, T. (2009a). 8 ways of learning. Retrieved from: http://8ways.wikispaces.com.

——(2009b). Aboriginal pedagogies at the cultural interface. EdD thesis, James Cook University, Townsville, Qld. Retrieved from: http://eprints.jcu.edu.au/10974.

# 18

# STUDIES OF ASIA AND AUSTRALIA'S ENGAGEMENT WITH ASIA

*Deborah Henderson*

## Learning objectives

After reading this chapter, you should be able to:

- understand why young Australians should study the cross-curriculum priority, Asia and Australia's engagement with Asia, in the *Australian Curriculum: HASS*
- understand how this cross-curriculum priority is represented and structured in the *Australian Curriculum: HASS*
- identify the ways in which the general capabilities can be used to foster knowledge, understanding and skills about Asia and the development of Asia capability
- appreciate how engagement with the countries of the Asia region can be developed in educational settings.

## INTRODUCTION

The Asia region is critically important for Australia's long-term future as people-to-people links through education and cultural exchange, business, trade, defence, migration and tourism continue to increase. Accordingly, Asia and Australia's engagement with Asia is identified as one of three cross-curriculum priorities in the Australian Curriculum. Referred to as the 'Asia priority', this cross-curriculum priority provides opportunities for learners to investigate, understand and recognise the diversity within and between the peoples and countries of the Asia region as well as the diversity within communities in Australia. In doing so, learners from the early years and F-6/7 can develop some knowledge and understanding of Asian societies, cultures, beliefs and environments, and the connections between the peoples of Asia, Australia and the rest of the world. Such knowledge and understanding, when linked with the Australian Curriculum's general capabilities, provides learners with opportunities to develop those skills required to communicate and engage with the peoples of the region who are 'different' from yet 'similar' to them. Referred to as 'Asia literacy', and more recently as 'Asia capability', this combination of knowledge, understanding and skills prepares learners for the challenges of living, studying and working in the region.

This chapter explores how studies of Asia and Australia's engagement with some of the countries and cultures in this region can be taught in ways that foster intercultural understanding in educational settings as part of a future-focused curriculum. It offers strategies for learning about and engaging with diverse cultures that go beyond the instrumentalism of national economic and security interests in Asia, by exploring how learners can be encouraged to recognise commonalities and differences as well as appreciate and empathise with the lived experiences of diverse peoples and local communities in Australia and Asia. Put simply, this chapter argues that study of Asia and Australia's engagement with Asia matters. Learners need to understand their own cultural traditions, values and beliefs as well as engage with the experiences and ideas of others. This form of Asia capability will enable them to navigate the multiplicity of 21st-century intercultural relations as local, regional and global citizens.

# WHY YOUNG AUSTRALIANS SHOULD STUDY ASIA AND AUSTRALIA'S ENGAGEMENT WITH ASIA

In 2012, an Australian Government White Paper (Commonwealth of Australia 2012, p. 1) stated:

> The Asian century is an Australian opportunity. As the global centre of gravity shifts to our region, the tyranny of distance is being replaced by the prospects of proximity. Australia is located in the right place at the right time – in the Asian region in the Asian century.

In outlining why Asia matters for Australia's future, the White Paper also noted that Asia would soon be the world's largest producer of goods and services, as well as the world's largest consumer of them and 'home to the majority of the world's middle class' (Commonwealth of Australia 2012, p. 1). Other factors indicate why the Asia region is too significant to ignore. Asia comprises 30 per cent of the earth's land and 60 per cent of the world's population. Two of the world's most populous nations (China and India) and two of the world's superpowers (Japan and China) are located in Asia. The world's second-largest economy (Japan) and the two fastest-growing economies (China and India) are also part of the region. Furthermore, the greatest diversity of belief systems, including those of Indonesia, Australia's closest neighbour and the world's largest Muslim nation, are located in this region.

Given these factors, it is somewhat surprising that the agreed policy that informs the Australian Curriculum and all other national and state/territory initiatives, the *Melbourne Declaration on Educational Goals for Young Australians* (Melbourne Declaration; MCEETYA 2008), marked the first time that the study of Asia was prioritised in a national statement of goals for schooling in Australia. Indeed, the Melbourne Declaration noted that 'Australians need to become "Asia-literate" engaging and building strong relationships with Asia' (MCEETYA 2008, p. 4).

Yet until the 1990s, school curricula in Australia were dominated by a focus on Western knowledge, customs, traditions and practices, with few opportunities to learn about the peoples and countries of Asia (Henderson 2012, 2015). This is despite the fact that for more than 50 years academics and government officials argued that teaching Asian studies and languages was essential for Australia's national interest. For example, the 1970 Auchmuty Report identified the need for Asian studies to be accorded 'parity of esteem' (Auchmuty 1970, p. 90) with the study of European languages and cultures in the Australian education system and that it was in Australia's national interest to 'challenge the prevailing **Anglocentric traditions** that dominated Australian intellectual and cultural life' (Henderson 2003, p. 27). The inclusion of Asia and Australia's engagement with Asia as one of the three cross-curriculum priorities offers many opportunities to rebalance the learning of young people so they can understand more about the region in which Australia is located.

> **Anglocentric traditions**: place an emphasis on English historical and cultural traditions and their influence in shaping Australian attitudes, beliefs and world views. There is also the assumption that English culture is superior to other cultures.

Another important reason why the Asia priority matters for young Australians is that Australia's demography is undergoing one of the most significant changes in its history. Forty per cent of migrants to Australia now come from Asia, notably from China, India, Vietnam and the Philippines (ABS 2016). In providing opportunities for young people to learn about Asia and its peoples, as well as Australia's own multicultural communities, the Australian Curriculum also reflects the diversity of Australia's people, and is inclusive of all Australians' backgrounds and experience. While the Asia and Australia's engagement with Asia priority provides a regional context for all learning in the curriculum, it has particular importance for Humanities and Social Sciences (HASS). Educators can devise a range of opportunities for learners to inquire into Asian content in the F-6/7 HASS sub-strands of History, Geography, Economics and Business, and Civics and Citizenship, and they can also draw from the general capabilities to enrich teaching and learning. Prior to exploring these exciting opportunities, it is necessary to briefly consider what is meant by Asia literacy and why some consider it to be problematic.

## Exploring the notion of Asia literacy

The concept of Asia literacy, first coined by the Asian Studies Council (1988) in its recommendations for a national strategy for studies of Asia in Australia, is now a shorthand term encompassing knowledge, understandings, a range of skills and a set of social practices. Asia literacy builds on some of the features identified in the Australian Curriculum's general capability of literacy whereby learners develop the capability to make meaning, present ideas and opinions, interact with others and participate in activities at school and in their lives beyond school. However, Asia literacy also depends on acquiring some discrete knowledge and intercultural capabilities. Of the four definitions of literacy provided in UNESCO's (2006a) fourth annual Education for All Global Monitoring Report, *Literacy for Life: Education for all*, two have significance for conceptualising Asia literacy. These are *literacy as a learning process* and *literacy as applied, practised and situated*. We will explore these possibilities in this chapter.

The most contentious aspects of Asia literacy relate to the knowledge component. It could be argued that the Australian Curriculum presents an unproblematic, static definition of Asia, whereby it is defined by geographical, historical, cultural, religious and language boundaries within the three sub-regions of North-East Asia, South-East Asia and South Asia (ACARA 2018b). Excluded from this definition are those countries known as the Middle East and those in the Asia-Pacific region. Rizvi (2015) contends that such static definitions are inadequate,

**homogenous 'Other'**: a tendency to assume that people of 'other' cultures who are 'different' to the observer are all the same and frozen in time. When this expression is used in relation to studies of Asia, the implication is that Asians have no distinguishing cultural features and ignores the fact that all cultures are dynamic.

and construct Asia as the **homogenous 'Other'**, thus they are not representative of the ways in which cultures are dynamic, evolve and change. By extension, Rizvi's (2015) argument suggests that this positioning of Asia-related knowledge *limits learning processes*. Similarly, Chen (2010) observes in broad terms that Asia has been historically constituted through colonial, imperial and other Western-centric practices that assume Western knowledge or views are superior to those of other cultures. He conceptualises Asia as method – a process that 'sees Asia as a product of history, and realises that Asia has been an active participant in historical processes' (Chen 2010, p. 215).

Such theoretical positions remind us that, as HASS educators, we need to challenge imperial and Orientalist (Said 1978) legacies that position Asia as exotic and/or inferior to the West. Instead, educators need to provide opportunities for learners to critique reified or stereotyped images and representations of Asian peoples and cultures. Educators also need to provide opportunities for learners to engage with a balance of contemporary and traditional cultural representations and consider how people from the regions have been powerful, independent and productive shapers of their own histories, cultures and environments. This form of Asia literacy encompasses literacy as *applied, practised and situated*. We will explore some possible ways to interpret and work from the curriculum to foster this form of Asia literacy in HASS.

## HOW THE ASIA PRIORITY IS REPRESENTED AND STRUCTURED IN THE HASS CURRICULUM

Following concerns about an overcrowded curriculum, the *Australian Curriculum: HASS* may now be implemented as a combined F–6 program or as an F–7 program. As discussed in earlier chapters, the F–6/7 curriculum is organised into two interrelated strands: knowledge and understanding, and inquiry and skills. Although studies of Asia are not explicitly identified in the 'key ideas', there are many opportunities to embed Asia-related content in the HASS sub-strands of History, Geography, Civics and Citizenship, and Economics and Business. Similarly, educators can draw from the general capabilities to enhance Asia-related learning. In the revised version of the curriculum, some of the explicit links to embedding Asia content in the sub-strands are removed; however, by carefully reflecting on the content descriptors, educators can enrich and extend learning to build knowledge and understanding about Asia. The Spotlight on HASS education feature explores how Reece, a final year preservice teacher, embedded Asia-specific content as he taught learners in the early years during his teaching placement.

In the following Spotlight on HASS education, Year 6 learners explore links with China through a focus on Australia in the past and present and its connections with a diverse world. In this case, educators devised learning sequences from the History sub-strand content descriptor, Stories of groups of people who migrated to Australia since Federation (including from ONE country of the Asia region) and reasons they migrated (ACHASSK136); and the Geography sub-strand content descriptor, Australia's connections with other countries and how these change people and places (ACHASSK141).

# REECE'S EXPERIENCE IN EMBEDDING STUDIES OF ASIA IN HASS

Reece worked with Prep (or Foundation) learners in a multicultural educational setting to explore 'My personal world' via the Geography sub-strand content descriptor: The places people live in and belong to, their familiar features and why they are important to people (ACHASSK015); and through the History sub-strand content descriptor: How the stories of families and the past can be communicated, for example, through photographs, artefacts, books, oral histories, digital media and museums (ACHASSK013).

As five of the Prep learners were of Chinese origin, Reece decided to select a specific country as a starting point and devote several days to exploring aspects of Australia's Chinese migration and heritage via the ideas of family, journeys and festivals. Reece introduced the activities by reading the picture book, *Shanyi Goes to China*, written by Sungwan So (2009). In this story, learners are invited to accompany Shanyi on her journey to China to explore the country where her parents were born. During her travels, Shanyi visits relatives throughout China and has the opportunity to explore a fishing village, eat dim sum, observe several festivals and learn to write her name in calligraphy, among other activities. At key stages in reading the narrative, Reece paused and referred to a large world map to indicate how far the places Shanyi visited were from Australia. Reece also provided time for learners to use their iPads to search for the villages and towns Shanyi visits via Google Earth.

Following this activity, Reece employed an **engage**, **explore** and **reflect** strategy to encourage learners to explore different Chinese celebrations, holidays and festivals. To enrich his planning, Reece drew from the Hoopla Doopla curriculum resource package for ideas on how to use its resources in the classroom to explore the Dragon Boat Festival.

To consolidate learning, Reece used a class set of big books, *Snapshots of Asia: China* (Commonwealth of Australia 2001). Parents and carers were invited to spend an afternoon with pairs of learners and guide them through the big book about China with topics ranging from Getting About to Our Environment, Going Shopping, Playing Games and Having Fun Cooking, among others. Later that afternoon, Reece, some of the parents and carers, and learners prepared, cooked and ate a Chinese meal. The final activity involved some quiet time for the children to reflect on their learning and to create a picture that captured something they'd learnt about China that was special to them. In his reflective log, Reece noted, 'It was so encouraging to see the willingness of children to learn about China, to experiment and to get excited about their learning. I was especially touched to see the drawings they created and how positive and happy the images were.'

**engage**: educators need to engage learners by capturing their curiosity and interest, and giving them opportunities to demonstrate their prior knowledge. This strategy helps learners make connections between prior knowledge and new ideas.

**explore**: educators need to devise activities that provide learners with a range of opportunities to explore the content/concept/skill being taught. This enables them to engage with problems and describe them in their own words, and helps them to acquire a common set of experiences to share with their peers.

**reflect**: learners need time to reflect on their learning and to clarify their understandings, both as individuals and in groups. When they are encouraged to reflect on the insights they have gained and on things they have started to make sense of and understand, they become more aware of their own learning processes.

# THE GILBERT RIVER GOLDFIELD

In a Far North Queensland primary school, located near the place where Chinese immigrants mined the Gilbert River goldfield from 1870, learners in Year 6 explored what life was like for the Chinese miners who came to Australia. They examined the National Museum of Australia website and studied the *Harvest of Endurance*, a 50 metre-long scroll that represents two centuries of Chinese contact with, and emigration to, Australia. For example, in pairs, learners explored the panel (Figure 18.1) that depicts Chinese miners using a sluice box and puddling mill to search for gold.

FIGURE 18.1 *Harvest of Endurance*, depicting Chinese miners

**represent**: learners need to represent their learning in concrete forms. This could involve constructing a diagram, map and/or timeline, completing a 'looks like-feels like-sounds like' pro forma or Y-chart, drawing an image or creating a collage.

**report**: educators need to seek out, value and use questions from learners, as well as themselves, to embed inquiry to guide reporting strategies. Reporting to peers provides opportunities for learners to consolidate and extend their learning in a non-threatening environment.

During this unit of work, learners researched their community's local history, retraced the journey of some miners from their place of origin in Guangdong province, south-east China, and mapped the physical terrain around the Gilbert River to reconstruct a Chinese mining camp. They also researched the traditional customs the Chinese miners brought with them to Australia. Guided by a reflect, **represent**, **report** process, learners organised a Chinese Lantern Festival Day as the culmination of their term's work. Local and extended members of the community were invited to join in the festivities, which included sharing food, performing traditional Chinese celebratory dances and a community parade around the school holding the Chinese paper lanterns learners had made. In the school hall, learners established learning posts to showcase, or report, their knowledge, understanding and skills; community members were invited to view student-produced maps, timelines, artworks, poetry and short stories about the Chinese miners together with representations of some of the myths and stories behind the Lantern Festival.

These spotlights offer insights into the ways in which HASS can provide rich learning opportunities that serve as building blocks to developing knowledge of the history, cultures and societies of countries in Asia. Both examples also embed some key ideas about the Asia priority and these important ideas are discussed next.

## Key organising ideas

The Asia priority has been developed around three key concepts: Asia and its diversity, the achievements and contributions of the peoples of Asia, and Asia–Australia engagement. According to the curriculum:

> The first key concept highlights the diversity within and between the countries of the Asia region, from their cultures, societies and traditions through to their diverse environments and the effects of these on the lives of people. The second concept examines the past and continuing achievements of the peoples of Asia, identifies their contribution to world history and acknowledges the influences that the Asia region has on the world's aesthetic and creative pursuits. The third concept addresses the nature of past and ongoing links between Australia and Asia, and develops the knowledge, understanding and skills that make it possible to engage actively and effectively with peoples of the Asia region. (ACARA 2018a)

There are numerous ways in which educators can explore these ideas. With reference to engaging with the first key idea, learners require opportunities to understand the ways in which the peoples and countries of Asia are diverse in ethnic background, traditions, cultures, belief systems and religions. They also need to appreciate the connections and interrelationships between people and the diverse environments in Asia, and how these affect the region and have global implications. For example, young learners can explore sustainability challenges prompted by deforestation, the destruction of habitats and the unsustainable production of goods sourced in Asia and sold in Australia, such as palm oil and sugar, among other topics for inquiry.

---

Consider how you could add to the possibilities for exploring the key idea described above. Reflection

---

The second key idea enables learners to investigate some of the contributions and achievements of people from the Asia region in relation to traditional and contemporary artists and musicians, philosophers such as Confucius, human rights activists, environmentalists and politicians. Older learners can consider how Asia influences aesthetic and creative pursuits within Australia, such as the Asia Pacific Triennial of Contemporary Art (APT) held in the Gallery of Modern Art (GOMA), Brisbane. This exhibition of contemporary art from the Asia region offers cross-cultural insights via art, film, Children's Art Centre projects and a public program of talks and workshops.

By exploring some of the different aspects of Asia–Australia engagement, as emphasised in the third key idea, learners can discover how Australians of Asian heritage have influenced Australia's history and how they continue to shape its culture and society.

Learners can also find out about the ways in which Australians play a significant role in social, cultural, political and economic developments in the Asia region. For example, Governor-General Sir Peter Cosgrove served as commander of the International Force for East Timor (INTERFET), which oversaw the peacekeeping mission in East Timor from 1999 as it transitioned to independence. Learners can inquire into how Australians working in non-government organisations such as UNICEF, UNESCO, World Vision and Save the Children perform vital tasks in response to natural disasters, and the challenges of war and famine in the region.

## USING THE GENERAL CAPABILITIES TO FOSTER KNOWLEDGE, UNDERSTANDING AND SKILLS ABOUT ASIA AND THE DEVELOPMENT OF ASIA CAPABILITY

The Australian Curriculum uses the term 'capability' to encompasses a range of knowledge, skills, behaviours and dispositions. The general capability of intercultural understanding is of particular significance for the Asia priority, as developing learners' intercultural understanding is fundamental to education in a diverse and interconnected world. The capacity to engage with people who seem different lies at the heart of intercultural understanding (Banks 2004) and involves young people learning how to value and critically reflect on their own cultural perspectives and practices, and those of others, through their interactions with people, texts and contexts across the curriculum. Australian pioneer in intercultural learning David Dufty and his colleagues (Dufty et al. 1973, p. 2) put it this way:

> we are all conditioned by our culture . . . we tend to judge other cultures by our own standards and . . . to be culturally mature we need to be able to understand and appreciate at least one other culture in some depth and to be able to imagine with some accuracy how others view their world: in other words, to develop an intercultural perspective – to try seeing it their way as well as our own way.

In the Australian Curriculum, the intercultural understanding general capability comprises three interrelated organising elements, each of which contains several sub-elements. The organising elements are: recognising culture and developing respect; interacting and empathising with others; and reflecting on intercultural experiences and taking responsibility (ACARA 2018b). Table 18.1, adapted from an earlier version of the curriculum, illustrates how each organising element is divided into sub-elements, which provide useful elaborations to aid planning. Educators will find the learning continuum devised by ACARA, accessible via a PDF link, helpful in planning for and monitoring their learners' intercultural understanding: https://www.australiancurriculum.edu.au/media/1075/general-capabilities-intercultural-understanding-learning-continuum.pdf.

There is evidence to indicate that school principals and educators value the social capacity building that occurs when studies of Asia foster intercultural understanding in the curriculum, and more broadly in their school community. In a survey of 1471 teachers

**TABLE 18.1** ORGANISING ELEMENTS AND SUB-ELEMENTS FOR INTERCULTURAL UNDERSTANDING

| Organising element | Sub-elements |
| --- | --- |
| Recognising culture and developing respect | <ul><li>Investigate culture and cultural identity</li><li>Explore and compare cultural knowledge, beliefs and practices</li><li>Develop respect for cultural diversity</li></ul> |
| Interacting and empathising with others | <ul><li>Communicate across cultures</li><li>Consider and develop multiple perspectives</li><li>Empathise with others</li></ul> |
| Reflecting on intercultural experiences and taking responsibility | <ul><li>Reflect on intercultural experiences</li><li>Challenge stereotypes and prejudices</li><li>Mediate cultural differences</li></ul> |

Source: ACARA 2018c

and 481 principals in Australia, which sought their views on Asia capability, 72 per cent of respondents noted that fostering intercultural understanding was a key reason for focusing on Asia in the curriculum (Halse et al. 2013). Of note was the following finding:

> Teachers said they hoped that teaching and learning about countries in Asia would help counter 'racist generalisations that stifle thinking' and help to alleviate 'fear and xenophobia'. On the other hand, other teachers said that an Asian focus in their teaching helped students from Asia to learn, understand, embrace and celebrate their own histories and heritages. (p. 64)

The survey also found that 73 per cent of educator respondents thought that a key feature of the 'Asia-literate teacher' was effectiveness in building intercultural understanding through teaching practices and dispositions and behaviours such as being 'accepting', 'open-minded', 'compassionate', 'flexible', 'adaptable', 'forward thinking', 'outward looking', 'culturally inquisitive', 'non-judgemental' and having 'a strong sense of justice' (Halse et al. 2013, p. 65).

In broad terms, Asia capability and intercultural understanding also contribute to the development of global citizenship and global competence. The Organisation for Economic Co-operation and Development (OECD 2018, p. 4) refers to global competence as a multidimensional capacity that, among a range of attributes, enables young people to 'understand and appreciate different perspectives and world views, interact successfully and respectfully with others, and take responsible action toward sustainability and collective well-being'.

The general capabilities of personal and social, critical and creative thinking and ethical understanding all have relevance to fostering studies of Asia and intercultural understanding in topics for inquiry in HASS. In the next section, the information and communication technology (ICT) capability is discussed with reference to the Asia Education Foundation's (AEF) Bridge Program. It provides some wonderful examples of how learners and educators can use ICT to make meaningful connections with their peers in Asia.

# Developing engagement with the countries of the Asia region in educational settings

There are a range of ways in which young learners can be authentically engaged in learning about the peoples and cultures of Asia within and beyond the school. However, educators need to be mindful that purposeful, in-depth and sustained studies produce the most valuable learning. One-off 'Asia festivals' or 'food days', for example, that are not linked to Asia-related learning in a HASS unit, usually produce surface-level learning that lacks meaning. Research suggests that the school programs most effective at achieving inter-cultural understanding include both skills-based and knowledge-based deep learning (Asia Education Foundation 2006). Once schools move beyond a 'knowledge-about-cultures' approach to a focus on inquiry and on engaging with people of diverse cultures, students can develop deeper understandings of culture (Hassim 2013). Furthermore, the Asia Education Foundation (2006, p. 10) contends that when schools offer studies of Asia in course content 'across the curriculum with a balance between in-depth, sustained studies and broader, more general studies that explore themes, topics or issues in conjunction with whole school planning', they foster authentic relationships that contribute to the development of intercultural understanding.

This sort of learning is central to education in an increasingly diverse and intercon-nected world. Australian educators have consistently argued for the need to place more emphasis on Asia and the world in school curricula (Curriculum Corporation 2008). The capacity to relate well with diverse others is recognised internationally as an important 21st-century global skill (OECD 2018) and this capability lies at the core of intercultural understanding. Within their local community, schools can forge partnerships through whole-of-school approaches that involve local community members of Asian descent. Examples of these initiatives include family history programs in which a learner's parent, grandparent or family friend shares their immigration story at school and brings with them photographs or objects that help tell their story. Other options might include establishing an Asian artist-in-residence program, or a traditional music or writer-in-residence program, a traditional craft-making club, such as batik, and performing arts events to prompt community collaboration.

Purposeful encounters during site visits, such as those organised via school-based study tours, sister-school collaborations and homestays with a sister-school family, are powerful ways to prompt further learning about Asia. Virtual experiences can also be most effective for fostering knowledge and intercultural understanding about the region. For example, the ICT general capability offers exciting opportunities for learners to access, create and communicate information and ideas. ICT capability involves students acquiring skills to make the most of the digital technologies available to them, and learning how to adapt to new ways of doing things as technologies evolve while also being mindful of limiting the risks to themselves and others in a digital environment.

## The BRIDGE program and ICT capability

The Building Relationships through Intercultural Dialogue and Growing Engagement (BRIDGE) program is an internationally acclaimed AEF initiative that establishes school partnerships between educators, learners and school communities across the Australia and the Asia region. BRIDGE participants collaborate on various projects, practise language skills and develop friendships with learners at their partner school. These authentic collaborations between educators and learners across Australia and Asia offer rich insights into developing Asia capability (Asia Education Foundation 2013).

BRIDGE projects can involve learners in Australia and Asia sharing learning with their peers in reciprocal ways. These virtual collaborations can include individual and group program presentations via videoconferencing and digital storytelling. With reference to the latter, learners can create digital stories to introduce themselves to each other and share information about their respective families, and they can also video virtual school and local area tours to share with their partner students. Another successful BRIDGE strategy involves the publication of a bilingual book resulting from the sharing of stories across Asia and Australia about students' daily lives. Learners can use video, digital photography and Wikispace to document partnership activities and tell their 'School Partnership Story'. Similarly, learners can virtually travel to each other's countries on Travelbugs and collaborate to write articles about places, people and practices.

In school-based educational settings, learners in the early primary years can write penpal letters and share 'My Place' PowerPoint presentations, and they can share their learning about selected topics, such as wayang puppets and NAIDOC week. Educators can create, compile and share teaching resources with their partner colleagues in the region to support learning about specific issues and topics, such as videos and unit plans, and make these available on the school partnership Wikispace. The success and reach of the BRIDGE program is evidenced by the fact that in 2018, BRIDGE school partnerships involved 764 schools in Australia and Brunei, Cambodia, China, India, Indonesia, Laos, Malaysia, Myanmar, the Philippines, Singapore, South Korea, Thailand and Vietnam, as shown in Figure 18.2 (Asia Education Foundation 2018).

FIGURE 18.2   **BRIDGE school partnerships program**
Source: Asia Education Foundation 2018

# EMBEDDING STUDIES IN ASIA VIA INQUIRY IN HASS

Many Australian schools use explicit planning to ensure studies of Asia are embedded across the learning areas. In HASS, an inquiry-based approach to teaching and learning (Murdoch 2005, 2017) to promote Asia capability places emphasis on posing questions and encouraging young people to be active learners (see Chapter 11). This approach goes beyond awareness raising and information sharing and provides opportunities for young learners to critically engage with regional issues, such as the rise in endangered species and food scarcities due to deforestation, overfishing and pollution. Young people are passionate about the sustainability of the environment (United Nations 2016), and Sustainability is one of the Australian Curriculum's cross-curriculum priorities. Human rights concerns such as access to education, child labour and people smuggling also matter to young learners.

One of the well-known benefits of an inquiry approach is that it enables learners to connect knowledge, understanding and skills so that, as they move through the process of inquiry, they can integrate concepts, content and skills from HASS disciplines and subjects and express their developing ideas and initial understandings. The role of the educator is critical to designing the processes and activities that promote this sort of learning to ensure that intercultural understanding can be developed (UNESCO 2006b). When planning a HASS inquiry unit to embed studies of Asia and foster intercultural understanding, it is important to select an Asia-related topic that will be interesting and relevant to learners, and that will enable them to make connections to their lives.

The HASS sub-strands include a range of skills – questioning, researching, analysing, evaluating and reflecting, and communicating – and the curriculum makes clear that learners are expected to apply these skills to investigate events, developments, issues and phenomena, both historical and contemporary, as they engage in considered and intentional inquiry. It is also critical that, when applied to topics and issues about Asia, this sort of learning involves some form of action or participation so it is authentic and transformative. Transformative learning requires learners to search for and make meaning from their experiences. This meaning, in turn, guides understanding and action (Mezirow 1990) whereby 'knowledge results from the combination of grasping and transforming experience' (Kolb 1984, p. 41). A future-focused curriculum requires transformative approaches to teaching and learning so young people can draw from their knowledge, understanding and skills in ways that actively involve them 'in building solutions' (Curriculum Corporation 2008, p. 1) to the issues and challenges they have investigated.

## EDUCATOR TIP

You may feel more knowledgeable about framing inquiry in one discipline such as History. However, for learners to be successful you need to facilitate, motivate and direct inquiry-based learning across all areas of HASS. Kath Murdoch's (2017) blog provides some useful strategies for teaching to 4–12 year olds via inquiry that are also relevant to fostering Asia capability in HASS. Go to: http://www.kathmurdoch.com.au/blog/2017/11/25/the-art-of-inquiry-10-practices-for-the-inquiry-teacher.

Consider another lens to examine the ways in which learners' lives are connected to the Asia region by examining the links between studies of Asia and developing global perspectives in school curricula. Access *Global Perspectives: A framework for global education in Australian schools* (Curriculum Corporation 2008): http://www.globaleducation.edu.au/verve/_resources/GPS_web.pdf.

In this document, refer to the five learning emphases, which encapsulate some of the recurring themes that can also be encountered meaningfully in studies of Asia. These are interdependence and globalisation, identity and cultural diversity, social justice and human rights, peace building and conflict resolution, and sustainable futures. Reflect on the fact that each learning emphasis has a spatial as well as a temporal dimension. The spatial dimension refers to 'overlapping local and global; social and natural communities which describe interdependence, influence identity and ability to make change' (Curriculum Corporation 2008, p. 5). The temporal dimension relates to the context whereby 'connections between the past, present and future in the dynamic and changing world which influences identity and interdependence of people and their ability to respond to global issues' (p. 5).

How might you draw from the Global Perspectives Framework to enrich your approach to studies of Asia in an educational setting? Suggest at least three possibilities.

# CONCLUSION

This chapter has explored some of the reasons why the Asia region is significant for Australia and why learning about Asia and the development of Asia literacy, or Asia capability, matters for learners. It examined how the cross-curriculum priority, Asia and Australia's engagement with Asia, is represented and structured in the *Australian Curriculum: HASS* from Foundation to Years 6/7, as well as some of the ways in which the general capabilities can be used to foster knowledge, understanding and skills for Asia capability. In discussing how Asia engagement can be developed in educational settings, within and beyond the school, the chapter has advocated a range of approaches that emphasise authentic learning through whole-of-school and community-based learning. It has also examined the rich possibilities of virtual engagement using digital technologies by highlighting the achievements of the Asia Education Foundation's BRIDGE program. The chapter concluded by advocating for inquiry-based learning in units of work that embed the Asia priority in ways that draw from and integrate the F-6/7 HASS sub-strands and connect young people to issues and concerns that matter to them as citizens.

## REVIEW QUESTIONS

1.  What are some 'instrumental reasons' why young people should learn about the Asia region? Provide two reasons.

2.  Why is it important for educators to go beyond instrumentalism and develop intercultural understanding through studies of Asia with learners in HASS? Provide two reasons.

3.  How can studies of Asia and intercultural understanding be developed through HASS within a school?

4.  How can studies of Asia and intercultural understanding through HASS be developed outside a school?

5.  In what ways can the development of Asia capability be transformative for learners?

## LEARNING EXTENSION

1.  Go to the BRIDGE school partnership videos at: http://www.asiaeducation.edu.au/bridge. Investigate how BRIDGE supports learners' skills through authentic interaction with peers. See ways in which school partnerships are collaborating and sharing learning experiences and reflect on how you might implement some of these ideas with learners in your own classroom.

2.  Go to the Immigration Museum's (Melbourne) School programs and resources website at: https://museumsvictoria.com.au/immigrationmuseum/learning/school-programs-and-resources. Access the Pack Your Bags page, which provides opportunities for children in Years 2 to 4 to explore migration and cultural diversity through stories told with objects, artefacts and costumes. Select a specific year level from Years 2 to 4. Consider how you might adapt at least two of the museum's suggested pre-visit activities and two of the post-visit activities to meaningfully engage learners who have English as an additional language/dialect (EAL/D), and who are unable to physically visit the museum, about the nature of the migration experience to Australia.

## REFERENCES

ABS (Australian Bureau of Statistics). (2016). *Census of Population and Housing: Reflecting Australia – Stories from the Census, 2016*. Retrieved from: http://www.abs.gov.au/ausstats/abs@.nsf/Lookup/by%20Subject/2071.0~2016~Main%20Features~Cultural%20Diversity%20Article~60.

ACARA (Australian Curriculum, Assessment and Reporting Authority). (2018a). *Australian Curriculum: F-10, v8.3*. Asia and Australia's engagement with Asia. Retrieved from: https://www.australiancurriculum.edu.au/f-10-curriculum/cross-curriculum-priorities/asia-and-australia-s-engagement-with-asia.

——(2018b). *Australian Curriculum: F-10, v8.3*. Intercultural understanding. Retrieved from: https://www.australiancurriculum.edu.au/f-10-curriculum/general-capabilities/intercultural-understanding.

——(2018c). *Australian Curriculum: F-10, v8.3*. Intercultural understanding learning continuum. Retrieved from https://www.australiancurriculum.edu.au/media/1075/general-capabilities-intercultural-understanding-learning-continuum.pdf.

Asia Education Foundation. (2006). *The National Statement for Engaging Young Australians with Asia in Australian Schools*. Retrieved from: http://scseec.edu.au/site/DefaultSite/filesystem/documents/Reports%20and%20publications/Publications/Cultural%20inclusion%20and%20ATSI/National%20Statement%20for%20Engaging%20Your%20Austrlians%20with%20Asia.pdf.

——(2013). *Achieving Intercultural Understanding Through the Teaching of Asia Perspectives in the Australian Curriculum: English and History*. Melbourne: Asia Education Foundation.

——(2018). BRIDGE School partnerships: Participating countries. Retrieved from: http://www.asiaeducation.edu.au/programmes/school-partnerships/participating-countries/participating-countries.

Asian Studies Council. (1988). *A National Strategy for the Study of Asia in Australia*. Canberra: AGPS.

Auchmuty, J.J. (1970). *The Teaching of Asian Languages and Cultures*. Canberra: AGPS.

Banks, J.A. (2004). Multicultural education: Characteristics and goals. In J.A. Banks & C.A.M. Banks, eds, *Multicultural Education: Issues and perspectives*. Hoboken, NJ: John Wiley & Sons, pp. 3–30.

Chen, K.H. (2010). *Asia as Method: Toward deimperialization*. Durham, NC: Duke University Press.

Commonwealth of Australia. (2001). *Snapshots of Asia: China*. Access Asia Series. Canberra: DEETYA.

——(2012). *Australia in the Asian Century*. *White Paper*. Retrieved from: http://www.defence.gov.au/whitepaper/2013/docs/australia_in_the_asian_century_white_paper.pdf.

Curriculum Corporation. (2008). *Global Perspectives: A framework for global education in Australian schools*. Carlton South, Vic.: Education Services Australia. Retrieved from: http://www.globaleducation.edu.au/verve/_resources/GPS_web.pdf.

Dufty, D., Sawkins, S., Pickard, N., Power, J., Bowe, A., et al. (1973). *Seeing It Their Way: Ideas, activities and resources for intercultural studies and looking around corners: The intercultural explorer's guide*. Sydney: Reed Educational.

Halse, C., Kostogriz, A., Cloonan, A., Dyer, J., Toe, D. & Weinmann, M. (2013). *Asia Literacy and the Australian Teaching Workforce*. Melbourne: Education Services Australia.

Hassim, E. (2013). *An 'intercultural understanding' view of the Asia priority: Implications for the Australian Curriculum*. Centre for Strategic Education Occasional Paper, 131 (July).

Henderson, D. (2003). Meeting the national interest through Asia literacy: An overview of the major themes and debates. *Asian Studies Review*, 27(1), 23–53.

——(2012). Thinking about Australia and its location in the modern world in the Australian Curriculum: History. *QHistory*, annual edn, 24–33.

——(2015). Globalisation and national curriculum reform in Australia: The push for Asia literacy. In J. Zajda, ed., *Second International Handbook on Globalisation, Education and Policy Research*. Dordrecht: Springer, pp. 633–47.

Kolb, D.A. (1984). *Experiential Learning: Experience as the source of learning and development*. Englewood Cliffs, NJ: Prentice Hall.

MCEETYA (Ministerial Council on Education, Employment, Training and Youth Affairs). (2008). *Melbourne Declaration on Educational Goals for Young Australians*. Retrieved from: http://www.curriculum.edu.au/verve/_resources/National_Declaration_on_the_Educational_Goals_for_Young_Australians.pdf.

Mezirow, J. (1990). How critical reflection triggers transformative learning. In J. Mezirow & Associates, eds, *Fostering Critical Reflection in Adulthood: A guide to transformative and emancipatory learning*. San Francisco, CA: Jossey Bass, pp. 1–20.

Murdoch, K. (2005). *Take a Moment: 40 frameworks for reflective thinking*. Melbourne: Seastar Education.

——(2017). The art of inquiry: 10 practices for the inquiry teacher. Retrieved from: http://www .kathmurdoch.com.au/blog/2017/11/25/the-art-of-inquiry-10-practices-for-the-inquiry-teacher.

OECD (Organisation for Economic Co-operation and Development). (2018). *Preparing Our Youth for an Inclusive and Sustainable World. The OECD PISA global competence framework*. Retrieved from: https://www.oecd.org/education/Global-competency-for-an-inclusive-world.pdf.

Rizvi, F. (2015). Learning Asia: In search of a new narrative In C. Halse, ed., *Asia Literate Schooling in the Asian Century*. Abingdon: Routledge, pp. 56–69.

Said, E.W. (1978). *Orientalism*. New York: Random House.

So, S. (2009). *Shanyi Goes to China (Children Return to their Roots)*. London: Francis Lincoln Children's Books.

UNESCO (United Nations Educational, Scientific and Cultural Organization). (2006a). *Education for All Global Monitoring Literacy for Life: Education for all, fourth annual report*. Paris: UNESCO.

——(2006b). *UNESCO Guidelines on Intercultural Education*. Paris: UNESCO.

United Nations. (2016). 17 sustainable development goals (SDGs) of the 2030 Agenda for Sustainable Development. Retrieved from: http://www.un.org/sustainabledevelopment/development-agenda.

# EDUCATING FOR SUSTAINABILITY: THEORETICAL AND PRACTICAL INSIGHTS FOR PRESERVICE EDUCATORS

*Kathryn Paige, David Lloyd and Samuel Osborne*

**19**

## Learning objectives

After reading this chapter, you should be able to:

- engage with ideas for living sustainably and understand the need to shift the way people live towards greater sustainability
- reflect on the value of connecting students to holistic understandings of place with particular reference to Aboriginal and Torres Strait Islander knowledges, perspectives and histories
- develop an understanding of the principles of an educating for sustainability (EfS) framework to plan learning experiences
- incorporate a range of EfS pedagogical practices into classroom experiences
- take an activist role in EfS in both professional and personal life.

## INTRODUCTION

Building sustainable futures through education requires us to understand the world through a **transdisciplinary curriculum** that addresses pressing global concerns in a consumerist society. The most important challenge for **educating for sustainability (EfS)** in schools and the community is having its transdisciplinary nature understood and valued. This chapter starts by describing the need for humans to shift the way they live towards greater sustainability, followed by an overview of why it is important to connect learners to the natural world, and particularly the place where they live. We use a set of guiding principles informed by a transdisciplinary approach in science education where EfS has strong connections to the cross-curriculum priorities of Sustainability and Aboriginal and Torres Strait Islander histories and cultures. The chapter concludes by sharing practical suggestions for preservice and early career educators.

**transdisciplinary curriculum:** an approach that focuses on the exploration of a relevant issue or problem that integrates the perspectives of multiple disciplines in order to connect new knowledge and deeper understanding to real-life experiences

**educating for sustainability (EfS):** learning that links knowledge, inquiry and action to help learners build a healthy future for their communities and the planet

## ENGAGING WITH IDEAS FOR LIVING SUSTAINABLY

We are living in a world where human impacts are changing the earth's environment significantly and, in some cases, irreversibly. Lowe (2014, p. 183) asserts that 'human civilization now faces a crisis. It is clearly impossible for all humans to use resources at the level of contemporary Australians'. Costanza (2012) describes this period in history as the 'Anthropocene', an era in a full world where humans are dramatically altering the ecological life support system. Francoeur (1976, p. 127) argues that for 'most people the changes that loom on our horizon are so psychologically traumatic that there is an often-expressed wish to not even hear, let alone think, about what may lie ahead'.

We can live for the present moment and block out undesirable futures images. The alternative, as suggested by Citraningtyas (2010, p. 190), is to allow this greater awareness of vulnerability to give us the strength to change and to live sustainably; that is, within planetary boundaries (Rockström 2015), the boundaries outside of which the earth as we know it changes radically.

Sustainability needs to be considered from multiple perspectives, and this must include the needs and rights of all species: 'Preserving life on Earth in some form is the challenge for, and responsibility of, humankind now' (Lovelock 2014, p. xvi). Doppelt (2008, p. 67) argues that

> the crises that humanity faces today are very much of our own making. More than anything, climate change and today's other pressing sustainability challenges result from a lack of mindfulness and false feedback mechanisms, that is erroneous and incomplete core beliefs, assumptions and automatic thoughts.

This observation requires an approach to education that starts with learners' understandings, crosses discipline boundaries, includes knowing (cognitive), feeling (affective) and doing (intentional), and seeks to ensure we stay within planetary boundaries for the wellbeing of all the earth's species. This is where informed and authentic engagement with the cross-curriculum priority of Aboriginal and Torres Strait Islander histories and cultures can reposition learners' engagement with knowledges and the environment in powerful ways. This is an opportunity to make links to:

- Indigenous relationships to land and sustainable practices (epistemology, cosmology, ontology, axiology)
- Indigenous knowledges as holistic as opposed to 'disciplined' and segmented approaches
- the place of Indigenous histories and knowledges in place-based transdisciplinary education for sustainability programs.

Torres Strait Islander scholar Martin Nakata (2007) explains that Indigenous knowledges are retained, shared and enacted as a whole. It is Western science and education that seek to compartmentalise, or place 'discipline' knowledge into subjects, faculties and so on. Like many other Indigenous scholars globally, Nakata argues that decolonial approaches to education, knowledge and place are needed to pursue justice and reconciliation, where a more nuanced engagement with the foundations of knowledge gives rise to transformative possibilities through education, society and the landscapes and seas within which we are located (Rigney 1999; Smith 1999).

In social science terms, Indigenous knowledges are underpinned by Indigenous ways of knowing (epistemology), being (ontology) and doing (axiology) (Arbon 2008; Martin 2008).

In the context of sustainability and the environment, engaging with Aboriginal and Torres Strait Islander stories and storytellers, songs and languages, communities and cultures repositions young people to engage with Aboriginal perspectives and practices for sustainable interaction with land, natural resources and each other. It is important that educators move away from stories *about* Aboriginal and Torres Strait Islander peoples and experiences and ensure that Aboriginal and Torres Strait Islander accounts are shared in context and on their own terms. This approach provides a logic and lens for multidisciplinary engagement with EfS pedagogies and enables learning opportunities for learners towards reconciliation and justice. It should allow learners to understand that interdisciplinary engagement with the land, seas and natural resources have contributed towards a respectful and sustainable relationship with the earth and is an approach that can be taken up in schools and communities today.

While we can only ever live in the present moment, we should do so with an eye on where we have come from and the successes and failures we have experienced so that we do not repeat the same mistakes over and over, and set goals for the future and work towards them. Consider in what ways your goals could be informed by patterns and laws – physical, ecological, cultural, social and so on (a transdisciplinary approach) – where there is learning from the past and taking appropriate action based on your future visions.

## THE VALUE OF CONNECTING LEARNERS TO PLACE

The EfS approach advocated in this chapter is one that values learners' interests and concerns, cuts across discipline boundaries and values equally the knowing (cognitive), the connecting (affective) and the doing (intentional); that is, it is a transdisciplinary approach. The ideas behind transdisciplinary learning are reflected in the thinking of educational pioneers like John Dewey, Maria Montessori and Rudolf Steiner, who insisted on cultivating the moral, emotional, physical, psychological and spiritual dimensions of the learner; that is, their broader life skills and values (Gidley 2016). A *transdisciplinary pedagogy* not only values the understanding of the situation under study but also the requirement of active engagement to bring about a preferred future and taking an active part in the change process (Hodson 2003; Lloyd & Wallace 2004; Paige & Lloyd 2016). From a Western knowledge and pedagogical perspective, this work has strong synergies with Indigenous knowledges and pedagogies described above and provides opportunities to engage in the cross-curriculum priorities of Sustainability and Aboriginal and Torres Strait Islander histories and cultures within a range of subject areas including HASS, science, maths and the arts.

A transdisciplinary pedagogy uses many disciplines *and* the grounded, local knowledge and needs of those in a particular social setting to approach a problem (Balsiger 2004; Després, Brais & Avellan 2004). Balsiger (2004, p. 407) states that transdisciplinarity is an approach to understanding the world with a strong orientation towards societal/

environmental problems. The following quote identifies the interconnectivity of the elements of the natural world and humans' impact on it:

> The single most important thing to try to understand is that all things are connected. The air we breathe, the water we drink, the food we eat, the clothes we wear, the place we live in our home and environment (all the plants, animals and living things around us), the energy we use, our family and friends they are all interconnected. Small changes now might have huge consequences in the future. We need to re-connect ourselves to the earth, to nature, to the systems that enable us to live. (Education for Sustainability and Global Learning 2012)

To once again draw the links, Indigenous knowledges are framed within cultural, spiritual and religious terms of connection, which order responsibility for sustainable and continuing connections to Country/Place (the land and its associated sites and stories). These are shared and continued through an education model incorporating story, song, dance, art, embodied (re)enactment, law/lore and culture, kin and connections to nature (such as totems) and so on. But these are not 'disciplined' (Nakata 2007) into science, legal studies, history, social studies, language and the arts. Further, these concepts are brought together through singular (transdisciplinary) concepts of 'knowledge' (Pratt et al. 2018). Osborne (2017) explains that working from Aboriginal language concepts, such as the term *kulini* in Pitjantjatjara, an Australian language of the Western Desert, better positions educators and researchers for ethical engagement in Indigenous contexts.

**ecojustice**: seeks to preserve and, where appropriate, enhance ecological wellbeing and the integrity of the ecological commons – the 'properties' of the earth that sustain all life

In the next section, we first describe a set of EfS principles for preservice and early career educators and then provide examples of how a transdisciplinary pedagogy can be used to address social and environmental issues towards what we term '**ecojustice**'.

## EDUCATOR TIP

Proactive learning values the issues and concerns learners bring to the classroom and their current understandings. Build on this by looking at what others think (transdisciplinary knowing) and then develop with learners actions they would like to take, what they could do, what they will do and how they will do it. Conduct an evaluation.

# PLANNING LEARNING EXPERIENCES AROUND THE PRINCIPLES OF EfS TOWARDS ECOJUSTICE

Teacher education programs contribute to ecojustice learning by introducing and making explicit the necessary attitudes and ethical commitments towards sustainability, such as valuing all aspects of the earth's systems, and behaving accordingly through the preservice courses to rehearse and embed key understandings and mobilise learner participation (Ferreira, Ryan & Davies 2015). Learning activities structure and enable direct actions that are essential for healthy, resilient communities and ecosystems.

As discussed earlier, Sustainability is one of the three cross-curriculum priorities in the Australian Curriculum (ACARA 2018), aimed at ensuring learners engage effectively in a global world and contribute to a more just Australian society through social, intellectual and creative pursuits. Sustainability is to be woven through learning areas. Key statements included in this cross-curriculum priority are 'Sustainable patterns of living meet the needs of the present without compromising the ability of future generations to meet their needs' and 'Sustainability education is **futures-oriented**, focusing on protecting environments and creating a more ecologically and socially just world through informed action' (ACARA 2018).

**futures-oriented**: images of futures powerfully affect what people believe and how they respond in the present. Futures work has a special responsibility to ensure that all members of a learning community are prepared for and proactive about their future.

Over several decades of working in EfS, we have developed a framework of seven principles that we believe contribute towards an ecojustice education (see Table 19.1). The first principle is about identifying and challenging the assumptions that direct our thoughts and behaviours. This includes challenging deep-seated ideologies of consumerism, individualism, growth, development and progress, and relearning the values central to living well with sufficient resources, in humility and with respect, within a whole-earth community. The second principle is to encourage the development of a community of learners with a common disposition to valuing with compassion natural and human systems (the cultural commons) compatible with and within them, in the geosphere and biosphere, and elements of the noosphere (i.e. the sphere of human thought) (Teilhard de Chardin 1955) supportive of natural. This means promoting 'knowing our place' – where we 'fit' as earth citizens into the structure of things. The third principle invites participants to engage collaboratively in enhancing socially and ecologically just and sustainable communities of people and other living things, and the physical systems on which they depend. The fourth principle aims for educators to act as ecojustice role models in their personal lives and in educational communities, and encourage learners to do likewise. The fifth principle aims for the development of ways of thinking, feeling and acting with eco-social wisdom in places that humans inhabit, recognise and relate to, a wisdom that necessarily includes ecological systems thinking and scientific knowledge, skills and practices using transdisciplinary planning. The sixth principle seeks to develop a respect for long-term rather than short-term thinking, through historical and futures studies that introduce learners to the traditions of past and future communities that have or will have worldview values that respect all aspects of the earth's systems. The seventh principle provides opportunities for learners to reflect critically on what they have learnt, the impact their learning has had on their perspectives, and how this could influence their future behaviour (Paige, Lloyd & Smith 2016).

Table 19.1 provides some examples of pedagogical practices that connect to each of the seven principles that can be implemented in third- and fourth-year preservice placements and early career education.

| **TABLE 19.1**   ECOJUSTICE PRINCIPLES FOR TEACHER EDUCATION PROGRAMS | |
|---|---|
| **Ecojustice education principles** | **Examples of practice** |
| 1. *Identify and challenge* current world view values and behaviours. | <ul><li>Carbon and water footprints</li><li>Pledge of Green</li><li>Product life-cycle analysis</li><li>Visiting/taking part in environmentally connected businesses/institutions</li></ul> |
| 2. Develop a *community of learners* with a disposition to value with compassion natural and human systems (the cultural commons) in the geosphere and biosphere, and elements of the noosphere supportive of natural systems. | <ul><li>Extended field trips</li><li>Excursions in natural/wild places</li><li>Participation in citizen science projects</li><li>Working with community gardens</li></ul> |
| 3. Invite learners to *engage* collaboratively in working towards socially and ecologically Just and sustainable communities. | <ul><li>Placed-based experiences</li><li>Volunteering in community and spontaneous gardening</li><li>Pledge of Green</li></ul> |
| 4. Assist learners in their development as *role models* who value the commons – i.e. the cultural and natural resources accessible to all members of a society, including natural materials such as air, water and a habitable earth – as well as partnerships, quality of life and material adequacy. | <ul><li>Arts projects</li><li>Policing electric lighting and managing school recycling</li></ul> |
| 5. Promote learners' acquisition of *eco-social wisdom* – ways of thinking, feeling and acting within places that they inhabit. | <ul><li>Transdisciplinary planning for learning</li><li>Carbon and water footprints</li><li>Volunteering with Trees For Life and other community environmental groups</li></ul> |
| 6. Help learners to develop a respect for long-term rather than short-term thinking through historical and *futures* studies. | <ul><li>Future scenario writing and futures planning and enacting</li><li>Engaging Indigenous knowledges, narratives and perspectives through community engagement, quality digital and other resources</li></ul> |
| 7. Provide opportunities for learners to *reflect critically* on what they have learnt. | <ul><li>Pledge of Green</li><li>Future scenarios presentations and conversations</li><li>Application of learning as members of community charity and environmental groups</li></ul> |

# INCORPORATING EfS PEDAGOGICAL PRACTICES INTO CLASSROOM EXPERIENCES

To ensure preservice and early career educators understand and internalise EfS, they need ongoing exposure to ideas in a range of disciplines. The notion of 'slow pedagogy' raised by Payne and Wattchow (2009, p. 16) 'allows us to pause or dwell in spaces for more than fleeting moments and therefore encourages us to attach to and receive meaning from that place'. It supports connections to place through experiential learning.

This chapter provides examples of practice that are focused on EfS. We illustrate this by describing some enabling pedagogical practices that contribute to the enormous task of 'unlearning' (Jucker 2004, 2014) and attempt to 'reculturalise' preservice educators so that by graduation they better understand the principles of ecojustice, enabling them to incorporate aspects of ecojustice in their early teaching experiences.

We posit the following nine EfS ideas in teacher education and then examine each one in detail:

1. Place-based in urban ecological setting
2. A place in time
3. Future scenarios
4. Pledges
5. Indigenous perspectives
6. Transdisciplinary
7. Citizen science
8. Creativity/arts
9. Spontaneous gardening
10. YGAP/single-use containers.

## 1. Place-based in urban ecological setting

In this pedagogical practice, educators are encouraged to work collaboratively on voluntary community projects that deliver sustainability outcomes; for example, learning about places of conservation such as zoos and botanic gardens, and places associated with sustainability practices, such as recycling depots, carbon offsetting companies, community gardens, and government or public institutions such as SA Water. The place-based education experience involves spending between three and 10 days in an urban ecological setting. The experience culminates in a rich assessment task involving constructing a digital narrative. Voluntary work undertaken can include removing non-indigenous plants in coastal dunes; cooking food from ingredients sourced from the school kitchen garden; attending workshops about propagating trees from seeds with Trees for Life; or leading beach walks at a marine discovery centre. There is an expectation that preservice educators will contribute in an educational sense, by **paying it forward** through developing websites and pamphlets. Taking part in service learning activities helps educators to develop a framework of thinking against which they can judge issues of social and ecological justice (Paige, Lloyd & Smith 2016).

**paying it forward**: describes the beneficiary of a good deed repaying it to others instead of to the original benefactor

## 2. A place in time

A place in time is a transdisciplinary sequence of workshops that is the culmination of the learning in the third-year science curriculum course. Previous to this sequence, preservice educators have used a science lens when undertaking soil science workshops investigating the properties of soil such as colour, pH levels and porosity, and exploring the characteristics of vertebrates and invertebrates. To be reflective of transdisciplinary learning, the topic needs to incorporate more than one discipline area and be issue based. Linking to HASS, the issue is preservice educators developing a sense of belonging to place (ACARA 2018). This theme is particularly relevant due to complex work/study timetables, online learning/ time attached to technology and lack of time spent in the natural world.

A place in time begins by locating indigenous plants in the campus grounds and developing connections to place through using all of the senses: smell (e.g. describing smells associated with the plant), touch (e.g. does it matter which part of the body is used to touch the plant?), texture (e.g. using crayons and paper to make rubbings of woody stems, dead leaves) and sound (e.g. finding a space near the plant/s, sitting quietly and listening for a range of sounds, and recording them on an aural map).

A significant tree is selected and, by visiting regularly over a three-week period, small changes in the tree and its environment are observed. The key concept of interdependence between the tree and animals is a particular focus.

A sustainability lens to explore place focuses on four key components:

1. Spaceship earth activities (Van Matre 1990); two examples are: 'Find a piece of natural detritus and piece of human detritus, and consider where they come from' and 'Build a national park 2 cm x 2 cm. Find interesting things that will fit. Put up small flags to identify what is significant.'

2. Using possible futures drawing of the tree site as a starting point to write a 100-word futures scenario set 20 years from now. Consider the physical and biological aspects of place, the social and cultural aspects of place, and the spirit of place.

3. Indigenous perspectives. When projected into an investigation such as a place in time, questions like the following are raised: What was this place like before the university was built? What species of plants and animals were there? Where are the locations of constellations and stars? What materials in the place could have been used for tools, games and toys, and food? Are there any remnants of natural bush?
(Paige, Lloyd & Chartres 2008).

**ecological footprint**: the impact of human activities measured in terms of the area of biologically productive land and water required to produce the goods consumed and to assimilate the wastes generated

4. Taking action. What is possible? Examples include investigating whether the tree is deemed 'significant' according to local council guidelines, and which indigenous sedges and grasses should be planted to encourage butterflies and bees on campus. Exploring **ecological footprints** and organisations such as FairShare International are other useful starting points. They provide opportunities for personal action for people living in the minority world.

## 3. Future scenarios

Social and ecojustice issues require action in the present that is well informed by where we have come from (history of the past) and where we want to go (history of the future – futures studies). Because images of futures powerfully affect what people believe and how they respond in the present, futures work has a special responsibility for ensuring that members of learning communities are prepared for and proactive about their future (Hutchinson & Herborn 2012; Lloyd 2011, 2014; Masini 2013). To live ethically in the present requires people to understand that decisions made in the present moment influence what the future can become. This is true for personal, collective and world futures. With this in mind, exploring opportunities to develop integral (personal, cultural, social, material and ecological) futures scenarios will help educators to bring together their understandings of, and visions for, a sustainable world (Lloyd 2010, 2014; Paige & Lloyd 2016).

## 4. Pledges

Preservice educators are required to make an environmental pledge at the beginning of the semester. The aim is for them to select an aspect of their life in which they can make some reduction in resource use. Key areas include reducing water consumption; buying fresh rather than processed food; reducing distances travelled by car by using public transport and car-pooling; and avoiding the use of single-use containers. Having identified the pledge, data are collected and recorded and at the end of the semester consequences are reported to the class (Paige 2014, 2016).

### PLEDGES

My pledge was to drop my cost of fuel from $80 a week to roughly $40 a week, saving myself money and the environment as well. To achieve this, I rode my pushbike to university once a week and car-pooled with friends. In the end, I spent: $530 rather than $1120. So, from this pledge I saved myself $590 in fuel expenses. (Preservice educator 1)

After setting the timer for seven minutes, I began shortening my showers and ended up spending about five minutes in the shower compared with my 10–15 minutes at the start of the pledge. This reduction meant that I was only using 315 litres compared to the 576 litres per week. (Preservice educator 2)

At the end of 12 weeks I had totalled 50 water bottle fill-ups, saving me a total of $140. That is 50 plastic bottles that did not go to the dump and create more landfill. (Preservice educator 3)

We encourage all educators to make a similar environmental pledge to demonstrate their commitment to sustainability to learners.

SPOTLIGHT ON HASS EDUCATION

## 5. Indigenous perspectives

During the first three years of the teacher education program, preservice educators engage with Aboriginal and Torres Strait Islander histories, knowledges and perspectives. This happens through engaging with literatures written by Indigenous scholars and local community narratives and experiences through written texts, film and digital media, and working with local community Elders and community members (O'Keeffe, Paige & Osborne 2018). From this growing foundation of theoretical knowledge and experience, preservice educators are introduced to Aboriginal ways of knowing within the context of place-based learning; for example, learning about local Indigenous (Kaurna) calendars that order seasons and engagement with nature, or by identifying sites of natural and cultural significance to Kaurna people on campus that would otherwise remain overlooked or hidden within dominant culture narratives about place, history and the environment.

By acknowledging the epistemological, ontological, axiological and cosmological components that frame both Indigenous and non-Indigenous histories and systems of knowledge, a more nuanced understanding emerges in the exploration of Indigenous histories and perspectives. For example, preservice educators learn about the Indigenous night sky which, coupled with a non-Western view of geometry and the constellations, provides Indigenous peoples with a natural calendar and compass, but also draws on ancient and continuing narratives highlighting cosmological/epistemological entanglements where story and science intermingle across both Indigenous and Western knowledge spaces (Curnow & Paige 2006; Nakata 2011; O'Keeffe, Paige & Osborne 2018). This process has great value in orienting preservice educators to 'other' ways to know, be and do, as well as providing contemporary and continuing examples of integrated knowledges at work with the local ecology, as working from Indigenous knowledges and experiences can inform integrated models of engaging with the environment towards ecojustice.

**Reflection**

Take a moment to reflect on your own understandings from your upbringing about 'land'. For example, 'What is land for and how is it used and useful to human populations?' What are some of the key ideas relating to land (or Country) that bring the cross-curriculum priorities of Sustainability and Aboriginal and Torres Strait Islander histories and cultures together? Are there shared ideas on which learners need to reflect to inform local community actions towards ecojustice within an EfS framework?

## 6. Transdisciplinary examples

In preparation for undertaking fourth-year final placement, preservice educators plan one transdisciplinary inquiry unit, using at least two different ways of knowing to describe 'the valued learning' and 'how the learners will engage with the valued learning' and to respond to the question, 'How do you know what the learners have learnt?' For the transdisciplinary unit, preservice educators must identify the issue/topic, an essential question, the key HASS, science and mathematics concepts, Indigenous perspectives within the topic, desired learning outcomes and the sequence of learning experiences (incorporating the inquiry process). Preservice educators are also required to address possible ethical action and social responsibility at the local school level, and demonstrate how it connects to learners' life worlds.

Table 19.2 identifies examples of issues-based topics that are connected with preservice educators' interests, expertise and concerns. They require historical, geographical, scientific and mathematical background knowledge. The essential questions help focus the key concepts, skills and values that need to be addressed during the unit. As Jacobs states, an essential question 'is an exceptional tool for clearly and precisely communicating pivotal points of the curriculum' (Jacobs 1997, cited in Chiarelott 2006, p. 13).

**TABLE 19.2   TRANSDISCIPLINARY ISSUES-BASED TOPICS AND ESSENTIAL QUESTIONS**

| Issue/topic | Essential question |
| --- | --- |
| Ocean pollution | How does human activity, such as pollution, affect the ocean's ecosystems? |
| Light pollution | How has light changed the way you live? What impact does light pollution have on our environment? What actions can we take to minimise the light pollution in our home, school and community? |
| Biodiversity in schoolyard | How much does our local school environment currently support biodiversity? What can we do to support biodiversity in our school and local communities? |
| Depletion of seagrasses | Why is the seagrass along the coastline disappearing? |
| Ecological footprints | What impact am I having on the environment? How can I reduce this impact, particularly in regard to waste management? |
| Food | Where does food come from? How much of what we eat is locally produced? |
| Packaging of everyday materials | How can we help to limit the impact that packaging (particularly plastics) has on our environment? |
| Soil erosion | What is erosion and what are the key causes of it? How can we identify an area of erosion in the school and prevent further erosion? |
| Weather and data | How can chance and data help explain the weather? |

The following Spotlight on HASS education is one preservice educator's reflection on her transdisciplinary unit, the action that could be taken and how opportunities for learners to develop sustainability skills were provided. In the example Lucy, who taught part of the sequence to her Year 4 class during her final placement, describes how the action involved a reduction in light pollution. It is intended for learners to develop a higher-order level of thinking about light technology and its impact on the planet. Young people learn that while light technology has provided many benefits and made our lives more comfortable, there are also consequences, specifically light pollution, and society needs to find a harmonious balance between the benefits of light technology and the impacts of light pollution on the environment. This example can be applied by all educators being responsive in their contexts.

The science understanding is focused on how light travels, light as a form of energy and light sources. The knowledge and understanding strand of History is evident through learners exploring the inventions of the mirror (Ancient Egyptians and Romans), the lighthouse, and the light bulb in the 19th century. The mathematics focus is on the concept of angle and representation in drawings of the direction in which light rays travel and angle of light scatter as well as reflection, mirror images and symmetry. Another mathematical aspect is managing data collected from light

## LIGHT POLLUTION

Through studying the impact of light pollution on our wildlife, and the economic costs of light pollution in terms of wasted electricity and carbon dioxide emissions, learners can see how everyone – themselves, their families, the school and the wider community – has an impact on the planet and that everyone can take responsibility for their own actions by taking steps towards reducing the negative effects of light pollution on our environment.

Learners are encouraged to take local action through initially conducting a school audit on the lighting used and light pollution created by the school. Learners can suggest alternative light fittings to minimise the light pollution of the school. Next, they are encouraged to do either an audit of the local community or of their home, and write a letter to a council member or create a pamphlet to send home to all parents/carers detailing ways to minimise the effects of light pollution around the house. The slogan: Think globally, act locally! (Reflection by Lucy, preservice educator)

sources when completing a school audit. The EfS issue is about reducing light pollution. This illustrates a transdisciplinary unit that resulted in some personal action by the learners.

Local action evident in the transdisciplinary unit and the importance placed on activism and learner agency is supported by Bencze, Sperling and Carter (2012). The aim is for the actions to be initiated by learners' experiences and that through collaborative planning in small groups there is a responsibility for taking small steps towards sustainable practices. It is not always easy to balance an ethical approach and empower learners to adopt environmentally aware practices in the classroom. Action-oriented outcomes can be controversial and educators need to be mindful of time available and of 'hearing' learners' voices to avoid indoctrination (Jickling 2009). Transdisciplinary units provide an opportunity to be adventurous when constructing curriculum.

Preservice educators engaging in planning transdisciplinary units at university will not always see these units in schools during placement. As future leaders educating the next generation, it is important that educators do not merely replicate what they see but take a contemporary and leading-edge perspective in curriculum planning (Paige 2014).

## 7. Citizen science

Citizen science involves professional researchers engaging the public to collect data within a cooperative framework of research and education (Cooper et al. 2007; Phillips 2007). There are many examples of citizen science projects in South Australia, each focusing on an iconic species: Operation Blue Tongue (2007), Operation Possum (2008), Operation Magpie (2009), Operation Spider (2010), Operation Koala (20015/16) and Cat Tracker (2015/16). There are also national and international examples such as Birds in the Burbs and Frogwatch. These projects provide opportunities for educators and learners to collect data about local species. The example in the Spotlight on HASS education involves the reflective description of one final placement experience.

## OPERATION MAGPIE

During the last three weeks of my final practicum, I taught three Operation Magpie lessons. I was also concurrently undertaking an inquiry into one area of my pedagogy, which focused on incorporating literacy strategies into hands-on science learning experienced within a Year 6 classroom. Operation Magpie and citizen science provided me with the context in which I could implement literacy strategies.

As time constraints only enabled me to teach three lessons, my interactive teaching sequence was dramatically cut short to simply engaging learners and exploratory activities. The first lesson engaged learners with the topic of magpies and the notion that, despite daily magpie sightings, there is much to learn about this feathered creature.

Each learner was asked to draw and annotate an image of a magpie. All the pictures were placed on the board, then an open class discussion began, analysing the wide variety and somewhat humorous adaptations of magpies. This discussion assessed the learners' prior knowledge, which led to the identification of specific magpie characteristics. Pictures of magpies were shown and learners were required to redraw their magpie, this time using their newly gained knowledge.

The second and third lessons provided learners with the exploratory activity of observing magpies within their school grounds using binoculars. I implemented the literacy strategy of learners drawing up their own results table instead of using an online version. Clear instructions were given on how to use the binoculars correctly and the learners headed outside. It took some time before they realised, through subtle leading, that in order to observe a magpie the best approach is to sit down quietly and wait, not charge at the poor bird hoping it will stay still. Learners then expressed their results in written form and communicated them to the class.

Now, as a beginning educator, I would definitely teach this process again, more thoroughly and allowing for greater learner investigation. I feel Operation Magpie, and citizen science, provided me with an excellent platform to engage learners with their surroundings and make connections with something greater than themselves.

## 8. Creativity/arts

Learning situations in outdoor or nature-based settings offer opportunities for construction of wildlife representations through drawing and photography, much like nature journaling (Warkentin 2011), or towards expressive responses to nature experiences and reflections in simple poetic forms. There are many opportunities to incorporate an artistic focus to enhance teaching and learning about the impact of society and culture. Murals depicting local fauna and flora, and night sky and museum boxes can be constructed with the help of professional artists (Paige & Whitney 2008). An early career educator who had experienced artwork in nature on geological field trips as part of his university degree implemented and wrote about similar experiences with his class (Whitney, Sellar & Paige 2004). Using a creative lens is also a component of the transdisciplinary unit of work, A place in time, described earlier, where preservice educators sketched a tree, made crayon rubbings of leaves and bark, and explored the idea of natural sculptures (Paige, Lloyd & Chartres 2008).

A further example involved learners working with artists to represent the key principles underpinning educating young adolescents. The key principles of futures thinking, EfS, place-based learning, social justice, equity, and wellbeing and relationships were represented by drawings that were the basis of metal cutouts that covered the breezeway between two buildings.

## 9. Spontaneous gardening

Spending some time to find a place that needs 'greening' is a proactive way to end a semester. Learners turn up with plants, spades, compost and watering cans, and planting is undertaken across available spaces. It is a collegial act of green that is appreciated for months to come by everyone walking past – until the summer dry hits. There is a sense of fun and a feeling of making a direct difference to the local environment. This type of spontaneous, or 'guerrilla', gardening is often referred to as a favourite part of the semester. We know that many beginning educators have undertaken similar seeding projects with learners. It is interesting that the first year we undertook spontaneous gardening, we turned up with beanies and gardening equipment, meeting in a car park on campus on a Sunday afternoon – all a bit unsure about how others would view what we were doing, Now that we do it on a Thursday afternoon in full view of staff and learners, many passers-by make comments such as, 'So it is *you* guys'. It is a small act but a powerful one.

Goodall (2014) writes about random acts of gardening in *Seeds of Hope* as a way to brighten dreary neighbourhoods, and Richard Reynolds provides many examples on the website: http://www.guerrillagardening.org. There are lots of opportunities on a small scale in school grounds or on a bigger scale working with local councils (Paige, Lloyd & Smith 2016).

## 10. YGAP/single-use containers

Modelling ecojustice practices at work is part of the process of being an environmental advocate (Kopnina 2014). Examples include: taking one's own coffee cup to the coffee shop; bringing water in a reusable container; organising recycling containers and encouraging learners to use them; bringing litter-free lunches; organising donations boxes for food at Christmas; collecting 5-cent coins for YGAP, which an International Development not-for-profit with an innovative approach to poverty alleviation; using the stairs and not the lift; catching public transport where possible; and reducing the amount of printing done and using double-sided printing (Paige, Lloyd & Smith 2016).

## EDUCATOR TIP

Instigate an environmental pledge at an individual or class level. Ideas include litter-free lunches and walking to school (collect data about how many kilometres the class has walked/ reduced carbon emissions). Look for opportunities with learners as they arise during the year to pay-it-forward. Examples include collecting 5-cent pieces for YGAP, using recyclable containers to reduce landfill and establishing a butterfly garden.

# CONCLUSION

This chapter has emphasised that early career educators need to think about and take on board the key issues raised around educating for sustainability. Revisiting or keeping in the foreground the ecojustice principles as learning experiences are planned helps to ensure a difference is made in the lives of learners in today's classrooms. An important feature of EfS is connecting learners to the natural world and undertaking ethical action in local places. We encourage a connection to place in the first instance, go outside, look up with amazement at the night sky, and wonder about what invertebrate is leaving holes in the leaves and the potential impact on the local environment of a reduction in the bee population. Then introduce and connect learners wherever and in as many ways as possible to their local environment. An emotional connection to place will endure for a lifetime. Four key EfS messages are:

1. the importance of connection to place – virtual experiences aren't a substitute
2. to ensure curriculum decisions include transdisciplinary learning that value local and real life examples
3. being mindful of your ecological footprint
4. that empowerment comes through action.

There are many examples of EfS within schools: litter-free lunches, water analysis, adopting a part of the schoolyard for planting, and working with community on sustainable projects. Educators can promote EfS by becoming informed, using their imagination and connecting to issues locally. In conclusion, we refer you to David Suzuki (2010), who says that if you are connected to the natural world then you are more likely to look after it.

## REVIEW QUESTIONS

1. What are starting points for transdisciplinary topics?
2. How can you become proactive with learners to guard against them becoming overwhelmed by environmental problems?
3. How can you create networks in the local community in order to be proactive and make a positive difference?
4. What strategies are available for invoking a futures perspective in the classroom?
5. How can educators take learning beyond the classroom to include the wider community and act on ecojustice and social justice issues?
6. How can you ensure that learners develop subject-specific cognitive frameworks and value the ideals of transdisciplinary learning?

## LEARNING EXTENSION

Your task is to select something in your community in which you have an interest – for example, a nursing home, refugee association, environmental action group or native roadside vegetation. It needs to be something that is marginal in your area and not connected to targeted funding. Talk to people at the local level, interview elders and digitally (interview, photographs) record their story to share. The aim is to focus on an aspect of the community looking at something or a group that is disconnected and think about the question: 'What would it take for that person/element to be reconnected to their community?'

## REFERENCES

ACARA (Australian Curriculum, Assessment and Reporting Authority). (2018). *Australian Curriculum: Humanities and Social Sciences, v8.3*. Retrieved from: http://australian-curriculum.org/humanities-and-social-sciences.

Arbon, V. (2008). *Arlathirnda Ngurkarnda Ityirnda: Being-knowing-doing, de-colonising Indigenous tertiary education*. Brisbane: Post Pressed.

Balsiger, P.W. (2004). Supradisciplinary research practices: History, objectives and rationale. *Futures*, 36, 407–21.

Bencze, L., Sperling, E. & Carter, L. (2012). Students' research-informed socio-scientific activism: Re/visions for a sustainable future. *Research in Science Education*, 42(1), 110–29.

Chiarelott, L. (2006). *Curriculum in Context: Designing curriculum and instruction for learning in context*. Belmont, CA: Thomson Wadsworth.

Citraningtyas, T. (2010). Beyond resilience in the face of disaster: Transforming adversity by transforming ourselves and our system. In S. Cork, ed., *Resilience and Transformation: Preparing Australia for uncertain futures*. Melbourne: CSIRO, pp. 189–96.

Cooper, C.B., Dickinson, J., Phillips, T. & Bonney, R. (2007). Citizen science as a tool for conservation in residential ecosystems. *Ecology and Society*, 12(2), Article 11.

Costanza, R. (2012). The value of natural and social capital in our current full world and in a sustainable and desirable future. In M.P. Weinstein & R.E. Turner, eds, *Sustainability Science: The emerging paradigm and the urban environment*. New York: Springer, pp. 99–109.

Curnow, P. & Paige, K. (2006). The cosmic story board. *Teaching Science*, 52(2), 36–40.

Després, C., Brais, N. & Avellan, S. (2004). Collaborative planning for retrofitting suburbs: Transdisciplinarity and intersubjectivity in action. *Futures*, 36(4), 471–86.

Doppelt, B. (2008). *The Power of Sustainable Thinking*. London: Earthscan.

Education for Sustainability and Global Learning. (2012). Homepage. Retrieved from: http://esd.escalate.ac.uk.

Ferreira, J.A., Ryan, L. & Davies, J. (2015). Developing knowledge and leadership in pre-service teacher education systems. *Australian Journal of Environmental Education*, 31, 194–207.

Francoeur, R.T. (1976). Human nature and human relations. In R. Bundy, ed., *Images of the Future: The twenty-first century and beyond*. New York: Prometheus, pp. 125–34.

Gidley, J.M. (2016). *Postformal Education: A philosophy for complex futures*. Dordrecht: Springer.

Goodall, J. (2014). *Seeds of Hope: Wisdom and Wonder from the World of Plants*. New York: Grand Central Publishing.

Hodson, D. (2003). Time for action: Science education for an alternative future. *International Journal of Science Education*, 25(6), 645–70.

Hutchinson, F.P. & Herborn, P.J. (2012). Landscapes for peace: A case study of active learning about urban environments and the future. *Futures*, 44, 24–35.

Jickling, B. (2009). Sitting on an old grey stone. Meditations on emotional understanding. In M. McKenzie, P. Hart, H. Bai & B. Jickling, eds, *Fields of Green: Restorying culture, environment, and education*. Cresskill, NJ: Hampton Press.

Jucker, R. (2004). Have the cake and eat it: Ecojustice versus development? Is it possible to reconcile social and economic equity, ecological sustainability, and human development? Some implications for ecojustice education. *Educational Studies: A Journal of the American Educational Studies Association*, 36(1), 10–26.

——(2014). *Do We Know What We Look Like? Reflections on learning, knowledge, economics, community and sustainability*. Newcastle on Tyne: Cambridge Scholars Publishing.

Kopnina, H. (2014). Future scenarios and environmental education. *The Journal of Environmental Education*, 45(4), 217–31.

Lloyd, D. (2010). Futures scenario construction around contemporary issues: Tertiary students' perceptions of their value. *The International Journal of Environmental, Cultural, Economic and Social Sustainability*, 6(4), 85–106.

——(2011). Connecting science to students' lifeworlds through futures scenarios. *The International Journal of Science in Society*, 2(2), 89–104.

——(2014). Futures, wellbeing and flourishing communities. *The International Journal of Social Sustainability in Economic, Social, and Cultural Context*, 9(4), 41–53.

Lloyd, D. & Wallace, J. (2004). Imaging the future of science education: The case for making futures studies explicit in student learning. *Studies in Science Education*, 40, 139–78.

Lovelock, J. (2014). *A Rough Ride to the Future*. London: Akkan Lane.

Lowe, I. (2014). Wild law embodies values for a sustainable future. In M. Maloney & P. Burdon, eds, *Wild Law – In practice*. Abingdon: Routledge, pp. 3–16.

Martin, K. (2008). Childhood, lifehood and relatedness: Aboriginal ways of being, knowing and doing. In J. Phillips & J. Lambert, eds, *Education and Diversity in Australia*. Sydney: Pearson Education, pp. 127–40.

Masini, E.B. (2013). Intergenerational responsibility and education for the future. *Futures*, 45, S32–S37.

Nakata, M. (2007). *Disciplining the Savages: Savaging the disciplines*. Canberra: Aboriginal Studies Press.

——(2011). Pathways for Indigenous education in the Australian curriculum framework. *The Australian Journal of Indigenous Education*, 40, 1–8.

O'Keeffe, L., Paige, K. & Osborne, S. (2018). Getting started; Exploring pre-service teachers' confidence and knowledge of Aboriginal culture. *Australian Journal Teacher Education*, forthcoming.

Osborne, S. (2017). Kulini: Framing ethical listening and power-sensitive dialogue in remote Aboriginal education and research. *Learning Communities: International Journal of Learning in Social Contexts*, 22, 26–37.

Paige, K. (2014). Sustainability practices in a fourth year mathematics and science pre-service primary/middle pathway course. *The International Journal of Environmental, Cultural, Economic, and Social Sustainability*, 9(4), 2–16.

——(2016). Educating for sustainability: Environmental pledges as part of tertiary pedagogical practice in science teacher education. *Asia Pacific Journal of Teacher Education*, 45(3), 285–301.

Paige, K. & Lloyd, D. (2016). Use of future scenarios as a pedagogical approach for science teacher education. *Research in Science Education*, 46(2), 263–85.

Paige, K., Lloyd, D. & Chartres, M. (2008). Moving towards transdisciplinarity: An ecological sustainable focus for science and mathematics pre-service education in the primary/middle years. *Asia-Pacific Journal of Teacher Education*, 36(1), 19–33.

Paige, K., Lloyd, D. & Smith, R. (2016). Pathway to 'knowing places' – and ecojustice: Three teacher educators' experiences. *Australian Journal of Environmental Education*, 32(3), 260–87.

Paige, K. & Whitney, J. (2008). Vanishing boundaries between science and art: Modelling effective middle years of schooling practice in pre-service science education. *Teaching Science*, 54(1), 42–4.

Payne, P. & Wattchow, B. (2009). Phenomenological deconstruction, slow pedagogy and the corporeal turn in wild environmental/outdoor education. *Canadian Journal of Environmental Education*, 14, 15–32.

Phillips, T. (2007). NestWatch & Virtual NestWatch: An intersection of science, education, conservation, technology. In C. McEver, R. Bonney, J. Dickinson, S. Kelling, K. Rosenberg & J. Shirk, eds, *Proceedings of the Citizen Science Toolkit Conference*. Ithaca, NY: Cornell Laboratory of Ornithology, pp. 37–46.

Pratt, Y., Louie, D., Hanson, A. & Ottmann, J. (2018). Indigenous education and decolonization. In *Oxford Research Encyclopedia of Education* January, 1–32, doi: 10.1093/acrefore/9780190264093.013.240.

Rigney, L. (1999). Internationalization of an Indigenous anticolonial critique of research methodologies: A guide to indigenist research methodology and its principles. *Wicazo Sa Review*, 14(2), 109–21.

Rockström, J. (2015). Bounding the planetary future: Why we need a great transition. In *Great Transition Initiative*, April. Retrieved from: http://www.greattransition.org/publication/bounding-the-planetary-future-why-we-need-a-great-transition.

Smith, L. (1999). *Decolonizing Methodologies: Research and Indigenous Peoples*. London: Zed Books.

Suzuki, D. (2010). *The Legacy: An elder's vision for our sustainable future*. Sydney: Allen & Unwin.

Teilhard de Chardin, P. (1955). *The Phenomenon of Man*. London: Fontana Books.

Van Matre, S. (1990). *Earth Education: A new beginning*. Warrenville: Institute of Earth Education.

Warkentin, T. (2011). Cultivating urban naturalists: Teaching experiential, place-based learning through nature journaling in Central Park. *Journal of Geography*, 110, 227–38.

Whitney, J., Sellar, S. & Paige, K. (2004). Science art and teaching: Making connections. *Teaching Science*, 50(4), 25–9.

# PART V
# HASS for all learners

# VALUES EDUCATION AND SOCIAL JUSTICE

*Tace Vigilante*

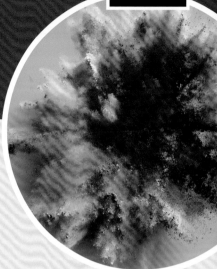

## Learning objectives

After reading this chapter, you should be able to:

- recognise values education as an integral component of the educational goals for schooling and the Australian Curriculum
- discuss the role of Humanities and Social Sciences (HASS) in developing ethical understanding and critical and creative thinking, two of the general capabilities in the Australian Curriculum
- appreciate the crucial role of ethical inquiry in values education
- understand the benefits of the community of inquiry approach in developing ethical understanding and critical and creative thinking in HASS
- work with a clear concept of social justice and recognise this concept as a core component of values education
- apply principles of ethical reasoning in a HASS community of inquiry discussion.

## INTRODUCTION

The subject areas that form the HASS learning area are founded on and around 'values', and values underpin everything we do in educational settings. This is not surprising, given that values are at the core of our thinking and actions (Aspin 2000). As human beings, we have core values to which we subscribe – things that we think are of importance and of worth. As an example, consider the values listed by Burgh, Field and Freakley (2006, p. 44): friendship, security, health, education, beauty, art and wealth. We may think that holding one or more of these values would not lead to a good life; that is, we may disagree that each of these values is of importance. The point, however, is that 'Everyone has values, but there is not universal agreement about what is valuable' (Freakley, Burgh & Tilt-MacSporran 2008, p. 8). *Values education* is essential in a participatory democracy as it involves people joining together to inquire into what is of value amid diversity, in the quest for a just society (Freakley, Burgh & Tilt-MacSporran 2008).

In 2005, the *National Framework for Values Education in Australian Schools* (Commonwealth of Australia 2005) identified a set of nine values that are considered foundational to developing citizens who have the necessary knowledge, understanding, skills and values for a productive and rewarding life in an educated, just and open society (Education Council

1999). Since then, the goal of developing active and informed citizens and the importance of values and ethical understanding in achieving this has been reinforced by the *Melbourne Declaration on Educational Goals for Young Australians* (Melbourne Declaration; MCEETYA 2008) and the Australian Curriculum (ACARA 2018a).

There are two questions often asked about values education: 'Whose values should be taught?' and 'How do we teach in this area without pushing our own values onto our learners?' In this chapter, community of inquiry and, in particular, community of *ethical* inquiry, will be explored as a means of structuring meaningful inquiry under the umbrella of HASS; inquiry that empowers learners, including very young learners, to think critically about issues pertaining to values, ethics and social justice in a safe environment while avoiding indoctrination.

# VALUES EDUCATION

**values inquiry**: thinking about what matters and what is important to us – what we value

In the broadest terms, values education is concerned with finding meaning in life. **Values inquiry** is thinking about what matters and what is important to us – what we value (Burgh, Field & Freakley 2006). Making value judgements about living a good a life is essential in leading a good life. Or to put it another way, 'Values education is an important aspect of living well' (Freakley, Burgh & Tilt-MacSporran 2008, p. 1).

As value judgements centre around what is good and bad, and right and wrong, they are at the heart of assessing what it means to live well. For this reason, values education is very much a part of the moral domain of education, which can be considered as having an overarching aim of fostering an *ethical disposition* in learners. There are many variations on achieving this aim; however, all credible forms of values education, including primary ethics, character education and philosophy for children, for example, share the common and broad objectives of developing ethically minded young people with the aim of producing good citizens who act with moral and ethical integrity. As suggested by Knight and Collins (2006, p. 320), it has long been argued that education should have both individual and social ends:

> In the West, the argument goes back at least to Plato's Republic. This tradition identifies the social end with the development of a just democracy, so that the fundamental goal of education is seen as one of equipping individuals to function optimally as members of a just democracy.

This aim is articulated in the Melbourne Declaration: 'Active and informed citizens ... act with moral and ethical integrity' (MCEETYA 2008, p. 8; see Chapter 23 for more on active and informed citizens). Also expressed in this document are the ways in which values and value judgements permeate almost all facets of what is considered essential for a confident and creative individual (p. 8):

- develop personal values and attributes such as honesty, resilience, empathy and respect for others
- have the knowledge, skills, understanding and values to establish and maintain healthy, satisfying lives

- have the confidence and capability to pursue university or post-secondary vocational qualifications leading to rewarding and productive employment
- relate well to others and form and maintain healthy relationships
- be well prepared for their potential life roles as family, community and workforce members
- embrace opportunities, make rational and informed decisions about their own lives and accept responsibility for their own actions.

## Values in HASS

Read through the introduction and aims of the HASS curriculum. Brainstorm the values that you think are embedded in this view of the HASS learning area. Discuss with your peers whether you agree with what is being valued. Consider whether you think the aims are consistent with your idea of preparing young people to live a good life.

   If you could summarise the aim of the HASS learning area in one or two sentences, what would it be?

The HASS curriculum area privileges inquiry and the foundations of thinking, and it is important to consider what kind of inquiry is required to develop the general capabilities of ethical understanding and critical and creative thinking skills associated with the aim of developing *good*, active and informed citizens. The following sections describe a process of collaborative, discussion-based ethical inquiry that has the potential to accomplish this aim.

It is essential to understand why we engage in inquiry, and do not simply require learners to memorise a set of Australian values. The reason is simple: rote learning or the uncritical promotion of a set of values is unlikely to achieve the goals of developing the critical and creative thinking skills required for active and informed citizens in a participatory democracy such as Australia. As Cassidy (2007, p. 158) argues, 'We cannot consider moral issues by simply doing as we are told by the power or authority in charge – this is the case both in schools and the wider world, both for school pupils and those outside formal education'. Essentially, requiring the uncritical adherence to a list is asking learners to behave in line with an authority rather than to imbue critical thinking based on the evaluation of reasons. Such an approach fundamentally relies on indoctrination to inform citizens' thinking and actions.

**Indoctrination**, which in an educational context can be defined as implanting the educator's (or institution's) values in the minds of learners, is a practice educators must be careful to avoid. This form of values education is dangerous as it undermines the very basis of a democracy and is inconsistent with the goals of HASS, which aim to foster democratic principles, understandings and actions. Knight and Collins (2006) put it well with the following analogy: 'Equipping students with a set of values is not in itself

**indoctrination**: in an educational context can be defined as implanting the educator's (or institution's) values in the minds of learners, and is a practice educators should avoid

sufficient to develop their capacity to exercise moral judgement, just as equipping students with the rules of football is not in itself sufficient to develop their ability to play football.'

Inquiry that aims to develop ethical understanding has to involve more than factual questions (see Chapter 11). Learners need opportunities to discuss ideas and, crucially, ethical ideas. Yet when Collins and Knight (2007) reviewed classroom questioning practices, including questions from within the HASS learning area, their conclusion was that very few ethical questions were raised in the educational setting by either educators or learners. Instead, it was their view that classroom questions were dominated by questions that required learners to clarify or recall facts acquired through research-based activities.

Although, on the whole, educators seem to like the idea of including discussion in their lessons, more traditional forms of whole-class interactions remain prominent in educational settings. Such interactions are characterised by Hargraves et al.'s (2003, cited in Lyle 2008) whole-class dialogue, which is dominated by a process of 'Recitation' involving: 'Initiation' (by educator to individual learner), 'Response' (by individual learner to educator) and finally 'Feedback' (by educator to individual learner). Such pedagogical practice, according to Lyle (2008), supports traditional educational setting power relationships, with the transmission of pre-packed knowledge as the goal. This form of whole-class dialogue is distinct from, and contrasts with, the goal of developing the ethical understanding and critical and creative thinking that are outlined as part of values education in this chapter. We can see here that relying on a process of recitation as a form of dialogic teaching to foster ethical understandings amounts to little more than indoctrination.

## Value judgements: ethical reasoning

Values education requires more than listing a set of aspirational values and then identifying any disparities with our lived experiences. It is about critically considering both what we aspire to and what we actually do (Freakley, Burgh & Tilt-MacSporran 2008, pp. 1–2). We can put what we value to the test, 'in discussion with others, employing the actions of thinking, reasoning and evaluating to arrive at expressions of rational commitment that can then be further tested in everyday activity' (Freakley, Burgh & Tilt-MacSporran 2008, pp. 1–2).

'Valuing therefore requires value judgements' according to Burgh, Field and Freakley (2006, p. 44), who further cite Lipman (1988, p. 56):

> By examining the grounds and consequences of particular values, value inquiry moves away from subjectivity towards objectivity in assessing what is important or worthwhile, whether the values in question be aesthetic, political, environmental, ethical, social or any other of the countless categories in which values fall.

We began the chapter by including the goals of values education and emphasised the word 'good' when referring to good citizens' 'moral integrity'. This is because what is considered a 'good' citizen is somewhat contentious. Equally contentious can be what is considered as acting with 'moral integrity'. We say 'somewhat' because, although there is definitely disagreement around these terms, there are also widely accepted processes that allow us to evaluate the rightness or wrongness of one's actions. These processes, or ethical theories, can be found in the theories of moral philosophy on the one hand and ethical reasoning on the other.

Ethical reasoning involves the ability to analyse arguments, and this is a fundamental component of critical thinking (Rachels 2009, p. 12). According to Rachels (2009, p. 12), the first task of analysing an argument is to get the facts straight. Part of determining the facts is to acknowledge any bias in the argument. Next, ethical principles can be introduced and assessed. Examples of moral principles include 'avoid doing harm', 'act in the common good', 'refrain from using people as mere means to our own ends' and 'treat others as you would like to be treated'. This is clearly not an exhaustive list and there is more on this in the last section of this chapter, which looks at Knight and Collins' ETHIC model (Knight & Collins 2010). From here, Rachels states that good ethical reasoning should include a commitment to impartiality, which means that everyone is treated alike – no one is favoured. To sum this up, Rachels (2009, p. 13) suggests that impartiality forbids treating one person worse than another where there is no good reason to do so. This, for example, explains why certain forms of discrimination such as racism and sexism are wrong.

In addition, and in concert with this aim, values education is often associated with justice in society, and here there is a clear connection with questions of social justice.

## Social justice

Social justice is usually associated with ideas of equity and equality. The conditions that make a just society are contested and concerned with the distribution and achievement of goods pertaining to a good life. Assessing who is doing well and flourishing within a society, and who is not, is an evaluation of justice. Nussbaum (1995, 1999, 2000, 2005) argues that the justness of a society can be evaluated in terms of the opportunities each individual has to exercise their own important and valued capabilities. Sen (1995, p. 31) makes a similar point: for him social justice is determined by the freedom a person has to choose to live the 'kind of life he or she has reason to value'. Therefore, it can be considered unjust where there is a disparity between a group's opportunities to choose to exercise important human capabilities. For the Curriculum Council, social justice is defined as follows:

> Social justice supports the fair and equitable treatment of all people and aims to protect them from discrimination because of race, gender, age and ability etc. The concepts of social justice are codified in the form of human rights, international commitments to protect civil and political rights, economic, social and cultural rights. Education about social justice and human rights allows students to understand the importance of treating people equitably and the responsibilities we all have to protect the rights of others. (AAID 2008, p. 10)

While this social aim of education focuses on the crucial role that individuals play in the construction of a just society, writers from within the field of social justice education are equally concerned with achieving equitable and quality education for *all* learners. As prominent social justice education theorist Lee Ann Bell (2007, pp. 3–4) explains:

> [S]ocial justice education is both a process and a goal. The goal of social justice education is full and equal participation of all groups in society that is mutually shaped to meet their needs. Social justice includes a vision of society in which the distribution of resources is equitable and all members are physically and psychologically safe and

secure. We envision a society in which individuals are both self-determining (able to develop their full capacities), and interdependent (capable of interacting democratically with others).

SPOTLIGHT ON HASS EDUCATION

## THE EARLY YEARS

The foundations of social justice and inquiry learning can be developed in early years programs, with three to five year olds, for example, through the use of carefully selected picture books that invite inquiry into the notions of equality through developing understandings of others as similar to themselves. The picture books *Around the World: Hair* by Kate Petty (2006) and *Whoever You Are* by Mem Fox (1998) lend themselves to exploring the idea of a *common* humanity. Both children's books can be read to young learners, and questions around differences as well as similarities, with a focus on the important aspects of being human that we share in common, can be discussed. For more resources using picture books, see *Books into Ideas* (Sprod 1993), *Teaching Philosophy with Picture Books* (Murris 1992) and *Philosophy with Kids, Books 1–4* (DeHaan, MacColl & McCutcheon 1995).

## Value judgements and ethical reasoning in HASS

Value judgements are an important aspect embedded in HASS and can be a deeply engaging and enlivening experience. Young learners can ask ethical questions and meaningfully discuss them. Cam (2012, p. 22) provides the following examples of questions eight-year-old children raised after reading *The Boy Who Cried Wolf*:

- Is a lie being unfaithful?
- Can a lie be considered cheating somebody?
- Do you agree that a lie and trick are the same thing?
- Are magicians liars?

Ethical reasoning and evaluation can be a genuine force in making the HASS curriculum come alive. As HASS is founded on values, it is brimming with opportunities to foster ethical reasoning and understandings. Consider some of the following themes and topics suggested by Collins (2010, p. 4) that raise ethical issues and are central to the HASS learning area:

- Is it OK to clear the world's rainforests?
- Is it ever OK to keep wild animals in cages?
- Should Aboriginal and Torres Strait Islander peoples be compensated for past wrongs?
- How should water from the Murray-Darling River system be allocated?
- Is it ever acceptable to mandatorily detain asylum seeker?
- To what extent are we obliged to help others, including those we will never know?

The abundant ethical questions that can be raised in HASS mean educators need to know how to attend to ethical issues in a way that will foster the development of ethical understanding while avoiding the pitfalls of values education outlined earlier. Focusing on developing critical and creative thinking, as required by the Australian Curriculum general capabilities (ACARA 2018b), is in clear contrast to the practices of recitation and indoctrination and it is in the philosophy for children's community of inquiry approach that a robust educational practice can be found, with a focus on critical thinking-based values education within HASS (for more a systematic review, see Trickey & Topping 2004).

# THE COMMUNITY OF INQUIRY APPROACH

The philosophy for children movement (also known as P4C) began with the work of Matthew Lipman and colleagues at Montclair University in the United States (Murris 2008). The program was established primarily in response to what Lipman considered a failing of educational settings to effectively develop thinking skills fundamental to both individual and common good (Lipman 2003). The core business of philosophy for children for Lipman was to promote the improvement of three aspects of thinking: critical, creative and caring (Lipman 2003). More recently, Haynes and Murris (2012) have updated this list to include a fourth aim of collaborative thinking. This type of critical, creative, caring and collaborative thinking is required to develop the general capability of ethical understanding in HASS as part of values education. The *philosophy for children movement* is concerned with rational reflection on questions of human importance at the levels of the individual and society (Van der Leeuw 2009, cited in Vansieleghem & Kennedy 2012).

The educational method known as *community of inquiry* can be described as a core pedagogical practice for facilitating philosophical inquiry with young people (Murris 2008; Splitter & Sharp 1995). It has been described in this way: 'As a practice, Community of Philosophical Inquiry encourages individuals to challenge their own assumptions and the assumptions of others. Furthermore, it has been claimed that this type of inquiry promotes 'moving society to that of community as there would be a common and understood goal or purpose- that of the betterment of society for all its members' (Cassidy 2007, p. 135).

Lipman (2003, p. 94) argues that education that revolves around inquiry is character-ised by 'non-adversarial deliberations, shared cognitions, the cultivation of literacy and philosophical imagination and the encouragement of deep reading, and the enjoyment of dialogical texts'. Moreover, Lipman's account of a community of inquiry includes the following features: inclusiveness, participation, shared cognition, face-to face relationships, the quest for meaning, feelings of social solidarity, deliberation, impartiality, modelling, thinking for oneself, challenging as a procedure, reasonableness, and the reading, the questioning and the discussion (pp. 95–100). It involves 'a group of people used to thinking together with a view to increasing their understanding and appreciation of the world around them and of each other' (SAPERE 2010, n.p.).

Typically, a community of inquiry involves a group of learners sitting together in a circle facing one another, the educator among them as both facilitator and co-inquirer. Splitter and Sharp (1995, p. 18) describe the necessary attributes as follows: 'We would see a physical configuration which maximizes opportunities for participants to communicate with, and behave democratically toward, one another.' For example, a class could be sitting in a circle discussing the question: 'Whose responsibility is it to save water?'

# EDUCATOR TIP

## DISCUSSION VERSUS DEBATE

In a community of inquiry discussion, the objective is to progress in our thinking on a question or topic rather than debate the question or topic with the objective being to win.

SPOTLIGHT ON HASS EDUCATION

## ACTIVITY: EXPLORING VALUES AND ETHICS

The types of questions that centre on values and ethics within HASS are numerous, so educators need to be able to highlight opportunities to explicitly explore them. The following activity will help you with the process.

- Select one of the HASS curriculum areas by discipline and age group and construct an inquiry question that you think will invite learners to foster ethical reasoning.
- Consider the following questions and discuss a topic and indicator with which you could align the question or topic:
  - Is it ever OK to cage animals?
  - Is logging of old-growth forests OK?
  - Whose responsibility is it to save water?
  - Is it OK to buy products that contain palm oil?
  - Should we care for the environment?
  - Should we know where our food comes from?

  (Hint: topics could include themes of food, industry and the environment.)
  - Is it ever OK to lie?
  - What does it mean to be a good friend?
  - Who should care for our local park?
  - Whose interests should politicians consider?
  - Is it ever OK to discriminate against a person based on their gender, race or culture?
  - Whose responsibility is it to care for the homeless?
  - Should all people have the right for their basic needs to be met?
  - Should we care for those who live in developing nations?

  (Hint: topics could include themes of friendship, community and human rights.)

McCall, like others in the field of philosophy for children, asserts that 'people are capable of reasoning by virtue of being human beings, but to be proficient takes practice' (McCall 1991, p. 38, cited in Cassidy 2007, p. 121). Opportunities for learners to practise their reasoning by discussing questions that matter and do not have ready-made answers are available through inquiry in the key learning areas of the Australian Curriculum. As has been noted, HASS offers many opportunities for inquiry, particularly ethical inquiry.

# EDUCATOR TIP

## PREPARING THE GROUP

The following guide on conducting a community of inquiry was developed by Museums Victoria:

- Discuss with learners what the process is about and how supportive and respectful behaviour will make it successful.
- This is a thinking process that can challenge assumptions and preconceived ideas. It may be that you need to change your mind.
- It is *not* about winning an argument.
- It *is* about thinking more deeply about matters of importance to you as a member of the community.
- A sense of community is essential – sharing, support and respect for all.
- Differences are an important part of the process. Accept that others may disagree with you. Conflict and mistakes made in good faith are opportunities for learning and growth (Museums Victoria 2008, p. 10).

As facilitator, the educator provides some stimulus for inquiry; this may be a story or segment of a story (as with Lipman's novels) or picture book, or it could be a visual stimulus (photograph, painting, clip from a video or television, etc.); all these resources are common in most educational settings.

In the case of a social justice education program any of these stimulus materials could be presented, depending on the theme or understanding to be developed through the inquiry. Whatever the form, stimulus materials are used to provoke learners' interest and curiosity in a particular theme or set of themes and to prompt them to raise questions related to the theme(s). This set of questions, which will likely include both factual and philosophical questions, then forms the basis of the inquiry. (Philosophical questions are taken to be questions that cannot be answered solely by research but need to also be thought through for oneself.) Learners categorise and sequence the questions to plan aspects of their inquiry, with help from the facilitator where required, including determining whether it may be necessary to answer some factual questions in order to make progress with the philosophical questions. The group then selects and begins discussing one of the questions. This is an important step in the process as it sets up the community to own the inquiry. As Haynes and Murris (2012, p. 52) assert, '[o]wnership of the initial questions about a picture book narrative [for example] opens up possibilities for learners to express the ideas *they* will engage in and respond to the thinking of the others in the community'.

To assist in the inquiry process, the facilitator/educator may use a discussion plan or exercises (such as those found in Lipman's numerous teaching manuals), or may themselves prepare a series of questions for learners to consider and discuss. The discussion generally follows a process in which learners reflect on the questions raised and respond to one another, putting forward their view and associated reasons as they collaboratively try to make progress in answering the questions. As described by Lipman (2003, p. 20), 'a community of inquiry attempts to follow the inquiry where it leads rather than be penned in by the boundary lines of existing disciplines'. The facilitator's role is crucial in that they must support the discussion process by asking for clarification and reasons, asking further questions, summarising and evaluating points made, as well as helping the learners to do so, and assisting learners in deciding how the next discussion should begin. It is important to note here that learners are given the opportunity to discuss their ideas. This is an empowering pedagogy and quite different from dialogue dominated by a process of recitation.

## Discussion avoiding rhetorical questions

Part of a community of inquiry approach is to uncover any assumptions held. This means that critically engaging in a community of inquiry involves identifying and challenging assumptions within classroom discussions. Rhetorical questions are not often helpful in progressing the discussion/line of inquiry because, by definition, they have an expected answer. Rhetorical questions can be useful in some contexts (e.g. in speeches) but the purpose of the community of inquiry discussion is quite different from that of a speech. It is better to phrase the point (or premise) as a statement to avoid making unnecessary assumptions.

Crucially, however, group discussion and dialogue must be conducted within a supportive, safe and respectful environment (Griffin 1997). Museums Victoria's (2008) guidelines for conducting a community of inquiry (see the Educator tip earlier) provide a basis for a safe and supportive learning environment:

> The process promotes critical thinking and requires members of the group to show respect for each other. It attempts to produce better thinkers and more caring members of society, who accept differences and at the same time, submit conflicts to reasonable scrutiny.

> All participants are expected to respect one another as thoughtful people who together seek to better understand the issue at hand.

> So, a community of inquiry works best when the group agrees that:
> - The thinking they will do will be:
>   - *caring* (each member is an integral member of the community),
>   - *creative* (new ideas will be sought and encouraged),
>   - *critical* (good reasons need to be given for ideas and opinions).

- They can all make mistakes, acknowledge them and are willing to be corrected.
- All challenges made by learners in a community of inquiry are to the ***ideas*** expressed – not to the ***people*** expressing the ideas. (pp. 10–11)

Guidelines such as these and those listed below can be used in preparing learners for a productive discussion:

- Be prepared to take part in the discussion.
- Only one person is to speak at a time.
- There is a need to ask questions.
- Deep listening is the key to the process.
- Give reasons for any opinion you express.
- Check assumptions, reasoning, evidence – your own as well as those of others.
- Define and discuss points of difference as well as points of agreement.
- Ask others for reasons, definitions, evidence, examples and assumptions if necessary.
- Admit when you disagree with something that you may have agreed with earlier.

## EDUCATOR TIP

### FORMULATING GUIDELINES

Guidelines for discussion can be developed and agreed as a group. This should be done before the first discussion begins and can be referred to before any subsequent discussions. The agreed-upon guidelines can include visual cues to be displayed during discussions.

# COMMUNITY OF ETHICAL INQUIRY IN HASS

At a minimum, educators want to know that learners are being guided in the community of inquiry to consider important elements of reasoned ethical decision-making. Knight and Collins (2010) developed a guide for ethical decision-making with what they have coined the 'ETHIC' model. An important focus of the community of inquiry is to ascertain and evaluate the relevant facts of the theme or issue under consideration. As Knight and Collins (2010) put it:

> Reasoned ethical decision making ... requires that the agent take the relevant facts into account; that is, that she gather information relevant in the determination of the likely effect of her actions on others. The following sets out aspects that should be considered as part of the ethical decision-making process within a community of inquiry:
> - **E**qual consideration of the interests of all of those (at least all those humans) affected by one's actions and emphasising with others;
> - **T**hinking (logical reasoning) for oneself;
> - **H**arm; recognising harm and weighing up the relevant harm to all involved;

- **I**nformation; getting the factual information correct and lastly;
- **C**ircumstances; taking the circumstances into account. (p. 4)

Knight and Collins (2010) argue that attending carefully to these elements provides a sound basis on which to help learners make well thought-through ethical decisions. The authors argue that the model provides a process that can be used as a guide for educators (and preservice educators) during community of inquiry discussions. They also note that it is not intended as a step-by-step procedure; instead, the model promotes consideration of important aspects of widely accepted procedures for dealing with ethical questions. Knight and Collins (2010, p. 5) add that 'to have learners act ethically, that is to act in the broad social interest, it is essential that learners are introduced to the elements of and procedures'.

## Planning for ethical inquiry

It is important that the inquiry questions are relevant to the lives of learners. Learners will not engage in a community of inquiry 'unless the problem or issue under discussion touches upon their interests, fires their imagination or otherwise moves them' (Cam 1995, p. 18). In considering the inquiry questions that will guide a learning sequence, educators start with the content, skills and understandings that they want to develop, listing what learners will be able to know, do and understand and act on at the end of the sequence. An overarching inquiry question can be used to guide the learning activities. For example, the Stolen Generations is an important social justice topic that relates directly to the HASS learning area. Below are the inquiry questions that are used in the Reconciliation South Australia Stolen Generations Education Pack (2008, p. 3). The four guiding questions for teaching and learning activities are:

1. What impact has the removal of Aboriginal and Torres Strait Islander children had on Indigenous Australians and the broader Australian community?
2. Is Australia a 'fair' place today for all Australians?
3. Should all Australians contribute to Reconciliation and what actions could be taken?
4. Do you choose to take action? If so, what actions do you choose to take?

## Selecting stimulus materials

The HASS educator has an important role in selecting learning and stimulus materials. The intended purpose of the materials is to provide a stimulus for inquiry-based discussion. The stimulus must be sufficiently provocative to create the grounds for inquiry questions to result. As Lipman (2003, p. 94) asserts, 'for there to be inquiry there must be some doubt that all is well, some recognition that one's situation contains troubling difficulties and is somehow problematic'. Murris (2008, p. 677) is clear on this point: 'in line with the pedagogy (P4C), starting points for enquiry need to be selected carefully for their power to express ambiguity, to produce puzzlement, or to evoke deep responses'.

A sequence of learning can be developed by the educator, with the benefit of this approach being that the educator can link the inquiry to relevant HASS topics and outcomes (Echeverria & Hannam 2016). Inquiry questions can then be used to guide the unit of learning. Alternatively, with the educator scaffolding the process, inquiry questions can be developed by the learners. It is important for the educator to build opportunities into the sequence of learning for thinking about and discussing both the factual and ethical aspects relating to the inquiry questions (Collins 2010).

Having prepared questions ready for discussion in the form of a discussion plan is recommended. 'These may form an extension to questions that learners have already raised in an earlier lesson, they may be designed to ensure that certain aspects of a topic are covered or they merely act as prompts to refocus discussion or rekindle it when things begin to flag' (Cam 2012, p. 71). Cam describes two types of discussion plans used in a community of inquiry discussion. The first is a sequential discussion plan, which is characterised by following a series of questions in order:

- Each question builds upon those that came before.
- A consecutive set of questions may proceed from the specifics of a text or other stimulus to a broader or more comprehensive consideration of some problem or issue.
- It may start from things that are already familiar to learners and then connect up their experience with things they are only just beginning to explore, or it may begin with questions that consist of a relatively simple or clear-cut answer and advance to ones where the going is more difficult or uncertain (Cam 2012, p. 72).

The second, Cam (2012) explains, is a list of questions that can be asked in any order with the aim of considering alternatives, and differing viewpoints, helping to define or categorise the concept under review. There are now many prepared educator materials designed for use in a community of inquiry. As a beginner to the community of inquiry approach, it is recommended to use such prepared materials, as these materials will provide confidence in the approach and ensure that the discussion is structured and working towards making progress on an idea or inquiry question. For a detailed example of how the community of inquiry has been used within the HASS learning area, see Collins (2010).

## EDUCATOR TIP

### YOU DON'T NEED TO REINVENT THE WHEEL

One strategy for planning an inquiry is to first consider the values or ethical question or theme that you wish to raise within your learning sequence and then search for the topic in the philosophy for children materials, of which there is a great many, including *Values Education in Schools: A resource book for student inquiry* by Freakley, Burgh and Tilt-MacSporran (2008) and *Teaching Ethics in Schools: A new approach to moral education* by Cam (2012).

## CONCLUSION

Values education within HASS is aimed at developing *good*, active and informed citizens. In summary, values education should involve learners having opportunities to think critically and develop their own ethical understanding through engaging in critical and creative thinking. The community of inquiry approach provides educators with a pedagogy that has the potential to empower learners by discussing questions that matter and do not have ready-made answers, including questions around social justice. It is also important that the conditions for a supportive, safe and respectful learning environment, such as sitting in a circle and adhering to agreed-upon guidelines, are in place to allow for a productive ethical inquiry discussion. Planning ethical inquiry involves devising or selecting the inquiry questions with or for the learners and then locating or developing a discussion plan that will help learners to think critically about ethical issues that are presented throughout the topic.

## REVIEW QUESTIONS

1. Value judgements centre around what is good and bad, right and wrong. What are some ethical principles that are widely accepted for evaluating the rightness or wrongness of one's actions?

2. Values education has the objective of developing what kind of person?

3. Why is ethical inquiry argued to be the preferred approach to values education?

4. Explain social justice and social injustice.

5. What are aspects that should be considered as part of the ethical decision-making process within a community of inquiry?

## LEARNING EXTENSION

Reflect on your own primary school and secondary school experiences of HASS:

- What was the focus?
- What do you remember learning about?
- How was the learning structured?
- What were the pedagogies that were used?
- Did the pedagogies achieve the desired ethical understanding required for HASS?
- Look up the philosophy materials available online and in your library and locate a discussion plan that could be used in a HASS topic of learning. Some good starting points online are Federation of Australasian Philosophy in Schools Associations (FAPSA; http://fapsa.org.au/resources), SAPERE (https://www.sapere.org.uk/Default.aspx?tabid=270) and The Philosophy Club (https://thephilosophyclub.com.au).

## REFERENCES

AAID (Australian Agency for International Development). (2008). *Global Perspectives: A framework for global education in Australian schools*. Carlton, Vic.: Education Services Australia. Retrieved from: http://www.globaleducation.edu.au/verve/_resources/GPS_web.pdf.

ACARA (Australian Curriculum, Assessment and Reporting Authority). (2018a). *Australian Curriculum: Humanities and Social Sciences F-10, v8.3*. Retrieved from: https://www.australian curriculum.edu.au/f-10-curriculum/humanities-and-social-sciences/hass.

——(2018b). *Australian Curriculum: Humanities and Social Sciences, v8.3*. General capabilities. Retrieved from: https://www.australiancurriculum.edu.au/f-10-curriculum/general-capabilities.

Aspin, D. (2002). An ontology of values and the humanisation of education. In S. Pascoe, *Values in Education*. Canberra: Australian College of Educators.

Bell, L.A. (2007). Theoretical foundations for social justice education. In M. Adams, L.A. Bell & P. Griffin, eds, *Teaching for Diversity and Social Justice*. New York: Routledge, pp. 1–14.

Burgh, G., Field, T. & Freakley, M. (2006). *Ethics and the Community of Inquiry: Education for deliberative democracy*. Melbourne: Thomson Social Science Press.

Cassidy, C. (2007). *Thinking Children*. New York: Continuum.

Cam, P. (1995). *Thinking Together: Philosophical Inquiry for the Classroom*. Sydney: Primary English Teaching Association and Hale and Iremonger.

——(2012). *Teaching Ethics in Schools: A new approach to moral education*. Melbourne: ACER.

Collins, C. (2010). Thinking together about questions that matter in the SOSE classroom. *The Social Educator*, 28(3), 5–10.

Collins, C. & Knight, S. (2007). The role of dialogue-based ethical inquiry in education for just democracy: An intervention study. In *13th International Conference on Thinking, Sweden, June, Proceedings*, 1(21).

Commonwealth of Australia. (2005). *National Framework for Values Education in Australian Schools*. Canberra: Department of Education, Science and Training.

DeHaan, C., MacColl, S. & McCutcheon, L. (1995). *Philosophy with Kids, Books 1–4*, Melbourne: Longman.

Echeverria, E. & Hannam, P. (2016). The community of philosophical inquiry (P4c): A pedagogical proposal for advancing democracy. In M.R. Gregory, J. Haynes & K. Murris, eds, *The Routledge International Handbook of Philosophy for Children*. Abingdon: Routledge, pp. 3–10.

Education Council. (1999). *The Adelaide Declaration on National Goals for Schooling in the Twenty-First Century*. Retrieved from: http://www.scseec.edu.au/archive/Publications/Publications-archive/The-Adelaide-Declaration.aspx accessed 1–12–17.

Fox, M. (1998). *Whoever You Are*. Sydney: Hodder Headline.

Freakley, M., Burgh, G. & Tilt-MacSporran, L. (2008). *Values Education in Schools: A resource book for student inquiry*. Camberwell, Vic.: ACER Press.

Griffin, P. (1997). Facilitating social justice education courses. In M. Adams, P. Griffin & L.A. Bell, eds, *Teaching for Diversity and Social Justice: A source book*. New York: Routledge pp. 279–98.

Haynes, J. & Murris, K. (2012). *Picturebooks, Pedagogy and Philosophy*. New York: Routledge.

Knight, S. & Collins, C. (2006). The Australian Values Education Framework: No justification required? *Critical and Creative Thinking: The Australasian Journal of Philosophy in Education*, 14(2), 32–49.

——(2010). *ETHIC: A procedure for ethical decision making within Society & Environment*. The Social Educators' Association of Australia, Biennial Conference, Adelaide.

Lipman, M. (1998). *Philosophy Goes to School*. Philadelphia, PA: Temple University Press.

——(2003). *Thinking in Education*. New York: Cambridge University Press.

Lyle, S. (2008). Dialogic teaching: Discussing theoretical contexts and reviewing evidence from classroom practice. *Language and Education*, 22(3), 222–40.

MCEETYA (Ministerial Council on Education, Employment, Training and Youth Affairs). (2008). *Melbourne Declaration on Educational Goals for Young Australians*. Retrieved from:

http://www.curriculum.edu.au/verve/_resources/National_Declaration_on_the_Educational_
Goals_for_Young_Australians.pdf.

Murris, K. (1992). *Teaching Philosophy with Picture Books*. London: Infonet.

——(2008). Philosophy with children, the stingray and the educative value of disequilibrium.
*Journal of Philosophy of Education*, 42(3–4), 667–85.

Museums Victoria. (2008). Teacher notes. Community of inquiry. Melbourne Museum,
pp. 10–11.

Nussbaum, M.C. (1995). Human capabilities, female human beings. In M.C. Nussbaum,
J. Glover & World Institute for Development Economics, eds, *Women, Culture, and
Development: A study of human capabilities*. Oxford: Clarendon Press.

——(1999). *Sex and Social Justice*. New York: Oxford University Press.

——(2000). *Women and Human Development: The capabilities approach*. New York: Cambridge
University Press.

——(2005). *Frontiers of Justice: Disability, nationality, species membership*. Cambridge, MA:
Belknap Press of Harvard University Press.

Petty, K. (2006). *Around the World: Hair*. Princeton NJ: Two-Can Publishers.

Rachels, J. (2009). The challenge of cultural relativism. In S.M. Cahn, ed., *Exploring Ethics:
An introductory anthology*. New York: Oxford University Press, pp. 34–46.

Reconciliation South Australia (2008). Stolen Generations Education Pack. Retrieved from:
http://www.reconciliationsa.org.au/for-schools/education-packs.

SAPERE (2010). Community of inquiry. Retrieved from: https://www.sapere.org.uk/default.aspx?
tabid=76.

Sen, A. (1995). *Inequality Reexamined*. New York: Russell Sage Foundation.

Splitter, L. & Sharp, A.M. (1995). *Teaching for Better Thinking: The classroom of community of
inquiry*. Melbourne: ACER.

Sprod, T. (1993). *Books into Ideas*. Melbourne: Hawker Brownlow.

Trickey, S. &. Topping, K.J. (2004). 'Philosophy for children': A systematic review. *Research Papers
in Education*, 19(3), 365–80.

Vansieleghem, N. & Kennedy, D. (2012). Introduction: What is philosophy for children? In
N. Vansieleghem & D. Kennedy, eds, *Philosophy for Children in Transition: Problems and
prospects*. Hoboken, NJ: Wiley-Blackwell.

# CULTURALLY RESPONSIVE PEDAGOGY: RESPECTING THE DIVERSITY OF LEARNERS STUDYING HASS

*Dylan Chown*

## Learning objectives

After reading this chapter, you should be able to:

- explain and advance broad notions of citizenship characterised by equity and justice recognising learners' cultural and religious diversities and ways of knowing as assets for teaching and learning
- understand and appreciate the value of learners' diverse cultural and religious knowledges through promoting the general capability of intercultural understanding
- apply culturally responsive pedagogical strategies inclusive of all learners to maximise Humanities and Social Sciences (HASS) engagement and learning outcomes
- plan and implement learning experiences/lessons that employ culturally responsive pedagogies and support HASS learning for broad and inclusive notions of citizenship.

## INTRODUCTION

Educators within contemporary Australian educational settings are increasingly being called on to enact their pedagogy in multicultural classrooms, yet pedagogies tend to remain oriented towards a narrow learner cohort (Hattam 2017; Preger & Kostogriz 2014). Meaningful inclusion of culturally and religiously diverse learners not only focuses on what is being taught or what knowledge is privileged, but is concerned with how it is taught and from whose perspective. Importantly, it prioritises what learners bring to educational settings – their diverse knowledge(s), languages, values and beliefs; all of which are embedded in their ways of knowing, being and doing informed by their cultural and religious traditions. Sometimes normative educational practices are rooted in philosophies not inclusive of diverse **epistemologies** or **cosmologies** (Memon & Zaman 2016) for learners who identify with cultural, religious and spiritual traditions. When epistemological diversity, including learners' knowledge(s) or ways of knowing, is excluded or minimised and pedagogy is not responsive in using these assets for teaching and learning, culturally diverse learners face additional challenges around issues of identity, sense of belonging and their overall educational experience, compromising equitable and just notions of citizenship in Australian educational contexts.

**epistemology:** refers to the study of knowledge, or how we know what we know

**cosmologies:** understandings about the origin and evolution of the universe

**world view:** beliefs about fundamental aspects of reality that inform one's perceiving, thinking, knowing and doing (Abdullah & Nadvi 2011)

This chapter aims to support educators in enacting culturally responsive pedagogy, including consideration of learners' **world views**, knowledge(s) and ways of knowing, as well as respect for identities and backgrounds as meaningful sources for optimal learning, while simultaneously holding high expectations of them all (Klump & McNeir 2005). Culturally responsive pedagogy is essential if educators are to promote equity and excellence for all learners, such that they can become successful, confident and creative individuals who develop into active and informed citizens, as set out in the *Melbourne Declaration on Educational Goals for Young Australians* (Melbourne Declaration; MCEETYA 2008). In this chapter, educators will be challenged to examine epistemological and pedagogical diversity in HASS teaching and learning, to further develop learners' knowledge, values and beliefs towards engaged and informed citizenship. In building on Chapter 17, which focused on inclusion of Aboriginal and Torres Strait Islander learners in educational settings, this chapter will link concepts and understandings to a case study of the increasing Muslim learner population. The key learnings have implications that are transferable across cultural and religious communities.

## ADVANCING BROAD NOTIONS OF CITIZENSHIP CHARACTERISED BY EQUITY AND JUSTICE

In a multicultural country such as Australia, educational contexts are important sites that 'create and recreate citizens and the nation' (Abowitz & Harnish 2006, p. 664). Learners studying HASS are encouraged to develop critical perspectives of citizenship by exploring histories, human geographies and political influences (Abowitz & Harnish 2006). A critical perspective allows narrow conceptualisations of and potentials for citizenship to be challenged and broadened in favour of more inclusive notions underscored by equity and justice. How citizenship is framed and advanced can lead to the marginalisation of learners and their knowledge(s), ways of knowing, languages, values and beliefs. Therefore, critical reflection about how educators frame and advance citizenship in educational settings is paramount. A more nuanced understanding of notions of inclusion and diversity is required if all learners are to engage and practise active citizenship in HASS.

### The rationale for a focus on cultural and religious diversity of learners

It is necessary to understand why there is attention on learners' cultural and religious backgrounds and ways of knowing, and why this is central to HASS education.

An important starting point is that all educators have the responsibility to 'know [their] students and how they learn', and demonstrate teaching strategies 'responsive to learning strengths and needs of students from diverse linguistic, cultural, religious and socio-economic backgrounds' (AITSL 2015). Interestingly, in the case of Muslim learners, O'Donnell, Davis and Ewart (2017) reveal that 70 per cent of Australians who do not identify as Muslim acknowledge that they know little to nothing about Islam or Muslims, a finding similar to the knowledge gap identified by social geographer Kevin Dunn in his 'seminal analysis of attitudes towards Islam in Australia' (Dunn 2004; O'Donnell, Davis &

Ewart 2017, p. 42). To date, little is known about the knowledge and preparedness of educators in relation to effectively teaching Muslim learners. The knowledge implied here is beyond decontextualised knowing about Islam and Muslims or cultural and religious traditions of diverse learners generally; rather, it relates more to educators' orientations in light of 'othering' discourses and political tensions around 'recognition and misrecognition, inclusion and exclusion, democracy and coercion, homogenization and pluralism' (Preger & Kostogriz 2014, p. 157). Understanding the impact of these discourses and tensions on the deep knowledge of pedagogical strategies responsive to the 'learning strengths and needs' of learners from 'diverse linguistic, cultural, religious and socioeconomic backgrounds' (AITSL 2015) is essential.

Culturally and religiously diverse learners represent a vulnerable cohort on account of normative pedagogies that can sideline religion, faith and spirituality, devalue their sociocultural-religious capital (Bourdieu 1986) and fail to recognise or benefit from their knowledge(s). Returning to the example of Muslim learners as a vulnerable cohort, additional factors relate to broader marginalisation or silencing of Muslim 'ways of knowing and the humanizing Muslim voices that derive from them' that are overshadowed by a dominant meta-narrative of Islam and Muslims (Stonebanks 2008, p. 293). This positions Muslims as antithetical to the West, contributing to the rise of Islamophobia in Australia (Briskman et al. 2017). The complexities of these related factors can lead to enforced silence (Aly & Green 2008) and, as in the case of cultural religiously diverse learners generally, compromise identity, belonging and citizenship, especially for young peoples in Australian educational settings.

As an educator, how exempt are you from the power of the dominant discourse on marginalised learners' cultural and religious identities and ways of knowing that you, along with your learners, consume (Stonebanks 2008)?

As a HASS educator, you have a choice 'to be a tacit agent of reproduction or a critical educator of transformation' (Stonebanks 2008, p. 318). The negative discourse and narrative surrounding Islam and Muslim learners are a prime example of how some marginalised culturally and religiously diverse learners 'must learn to negotiate within schools and classrooms that pay little attention to their knowledges, perspectives, or humanity' (Stonebanks 2008, p. 318). This chapter challenges you to redress these inequities.

## Funds of knowledge of cultural and religious learners

**Funds of knowledge** is an expansive concept that can include a recognition of learners' identities, cultural, religious and linguistic capital, and lifeworld knowledges, including ways of knowing. These are all viewed as assets for teaching and learning. Educators are encouraged to consider how funds of knowledge can extend responsive pedagogy for culturally and religiously diverse learners. Funds of knowledge invoke not only 'knowledge contents' (cultural and religious accumulated artefacts, skills, rituals and lore) from learners' banks of cultural and religious assets, but

**funds of knowledge:** an expansive concept that can include a recognition and availing of learners' identities, cultural, religious and linguistic capital and lifeworld knowledges, including ways of knowing. These are all viewed as assets for learning and educator pedagogies.

**lifeworld pedagogies:**
informal and formal ways of
teaching and learning from
which learners benefit within
their lives outside of formal
schooling, often drawn from
faith, family and community
traditions, beliefs, values and
norms that offer agency for
integrated teaching and
learning in learners'
schoolworlds

'lifeworld pedagogies' (integrated ways of teaching and learning from faith, family and community) described by Zipin (2009) as 'funds of pedagogy'. Funds of knowledge in this chapter thus constitute both knowledge contents and, more so, ways of knowing from diverse learners' lifeworld knowledges, viewing these as learning assets (Zipin 2009). When educators are responsive to learners' funds of knowledge, learners will find that their ways of knowing hold value and that they can transact with knowledge within the education setting for deeper learning (Zipin 2009). Pedagogy is more responsive to learners, as it bridges the gap between the ways of teaching and learning that learners experience and engage with their culture and faith within their homes, families and communities. It can also lead to an enrichment of the HASS curriculum through more meaningful inclusion of learner identities and greater application in learners' lives (Zipin 2009).

## Broader sociopolitical environment and culturally and religiously diverse learners in Australian educational settings

**critical educator:** one who
strives towards
transformation within a
paradigm of justice
promoting greater equity,
social justice and positive
social change through
collective human capacity

It is important to understand the role **critical educators** of HASS can play in preventing and/or redressing negative discourses through fostering positive self-identities and making curriculum decisions that help *all* learners digest the complexities of social cohesion and genuine pluralism. For this to occur, this chapter emphasises reflection on educator orientation, and the enactment of curriculum through pedagogy and the creation of transformative classroom spaces. As we have seen, pedagogy cannot be separated from politics, as it reflects policy and demands that educators are aware of the need for pedagogical diversity to advance broad and just notions of citizenship for all learners so they can be active and engaged.

While highlighting culturally and religiously diverse learners of HASS, there is a reciprocal relationship with this chapter's objectives and all learners in HASS educational settings. HASS 'encompasses the knowledge and understandings of history, geography, civics and citizenship, and economics and business, [giving] students a deep understanding of the world they live in from a range of perspectives, past and present, and encourages them to develop an appreciation and respect for social, cultural and religious diversity' (ACARA 2018a). To achieve this goal in a 'world that is increasingly culturally diverse and dynamically interconnected, it is important that students come to understand their world, past and present, and develop a capacity to respond to challenges, now and in the future, in innovative, informed, personal and collective ways' (ACARA 2018a). This demands that learners think in more integrated ways, avoiding presumptions and premature conclusions while recognising interconnections for enhanced interdependency – in other words, learning to be system thinkers (Strauss & Corbin 1990, p. 5).

As indicated in this chapter's case study, educators are educating increasing numbers of Muslim learners in Australian classrooms, reflective of the increase of Muslim people from 2.2 to 2.6 per cent of the total population (ABS 2016; Buckingham 2010). Since the 2000s, Muslim learners have been the subject of scrutiny and judgement on account of broader social 'othering' (Preger & Kostogriz 2014), facing complex challenges in relation to bullying, bigotry, identity, belonging, self-worth and exclusion (Briskman et al. 2017; Mansouri & Trembath 2005; Pe-Pua et al. 2010). Political and media discourses have thrust issues of national identity to the forefront, and this has had significant implications for further othering of Muslim Australians, particularly since 9/11 (Briskman et al. 2017). In turn, this has caused some to question the compatibility between wider Australian values and those held by Muslims (Briskman et al. 2017), with a telling impact on Muslim learners in educational settings (Jones 2013). Preger and Kostogriz (2014) argue that what has been missing in this sociopolitical environment is **relationality**, beginning with respect and recognition and implying **reciprocity** in the form of robust and respectful debates on issues of national significance. This critique is instructive for learners of HASS as they prepare to be 'well placed to contribute to Australia's ideas of a cohesive society, sustainable environment, productive economy and stable democracy' (ACARA 2018c).

> **relationality**: involving affective exchanges for relating to one another through purposeful action for potential to transform people, communities and societies (Zembylas 2015)
>
> **reciprocity**: the practice of exchanging things (e.g. dialogue, experience or knowledge) between people(s) (with embodied respect) for mutual benefit, mutual understanding and the possibility of mutual transformation

Islamophobia is often contested, minimised or dismissed, due partly to its complexity. It has been defined as 'anti-Muslim (the people) and anti-Islam (the religion) sentiments' (Zaidi 2017), possibly overlapping with 'racism, xenophobia, anti-religious, and anti-immigrant views' (Cesari 2011, p. 24). While embedded in racist ideologies, Islamophobia is also fanned by the presumption that Islam is inherently connected, and therefore conflated, with terrorism (Briskman et al. 2017).

Muslim learners represent a prime case study of the importance of recognising culturally and religiously diverse learners in Australian educational settings. Therefore, it is crucial that educators provide learning experiences that enable differences to be mediated through mutual respect and dialogue where misconceptions are critically analysed – something that aligns closely with the HASS learning area.

## EDUCATOR TIP

As an educator, you are encouraged to reflect on the important distinction between drawing attention to learners on account of difference and providing a safe space where dialogue can engage with difference through respect for learners' identities, voices, perspectives and ways of knowing. By doing so, you can take an active role in creating a safe, transformative environment where all learners' identities and knowledges are valued and diverse voices and perspectives can be heard.

## Limitations of diversity and inclusion discourse

In advancing notions of citizenship that are characteristically equitable and just, it is important that HASS educators think about how they will accommodate equity and justice in their settings, if all learners are to be empowered to 'actively shape their lives', 'value their belonging in a diverse and dynamic society' and 'positively contribute locally, nationally, regionally and globally' (ACARA 2018c). It is also imperative that educators reflect on the limitations of diversity and inclusion discourse for marginalised members of society and, in turn, the microcosm that is the learning context. This entails a recognition and acknowledgement of the connections between identity and citizenship and their association with aspects such as 'culture, language, religion, and spirituality' (Zaidi 2017).

Social inclusion and social exclusion have become politically attractive concepts (Preece 2001), with the latter being a complex process entailing power and dominant values that marginalise the values, identities and experiences of different social groups (Preece 2001). Barry (1998, p. 9) cautions that social inclusion can be 'culturally defined, economically driven and politically motivated'. Inclusion, when reduced to a process of normalising people, can overlook or fail to recognise the knowledges, identities and experiences and their intimate ties to the aspects mentioned above (Zaidi 2017) that lead to a transformative classroom (Preece 2001; Stonebanks 2008); that is, a classroom that promotes learners' 'deep understanding of the world they live in from a range of perspectives, past and present, and encourages them to develop an appreciation and respect for social, cultural and religious diversity' (ACARA 2018c). Indeed, the 'process of awakening one's identity and voice is essential for the development of skills for critical engagement and participation' (Goduka 1998, p. 49).

Education that is transformative promotes broad conceptualisations of citizenship characterised by equity and justice and demands learning experiences that are liberating rather than reinforcing the status quo (Preece 2001). This challenges HASS educators to acknowledge learners' identities as an integral aspect of learning; rather than seeing learner deficits. It recognises that culturally and religiously diverse learners have a 'bank of socio-cultural resources at their disposal' (Preger & Kostogriz 2014, p. 162). All learners become 'well placed to contribute to Australia's ideas of a cohesive society, sustainable environment, productive economy and stable democracy' (ACARA 2018c).

## EDUCATOR TIP

The following activity captures a 'dialogue' between *diversity*, *inclusion*, *equity* and *justice* (Stewart 2017, para. 10). Engaging in such dialogue promotes equity, justice and proactive citizenship.

You are commencing a new educational role with a new cohort of learners. Begin by asking yourself these questions before you start your planning:

| | |
|---|---|
| **Diversity asks**: | Who's in the room? |
| **Equity responds**: | Who's trying to get in the room but can't, and whose presence in the room is under constant threat of erasure? |
| **Inclusion asks**: | Have everyone's ideas been heard? |
| **Justice responds**: | Whose ideas won't be taken seriously because they aren't in the majority? |
| **Inclusion asks**: | Is this environment safe for everyone to feel like they belong? |
| **Justice challenges**: | Whose safety is being sacrificed and minimised to allow others to be comfortable maintaining dehumanising views? |

# Conceptualisations of citizenship in HASS

'Education needs to aim to do more than prepare young people for the world of work; it needs to equip students with the skills they need to become active, responsible and engaged citizens' (OECD 2018, p. 4). To advance broad notions of citizenship for learners in HASS, characterised by equity and justice, it can be useful to reflect on two orientations for framing citizenship: 'citizenship as status' versus 'citizenship as practice' (Heilman 2006; Zembylas 2010). Examples of discourse within a status frame comprise the espousing of nationalism or love of one's country as an exclusive community (Zembylas 2010), hyperemphasis on the rights of citizenship (Abdi 2014) or conditional citizenship for those who 'do the right thing' (Zembylas 2010). This is of particular importance to learners in Australia who are marginalised or 'othered' when citizenship is framed as 'status' (Heilman 2006), as reflected in this chapter's case study about Muslim learners. As an example, Aly and Green (2008, para. 5) argue that, within a status frame, 'Muslim citizens run the risk of being construed as "un-Australian" when they articulate their concerns or opinions'. This has resonance for culturally and religiously diverse learners generally.

Citizenship as practice, however, expands the scope of citizenship and includes empathy and care for those who are marginalised (Zembylas 2010). The notion of empathy and care for the marginalised through education policy, curriculum and pedagogy, in relation to citizenship in HASS, reorganises learning contexts in order to foster affinity between individuals (Zembylas 2010), rather than sameness or compliance within dominant values and groups. The task of HASS educators, in enacting the Civics and Citizenship sub-strand, and the HASS curriculum more broadly, is to develop a transformative space for encounter, relationality, empathetic engagement and respectful dialogue, and to identify the pedagogical strategies that lead to this (Zembylas 2010). Epistemological and **pedagogical diversity** is therefore essential for HASS learners to account for in their educational settings.

> **pedagogical diversity**: refers to both culturally responsive pedagogy broadly and recognition of how this can be shaped by learners' lifeworld pedagogies

Part of the role of reflective practitioners is to critically reflect on their approaches to pedagogy and curriculum as well as their orientation within the educational setting. Culturally responsive pedagogy offers a useful framework for accounting for the complexities of inclusion and exclusion, and the practice of engaged and proactive citizenship. This enables learners to hear and benefit from the humanising voice of their stories, histories and knowledges, and draw on these in shaping solutions to shared issues and concerns (Preece 2001). Education 'should confer the power to arrest fragmentation, resolve conflict and transcend narrow definitions of identity' (Hanezell-Thomas 2018, p. 7).

In promoting justice and equity, reflect on your own belief systems in relation to dominant values and how you may have been normalised within them. Consider:

Reflection

1. What values do you bring to an educational setting?
2. How are your values situated in relation to dominant societal values?
3. What shapes your own belief system?
4. Are you prepared for learners who do not share a common belief system?
5. What is your appetite for accepting and embracing difference?
6. How do you reconcile difference with Australia's ideas of a cohesive society, sustainable environment, productive economy and stable democracy?

Given the major concepts within HASS and the overall intent of the learning area, it is a prime site for doing this.

## EDUCATOR TIP

Educators who model care and empathy as a democratic process in their learning environment ensure marginalised learner identities and narratives are given voice and humanised, allowing all learners to engage in the practice of critical citizenship for justice – citizenship that may challenge the status quo and invoke positive change (Zembylas 2010).

**critical citizenship**: the development of critical learners committed to care and empathy as democratic processes engaged in the practice of citizenship for justice (Zembylas 2010)

# VALUING THE DIVERSITY OF LEARNERS' CULTURAL AND RELIGIOUS KNOWLEDGES

In aiming to have understanding and appreciation for the diversity of learners in educational settings, it is important for educators to recognise that they are not expected to be an expert on all things to do with all learners' cultures and religions. Increasing understanding and appreciation, however, offers multiple benefits. It assists critical educators to be active agents of transformation in redressing inequities faced by learners. It assists educators to better understand the scope of learners' funds of knowledge, allowing them to support learners to attain better learning outcomes in HASS. More broadly, they can add to efforts to promote intercultural understanding among all learners for reciprocal mutual understanding and thus mutual transformation (Hanezell-Thomas 2018), in line with the aims of the Australian Curriculum general capability of intercultural understanding: 'Intercultural understanding is an essential part of living with others in the diverse world of the twenty-first century. It assists young people to become responsible local and global citizens, equipped through their education for living and working together in an interconnected world' (ACARA 2018b).

## Intercultural understanding

The intercultural understanding capability (ACARA 2018b) outlines important implications for educators of HASS; for example, educators can assist learners in making connections between their own worlds and the worlds of others, sharing commonalities and mediating difference, and developing their abilities to communicate and to analyse intercultural experiences critically. As stated in the Australian Curriculum (ACARA 2018a), intercultural understanding aims to cultivate values and dispositions such as curiosity, care, empathy, reciprocity, respect and responsibility, open-mindedness and critical awareness, and supports new and positive intercultural behaviours. Three broad dispositions capture this: expressing empathy, demonstrating respect and taking responsibility (ACARA 2018a).

Within the case study of Muslim learners, negative and inaccurate perceptions and assumptions about Muslims in Australia not only give rise to stereotypes; they can present a barrier to engaging Muslim learners in HASS and compromise intercultural understanding for all learners. Common perceptions that educators and learners must critically reflect upon and challenge include that Muslims are a monolithic community, predominantly new arrivals, follow backward and outdated cultural practices and wish to impose these practices on others, follow a religion (Islam) that is alien to mainstream Australian society (Buckley 2012, p. 22), and are incompatible with democracy and Western values and secular modernity (Abdalla 2010). These perceptions tend to manifest in assumptions that Muslims are typically 'homogenous, foreign, newly arrived, anti-Western and insular' and 'position the culture and values of Muslims and Islam as contradictory to the culture and values of Australia society and the West in general' (Buckley 2012, p. 22).

Genuine pluralism and intercultural understanding are a 'truth seeking encounter, a 'process of mutual transformation' that goes beyond trying to 'understand the "other"' but reaches out to a new level of mutual self-understanding' (Hanezell-Thomas 2018, p. 12). The 'fostering of relationship is at the core of that encounter' and one of the most important ways to develop relationality is in the HASS space (p. 12). The 'human' contained within the term 'Humanities' in HASS offers a clue to its immense value, for education 'should confer the power to reach for a universal vision of excellence which encompasses truth, meaning, purpose and what it means to be fully human' (p. 13).

In educational settings, learners can engage with the plurality of diverse cultural and religious identities and communities in ways that recognise commonalities and differences, create connections and cultivate mutual respect (ACARA 2018b). What educators of HASS can take into account is that there are distinctions within distinctions, that communities are complex and changing, and for these reasons the key message is not to 'box' or 'label' learners, but rather empower individual learners to define themselves.

## CULTURALLY RESPONSIVE PEDAGOGICAL STRATEGIES TO MAXIMISE LEARNING OUTCOMES WITHIN HASS

Culturally responsive pedagogy is underpinned by justice for a just education – something that echoes the core values of HASS education. Being culturally responsive can be framed as a process whereby one gains respect for, and thus utilises as assets, the diversity of cultural and religious identities (Zaidi 2017), characteristics, experiences, perspectives and funds of knowledge (Zipin 2009) as enablers to teach learners (Rychly & Graves 2012). While commonly also including concepts such as values, traditions and language, it can be further expanded to include communication, learning styles and relationship norms (Gay 2002). Culturally responsive pedagogy, however, is not only relevant solely for culturally diverse learners. This chapter also frames culturally responsive pedagogy around equity and justice, and the idea that it can be responsive to all learners, facilitating reciprocal benefits for mutual transformation and respect and greater agency in the learning process. This has a clear synergy with HASS, which aims to give learners 'a deep understanding of the world they live in from a range of perspectives, past and present, and encourages them to develop an appreciation and respect for social, cultural and religious diversity' (ACARA 2018a). Encapsulating broad notions of citizenship and intercultural understanding, Hanezell-Thomas (2018) invokes a form of education that confers power to change oneself, society and the world in which learners live.

## ONE SIZE DOES NOT FIT ALL

A lecturer narrates an episode with a preservice educator in her cohort. The preservice educator was to embark on her first practicum experience, her first encounter as an educator with learners in an educational setting. She was essentially looking for a shortcut. She said, 'I know we have been engaging in all this theory and all this reflection on practice, but please just tell me the top ten things I need to know or do to be a good educator.' The lecturer, being experienced, said, 'Sure, you want just the top ten?' 'Yes, just give me the top ten and I will just focus on these.' The lecturer offered a wry smile and responded, 'For which student?'

As we turn to explore considerations for HASS educators, it is important to emphasise that this section does not seek to provide a one-size-fits-all blueprint for teaching culturally and religiously diverse learners. This is counter to the idea of culturally responsive pedagogy. As this Spotlight reinforces, all learners are unique and different, so knowing learners and how they learn (AITSL 2015) begins through encounter, relationship building and dialogue (Hanezell-Thomas 2018). It involves an openness to learn with and from the learner, and to foster learning from learner to learner in the educational setting, recognising the diversity that learners bring to the setting.

## Considerations for HASS educators

As educators in HASS, you are encouraged to consider the following:

- That you view yourself both as an educator and researcher, learning with and from your learners as you engage in the enquiry journey with them.
- That you recognise that you are not the only expert in the setting and learners bring their own expert knowledge (Delpit 1988).
- That you engage learners as researchers in inquiries that are relevant to their lifeworlds and the social issues that concern them locally, regionally and globally (Hattam, Sawyer & Gannon 2018).
- That you continually develop your capabilities to negotiate policy contexts, mandated knowledges and how these intersect with the lifeworlds and knowledges that learners bring to the learning environment (Hattam, Sawyer & Gannon 2018).
- That you develop confidence in decision-making in the context of your educational setting with a level of co-construction of curriculum (Delpit 1988; Hattam, Sawyer & Gannon 2018) and negotiation of pedagogy with learners informed by funds of knowledge and respect for their ways of knowing (Zipin 2009).

- That you are prepared to take up the role as a critical educator – more specifically a socially and ethically critical educator (Wrench & Garrett 2015) who is committed to a transformative classroom that is emancipatory and empowering (Preece 2001) for all learners, including those who are marginalised (Stonebanks 2008).

- That as a reflective practitioner you reflect on your own beliefs, values and orientations. What do you bring to the classroom? What are your biases? Like a good researcher, are you willing to disclose and acknowledge these for learners (Stonebanks 2008)?

## Culturally responsive pedagogical strategies

Key pillars or principles of culturally responsive pedagogy that you may consider as a HASS educator as you frame how this pedagogy will look in your educational setting include the following:

- Care and empathy as a democratic practice is modelled by you and is evident to all learners (Zembylas 2010), ensuring marginalised identities and narratives are given voice and humanised (Stonebanks 2008).

- Curriculum is inclusive of many voices, contributions and histories, highlighting interconnectedness, and promoting genuine pluralism and intercultural understanding.

- All learners are engaged in the practice of citizenship (Zembylas 2010) for justice that is applied to solving relevant social, cultural, civic, environmental and political challenges.

- Recognition of and respect for learners' funds of knowledge (Zipin 2009) that learners bring to the learning environment, is characterised by:
  - inclusion of learners' identities, allowing learners to identify themselves
  - recognition and respect for learners' cultural, religious and linguistic capital as assets for learning (Stonebanks 2008; Zipin 2009)
  - commitment to getting to know the lifeworlds of learners, including lifeworld pedagogies as integrated ways of teaching and learning from faith, family and community (Zipin 2009)
  - ways of knowing (Stonebanks 2008; Zipin 2009) employed to transact with knowledge in the educational setting for deeper learning (Zipin 2009).

These pillars or principles are by no means exhaustive; rather, they provide the foundation for educators to frame what culturally responsive pedagogy can look like in the educational setting with learners. Educators of HASS will see how these can be expanded practically in the following section.

## EDUCATOR TIP

As a culturally responsive educator, you have the opportunity to actively engage learners as researchers, giving voice and agency to learners' expert knowledges in transformative inquiries about the interests, priorities, dilemmas and challenges that shape them and their world – locally, regionally and globally.

# STRATEGIES FOR SUPPORTING HASS LEARNING FOR BROAD AND INCLUSIVE NOTIONS OF CITIZENSHIP

Culturally responsive pedagogy foregrounds equity and justice for all learners. Learners of HASS will be introduced to examples of learning experiences and lessons employing culturally responsive pedagogy, explicitly highlighting and emphasising how these can purposefully engage all learners.

## The Yarning Circle – *Nga Tana Lui Dha* (the great learning circle of life)

Learning experiences and lessons in this chapter will draw from the Yarning Circle – *Nga Tana Lui Dha* model, which is a protocol and a process enabling learners to come together in equal status to listen to each other's stories and perspectives (Bennet 1997). The model adopted here recognises the need for a diversity of cultural expressions, inclusive of traditions, beliefs, values and languages, acting as a cultural lens or filter (Bennet 1997). It is in alignment with inquiry-based learning but provides an ideal model for considering cultural diversity, including learners' cultural and religious backgrounds and language knowledges and ways of knowing. It engages learners as researchers and facilitates respectful relationships or relationality in educational settings, as well as reciprocity, as learners draw on their funds of knowledge, share knowledge and search for new knowledge (OECD 2018) and take on individual and collective responsibility in trialling solutions to real-world issues locally, regionally and globally (ACARA 2018a).

### About the Yarning Circle – *Nga Tana Lui Dha*

The Yarning Circle – *Nga Tana Lui Dha* (the great learning circle of life) is the invention and lifework of 'Goorie Woman', recognised Elder and direct descendant of the Kullali Peoples (of South-West Queensland) and Wakka Wakka and Gubbi Gubbi Peoples (of South-East Queensland), Aunty Debra Bennet. The Yarning Circle – *Nga Tana Lui Dha* also incorporates the Indigenous Research Agenda from Professor of Education and Maori Development, Linda Tuiawi Smith, '*Ngati Awa* and *Ngati Porou*' (Smith 2012). The Yarning Circle – *Nga Tana Lui Dha* promotes transformative elements for learners based on self-awareness and self-determination, also providing agency for the humanising of voices and narratives of marginalised peoples, and peoples negotiating the impact and experience of colonisation such as the many Muslim peoples who have migrated to Australia. 'The dynamic wisdom of The Yarning Circle – *Nga Tana Lui Dha* concepts are not unique to Aboriginal peoples or any specific culture, gender or age. They contain global truths, which is why this process is so translatable across cultures as a transformative model and a tool for critical thinking' (Bennet 1997, n.p.).

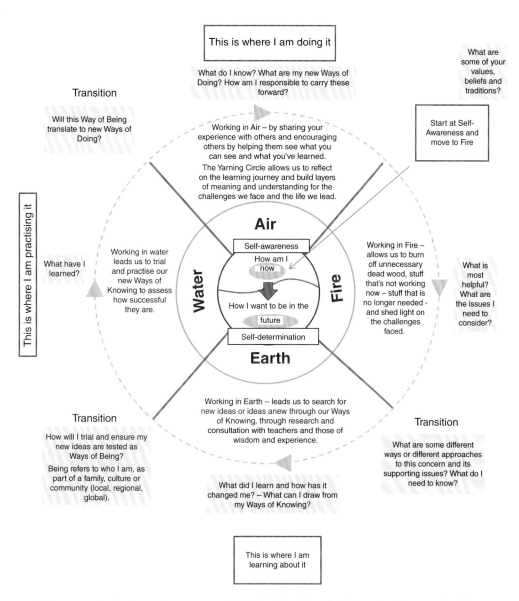

FIGURE 21.1 Exploring issues in the Yarning Circle – *Nga Tana Lui Dha* (the great learning circle of life)
Source: Bennet 1997

## Taking the journey around the Yarning Circle – *Nga Tana Lui Dha*

The Yarning Circle – *Nga Tana Lui Dha* functions as a compass. It has as its central focus the work of self-awareness, which is about 'knowing the self' by working through the milestone stages that include elements of *fire*, *earth*, *water* and *air*. These transitions are powerful metaphors for life (Bennet 1997).

The Yarning Circle – *Nga Tana Lui Dha* depicts a journey of learning and self-discovery that empowers the individual and the community. Ultimately it leads to self-determination so each person is able to take leadership of their own life and encourage others, family and community to take the journey (Bennet 1997). It also offers an accessible tool to apply the 'three dispositions – expressing empathy, demonstrating respect and taking responsibility – [as] have been identified as critical to the development of Intercultural Understanding in the Australian Curriculum' (ACARA 2018b).

By utilising the Yarning Circle – *Nga Tana Lui Dha* as a compass, filter or tool to help learners think about issues and make decisions (Bennet 1997), the process becomes a part of learners' lifeworlds as an extension of learning in their educational settings (see Figure 21.1). It is important to note that learners can and will move back and forth between the milestones while trialling a new idea or a new solution, or working through a complex or wicked challenge until, individually and collectively, the right knowledge and the right approach or 'fit' has been found. At this point it becomes a 'good fit' because 'learners have worked at it in each milestone ... and now it can become incorporated into learners' lifestyles ... their "*Way of Doing*"' (Bennet 1997, n.p.). In other words, it can assist educators in enacting pedagogy that works with the HASS curriculum to develop both what knowledge learners ought to know and what learners ought to be and become (Lingard 2017). As shared by Aunty Debra (Bennet 1997, n.p.), 'We travel the great circle many times in a lifetime. Our life journey spirals back over itself in ever deepening concentric layers of experience as we move towards the meaning we make of our lives ultimately evolving spheres of wisdom.'

## Using the Yarning Circle – *Nga Tana Lui Dha* in teaching

The Yarning Circle – *Nga Tana Lui Dha* can be used in small groups of learners or with the entire class. The strategy works well when learners are asked to reflect on their values, beliefs and traditions in the self-awareness milestone at the outset of an inquiry and read or view, for example, a range of short vignettes, websites or case studies on one topic in the earth milestone element. The aim is to provide opportunities for learners to draw on their own cultural and religious assets and funds of knowledge as well as hear others' points of view and discuss more deeply what they have read in preparation for writing.

To take the journey around the Yarning Circle – *Nga Tana Lui Dha*:

- Begin in the centre circle (self-awareness milestone element). Ask learners what resources can they draw on for this activity. Greater self-awareness allows greater understanding of other perspectives and other people's resources. Ask learners to reflect on these and identify useful resources and ways of knowing from which they can benefit.

- Identify with learners (co-construct) the focus questions in the Fire milestone element. What do we already know? What resources are useful for this inquiry? What do we need to know? What do we need to ask or find out?

- Provide access to a range of sources for learners to use in the Earth milestone element. These may include images, websites, case studies or excerpts from texts. Provide learners time to read or view and understand the texts. Clearly state the focus question.

- Direct learners to pairs or groups based on their inquiry. Ask learners to continue their journey around the Yarning Circle – *Nga Tana Lui Dha* together.

**TABLE 21.1** MILESTONE ELEMENT ORDER, TRANSITIONS AND CHARACTERISTICS (WITH 'TEACHER TALK') AT EACH MILESTONE

| Milestone elements | Transitions | Characteristics of each milestone |
|---|---|---|
| Self-awareness | *This is where the process begins* | How are you now? How do you identify yourself? What are some of your values, beliefs and traditions? |
| Fire | *This involves unpacking* <br> *Stepping stone to Earth* | Means to shed light on the situation; to unpack and sometimes to burn off dated or unhelpful ways. <br><br> *How can you identify beneficial knowledge and skills to carry forward (like a firebrand – illuminating the path)?* |
| Earth | *This is where transformation occurs* <br> *Stepping stone to Water* | Means to dig deeper through research; to search for old and new wisdom. <br><br> *What are your deep knowledges, your values (your foundation – as in the earth underneath your feet)? How can you retrieve your traditions and your ways passed on to you as well as search for new ones?* |
| Water | *This is a reflective practice* <br> *Stepping stone to Air* | Means to test; to put into practice; finding stillness and reflecting *(as water does)* on what you have learnt and what you now know. <br><br> *What do I know? What was learnt while working through previous milestones of Fire and Earth?* |
| Air | *Leadership – owning responsibility* <br> *Stepping stone to self-awareness and self-determination* | Means to report on it; refers to a leadership level; your responsibility to accurately represent your learning through acknowledging how you got there *(understanding the big picture as in a birds' eye view)* – system thinkers! <br><br> Air also involves a 'peak experience', an 'aha' moment. It could be learning a new habit or refining an old habit, which might happen quickly or it could be a deeper realisation of who you are and how you can contribute that takes longer. <br><br> *How do you represent your communities (local, regional, global), your family, your school, yourself?* |
| Self-determination | *This means learners have taken one journey around the great circle – they may take others* | How do you want to be in the future? Where can you contribute? Where can you be of benefit? |

- Ask learners to identity solutions and strategies in the Water milestone element supported by evidence or trialled if relevant.
- Learners provide justification and present these as recommendations in the Air milestone element.
- Learners reflect on these in the centre circle, concluding with implications and how they are responsible for what they have learnt in previous milestone elements.
- Learners record key points at each milestone element and present these to the class.
- The educator's role is to time-keep and assist learners in capturing key points so they can refer to these in the follow-up writing activity.

## EDUCATOR TIP

Engage learners in a discussion by taking a journey around the Yarning Circle – *Nga Tana Lui Dha*, allowing them to identify relevant topics or issues of interest to them, and co-constructing the inquiry learners will explore individually, either as a learning experience or as an assessment piece.

### Identity

Culturally responsive pedagogy involves getting to know learners' identities, including their multiple identities as well as their lifeworlds. One of the most empowering yet simplest ways to do this is to ask learners to identify themselves. While this can be done in many ways, one strategy is to explore it via the Yarning Circle – *Nga Tana Lui Dha*, initially focusing on the centre circle and taking the journey around each of the elements, before returning to the inner circle. This self-reflection stimulates a greater sense of self-awareness and provides a safe transformative space that gives voice to learners' identities, stories and ways of knowing. It can also be a cornerstone to building relationality and reciprocity through empathy and care for all learners in the classroom (Zembylas 2010) and the space for learners to add to new knowledge of selves and of issues and new 'ways of doing' (Bennet 1997).

## EDUCATOR TIP

Conduct and reflect on the following learning challenge: 'Dear researchers (learners), I want you to go home and talk with your parents, families and trusted others about your name. Come back and share – tell us about your name.'

Names hold many meanings, carry traditions and languages, tell stories and shape identities. In diverse classrooms, giving voice to marginalised identities humanises all learners and demonstrates respect for values, beliefs, traditions, languages and ways of knowing. For learners who identify as Aboriginal or Torres Strait Islander people, it can reveal important information about family, community and cultural knowledges as well as various responsibilities. For all learners, their name allows them to identify themselves in ways that valuable cultural and religious banks are viewed as assets. Importantly, the activity in the Educator tip provides an opportunity for the educator to get to know the lifeworlds of learners, which can assist in ongoing culturally responsive pedagogical approaches in the educational setting.

There are several ways to scaffold and assist learners, depending on their age, to unpack and share their names. One way is for the educator to model this for them. Another is to provide task cards with guiding reflective questions for each milestone of the Yarning Circle – *Nga Tana Lui Dha*. Learners can also trial this process in pairs, with each pair taking time to analyse and synthesise what they have heard via the milestone guiding questions. As an extension, learners can refine their story orally or in text and share it as a class.

## THE YARNING CIRCLE – *NGA TANA LUI DHA*: IDENTITIES, WAYS OF KNOWING, SHARED VALUES AND ACTIVE CITIZENSHIP

**Topic:** Year 7 learners identify the ideas, values and principles that underpin the institutions and processes in Australia's political and legal systems. They explain the diverse nature of Australian society and identify the importance of shared values in contemporary Australian society.

Learners formulate significant questions to investigate Australia's political and legal systems. They locate, collect and organise useful information from a range of primary and secondary sources. They examine sources to determine their origin, purpose and reliability and to identify and describe values and perspectives. They evaluate and synthesise information to draw conclusions. When planning for action, learners take into account multiple perspectives to develop solutions to an issue. They reflect on their learning to identify ways in which they can be active and informed citizens by presenting ideas, viewpoints, explanations and conclusions in a range of communication forms that incorporate source materials, citations, and Civics and Citizenship terms and concepts.

### Curriculum content descriptions

How groups, such as religious and cultural groups, express their particular identities; and how this influences their perceptions of others and vice versa (ACHASSK198) (ACARA 2018a).

Elaborations:

- Investigating how and why different Aboriginal and Torres Strait Islander communities are maintaining and developing their identities and what this means for Australia as a whole

SPOTLIGHT ON HASS EDUCATION

- Discussing how belonging to a religious or cultural group can provide a sense of belonging and how this group membership can shape an individual's identity
- Identifying the different ways that cultural and religious groups express their beliefs, identity and experiences (e.g. through customs, practices, symbols, language, traditions and art, and virtual communities)
- Discussing how stereotypes are linked with people's cultural identity (e.g. clothes, accent/language, media representations)
- Considering how Australia's location in the Asia region influences interactions between Australians and those living in the region.

## EDUCATOR TIP

In identifying and respecting the different ways that cultural and religious groups express their beliefs, identity and experiences, manifesting in customs and symbols, it is important to move beyond appreciation premised on 'exoticness' and connect these with ways of knowing, being and doing and as assets for the practice of Civics and Citizenship and classroom engagement in HASS generally.

## CONCLUSION

This chapter has provided knowledge, skills and understandings for educators to adopt culturally responsive pedagogies that support learners studying HASS. Transformative educational settings and pedagogy within the disciplinary area of HASS provide great potential for all learners to engage in the practice of citizenship. Greater understanding of and appreciation for the diversity of learners in Australian educational settings engage critical educators in genuine pluralism, social cohesion and greater intercultural understanding, leading to mutual understanding and mutual transformation. Pillars or principles of culturally responsive pedagogy given agency here in the Yarning Circle – *Nga Tana Lui Dha* expand all learners' understandings and engage them in deep, critical thinking. Insight gained from HASS develops learners into active and informed citizens who will contribute to a just and empathetic society. Educators' knowledge and commitment to culturally responsive pedagogy can form a strong basis from which to teach all learners in HASS.

## REVIEW QUESTIONS

1. Why is it important for educators to model care and empathy as a democratic process in the learning environment?
2. Explain concepts of relationality, reciprocity and mutual understanding in relation to the development of intercultural understanding.

3. What are the benefits of drawing on culturally and religiously diverse learners' funds of knowledge in teaching and learning in HASS? Support each benefit with an example of how you can include this in the educational setting through your pedagogical practice.

4. What pillars or principles can educators draw from in formulating what culturally pedagogy for learners may look like in the educational setting?

## LEARNING EXTENSION

1. Write a reflective piece to connect personal change and the responsibility to practise engaged citizenship.

2. Write a persuasive piece that addresses an issue of social justice for a marginalised group and highlight personal and collective direct action within the practice of citizenship.

## ACKNOWLEDGEMENT

Cultural Custodian, 'Goorie Woman', recognised Elder and direct descendant of the Kullali Peoples (of South-West Queensland) and Wakka Wakka and Gubbi Gubbi Peoples (of South-East Queensland), Aunty Debra Bennet is acknowledged here for sharing her invention and lifework, the Yarning Circle – *Nga Tana Lui Dha* (the great learning circle of life). The author offers sincere gratitude and appreciation for allowing educators and learners of HASS to benefit from the dynamic wisdom of this model, protocol and process.

## REFERENCES

Abdalla, M. (2010). Muslims in Australia: Negative views and positive contributions. In H. Rane, J. Ewart & M. Abdalla, eds, *Islam and the Australian News Media*. Melbourne: Melbourne University Press.

Abdi, A.A. (2014). Critical global citizenship in K–12 classrooms. In D. Montemurro, M. Gambhir, M. Evans & K. Broad, eds, *Inquiry into Practice: Learning and teaching global matters in local classrooms*. Toronto: Ontario Institute for Studies in Education of the University of Toronto.

Abdullah, M. & Nadvi, M.J. (2011). Understanding the principles of Islamic world-view. *Dialogue*, 6(3), 268–89.

Abowitz, K.K. & Harnish, J. (2006). Contemporary discourses of citizenship. *Review of Educational Research*, 76(4), 653–90.

ABS (Australian Bureau of Statistics). (2016). 2016 Census: Religion. Retrieved from: http://www.abs.gov.au/AUSSTATS/abs@.nsf/mediareleasesbyReleaseDate/7E65A144540551D7CA258148000E2B85?OpenDocument.

ACARA (Australian Curriculum, Assessment and Reporting Authority). (2018a). *Australian Curriculum: Humanities and Social Sciences, v8.3*. Retrieved from: http://australian-curriculum.org/humanities-and-social-sciences.

——(2018b). *Australian Curriculum: Humanities and Social Sciences, v8.3*. Intercultural understanding. Retrieved from: https://www.australiancurriculum.edu.au/f-10-curriculum/general-capabilities/intercultural-understanding.

——(2018c). *Australian Curriculum: Humanities and Social Sciences, v8.3*. Rationale. Retrieved from: https://www.australiancurriculum.edu.au/f-10-curriculum/humanities-and-social-sciences/hass/rationale.

AITSL (Australian Institute for Teaching and School Leadership). (2015). *Australian Professional Standards for Teachers*. Retrieved from: https://www.aitsl.edu.au/docs/default-source/general/australian-professional-standands-for-teachers-20171006.pdf?sfvrsn=399ae83c_12.

Aly, A. & Green, L. (2008). 'Moderate Islam': Defining the good citizen. *M/C Journal*, 11(1). Retrieved from: http://journal.media-culture.org.au/index.php/mcjournal/article/view/28.

Barry, M. (1998). Social exclusion and social work: An introduction. In M. Barry & C. Hallett, eds, *Social Exclusion and Social Work. Issues of theory, policy and practice*. Lyme Regis: Russell House, pp. 1–25.

Bennet, D. (1997). Dynamic wisdom of the Yarning Circle. Making meaning in changing times. Workshop materials. Materials provided courtesy of the author.

Bourdieu, P. (1986). The forms of capital. In J. Richardson, ed., *Handbook of Theory and Research for the Sociology of Education*. Westport, CT: Greenwood Press, pp. 241–58.

Briskman, L., Iner, D., Krayem, G., Latham, S., Matthews, Z., Pearson, C., … Zayied, I. (2017). *Islamophobia in Australia 2014–2016*. Sydney: Charles Sturt University. Retrieved from: https://researchoutput.csu.edu.au/en/publications/islamophobia-in-australia-2014-2016.

Buckingham, J. (2010). *The Rise of Religious Schools*. Sydney: The Centre for Independent Studies.

Buckley, A. (2012). The first Islamic museum of Australia: Challenging negative assumptions of Muslims in Australia through art, heritage and discovery. *La Trobe Journal*, 89, 20–35.

Cesari, J. (2011). Islamophobia in the West: A comparison between Europe and the United States. In J. Esposito & I. Kalin, eds, *Islamophobia: The challenge of pluralism in the 21st century*. New York: Oxford University Press, pp. 21–43.

Delpit, L.D. (1988). The silences dialogue: Power and pedagogy in educating other people's children. *Harvard Educational Review*, 58(3), 280–98.

Dunn, K.M. (2004). *Attitudes Towards Islam in Australia, Report for the Australia-Indonesia Institute*. Sydney: Geography Department, University of New South Wales.

Gay, G. (2002). Preparing for culturally responsive teaching. *Journal of Teacher Education*, 53, 106–16.

Goduka, I.N. (1998). Educators as cultural awakeners and healers. *South African Journal of Higher Education*, 12(2), 49–59.

Hanezell-Thomas, J. (2018). *The Power of Education*. London: International Institute of Islamic Thought.

Hattam, R. (2017). Diversity, global citizenship and the culturally responsive school. In I. Davies, et al., eds, *Palgrave Handbook of Global Citizenship and Education*. London: Palgrave, pp. 257–75.

Hattam, R., Sawyer, W. & Gannon, S. (2018). Reclaiming educational equality: Towards a manifesto. In S. Gannon, R. Hattam & W. Sawyer, eds, *Resisting Educational Inequality: Reframing policy and practice in schools serving vulnerable communities*. London & New York: Routledge, pp. 294–301.

Heilman, E. (2006). Critical, liberal, poststructural challenges for global education. In A. Segall, E. Heilman & C. Cherryholmes, eds, *In Social Studies – the next generation: Re-searching in the postmodern*. New York: Peter Lang, pp. 189–208.

Jones, P. (2013). Islamic schools in Australia. PhD thesis, University of New England.

Klump, J. & McNeir, G. (2005). *Culturally Responsive Practices for Student Success: A regional sampler*. Portland, OG: Northwest Regional Educational Laboratory. Retrieved from: http://educationnorthwest.org/sites/default/files/culturally-responsive-practices.pdf.

Lingard, B. (2017). Keynote address. Australian Curriculum Studies Association Biennial Conference, October, Sydney.

Mansouri, F. & Trembath, A. (2005). Multicultural education and racism: The case of Arab-Australian students in Australia. *International Education Journal*, 6(4), 516–29.

MCEETYA (Ministerial Council on Education, Employment, Training and Youth Affairs). (2008). *Melbourne Declaration on Educational Goals for Young Australians*. Retrieved from: http://www.curriculum.edu.au/verve/_resources/National_Declaration_on_the_Educational_Goals_for_Young_Australians.pdf.

Memon, N.A. & Zaman, M. (2016). *Philosophies of Islamic Education: Historical perspectives and emerging discourses*. New York: Routledge.

O'Donnell, K., Davis, R. & Ewart, J. (2017). Non-Muslim Australians' knowledge of Islam: Identifying and rectifying knowledge deficiencies. *Journal of Muslim Minority Affairs*, 37(1), 41–54.

OECD. (2018). *The Future of Education and Skills: Education 2030*. Paris: OECD. Retrieved from: https://www.oecd.org/education/2030/E2030%20Position%20Paper%20(05.04.2018).pdf.

Pe-Pua, R., Gendera, S., Katz, I. & O'Connor, A. (2010). *Meeting the Needs of Australian Muslim Families: Exploring marginalization, family issues and 'best practice' in service provision*. Sydney: Social Policy Research Centre, University of New South Wales.

Preece, J. (2001). Challenging the discourse of inclusion and exclusion with off limits curricula. *Studies in the Education of Adults*, 33(2), 201–16.

Preger, M. & Kostogriz, A. (2014). Multiculturalism, schooling and Muslims in Australia: From orientation to a possibility of hospitable education. In A.W. Ata, ed., *Education Integration Challenges: The case of Muslims in Australia*. Melbourne: David Lovell Publishing, pp. 157–66.

Rychly, L. & Graves, E. (2012). Teacher characteristics for culturally responsive pedagogy. *National Association for Multicultural Education*, 14(1), 44–9.

Smith, L.T. (2012). *Decolonizing Methodologies: Research and indigenous peoples*, 2nd edn. Dunedin: Otago University Press.

Stewart, D.-L. (2017). Colleges need a language shift, but not the one you think (essay). Retrieved from: https://www.insidehighered.com/views/2017/03/30/colleges-need-language-shift-not-one-you-think-essay?width=775&height=500&iframe=true.

Stonebanks, C.D. (2008). An Islamic perspective on knowledge, knowing, and methodology. In N.K. Denzin, Y.S. Lincoln & L.T. Smith, eds, *Handbook of Critical Indigenous Methodologies*. Thousand Oaks, CA: Sage, pp. 293–321.

Strauss, A.L. & Corbin, J.M. (1990). *Basics of Qualitative Research: Grounded theory procedures and techniques*. Thousand Oaks, CA: Sage.

Wrench, A. & Garrett, R. (2015). Emotional connections and caring: Ethical teachers of physical education. *Sport, Education and Society*, 20(2), 212–27.

Zaidi, R. (2017). *Anti-Islamophobic Curriculums*, vol. 1. New York: Peter Lang.

Zembylas, M. (2010). The ethic of care in globalized societies: Implications for citizenship education. *Ethics and Education*, 5(3), 233–45.

——(2015). *Emotion and Traumatic Conflict: Reclaiming healing in education*. New York: Oxford University Press.

Zipin, L. (2009). Dark funds of knowledge, deep funds of pedagogy: Exploring boundaries between lifeworlds and schools. *Discourse: Studies in the Cultural Politics of Education*, 30(3), 317–31.

# HASS FOR EVERYONE: INCLUSIVE APPROACHES RESPECTFUL OF LEARNER DIVERSITY

*Deborah Price and Deborah Green*

## INTRODUCTION

All young people have rich histories, connections to space, place and significant events, which fuel their curiosity about the world in which they live and provide an excellent platform from which powerful HASS learning experiences can be developed. The HASS curriculum, as presented in the Australian Curriculum, provides flexibility for educators to link learning to young people's lifeworlds and experiences through culturally responsive and inclusive pedagogies. This chapter challenges you to place learners and contexts at the centre of planning, using co-design principles that value young people's voice, histories, capabilities and connections with people and place in HASS planning, teaching and assessment. All educational settings are enriched with a diversity of learners, who need to be involved in learning designs from the outset, rather than having their diverse needs planned for after the event. Such universal design approaches to learning need to be embedded from the early years of education.

For the context of this chapter, the term 'diverse learners' refers to all learners, inclusive of gender, ability, culture, religion, age and so forth. A deliberate effort is made to model inclusive principles in a way that places the focus on learners' capabilities – that is, *what they can do and be* (Nussbaum 2003; Price 2015, 2016; Sen 1985) – rather than being driven by stereotypical, medicalised characteristics and labels that tend to marginalise and exclude learners from educational opportunities (Price & Slee 2018; Reddington & Price 2017, 2018; see also Chapter 21). The educator has a vital role in promoting inclusive principles, and the affordances of applying UDL and differentiated learning will be addressed. This may initially be challenging for educators. However, in applying co-design principles to learning experiences, all learners can feel valued, have access to learning, and be meaningfully engaged in age-appropriate and contextual education. For this to be achieved, it is important to begin by understanding foundational inclusive educational principles.

## INCLUSIVE PRINCIPLES

Forbes (2007, p. 67) describes the current Australian view of an 'inclusive school as a place where everyone belongs, is accepted, and where special education needs students are supported and cared for by their peers and other members of the school community'. She argues that inclusion also needs to address the processes and learning environments required 'to achieve authentic educational outcomes for all students' (p. 67).

Price and Slee (2018, p. 222) contest that all learners need to be engaged purposefully in relevant learning so that they can progress academically and developmentally. They explain that to be truly inclusive relies on curriculum design that is more than rewriting or adapting syllabi and tests. 'It requires a much more expansive view of curriculum, a view that recognises that the challenge is not just making additional curriculum for different cohorts.' As Hyde (2017, p. 355) identifies, the cyclical process of inclusion requires the right balance between 'provision of high levels of differentiation of services and support to the needs of the specific individual, and the degree of uniformity that is maintained across a system and school community to ensure that funds are distributed appropriately and that the rights of all are preserved'.

## PHILOSOPHY OF ENGAGEMENT

As I nervously entered my first classroom of 23 children aged five to eight years in a regional country town in Australia, the sense of responsibility for shaping their academic achievement and holistic development as respectful and productive citizens was naturally daunting. My orientation days had immersed me in profiles of learners with low academic performance, non-verbal, low intellectual functioning, speech difficulties, health issues, diverse cultures, aggressive behaviours, complex home environments, low socio-economic status, those under the guardianship of the minister, trauma affected, and a whole comorbidity of issues. Coupled with this was the background that the previous educator had left due to stress. On the eve of entering the class, I felt overwhelmed by the deficit/negative profiles created and began questioning, what each of these young people's lifeworlds, abilities, interests, dreams and skills might be. So my planning began with an inclusive philosophy of engaging all learners in contributing to the design and choices of learning activities that began with exploring their rich histories, connections to places and people and current experiences

**SPOTLIGHT ON HASS EDUCATION**

of the world they inhabited. The HASS curriculum provided a framework to pursue this focus through capturing their knowledge, values and beliefs as citizens, which was underpinned by an inclusive philosophy and **capabilities perspective** of what young people can do and be (Nussbaum 2003; Price 2015, 2016; Sen 1985). From that initial moment in teaching, I committed to plan for *all* learners from the outset, rather than making adjustments to the plan to accommodate diversity. What culminated was a community of engaged young people with a strong sense of and respect for their identity. What are the inclusive principles that you apply in your educational philosophy and practice?

**capabilities perspective:** focuses on what young people can do and be

## Principles to guide inclusive teaching and education

A range of inclusive principles have informed educational policy, and educators will continually be challenged to incorporate and transform these in their practice. A summary of some key principles (albeit by no means exclusive) is provided below:

- Social justice and human rights – recognises learners as being people first, making decisions about themselves and equitable rights to education (Foreman 2017).
- All children are learners and can learn (Foreman 2017).
- Provision of least restrictive environments for learning (Foreman 2017); providing choice of most appropriate learning environments to the learner and parent/carer.
- Positive school/site, leadership, educator, community attitudes towards all learners, where diversity is valued (Hyde 2017).
- Provision of access and participation, collaborating for better learner outcomes with all stakeholders, delivering responsive programs and services, matching pedagogy with each learner's needs (DET WA 2004; Hyde 2017).
- Quality educators with the knowledge, skills and understandings to promote inclusion (Hyde 2017).
- Involve learners in co-designing learning opportunities.
- Learners are agents in making decisions, problem-solving and goal-setting.
- Value learners' lifeworlds, communities, contexts and experiences.

**Reflection**

Take the time to consider the inclusive principles that you exhibit in your everyday thinking, actions and communication. How do these influence your teaching, pedagogy and assessment? How do you take the lead in advocating inclusive principles?

For HASS educators, the opportunities to promote positive attitudes among learners as active, informed and productive citizens are immense. We now turn to explore the educator's role in promoting inclusive principles within the HASS learning area.

# RESPONSIBILITY IN APPLYING INCLUSIVE PRACTICES TO THE HASS LEARNING EXPERIENCE

In Australia, the drive to increase learner outcomes from a commitment to raise educator quality is promoted in the Australian Professional Standards for Teachers (APST; AITSL 2015). The first of these standards outlines an educator's responsibility to 'know students and how they learn' with Standard 1.3 addressing learners with diverse linguistic, cultural, religious and socio-economic backgrounds. Graduates are expected to 'demonstrate knowledge of teaching strategies that are responsive to the learning strengths and needs of students from diverse linguistic, cultural, religious and socioeconomic backgrounds' (AITSL 2015). In addition, the professional standards outline educators' responsibilities to know all learners, including those with disabilities, by ensuring their teaching and learning is responsive. So how do HASS educators specifically incorporate their knowledge of young people in meeting the *Australian Curriculum: HASS* content requirements and achievement standards within their diverse settings?

The Australian Curriculum website provides a process for designing learning experiences to meet the needs of all learners, as shown in Figure 22.1.

**Using the Australian Curriculum to meet the learning needs of all students**

Teachers refer to the Australian Curriculum learning area content that aligns with their students' chronological age as the starting point in planning teaching and learning programs.

Teachers take account of the range of their students' current levels of learning, strengths, goals and interests, and personalise learning where necessary through adjustments to the teaching and learning program, according to individual learning need, by:

- drawing from learning area content at different levels along the Foundation to Year 10 sequence to personalise age-equivalent learning area content
- using the general capabilities and/or cross-curriculum priorities to adjust the learning focus of the age-equivalent learning area content
- aligning individual learning goals with age-equivalent learning area content.

Teachers assess students' progress through the Australian Curriculum in relation to achievement standards. Some students' progress will be assessed in relation to their individual learning goals. Approaches to assessment and reporting will differ across the states and territories.

FIGURE 22.1   Meeting diverse learning needs
Source: ACARA 2018

In the context of teaching in the HASS learning area, how are inclusive principles reflected in ACARA's approach to meeting the learning needs of diverse learners (see Figure 22.1)? What are the strengths of this approach? What would you do differently? Why?

Educators across the globe have questioned national curriculum design efforts, particularly the relationship between an official curriculum and meeting the learning needs of every learner (Price 2015; Price & Slee 2018). In the above approach, we suggest that it is important that all HASS learning experiences are personalised and related to young people's interests, experiences, skills and lifeworlds. This should be the intent from the outset. Beginning planning from the HASS achievement standards and learning area content descriptors aligned with the learner's chronological age is respectful of their identity. It is then, however, possible to differentiate learning activities according to developmental needs to ensure that all learners are engaged and successful. Before turning to explore UDL and differentiation within HASS, it is important that educators recognise their responsibility in curriculum design, pedagogy and assessment. Within the scope of this chapter, we address curriculum and pedagogy separately to support understanding, keeping in mind that curriculum, pedagogy and assessment are interrelated and form the whole educational package.

## Educator responsibility: inclusive HASS curriculum design

As a HASS educator, it is important to keep in mind that the term 'curriculum' refers not only to specific planned activities, but to all planned and unplanned 'interactions, experiences, routines and events' that occur in either early learning settings (ACECQA 2011, p. 203; DEEWR 2009, p. 9) or primary years contexts. The written text of any curriculum is only the intended curriculum (Reid 2018); therefore, it is the educator's responsibility to have a solid knowledge of the curriculum and then enact this so that all learners can be included and succeed. That is, the HASS learning area in the Australian Curriculum is a guide and the educator's role is to make it dynamic, inclusive and contextual for *all* learners in the setting. The educator begins by looking at the community to which learners belong and to which they are connected, and the spaces and places with which they identify and interact. What can they share with their peers and how can they learn from each other's communities? Having deep knowledge of learners' lifeworlds enhances the educator's ability to locate the most relevant HASS curriculum concepts and content that builds on learners' prior knowledge and communities. This is the point at which to look at the age-appropriate sub-strands of History, Geography, Civics and Citizenship, and Economics and Business, and identify concepts both within and across the sub-strands that can be potential options for learners to frame an inquiry.

At this time, it is important to identify the learning outcomes and parameters of the learning experience/unit of work, which facilitates scope for learner choice, developmental level, culture and prior knowledge, skills and understandings. For example, to respect each learner's identity and self-efficacy, a learner in Year 6 who has been identified as operating at a Year 2 developmental level needs to be included in the age-appropriate HASS concept, yet the content, pedagogy and assessment may need adaption. Their inquiry will reflect their age-appropriate content descriptor, yet the achievement standards will align to their individual learning goals.

To demonstrate this, let's look at a Year 6 class, which may be learning about the contribution of individuals and groups to the development of Australian society since Federation (ACHASSK137), where the achievement standard may be adapted to align more closely to Year 2. For example, the achievement standard for Year 6 is:

> By the end of Year 6 students explain the significance of an event/development, an individual or group. They identify and describe continuities and changes for different groups in the past. They describe the causes and effects of change on society. They compare the experiences of different people in the past. (ACARA 2018)

As the achievement standards are sequential over years, this achievement standard can be adapted in the following way:

> Students explain the significance of an event/development, an individual and/or group by describing a person or group of significance in the community. They identify how and why the lives of people or groups have changed over time while others have remained the same and how this has contributed to Australian society.

To achieve this, learners need choice and a range of differentiated approaches to communicate their explanation, which aligns with their skills and abilities; for example, written, visual, multimodal, digital, verbal, etc., as described later in this chapter. This supports their ability to be assessed on their content knowledge and learning, rather than being restricted by the mode of expression.

Educators will also work with learners, their families/carers and broader support personnel, with individualised plans including individual education plans and negotiated education plans. The educator's responsibility is to collaborate with all stakeholders to plan appropriate curriculum goals with high, yet achievable expectations. Collaborative goal setting provides opportunities to learn more about learners' lifeworlds so that curriculum design is responsive and aligned to learners' needs and values, and family/carer perspectives.

## EDUCATOR TIP

Remember, all learners can learn and achieve. Linking 'official curriculum' with learners' communities and lifeworlds provides the starting point for curriculum design. This promotes an inclusive platform for learning, and connects curriculum to prior knowledge, skills and understandings, thus motivating learners as their community is respected and curriculum is contextual. *Your responsibility is to inclusively enact the curriculum.*

# Educator responsibility: inclusive HASS pedagogy

Educators are continually challenged to deliver a mandated overcrowded curriculum, be accountable to staff, systems and parents/carers for high achievement outcomes for all learners and have increased evidence to support such outcomes. Given such pressure, and governance and compliance requirements, we caution educators not to fall into the trap of teaching a narrow curriculum through outdated pedagogies that fail to engage young learners. Within Australia, we are experiencing an 'unspoken crisis' (Cuervo & Wyn 2016), with an increasing number of young people disengaging from education and employment (Vinson et al. 2015). These young people are engaging in 'learning at not-school' education alternatives (Sefton-Green 2013). We contend that it is our responsibility as educators to design and enact curriculum to re-engage learners, with HASS providing an ideal vehicle to achieve this. As educators of HASS, we need to promote turnaround pedagogy to engineer curriculum redesigns that make a difference by viewing learners as young people of promise to disrupt the cycle of failure (Comber & Kamler 2004; Price 2015). Employing inclusive pedagogies involves having positive educator self-efficacy and attitude; focus on progression and achievement; and equity, flexibility, access and choice (Price 2015).

**Reflection**

Draw on any educational setting experiences, whether your own education or professional experience placements, volunteer roles or current educational teaching roles. What pedagogies did educators use that sparked learners' curiosity, energy, focus, questioning and action? Were there any pedagogies that positively impacted all learners in the group? If so, what were they? How did the educator adapt pedagogies to include a diversity of learners? This includes ability, Aboriginal or Torres Strait Islander background, culture, gender, religious beliefs, migrants and refugees; that is, all learners in the educational setting.

Did these pedagogies need to be different according to these traditional categories of diversity or could they have been appropriate across diversity groups?

## Culturally responsive pedagogy

When planning learning experiences, rather than being solely focused on delivering the intended curriculum, it is argued that we should begin with the culture of the learners, drawing on their cultural strengths and those of their families and communities (Castagno & Brayboy 2008). Building on Chapter 21, culturally responsive pedagogy reinforces that culture counts, power is shared and learning is interactive with dialogic connectedness (Bishop et al. 2007a, 2007b; Villegas & Lucas 2002a, 2002b). As educators, our overarching aim should be to promote the view that every learner needs to be proud of who they are, drawing upon Chris Sarra's Stronger Smarter initiative (Stronger Smarter Institute 2018) to improve educational outcomes for Aboriginal and Torres Strait Islander students. This involves professional accountability and responsibility for change; a strength-based approach; embracing a positive Indigenous student identity (Strong and Smart); and building high-expectations relationships (Stronger Smarter Institute 2018). See the following link for further details: http://strongersmarter.com.au/resources/high-expect ations-relationships/stronger-smarter-approach-position-paper.

In your educational role, what evidence of culturally responsive pedagogy have you found – that is, evidence of high intellectual challenge, strong connection to students' lifeworlds, recognition of cultural difference as a positive asset and active orientation? How effectively does your educational setting advocate welcoming and openness to difference, points of view, uncertainty, suspension of judgement, integrity and attention to personal thought?

While all curriculum requires culturally responsive pedagogy as a mode of delivery, increased emphasis on arts-based and embodied pedagogies offers increased opportunity to connect with the increasing numbers of disengaged and diverse learners in every educational setting.

## Creative body-based pedagogy

It is important to recognise that creative industries and arts-based pedagogies provide significant benefit in promoting young people's health, wellbeing, education, employment and citizenship. While educators aim to provide innovative and novel approaches to curriculum design, pedagogy and assessment, often traditional educator-directed pedagogies can be the fallback position, as they are driven by prescriptive curriculum and compliance requirements. These pedagogies can often exclude a significant number of learners who exhibit diverse knowledge, skills and understandings. Therefore, the challenge for educators is to provide opportunities to demonstrate how creative arts-based pedagogies afford optimal learning outcomes through facilitating artistic expression and embodied and sensory experiences. Approaches such as role play can help to enhance understandings of and empathy about what things were like in the past. Furthermore, the combined value of the social capital and creative artistic abilities that young citizens bring to their local community and broader society empowers them as transformative agents of change when provided with the tools, resources, space and opportunities to develop creative responses to societal issues (Price et al. 2016). Information and communication technology (ICT) offers innovative opportunities for learners to more fully engage in the curriculum and to communicate through creating photo stories, digital narratives and movies, podcasts and websites, while body-based pedagogies afford extended kinaesthetic and affective forms of engagement. Educators might think about the interdisciplinary and intradisciplinary concept of HASS and consider how to employ some of these approaches in HASS so that all learners are engaged and included.

Katie Dawson has pioneered **drama-based pedagogy (DBP)**, whereby learners are engaged in active and dramatic approaches to promote learning across academic (analysis, synthesis, transfer and problem-solving), affective (emotional, social and cultural curriculum) and aesthetic (art making,

**drama-based pedagogy (DBP):** learners are engaged in active and dramatic approaches to promote learning across academic (analysis, synthesis, transfer and problem-solving), affective (emotional, social and cultural curriculum) and aesthetic (art making, meaning making and creating through sensory experiences) spheres (Dawson 2018; Dawson & Lee 2018)

meaning making and creating through sensory experiences) spheres (Dawson 2018; Dawson & Lee 2018). This is achieved within a community of learners engaging in dialogic meaning making, an interactive exchange between people and their environment, with a focus on listening, reflecting, responding and building upon. In aligning with the HASS curriculum, this pedagogy draws on learners' imagination and memory to create beyond themselves; understand alternative perspectives and ideas; make sense of things and provide an embodied demonstration of cultural experiences and social interaction through the body and mind (Dawson 2018; Dawson & Lee 2018).

The DBP strategy categories include:

- *activating dialogue*: through multimodal (verbal, written and/or embodied) dialogic approaches to analyse and synthesise participants' understanding in relationship to a larger inquiry
- *game as metaphor*: strategies that use group games to develop mind/body awareness, rehearse pro-social skills and explore elements of storylike character, setting and conflict; for example, something that can be employed to help learners explore the First Fleet and world wars
- *image work*: strategies that use an object or the body to represent an idea, feeling, character, relationship, force, setting or situation
- *role work*: strategies that invite participants to think, dialogue, problem-solve and 'act' either as themselves or as someone else in response to a set of imagined circumstances. This strategy links closely with the aims of the HASS curriculum, particularly that of Civics and Citizenship and History, where learners are asked to stand in another's shoes (Dawson 2018; Dawson & Lee 2018).

**Reflection** How might you apply body-based pedagogies that recognise the diversity of learners across cultures, genders, abilities, geographic locations and so forth to engage them in the HASS learning areas (History, Geography, Civics and Citizenship, and Economics and Business)? For example, how might this pedagogy increase HASS curriculum access and engagement for learners with a physical, social/emotional, cognitive, developmental or sensory disability?

## EDUCATOR TIP

Beginning planning with a range of pedagogies, including creative arts modes, offers all learners choice about how they engage with learning from the outset, rather than needing to make adjustments after the program is implemented. This makes all learners feel valued for their abilities, skills and interests, and that diversity is embraced.

Creative and drama body-based pedagogies have been suggested to be highly applicable for implementation across curriculum learning areas, cross-curriculum priorities and general capabilities. Within the context of HASS, the following examples are provided:

- Explore events leading up to major historical moments such as World War I or the arrival of the First Fleet in Australia.
- Enact struggles over policies such as slavery or apartheid, as well as governmental representation and the right to vote.
- Debate controversies over taking care of rainforests, endangered species, habitat or drinking water.
- Learn language and practise techniques to resolve conflicts, improve self-esteem, combat racial or gender stereotypes, manage anger (Dawson 2018).

Giving young people opportunities to have a say and represent their interests is seen as key to ensuring they became productive, engaged citizens while contributing to their identity and wellbeing (Carter et al. 2018). As described earlier in this chapter, the intended curriculum is just the starting point and the educator's role is to make decisions regarding how curriculum is reflective of learners' lifeworlds and the pedagogies used to enact this curriculum. Culturally responsive and creative body-based pedagogies are just two approaches that aim to promote inclusion and belonging through providing artistic spaces for developing each learner's identity and self-concept (Hall 2010). Providing these opportunities at the beginning of programming is fundamental to achieving authentic inclusion.

## UNIVERSAL DESIGN FOR LEARNING IN HASS

HASS learning experiences need to be underpinned by a **universal design for learning (UDL)** philosophy, which ensures that all learners have the opportunity to learn, pursue their interests, build on their strengths and achieve. Learning experiences have multiple entry points that build on prior knowledge and experiences, with a diverse range of pedagogies and assessment approaches to demonstrate learning and skills.

**universal design for learning (UDL):** multiple ways of teaching and learning that provide all learners with access to resources, engagement in learning and opportunities to demonstrate what they know on an equitable basis. It is not just one way of teaching, learning and assessing.

In meeting the learning needs of all young people 'UDL is an orientation to instructional design that aims to anticipate learner diversity and presumes the school's responsibility to take learner variation into account from the start' (Baglieri & Shapiro 2017, p. 179; Rose & Meyer 2002). Baglieri and Shapiro (2017, p. 180) articulate that rather than adjusting and accommodating, teaching needs to be conceptualised as offering a 'spectrum of possibility' whereby curriculum is viewed as flexible and 'to be crafted for diverse needs from the beginning'. This can be addressed across lesson planning and contextualising content, task analysis, scaffolding, explicit and direct instruction, guided discovery learning, cooperative learning and embedding ICT in the learning experience. From the outset of designing learning opportunities, they need to connect to learners' lifeworlds, be accessible to every learner and be flexible in meeting individual learning needs. The Spotlight on HASS education provides two examples of initial learning experiences that employ a universal design inclusive of diverse learners.

PART V HASS FOR ALL LEARNERS

SPOTLIGHT ON HASS EDUCATION

## DAILY LIFE IN THE EARLY YEARS

Year 1 learners are required to develop understandings of how some aspects of daily life have changed and/or stayed the same over time. To achieve this, I asked the Year 1 class to watch the ABC video *Children's Games* (Episode 13; https://www.myplace.edu.au/teaching_activities/1888/1/childrens_games.html). This video illustrates children in 1888 playing 'blind man's bluff'.

At the conclusion, questions were asked, such as:

- What games were they playing in the clip?
- Are any of these similar to games that you play now?
- What more would you like to know about the games that were played in the past?

Using their responses, learners can develop their own inquiry focus and connect with their lifeworlds by drawing on the games played in their cultures and communities. The learning experience is open and flexible to support individual learning goals through varying content, pedagogy and assessment.

## DAILY LIFE IN THE PRIMARY YEARS

In Year 5, learners start to explore the reasons why people migrated to Australia and the experiences and contributions of a particular migrant group within a colony (ACHASSK109). At the commencement of the four-week unit of work, I wanted to determine what learners already knew. Therefore, I asked them in small groups to create a 'word splash' poster that detailed what they already knew, what they had either seen or read in the media and how they felt about migration. We then read *Refugees* by David Miller (2005), which uses ducks to illustrate the misadventures that they experienced when trying to find a new place to live. To help learners to understand the concept of cause and effect, I asked them to think of the main events in the story that impacted on the wellbeing of the ducks. We then visited the National Maritime Museum website (https://www.anmm.gov.au/discover/online-exhibitions/waves-of-migration/immigration-stories), where learners could choose a migrant to study. This enabled them to explore people from their own cultures and backgrounds or areas of interest, and to develop their own questions for further research.

## EDUCATOR TIP

Universal design respects all learners, their backgrounds, strengths and interests. From the outset of planning, learning experiences engage all learners, rather than teaching to the middle of the cohort and then making changes in an attempt to include everyone. As Tomlinson and Imbeau (2010) suggest, fair education involves equitable opportunity for all learners to grow and succeed.

Reflect on an age group of learners with whom you are currently working. How are you already employing universal design and how might you improve? What do you see as the benefits and challenges of employing UDL in your setting? How might you address these challenges?

# DIFFERENTIATION IN HASS

As educators work to apply UDL principles in planning, pedagogy and assessment, **differentiation** can support these principles as they are a response to individual learners' needs. The APST outlines explicit responsibility for differentiation of learning. HASS educators need to address Standard 1.5: Differentiate teaching to meet the specific learning needs of students across the full range of abilities (AITSL 2015), and 'demonstrate knowledge and understanding of strategies for differentiating teaching to meet the specific learning needs of students across the full range of abilities' (AITSL 2015).

**differentiation**: provides learners with opportunities to learn, accommodating different starting points, different experiences, working at different rates, and varying information processing, and providing different support in achieving learning outcomes

When differentiating, an educator's belief centres around every learner having the opportunity to learn common content. However, every learner has a different starting point, brings different experiences to connect learning, works at a different rate, has a variety of ways to process information and requires different support in achieving their learning outcomes (Tomlinson & Imbeau 2010). To ascertain a learner's starting point, assessing readiness provides current knowledge, understanding and skill in relation to the objectives or demands of a specific task (Jarvis 2015). This supports the educator in allocating flexible groupings with learners with similar skills and prior knowledge of a concept. Readiness is fluid and can change, depending on each topic or skill the learner is about to undertake. The educator also needs to take into account the interests of the learner and their learner profile. This supports differentiation across content, process and product.

To support differentiation, Westwood (2016) describes how the curriculum content doesn't need to be changed drastically as it can be covered by all learners. However, learning activities may need differentiation to accommodate learner skills, abilities and prior knowledge, with varied support for individuals.

The Australian Curriculum (ACARA 2018) expresses the importance of catering for learners living with a disability and using appropriate adjustments. However, these learners must have access to the 'same opportunities, and choices as students who do not have a disability'. Reasonable adjustments are needed, such as 'drawing from learning area content at different levels along the Foundation to Year 10 sequence to personalise age-equivalent learning area content' (ACARA 2018) according to their developmental needs. This gives learners an opportunity to be involved in high-quality curriculum and aims to expand their knowledge and understanding of a broad range of learning areas, in a program that has been personalised to cater for their particular needs (Tomlinson 2014; see Figure 22.2).

FIGURE 22.2   A student with visual impairment explores the globe

Reflect on the Spotlight on HASS education for the early years and primary years learning experiences. How might you apply differentiation inclusive of learners with a disability? How can you assess their readiness? What flexible grouping might you arrange? How might you differentiate content, process and product? What content enhancements might you integrate?

## EDUCATOR TIP

When differentiating, be mindful of inclusive and universal design principles, particularly advocating that all children are learners who can learn. As an educator, work with learners, and engage their voice and decision-making in personalising and contextualising learning experiences. Co-designing learning experiences with young people is increasingly being used to authentically promote their voice and agency in their own learning.

## CO-DESIGNING HASS LEARNING EXPERIENCES

Learners who may fall into traditional categories of disadvantage, due to disability, culture, religion, gender, Aboriginal or Torres Strait Islander background, or socio-economic status, for example, have often been taught mainstream curricula that have been adapted from mainstream normative curricula. Further to this, they traditionally have received less opportunity to contribute to curriculum and assessment design. In challenging this approach, educators need to support learners in developing skills as co-designers of their learning experiences, premised on the idea that:

> Participatory experience is not simply a method or set of methodologies, it is a mindset and an attitude about people. It is the belief that all people have something to offer to the design process and that they can be both articulate and creative when given appropriate tools with which to express themselves. (Sanders 2002)

In promoting Civics and Citizenship within the HASS curriculum, the notions of co-creation, co-design and co-production by collaborative, cooperative and community-centred approaches to creating social good lead to more effective services and greater social impact (Murray, Vanstone & Winhall 2006). Many learners with diverse needs have often been spoken for and decisions made about them, without them. The notion of co-creation challenges this 'power-over' model as it involves the systematic process of creating new solutions *with* people, not *for* them; involving citizens and communities in policy and service development (Bason 2010). In building on this, involving learners in **co-design** is 'the process of designing with people that will use or deliver a product or service' (Murray, Vanstone & Winhall 2006). These authors further explain how it needs to be person-centred,

**co-design**: the process of designing with others

start with a desired end, have practical real-world solutions, and make ideas, experiences and possibilities visible and tangible, with inclusive processes that draw on many perspectives, people, experts, disciplines and sectors (Murray, Vanstone & Winhall 2006). In connecting the HASS curriculum to contextual community issues, co-design opportunities offer learners authentic real-world contexts in which to apply their problem-solving skills, local knowledge and creativity. It also supports building their identity in contributing to society. The Spotlight on HASS education provides an example of applying co-design principles.

## ABORIGINAL HISTORIES, STORIES AND WAYS OF LIVING

As part of our school's reconciliation plan we were lucky enough to have an Elder from our local Aboriginal community speak to the children. The Elder provided a very engaging, rich recollection of histories, stories and ways of living. Learners were full of questions, some of which the Elder had time to answer and others that they were left to ponder. Upon returning to my Year 4 classroom, I was keen to know what learners had got from the presentation but also, more importantly, what they were interested in learning more about. Many wanted to know about the Dreamings that were presented and others wondered what life was like for Aboriginal peoples before the arrival of Europeans. With this in mind, I helped learners form groups with others who were also interested in similar topics. This enabled mixed-ability groups to be formed from basic interests, thus promoting a community of learners. Groups were then set the task of thinking about what this unit of work might look like for them, how they would research the information needed, what resources they might need and how their work should be assessed. This co-design approach provided learners with an opportunity to foster understandings about areas in which they were interested and develop in their own way, while providing a sense of power and ownership over their learning.

SPOTLIGHT ON HASS EDUCATION

While applying UDL, differentiation, inclusive curriculum and pedagogy are foundational to developing learners' HASS knowledge, skills and understandings, the key is to apply these inclusive principles in the early learning years.

# INCLUSIVE HASS LEARNING EXPERIENCES BEGIN IN THE EARLY YEARS

**inclusive practice**: in the EYLF, supportive learning environments that are 'vibrant and flexible spaces that are responsive to the interests and abilities of each child' (DEEWR 2009, p. 15)

The Early Years Learning Framework (EYLF; DEEWR 2009) describes **inclusive practice** in the description of supportive learning environments as 'vibrant and flexible spaces that are responsive to the interests and abilities of each child. They cater for different learning capacities and learning styles and invite children and families to contribute ideas, interests and questions' (DEEWR 2009, p. 15).

From the outset of children's educational journey and life experiences, the educator's responsibility and influence are significant, and their philosophy needs to reflect inclusive principles to guide their interactions and approach to learning. As Barnes (2012, p. 1) challenges us: 'The philosophy is the "why" behind your work with children, their families and each other. It is the combination of your beliefs, values and hopes for the educational program that you provide and its outcomes. When children are assigned to traditional categories in their early years (such as the following example of children with disabilities), educators need to challenge their own philosophy through reflective questions such as:

- What is my understanding of the term 'disability'?
- What are my attitudes towards children who have a disability?
- Why do I believe it is important to include children who have a disability in the setting?
- Who will benefit from this, and how?
- What does current research tell us about children who have a disability and their inclusion in early learning settings? (Owens 2012)

These questions can also be used to clarify and challenge families and individuals in relation to their values and beliefs regarding the inclusion of diverse learners. Building positive and inclusive philosophy as an educational community from the beginning years maximises learning, wellbeing and citizenship for every young learner.

# CONCLUSION

All learners have rich histories and curiosity about their world. Inclusive philosophy places learners at the centre of HASS planning, teaching and assessment, through using universal, differentiation and co-design principles that value young learners' voices, histories, capabilities and connections with people and place. All educational settings are enriched with a diversity of learners, and the educator's responsibility is to ensure learners are actively involved in learning designs from the outset, rather than having their diversity of needs planned for after the event and as an added-on curriculum.

## REVIEW QUESTIONS

1. List five inclusive principles.

2. What does culturally responsive pedagogy aim to reinforce for learners?

3. What are the Stronger Smarter initiatives to improve educational outcomes for Aboriginal and Torres Strait Islander students?

4. Name and describe the four drama body-based pedagogy strategies?

5. How might an educator apply UDL with supports and accommodations into the original mode of teaching to make instruction accessible for all learners?

## LEARNING EXTENSION

Your beliefs, values and attitudes are paramount to your approach to teaching. Write a short (150-word) position statement about your beliefs on inclusion, differentiation and universal design.

   OR

Having read this chapter, compose your own definitions of what differentiation and universal design are. Provide an example of each that you have witnessed, practised or heard about. Justify why you think the chosen strategies or pedagogy are examples of differentiation or UDL.

## REFERENCES

ACARA (Australian Curriculum, Assessment and Reporting Authority). (2018). *Australian Curriculum: F-10, v8.3*. Student diversity. Retrieved from https://www.australiancurriculum .edu.au/resources/student-diversity.

ACECQA (Australian Children's Education and Care Quality Authority). (2011). *Guide to the National Quality Standard*. Sydney: ACECQA.

AITSL (Australian Institute for Teaching and School Leadership). (2015). *Australian Professional Standards for Teachers*. Retrieved from: https://www.aitsl.edu.au/docs/default-source/general/ australian-professional-standards-for-teachers-20171006.pdf?sfvrsn=399ae83c_12.

Baglieri, S. & Shapiro, A. (2017). *Disability Studies and the Inclusive Classroom: Critical practices for embracing diversity in education*, 2nd edn. London: Routledge.

Barnes, H. (2012). NQS PLP e-Newsletter no. 28: Revising the service philosophy. Canberra: ECA.

Bason, C. (2010). *Leading Public Sector Innovation: Co-creating for a better society*. Chicago, IL: University of Chicago Press.

Bishop, R., Berryman, M., Cavanagh, T. & Teddy, L. (2007a). *Te Kotahitanga Phase 3 Whanaungatanga: Establishing a culturally responsive pedagogy of relations in mainstream secondary school classrooms*. Wellington: Ministry of Education.

Bishop, R., Berryman, M., Powell, A. & Teddy, L. (2007b). *Te Kotahitanga: Improving the educational achievement of Māori students in mainstream education phase 2: Towards a whole school approach*. Wellington: Ministry of Education.

Carter, J., Stehlik, T., Comber, B. & Price, D. (2018, under review). Hanging out in the city of tomorrow: Music and arts in the lifeworlds of young people. *Journal of Youth Studies*.

Castagno, A.E. & Brayboy, B.M.J. (2008). Culturally responsive schooling for indigenous youth: A review of the literature. *Review of Educational Research*, 78(4), 941–93.

Comber, B. & Kamler, B. (2004). Getting out of deficit: Pedagogies of reconnection. *Teaching Education*, 15(3), 293–310.

Cuervo, H. & Wyn, J. (2016). An unspoken crisis: The 'scarring effects' of the complex nexus between education and work on two generations of young Australians. *International Journal of Lifelong Education*, 35(2), 122–35.

Dawson, K. (2018). Drama-based instruction: Activating learning through the arts! Retrieved from: http://dbp.theatredance.utexas.edu/about.

Dawson, K. & Lee, B.K. (2018). *Drama-based Pedagogy: Activating learning across the curriculum*. Chicago, IL: University of Chicago Press.

DEEWR (Department of Education, Employment and Workplace Relations). (2009). *Belonging, Being and Becoming: The Early Years Learning Framework for Australia*. Canberra: DEEWR.

DET WA (Department of Education and Training, Western Australia). (2004). *Building Inclusive Schools: Pathways to the future*. Updated 2016. Perth: Department of Education and Training.

Forbes, F. (2007). Inclusion policy: Towards inclusion: An Australian perspective. *Support for Learning*, 22(2), 66–71.

Foreman, P. (2017). Introducing inclusion in education. In P. Foreman & M. Arthur-Kelly, eds, *Inclusion in Action*, 5th edn. Melbourne: Cengage Learning.

Hall, E. (2010). Spaces of social inclusion and belonging for people with intellectual disabilities. *Journal of Intellectual Disability Research*, 54, 48–57.

Hyde, M. (2017). Creating inclusive schools. In M. Hyde, L. Carpenter & S. Dole, eds, *Diversity, Inclusion and Engagement*, 3rd edn. Melbourne: Oxford University Press.

Jarvis, J.M. (2015). Inclusive classrooms and differentiation. In N. Weatherby-Fell, ed., *Learning to Teach in the Secondary School*. Melbourne: Cambridge University Press, pp. 154–72.

Miller, D. (2005). *Refugees*. Melbourne: Lothian.

Murray, R., Vanstone, C. & Winhall, J. (2006). *RED Report 01: Open Health*. London: Design Council. Retrieved from: http://www.designcouncil.info/mt/RED/health.

Nussbaum, M. (2003). Capabilities as fundamental entitlements: Sen and social justice. *Feminist Economics*, 9(2–3), 33–59.

Owens, A. (2012). NQS PLP e-Newsletter no. 38: Curriculum decision making for inclusive practice. Canberra: ECA. Retrieved from: https://lo.unisa.edu.au/pluginfile.php/1446164/mod_resource/content/1/NQS_PLP_E-Newsletter_No38.pdf.

Price, D. (2015). Pedagogies for inclusion of students with disabilities in a national curriculum: A human capabilities approach. *Journal of Educational Enquiry*, 14(2), 18–32.

——(2016). Wellbeing in disability education. In F. McCallum & D. Price, eds, *Nurturing Wellbeing Development in Education: From little things big things grow*. London: Routledge, pp. 40–71.

Price, D., Comber, B., Tedmanson, D., Sharpe, C., Andrew, J., Sellar, B., Carter, J., Zufferey, C., MacGill, B. & Stehlik, T. (2016). *Youthworx Alliance, Re-engaging Youth in Learning and Work through Film-making: A collaborative investigation*. Adelaide: University of South Australia: Research Themes Investment Scheme – Seed Funding (RTIS) Grant.

Price, D. & Slee, R. (2018). An Australian Curriculum that includes diverse learners: The case of students with disability. In A. Reid & D. Price, eds, *The Australian Curriculum: Promises, problems and possibilities*. Canberra: Australian Curriculum Studies Association.

Reddington, S. & Price, D. (2017). Trajectories of smooth: The multidimensionality of spatial relations and autism spectrum. *International Journal of Inclusive Education*, 1–13.

——(2018). Pedagogy of new materialism: Advancing the educational inclusion agenda for children and youth with disabilities. *Disability Studies Quarterly*, 38(1), 1021–42.

Reid, A. (2018). The journey towards the first Australian Curriculum. In A. Reid & D. Price, eds, *The Australian Curriculum: Promises, problems and possibilities*. Canberra: Australian Curriculum Studies Association, pp. 3–18.

Rose, D. & Meyer, A. (2002). *Teaching Every Student in the Digital Age: Universal design for learning*. Alexandria, VA: ASCD.

Sanders, L. (2002). MakeTools. Retrieved from: http://www.maketools.com/papers.html.

Sefton-Green, J. (2013). *Learning at Not-School*. Cambridge, MA: MIT Press.

Sen, A. (1985), *Commodities and Capabilities*. Amsterdam: North-Holland.

Stronger Smarter Institute. (2018). Stronger Smarter approach: Position paper. Retrieved from: http://strongersmarter.com.au/resources/high-expectations-relationships/stronger-smarter-approach-position-paper.

Tomlinson, C.A. (2014). Good curriculum as a basis for differentiation. In *The Differentiated Classroom: Responding to the needs of all learners*, 2nd edn. Alexandria, VA: ASCD, pp. 60–79.

Tomlinson, C. & Imbeau, M. (2010). An invitation to be part of a vision: Talking with students, parents and other educators about differentiation. In *Leading and Managing a Differentiated Classroom*. Alexandria, VA: ASCD, pp. 43–68.

Villegas, A.M. & Lucas, T. (2002a). *Educating Culturally Responsive Teachers*. Albany, NY: State University of New York Press.

——(2002b). Preparing culturally responsive teachers: Rethinking the curriculum. *Journal of Teacher Education*, 53(13), 20–32.

Vinson, T., Rawsthorne, M. with Beavis, A. & Ericson, M. (2015). *Dropping Off the Edge: Persistent communal disadvantage*. Melbourne and Canberra: Jesuit Social Services/Catholic Social Services Australia.

Westwood, P. (2016). *What Teachers Need to Know About Differentiated Instruction*. Melbourne: Australian Council for Educational Research.

# PART VI

# Community and global connections

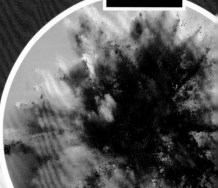

# USING COMMUNITY RESOURCES TO DEVELOP ACTIVE AND INFORMED CITIZENS

**23**

*Jann Carroll*

## Learning objectives

After reading this chapter, you should be able to:

- understand active and informed citizenship
- identify useful community resources to support the teaching of Humanities and Social Sciences (HASS)
- understand the advantages and disadvantages of using community resources in HASS
- apply authentic and experiential learning to develop active and informed citizens
- plan effective units of work using inquiry learning models and community resources.

## INTRODUCTION

What does it mean to live a good life? Philosophers through the ages such as Aristotle, Plato, Immanuel Kant and Friedrich Nietzsche have wrestled with what it means to be a good citizen and live a good life. More recently, Howard Gardner applied his thinking to the skills that future generations need to synthesise and communicate complex ideas, respect human differences and fulfil the responsibilities of work, life and citizenship. He identified 'five minds for the future', one of which is the ethical mind. To be ethically minded calls upon citizens to know their rights and responsibilities, actively contribute to the good of society and foster citizenship within and between communities. Communities encompass the family, educational setting, workplace, nation and global community (Gardner 2008). It is through contributing to others as active and informed citizens that meaning is acquired.

This chapter extends the ideas presented in Chapter 9 by explaining what it means to be an active and informed citizen and how educators can use community resources, such as museums and national institutions, to teach the Civics and Citizenship curriculum using an inquiry approach. Reynolds (2014) defines inquiry learning as a sequence of activities to guide learners through meaningful social investigation to develop deep understanding of complex issues. Inquiry learning is based on effective pedagogy and there are many approaches. Using a constructivist approach, learners and educators construct meaning through social interaction, engaging in authentic learning experiences to build understanding of the interconnections among facts and concepts. For learners of all ages, learning happens through action or doing, and is effective in developing active and informed citizens (Tomlinson & McTighe 2006).

**Reflection** Reflect on what it means to live a life for others or a meaningful life. Search online for Hugh Mackay's book or videos, *The Good Life* (2013), to build your understanding.

# DEVELOPING ACTIVE AND INFORMED CITIZENS THROUGH SCHOOLING

'I wonder why we have different political parties and why that is important to the way in which governments function?' This question was the result of a finding-out session (Murdoch 1998) at the commencement of a unit of work on democracy in an upper primary classroom. The goal for the term was to teach the fundamentals and effects of democracy while providing learners with as much lived experience as possible to enhance understanding. This links to the central concept of creating active and informed citizens, which is a goal of the *Australian Curriculum: Civics and Citizenship* (ACARA 2018b).

Educational settings play a key role in developing active and informed citizens. Educators serve as crucial role models and are charged not only with delivering learning through the curriculum, but also the values, attitudes and dispositions their learners need for becoming effective citizens. Additionally, if learners see that knowledge and skills acquired in the classroom have value and application beyond the classroom – perhaps through community service – they are more likely to enjoy learning and find it meaningful, thus becoming lifelong learners and good citizens who are aware of their roles, rights and responsibilities (Gardner 2008; Wiggins & McTighe 2005, 2011).

The need for active and informed citizens can be understood through sociological theories, which aim to explain and make sense of the social world and social behaviour. One such theory is structural functionalism, of which Émile Durkheim, Auguste Comte, Talcott Parsons and Robert Merton are key theorists (see Connell et al. 2014); it views society as a system of interrelated parts. These interrelated parts, or structures, such as the educational setting, the family, business, government and religious organisations, serve to integrate and teach citizens to act out the roles, norms and values that maintain a socially ordered society. Functionalists rely on institutions teaching and forming citizens so that they can contribute positively to the overall functioning of society and build **social capital** (Carl et al. 2012). A concrete example is found in the *Melbourne Declaration on Educational Goals for Young Australians* (Melbourne Declaration; MCEETYA 2008), which has two overarching goals: first, that Australian educational settings

**social capital:** the networks of relationships among people who live and work in a particular society, enabling that society to function effectively

promote equity and excellence; and second, that all young Australians become successful learners, confident and creative individuals, and **active and informed citizens**. The Early Years Learning Framework (EYLF) also supports the second goal by providing the foundation to ensure all children are connected with and contribute to their world (Outcome 2; DEEWR 2009).

**active and informed citizen**: one who acts with moral and ethical integrity, appreciates Australia's social, cultural, linguistic and religious diversity, and has an understanding of Australia's system of government, history and culture

The goals for young Australians are to be achieved both through the EYLF and the *Australian Curriculum: Civics and Citizenship* with the following aims:

- a lifelong sense of belonging to and engagement with civic life as an active and informed citizen in the context of Australia as a secular democratic nation with a dynamic, multicultural, multi-faith society and a Christian heritage. In early childhood settings, this can be achieved through promoting a sense of belonging and identity within the setting and with the broader community (EYLF Outcome 1).

- knowledge, understanding and appreciation of the values, principles, institutions and practices of Australia's system of democratic government and law, and the role of the citizen in Australian government and society. In early childhood settings, young children are taught the importance of rules, of respect and cooperation and how to participate positively through play to build reciprocal relationships with their peers and carers (EYLF Outcome 2).

- skills, including questioning and research; analysis, synthesis and interpretation; problem-solving and decision-making; communication and reflection, to investigate contemporary civics and citizenship issues and foster responsible participation in Australia's democracy. In early childhood settings, exploration, discovery, questioning and predicting are encouraged to learn about the environment and others (EYLF Outcome 3).

- the capacities and dispositions to participate in the civic life of their nation at the local, regional and global level and as individuals in a globalised world (ACARA 2018a). In early childhood settings, children are given opportunities to develop dispositions for learning, such as curiosity, as well as skills such as problem-solving and inquiry alongside opportunities to communicate verbally, non-verbally and through information and communication technology (ICT) that set them up for success in civic life (EYLF Outcomes 4 and 5) (DEEWR 2009).

Furthermore, the rationale of the Civics and Citizenship curriculum rests on learners developing skills of inquiry, values and dispositions that enable them to be active and informed citizens, and to question, understand and contribute to the world in which they live. It aims to reinforce learners' appreciation and understanding of what it means to be a citizen and to contribute to an evolving and healthy democracy that fosters the wellbeing of Australia as a democratic nation (ACARA 2018b). In the words of Ralph Nader, 'Citizenship is not some part-time spasmodic affair. It's the duty of a lifetime' (cited in Gardner 2008, p. 135).

## EDUCATOR TIP

Download and read the EYLF and then visit a preschool or childcare centre to identify strategies and ideas that early years educators are using to create democratic learning environments. Identify how teachers in Years 3–6 enact the Civics and Citizenship curriculum in their classroom practices. Critically reflect on what is effective in light of the information in this section on developing active and informed citizens through schooling.

# COMMUNITY RESOURCES TO SUPPORT THE TEACHING OF HASS

**community resource**: an institution that can be visited, either virtually or actually, as a site of inquiry to support authentic and experiential teaching and learning in HASS

For the purposes of this chapter, a **community resource** is defined as an institution that can be visited as a site of inquiry to support teaching and learning in HASS. Community resources include museums, galleries, public buildings and significant natural sites, such as botanic gardens, that can be visited either virtually or in person, the National Museum of Australia, Parliament House in Canberra or the British Museum in London. Community resources provide opportunities for learners to engage in authentic learning through active participation and are valuable for supporting educational endeavours. Community resources have been established to create a shared experience where people in the community can participate in a learning environment that is organised and aesthetically pleasing, through visual, auditory and informational modes.

## Types of community resources

Social and cultural community resources include museums, such as the National Museum of Australia, with its emphasis on Indigenous history and Australian life past and present, and the National Film and Sound Archive of Australia, with an emphasis on cultural artefacts that have shaped Australia. The Australian War Memorial and the Sydney Jewish Museum include perspectives on war and the effects of war. Sovereign Hill near Ballarat in Victoria provides insights on the gold rush and early settlement, and the Powerhouse Museum in Sydney lends understanding to how far Australia has come in becoming a world-class contributor to innovation. The Tasmanian Museum and Art Gallery, Hobart, aims to engage learners with exhibitions with direct links to curriculum. Public libraries such as the National Library in Canberra and state/territory libraries offer special exhibits from around the world and Trove, which is an extensive collection of archived materials, online. The National Gallery of Australia, Portrait Gallery and Museums of Modern Art such as QAGOMA in Brisbane and MoNA in Hobart provide special exhibitions of national and international work that provide perspectives on civic life through art.

Community resources such as Parliament House, the Museum of Australian Democracy, the High Court of Australia and state or territory government buildings become places to learn about the role of the legislature, judiciary and administrative aspects of government and how democracy functions in practice. The Old Melbourne Gaol and the Adelaide Gaol provide a fascinating look at the judicial processes of Australia's early history where learners can dress up and participate in role plays. Natural outdoor community resources such as botanic gardens and arboretums provide insight into the influence of humans on the planet and the ways in which symbiotic, rather than competitive, cohabitation can be facilitated. More informal and free community resources available for authentic learning experiences include a walk around the local suburb or park, or a visit to a local monument commemorating the community's contribution to the world wars. Planned visits to a range of community resources provide authentic opportunities, involving real people, to create relevant learning experiences for those who visit (Marsh & Hart 2011; Reynolds 2014).

Community resources are available to local, national and international visitors. However, recent advances in technology enable access to many of these resources without having to step inside a building. Virtual visits are a major advantage for educators in remote areas or those with limited time and budgets. Digital connection to museums affords continuous learning opportunities beyond the educational setting. An example is the unprecedented digital access to the Smithsonian Institution in Washington, DC, the United Nations Museum in Geneva, and the National Museum of Australia in Canberra. Institutions have embraced digital redesign and curation to provide additional options for pedagogical and educational purposes (Marsh & Hart 2011). Whether visiting virtually or in person, educational officers are on hand to develop and implement a range of programs that promote inquiry and hands-on experiences, and pose questions that ignite discussion and interest (Marsh & Hart 2011).

Learners and educators have infinite learning resources at their fingertips via these developments in technology. Most community resources support the use of digital technology through interactive and hands-on learning while within the walls of the institution. For example, learners can participate through accessing information via QR codes, interactive displays or photo galleries with embedded information that link to a smartphone or iPad. Learners can in turn be curators and creators of their newfound understanding, employing apps such as Piktochart or ChatterPix for the creation of their own digital artefact (see Chapter 25). Either virtually or physically, community resources enable learners to be exposed to information-rich and culturally diverse environments, and experience hands-on inquiry learning.

Community resources offer a treasure trove of on-site education programs for educational sites, educator resources and professional development to assist educational sites to achieve curriculum aims. Australian community resources have links to curriculum and the cross-curriculum priorities, and apply a **world history approach** to their collections. From a geographical point of view, the *Australian Curriculum: Geography* aims to ensure that learners develop as informed, responsible and active citizens who can contribute to the development of an environmentally and economically sustainable and socially just world (ACARA 2018b). For example, the National Museum of Australia and the National Geographic Museum in Washington, DC, both have extensive online resources to support inquiry learning in human and natural geography.

**world history approach:** equips learners to understand Australian history within the context of world events as well as that which is unique to Australia

## EDUCATOR TIP

Survey the parents/carers of learners for their areas of expertise and invite them into the educational setting. For example, a parent/carer who is an Aboriginal Elder, historian, politician, environmentalist or scientist can share artefacts, stories and examples before or after a visit to a community resource. Survey learners to find out where their interests lie and match these to relevant community resources.

# EVALUATING THE USE OF COMMUNITY RESOURCES

## Advantages of using community resources to teach HASS

Experiential and authentic learning within the community engages learners with real issues and events of the past that are relevant to their lives (Marsh & Hart 2011). Community resources to teach HASS:

- provide an immersive context for learners' inquiry questions (Marsh & Hart 2011)
- enable learners to construct their own knowledge by connecting new knowledge with previous knowledge (Reynolds 2014)
- reinforce HASS concepts through experiences that cater for all: learners are encouraged to handle artefacts; and visual and auditory experiences provide authentic demonstrations and scenarios, expert voices and perspectives, showcasing multiple intelligence theory (Gardner 1993)
- provide rich examples of Australian history from Indigenous origins, through to settlement histories and immigration, war efforts, and past and present international engagements (Tudball & Forsyth 2009)
- provide lived examples, as opposed to limiting learning to textbooks and in-class examples (Marsh & Hart 2011)
- provide durable experiences that encourage the development of citizens who are willing and able to take responsibility for their community now and into the future
- facilitate lifelong learners by providing a rich experience on which to base further education – learners are often more engaged in the classroom if they have a genuine interest from personal experience of a concept (Cullen 2005)
- enable learners to take on more responsibility for their own learning if their curiosity is piqued; for example, including a visit to a community resource as part of a structured learning plan provides an opportunity to influence knowledge development in the educational setting and at home in an authentic way

- allow learners, through investigation, to explore value-laden issues that enable consideration of a vision of the future (Reynolds 2014)
- provide opportunities for learners whose families do not have the resources (time, money, interest) to engage in different learning experiences beyond the educational setting.

## Limitations of using community resources to teach HASS

As authentic learning has influenced the need for an integrated curriculum, focus on pedagogies within curriculum areas must be carefully planned for History, Geography, and Civics and Citizenship to be taught effectively and authentically (Reynolds 2014). When determining a community resource visit, careful planning must occur. Educators must have strong content knowledge and sound **pedagogical reasoning** (Shulman 1987) to determine effective curriculum integration and the purpose of a community resource visit. Educators must also consider the timing of the visit (when in the term, for how long), plus associated costs, transport, permissions and personnel required, and disability access, to ensure success. Most educational settings require a risk assessment, which relies on the educator visiting the community resource prior to the class visit to establish suitability.

**pedagogical reasoning**: teaching strategies that transform knowledge into understanding as part of disciplined inquiry and planning

Community resources provide a range of appropriate materials to support pre- and post-visits for learners through education resource centres and public websites. This provides access for those who cannot attend due to geographical or financial constraints. For example, Parliament House in Canberra has designated online education resources that directly support school visits yet can stand alone for school groups that are unable to attend. However, navigation through the webpage requires time and patience on the first visit and educators need to ensure they are efficient in the navigation before introducing the website to learners. The Australian War Memorial provides 'Memorial Boxes', which can be delivered to educational settings filled with real and replica uniforms, artefacts and fact sheets. Again, educators must have provided the background knowledge for learners to make the most of the treasure they are handling.

Educators are required to carefully consider the Australian Curriculum or EYLF and educational scope and sequence documentation when planning their programs. Visits, either virtually or in person, need to connect to learning in the classroom to ensure relevancy. Explicit connections and learning intentions need to be established so that learners have the capacity to create understanding that can be transferred into action. Scaffolding of learning is vital to ensure learners have the requisite background knowledge prior to the visit. Educators also need to ensure learners understand the purpose of the visit and are equipped with the necessary skills to collect and synthesise information gained through the visit. Otherwise, learners are liable to find themselves distracted and disconnected from the learning that was intended. Additionally, learners require the skills of self-direction, critical thinking and discernment as they engage with the displays to ascertain the value for their learning. The skills of critical reflection and meaning making must accompany the post-visit experience as educators structure activities to enhance the community resource excursion. Explicit connections, inquiry skills such as comparison, and analysis and synthesis with the view to taking action as informed citizens make visits to community resources meaningful, both personally and pedagogically. Clearly there is much to be taught by way of basic skills, scaffolded and understood in order to ensure that a visit to a community resource is fruitful.

## PMI INQUIRY STRATEGY

Identify a community resource that links to a topic learners are undertaking. Complete a PMI (plus, minus, interesting) chart as a tool to find out about the resource and the value it will bring to learners.

**Reflection**

What do you need to focus on to prepare learners for a successful inquiry learning experience at your chosen resource? What activities will you plan to consolidate their learning?

# CONTRIBUTION OF COMMUNITY RESOURCES TO LEARNING

Community resources open the doors to a learning space with infinite possibilities and promote inquiry learning. As mentioned earlier, inquiry learning is based on constructivist theory. Godinho (2016) identifies constructivism as learning that occurs when learners actively engage to make sense of, and construct, new knowledge with the big picture in mind. Excursions to community resources and opportunities to participate in interactive workshops enable connections to the real world using a constructivist approach. For example, the Parliamentary Education Office at Parliament House in Canberra runs workshops for learners from Years 5–9, and for preservice educators, from around Australia. Programs include 'How Parliament Makes Decisions', 'Democracy' and 'The History of

Federal Parliament'. Learners participate in role plays, see Parliament in action in the Chambers and take a behind-the-scenes tour of Parliament House. All learning is linked to the Australian Curriculum and there are many educator resources to use in the classroom. The staff can also tailor a visit. See http://www.peo.gov.au for more information.

## Authentic learning

Research suggests that the most effective way to teach HASS is for learners to develop understandings, processes and reasonings with 'real-world, hands-on' approaches through authentic learning experiences (Reynolds 2014). Authentic learning experiences enable learners to develop their social and cognitive skills, both of which are necessary to become active and informed citizens.

To become active and informed citizens capable of participating in and developing Australia in a competitive, globalised environment, authentic learning opportunities are vital. Authentic learning is defined as learning through quality teaching and planning that can be applied to the world outside the educational setting (Reynolds 2014) and has value beyond the educational setting (Wiggins & McTighe 2005, 2011). Ideally, the learning will be closely related to circumstances, events and actions in the world. Authentic learning gives meaning and purpose to learner endeavours creating self-motivated and self-directed learners, and involves real and genuinely important issues (Reynolds 2014). An example is a visit to the Museum of Australian Democracy (MOAD), which is housed in Old Parliament House in Canberra. MOAD has informative, accessible, topical exhibitions on democracy and key historical events of national significance. See more at https://www.moadoph.gov.au/whats-on.

Authentic learning provides opportunities for learners to wrestle with real-world problems to actively construct their own understanding, often collaboratively, using higher-order thinking over sustained periods of time (Lowe 2016). Learners require the skills of self-discipline, collaboration, creativity, flexibility and desire for a deeper understanding of important matters of society (DEEWR 2009; Laur 2013). The benefits translate to increased motivation to develop deeper understanding of the content and afford learners the opportunity to address complex problems, and think and act like professionals (Herrington, Parker & Boase-Jelinek 2014).

Authentic learning experiences foster the development of self-regulation and critical thinking skills to develop confident and involved learners (DEEWR 2009). At a community resource, children are expected to participate and manage their behaviour. According to Power et al. (2009), out-of-school activities enhance learners' cognitive, affective and social outcomes. Additionally, out-of-school learning is particularly important for learners from low socio-economic backgrounds as they tend to have fewer resources at home to supplement their schoolwork (Power et al. 2009). Some educators are averse to or unable to facilitate excursions to community resources and advocate for the value of 'virtual field trips' or e-learning. As discussed in this chapter, online and mobile technologies enable educators to easily create cost-effective experiences, while providing similar educational benefits as a physical excursion. However, just as enjoying the thrill and atmosphere of a

**experiential learning:** the process by which learners create understanding and knowledge through experience and action using Kolb's (1984) model

sporting contest in a stadium is not comparable to watching it on television, visiting a community resource in person is preferable to vicariously experiencing it through a smartboard in the educational setting.

## Experiential learning

Kolb (1984) used the work of Dewey to conceptualise his experiential learning theory. **Experiential learning** theory rests on social constructivism (Vygotsky 1978) and active learning theory (Piaget & Cook 1952). Kolb (1984, p. 38) defines learning 'as the process whereby knowledge is created through the transformation of experience'. The four stages of experiential learning are: first, a concrete experience (or 'do'); second, observation and reflections (or 'observe and reflect'); third, forming abstract concepts (or 'think'); and fourth, active experimentation (or 'plan') (see Figure 23.1).

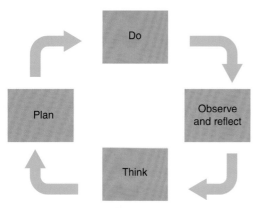

FIGURE 23.1    Experiential learning cycle

## EXPERIENTIAL LEARNING STRATEGY

Experiential learning theory can be applied to a visit to a community resource as follows. This example is based on Parliament House in Canberra and links to the Civics & Citizenship curriculum (Year 6 ACHASSI130 and ACHASSK143–48).

1. Concrete experience/'do': Learners visit Parliament House and participate in role plays to learn how Parliament makes a decision and bills are debated to become law through the Committee system.

2. Reflective observation/'observe': Learners watch and reflect upon the work of Parliamentarians in the House of Representatives and/or the Senate, view question time and engage with resources on the Parliamentary Education Office website.

3. Abstract conceptualisation/'think': Back in the classroom, learners identify issues relating to their educational site or community, inquire, research and collect evidence from primary and secondary sources to support their position. Using their experience of role plays and how elected representatives use the Committee system, learners debate the merits of their issue and seek ways to implement a change; for example, action to support a marginalised group in their community or raising awareness with their local member to make improvements to their suburb.

4. Active experimentation/'plan': Learners create an action plan to resolve the issue and to take action in their community as part of an authentic learning experience (Holman, Pavlica & Thorpe 1997; Kolb 1984).

How can you implement the experiential learning strategy in a preschool setting? Choose a topic and plan two play-based activities for 'do, observe and reflect, think and plan' on a relevant topic, then implement and critically reflect on the depth of learning.

Reflection

# INQUIRY LEARNING THROUGH COMMUNITY RESOURCES

Inquiry learning is a highly effective method for teaching HASS. Inquiry learning enables learners to be active participants in their learning through learner-directed investigations, facilitated by educators (Murdoch 1998). The focus of inquiry learning is on the acquisition of broad concepts through open-ended tasks rather than restricting focus to the curriculum descriptors or what the educator deems important (Murdoch 1998). Inquiry learning provides learners with the opportunity to explore their history, identity, place in the world and power to influence it, alongside core geographical skills such as place, space, interconnections and sustainability (ACARA 2018c). Providing learners with directed choice to investigate a breadth of key concepts, guided by their own curiosity, provides rich learning and deep understanding of matters important to all people of the world and encourages active citizenship (DEEWR 2009; Reynolds 2014).

There are many models to assist with learning the skills of inquiry. Learners who have a clear idea of the purpose of their visit to a community resource and how it links with classroom learning along with key inquiry skills will be effective inquirers. Community resource visits provide plenty of **teachable moments** sparked by curious questions and stimulus displays, which enable practical and authentic application of inquiry learning.

This section highlights two useful models for planning inquiry learning: understanding (backwards) by design; and the integrating socially inquiry model.

**teachable moment:** an unplanned teaching opportunity that arises out of either an experience in the classroom or in a community resource. It occurs when educators create and take advantage of the right inquiry conditions for learners to wonder and be curious.

## Understanding by design (UbD)

**Understanding by design (UbD)** is a planning tool for inquiry learning, rather than a prescriptive program or philosophy of education. The premise on which UbD (also known as backwards design) is based is that learning is enabled through the opportunity to work with, play with, investigate and use key ideas and make connections to generate understanding. Wiggins and McTighe (2005, p. 4) provided the UbD model to assist educators to answer the question, 'How do we make it more likely – by our design – that more learners really *understand* what they are asked to learn?'. Therefore, UbD is an approach to designing a unit that begins with the end in mind and designs backwards to the end to facilitate learner understanding. Inquiry learning is much more than designing units – it involves deep reflection, commitment to the process of learning, meaning making and the ability to make connections for new understanding.

**understanding by design (UbD):** an inquiry planning model established by Wiggins and McTighe (2005). Key terms are *big ideas* and *desired results,* which include authentic assessment tasks.

Planning with UbD requires educators to plan as follows:

*Stage 1: Big ideas* = a concept, theme or issue that gives meaning and connection to discrete facts and skills and creates the direction and goal for learning.

*Stage 2: Desired results* = experiences, assessment and assignments that demonstrate understanding of what a learner knows and can do, based on curriculum. To demonstrate understanding, a learner is able to synthesise information, transfer and use or apply what they have learnt in realistic tasks and settings. Bloom's revised taxonomy will assist in setting tasks that enable learners to engage in higher order thinking (see Krathwohl 2002).

*Stage 3: Plan learning experiences* = deciding on the sequence of teaching and learning experiences to equip learners to engage with, develop and demonstrate the desired results and understanding. A key part of planning effective learning is the inclusion of authentic learning experiences and authentic or real-world assessment.

**Reflection** What challenges might you encounter in planning using UbD?

## The integrating socially inquiry model

Developed by Julie Hamston and Kath Murdoch (1996), the integrating socially inquiry model adopts a heavily learner-led approach and describes six stages of learning: tuning in, preparing to find out, sorting out, going further, making connections and taking action. The social aspect is based on a constructivist view of learning relating to the work of Dewey (1938), Bruner (1966), Piaget and Cook (1952) and Vygotsky (1978), whose research suggested that learning with others around us can expand our capabilities as our zone of proximal development broadens to incorporate not one, but multiple perspectives. Inquiry learning in this model is interactive and understanding is constructed with others rather than relying solely on transmission from educator to learner (Preston, Harvie & Wallace 2015). In the early years, play-based learning enables discovery, creation, improvisation and imagination to develop understanding (DEEWR 2009, p. 5).

More recently, Murdoch (2015, p. 21) defined the role of the inquiry educator as follows:

1. Create flexible, equitable learning environments where learners have guided choice and independence in learning.

2. Situate inquiry learning in authentic contexts, linked to real purposes and audiences to assist learners to connect to the world beyond the educational setting.

3. Position learners as inquirers through effective open-ended questions or problems to promote deep thinking and develop questioning skills.

4. Provoke, model and celebrate curiosity through sharing interesting artefacts, images and stories. All community resources have an abundance, both materially and virtually.

## EDUCATOR TIP

Investigate the following texts by Grant Wiggins, Jay McTighe and Kath Murdoch for more depth and excellent examples and ideas. See also the community resources listed in the Learning extension at the end of this chapter.

- Wiggins, G. & McTighe, J. (2005). *Understanding by Design*, expanded 2nd edn. Alexandria, VA: ASCD.
- Wiggins, G. & McTighe, J. (2011). *The Understanding by Design Guide to Creating High-quality Units*. Alexandria, VA: ASCD.
- Murdoch, K. (2015). *The Power of Inquiry*. Melbourne: Seastar Education.
- Kath Murdoch website at http://www.kathmurdoch.com.au.

# CONCLUSION

This chapter has provided an explanation of the term 'active and informed citizen' and strategies for educators to use community resources and inquiry learning to achieve the goals of the Civics and Citizenship curriculum. Educators are role models for, and shapers of, future generations of active and informed citizens who will need to contribute positively to the effective functioning of a democratic society. The impact of globalisation, swift technological change and increased migration has created a need for learners to have the values, skills and attitudes to work for the common good and improve the quality of life for all in their communities and beyond. Including authentic, experiential learning opportunities, such as visiting a community resource, as part of a well-planned inquiry unit is effective pedagogy and lays the foundation for successful Civics and Citizenship education.

## REVIEW QUESTIONS

1. What role do educators play in creating active and informed citizens?
2. Evaluate the quote 'Citizenship is not some part-time spasmodic affair. It's the duty of a lifetime' (cited in Gardner 2008, p. 135) and justify your answer with examples.
3. Define what is meant by a community resource.
4. Identify five community resources in your area and relevant curriculum descriptors to support a visit to them.
5. What do educators need to take into consideration when planning an effective visit to a community resource?

## LEARNING EXTENSION

Select an area of the HASS curriculum and one of the community resources listed below. Explore the website and create a series of three lessons that includes a visit to your chosen resource using an inquiry learning model discussed in this chapter.

## Community resources

| Community resource | Location | Website address |
| --- | --- | --- |
| Australian War Memorial | Canberra, ACT | https://www.awm.gov.au |
| Immigration Museum | Melbourne, Vic. | https://museumsvictoria.com.au/immigrationmuseum |
| Islamic Museum of Australia | Melbourne, Vic. | https://islamicmuseum.org.au |
| Museum of Australian Democracy | Canberra, ACT | https://www.moadoph.gov.au |
| National Museum of Australia | Canberra, ACT | http://www.nma.gov.au |
| Parliamentary Education Office at Parliament House | Canberra, ACT | https://www.peo.gov.au |
| Sydney Jewish Museum | Sydney, NSW | https://sydneyjewishmuseum.com.au |
| Tasmanian Museum and Art Gallery | Hobart, Tas. | http://www.tmag.tas.gov.au/learning_and_discovery |
| UN Live Museum | Geneva, Switzerland | www.unlivemuseum.org. See Information for educators and take a virtual tour. |

## REFERENCES

ACARA (Australian Curriculum, Assessment and Reporting Authority). (2018a). *Australian Curriculum: Humanities and Social Sciences F-10, v8.3.* Civics and Citizenship. Aims. Retrieved from: https://www.australiancurriculum.edu.au/f-10-curriculum/humanities-and-social-sciences/civics-and-citizenship/aims.

——(2018b). *Australian Curriculum: Humanities and Social Sciences F-10, v8.3.* Civics and Citizenship. Rationale. Retrieved from: https://www.australiancurriculum.edu.au/f-10-curriculum/humanities-and-social-sciences/civics-and-citizenship/rationale.

——(2018c). *Australian Curriculum: Humanities and Social Sciences F-10, v8.3.* Geography. Retrieved from: https://www.australiancurriculum.edu.au/f-10-curriculum/humanities-and-social-sciences/geography.

Bruner, J. (1966). *The Culture of Education.* Cambridge, MA: Harvard University Press.

Carl, J., Baker, S., Scott, J., Hillman, W. & Lawrence, G. (2012). *Think Sociology.* Melbourne: Pearson Australia.

Connell, R., Welch, A., Vickers, M., Foley, D., Bagnall, N., Hayes, D., Proctor, H., Sriprikash, A. & Campbell, C. (2013). *Education, Change and Society*, 3rd edn. Melbourne: Oxford University Press.

Cullen, M. (2005). Enhancing multiple intelligence through museum visits. *The Journal of the Science Teachers' Association of Western Australia*, 41(3), 27–9.

DEEWR (Department of Education, Employment and Workplace Relations). (2009). *Belonging, Being and Becoming: The Early Years Learning Framework for Australia.* Canberra: DEEWR.

Dewey, J. (1938). *Logic: Theory of Inquiry*. New York: Holt and Co.

Gardner, H. (1993). *Multiple Intelligences: The theory in practice*. New York: Basic Books.

——(2008). *5 Minds for the Future*. Boston, MA: Harvard Business Press.

Godinho, S. (2016). Planning for practice: Connecting pedagogy, assessment and curriculum. In R. Churchill, S. Godinho, N. Johnson, A. Keddie, W. Letts, K. Lowe, . . . M. Vick, *Teaching: Making a difference*, 3rd edn. Brisbane: Wiley, pp. 210–49.

Hamston, J. & Murdoch, K. (1996). *Integrating Socially: Planning integrated units of work for social education*. Melbourne: Eleanor Curtain.

Herrington, J., Parker, J. & Boase-Jelinek, D. (2014). Connected authentic learning: Reflection and intentional learning. *Australian Journal of Education*, 58(1), 23–35.

Holman, D., Pavlica, K. & Thorpe, R. (1997). Rethinking Kolb's theory of experiential learning in management education. *Management Learning*, 28(2), 135–48.

Kolb, D. (1984). *Experiential Learning: Experience as the source of learning and development*. Englewood Cliffs, NJ: Prentice-Hall.

Krathwohl, D. (2002). A revision of Bloom's taxonomy: An overview. *Theory into Practice*. Routledge. 41(4), 2121–218.

Laur, D. (2013). *Authentic Learning Experiences: A real world approach to project-based learning*. New York: Routledge.

Lowe, K. (2016). Assessment, feedback and reporting. In R. Churchill, J. Mackay, M. Nagel & others, *Teaching: Making a difference*. Brisbane: Wiley, pp. 420–78.

Mackay, H. (2013). *The Good Life: What makes a life worth living?* Sydney: Pan Macmillan.

Marsh, C. & Hart, C. (2011). *Teaching the Social Sciences and Humanities in an Australian Curriculum*, 6th edn. Sydney: Pearson Australia.

MCEETYA (Ministerial Council on Education, Employment, Training and Youth Affairs). (2008). *Melbourne Declaration on Educational Goals for Young Australians*. Retrieved from: http://www.curriculum.edu.au/verve/_resources/National_Declaration_on_the_Educational_Goals_for_Young_Australians.pdf.

Murdoch, K. (1998). *Classroom Connections: Strategies for integrated learning*. Melbourne: Eleanor Curtain.

——(2015). *The Power of Inquiry*. Melbourne: Seastar Education.

Piaget, J. & Cook, M. (1952). *The Origins of Intelligence in Children*. New York: International University Press.

Power, S., Taylor, C., Rees, G. & Jones, K. (2009). Out-of-school learning: Variations in provision and participation in secondary schools. *Research Papers in Education*, 24(4), 439–60.

Preston, L., Harvie, K. & Wallace, H. (2015). Inquiry-based learning in teacher education: A primary humanities example. *Australian Journal of Teacher Education*, 40(12/6), 73–85.

Reynolds, R. (2014). *Teaching the Humanities and Social Sciences in the Primary School*. Melbourne: Oxford University Press.

Shulman, L. (1987). Knowledge and teaching: Foundations of the new reform. *Harvard Educational Review*, 15(2), 1–22.

Tomlinson, C.A. & McTighe, J.(2006). *Integrating Differentiated Instruction & Understanding by Design: Connecting content and kids*. Alexandria, VA: ASCD.

Tudball, J. & Forsyth, A. (2009). *Effective Practice in Civics and Citizenship Education: A guide for pre-service teachers*. Canberra: Australian Department of Education, Employment and Workplace Relations.

Vygotsky, L. (1978). *Mind in Society: The development of higher psychological processes*. Cambridge, MA: Harvard University Press.

Wiggins, G. & McTighe, J. (2005). *Understanding by Design*, expanded 2nd edn. Alexandria, VA: ASCD.

——(2011). *The Understanding by Design Guide to Creating High Quality Units*. Alexandria, VA: ASCD.

# UNCOVERING HIDDEN GEMS IN THE COMMUNITY

*Mandi Dimitriadis*

24

## Learning objectives

After reading this chapter, you should be able to:

- define what is meant by the term 'community' in relation to learners and educational settings
- understand the importance of community in ensuring holistic, authentic and connected learning experiences for learners
- understand a range of resources available within the local community to support Humanities and Social Sciences (HASS) teaching and learning
- explain how resources found within the local community can help educators address learning outcomes in the *Australian Curriculum: HASS* and Early Years Learning Framework (EYLF)
- understand how to work with community members and organisations to design effective HASS learning experiences for learners.

## INTRODUCTION

HASS is the study of human behaviour and interaction in social, cultural, environmental, economic and political contexts (ACARA 2018). The communities to which learners belong provide the context in which they develop their own values, attitudes, identities and knowledge, as well as affording authentic, relevant environments in which to learn.

Learning in HASS subjects is usually characterised by inquiry-based learning; collecting, organising, **analysing** and synthesising information, and research (Gilbert & Hoepper 2017). By their nature, these forms of learning involve and depend on reliable, useful and relevant data and information sources. Effective educators know how to select and help their

> **analyse**: to examine something methodically to interpret, explain or understand it

learners access age-appropriate and suitable resources to support their inquiries, investigations and research. Rather than being provided with ready-made information, inquiry and research-based learning involves learners actively seeking, locating, interpreting, analysing, synthesising, representing and communicating information, evidence and data to inform a HASS inquiry, answer a research question or examine a topic from a range of perspectives. Resourceful educators and learners can capitalise on a wealth of resources available in their local communities to enrich their learning. Most communities feature museums and other collections, significant cultural, heritage and natural sites, as well as groups and individuals with extensive knowledge, stories and experiences that represent valuable learning resources for learners of all ages. This chapter explores some of the resources that can be tapped into, often free of charge, and sometimes in the most unlikely places.

# COMMUNITY AND LEARNING

Children develop and learn within connected communities and networks rather than solely within separate contexts such as families and schools. From before we are born, we become members of communities, including families, cultural groups, neighbourhoods and wider communities. Our communities are usually determined by the geographical locations in which we live, learn and work. However, the concept of community means so much more than a collection of people. To belong to a community means to be connected to others through relationships, needs and interdependencies.

This sense of belonging is identified by Maslow (1954) as a universal human need. Belonging to a community promotes a belief that members matter to one another and to the group as a whole and leads to a shared faith that members' needs will be met (McMillan & Chavis 1986). The EYLF (DEEWR 2009) reminds us that knowing where and with whom we belong is integral to human existence.

If we view learning as a lifelong endeavour that begins at birth and involves the cognitive, physical, emotional, spiritual and social development of a person (Chapman & Aspin 1997), then we cannot easily separate a learner's life into compartments such as home, school and community. The socio-ecological model of human development (Bronfenbrenner 1979) places children at the centre of a community system. This community system embodies the social, political, cultural and economic environment that influences a child's development and wellbeing.

Effective educators nurture a sense of belonging in their learners and ensure that learning builds upon and is connected to the resources, skills, knowledge, values and goals that learners develop in their homes and communities (Hiatt-Michael 2001). The importance of community in education is widely recognised, researched and discussed. A quick Google search returned over 74 000 000 articles about community and education. The *Melbourne Declaration on Educational Goals for Young Australians* (Melbourne Declaration; MCEETYA 2008) identifies partnerships between students, parents, carers and families, the broader community, business, schools and other education and training providers as being mutually beneficial to all parties and leading to increased learner engagement and achievement.

The Glossary of Education Reform (Great Schools Partnership 2014) defines school community as the various individuals, groups, businesses and institutions that are invested in the welfare and vitality of a school and its community. Partnerships between educational sites and their communities can include:

- families and other members of learners' communities being seen as equal partners in learning through active involvement in learning activities and effective two-way communication. The active engagement of families in their children's learning has been shown to have a significant impact on learners' self-esteem, school attendance and academic learning outcomes (Epstein et al. 2002).

- learning programs that combine resources and expertise of both the educational site and the wider community. These may include school gardening programs, programs based on specialist knowledge and skills held within the community, and health and wellbeing initiatives.

- partnerships with industry, where schools and industry create and adapt knowledge for the workplace with specific content, skills and dispositions, including work skills and work experience programs (Capasso, Dagnino & Lanza 2005)

- models where educational sites view their communities as partners with shared visions, goals and moral purpose (Fullan 1999), who are consulted and involved in decision-making at various levels

- projects that combine resources to provide infrastructure and improvements that serve both educational sites and the broader community, such as libraries, sporting facilities and theatres

- educational sites operating as learning communities in themselves, where educational leaders purposefully combine individual elements of community, such as shared purpose, respect for difference, communication, collaboration, trust, efficacy, equity, democracy and cohesion to create flourishing systems where all learners thrive and succeed (Cooper & Boyd 2018; Serigiovanni 1994)

- educators empowering learners to become effective members of the communities they belong to. The crucial role that educators play in helping learners develop as active and informed citizens and the value community resources can add is discussed in detail in Chapter 23.

- educators designing and embracing opportunities for learners to be involved in authentic community-based learning and projects that encompass issues and contexts in the local community (Bailey 1998)

- opportunities to take learning outside the classroom and to take advantage of places and spaces in learners' own communities (Neil 2006). This can include the facilitation of learning in natural outdoor venues such as parks, waterways and reserves.

- accessing resources within the community to support learning outcomes and provide rich, connected learning experiences. The remainder of this chapter will explore ways in which educators can access and use community resources.

## RESOURCES IN THE LOCAL COMMUNITY

Engaging with community resources can be highly beneficial to learning. In his report on cultural education, Darren Henley (2012, p. 8) states:

> Cultural organisations and venues (such as museums, galleries, concert halls, theatres, cinemas and heritage sites) offer children and young people the opportunity to visit places of specific interest, which can deepen their understanding of the world around them and provide fresh insight into their studies.

The stories to be told in each community are as unique as the communities themselves. Every community is different and will have different resources, depending on its size, population, history, geography and cultural heritage. However, there are some common places educators can start looking to uncover the gems in their local communities.

## Museums, galleries and collections

**community museum**: a museum that exhibits a social history of a local area or an ethnic group

**artefact**: something made or shaped by humans for their use, such as a stone tool, metal sword, letter or plastic toy, usually of historical interest

**social history**: history that concentrates on the social, economic and cultural activities and lives of groups of people

Most cities, country towns and regional centres have a **community museum** of some kind (Figure 24.1). These are often staffed by volunteers and are usually very reasonably priced, or even free, to visit. A community museum will feature **artefacts**, exhibitions, displays, photographs and collections of interesting objects. They are often **social history** museums, meaning they exist to conserve and display records of how people lived in the past. Community museums can be great places to find information and history about specific people and groups in the community, but their collections can e more generalised information and insights about social patterns from a particular era. For example, a museum might have an area set up as an 1800s schoolroom that exhibits past records and artefacts from local schools, but will be useful in helping learners to understand education from that time at a broader, more general level. Museums are often organised into themes, galleries or exhibitions, depending on their available collections and the role of the museum and the community it represents. For example, the Immigration Museum in Melbourne holds collections and exhibitions that tell the stories of people who have migrated to Victoria from over 200 different countries.

FIGURE 24.1 **Museums can help learners understand how people lived in the past.**

**archives**: a collection of historical documents or records providing information about a place, institution or group of people

## Archives and records

Besides community museums, there are many places that hold records and **archives** that might support particular inquiry questions or research topics.

National and state-based authorities hold enormous amounts of information about government, law, history, births, deaths, marriages, migration, war, economic issues, photographs, newspapers, art collections and any other type of information that is considered important to be conserved and protected for the nation's people. The National Archives of Australia has offices and reading rooms in all Australian capital cities, as well as online facilities that allow access to tens of millions of items, and includes records about immigration, military service, transport, Indigenous Australians, science and the environment (National Archives of Australia 2018). Useful records and archives are also held in many local councils, community facilities, organisations and businesses. The owners or trustees of these records are often able to allow access to whole collections or specific documents on request. **Documents** held might include maps, shipping and migration records, newspapers, financial ledgers, employment records, school records, farming records, weather events, photographic collections, real estate records, legal proceedings, government activities, community events or war documents.

**document**: a piece of written, printed or electronic matter that provides information or evidence or that serves as an official record

## Libraries

Public, private, school and community libraries are probably the most obvious source of information to support research and inquiry-based learning. However, most libraries have a lot more to offer than the books displayed on their shelves. They may have special collections of older, more fragile items in storage or behind the scenes. They might also look after collections of newspapers, maps, records and photographs that can be accessed on request. Staff in libraries can also be valuable sources of information and often have specific roles, such as local history or genealogy officer.

## Community organisations

There are many organisations within a community that can provide sources of information, knowledge and expertise to support learning. Organisations such as the National Trust and state/territory history trusts are specifically entrusted with the protection, preservation and promotion of Indigenous, natural and historical heritage. For example, 'The National Trust has over 180 places for you to visit around Australia. They range from stately historic homes in the heart of the city to beautiful nature reserves. Each place has its own special story to discover' (National Trust Australia 2018).

Other local groups with extensive knowledge, records and expertise include local Aboriginal or Torres Strait Islander Elders and groups, local and family history groups, environmental groups, the Returned and Services League of Australia (RSL), sporting associations, cultural organisations and enthusiast groups. These groups may also run competitions, festivals and events in which learners can participate and that they can contribute to as community members.

## Tours and trails

Most communities have self-guided tours, walks or trails that the public can access by foot or car. These might include guided notes and maps available from an information centre,

**interpretation:** an explanation of the past, for example, about a specific person, event or development made by examining sources

signposts and information at key points, specific sites that can be accessed with a key when the tour is booked or supplementary information offered through an app or website. Tours, walks and trails may have a specific focus, such as Indigenous history, native flora and fauna, local history or historic houses. There may also be guided tours available in the local area with a guide who can lead learners, offer information and help to **interpret** what is seen.

## Significant sites

Natural and built sites in local communities can provide useful, accessible and free primary sources and experiences to support learning. Natural geographical features and sites such as waterways, parks, rock formations and reserves are ideal sites for geography fieldwork as well as providing authentic contexts for research about the history, people and culture of a local community.

Learners can learn a lot about a community's history and heritage by looking at the remains of the past. This includes old houses, shops and other buildings whose purpose may have changed over time, and artefacts such as old machinery and vehicles. History and heritage are also represented in objects such as war memorials, cemeteries, statues, signage, plaques, memorial gardens and public artworks.

## Community members

One of the richest resources in a community is the people themselves. Community members, especially those who have lived in an area for a long time, have a wealth of stories and memories that can provide valuable insights, perspectives, experiences and knowledge to help inform learners' inquiries and answer their research questions. There are many people who may be willing to talk to learners about topics such as war experiences, memories of living in the area, accounts of key events and changes in the community or migration stories. People with specific expertise or interest in a range of topics are also often keen to have a genuine audience with which to share their stories and knowledge. People living in aged-care or retirement facilities may be especially willing and able to meet with learners and share their memories, stories and experiences.

## EDUCATOR TIP

It is important to remember that learners are community members themselves and can play an active role within their own communities. This helps learners to develop as active and informed citizens as well as helping them to develop the relevant knowledge, understandings, concepts and skills described in the HASS curriculum. Find out what opportunities are available in the community for learners to volunteer to be involved in.

## THE MIGRANT EXPERIENCE

Consider the value of involving community members in an inquiry about the experiences of migrants in this example.

Kyle, a Year 6 learner who lives a transient lifestyle with his family and has already attended five different primary schools, recently developed a new sense of belonging when he met Joan, a resident in an aged-care facility located behind his current school. Kyle and a small group of classmates had developed a series of interview questions to find out about Joan's experiences as a migrant to Australia from England in the 1950s. Kyle was behind the camera filming one of his classmates conduct the interview when he heard Joan describe the suburb she lived in with her young family when she first arrived in Australia. Kyle had lived in the same suburb for two years and was fascinated to hear that, when Joan lived there, the suburb had no sealed roads, no shopping centre and no public transport. Kyle was especially interested in Joan's memories of door-knocking in the neighbourhood with a baby in a pram and two preschoolers in tow to collect signatures to support the opening of a primary school in the local area – the school that Kyle would eventually attend more than 60 years later. Kyle asked to return later to continue the conversation with Joan, who had in the meantime located photographs of the house and suburb she lived in and old school records.

How can learners be supported to evaluate community records for relevance and usefulness, and identify the point of view they represent?

Reflection

## USING COMMUNITY RESOURCES TO SUPPORT HASS LEARNING

By having clear learning intentions in mind, educators can design rich, engaging, purposeful and meaningful learning experiences that are enriched by community organisations, sites and people. Drawing from curriculum expectations, educators need to be explicit about the skills, concepts, knowledge and understandings they want learners to develop as a result of accessing or interacting with a community resource.

The *Australian Curriculum: HASS F-10* has a strong focus on personal, local, regional, state and national contexts, which makes the local community an obvious place to start when looking for resources and information for learners to engage with (ACARA 2018). To address ACHASSK044 with Year 2 learners, for example, the class might visit a community museum featuring a collection of household items from the past, to learn how daily chores were carried out without access to electricity and to investigate how changes in technology have impacted daily life. Similarly, Year 6 learners might connect with members of the community or local cultural groups to explore the experiences of migrants to Australia after Federation (ACHASSK136).

Local knowledge held within a community can be invaluable in allowing learners to engage in inquiry-based learning through exploring relevant contexts and considering a range of perspectives. For example, a Year 7 educator leading an inquiry about water might invite local Aboriginal or Torres Strait Islander Elders to explain the significance of local waterways for the culture and way of life of local language groups (ASCHASSK186). The same inquiry might see a local water quality control officer meet with learners to provide data on the quality and variability of local water resources compared with other parts of Australia and other continents (ACHASSK184).

All HASS subjects in the Australian Curriculum include a focus on inquiry and discipline-specific skills that learners should develop through their engagement with the knowledge and concepts in the curriculum.

Resources within communities can provide authentic contexts and audiences for learners to practise, develop and apply skills across all HASS subjects. Year 1 learners might, for example, prepare interview questions to ask parents/carers and grandparents about their school experiences as children. They might visit a community museum with an old schoolroom exhibition and use the primary sources in the exhibition to make comparisons about school life in the past and present.

# COMMUNITY RESOURCES IN EARLY CHILDHOOD SETTINGS

The EYLF (DEEWR 2009) is underpinned by the view that children experience life through being, belonging and becoming, and that they are connected, from before birth, to family, community, culture and place. Connections to community are fundamental to how children learn in early childhood settings. Early childhood educators create learning opportunities and environments that support learners to develop their own interests and construct their own identities and understandings of the world. As discussed earlier in this chapter, a sense of belonging is key to the concept of community.

Early childhood settings provide safe secure environments in which learners can explore, learn and develop their physical, social, emotional, cognitive and spiritual identities (EYLF Outcome 1). Through play and relevant experiences (Figure 24.2), early childhood educators provide opportunities for children to investigate ideas, complex concepts and ethical issues that are relevant to their lives and their local communities (EYLF Outcome 2). For example, learners might visit a creek in the local area to help a volunteer organisation plant native plants to attract butterflies back to the area.

FIGURE 24.2   Learners applying geographical fieldwork skills in their local community

## EDUCATOR TIP

If you feel the need to deepen your own content knowledge of a particular HASS topic, there may be someone in the local community who would be happy to share their knowledge and expertise.

# WORKING WITH COMMUNITY MEMBERS AND ORGANISATIONS

So far, we have established that communities hold a wealth of resources that can help learners develop the skills, concepts, knowledge and understandings that underpin HASS learning. Although the museums, organisations, sites and people in a local community represent a significant resource for learning, it is the way learners interact with them that makes the difference. Educators play a key role in designing learning experiences that facilitate learning outcomes. We will now explore some key factors educators need to consider when selecting and working with community resources.

## Working with community museums

As well as welcoming self-guided visits, many community museums also offer guided tours, education programs and resources specifically designed to cater for education groups.

Museums are usually staffed by paid or volunteer officers and guides who have a wealth of knowledge, experience and passion for the collections and stories housed within the museum. These people are not usually educators – although a retired educator might be enjoying a post-school career as a museum guide – but they generally are keen to help young people with their learning. When approaching a museum, it is important, as the educator, to remember the purpose of the museum visit and the learning outcomes to be achieved. The museum staff know their museum, and the educator knows the learners and curriculum, and a successful museum learning experience requires effective communication between both parties. The educator begins by finding the right person to whom to speak – for example, the museum might have an education officer or volunteer in charge of coordinating visits. The educator explains the learning focus to the museum officer and asks for their help in designing a relevant and successful museum visit. If the programs offered by the museum do not meet the specific learning needs, the educator should not be afraid to ask for or suggest an alternative experience. Most museums welcome educators to visit prior to a school visit and do not charge educators for this service. During the pre-excursion visit, the educator should speak to the staff at the museum, who can recommend relevant sections of the museum and provide more information, and should also look around the museum. Museums usually only have a small percentage of their collections on display and the officer might be able to suggest other useful artefacts, photo collections and objects that might be relevant to learning.

## EDUCATOR TIP

Before visiting a museum, library or other facility with learners, make sure you find out any specific rules or guidelines to ensure that learners are well prepared to behave responsibly and appropriately during the visit. For example, museums may have policies that limit photography, areas that are not for public access or copyright guidelines for using certain documents.

## Learners as interviewers

As active participants in their own communities, learners continually construct knowledge and make their own meaning through the experiences and interactions they have with people and places within their communities. As they develop as active and informed citizens, learners participate in their communities by contributing, questioning and understanding the world in which they live.

Chapter 23 explored ways educators and communities can work together to help learners develop as active and informed citizens. Another way that learners can interact effectively and learn from members of their communities is to develop their skills as active listeners and interviewers. Interviewing community members or inviting guest speakers can be a great way for learners to gather information and explore a range of perspectives (Figure 24.3). However, an interview can only ever be as good as the questions asked, and learners need to be well prepared and organised prior to meeting a guest speaker or

FIGURE 24.3   Interviewing family and community members is a great way to uncover different perspectives about the past.

attending an interview with a community member. Conducting interviews that elicit useful information and responses requires specific skills and considerations. Whether working with young learners who are interviewing family members or adolescents recording oral histories of war veterans, it is important that the educator helps learners to develop the skills needed to conduct   effective interviews (Yow 2005). There are some excellent resources available to help learners develop skills as interviewers and recorders of oral histories, including those that can be downloaded from the websites of the Australian War Memorial and the Department of Environment and Conservation (NSW).

Educators should consider the following points when asking learners to interview community members:

- Select interview subjects who can add relevant information or insights to the research topic.
- Choose equipment and strategies for recording the interview. Learners will need to decide, for example, whether to use a digital voice recorder, take written notes or have someone film the interview.
- Ensure the person being interviewed knows what to expect and has time to prepare. It is a good idea to provide the questions to be asked well in advance of the interview and to encourage the interviewee to bring any props such as photographs and documents that might be relevant.
- Develop relevant and effective research questions. It is usually best to ask open-ended questions that begin with words such as what, where, when, why, who and how.
- Conduct the interview so that the interviewee feels comfortable. Learners will need practice in conducting interviews that are conversations rather than a list of questions.
- Transcribe, edit and use information obtained during interviews in ways that add value to learners' research topics or inquiries.

Reflection: Consider the merit of interviewing two or more people on the same topic to help learners explore multiple perspectives and develop skills in analysing, interpreting and synthesising information.

## Heading outside the educational setting

Incorporating community resources into teaching and learning programs often means leaving the educational setting for an excursion, field trip or visit. We all remember the excitement of going on an excursion and enjoying the break from the normal routine. Of course, learners will want to enjoy an engaging and stimulating learning experience. However, it is essential that learners understand that the excursion is an important part of their learning and know the purpose of the experience. Learners need to know what to expect in terms of the activities in which they will be engaged and how the visit fits with their learning. For example, rather than an 'afternoon off to visit a museum', learners will need to understand they are visiting the museum to collect evidence about how technology has changed over time. Learners could be involved in planning the excursion and designing aspects of the activities they think will help meet their learning outcomes. Many venues provide useful materials on their websites for planning excursions. Learners need to be prepared before the museum visit or field trip. For example, they might be required to develop a series of interview questions or design a chart for recording data during Geography fieldwork. To make the most of the experience, it is important for learners to be accountable for the learning they do during the excursion and to know that the activities will be followed up in the educational setting (Fisher & Binns 2016). Rather than being one-off outings, these types of experiences need to have a clear purpose and be connected to an inquiry or research project in which learners are engaged.

## EDUCATOR TIP

When planning to take learners out of the educational context for an excursion or fieldwork, be sure to check your school or sector's policies and procedures for leaving the learning environment. This includes first aid, risk assessments, supervision ratios and parent/carer consent. Every state and sector will have its own policies and guidelines regulating school camps and excursions, which can be downloaded from the appropriate websites in your state.

Reflection: What considerations might be necessary to ensure that learner interactions with community members are sensitive, appropriate and ethical?

# CONCLUSION

This chapter has highlighted the importance of developing rich learning partnerships with learners' local communities to promote a sense of belonging and connect learning to learners' lives and experiences. It is beneficial to draw on community resources to support teaching and learning in HASS subjects. The inquiry-based nature of learning in HASS depends on access to relevant information and reliable primary and secondary sources. Local museums, archives, organisations, sites and community members can be valuable sources to support inquiry-based HASS learning. As active HASS learners, learners can engage with their communities as researchers, interviewers, analysers, interpreters, synthesisers, communicators and problem-solvers, while developing into active and informed citizens with a strong sense of identity.

## REVIEW QUESTIONS

1. What might you expect to find in a community museum?
2. Why might you want learners to access documents and records held in the community?
3. How can a static site such as a building or waterway be considered a useful teaching resource?
4. Why should you speak with museum staff when planning a visit?
5. How can you support learners to conduct successful interviews?

## LEARNING EXTENSION

Investigate resources within your own community (or the community of an educational site with which you are working) that could support a range of HASS learning activities and topics. Compile a directory of the resources you locate. Include key contact details, a description of the resources and some examples of how they might be useful. As a starting point, visit the National Trust website and find out whether it has any sites in your area: https://www.nationaltrust.org.au. Add to your directory over time as you continue to uncover hidden gems in the community.

## REFERENCES

ACARA (Australian Curriculum and Reporting Authority) (2018). *Australian Curriculum: Humanities and Social Sciences F-10, v8.3*. Retrieved from: https://www.australiancurriculum.edu.au/f-10-curriculum/humanities-and-social-sciences/hass.

Bailey, R. (1998). *Teaching Values and Citizenship Across the Curriculum: Educating children for the world*. London: Routledge Falmer.

Bronfenbrenner, U. (1979). *The Ecology of Human Development: Experiments by nature and design*. Cambridge, MA: Harvard University Press.

Capasso, A., Dagnino, G.B. & Lanza, A. (eds). (2005). *Strategic Capabilities and Knowledge Transfer Within and Between Organizations*. Cheltenham: Edward Elgar.

Chapman, J. & Aspin, D. (1997). *The School, the Community and Lifelong Learning*. London: Cassell.

Cooper, C. & Boyd, J. (2018). *Schools as Collaborative Learning Communities*. Launceston: Global Learning Communities International Office.

DEEWR (Department of Education, Employment and Workplace Relations). (2009). *Belonging, Being and Becoming: The Early Years Learning Framework for Australia*. Canberra: DEEWR.

Epstein, J.L., Sanders, M.G., Simon, B.S., Salinas, K.C., Jansorn, N.R. & Van Voorhis, F.L. (2002). *School, Family, and Community Partnerships: Your handbook for action*, 2nd edn. Thousand Oaks, CA: Corwin Press.

Fisher, C. & Binns, T. (2016). *Issues in Geography Teaching*. Abingdon: Routledge.

Fullan, M. (1999). *Change Force: The sequel*. London: Falmer Press.

Gilbert, R. & Hoepper, B. (2017). *Teaching Humanities and Social Sciences: History, geography, economics and Citizenship in the Australian Curriculum*, 6th edn. Sydney: Cengage Learning.

Great Schools Partnership. (2014). The Glossary of Education Reform. Retrieved from: https://www.edglossary.org.

Henley, D. (2012). *Cultural Education in England*. London: Department for Education.

Hiatt-Michael, D. (2001). Schools as learning communities: A vision for organic school reform. *School Community Journal*, 11(2), 93–112.

Maslow, A. (1954). *Motivation and Personality*. New York: Harper.

MCEETYA (Ministerial Council on Education, Employment, Training and Youth Affairs). (2008). *Melbourne Declaration on Educational Goals for Young Australians*. Retrieved from: http://www.curriculum.edu.au/verve/_resources/National_Declaration_on_the_Educational_ Goals_for_Young_Australians.pdf.

McMillan, D. & Chavis, D. (1986). Sense of community: A definition and theory. *Journal of Community Psychology*, 14(1), 6–23.

National Archives of Australia. (2018). Welcome to the National Archives. Retrieved from: http://www.naa.gov.au/about-us/index.aspx.

National Trust Australia. (2018). Places SA. Retrieved from: https://www.nationaltrust.org.au/ places-sa.

Neil, J. (2006). *Experiential Learning & Experiential Education: Philosophy, theory, practice and resources*. Canberra: University of Canberra.

Serigiovanni, T. (1994). *Building Community in Schools*. San Francisco, CA: Jossey-Bass.

Yow, V.R. (2005). *Recording Oral History: A guide for the humanities and social sciences*. London: Rowman and Littlefield.

25

# ENHANCING HASS LEARNING WITH TECHNOLOGY

*Mandi Dimitriadis*

## Learning objectives

After reading this chapter, you should be able to:

- explain ways that technology can be embedded in Humanities and Social Sciences (HASS) learning tasks at different levels based on the substitution, augmentation, modification and redefinition (SAMR) model
- understand how learners develop information and communication technology (ICT) capability in the context of the *Australian Curriculum: HASS*
- analyse the role technology plays in enhancing learning in a range of HASS learning activities.

## INTRODUCTION

Young people are learning in a digitally connected world where rapid advancements in technology are impacting the way people communicate and live their lives. Technology is changing the way learners access, apply and demonstrate their learning. HASS educators need to embrace this learning context and understand that the world young people are learning about, and learning in, is a globally connected and highly technological one. The impact of technology on learning and educator practice has been widely researched and recognised in education circles. Education technology refers to the tools learners have available to support learning. This includes information technology, software and other digital tools, hardware tools, social media and communication devices. It is clear that although technology has the potential to positively change the way young people learn, the role of the educator is crucial in ensuring that technology is used in ways that improve learning outcomes. The SAMR model (Puentedura 2013) is a well-researched and widely accepted framework for supporting educators to embed technologies into teaching and learning. In this chapter, we will use the SAMR model to explore ways that educators can activate the power of technology to engage learners in relevant, meaningful and rigorous HASS learning.

## EMBEDDING TECHNOLOGY IN LEARNING TASKS

The use of technology presents many opportunities to enhance learning in HASS by influencing the ways learners engage with ideas and new information, develop and apply knowledge and concepts, communicate and respond, and demonstrate their learning. However, it is not the technology alone that impacts on learning. Educators play an essential role in selecting technology to use and design learning tasks that integrate technology in meaningful ways. When educators are designing learning tasks, they need to have clear intentions about what they want learners to be able to do, know and understand as a result of engaging in the task.

## The SAMR model

The substitution, augmentation, modification and redefinition (SAMR) model, developed by Dr Ruben Puentedura (2013), describes levels at which technology can be integrated into the learning experiences educators design for their learners. The model articulates four different levels: substitution, augmentation, modification and redefinition. Understanding these levels helps guide educators to intentionally integrate technology into their teaching and learning. The model articulates the hierarchical use of technology to enhance learning outcomes, with each level of the model leading to an increasingly deeper cognitive engagement in learning and a more sophisticated use of technology as a facilitator of learning. The model provide a framework for the intentional integration of technology into task design.

The SAMR model challenges educators to use technology in ways that transform learning and provide learning opportunities that would not be as effective, or even possible, without the use of technology (Kimmons 2016).

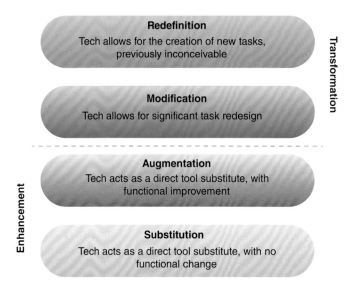

FIGURE 25.1 **The SAMR model**
Source: Dr Ruben Puentedura, http://www.hippasus.com/rrpweblog.

We will now look at each level of the SAMR model and its place in learning tasks.

### Substitution

The substitution level involves the replacement of one technology with another. There is no change to the task learners are being asked to engage in, other than the tool they are required to use. For example, an educator might ask learners to write a description of a significant historical event using Microsoft Word rather than paper and pencil. The task – writing a description – is the same, but the tool is different.

## Augmentation

The augmentation level still involves the substitution of one tool for another but allows for improved or increased functionality in the learning experience. For example, learners use Google Docs instead of Microsoft Word to write their descriptions of significant historical events. The task remains the same, but learners can take advantage of the extra functions Google Docs provides, such as auto-saving and **cloud-based** sharing.

**cloud-based**: a software platform or service hosted in a remote location that can be accessed freely and used anywhere via internet access

## Modification

At the modification level, learners are not asked to do the same task using different tools, but are presented with redesigned tasks where technology changes how they engage in their learning. For example, learners use Google Docs to write collaboratively about significant historical events or to give each other feedback on their writing using the commenting feature. At this level, technology is being used more effectively and is beginning to transform the way young people learn.

## THE SAMR MODEL

Year 6 learners from two different continents benefited from technology being used at the redefinition level of the SAMR model when their classes connected for a cross-cultural design challenge. Learners were asked to help each other learn more about their respective countries, Australia and Iran, in a collaborative project based on built and natural environments and heritage.

The learners in both classes began by generating as many ideas as they could about buildings and structures that have cultural, historical, geographical, social or economic significance in Iran and Australia. These long lists were then narrowed down to a group of five or six ideas that learners thought would help the other learners develop a balanced and illustrative view of important features and characteristics of each country. These included Australia's Parliament House and the Melbourne Cricket Ground, and the Great Tomb of Pasargad Cyrus and the Tehran Milad Tower in Iran.

Learners then used 3D modelling software to design models of the buildings and structures. They researched information and images online to make sure their models were architecturally and spatially accurate. Once the designs were completed, the design files were exchanged with the other class via email, and 3D printed. Learners connected through video conferencing to observe their own designs being 3D printed across the world. They shared information about the buildings and structures during the video conference and in an online chat room.

Each class created a virtual exhibition featuring the models using a range of online tools to communicate what they had learnt about the significance of the buildings and structures to Australia or Iran.

SPOTLIGHT ON HASS EDUCATION

## Redefinition

Ultimately, technology can be used to redefine the way young people learn. At this level, learners are engaged in learning tasks that would not be possible, or even conceivable, without technology. For example, learners might compare their descriptions of a significant event with descriptions of the same event written by learners in another part of the world. They might connect with each other using a live chat and discuss their different perspectives on the historical event. They might then use the recorded chat as part of a podcast or publish it on the class website.

The SAMR model is presented as a hierarchy, with 'redefinition' being the most sophisticated and desirable use of technology in a learning task. However, this does not mean that educators should never use technology for substitution or augmentation. These can be perfectly valid uses of technology, depending on the nature of the task, the intentions of the educator and the intended learning outcomes.

**Reflection**

Consider a learning experience you have recently planned for learners. How might you use the SAMR model to integrate or enhance the use of technology in the task?

These guiding questions might help you apply the SAMR model to your learning task.

- *Substitution:* What will I gain by replacing a low-tech tool with a high-tech tool? Or an older technology with a newer one?
- *Augmentation:* Have I added an improvement to the task that could not be achieved with the low-tech or older technology?
- *Modification:* How has my original task been modified? Does my modification fundamentally depend on the new technology?
- *Redefinition:* What is my *new* task? Will any aspect of the original task be retained? How is the new task uniquely made possible by the new technology?

## EDUCATOR TIPS

It can be overwhelming for learners to be introduced to too many new ideas at once. If you are introducing new ideas and information, use digital or non-digital tools with which learners are already familiar, and allow them to practise with information and concepts they already understand.

## TECHNOLOGY IN THE EARLY YEARS LEARNING FRAMEWORK

The Early Years Learning Framework (EYLF; DEEWR 2009) is underpinned by a deep understanding about how children learn. It promotes a holistic, play-based approach that interweaves learners' physical, social, emotional, personal, spiritual, creative, cognitive and linguistic development. Technology can play a key role in enhancing learning in the early years. Educators can use technology to help learners express their personalities and uniqueness; be curious and creative; make connections between prior experiences and new learning; actively construct their own understandings; and recognise their agency and capacity to initiate and lead learning.

The EYLF presents many ways for using technology to enhance learning outcomes. The following two learning outcomes specifically identify the role technology can play in enhancing the learning experiences that educators design for learners.

> Outcome 4: Children are confident and involved learners. Children resource their own learning through connecting with people, technologies and natural and processed materials.

> Outcome 5: Children are effective communicators. Children use information and communication technologies to access information, investigate ideas and represent their thinking. (DEEWR 2009)

Young learners need opportunities to experiment with different technologies and to explore the purpose and functions of a range of tools and media. Educators can facilitate these opportunities by providing access to a range of technologies, integrating technologies into play experiences and helping learners develop skills and techniques for using technologies to explore new information and represent their ideas. Some examples are:

- A range of telephones from different eras are added to a play area as props for learners to experiment with and pose questions about everyday uses of technology.

- An educator supports learners to use an internet search to find images and information about a particular animal in which the learners are interested. An image could be projected into the play area for learners to interact with.

- Learners are showing how they can use an iPad to take photos during a walk in the local community. They then use simple editing software to narrate a story and share their experience.

# TECHNOLOGY IN THE AUSTRALIAN CURRICULUM

HASS curricula around the world are increasingly embracing the role that technologies can play in enhancing learning as well as recognising the need for learners to develop skills and confidence using current and emerging technologies (Eady & Lockyer 2013; Hanover Research 2014).

The *Australian Curriculum: HASS* aims to develop the capacity of learners to use inquiry methods and skills, including questioning, researching using reliable sources, analysing, evaluating and communicating (ACARA 2018b). Technology provides many opportunities and applications for helping learners develop these skills.

**Information and communication technology (ICT)** capability is identified in the Australian Curriculum as one of seven general capabilities considered key to equipping young people with the knowledge, skills, dispositions and

**information and communication technology (ICT):** a broad term describing the range of available technological tools and resources used to communicate, and to create, disseminate, store and manage information

behaviours needed to successfully live and work in the 21st century (ACARA 2018a; refer also to Chapter 16).

Working with current and emerging technology, learners develop capabilities in accessing and managing information, creating and curating information, presenting, problem-solving, reasoning, decision-making, communication and creative expression. To develop this capability, learners work independently and in collaboration with others to conduct research, create **multimedia** information products, analyse data, design solutions to problems, control processes and work with a range of devices.

**multimedia**: content that is presented in a combination of different forms such as text, audio, images, animation, videos and interactive content

> Students develop knowledge, skills and dispositions around ICT and its use, and the ability to transfer these across environments and applications. They learn to use ICT with confidence, care and consideration, understanding its possibilities, limitations and impact on individuals, groups and communities. (ACARA 2018c)

HASS presents many opportunities for learners to develop ICT knowledge, skills and dispositions in authentic, engaging contexts.

## ICT capability in HASS F-6/7

The Australian Curriculum provides a holistic, integrated approach to teaching HASS in F-6 (and F-7 in contexts where Year 7 learners are in primary settings), which encompasses the specific discipline knowledge and understandings of History, Geography, Civics and Citizenship, and Economics and Business. Learners develop ICT capability within the HASS context by working independently and in groups to pose questions, research, analyse, evaluate and communicate information, concepts and ideas about people, places, events and contexts of the past, present and future. Learners develop as responsible ICT users with the ability to use **social media** and other digital tools by reflecting on online safety and ethical protocol for using ICT.

**social media**: websites and applications that enable users to create and share content or participate in social networking

HASS also allows young people to learn about the impact of technological developments over time and place (ACARA 2018c). Examples include:

- Learners have immersive experiences of other times and places by exploring multimodal resources such as the ABC's My Place website.
- Learners compare and analyse digitised objects according to specific criteria. They might compare digitised images of old toys and draw conclusions about the materials used to make toys over time or go on virtual walks in different places to observe and compare geographical phenomena.
- Learners use 3D modelling software to create 3D printed models. For example, students investigate heritage buildings in their local area and design their own models of buildings inspired by the architectural features of 19th-century buildings.
- Learners investigate Australia's preferential voting system by conducting a mock election in their class and use the Australian Electoral Commission's online voting tool to collate, calculate and scrutinise the results.

## ICT capability in the middle years

ICT capability fostered in the early childhood and primary years informs ICT development in later schooling. Learners develop ICT capability in all areas of the *Australian Curriculum: HASS 7-10*. In History, technology is an important tool in helping learners to engage in historical thinking and develop inquiry skills. Thanks to the Internet, learners can now readily access a huge range of sources to support their research, including digitised documents, archives, museum collections and images. ICT capability is developed as learners critically analyse evidence; communicate to present and represent their learning; and collaborate with others to discuss, debate and co-construct their knowledge (ACARA 2018c).

ICT capability is developed in Geography learning when learners locate, select, evaluate, communicate and share information using **digital technologies** and **spatial technologies**. Geography learning in particular has been enhanced by recent developments in spatial and Global Positioning System (GPS) technologies (Queensland Government 2018). Geography educators are now able to give learners access to sophisticated, authentic, interactive and engaging tools for collecting, representing, communicating and responding to geographical data. These tools are especially applicable to fieldwork, which the Australian Curriculum recognises as an important factor in Geography learning (ACARA 2018c).

**digital technology**: any electronic tool, system, device or resource that generates, stores or processes data

**spatial technology**: any software that interacts with real-world locations; includes the Global Positioning System (GPS), Geographic Information Systems (GIS), Global Navigation Satellite Systems (GNSS) and remote sensing

Geographical thinking also helps learners develop ICT capability by examining the impact technology has on places, economic activities and people's lives.

Civics and Citizenship learning can be enhanced with technology by providing effective tools for collecting and analysing data, facilitating decision-making and presenting evidence-based arguments for a specific course of action. Learners develop ICT capability by using internet resources and social media to collaborate with others to share information and build consensus on political, legal and social issues (ACARA 2018c).

Learners develop ICT capability in Economics and Business by accessing reliable and authentic sources of data and tools for applying economics and business knowledge, skills and concepts. Digital technologies provide both investigative and creative tools for learners to create, communicate and present Economics and Business data and information for a variety of reasons and audiences (ACARA 2018c). Some examples are:

- Learners use virtual museum exhibits and other online resources to research the life of a significant person from an ancient society and explain their contributions and legacies. They might join an online forum and discuss and compare the significance of leaders from a particular ancient society and then prepare an oral presentation supported by audiovisual materials to communicate their learning with their class.

- Learners collect, record, evaluate and represent relevant data to inform a geographical inquiry about drought. They might collect rainfall data from the Bureau of Meteorology's website and represent this using online graphing tools. They might also use the GPS to make a map of features of a landform.

- Learners work in groups to propose a mock referendum to change the Australian Constitution. They can use statistical databases to analyse data and identify patterns and trends. They then use digital tools to facilitate democratic processes to reach consensus on a course of action.

- Learners apply Economics and Business knowledge, skills and concepts in real-life situations. Learners may, for example, be required to establish a small business in collaborative groups and use budget-management software to manage their business.

Reflection    How might educators ensure that learners are developing ICT capability and achieving HASS learning outcomes at the same time? What assessment techniques might be useful?

## EDUCATOR TIP

Social media can be used in engaging ways to support learning and communication. Be sure to adhere to your educational setting or sector's rules and policies regarding the use of social media, and ensure learners know how to be safe in online environments.

# TYPES OF TECHNOLOGY AND THEIR APPLICATIONS TO HASS LEARNING

Earlier in this chapter, we established that technology has the potential to enhance the way young people learn in HASS. We also discussed how the way educators and learners use technology is more important than the technology itself. Of vital importance is the intentionality educators bring to selecting both the type of technology they provide for learners, and the processes and activities they ask learners to engage in with the technology. Different types of technologies are best suited to different types of learning activities and purposes. It is all about choosing the right tools for the right job!

By considering the range and nature of technology tools and resources available to educators, we can begin to understand the decisions educators need to make regarding both the selection of technology and the design of tasks learners will use the technology to engage in (Hew & Brush 2006). The design of a task directly impacts on the way learners engage in learning, so it is important for educators to consider the purpose and desired outcome of the task. Educators need to consider the knowledge, skills and understandings they want learners to develop, as well as the processes and learning behaviours learners will use in the task. This means being clear about what learners are being asked to do, how they are being asked to work, and which tools, materials and resources they are being asked to use.

Diana Laurillard (2012) identifies six types of learning, and specific activities that can facilitate them. Selection of specific technologies and integration strategies can be guided by being clear about whether the purpose and expected learning mode of the task is acquisition, investigation, discussion, collaboration, practice or production.

We will now look at each of these activity types, the technology that supports them and how integrating these technologies into HASS learning tasks can enhance learning outcomes and engagement.

## Acquisition

Learning through acquisition is what learners do when they are listening to a lecture, reading a book, viewing a video, watching a demonstration or downloading information from a website.

Types of technology that support learning through acquisition include multimedia resources, digital documents, podcasts, websites, e-books, blogs, webcasts, animations, virtual reality and videos. Examples include:

- Learners view historical footage from a museum archive to gain primary source information about an historical event; for example, footage of World War I trench warfare or Martin Luther King Jr's famous 'I Have a Dream' speech.

- Learners access images of different types of homes and incorporate these into their role play activities.

- Learners visit virtual walkthroughs of significant places showing geographical features.

- Learners access records online such as Census data or Bureau of Meteorology statistics.

- Learners scan **Quick Response (QR) codes** that the educator has prepared to access and read relevant web articles or view Google Earth locations.

> **Quick Response (QR) codes**: a machine-readable code consisting of an array of black and white squares, typically used for storing URLs or other information for reading by the camera on a smartphone or tablet

## Investigation

Learning by investigation is what learners do when they compare, analyse, evaluate and critique information, texts and other content related to concepts and ideas being taught. Investigation skills are a core focus of the inquiry and skills strand in the *Australian Curriculum: HASS*. These types of skills also relate to Outcome 4 of the EYLF: Children are confident and involved learners.

Types of technology that support learning through acquisition also support learning through investigation. These include multimedia resources, digital documents, podcasts, websites, e-books, blogs, webcasts, animations, virtual reality and videos. Investigation often follows acquisition, where learners think about and respond to the information they gain through acquisition. Examples include:

- Learners use online archives to locate and compare different versions of the same event. For example, learners might compare and analyse the perspectives represented in two digitised newspaper articles about Australia's involvement in the Vietnam War.

- Learners compare and critique two websites about the same topic in terms of accuracy, reliability, usefulness and impartiality.

- Learners use digital tools to collect and analyse data. For example, learners use a GPS tracking app on an iPad to trace the routes related to a World War II study to create a spatial narrative trail.

- Learners compare images of two different places their friends have been to on holidays.

## Discussion

Learning through discussion is what happens when learners are required to articulate their ideas and questions, and to challenge and respond to the ideas and questions of others, including their peers and educators. Learning by discussion is clearly defined in the inquiry and skills strand where learners evaluate, reflect on and communicate their learning. This type of learning is also key to learners developing the skills described in Outcome 5 of the EYLF: Children are effective communicators.

**forum:** an online discussion site where users can hold conversations in the form of posted messages; also known as a message board

**chat room:** an area on the Internet or other computer network where users can communicate, usually on a particular topic

Types of technology that support learning through discussion include **forums, chat rooms**, social media, wikis, web-conferencing tools and shared drives. Examples include:

- Educators set up a chat room in a safe environment such as Teach-Meet and ask learners to join an online chat about the effects of climate change.

- Web- or video-based conferences are a great way to facilitate dialogue between learners and can be used to connect learners from other classes, educational settings or parts of the world to discuss different points of view and perspectives on issues and topics.

## Collaboration

Learning by collaboration is what happens when young people are asked to learn in cooperation with others. Collaborative learning is often an extension of learning through discussion and might involve dialogue, discussion and debate as well as working together in groups to develop plans, learn together and achieve shared outcomes.

**mobile technology:** portable electronic equipment such as smartphones, tablets and small computers that can be used in different places and the technology associated with them

Types of technology that support learning through collaboration include forums, wikis, chat rooms, social media, shared drives, web-conferencing tools, **mobile technologies** and project management tools. Some examples are:

- Cloud-based platforms such as Google Drive are a valuable tool for facilitating collaborative research projects.

- Learners work in groups and use project management software such as Trello to plan and manage a project. For example, learners might be required to set up a small viable business as a team with a budget of $20.

- Learners use a social media platform such as Twitter or Facebook to pitch an idea for solving a problem the class has identified.

## Practice

Learning by practice is what learners do when they make adjustments to their actions by responding to feedback as they actively work towards the goal or outcome of the task. Feedback helps inform the learner's next action and make improvements. It can come from self-reflection, peer and educator feedback or feedback from the activity itself.

Types of technology that support learning through practice include models, simulations, games, online role-play activities, shared drives, interactive environments such as Minecraft, virtual reality and digital field trips (Figure 25.2). Examples include:

- Learners engage in a treasure hunt using QR codes which provide clues they need to solve in order to be directed to the next location.

- Learners apply their knowledge and understanding to play an online game; for example, the Gold Rush Game on the National Museum of Australia website.

- Learners play an age-appropriate online role-play game to engage in a particular historical period and apply their understanding by making decisions and interacting in a simulated 3D historical setting.

- Learners explore Australia's preferential voting system by conducting a mock election in their class and using the Australian Electoral Commission's online voting tool to collate, calculate and scrutinise the results.

FIGURE 25.2   Digital resources such as virtual tours can redefine the way learners engage with new ideas and information.

## Production

Learning through production is what learners do when they consolidate their current conceptual understanding and new learning by articulating, communicating and representing their learning and demonstrating how they have applied their learning in authentic contexts.

Types of technology that support learning through production include animation software, digital modelling tools, spatial and GPS technologies, hardware, slideshows, videos, **e-portfolios** and other digital creation tools. Examples include:

**e-portfolios**: an electronic portfolio of learner work collected over time and organised to demonstrate learning progress

- Learners use iMovie to construct a video journal of a geographical inquiry into floods in a region such as South-East Queensland. This could include images, video footage, representations of data collected and learner-created voiceovers explaining their responses and actions related to their inquiry. They could also use an application to create an e-portfolio.

- Learners use Weebly to build and manage a website for a small business they have established as part of an enterprise project. This might include a class blog to document the learning over the course of the project.

- Learners design a game or app using, for example, Scratch or Codea, that demonstrates what they have learnt and enables others to learn as well.

- Learners create an online timeline using a tool such as Dipity, Capzles or Timetoast that has video footage, images, captions and other information organised chronologically to show cause-and-effect relationships between historically significant events.

---

**SPOTLIGHT ON HASS EDUCATION**

## THE INTERNET AS AN EFFECTIVE TOOL

The rapid growth of the Internet has made all kinds of information readily accessible to learners. While this represents a wealth of resources to support learning, it is important that learners are taught how to locate, evaluate, use and interpret information safely and effectively. It is not enough to simply ask learners to research on the Internet or look up information on Google.

> Learners in this internet age don't need more information. The information already exists. What they need to know is how to efficiently and effectively use the massive amount of information available at their fingertips – to determine what's credible, what's relevant, and when its useful. (Ravindran 2016)

To use the Internet as an effective tool for HASS learning, learners need to be able to:

- learn how to search engines effectively, including the use of keywords and advanced search techniques

- know how to keep themselves safe in online environments, including the use of privacy settings and cybersafety practices. There are some very useful resources, that educators can use to help learners develop these skills, such as those developed by the eSafety Commissioner (Australian Government 2018).

- evaluate online sources of information in terms of reliability, relevance and bias
- use information ethically and responsibly by understanding plagiarism and copyright principles and how to acknowledge and reference information
- work with information and data in effective ways by using note-taking, synthesis, analysis and other digital literacy skills and techniques.

Read back over the examples included in this section and consider how technology is being used in each example in relation to the four levels of the SAMR model. How confident do you feel to use these tools in your own educational setting?

Reflection

## EDUCATOR TIPS

You don't need to have expert knowledge in all areas of HASS. Technology can help you to bring experts into your educational setting through webinars, video conferences, forums and podcasts.

## CONCLUSION

This chapter has outlined some of the ways in which educators can use technology to enhance learning in HASS. When selecting specific digital and non-digital tools to use in learning tasks, educators need to develop clear intentions on how the technology will be used by learners to achieve the intended learning outcomes of the task. Different types of technology are suited to different learning activities and educators play a key role in determining the level of sophistication in which learners engage with technology and the extent to which the technology supports deeper learning and higher-order thinking. Curriculum documents, such as the Australian Curriculum and EYLF, guide educators both in the integration of technology into HASS learning tasks and in helping learners develop ICT capability.

## REVIEW QUESTIONS

1. What is the purpose of the SAMR model?
2. What are the four levels of the SAMR model? Why are they represented as a hierarchy?
3. Why is ICT capability specifically included in the HASS curriculum?
4. What types of HASS learning activities can be enhanced with technology?
5. What types of technology are well suited to learning tasks that ask learners to collaborate with each other?

## LEARNING EXTENSION

Select a technology tool and give an example of a HASS learning task that uses this tool:

1. as a direct substitute for another tool

2. as a substitute for another tool, but with improved functionality

3. to significantly change the way learners engage with the task

4. to redefine the task, so that it could not be completed without the tool.

This learning extension is asking you to design a task at each of the levels of the SAMR model, using a particular technology tool. The tool you select for this activity might be a social media platform, a cloud-based sharing tool, a web-based app, a spatial technology or any other digital technology tool.

## REFERENCES

ACARA (Australian Curriculum and Reporting Authority). (2018a). *Australian Curriculum: F-10, v8.3*. General capabilities. Retrieved from: https://www.australiancurriculum.edu.au/f-10-curriculum/general-capabilities.

——(2018b). *Australian Curriculum: F-10, v8.3*. HASS introduction. Retrieved from: https://www.australiancurriculum.edu.au.

——(2018c). *Australian Curriculum: F-10, v8.3*. Information and communication technology (ICT) capability. Retrieved from: https://www.australiancurriculum.edu.au/f-10-curriculum/general-capabilities/information-and-communication-technology-ict-capability.

Australian Government. (2018). Office of the eSafety Commissioner, Canberra. Retrieved from: https://www.esafety.gov.au.

DEEWR (Department of Education, Employment and Workplace Relations). (2009). *Belonging, Being and Becoming: The Early Years Learning Framework for Australia*. Canberra: DEEWR.

Eady, M.J. & Lockyer L. (2013). *Tools for Learning: Technology and teaching strategies*. Wollongong: University of Wollongong, pp. 5–7.

Hanover Research. (2014). *Emerging and Future Trends in K–12 Education*. Washington, DC: Hanover Research, District Administration Practice.

Hew, K.F. & Brush, T. (2006). Integrating technology into K–12 teaching and learning: Current knowledge gaps and recommendations for future research. *Educational Technology, Research and Development*, 55(3), Education Module, p. 223.

Kimmons, R. (2016). *K-12 Technology Integration*. PressBooks. Retrieved from: https://k12techintegration.pressbooks.com.

Laurillard, D. (2012). *Teaching as a Design Science: Building pedagogical patterns for learning and technology*. New York: Routledge.

Puentedura, R.R. (2013). SAMR: Moving from enhancement to transformation. Retrieved from: http://www.hippasus.com/rrpweblog/archives/2013/05/29/SAMREnhancementToTransformation.pdf.

Queensland Government. (2018). Using spatial technologies in fieldwork. Retrieved from: https://www.qld.gov.au/education/schools/learningresources/spatial-education/pages/using-spatial-technologies-in-fieldwork.

Ravindran, R. (2016). Internet of things to internet of learning. Retrieved from: https://www.ibm.com/blogs/insights-on-business/education/internet-of-things-internet-of-learning.

# LIBRARIES AND LIBRARIANS: AT HOME WITH HASS

*Katie Silva*

## Learning objectives

After reading this chapter, you should be able to:

- investigate a cornucopia of sources and resources available from and through educational settings, public, state and national libraries
- exploit the knowledge, experience, skills and understanding offered by information literacy specialists
- formulate engaging and worthwhile Humanities and Social Sciences (HASS) learning units, lessons and experiences by collaborating with critical and creative thinking librarians.

# INTRODUCTION

The richness and importance of the HASS learning area pivots on the exploration and understanding of how we are human, our interactions with others and our journey as humans in the world. We are the authors and actors in the story of our past, present and future, captured in the published and unpublished texts that inform our learning in HASS. Writings, drawings, maps, data, images, reports, laws, journals, plays, poetry and **ephemera** are available as physical and online items because they have been collected, organised, preserved, curated and shared by **libraries** and **librarians**, and their colleagues in associated institutions in physical and digital spaces.

Many librarians are passionate about HASS in their own lives and the library profession has long been characterised as a champion of social justice, global awareness, empathy and equality. These qualities are evident across all the focus areas of HASS and offer an important partnership opportunity.

The Rationale for the HASS curriculum invites learners to 'understand their world, past and present, and develop a capacity to respond to challenges, now and in the future, in innovative, informed, personal and collective ways' (ACARA 2018b). This demands the use of culturally diverse resources (both physical and digital) and experiences. A major part of 'harnessing learners' curiosity and imagination' will be engagement with

**ephemera**: printed material such as posters, brochures, tickets and pamphlets originally meant to be discarded after use

**librarian**: the professionally qualified staff (used interchangeably with educator librarian) who identify, locate, select, acquire, organise and make available resources to meet the information, social and recreational needs of users

**library**: unless specifically stated, 'library' refers to the school library (information/resource centre) where educators and learners can access school resources, share their learning and interact with specialist staff

the thoughts, ideas, actions and lived experiences of the authors and creators of our past, present and future world through their words and images.

This chapter focuses on the possibilities and opportunities that libraries and librar-

FIGURE 26.1    Libraries, librarians and HASS: concepts that matter

ians can offer to support and enhance teaching and learning of HASS. While the content of this chapter is framed by the Early Years Learning Framework (EYLF), the ideas, experiences and strategies contained are applicable to all educational settings, regardless of curriculum, siteschool system and local context.

## LIBRARIES AS RICH SOURCES FOR HASS LEARNING AND LEARNERS

Libraries have always been places for intellectual pursuits, but most often as democratic institutions for sharing knowledge, sparking debate, inspiring critical and creative thinking and generating change and solutions. Libraries, therefore, are places that embody the central HASS big ideas of civics, citizenship, society, culture, local, national and global, communication, time, place and humanity.

It could be argued that the creation of libraries marks the transition between prehistory and history, when publishing began and as a place for valuing and sharing recorded knowledge. Our ideas and assumptions about libraries (and librarians) often depend on our own experiences. Sadly, literature and movies have often depicted libraries as institutions of regimented spaces and collections where 'nerds' seek sanctuary, overseen by strict disciplinarians in old-fashioned garb commanding patrons to be silent and solitary.

Many view libraries as less relevant now that learners and educators are assumed to have ubiquitous access to digital resources through the Internet on portable devices at school. However, this actually makes libraries more relevant as **curators** of targeted, accessible, available quality resources, and places of interest, inspiration, challenge, enjoyment, passion and complexity. At its best, a library is 'a dynamic interaction between physical and virtual sources of knowledge' (drhstringer 2014) that enriches HASS learning. Neil Gaiman (2013), author and champion of libraries, uses a democratic lens, explaining that:

**curators:** locate, select, organise and make available (often using online curation tools) quality resources that meet the needs of users

> Libraries are about Freedom. Freedom to read, freedom of ideas, freedom of communication. They are about education (which is not a process that finishes the day we leave school or university), about entertainment, about making safe spaces, and about access to information.

## School libraries

The school library is a physical space that should encompass all the elements of HASS. The library should be a welcoming space where educators and learners can meet, collaborate, research, learn and share (a social space). What it looks like, what it contains and how it is utilised will be dictated by local context. It is a place of and for HASS by being:

- a learning community resource that accommodates and respects diversity
- organised and managed to create a sustainable environment for authentic inquiry learning
- a people place for rich interactions to foster belonging, being and becoming.

Libraries are most effective in supporting teaching and learning, and academic success, when they are staffed by professionally accredited specialists who can support learning with their expertise. By providing access to a broad range of resources, learners can find and use the resources that are right for them.

## Public libraries

Building a strong relationship with the local public library extends opportunities to collaborate with local expertise and access the public library network in the relevant state/territory. Educators and educator librarians can build a collaborative relationship with librarians in public libraries and there are many instances where a joint-use library has both a school and public library function, which will be particularly useful when educators are customising units and themes to acknowledge local context. Early years settings can take advantage of the resources offered to extend their own collections to ensure that 'Children engage with a range of texts and gain meaning from these texts' (DEEWR 2009, p. 39).

Most public libraries will have a local history collection, often co-located with local councils, giving access to a number of resources to support the HASS learning areas: History, Geography, Civics and Citizenship, and Economics and Business.

## State/territory libraries

All state/territory libraries offer targeted education/school programs, with dedicated staff who develop programs, host visits and interact with educators online. These libraries have special collections that focus on the particular interests and issues relating to their context. Some collections may be digitised and available remotely, while others can be viewed on a visit.

### Legal deposit

It is a legal requirement that one copy of every item published in Australia must be deposited with the National Library of Australia and the relevant state or territory library. This applies to commercial publishers, private individuals, clubs, churches, associations, societies and organisations and, in some jurisdictions, this now applies to 'born-digital' material. Access to these materials may be possible, providing a unique window into a time, place or event. Educators could develop learning activities that ask learners, for example:

- What was the first telephone book like in your area? How did it change the way people communicated?

- Who are the authors that have published from your local community's perspective? What interests and experiences do they reflect?

- How do local newspapers show the development of communities? Are there particular issues or opportunities that have shaped the businesses and economies in your area?

- When were there elections in your state/territory? Are there posters and other election ephemera that indicate issues that were important to electors?

Each state/territory library has a website rich in resources that are worthwhile sources for educators and learners.

## National Library of Australia

The National Library of Australia (2018) describes its mission as being

> to ensure that documentary resources of national significance relating to Australia and the Australian people, as well as significant non-Australian library materials, are collected, preserved and made accessible either through the Library itself or through collaborative arrangements with other libraries and information providers.
>
> By offering a strong national focus in all that we do, and cooperating with others who share our goals, we support learning, creative and intellectual endeavour, and contribute to the continuing vitality of Australia's diverse culture and heritage.

By collecting, preserving, describing and digitising its collections, materials that align with resources required for teaching HASS can be located in the National Library. Although geographically remote for many, the vast array of materials in the library is accessible through its website, inter-library loan or its exceptional database, Trove. Available at http://trove.nla.gov.au, Trove offers access to both primary and secondary sources. Printed materials include books, newspapers, journals, articles and government gazettes; particular strengths are maps, pictures, photographs, music, sound and video, diaries and letters, objects and archived websites. Searches can be conducted for specific formats, availability, date ranges, languages and themes using the Advanced Search tool. Some examples of activities where the resources of the National Library can be used are:

- Compare a diary entry, newspaper article and government report to find different perspectives on an event for a History focus.
- Consider changes to a place through a sequence of maps, photographs and objects for a Geography focus.
- Explore an economic issue using data sets and business materials when exploring an Economics and Business topic.

Like other libraries, the National Library of Australia website offers how-to guides, digital resources and information on school and educator programs offered. All areas of HASS are supported across this broad database.

When did you last visit a library, other than at university? If it was some time ago, select a library with which you are unfamiliar and explore the services offered both online and by visiting in person. What has changed and what has remained the same? How could you use the library's services when planning learning experiences? Are library staff available in person and online? What expertise do they have that you would value?

# LIBRARIANS AT HOME WITH HASS

**referencing**: providing details of a resource according to recognised conventions to enable identification and location of the resource

Librarians are information and literature specialists who curate rich resources, offer 'big picture' thinking and collaboration, are experts in conducting and supporting inquiry learning, evaluating and **referencing** and the 'soft skills' that support HASS learners.

## Librarians know the curriculum

Librarians know the HASS curriculum and its context across all year levels and learning areas relevant to their setting. They have a deep understanding of how the different areas interconnect, and how the learning is sequenced across the years, making them excellent collaborators for planning and teaching. The team approach strengthens learning by respecting the many contexts of learning – the curriculum, state/territory, system, region and educational setting. In the Australian Curriculum, this includes the general capabilities and cross-curriculum priorities. In the Early Years Learning Framework (EYLF), librarians and educator librarians can help build 'children's understandings of concepts and the creative thinking and inquiry processes that are necessary for lifelong learning' (DEEWR 2009, p. 33).

For new educators, or those teaching HASS with little previous experience, it can be daunting to know what and how to teach. The experience and expertise of the librarian are invaluable in guiding and supporting educators to develop, teach and assess HASS learning.

It is their purpose for being in the educational setting. Acting as a sounding board, they help educators to explore ideas while avoiding the 'we've done that' syndrome. There are many excellent classics that educators love to use, but learners will be less enthusiastic about a text they have experienced before. The curriculum coordinator, learning leader, educator librarian or school principal may need to decide which year level uses Alison Lester's *Are We There Yet?* (Geography), Dr Seuss' *The Lorax* (Sustainability) or Shaun Tan's *The Arrival* (History) to prevent duplication; this can provide an ideal opportunity to ask the educator librarian for new title suggestions as inspiration.

## Librarians are curators of curiosity

Librarians are active collection builders who source print and digital resources that are engaging, appropriate and interesting to learners. They apply rigorous selection criteria to ensure high-quality resources are selected that are credible, accurate, appropriate, represent multiple perspectives, and accommodate and support diversity.

The best resources for any HASS learning experience will present information in a clear and readable format at an appropriate level, ensuring learners can easily navigate them. There will also be a range of materials that cater to the abilities of all learners and provide appropriate depth and breadth. In most cases, this can be provided by print, digital and multimodal resources.

While it might be tempting to go completely digital, it is worth noting that there are a number of studies and plenty of anecdotal evidence to indicate that we read differently on the screen from the way we read on the page. When researching using online sources, learners are most likely to scan and 'cherry pick' information that seems to match their perceived needs, limiting engagement with the complexities of a topic (Alexander 2017; Wolf 2018). Providing a variety of opportunities and contexts for research (e.g. quick fact checks, comparisons of time or place, different perspectives, primary and secondary sources, official versus personal accounts using data sets and following references) and different methods of communicating their understanding enhances both learning and achievement. Using a mixture of physical and digital resources focuses the learning on the content and context, and breaks the nexus between screens and entertainment that can inhibit learning. There is also intrinsic value in the tactile experience of physical items, considering the significance of primary sources being created, preserved and shared, particularly in the context of History.

## EDUCATOR TIP

You may find online resources such as unit and lesson plans that seem to match your needs. Some sites require you to purchase these. In most cases, the same content is available free of charge from reputable sources that acknowledge the original creator of the content. Collaborate with an educator librarian to locate appropriate source material and adapt it to your context.

Non-fiction texts designed for children often contain the visually stimulating engagement provided by online sources through their layout and design, while offering reliable information targeted at the age-appropriate level of the learners. Authors and the publishing industry in Australia have focused on producing quality materials that target the perceived needs of the Australian Curriculum and many of these resources will be available in school libraries. A number of titles and series now have digital versions and accompanying online content, which provides choice and support for the diversity required for learners. These texts can provide an excellent stimulus for engagement and inquiry.

Librarians know their collections, and are continually monitoring and reviewing new publications to select and acquire titles that support learning in their educational setting. They establish networks with local, national and international publishers and vendors and other libraries. Often these networks extend to authors and illustrators, providing opportunities for rich connections and potential visits to the school. Establishing and maintaining a strong information flow enables librarians and educators to collaborate in selecting and acquiring new resources. Educator librarians know the texts that have most often been used for particular units and encourage educators new to HASS to consider adding or replacing well-known titles to extend, update and diversify texts that refresh and reframe the learning experiences being provided. They also use their expertise to identify and locate primary sources using databases and networks.

## Librarians love literature

Everyone has experienced the power of a story that has inspired, challenged, amused, informed, comforted, extended, enraged or satisfied them. These stories usually come from the books we read as children, while some inspire the movies we watch. We are hard-wired to construct memories and understanding from the structure of a narrative. Neuroscientist and educator Judy Willis explains:

> Our brains seek and store memories based on patterns (repeated relationships between ideas). This system facilitates our interpreting the world – and all the new information we find throughout each day – based on prior experiences. (Willis 2017)

The wide range of resources used for HASS tell the story of a concept, idea, event, time, place or experience. Narratives are powerful learning tools which, when carefully selected, will engage learners in the current HASS topic, often providing a framework for a unit of work. Selection will be linked to learning intentions, perspective, content, developmental stage and purpose of the learning. Novels, picture books, graphic novels and short stories can be used with most age groups, and it should not be assumed that picture books are only suited to younger learners as adolescents can also gain valuable learning from them. The interplay between text and image enhances meaning making and is inclusive of all learners, as all elements interact to support the purpose of the book.

## PICTURE BOOKS FOR DIFFERENT LEARNING CONTEXTS

A group of preschool learners enjoy *Gary* by Leila Rudge and notice street signs with which they are familiar and different modes of transport. They make connections with their own trips between home and other familiar places, and recall stories of journeys. Other titles are shared and the librarian locates and shares signs and symbols that learners recognise and investigate within their community.

Older learners are focused on migration, using data to tease out the diversity of the Australian population. Many of them have moved from other countries or have family stories of migration, some of which are difficult to share. Exploring a range of picture books supports these learners to access different authentic experiences and perspectives, and make meaning from the impersonal data studied. Challenging themes such as displacement, conflict and rights are navigated successfully.

Sophisticated ideas and new perspectives can be negotiated and accessed by a broad range of abilities, particularly when supported by structured and focused discussions.

Educational settings in Australia reflect a wide diversity of cultures and experiences of both educators and learners. Many adults today grew up reading books that did not include their lived experience and presented more diversity in animal characters than human ones. Often due to their own backgrounds and interests, today's authors are more likely to represent more diverse communities and experiences in the characters, settings and storylines they write about. There are now specialised publishers that focus on titles representing the diversity of human experience, with major publishers also being more conscious of this aspect of their catalogue. Librarians take this into consideration when seeking and acquiring titles to diversify collections, providing opportunities to celebrate many important HASS themes such as the development of a particular area, the perspectives and experiences of different cultural groups during a historical event or the interactions between different groups that shape a style of government. This development in publishing and availability provides opportunities to reflect important ideas previously overlooked, inspiring and connecting learners in new ways.

Australia is privileged to have authors who have responded to the opportunity to write and publish high-quality literature with the curriculum in mind. There are now many wonderful works that represent Australia's history and geography. Librarians relish the opportunity to connect educators and learners to these works.

The specialist knowledge of librarians can be tapped for a range of titles matched to the needs and interests of learners. In the unique position of interacting with all learners in a variety of contexts across the curriculum and with a passion for promoting a reading culture and the joy of reading, these specialists can use their understanding and relationship with individual learners to connect texts to their specific circumstances. The power of the right book at the right time may generate enthusiasm and engagement in the learner, and support lifelong learning.

# Information literacy, ICT capability and digital citizenship

Librarians are important partners for educators and learners to develop the skills and resources needed for inquiry learning in HASS. Some of these skills are referred to as 'soft skills', which are applicable in most areas of learning and need to be taught explicitly. They all fit under the umbrella of **information literacy**, the set of lifelong learning skills required to locate, evaluate and effectively use information, and appear in the general capabilities – particularly in the ICT capability. In tandem with their teaching expertise, educator librarians can directly teach educators and learners or support educators to deliver activities that develop these skills and understandings. Developmental stages provide a framework to progress skills and understandings with the intention that learners develop the independence and critical skills required to be active, engaged citizens in a global community.

> **information literacy**: the set of lifelong learning skills required to locate, evaluate and effectively use information

## Planning searches and locating information

Younger learners will often use materials selected by educators in their learning experiences. It is appropriate for educators to explain how these materials were located and selected to avoid learners relying on materials 'magically appearing' in the educational setting. Orientation to non-fiction texts can include introduction to contents pages, indexes and glossaries, chapter headings, labels and text boxes, which are transferable concepts to other texts (including online). Learning how to search databases should commence by using controlled language on a library catalogue, progressing to a 'kid-friendly' search engine such as KidRex, Kiddle, Kids Search or KidsClick. It is highly recommended that searches are not framed as questions for academic purposes as the most likely results returned on these search engines are often less-reliable learner-created or commercial websites. More sophisticated search strategies and search engines can be taught as required.

## EDUCATOR TIP

If you have not yet registered to use Scootle (the national digital learning repository aligned to core areas of the Australian Curriculum), go to http://www.scootle.edu.au and do so. The resources on Scootle are curated by Education Services Australia and include interactive assessment, audio, photo and video resources, open-ended tools for creation, work samples, educator ideas and units of work. Learning paths can be created and shared with both the Scootle Community and learners. Invest some time in exploring the resources and features that will support and enrich your teaching.

## Selecting and evaluating sources

Regardless of the format of a possible information source, it is important to consider its appropriateness for meeting the required need. Print materials can be interrogated for language level, coverage, authority, currency and purpose. These concepts can then be extended to online resources, providing opportunities for learners to develop skills to assess suitability and appropriateness, and practise them. There are a number of website-evaluation tools available, and learning to use these is a fundamental skill for both educators and learners. Educator librarians can support educators in evaluating digital content. Wikipedia is not generally accepted as an authoritative source for academic work; it is usually written at an adult level and it is recommended, therefore, that Wikipedia not be cited as a source at school. For older learners, however, Wikipedia may be a useful introductory resource for a topic to establish an overview of unknown content, using the references provided to locate other sources.

Librarians encourage learners to verify information, regardless of the sources used, by confirming accuracy of information from other reputable sources such as government agencies, professional and community organisations and educational institutions. Of particular relevance to the HASS learning area is the necessity to identify the difference between 'fake news' and sources that offer a different but credible perspective. Identifying potential bias of sources based on the creator is becoming an important issue as educators and learners interact with people, places and events in a variety of settings. Using critical and creative thinking techniques and routines will assist learners to become informed citizens.

## Ethical use of sources

### Referencing

As identified in the Australian Curriculum, it is important that learners recognise and acknowledge intellectual property, and can indicate sources of information, using increasingly formal referencing conventions. To ensure consistency, the educator should use the referencing style that is expected at their educational setting. The School Libraries Association of South Australia (SLASA), for example, has created an easy-to-use online tool (available by annual subscription), called the Online Reference Generator, which supports the creation of accurate referencing at three levels (Junior, Middle and Senior School) for a huge range of resources, including print, digital, social media and others. Providing a URL with an image can be taught concurrently with copy/paste techniques as a starting point.

## EDUCATOR TIP

When preparing teaching and support materials, always acknowledge sources in the approved manner for your site. All learners need to understand the importance of giving credit to the original creators of a source and reference correctly for their stage of learning. Your modelling will establish the expectation that the recognition and acknowledgement of intellectual property, which appears in the ICT capability learning continuum, is always required.

## Copyright and fair use

Librarians are champions of **copyright** and fair use. They can be consulted to ensure compliance with legislation and changes that may occur, as the consequences of infringement can be legal and expensive. Educators must model fair use and ensure they frame assignments to encourage learners to create their own images and illustrations, use public domain resources or locate materials with **Creative Commons** searches. An excellent resource to bookmark is the 'Smartcopying: The official guide to copyright issues for Australian schools and TAFE' website at http://www.smartcopying.edu.au/information-sheets/schools, which offers guidance, support and resources.

## Note taking

Educator librarians teach note-taking skills, which enable learners to collect and understand concepts, ideas, data and information without **plagiarising**. Scaffolds such as mind maps (including online versions; e.g. Popplet), Venn diagrams for comparisons, lotus or fishbone diagrams or Cornell note taking for older students can be provided as organising frameworks for notes. Handwritten notes are preferred to avoid copying information verbatim, requiring learners to identify and process key ideas and assist retention of important learning. These notes can then be used effectively to create products with greater originality.

**copyright**: automatically assigned legal rights that protect the work of a creator to prevent others from profiting from their intellectual creation

**Creative Commons**: a voluntary system for creators to define and control how their work can be used and shared while respecting copyright

**plagiarising**: using or copying intellectual property of another without acknowledgement or permission as one's own work

## Digital citizenship

Librarians were early adopters of digital technologies, creating and developing databases to catalogue and integrate library collections, and they continue to be skilled and active users of such technologies. Library catalogues, databases and online resources can be used to find the best resources for an inquiry, regardless of the format of the material. Librarians are usually media specialists and operate in a variety of online spaces, including social media. This expertise is available to educators to frame appropriate behaviour and citizenship in online spaces. Collaborating and/or co-teaching digital citizenship before and as issues arise develops ethical use practices as learners interact locally, nationally, regionally and globally in HASS learning.

Preservice and early career educators can benefit from meeting with the educator librarian to take advantage of the support and expertise they can provide during placements and contracts. What important insights about your particular educational setting might an educator librarian offer you?

Reflection

# HASS WITH HEAD, HEART AND HANDS

The learning that sticks is the learning that matters, and HASS learning is a natural home for critical and creative thinking. An excellent outline of the kinds of thinking required appears on the Australian Curriculum website (ACARA 2018a). These modes of thinking are valued and prioritised by librarians, who can act as a critical professional support for educators in planning and delivering learning experiences and units. Because HASS focuses on human experiences, learners can find connections with their own lives and will be able to draw on these resources as they respond to challenges and opportunities that shape their futures.

Depending on the context, educator librarians can offer direct instruction, co-teach with educators individually or work with smaller groups for specific purposes. They are also an authentic audience for the products that learners create. If there is no librarian at the educational setting, the learning leader or teaching peers may fill this role.

Educators teaching an unfamiliar unit, perhaps for the first time, might use it as an opportunity to explore more unusual resources to pursue learners' passions, find the fascinating, challenge the curious and clarify the contested. Learning options encompassing creative products enable learners to demonstrate their learning in the library as a venue for displaying and sharing these products.

**SPOTLIGHT ON HASS EDUCATION**

## TRAVELLING ASIA

Reception (Foundation) learners are lining up to collect their boarding passes for today's learning adventure in the library. We have been visiting a different Asian country each week on our school 'airline' using Google Earth and they are excited to figure out today's destination, asking questions and reflecting on previous adventures (many of the countries we visit are reflected in learners' backgrounds, and some are based on local factors, guided by input from the educator and resources available in the school). As boarding passes are marked with today's destination, prior knowledge is activated ('I've been there!', 'X's family comes from that country') and predictions are made. Learners have already checked the local weather for their Science learning and will get a weather report before disembarking at our destination. The educator librarian and educator are co-pilots and tour guides. The flight is smooth and we have an opportunity to observe the physical features (Geography) of the country before landing. Before disembarking, we will learn some greetings in the local language (Languages) and read a picture book from, or set in, our country. On the ground, learners will greet a 'local', sometimes one of their peers, experience sights, sounds and smells (flag, images, books, music, food, artefacts and objects). Farewells are said and we board for the flight home. Learners journal their experiences by showing our destination on a map, recording highlights of the trip and deciding what clothing they would have needed. Discussion topics include 'I want to tell (parents/carers) about. . .', 'we can say hello to . . . in his/her own language', 'I was surprised that. . .', 'I want to see/do. . .'. Our learning has covered Geography, History, English, Science, Languages, literacy, ICT capability, critical and creative thinking, intercultural understanding, and Asia and Australia's engagement with Asia. It is a wonderful example of collaboration between educators and librarian, which learners remember and reminisce about.

The HASS learning area provides rich opportunities for innovative teaching and learning, which always need to be underpinned by developing and practising subject-specific knowledge and understanding and inquiry and skills. What could learners discover about their own and others' culture and community through the type of experience described in the Spotlight on HASS education?

# CONCLUSION

Libraries are a perfect home for HASS. A strong, supportive and collaborative partnership between educator librarians, educators and learners creates an intellectual and physical space, rich in inquiry, thinking, immersion and resources to fascinate, facilitate and engage educators and their learners. Libraries are places for intellectual pursuits, democratic institutions for sharing knowledge, sparking debate, inspiring critical and creative thinking, and generating change and solutions. They are a place for us to all be authors and actors of our collective and personal past, present and future, providing windows to our local, national, regional and global stories, and providing sites for sharing these stories.

## REVIEW QUESTIONS

1. Goal 2 of the *Melbourne Declaration on Educational Goals for Young Australians* includes the expectation that 'All young Australians become . . . active and informed citizens' (MCEETYA 2008), which is reflected in the Australian Curriculum and the EYLF. Libraries are institutions that serve their particular community as access points and disseminators of information. How could a visit to a public, state/territory or national library contribute to learners' understanding of Civics and Citizenship?

2. Unique resources for History can be accessed via the Trove website. What criteria would you use to establish whether an item was a primary or secondary source? Find an example of each for a topic of your choice.

3. Why is it preferable for learners to be involved in the selection process of resources from the library, rather than the educator collecting resources and taking them to the classroom? What transferrable skills can learners develop to become independent researchers?

4. Explain why referencing is essential. What are your responsibilities as an educator to model appropriate referencing techniques?

5. How can literature enrich HASS learning?

## LEARNING EXTENSION

Select a focus for a HASS unit you are likely to teach. Briefly identify the framing factors such as year level, driving idea, achievement standards and opportunities for cross-curricular engagement. Conduct a literature review to identify potential online, multimedia and print resources to support your unit.

- Analyse the selections you made.
- Identify any gaps about which you are concerned.

- Explain the benefits of using a range of resources and how they add value to your teaching and the learning.
- Devise a list of questions you would ask a librarian to enhance your suggested resources.

## REFERENCES

ACARA (Australian Curriculum, Assessment and Reporting Authority). (2018a). *Australian Curriculum: F-10, v8.3*. Critical and creative thinking. Retrieved from: https://www.australian curriculum.edu.au/f-10-curriculum/general-capabilities/critical-and-creative-thinking.

——(2018b). *Australian Curriculum: Humanities and Social Sciences F-10, v8.3*. Rationale. Retrieved from: https://www.australiancurriculum.edu.au/f-10-curriculum/humanities-and-social-sciences/hass/rationale.

Alexander, P.A. (2017). The enduring power of print for learning in a digital world. *The Conversation*, 4 October. Retrieved from: https://theconversation.com/the-enduring-power-of-print-for-learning-in-a-digital-world-84352.

DEEWR (Department of Education, Employment and Workplace Relations). (2009). *Belonging, Being and Becoming: The Early Years Learning Framework for Australia*. Canberra: DEEWR.

drhstringer. (2014). Redefining the school library for the 21st century. A Thought Piece, 28 January. Retrieved from: https://athoughtpiece.wordpress.com/2014/01/28/redefining-the-school-library-for-the-21st-century.

Gaiman, N. (2013). Neil Gaiman lecture in full: Reading and obligation. The Reading Agency, 14 October. Retrieved from: https://readingagency.org.uk/news/blog/neil-gaiman-lecture-in-full.html.

MCEETYA (Ministerial Council on Education, Employment, Training and Youth Affairs). (2008). *Melbourne Declaration on Educational Goals for Young Australians*. Retrieved from: http://www.curriculum.edu.au/verve/_resources/National_Declaration_on_the_Educational_Goals_for_Young_Australians.pdf.

National Library of Australia. (2018). Who we are. Retrieved from: http://www.nla.gov.au/about-us/who-we-are.

Rudge, L. (2016). *Gary*. Sydney: Walker Books Australia.

Willis, J. (2017). The neuroscience of narrative and memory. *Edutopia*, 12 September. Retrieved from: https://www.edutopia.org/article/neuroscience-narrative-and-memory.

Wolf, M. (2018). Our 'deep reading' brain: Its digital evolution poses questions. *Nieman Reports*. Retrieved from: http://niemanreports.org/articles/our-deep-reading-brain-its-digital-evolution-poses-questions.

# GLOBAL EDUCATION

*Andrew Peterson and Zea Perrotta*

**27**

## Learning objectives

After reading this chapter, you should be able to:

- understand what global education and global citizenship are
- know the core concepts, core knowledge and understandings, core skills and processes, and core attributes central to global education
- understand and analyse the importance of the participatory pedagogies for global education
- analyse connections between the Humanities and Social Sciences (HASS) curriculum and global education
- explore and analyse ways to connect learners' experiences of global education.

# INTRODUCTION

This chapter will introduce global education. While global education is not a subject in its own right in Australian educational settings, developing learners' understanding of **globalisation** and supporting them to become and be informed, responsible and active global citizens is an aim that sits across the Australian Curriculum. In this chapter, we engage with what global-isation means, as well as the ways in which learners in different educational settings learn about, and for, globally oriented citizenship. The chapter has three main sections. In the first, we set out what is meant

**globalisation**: usually refers to the ways in which the world is becoming increasingly interconnected through financial, economic, cultural, human and environmental processes

by the terms globalisation and global education, and introduce the concept of the globally oriented citizen. In the second, we set out the key building blocks of global education – concepts, knowledge and understandings, skills and processes and attributes. In the third, we explore pedagogical approaches to global education, as well as how global education connects to the curriculum from the early years to Year 10. We also consider how connections can be made across the various learning experiences that constitute global education.

# CHOCOLATE AND CHILD LABOUR

The following explains how a global education approach can be developed in HASS through the exploration of chocolate and child labour.

In a metropolitan co-educational primary school, the educator used the study of chocolate and child labour with a Year 7 class to promote critical thinking skills and an awareness of self as a member of a global, interconnected world. Chocolate is a topic to which learners can readily relate. It is a food that we tend to associate with enjoyment and luxury, and the topic of chocolate and child labour provides scope to explore real-world problems and look for pathways to an improved future.

Chocolate is produced from cocoa. Seventy per cent of the world's cocoa is produced in the African countries Côte d'Ivoire and Ghana. Chocolate farmers in these countries earn less than $2 per day, an income that is below the poverty line. To meet the demand for cheap labour, children are forced to harvest cocoa under dangerous conditions, including carrying heavy loads, using machetes and working with poisonous pesticides (Food Empowerment Project 2017).

The study of the chocolate industry serves to highlight the interconnections between Australian learners and the lives of unseen children in countries far away. It draws attention to global challenges such as inequalities in wealth and power, the exploitation of workers in developing countries, the ethics of buying chocolate produced under exploitative conditions, the impacts of consumer decisions on the livelihood of families in developing countries and the characteristics of global capitalism.

At the end of the unit, learners reported that the study of chocolate and child labour was challenging at times, as they were confronted with the harsh realities of child labour and the ramifications of their role in it as consumers of chocolate. However, the discussion that followed in the evaluating and reflecting phase was positive and energised, as learners were able to explore the power of their own actions as consumers and the ripple effect of their choices as global citizens living in an interconnected world.

Collectively, learners chose to run a campaign to raise awareness of the issues surrounding cocoa harvesting and the importance of supporting chocolate brands committed to the rights of children, such as Fairtrade chocolate. The campaign involved:

- production of an awareness campaign video to show at assembly and parent evening
- designing posters to be placed around the educational setting and the wider community; for example, the local library, supermarket, local community centres
- a letter-writing campaign to confectionary manufacturers in Australia run by learners for learners at lunchtime
- an ongoing 'Hot Choc Tuesday' fundraising event to sell Fairtrade hot chocolate to learners and staff.

The money raised by learners through their 'Chocolate and Child Labour' campaign was donated to World Vision. This resulted in a World Vision staff member visiting the educational setting to thank the class and speak at assembly. Table 27.1 illustrates links to each of the four strands in the HASS curriculum and the global emphases from *Global Perspectives: A framework for global education in global schools* (AAID 2008, p. 5).

**TABLE 27.1**   LINKS TO HASS CURRICULUM AND GLOBAL EMPHASES

| HASS | History | Geography | Civics and Citizenship | Economics and Business |
|---|---|---|---|---|
| Inquiry question | What have been the legacies of ancient societies and how has this influenced modern businesses such as chocolate factories? | What is the impact of chocolate factories on people and the environment? | How do the media influence social action for change? | How can ethical economies be encouraged? |
| Australian Curriculum Year 7 content description | Contacts and conflicts within and/or with other societies, resulting in developments such as the conquest of other lands, the expansion of trade, and peace treaties (ACHASSK175; ACARA 2018). | Factors that influence the decisions that people make about where to live and their perceptions of the liveability of places (ACHASSK188; ACARA 2017). | How values, including freedom, respect, inclusion, civility, responsibility, compassion, equality and a 'fair go', can promote cohesion within Australian society (ACHASSK197; ACARA 2018). | The ways consumers and producers interact and respond to each other in the market (ACHASSK199; ACARA 2017). |

Source: ACARA 2018

# UNDERSTANDING GLOBAL EDUCATION

If we are to teach young people about and for their role in an increasingly globalised world, it is essential that we think first about what the terms 'globalisation' and 'global education' mean. Both terms are contested, which means that while we may agree they exist and are important, there is disagreement about what each means and how it should be applied within educational settings. In this section we provide definitions of these key terms, and start to explore what they mean educationally.

What do globalisation and global citizenship mean to, and for, you? How do you experience globalisation and global citizenship? How might learners experience globalisation and global citizenship?

Reflection

# What is globalisation?

In general terms, globalisation refers to a range of processes, relationships and experiences that transcend the boundaries of individual nation-states and territories. Frequently, globalisation is understood to involve the following four elements, which often occur simultaneously and in relation with each other (a more detailed overview of these elements can be found in Peterson and Warwick 2014):

1. *Economic globalisation* – includes transnational/multinational corporations, trade systems, international financial and commercial systems, and global financial organisations such as the International Monetary Fund.

2. *Political globalisation* – includes supranational and intergovernmental organisations such as the United Nations and the International Court of Justice, as well as the rise of global civil society groups/non-governmental organisations that campaign and protest about particular issues around the world.

3. *Cultural globalisation* – includes the religions, cultures and ideas and the wide-ranging ways that culture is engaged with and experienced. Cultural globalisation can be viewed as an effect of international migration, as well as the result of increased flows of information through technology.

4. *Environmental globalisation* – includes changes to the environment brought about by globalisation, as well as the interconnectedness and interdependency of environmental issues such as climate change, water availability, energy, air pollution, food security and scarcity, and natural resource depletion.

## SPOTLIGHT ON HASS EDUCATION

### DEBATES ABOUT GLOBALISATION

Read the following quotation, which comes from the then Secretary-General of the United Nations, Kofi Annan (2000, p. 127):

> Throughout much of the developing world, the awakening to globalization's downside has been one of resistance and resignation, a feeling that globalization is a false God foisted on weaker states by the capitalist centres of the West. Globalization is seen, not as a term describing objective reality, but as an ideology of predatory capitalism.

Now read another quotation, this one from Joseph Stiglitz (2002, p. 5; emphasis in original), former Chief Economist at the World Bank:

> Those who vilify globalization too often overlook its benefits. But the proponents of globalization have been, if anything, even more unbalanced. To them, globalization ... *is* progress; developing countries must accept it if they are to grow and to fight poverty effectively. But to many in the developing world, globalization has not brought the promised economic benefits.

Is globalisation a positive process? What examples can you give of globalisation serving certain interests over others?

It is simply an empirical fact that most (if not all) people living today are affected in some way by globalisation. This does not mean, however, that globalisation is experienced by different people and different communities in similar ways. Indeed, and as the above quotation from Kofi Annan suggests, frequent criticisms of globalisation include that its influences and impact are felt in very inequitable ways and that it serves the interests of some at the expense of the interests of others. Consider the following:

> Globalization is getting more complex, and this change is getting more rapid. The future will be more unpredictable ... The last 40 years have been extraordinary times. Life expectancy has gone up by 25 years. It took from the Stone Age to achieve that. Income has gone up for a majority of the world's population ... and illiteracy has gone down, from half to about a quarter of people on Earth ... But there is an underbelly. There are two Achilles' heels of globalization. There is the Achilles heel of growing inequality – those that are left out, those that feel angry, those that are not participating ... The second Achilles heel is complexity – a growing fragility, a growing brittleness. What happens in one place very quickly affects everything else. This is a systematic risk, systematic shock. We've seen it in the financial crisis. We've seen it in the pandemic flu. It will become virulent and it is something we have to build resilience against. (Goldin 2009, n.p.)

As educators it is important that we take the globalisation discontents into account with learners to ensure that they are engaged not only with the positives of globalisation, but also with its resulting issues for justice – whether that be global justice, **social justice** or environmental justice. In addition, such engagement must take account of the ways in which young people are and can be citizens now *and in the future.*

**social justice**: commonly refers to the fair distribution of resources, power and opportunity within society

## WHAT IS GLOBAL EDUCATION?

In 2006, Mary Joy Pigozzi (2006, p. 1), then director of the Division for the Promotion of Quality Education at UNESCO, asserted that 'the need to attend to **global citizenship** education is essential'. This position has found support, with consistent and sustained focus on the importance of educating for global citizenship at the global level through, for example, the United Nations Secretary-General's *Global Education First Initiative* and the *2030 Agenda for Sustainable Development*. In Australia, the *Melbourne Declaration on Educational Goals for Young Australians* (Melbourne Declaration) (MCEETYA 2008, p. 9) established global education as a key focus for Australian schooling. The Melbourne Declaration aims for all young Australians to 'become successful learners, confident and creative individuals, and active and informed citizens', as well as 'responsible local and *global* citizens' (emphasis added).

**global citizenship**: connecting with the world in an informed, responsible and active way, seeking to challenge social injustices

Picture a 15-year-old learner sitting in an Australian classroom. Think about, and list, the ways in which globalisation may have affected that learner – within school, within their family life and within their community. Now think back to the time that learner was born, 15 years ago. Look again at your list and think about what either did not exist or has changed in important ways since their birth. Now think about 15 years from now. What other changes might globalisation have led to that would affect this learner?

How might educators working with learners in different settings seek to develop and implement global education? To start, educators must recognise that, as suggested in the introduction, global education is not a subject in its own right within the Australian Curriculum. Rather, global education is a dimension of learning that should permeate all aspects of education, including the curriculum, school ethos and values, and extra-curricular activities. This creates two particular challenges for global educators. The first is that global education within a particular educational setting is likely to be multifaceted and diffuse, making it hard for educators to always be precise and explicit with learners about when and how they are participating in global education. In short, global education within a setting might be everywhere and yet nowhere. The second is that global education might exist under a range of titles and, indeed, a single setting may use a number of different titles. Global education might consist of, or be called, any of the following: 'global learning', 'global citizenship education', 'global perspectives', 'global dimensions', 'international mindedness', 'development education', **human rights** education', 'peace education' and 'cosmopolitan education'.

**human rights:** the rights that all humans possess by virtue of their humanity

---

**Reflection**  Thinking about an educational site you know, which elements of its practice combine for global education? Are these various elements disparate or connected? What terms are used to frame global education within the site?

---

Accepting that no single definition is likely to cover all aspects and issues associated with globalisation and global education, the following description offered by the Global Education Project in Australia (AAID 2008, p. 2) offers a neat yet detailed appraisal of what global education encompasses:

> Twenty-first century Australians are members of a global community, connected to the whole world by ties of culture, economics and politics, enhanced communication and travel and a shared environment. Enabling young people to participate in shaping a better shared future for the world is at the heart of global education. It emphasises the unity and interdependence of human society, developing a sense of self and appreciation of **cultural diversity**, affirmation of social justice and human rights, building peace and actions for a sustainable future in different times and places. It places particular emphasis on developing relationships with our neighbours in the Asia-Pacific and Indian Ocean regions. Global education promotes open-mindedness leading to new thinking about the world and a predisposition to take action for change. Learners learn to take responsibility for their actions, respect and value diversity and see themselves as global citizens who can contribute to a more peaceful, just and sustainable world. With its emphasis not only on developing knowledge and skills but also on promoting positive values and participation, global education is relevant across all learning areas.

**cultural diversity:** the existence of a range of cultural and ethnic groups within a given society

As this definition makes clear, global education includes learning about the globalised world as well as learning for participation within it. As we explore in later sections, this focus on participation asks educators to think carefully about what education for global citizenship entails, and how they can support learners to develop appropriate knowledge, skills and dispositions to be effective change-makers on a global level.

To answer this question, we also have to think about whether it makes sense to talk about being a 'global citizen' at all, given that citizenship ordinarily refers to a relationship within a particular nation-state. In essence, the question goes back to the time in the 4th century BCE when the Cynic, Diogenes of Sinope, was asked from where he came and responded, 'I am a citizen of the world'. We would suggest that it makes sense to consider the global citizen as someone who is 'globally oriented' in their citizenship. We take the concept of 'globally oriented citizen' from the work of Bikkhu Parekh (2003) and, with adaptations, understand it to involve four elements:

1. Examining and responding to the effects of policies developed and enacted by one's national community to ensure they do not harm others.

2. Examining and responding to the policies and actions of other nations (and we would add to this transnational corporations and organisations).

3. An enacted commitment to work towards just communities across the world to develop peace and harmony.

4. Recognising that citizenship – including globally oriented citizenship – operates at an interpersonal, everyday level and requires us to practise kindness to each other, and to work with others in our various communities in hospitable ways (Peterson 2016; Peterson in press).

# THE BUILDING BLOCKS OF GLOBAL EDUCATION

We have already suggested that global education is best understood as an intention of the curriculum that sits within and across learning experiences within educational settings, including through institutional ethos and values, through the curriculum (learning areas, cross-curriculum priorities and general capabilities), and through extra-curricular activities (including community-based social action). In coming to grips with global education, it is essential to understand the core building blocks that comprise global education: core concepts, core knowledge and understandings, core skills and processes and core attributes.

## Global education: core concepts

In *Global Perspectives: A framework for global education in global schools* (AAID 2008, p. 5), the Australian Global Education project sets out five learning emphases – or concepts – that underpin global education:

1. *Interdependence and globalisation*: learning about the varied connections between people and the influence which we have on each others' lives.

2. *Identity and cultural diversity*: learning about our own identities and cultures, as well as being open to listen to and understand the identities and cultures of others.

3. *Social justice and human rights*: learning about global inequalities and the way that interests may be discriminated against, including respecting and standing up for the rights of others.

4. *Peace building and conflict resolution*: learning about ways that positive and sustainable relationships can be built and developed, including how conflict might be avoided or resolved.

5. *Sustainable futures*: learning about how we can work together to find and enact sustainable provision for our current and future needs.

As the Framework also highlights, each of these emphases has both a spatial and temporal dimension. The former refers to 'overlapping local and global, social and natural communities which describe interdependence, influence and ability to make change' (AAID 2008, p. 5). The latter refers to 'connections between the past, present and future in the dynamic changing world which influences identity and interdependence of people and their ability to respond to global issues' (AAID 2008, p. 5).

## Global education: core knowledge and understandings, and core skills and processes

To engage meaningfully and effectively with these core concepts, learners – from the early years to senior secondary – need to possess certain forms and levels of knowledge and understandings as well as the requisite skills to develop and apply them. Once again, the Global Perspectives Framework provides an insightful account of what the knowledge and understandings and skills and processes might be.

In terms of knowledge and understandings, the Framework (AAID 2008, p. 6) suggests that learners develop the following:

- An awareness of self as a member of interconnected and overlapping communities and how this influences responses to global issues.
- A recognition of social, political, economic and environmental links between people and between communities.
- A recognition and assessment of the range of perspectives and the temporal and global dimensions on a global issue or event.
- An understanding of the interdependence of all living things and that each has a value and the imperative of sustainability.
- An awareness of the role of economic development in overcoming poverty and raising living standards.
- An appreciation of diversity and the contributions of different cultures, values and belief systems.
- A discernment of the nature and impact of prejudice and discrimination, and capacity to challenge these positions.
- A familiarity with the universal and inalienable nature of human rights.
- A knowledge of causes of poverty, and inequality and ways to address it.
- An understanding of the causes and consequences of change and strategies available to manage change.

- An appreciation of the causes and effects of conflict, and the importance of conflict resolution and peace building.

- An appreciation of the importance of good governance.

- A recognition of the contested nature of global issues, and the importance of seeking an informed and balanced understanding.

Make a list of what you consider to be the 10 biggest current global issues. For each of the issues on your list, which elements of the knowledge and understandings would learners need to develop in order to engage with them? Would this differ between the early years, the primary years and the secondary years?

In terms of skills and processes, the Framework (AAID 2008, p. 6) suggests that learners develop a range of capacities, including those related to cooperation and diplomacy, conflict resolution, critical thinking, research and inquiry skills, expressing viewpoints supported by evidence, applying principles of equity and developing empathy for others.

## Global education: core attributes

Being and becoming a globally oriented citizen requires us not just to understand core concepts, or to learn core knowledge and understandings or core skills or processes. It requires us, as well, to think of ourselves as certain types of people – people who are willing and able to participate in dialogical relations with others in an attempt to share our own perspectives while listening to those of others. The connection between *dialogue* and *care* is crucial for this process. As Nel Noddings (2005, p. 23) suggests:

> Dialogue . . . connects us to each other and helps to maintain caring relations. It also provides us with the knowledge of each other that forms a foundation for response in caring . . . We respond most effectively as carers when we understand what the other needs and the history of this need. To receive the other is to attend fully and openly. Continuing dialogue builds up a substantial knowledge of one another that serves to guide our responses.

As part of its Making Caring Common Project, the Harvard Graduate School of Education (2014, p. 15) suggests that through dialogue, learners learn to 'zoom in' with their peers in ways that then enable them to 'zoom out' to consider the perspectives of, and to expand their care to, others:

> Children and youth need to learn to zoom in, listening closely and attending to those in their immediate circle, and to zoom out, taking in the big picture and considering multiple perspectives. It is by zooming out and taking multiple perspectives, including the perspectives of those who are too often invisible (such as the new kid in class, someone who doesn't speak their language, or the custodian), that young people expand their circle of concern and become able to consider the justice of their communities and society.

But what sorts of attributes enable learners to engage in dialogue and care in this way? The Global Education Framework (AAID 2008, p. 5) sets out the following values and attitudes:

- A sense of personal identity and self-esteem.
- A sense of community with the people around the world.
- Caring and compassionate concern for others.
- A recognition of shared responsibilities and a willingness to cooperate with others in fulfilling them.
- A commitment to upholding the rights and dignity of all people.
- A positive attitude towards diversity and difference.
- A willingness to learn from the experience of others.
- An appreciation of and concern for the environment and a commitment to sustainable practices.

**SPOTLIGHT ON HASS EDUCATION**

## TASK: ENGAGING WITH DIFFERENT PERSPECTIVES (AND AVOIDING A SINGLE STORY)

In this section we have emphasised the importance of dialogue in sharing our own perspectives and listening to the perspectives of others. Appreciating the perspectives of others is a central theme within a TED Talk given by Chimamanda Ngozi Adichie entitled 'The Danger of a Single Story' (Adichie 2009).

Visit http://new.ted.com/talks/chimamanda_adichie_the_danger_of_a_single_story. Watch the talk and think about how you might use the talk and its themes in your work with learners.

Reflection

The Global Education Project's *Thinking Globally: Global perspectives in the early years classroom* (AusAID 2008) sets out the potential benefits of engaging learners with global issues through the use of children's literature. Focusing on the age ranges with which you will be working, think about stories you have read that might provide a useful resource to engage learners with global issues.

# ORGANISING THE TEACHING AND LEARNING OF GLOBAL EDUCATION WITHIN AN EDUCATIONAL SITE

In this section we consider the various processes through which educational sites might teach global education. Given that global education is unlikely to feature as a distinct subject within the curriculum, individual sites are likely to combine a range of approaches to global education. It is important that, within these approaches, sites pay attention to how the various learning experiences connect to the official curriculum, whether that be the Early Years Learning Framework (EYLF; DEEWR 2009) or the Australian Curriculum (ACARA 2018). This section also focuses on how sites might look to draw explicit connections between the various elements of global education. To start this section, however, we will explore something that underpins all of the learning central to global education; namely, the establishment of a positive and conducive learning environment through participatory pedagogies.

## Participatory pedagogies for global education

For global education to succeed and thrive, educational sites and educators need to put certain processes into place. To be effective, these processes are likely to have certain common features, including strong and committed leadership and an understanding that preparation for global citizenship is central to the mission of the site. In addition, is the need to develop and enact particular pedagogical approaches, through which learners can develop the criticality, creativity and compassion required to become and be global citizens. Crucial within these, as the influential work of Graham Pike and David Selby (1999) reminds us, is the development of *world-mindedness* through pedagogies of *child-centredness*; that is, through pedagogies that start from learners' experiences and understandings and seek to help the development of appropriate attitudes and dispositions.

While there are several potential participatory pedagogical approaches that could be used to engage learners in global education, we follow Peterson and Warwick (2014) in viewing three as particularly appropriate:

1. **Issue-based learning**: A common approach within global education is to engage learners in issue-based learning, particularly given that research suggests young people hold an interest in a broad range of global issues (Holden 2007; Warwick 2008). These issues – from climate change to biodiversity – can provide educators with stimulus foci for exploring the core concepts of global education. Moreover, when taught through an active and participatory approach, issue-based learning can support learners to develop critical skills central to taking informed and appropriate action within and beyond their educational sites. Here again, dialogue-based approaches, such as the community of inquiry approach central to philosophy for children, can support learners to share their own perspectives while listening to those of others (see Chapter 12).

   **issue-based learning**: a teaching approach in which learners explore real-life issues of concern to themselves

2. **Problem-based learning**: Related to issue-based pedagogies is the idea of problem-based learning. Through problem-based learning, learners encounter real-world problems and work collaboratively and democratically to consider, explore and devise potential solutions. Learning in this way is a group exercise, involving learners in a creative process of action, reflection, communication and negotiation (Wildemeersch 2009). In so doing, problem-based learning provides learners

   **problem-based learning**: a teaching approach in which learners engage with real-life problems and work collaboratively to suggest possible solutions with the opportunity to apply constructive conflict-resolution strategies. Central to problem-based learning is educators setting up constructive controversy in learning environments and supporting young people to handle disagreements effectively through a cooperative problem-solving approach (see Johnson, Johnson & Tjosvold 2000).

3. *Service-learning:* This involves learners exploring a particular issue or theme, and then undertaking participatory social action projects that serve to engage, challenge or change an area of concern to themselves and their communities. A key part of service-learning is for learners to understand an issue, to take agreed and appropriate action with respect to the issue, and then to reflect on both the process and outcomes. In essence, the process of service-learning is cyclical, with learners then able to take further action (or not!) as a result of their reflections. Bringle, Hatcher and Jones (2011) suggest that international service-learning is a pedagogy ideally suited for active global citizenship in the 21st century, and point to its transformational potential for producing deep and lasting changes in learners' present and future lives.

Whichever participatory pedagogies the educator chooses to employ, a further two considerations are important to point out: *working with controversy* and *conceiving learning spaces*.

A challenge for educators teaching global education is that global issues are, by their very nature, often controversial. This recognition is important, and requires educators to think carefully about the ways in which a given global issue is contested, and how their awareness of the sensitivities involved can lead them, when working with controversy, towards an informed approach. In addition, **controversial issues** are often sensitive, drawing different emotive responses from different people and communities. Oulton, Dillon and Grace (2004, p. 415) advise that learners need to explore controversial issues, including 'how it is that individuals can apparently hold different perspectives on an issue', and concluding that introducing learners to 'multiple perspectives is therefore an essential part of the methods of teaching about controversial issues'.

**controversial issue**: an issue about which there is reasonable disagreement, and which may be sensitive to those who care about it

There are a wide variety of approaches that educators can take to engaging learners with controversial global issues. For example, Oxfam (2006) identifies a range of different roles that an educator can adopt with learners, including:

- *Impartial chairperson*: the educator seeks to ensure that a wide variety of viewpoints are represented either through learners' statements or stimulus material. In this role the educator refrains from stating their own opinion.

- *Objective*: the educator seeks to offer a balanced approach where they present learners with a wide range of alternative views without stating their own position.

- *Devil's advocate*: the educator adopts a provocative or an oppositional position to the one expressed by learners or the stimulus material. This helps to provide an atmosphere of challenge within the discussion and can prevent a sense of consensus quickly dominating the participants' exchanges.

- *Declared interest*: the educator makes their position known within the discussion but presents, or engages in considering, a variety of positions as objectively as possible.

Of course, educators – partly through the resources they use – are likely to employ different roles with learners, switching between them as the context, issue and climate and learner needs demand. Educators must also remember that, while they are expected to remain neutral regarding their own partisan views, they work within educational sites, educational systems and national laws that require them not to remain neutral on certain issues (such as racial discrimination). Planning for their own position regarding the issue at hand, and how this is or is not shared within the learning space, prior to engaging with learners is therefore crucial for the educator. In addition, educators must also consider the age range of the learners with whom they are working, taking account of the issues and depth of discussion that are appropriate. These considerations must always be guided by the key features and needs of the context in which the educator is working.

As well as paying attention to the controversial and sensitive nature of issues central to global education, educators must also think about the principles that underpin their practice. Peterson and Warwick (2014, p. 44) offer the following 10 educational principles for a child-centred approach to global education:

1. *holistic* – each learner's individual learning needs are met through attention being given to holistic aspects such as intellectual, moral, social and emotional development.
2. *personalised* – each learner is personally known; with attention to their cultural contexts, unique personal experiences and global learning preferences.
3. *flexible* – a range of learning spaces provide for small group, one to one and independent global learning.
4. *partnered* – all stakeholders are vital partners in the development and progress of global learning including learners themselves.
5. *equal* – each learner's contribution to the group's learning process is vital and of worth.
6. *convivial* – learning is facilitated by an immersion in a friendly and lively atmosphere, where global learners listen in order to understand each other, and are both encouraged and challenged.
7. *democratic* – all learners are involved in decision making processes within the global learning initiative.
8. *well-being based* – the educational action that forms the basis of global learning is underpinned by an active consideration of the well-being of others and the environment.
9. *rigorous* – the learning process is thorough, and is developed with close attention to being research informed and reflective.
10. *participative* – learners are actively involved in core elements of the educational process.

Thinking about an educational site with which you have engaged, which of these 10 principles were in evidence? How did they connect to global learning?

Reflection

## Connecting with the curriculum

While global education must be active and participatory if it is to fulfil its potentially transformational role, teaching and learning must also make solid and concrete connections to the formal curriculum. This is necessary to ensure that learning is rooted in the core concepts, and core knowledge and understandings set out in the previous section, and also supports learners to make connections between key aspects of the curriculum and their global education experiences.

### EXPLORING FAMILIES: JUNIOR PRIMARY

Learning about their own family, heritage and that of their peers contributes to learners' sense of identity and belonging, beginning the idea of active citizenship (ACARA 2018).

In Foundation HASS, the educator has commenced a unit of work on the topic of families. The school is a metropolitan, co-educational primary school, with a diverse community welcoming families from 38 different cultural backgrounds. The educator would like to actively promote learning opportunities to explore and celebrate cultural diversity in the educational setting.

The educator has set up a home corner to encourage children to explore family through imagination and play. Dolls that represent different races, genders and abilities are included, and the home corner utensils and clothing are from a variety of cultures (Reid-Nguyen 1999, p. 21). Valuing the cultural and social contexts of learners and their families is especially important in the early years as it sets learners up to explore worlds other than their own, and enables them to develop a strong sense of identity and wellbeing (DEEWR 2009, p. 14).

The reading corner is filled with books on family, with a range of cultures and family structures represented. It is important to consider how culturally inclusive the books and images in the learning environment are. What is valued in the learning environment sends a strong message, and can promote respect for diversity and inclusivity, or reinforce existing stereotypes (Reid-Nguyen 1999, p. 21).

In this learning activity, the educator uses a story to explore what families have in common. In the Australian Curriculum, this links to 'How stories of families and the past can be communicated...', specifically the elaboration 'Using images, learners' stories and stories from other places to explore what families have in common...' (ACHASSK013; ACARA 2018).

The educator reads the book *Mirror* by Jeannie Baker (2010), which tells the story of two little boys and their families – one from an inner-city family in Sydney, Australia, the other from a small, remote village in Morocco, North Africa. The book consists of two stories, designed to be read simultaneously side by side. Baker's collaged images serve to capture the different lifestyles, landscapes, clothing and activities of these two places. Yet, importantly, the story conveys that all families are essentially the same in that the characters care for each other; they need to belong, be loved and be part of a community.

Stories with global themes, set in other countries or written by people of different cultures, provide rich learning opportunities for learners to make links between their own experiences and those of others (AAID 2012). Stories can develop learners' insights into how different people live and view the world, thus developing historical understandings around empathy and perspectives.

After reading the picture book, the educator asks learners to identify the similarities and differences between the lives of the boys in Morocco and Sydney on the first few pages of the book (which show the two families waking up, having breakfast and preparing to go out). The educator uses a Venn diagram to record learners' responses (see Figure 27.1).

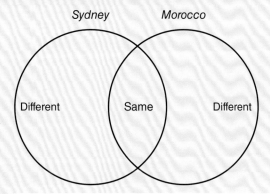

FIGURE 27.1   Venn diagram template to record similarities and differences

The discussion is lively, as learners keenly communicate the similarities and differences between the two families. This naturally leads to further discussion around learners' own experiences. The educator asks learners to pair up and share with one another what their own families do in the mornings (thus sharing their own stories).

Learners are then given a Venn diagram to record this information, which involves rich discussion as learners share and sort their own family experiences. Role play, collage and the creation of story maps are possible follow-up activities to further explore the important topic of family through story. Storytelling and storymaking with global themes provide a pathway to a range of meaningful learning activities that develop learners' understanding of diversity and cultural competence.

'Children learn about themselves and construct their own identity within the context of their families and communities. When children have positive experiences, they develop an understanding of themselves as significant and respected, and feel a sense of belonging' (DEEWR 2009, p. 20).

## EDUCATOR TIP

The possibilities of connections with the curriculum are almost endless, both in relation to the EYLF and the Australian Curriculum. As an educator, it is vital that you make use of the curricular documents – both official and those written within your settings – to inform and frame your planning. Make sure that you read, understand and actively use curriculum documents in your short-term, mid-term and long-term planning.

## Connecting the dots

The fact that global education is rarely taught as a stand-alone subject provides both opportunities and challenges for HASS educators. The flexibility and freedom provided by global education give educators great scope to introduce and explore aspects of global education in exciting and creative ways, engaging with learner interests and needs as they do so. One of the key challenges, however, is to support learners to make links between their global learning experiences so that they do not become fragmented. In other words, how do educators connect the dots between the various aspects of global education? We believe there are three interrelated ways in which such connections can be made in educational sites.

The first is to ensure that learners have a clear and consistent understanding of what it means to be a global citizen (or, as we prefer, a globally oriented citizen). Such a definition should underpin all global education activities and provide learners with a common touchpoint which they can bring to their various experiences of global education. The second is to connect global education to a key value within the school. This value might be something general, such as world-mindedness, or could be more specific, such as compassion or service; it can act as a unifying prism through which learners can make sense of and connect their learning. The third is to make sure that, wherever possible and appropriate, the global connects to the local. As Osler (2008, p. 22) states, global education

> requires us to re-imagine the nation … as cosmopolitan and to recognise local communities and the national community as cosmopolitan. It implies a sense of solidarity with strangers in distant places but it also requires solidarity, a sense of shared humanity and dialogue with those in the local community and the national community whose perspectives may be very different from our own.

International organisations, such as Oxfam, Amnesty International and Caritas, can play an important role in connecting learners to global issues through local action, as will be demonstrated through the learning extension task at the end of the chapter.

## EDUCATOR TIP

Key words/definitions are the cornerstone of understanding. Thinking of learners with whom you will be working as a HASS educator, devise a one-sentence definition of global citizenship that could act as a touchstone for global education experiences.

Reflection  Which values would you place as central to global education, and which do you think could provide a prism for connecting learner experiences?

# CONCLUSION

In this chapter we have suggested that, although it is not a stand-alone subject in the Australian Curriculum, global education represents a crucial element of learning for young people. Such learning is at its best when it is connected, creative and critical, underpinned by core concepts and knowledge and understandings, and supported through active skills and processes that connect learners with their locality and beyond. When taught well, global education synergises with multiple aspects of the HASS curriculum, and should be central to the work of HASS educators. Integral to teaching global education in HASS is the notion of perspectives – how learners can share their own perspectives and listen to those of others through dialogical learning experiences and encounters. Underpinning global education is a commitment to viewing young people as globally oriented citizens, both today and for the future.

## REVIEW QUESTIONS

1. What is globalisation?
2. What are the core components of global education?
3. What forms of learning are particularly apt for global education?
4. How does global education connect to the HASS curriculum?
5. How does global education connect to other aspects of curriculum and school life?

## LEARNING EXTENSION

Non-governmental organisations, such as Oxfam, Amnesty International and Caritas, are useful and productive sources of information and educational resources for global education. Visit the websites of three international organisations that work locally in Australia. Explore their educational resources and analyse how they present global education. How might these resources support you in your role as a HASS educator?

## REFERENCES

AAID (Australian Agency for International Development). (2008). *Global Perspectives: A framework for global education in Australian schools*. Melbourne: Education Services Australia. Retrieved from: http://www.globaleducation.edu.au/verve/_resources/GPS_web.pdf.

——(2012). Teaching strategies. Retrieved from: http://www.globaleducation.edu.au/teaching-and-learning/teaching-strategies.html.

ACARA (Australian Curriculum, Assessment and Reporting Authority). (2018). *Australian Curriculum: F-10, v8.3*. Retrieved from: https://www.australiancurriculum.edu.au.

Adichie, C.N. (2009). The danger of a single story. Ted Talk. Retrieved from: https://www.ted.com/talks/chimamanda_adichie_the_danger_of_a_single_story.

Annan, K. (2000). The politics of globalization. In P. O'Meara, H. Mohlinger & M. Krain, eds, *Globalization and the Challenge of a New Century: A reader*. Bloomington, IN: Indiana University Press, pp. 125–30.

AusAID. (2008). *Thinking Globally: Global perspectives in the early years classroom*. Melbourne: Education Services Australia.

Baker, J. (2010) *Mirror*. London: Walker Books.

Bringle, R., Hatcher, J. & Jones, S. (eds). (2011). *International Service Learning*. Sterling: Stylus.

DEEWR (Department of Education, Employment and Workplace Relations). (2009). *Belonging, Being and Becoming: The Early Years Learning Framework for Australia*. Canberra: DEEWR.

Food Empowerment Project. (2017). Child labor and slavery in the chocolate industry. Retrieved from: http://www.foodispower.org/slavery-chocolate.

Goldin, I. (2009). Navigating our global future. TED Talk. Retrieved from: http://www.ted.com/talks/ian_goldin_navigating_our_global_future.html.

Harvard Graduate School of Education. (2014). *The Children We Mean to Raise: The real messages adults are sending about values*. Harvard, MA: Harvard Graduate School of Education.

Holden, C. (2007). Young people's concerns. In D. Hicks & C. Holden, eds, *Teaching the Global Dimension: Key principles and effective practice*. London: Routledge.

Johnson, D.W., Johnson, R. & Tjosvold, D. (2000). Constructive controversy: The value of intellectual opposition. In M. Deutsch & P.T. Coleman, eds, *The Handbook of Conflict Resolution: Theory and practice*. San Francisco, CA: Jossey-Bass.

MCEETYA (Ministerial Council on Education, Employment, Training and Youth Affairs). (2008). *Melbourne Declaration on Educational Goals for Young Australians*. Retrieved from: http://www.curriculum.edu.au/verve/_resources/National_Declaration_on_the_Educational_Goals_for_Young_Australians.pdf.

Noddings, N. (2005). *The Challenge to Care in Schools: An alternative approach to education*, 2nd edn. New York: Teachers College Press.

Osler, A. (2008). Citizenship education and the Ajegbo report: Re-imagining a cosmopolitan nation. *London Review of Education*, 6(1), 11–25.

Oulton, C., Dillon, J. & Grace, M. (2004). Reconceptualizing the teaching of controversial issues. *International Journal of Social Science Education*, 26(4), 411–23.

Oxfam (2006). *Getting Started with Global Citizenship: A guide for new teachers*. Oxford: Oxfam.

Parekh, B. (2003) Cosmopolitanism and global citizenship. *Review of International Studies*, 29(1), 3–17.

Peterson, A. (2016). Global justice and educating for globally oriented citizenship. In A. Peterson, R. Hattam, M. Zembylas & J. Arthur, eds, *The Palgrave International Handbook of Education for Citizenship and Social Justice*. Basingstoke: Palgrave Macmillan, pp. 247–64.

——(in press). Asia literacy and the globally oriented citizen: Framing the moral dimension of educating for Asia literacy. In H. Soong & N. Cominos, eds, *Asia Literacy in a Global World: Securing Australia's future*. Dordrecht: Springer.

Peterson, A. & Warwick, P. (2014). *Global Learning and Education: Key concepts and effective practice*. Abingdon: Routledge.

Pigozzi, M.J. (2006). A UNESCO view of global citizenship education. *Educational Review*, 58(1), 1–4.

Pike, G. & Selby, D. (1998). *Global Teacher, Global Learner*. London: Hodder and Stoughton.

Reid-Nguyen, R. (1999). *Think Global: Global perspectives in the lower primary classroom*. Melbourne: Education Services Australia.

Stiglitz, J. (2002). *Globalization and Its Discontents*. Harmondsworth: Penguin.

Warwick, P. (2008). Apathetic or misunderstood: Hearing young people's voices within citizenship education. *Education Action Research Journal*, 16(3), 321–33.

Wildemeersch, D. (2009). Social learning revisited: Lessons learned from north and south. In A. Wals, ed., *Social Learning: Towards a sustainable world*. Wageningen: Wageningen Academic.

# PART VII
# Getting started

# EARLY CAREER TEACHING IN THE EARLY YEARS

*Steven Cameron*

## Learning objectives

After reading this chapter, you should be able to:

- understand early childhood pedagogy, including the critical importance of play and inquiry
- develop an awareness of the cycle of planning to inform teaching and learning
- recognise the importance of planning and engaging in ongoing professional development and dialogue that supports professional growth.

## INTRODUCTION

Early childhood education is both simple and complex. For early career educators, it can be challenging to navigate and orient themselves within the field. Increasing demands on, and accountability for, early childhood educators around the provision of a high-quality curriculum and clear learning outcomes for children are significant in their own right; however, for early career educators there is the added lack of clarity around the notion of what constitutes high-quality curriculum and learning outcomes.

In Australia, the Early Years Learning Framework (EYLF; DEEWR 2009) supports early childhood educators to shape their pedagogy, providing a high-quality early childhood curriculum in a holistic way that outlines what children's learning *could* look like, and not what it *will* look like. This is an important distinction, as it reinforces the notion that early childhood education must focus on context and not content; learning opportunities are influenced by the learner, and early childhood educators need to be aware of the role they adopt in supporting learning.

In a Humanities and Social Sciences (HASS) context, it is essential to view learning through an early childhood pedagogical lens, as learning is not segregated into subject areas within the early years; learning is viewed as holistic and interconnected (DEEWR 2009). For this reason, HASS should be viewed as part of the broader learning focus in early childhood education.

Play and inquiry have been singled out and further developed in this chapter both as powerful vehicles for learning and as cornerstones of high-quality early childhood pedagogy, with a focus on the planning cycle to inform teaching and learning, with descriptors to create conditions for high-quality learning for children.

This chapter highlights the importance of rigorous professional learning and reflective forums such as professional learning communities as processes that provide ongoing support for educators to reflect on their practice and pedagogy through identifying areas for growth.

# EARLY CHILDHOOD PEDAGOGY: YOUR WHY AND HOW

As noted, early childhood education is not content driven, but context driven. Bearing this in mind, early childhood pedagogy is fundamental, as it offers early childhood educators the flexibility and freedom to develop their pedagogy in a way that reflects the needs of the children, families and communities in which they work. For early career educators, developing an understanding of the context in which they work is critical as they hone their pedagogy. We all come to education with our own set of personal beliefs and values based on our lived experiences; however, we risk failing to contextualise learning for children if we proceed unaware of the unique characteristics of the communities in which we work (Rogoff 2003). It is therefore essential for educators to identify their core beliefs and align them with the context of the community in which they work. This gives rise to being able to define your 'why' – that which underpins all decisions and actions as an educator and enables you to continue to question your pedagogical practice: why you value working in the way that you do, and why your way of working makes a difference for learners. Reflecting on what aspects of your pedagogy lead you to act as you do should be central to your thinking. A focus on how you will act, informed by a clear idea of why, will enable you to ensure that your pedagogy mirrors your established beliefs and values.

## Play

As discussed in Chapter 13, play is the foundation of early childhood education. Children are intrinsically driven to play from the day they are born, and these experiences are central to shaping how they construct their view of the world and their place within it. Children build peer relationships, trial ideas and challenge their thinking through providing the time and place to engage in deep thinking, ask and answer questions and think critically about their learning, refining their awareness of their own strengths and abilities and building theories to explain their world (Hargreaves 2014). This makes play the perfect vehicle for HASS learning throughout the early years.

Learning experiences should provide children with multiple opportunities to engage in deep, extended play. As an educator, it is important to actively consider the role that you take while children engage in play, bearing in mind that play is intrinsically motivated; that is, it is not planned. This can be challenging for early career educators in the early years, as there are differing expectations for curriculum. Play is foundational within pre-school programs, but its visibility can vary between schools. Co-construction of learning requires the educator to fully immerse themselves in the experience and deeply engage with children, to potentially shine richer insight on their knowledge, skills and understandings. This enables the educator to respond to spontaneous play with intentionality and create conditions to enrich children's play through the **learning environments** they co-construct with children, the dialogue in which they engage and the provocations provided to extend and expand children's understandings about their world (DEEWR 2009).

There are rich opportunities for HASS learning through play, such as exploring different cultures through exposure to food, language, music, art and dance, and these opportunities enable children to develop their awareness and concepts of the world, as well as exposing them to the world view of others as they share their perspectives.

**learning environment**: responsive spaces that reflect the identities and context of those who engage within them

# EDUCATOR TIP

In your role as an early years educator, you can support children in developing cultural competence through intentional modelling of respectful dialogue about culture and diversity across cultural groups within their community.

## Inquiry-based learning

As discussed in previous chapters, inquiry goes far beyond answering a simple 'yes' or 'no' question. It is concerned with possibilities, more than with concrete outcomes – something children in the early years are extremely adept at generating naturally – thus offering educators a powerful vehicle to extend upon learning opportunities. Inquiry in early childhood should engage children to think about subject matter from multiple perspectives, rather than focus on one correct answer. This offers strong learning opportunities in HASS, as educators can foster children's natural curiosity and wonder about places, people and cultures through the generation of questions that seek to open their thinking and explore the possibilities, as opposed to one reality or way of thinking. Inquiry is the driver for this to occur (Murdoch 2015) and is a key tenet of learning in HASS.

A high-quality early childhood learning environment will be full of provocations for learning. It generates questions, promotes discussions, captures attention and sparks the imagination. The learning environment was described by Loris Malaguzzi (1993), founder and director of the municipal preschools in Reggio Emilia in Italy, as the 'third teacher' alongside adults and children due to the way in which it can influence learning by providing opportunities for children to engage in multiple inquiries about the world around them.

As an early career educator, take time to notice what is being reflected in your learning environment and what is being communicated implicitly to children and families through the learning environment you create. What your learning environment communicates to children will have a marked impact on the provocations it offers children as they generate their own wonderings for inquiry. Whose realities are reflected within the learning environment, and what impact does this have on children's learning?

Reflection

## TOY-FREE TUESDAY

Inquiry-based learning is a key feature of early childhood education and has clear links to both the EYLF and HASS learning area within the Australian Curriculum. Utilising inquiry in early childhood serves as an opportunity for children to explore a central idea from multiple perspectives and offers educators the opportunity to view HASS learning through a lens that is contextually relevant for children.

Early in my career, I worked at a preschool (with children between the ages of four and five) where over 50 per cent of the children were new arrivals to Australia, often with no or minimal English, and often from a refugee background. On one occasion, I noticed a group of children playing with some assorted rocks, with a child who had recently arrived from a refugee camp referring to them as 'toys'. This prompted several children to tell the child that they were rocks, and not toys.

I posed the question, 'What are toys?' to the group and collectively brainstormed the toys that we had available at the preschool, discussing how they were used and how they supported us to learn. My role as an educator was to continue to pose provocations to the children, ensuring that the dialogue was accessible for all children involved, and to challenge their thinking as they developed their idea of what makes a toy a toy.

As a group, we developed our own definition of what a toy was and applied it to the various resources available at the preschool. The children categorised the resources as either a 'toy' or 'not a toy', which led to one of the children posing their own question to the group: 'What if there were no toys at preschool?' This led to the commencement of 'Toy-Free Tuesday', where the only resources that were available to children for the entire day came from the non-toy list they had developed themselves. Resources such as paper, cellophane, cardboard, string, water and sticks became the only resources available. This led to another inquiry around the role of resources in supporting children's critical and creative thinking, as children experimented with each of the materials in an open-ended way, generating multiple possibilities for use through their play.

This example highlights the power of engaging in inquiry with children and using play as a research tool to support their inquiry. This not only shaped the development of their perspectives, but also myself as an early career teacher. It also served as a continual reminder that resources should support, not define, learning.

## EDUCATOR TIP

Some useful ways to maintain continual reflection on your practice are:
- Engage with families and community members regularly: how are the current needs of your community reflected in your pedagogy?
- Keep a journal and write in it at least weekly. Record your professional wonderings and reflect on shifts in thinking. This can be a powerful reflective process for

educators at any stage of their career; however, it is particularly powerful to track your evolving understandings as an early career educator.

- Reflect on how you currently resource learning opportunities for children. Is your current practice reflective of your pedagogy? Consider the role children take in resourcing decisions within the learning environment.

Your pedagogy should be influenced by the community in which you work. To what degree is your knowledge of the community evident in your pedagogy? How do you engage with stakeholders in your community to build your knowledge of your context?

## THE CYCLE OF PLANNING

How educators plan for children will heavily impact on the quality of the **learning outcomes** they achieve. Implementing a rigorous **cycle of planning** is essential, as it drives continuous pedagogical improvement for educators as much as learning outcomes for children. In my early teaching career, a model of plan/do/reflect was one that provided a clear format for planning. However, it quickly became evident that this was a deficient model with which to work, as the level of reflection was almost always shallow and did not always lead me to connect with my pedagogy. The release of the *Educators' Guide to the Early Years Learning Framework for Australia* (DEEWR 2010) offered a rigorous alternative – the early years planning cycle (Figure 28.1).

**learning outcomes**: the skills, knowledge or dispositions developed through experience

**cycle of planning**: the ongoing process of reflecting, questioning, planning and implementation to support children's learning

While this planning cycle almost mirrored the approach that I had been using, the addition of a questioning aspect within the cycle made a key difference in my practice, as it led me to reflect and act with a degree of intentionality, and to continuously realign my pedagogy with the learning needs of the children, site philosophy, my personal educational principles and beliefs, and the context of the local community (Taylor et al. 2006).

### Reflect/review

As a starting point, **reflection** always offers a rich space to explore what has occurred before, prior to planning, and where to head next. Reflection, particularly a focus on critical reflection, will enable you to consider how your view of each learner within your context has been constructed, and the rationale that drives the curriculum judgements and decisions you make for learners, both individually and as a cohort. This becomes a critical space to reflect on your impact as an educator, as you can still risk representing learners' reality through practice as opposed to a judgement that has been informed by children's voice, leading to a disconnect between core beliefs and pedagogical practice (Moore 2014).

**reflection**: a process of gathering information to support and inform learning

## Early years planning cycle
### *Belonging, Being and Becoming*

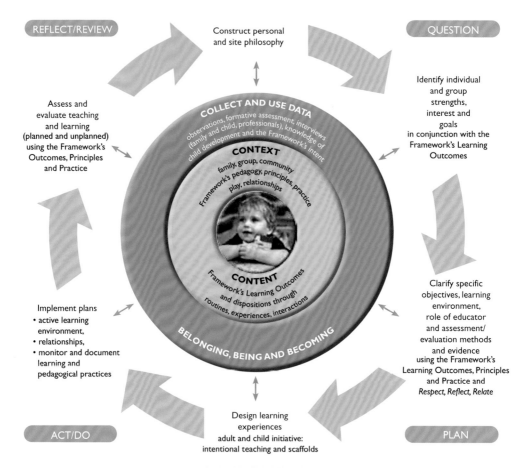

FIGURE 28.1   The early years planning cycle
Source: DEEWR 2010, p. 11

Reflecting on children's learning in this way enables educators to move beyond simple observations of what has occurred and towards a deeper understanding of other elements that impact learning. Reflecting on how the educator can shape and influence children's learning within learning environments is critical, as that influence extends to matters of curriculum and pedagogical leadership, how to manage behaviour, how to resource learning for and with children, the strategies engaged with to support learning and how to assess for learning (DEEWR 2010).

You can begin the reflect/review process by reflecting on a recent learning experience with a child and asking the following questions:

- What did I notice?
- What role did I take during this experience?
- What informed my resourcing decisions?

- Does what occurred within this learning experience add to or change what I know of the child? How do I know this?
- Did all elements of the learning experience align with my pedagogy?

Discussion with other members of the staff team will assist in shaping your thinking and serve as an additional layer of reflection. Reflections on teaching and learning must extend to questions around how this information will be used to plan for children's learning.

## Question

Questioning prior to planning for learning involves identification of learning goals and priorities for learners, which stems from the professional reflections and judgements of educators, informed by a range of data and aligned with key learning outcomes. The questioning aspect of the planning cycle offers an opportunity to reflect and position plans alongside pedagogy, linking with theoretical perspectives and how these have shaped the educator's knowledge of the child. It additionally serves as an opportunity to engage with families in a collaborative and meaningful way as the 'first educators' of their children. Families will often provide access to a wealth of information about their child's learning and prior knowledge, as well as their interests, skills and abilities. This serves to support the development of learning experiences that are both appropriate for that child and hold contextual relevance. Engaging families in the conversation about learning through the educator sharing their reflections and valuing families' knowledge (DEEWR 2010) is critical, as it adds an authenticity to HASS learning; this is because it is their realities that are presented as opposed to the educator's constructions and perceptions of their realities.

Key questions you could reflect upon during this aspect of the planning cycle are:

- What is my image of the child, and how does it impact on my professional judgements?
- What evidence is available that supports my professional judgements?
- How am I engaging collaboratively and meaningfully with families?
- How are children going to be involved in the planning and assessment for their learning? How will I ensure that their voice will be heard?

## Plan

Planning for learning should be reflective of the educator's core beliefs and pedagogy, contextualised by their knowledge of the learners as informed by their own judgements and information provided by families. The educator should be intentional in their thinking; that is, how will the learning experience, the educator's role within it and assessment for learning, or formative assessment (Rizvi & Lingard 2010), complement each other to support children's learning? You should try not to be too narrow in your focus; always bear in mind that children's engagement within a learning experience will often deviate from intended outcomes, and having preconceived notions of what a child will learn will create too many restrictions. Focus on creating the conditions for learning to occur, and while you may have set outcomes that you would like to achieve, be open to the unintended outcomes of the learning experience. Developing a broader goal and then refining how that goal will be met through consideration of the context will position learning experiences with far more relevance for each child.

The design, set-up and resourcing of the learning environment are also key considerations during this phase of the planning cycle. Your pedagogy should be highly visible through the learning environment, and influence set-up of the environment itself and the resourcing decisions made. In addition, this is where your knowledge of the child comes into play, as your planned goals/learning outcomes are strengthened by an environment that is contextually relevant and meaningful to learners and resourced in a way that will encourage deep engagement.

As an early career educator, it is important that your planning is deeply reflective to ensure you are designing learning opportunities with a clear intention. Some key questions to prompt your thinking in curriculum planning and designing learning experiences are:

- What goals/outcomes do I want to achieve through the learning experience? Are they narrow or broad?
- What data/evidence have I drawn on to support my professional judgement, and how is it reflected in the intended goals/outcomes?
- How will I engage families in the planning process?
- How will I communicate with families around the planned learning outcomes for children?
- What role will I adopt as an educator within the learning experience?
- What evidence of learner achievement will I collect to assess for learning? How will I collect the evidence?

## Act/do

As highlighted, the implementation of even the most considered learning experience will often deviate from intended outcomes; however, being clear about the intended outcomes is still crucial to how the educator implements a planned learning experience. Acting with intentionality in early childhood education complements learning through play and the spontaneous learning that occurs within the learning environment by providing children with provocations for learning that deepen their engagement with the experience.

Educators should have a clear idea of the role that they will take during the implementation of a planned learning experience. This links back to intentionality – that they have a clear idea of what opportunities for learning will be available to children through this planned experience, and what the educator's role will be within it. Educators should be flexible in their role and prepared to shift in response to the needs of children as they arise within the learning experience. While the educator may start by role modelling for children, they may quickly move to provide different provocations for learning through questioning or prompting learners to solve problems that arise throughout the learning experience (DEEWR 2009).

Because of the need for flexibility by the educator, how they plan to document children's learning may need to change. It is not always possible to document children's learning in minute detail, so the educator should be prepared to quickly capture the essence of the learning. This is another key reason why consideration needs to be given to how evidence of children's learning will be collected; if the plan requires the educator to be present and deeply engaged alongside children through questioning and reciprocal conversations, then the method of collecting data needs to reflect this role.

While implementing a planned learning experience, you should consider the following questions:

- What is my role within the learning experience, and does it need to change based on how it is unfolding?
- Does my intended method of documenting for children's learning need to change? What will my backup plan be?
- What will I document?
- How am I identifying and being responsive to the needs of children as they arise within the learning experience (i.e. resourcing)?

## EXAMPLE OF A PLANNED LEARNING EXPERIENCE

You notice a child at your preschool make comments to other children about the headscarves several children wear each day. The comments are general wonderings about why those children wear them. Based on your knowledge of your community, you know many of the families who attend your preschool identify as Sikh. In communication with the child's family, you discover that the child has asked their parents why the other children at preschool wear those 'hats' on their heads. In partnership with the child's family, you develop a goal for the child to broaden their knowledge, perspectives and appreciation of culture, with a specific focus on Sikh culture.

You then speak with some of the families who identify as Sikh about their cultural and religious beliefs. This is to develop your own awareness and seek their support and input into the design of learning experiences that will enhance the knowledge, appreciation and perspectives of children attending your site. Gaining this input provides an authenticity to learning through direct links to culture.

You plan several experiences to provide provocations for all children in the preschool around Sikh culture such as:

- child-led inquiry: 'Why do you think they wear them?'
- explicit teaching times such as small and large groups
- parent/carer discussions
- dress-ups of culturally specific clothes
- sharing of other aspects of the culture; for example, food, music, dance
- links to values, beliefs and language.

You plan to document children's initial thoughts through recording their thinking prior to any planned learning experiences to see how their understandings shift over time. During planned learning experiences, you use a range of methods, including photo reflections, your own notes, children's drawings and scribing their reflections, collation of answers to provocations and questions.

Following the implementation of your planned learning experience, you reflect on the evidence you have collected. How has the child's understanding changed throughout the learning experience? What had the greatest impact? What did the evidence suggest were the next steps to take? How will you highlight the learning that has occurred?

**SPOTLIGHT ON HASS EDUCATION**

## EDUCATOR TIP

Some useful tips when creating planned learning experiences are:

- Individual learning plans are useful tools for consolidating the evidence that informs teaching and learning for each child and links that information to goals and planned learning experiences. Augmenting these plans with reflections from families and children is a powerful way of planning in partnership for quality learning outcomes.

- Think about the role you will take in a learning experience before committing to a method of collecting evidence of children's learning. You will likely need to have multiple options available as you assume different roles within the learning experience.

- iPads or tablet devices are an excellent resource to support educators in capturing the essence of learning through typing or writing notes, or taking photos or making short films to reflect upon after the learning experience concludes.

## LEARNING FOR PROFESSIONAL GROWTH

Ongoing professional development provides a powerful support for enhancing pedagogical practice. As educators, we must continually challenge and stretch our thinking to refine our pedagogies through our contextual lens in order to continue to evolve practice to meet the diverse needs of learners. With this in mind, educators also need to consider the diverse nature of their own learning needs; one person's 'stretch' may be another's 'bread and butter'.

Continually reflecting on our own learning needs through the examination of what we know, what we need to consolidate and what the gaps are needs to be a critical and rigorous process in itself. Engagement in this reflective process and identification of goals are pertinent at all stages of the educator's professional career.

**professional learning**: learning experiences that impact and support reflections and shifts in pedagogy

As is the case with children, planning for our own **professional learning** needs should be viewed as a cycle where reflection is the book-end of each cycle. Our learning needs should be contextualised through consideration of prior knowledge, the context in which we work (i.e. community and site needs) as well as broader organisational goals, and align with our pedagogical approaches before we select goals and professional learning experiences and activities that will support professional growth.

**Reflection**    What are the key drivers of my professional learning?

This was a question that I asked myself regularly as an early career educator, and it is still one that has purpose in my reflections as an experienced educator. Engaging with this line of questioning as part of your reflections around your own learning will position your thinking in your pedagogical space as you begin to develop the next steps in your professional learning, and serve to reposition your professional learning priorities and refine your pedagogy (DEEWR 2010).

If we consider that our world view is a sociocultural construct that is shaped by our understanding and engagement within our world, then developing awareness through critical reflection on how our understandings have been constructed and continue to be influenced is pertinent to ongoing professional learning (Dahlberg, Moss & Pence 1999). Being mindful of how their own bias will shape professional learning and focus enables the educator to select learning goals that provide challenge and stretch. Educators must also be responsive to the ever-changing needs and demands of the field, through operating via unscripted pedagogies (Whitington, Thompson & Shore 2014).

Reflect on a recent professional learning experience, address these questions:

- What are my key beliefs, theories and values?
- Have these been reflected in recent professional learning experiences with which I have engaged?
- If not, what were the underlying beliefs, theories and values that underpinned the professional learning experience? How do those sit in relation to my views?
- How have my understandings evolved as a result of engaging in the professional learning experience?

Reflection

## Goal setting

Goal setting is about considering the outcome you want to achieve in your professional learning. What is the shift you are looking to enact, the belief you want to challenge or the practice you wish to consolidate? Educators should avoid attending numerous one-off professional learning opportunities or seeing professional learning as an 'event'; instead, it is best to view professional learning as part of a cycle, much like children's learning is viewed through the cycle of planning. Reflection will assist your thinking in firming up where your focus could sit. It is vital to set goals that provide a defined purpose and clear outcomes for your professional learning.

Some questions to consider when setting goals are:

- What is the focus of my professional learning?
- Why have I selected this focus?
- What broad outcome am I looking to achieve?
- How will achieving this goal lead to improvement as a professional?
- How will this goal lead to improved learning outcomes for children?

## Discernment

Not all professional learning opportunities will be relevant for your purpose. It is about finding the right opportunities, at the right time, to support your current thinking or achievement of a professional learning goal that has been set through reflection. Fullan and Quinn (2016) discuss the idea that traditional notions of professional development do little to address the gap that exists between professional learning programs for educators and learning outcomes for learners; the key issue is the fragmented nature of professional learning that focuses on 'fixing' teaching as opposed to a focus on sustained attention to smaller goals over a period of time. This highlights a need for professional learning to be goal driven, with a focus on developing changes over time to ensure sustained change in educational practice. In selecting which professional learning opportunities to engage in, you should consider the following questions:

- Who facilitates the professional learning, and what is their background?
- How does this professional learning opportunity differ from others with a similar focus/content?
- How will this professional learning result in sustained change in practice?
- Will this professional learning offer something different from what I have engaged with previously?
- What opportunities exist for collaboration and shared learning?

Discernment is all about carefully selecting the opportunities you will engage with. As an early career educator, you will have numerous opportunities to engage in professional learning, at times during paid release from your educational setting. It is important to maximise your learning by ensuring you are engaged with quality professional learning experiences that will both support you as a developing educator and translate into benefits for the children you teach.

---

**SPOTLIGHT ON HASS EDUCATION**

## A PROFESSIONAL DEVELOPMENT DAY TOO FAR

I am someone who is often frustrated rather than inspired by certain forms of professional learning, specifically one-off professional development (PD) days that deliver a blanket one-size-fits-all approach to teaching and learning, and assume that the act of sitting through the session will automatically equate to a shift in thinking. As an early career educator, I looked for any professional learning opportunity I could, and attended one around cultural awareness early in my career. The design brief was that the session would provide a comprehensive overview of 'cultural awareness', including how I could be a more culturally aware educator. The training offered a stereotypical overview of several cultures from across the world and concluded with the presentation of several stereotypical cultural resources for purchase at the conclusion of the training, all of which were not produced by their respective countries of cultural origin. I walked away from this professional 'learning' experience with no real shift in my thinking.

In discussions with my line manager, I was directed to consider how I instead engaged with the cultural wealth available within our context. Subsequent conversations with families yielded far more purposeful and contextually appropriate information than I could have hoped for, leading to many families donating items of cultural significance to my preschool and sharing aspects of their culture, such as music, clothing, art and dance, with the other children and families at the preschool. This experience is one that continues to reinforce that the value of contextualised learning is also applicable to adults. We need to consider what the intended impact of professional learning is as part of a targeted professional development planning cycle. As is the case with planning for children's learning, we must reflect upon and question our own goals for learning, prior to planning and connecting with professional learning experiences.

## EDUCATOR TIP

To enhance your own professional learning:

- Engage in a continuous reflective cycle around your own learning. Professional learning will be far more purposeful and lead to sustainable change if your goals for professional learning are aligned with your broader learning needs.
- Take the time to reflect upon your own learning.
- Engage in critical dialogue and reflection about your learning with friends or a mentor as a support to any formal workplace processes.

## CONCLUSION

For early career educators, navigating early childhood education can be a challenging proposition as there is no singular approach that will provide the same impact in a given context. Articulation of your core educational beliefs and values, development of your philosophy for teaching and learning, and alignment with your pedagogy will ensure that your teaching will always be driven with a clear sense of purpose – your 'why'.

The 'how' of your teaching practice should continue to be shaped by deep engagement with the curriculum, informed by a clear cycle of planning that leads you to reflect on children's learning and connect it purposefully to your context, acting with intentionality and augmented by your personal and professional commitment to improving your teaching practice.

## REVIEW QUESTIONS

1. Why is play the foundation of early childhood learning?
2. How does inquiry assist children in HASS learning?
3. What is pedagogy, and why is it important?

4.   What is the early years cycle of planning?

5.   What is the role of reflection in professional learning?

## LEARNING EXTENSION

Open-ended questions offer children powerful opportunities for inquiry as they can be answered in multiple ways. Asking children open-ended question such as 'Which colour is the heaviest?' will encourage them to explore the nature of the question itself to answer it. The focus is on possible answers, and not on reaching one correct answer or even an answer that everyone can agree on.

Design an open-ended question (unable to be answered with a simple 'yes' or 'no' response) that engages children to think about the question itself, and generate possible answers rather than one 'correct' answer. Attempt to answer your question in as many different ways as you can.

## REFERENCES

Dahlberg, G., Moss, P. & Pence, A. (1999). *Beyond Quality in Early Childhood Education and Care: Postmodern perspectives*. Philadelphia, PA: Taylor and Francis.

DEEWR (Department of Education, Employment and Workplace Relations). (2009). *Belonging, Being and Becoming: The Early Years Learning Framework for Australia*. Canberra: DEEWR.

——(2010). *Educators Belonging, Being and Becoming: Educators' guide to the Early Years Learning Framework for Australia*. Retrieved from: http://files.acecqa.gov.au/files/National-Quality-Framework-Resources-Kit/educators_guide_to_the_early_years_learning_framework_for_australia.pdf.

Fullan, M. & Quinn, J. (2016). *Coherence: The right drivers in action for schools, districts, and systems*. Thousand Oaks, CA: Corwin Press.

Hargreaves, V. (2014). Children's theorising about their world: Exploring the practitioner's role. *Australasian Journal of Early Childhood*, 39(1), 30–7.

Malaguzzi, L. (1993). History, ideas and basic philosophy. In C. Edwards, L. Gandini & G. Forman, eds, *The Hundred Languages of Children*, Norwood, NJ: Ablex.

Moore, D. (2014). Interrupting listening to children: Researching with children's secret places in early childhood settings. *Australasian Journal of Early Childhood*, 39(2), 4–11.

Murdoch, K. (2015). *The Power of Inquiry*. Melbourne: Seastar Education.

Rizvi, F. & Lingard, B. (2010). *Globalizing Education Policy*. New York: Routledge.

Rogoff, B. (2003). *The Cultural Nature of Human Development*. New York: Oxford University Press.

Taylor, S., Rizvi, F., Lingard, B. & Henry, M. (2006). *Educational Policy and the Politics of Change*, 2nd edn. New York: Routledge.

Whitington, V., Thompson, C. & Shore, S. (2014). 'Time to ponder': Professional learning in early childhood education. *Australasian Journal of Early Childhood*, 39(1), 65–72.

# EARLY CAREER TEACHING IN THE PRIMARY YEARS

**29**

*Deana Cuconits*

## Learning objectives

After reading this chapter, you should be able to:

- understand how to bridge connections between the curriculum and learning design
- evaluate ways in which you can direct your own ongoing professional learning to inform your teaching practice
- apply some practical ideas related to planning, programming and designing engaging learning experiences in the context of Humanities and Social Sciences (HASS) teaching
- recognise a range of effective pedagogies to engage learners in HASS and appreciate the role of materials, models, language and recording in scaffolding learners' understanding
- analyse a range of assessment strategies to enhance learner outcomes for learning, as learning and of learning.

## INTRODUCTION

Upon entering the teaching profession, new educators can become overwhelmed by the diversity of teaching demands, not least finding time and space to navigate an ever-evolving curriculum. The HASS learning area is complex, yet it provides scope to explore a rich and diverse range of concepts through time, place and space on a **global** scale.

**global**: relating to the whole world or an entire group of things

Through studying HASS, learners develop the ability to question, think critically, solve problems, communicate effectively, make decisions and adapt to change. This chapter aims to provide early career educators with practical steps to success for implementing effective and engaging HASS learning experiences in educational contexts for primary and middle years learners.

## STEP 1: START WITH THE CURRICULUM

*Build your understanding of what needs to be learnt before you start deciding how you will teach it.*

For optimal learner understanding, HASS must be taught in an intertwined manner and incorporate all four subjects (History, Geography, Civics and Citizenship, and Economics and

Business) rather than being taught in a segregated way. Educators must ensure that importance is shifted to skill development rather than individual concept knowledge. The most effective way to ensure that teaching is learner centred and outcomes focused is for educators to develop a strong understanding of the concepts outlined in the Australian Curriculum (see Chapter 5) (what learners will need to know) and make decisions aligned to these concepts, after consulting with learners about what they already know (ACARA 2018).

**investigation:** searching or inquiring to determine facts or information related to a real-world scenario

In planning, consider the inquiry questions, then the achievement standard, before searching externally for ideas. Before commencing your **investigation** of the curriculum, have all the information and necessary equipment close at hand. This method ensures you have optimal opportunity to investigate, while avoiding distractions by searching for things or needing to break your concentration to find a pencil or your notebook.

## What might I need?

The following tools should be at hand when you are planning:

- curriculum information
- A3 paper or a note-taking template if you like to organise your thoughts from the start
- pedagogical framework advice; for example, the Teaching for Effective Learning (TfEL) Framework (SA TfEL 2010; discussed later in the chapter)
- highlighters and markers
- sticky notes
- resources to inspire your own thinking, such as books and internet resources
- scheduled, uninterrupted time to organise your thinking.

It is important that you build a solid understanding of the previous year level's required skills and concepts to determine the suggested competency within each content area. This can be achieved by reading the previous year's curriculum to ascertain the knowledge base learners already have. When reading the curriculum, begin with the year level overview, followed by the achievement standard, key inquiry questions and content descriptors. The portfolios of learners' work samples are an excellent resource to gain an understanding of what learners' work should look like for each year level, as well as providing hints about the types of tasks you could plan for learners. This is a particularly useful resource for educators who are working with a year level with which they are unfamiliar.

## EDUCATOR TIP

Taking the time to develop authentic and real-world learning experiences and design them in such a way that invokes a sense of mystery and inquisitiveness, which will result in learners developing much deeper understandings of the content. Choose a topic that is relevant to your local context by utilising community resources such as the state/territory library or your local council.

# STEP 2: ENGAGE YOURSELF – YOU NEED TO LOVE THE CONTENT TOO!

*The most effective learning experiences for learners occur when the educator is visibly passionate and connected to the content themselves.*

Select a topic area that you know will enthuse learners, connect to their real-life worlds and enable **community engagement**. Make notes as you progress with your own learning in this area, and consider:

- What did you find new and interesting?
- What concepts were more challenging for you to understand?
- What resources did you find useful (keep a list on your USB in your 'HASS' folder of all the useful websites you visit).

**community engagement**: refers to the process of connecting and involving learners with community members or facilities

## A CHALLENGING CROWD

Early in my career, I taught a rather challenging class of Year 7s (in South Australia, Year 7 students are taught in the primary sector with one core teacher). I was so passionate about teaching HASS that I could hardly wait for our first lesson together. Our unit of work tackled the concepts outlined in the first depth study: Investigating our Ancient Past and the inquiry question: How do we know about the ancient past? The first lesson was on a Tuesday after lunch and I recall being met with a resounding groan, but this did not deter my enthusiasm. After this first lesson, it became clear that many of the learners perceived HASS as a compulsory subject that was aimed only at filling them with unimportant information that they would never use.

It became my mission to share with these learners some of the exciting possibilities in HASS learning. The next week we were scheduled to investigate archaeology. In my initial planning, I outlined that we would watch an excerpt of a documentary exploring the unveiling of the Egyptian tombs followed by an investigation of the many incredible artefacts found on the British Museum website. This lesson would have effectively exposed learners to all of the concepts I had intended to teach. However, I had a new goal; my aim was not to simply 'teach' the content – I wanted learners to deeply 'understand' it, to connect with it and make meaning from it. They needed to understand the 'why' of learning about archaeology and, more deeply, the 'why' of learning HASS.

I made my way to the local shopping centre and filled a basket with all sorts of objects – these were to become my 'artefacts', which would be buried in the sandpit. As the lesson began, I pulled out a box full of tools and brushes, showing them to the class and asking what they thought we might do with them. They came up with a whole range of suggestions and I left them to wonder as they followed me outside. We spent the next 30 minutes in the sandpit digging, brushing and carefully extracting artefacts of all shapes and colours – matchbox cars, cups, plates, toy animals and table tennis balls – using the techniques and strategies we had observed in the previous lesson in the video outlining the process of archaeological digging. I watched learners squeal with delight over a small plastic tiger and one of the most challenging learners reprimand his peer for trying to 'yank out' their buried treasure instead of carefully brushing the sand away like they were 'supposed to'.

As we headed back to class to pack up, this same learner ran up alongside me and asked whether we would be having HASS again that week.

**SPOTLIGHT ON HASS EDUCATION**

This scenario is a small example of how restructuring the delivery of a lesson, in response to the needs of the learners in your class, can positively engage learners and foster a deep connection with the content. This lesson reinforced the observations made by learners during an archaeology video by providing them with a concrete experience to explore various techniques. McInerney (2010) identifies the following key criteria that 21st-century educators ought to exemplify:

- Be flexible and responsive to learners' needs and interests.
- Inspire curiosity and critical analysis, building a mindset of lifelong learning.
- Be creative in their approaches to teaching, developing a culture of collaboration to engage learners in **higher-order thinking** and problem-solving.
- Develop learning programs that are connected to current events and enable opportunities to embrace teachable moments.
- Provide opportunities for learners to explore their learning in authentic contexts, while also involving learners in decision-making related to what, when and how they undertake their learning.

**higher-order thinking:**
involves learners undertaking tasks that require further cognitive processing

---

**Reflection**

As their educator, I was aware of the physical and cognitive needs of my cohort and, through observations made during the initial introduction to the topic, I altered the delivery of my lessons to connect with and engage learners. Possessing a strong understanding of the content enables educators to readily adapt and modify their pedagogy responsively.

- Discuss how you would follow up the lesson described in the Spotlight on HASS education.
- Reflect on your own practical experiences in the classroom, and consider a lesson you have observed or implemented that could have been restructured to promote maximum engagement for learners. What could you do differently?

---

## EDUCATOR TIP

One of the most important components of teaching is continuous reflection. I have never taught the same lesson twice – by this I mean that I always do something differently on the next occasion, whether altering the time allocations, changing the method of instruction, rephrasing the content or removing unnecessary elements. Reflection is not just a crucial step for learners to undertake in order to cement understanding; it is just as important for educators to consistently consider ways to enhance their practice.

# STEP 3: PLANNING AND PROGRAMMING – WORK BACKWARDS AND START WITH THE END IN MIND

*Educators know what they want to achieve before they start planning by using a cross-curriculum and outcomes-focused approach.*

There is no right way to plan or program lessons and it is normal to adapt and change as you go along – programs and unit plans ought to be working documents that are developed depending on what works. Reflect on what is important for you to know about the learning journey before you begin. These questions are useful to consider:

- What do I want learners to understand?
- What do I want learners to be able to do?
- How might I know if they have learnt these things?
- What does this group of learners need?
- What are these learners interested in?
- Which of these concepts connect to this inquiry?

Some educators require full lesson outlines, including question prompts and task sheets, in order to feel comfortable and prepared, whereas others prefer to use a brief outline with personalised notes alongside their curriculum guide. What is important is that the learning you have designed is clearly aligned to the expectations outlined in the curriculum, with clear consideration of pedagogical approaches in line with current educational research.

## EDUCATOR TIP

Beginning a learning experience with a clear understanding of the direction in which you are heading in terms of your year, term and weekly learning plans will ensure the skills and understandings towards which you are working are effectively and cohesively presented.

## Programming

There is a distinct difference between preparation and programming. Preparing for a lesson involves organising resources and ensuring the learning space is equipped for what the educator has planned. The physical organisation of equipment and resources can drastically affect the flow and pace of lessons and these factors need careful thought (Hoodless 2008). Consider the structure of the lesson, for example: will learners work collaboratively, will they be required to move around the room, what will they need access to? Structuring the teaching space to reflect the needs of the lesson prior to it beginning will ensure smooth implementation and transitions.

Programming is the overall development of a learning sequence; these sequences are designed to expose learners to the concepts outlined in the curriculum in a cohesive, consistent and logical order. Programming for HASS ought to be completed in three tiers: year overview, term overview and unit plan.

The first step in this tiered planning approach is to consider the whole picture; that is, what elements of the curriculum will be covered, when will they be covered, and what will the overarching focus for each term involve? A good place to start is with the inquiry questions for your year level, and these should become your 'themes'. From this brief year overview, educators will make decisions about how they will teach the content and pull this together in a term overview over 8–10 weekly sessions, followed by cohesive unit plans outlining the specific teaching strategies and learning outcomes.

## Planning with inquiry learning

The Australian Curriculum promotes the idea of inquiry-based pedagogy in the planning and teaching of HASS. However, educators' understanding and interpretation of inquiry learning is widely varied (see Chapter 11). A common misconception is that learners must develop their own learning investigations independently; that is, develop their own questions and then find their own sources for research. In the primary years it is particularly important that educators facilitate and closely guide the process of inquiry learning, preparing learners for secondary level HASS learning. The Australian Curriculum (ACARA 2018) stipulates that even at Year 7 in the area of inquiry and skills students will:

- Construct significant questions and propositions to guide investigations about people, events, developments, places, systems and challenges (ACHASSI152)
- Apply a methodology to locate and collect relevant information and data from a range of primary and secondary sources (ACHASSI153) (ACARA 2018).

Thus, following the construction of their own questions to *guide* the inquiry investigation that has been supplied by the educator, learners ought to be provided with appropriate primary and secondary sources for analysis. Therefore, the educator's role in scaffolding the inquiry process during the primary years is extremely involved, and it is not until Year 8 that learners must undertake these processes independently, as stipulated in the Australian Curriculum:

- Identify and locate relevant sources, using ICT and other methods (ACHHS151)
- Identify a range of questions about the past to inform a historical inquiry (ACHHS150) (ACARA 2018).

Kath Murdoch's (2010) inquiry learning model differs from the inquiry learning pedagogy often discussed in early childhood literature. In the early years, the role of the educator in implementing this model in HASS is perhaps even more crucial. Learners in the early years are making connections and forming new understandings at an incredibly rapid rate. They are rarely equipped with the vocabulary or knowledge of their own learning processes to effectively design the inquiry experiences that will provide them with the skills and understandings expected for their level of schooling. It is imperative that, while utilising early childhood pedagogy to build learners' understanding in areas of interest and passion, educators are developing learning programs that scaffold learners to obtain the outcomes outlined in the Australian Curriculum. As outlined by Murdoch (2010, p. 4), 'When students are given the choice of what they will pursue, how they will pursue it and how they will share their learning with others – they are challenged to use important skills in decision making, planning and problem solving.'

Figure 29.1 is a visual representation of Murdoch's inquiry learning model. Although it is presented as a flowchart, this model should be regarded as cyclical in nature and sections may need to be revisited or repeated during the learning experience. The model is one example of effectively structuring an inquiry learning program in HASS to ensure learners are exposed to the skills and content expected for their year level.

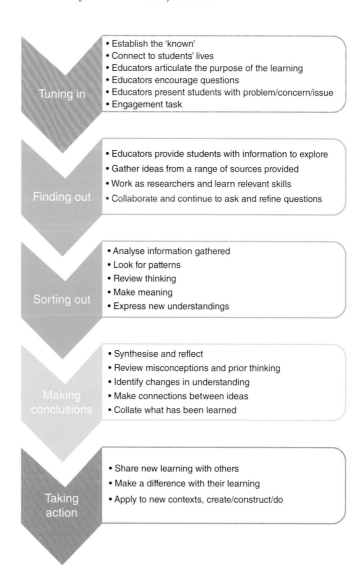

FIGURE 29.1 **Inquiry learning model**
Source: adapted from Murdoch 2010

# EDUCATOR TIP

Seek a mentor or colleague with whom you are able to plan and discuss learning resources. An experienced educator will be able to support you to answer any questions you may have, and perhaps save you time by assisting in creating resources or sharing their own resources with you.

## Learning design

It is important that educators carefully consider learning design and plan for HASS with assessment in mind; the accompanying website materials for this chapter provide an example sequence template that can be adapted and altered to suit different learning areas and year levels. A range of theoretical frameworks exist to support planning for educators, including the:

- understanding by design (UbD) framework (McTighe & Wiggins 1999), which is an example of backward planning design; that is, looking at the outcomes in order to design curriculum units of work, assessments and classroom instruction
- inquiry learning model (Murdoch 2010) (discussed earlier)
- Teaching for Effective Learning Framework (SA, TfEL 2010), which supports leaders and educators in working together to reflect on and develop quality learning and teaching; it provides an 'internal compass' for guiding designs for learning and decision-making about practice.

When educators plan prescriptively and purposefully, deeper learner outcomes are achieved and learner engagement is increased. Planning by design promotes higher-order thinking and enables cross-curriculum priorities and general capabilities to be embedded decisively within the learning sequence.

# EDUCATOR TIP

The taking action phase is particularly critical in the Geography learning area. Engaging students in Geography learning that is connected to a local context is easily accessible, yet often educators opt to focus on global contexts that have limited connection to learners. While this learning has its place, opportunities to explore real-world situations where learners have the potential to act on their findings and make a difference to their community are far too special to ignore.

## Integrating learning and cross-curriculum priorities

Drawing on concepts of disciplinary thinking, the Australian Curriculum identifies seven concepts that underpin HASS understanding as a whole. Educators must aim to embed these ways of thinking within the key ideas and conceptual understandings they develop across their annual HASS program. These concepts are outlined in Chapter 5.

HASS thinking for learners can often be described through a process of responding to questions that can be easily adapted or developed into more in-depth questions for inquiry. A basic framework is found in Mills (2013):

1. What happened?
2. When did it happen?
3. Why did it happen?
4. How did it happen?
5. Who was responsible?

This framework supports the thinking in this quote from Touhill (2012, p. 2): 'When learners reflect on what they have done in the past; plan for what they are going to do in the future; and have the opportunity to discuss, refine and modify their plans as they progress, their learning and thinking becomes far more complex.'

# STEP 4: IMMERSION AND ADVENTURE

*Learning should feel like an adventure, a never-ending journey of discovery.*

Here, 'immersion' refers to the learning experiences learners undertake with the educator as their guide. The richness of learning that is possible when learners are involved in negotiating and designing a learning experience that is relevant and authentic is truly inspiring. Creating authentic learning opportunities is possible when educators explore the connections between the curriculum concepts, as well as with their local community. Educators should consider:

- Where can I go for information or to further explore these concepts?
- Can I give learners access to firsthand experiences with this content?

The local council can be an excellent resource for local information relevant for learning in HASS (see Chapter 24).

## EDUCATOR TIP

Seek professional learning opportunities to expand your understanding of teaching, learning and local educational opportunities. Joining professional organisations such as the Geography Teachers' Association or History Teachers' Association is an excellent way to ensure you are aware of when such opportunities are occurring.

In all learning areas, it is crucial to teach to the learner's ability, not just their year level. For example, it would be ineffective to teach the idea of paragraphs in English before a child can write a sentence. It is the educator's responsibility to set up learners for success. You can do this by observing what learners need as you are working through the learning plan. If you provide a research task to introduce a concept to learners, you cannot expect them to be able to effectively interrogate their sources or know when they have found relevant information. Educators must provide sufficient prior experiences to learners before they can expect them to effectively research to consolidate their understandings. Educators must give learners access to year level-appropriate tasks *and* be prepared to scaffold and extend (differentiate) for those who need it.

**Reflection**

Reflect on times when you have presented new themes or inquiries to learners. How effectively have you engaged learners in this initial introduction?

Consider the inquiry process and critical thinking strategies. With these in mind, how might you modify your initial introduction?

## Practical tools for engagement

Displays can be used as an inexpensive teaching resource to engage and motivate learners without needing to spend a lot of time working through their ideas during class time. For example, a timeline can be constructed and displayed across the window depicting the period of time being investigated or an interactive display exploring artefacts used for open-ended questioning sessions, which could be extended throughout the sequence of lessons. The classroom atmosphere can be enhanced by these types of displays, which effectively bring into the classroom features of the outside world, linking learners' real-life worlds with their classroom learning (Hoodless 2008).

Guest speakers can be an engaging way to expose learners to the past, through hearing people talk about real-life memories and experiences. Speakers might talk about how their jobs have altered over time or how toys have evolved. Local groups associated with councils are often able to assist with finding suitable visitors to support oral history lessons (Hoodless 2008).

HASS teaching is brought to life in classrooms when educators feel that they are able to engage with the concerns they see as relevant in their current lives. Another incredibly useful pedagogical engagement tool is involving learners in decision-making. There is much research to suggest that when learners feel valued and connected to their school community they achieve higher-quality outcomes in all learning areas (e.g. see Bruner 1964; Erikson 1950; Sigel & Cocking 1977). Using engagement tools such as a mystery is a simple, yet highly effective, hook for learners to begin a learning journey in HASS. The mystery that is introduced to them can be presented in such a way that it promotes critical thinking and raises key inquiry questions.

## EXAMPLE ENGAGEMENT EXERCISE

This is an example of an inquiry based on the Ross Female Factory in Tasmania.

You discover a tattered, yellowing suit case with the name 'M.A. Clark' scrawled across it. When you open the case, you discover the following items:

- a map of Ross, Tasmania
- some rusty nails and thick yarn
- an 1850s-style bonnet
- six cracked 'olden-style' white buttons
- a small fraying Bible
- a torn front page from the Tasmanian newspaper *The Guardian* dated 22 May 1847
- the following short note.

*My Dear Fred,*

*It is with pleasure I now write these few lines to you with my sincere love, hoping you will not forget to send me five shillings as you know I had none when I was taken and you know it is of use to me in here. You can send it to me by the Priest, he will bring me anything you send.*

*Dear Fred I hope you will be steady till I come out as I intend to keep sober and steady and if you send a Memorial in you can get me out and go to [our] child in the Orphanage in town she is in town now.*

*Dear Fred send to me by Father Woolfrey I shall expect an answer by next Friday. Dear Fred I am surprised to think you should spend your hard earned money with that [other] woman old enough to be your Mother but I hope Dear Fred you know better for the future do not forget to write to me and send me some money I now conclude with my love to you.*

*Yours,*
*M.A. Clark.*
(Cranage et al. 2004)

## EDUCATOR TIP

Artefacts or objects such as briefcases or old envelopes are great tools for engaging learners with the concepts you are introducing.

Learners are immediately drawn in by the mystery of who these objects belong to, why they are in the case and how they may have ended up in there. The inquiry question that could be developed around this mystery may connect to the Year 6 curriculum: Australia as a Nation, or Year 2: Our past and present connections to people and places. Once learners have figured out the mystery connected to these particular artefacts, they can use the skills and ideas that they have learnt to further investigate what life was like during colonial Australia. This particular inquiry task can be modified and adapted to suit a range of different topics, including migration – the contents could include objects related to an immigrant's home for learners to understand where they have come from.

Educators can further enhance this learning experience by incorporating opportunities for learners to explore artefacts related to the subject content. Presenting sources of information can be made all the more exciting simply by placing the information in an envelope labelled 'Evidence Bag'. Learners instantly view themselves as detectives and investigators – active problem solvers rather than receptive participants. These types of strategies support active engagement for learners at all levels of schooling by presenting a challenge that involves discovery and investigation in an interesting and mysterious way.

Information and communication technology (ICT) provides a plethora of tools to enhance teaching and learning in HASS. For example, interviews can be conducted with archaeologists at the pyramids of Giza via Skype; learners can communicate and seek advice from interagency blogs; or they can investigate a carefully scaffolded WebQuest designed to enhance their learning. See also Chapter 25.

## EDUCATOR TIP

A WebQuest is an effective way for educators to encourage learners to explore concepts through well-scaffolded tasks that provide opportunities for independent research with robust sources that have been interrogated and approved prior to learner access. WebQuests are guided internet searches where learners collaborate to investigate problem-based scenarios. This method of investigation should support learners with establishing the skills required to identify relevant resources within the expanse of the World Wide Web. Structuring a WebQuest gives educators the opportunity to design tasks as rich, real and engaging challenges that are often developed using a free website generator. Common features of WebQuests include:

- an outline of the task
- a timeline for completion
- websites to consult
- an assessment rubric
- multiple-choice/short-answer questions
- customised puzzles.

# STEP 5: AUTHENTIC ASSESSMENT

Assessment is often labelled as one of the most challenging elements of early career teaching, yet it is one of the most important components of a teaching program. The UbD approach described in Step 3 encourages educators to begin with the end in mind; that is, to develop the final assessment task and then piece together the learning that will be required in order for learners to experience success in their summative task (refer to Chapter 15).

## Presenting a problem

Authentic assessment should be designed, where possible, around a real-world problem where learners can showcase and celebrate any new learning that has taken place. Summative assessment tasks can be developed to share the learning with other members of the school community and the learner's family.

### Example problem-based assessment task

When designing the assessment task, consider how the problem can be pitched to learners. For example, rather than writing an assessment requiring a 'poster' about one dynasty of ancient China, suggest to learners that the local museum Director has decided she would like to create a new exhibit exploring ancient China and present the following task.

> The Museum Director is unsure about which time periods, significant events and people should be showcased in her exhibition. I have offered to task my class with the job of working in teams to provide her with a portfolio or presentation of your choice outlining information regarding one of the dynasties we have explored in class. You should include artefacts, people, events and places that the Director would need to incorporate into her display. The exhibit will be designed to include displays on all five of the dynasties we have investigated. Your portfolio should also include a visual example of how your information and artefacts could be displayed.

## Designing assessment tasks

Carefully designing assessment tasks, such as the one described above, promotes the development of deeper learning experiences as learners immerse themselves in the role they have been tasked with and approach their learning in an **inquisitive** and investigative manner.

Another important element to consider when designing assessment is how you will provide the information to the learners. Learners should be provided with a task sheet that clearly outlines the requirements of the task, including numbered steps to scaffold the process. At the beginning of the task, learners should also have the opportunity to view and negotiate the **rubric** with the educator. Discussing the content of the rubric is a great way for learners to take ownership of their learning and responsibility for their outcomes.

**inquisitive:** having an intellectually curious disposition towards areas of unknown information

**rubric:** a scoring guide, in the form of a table, used to evaluate the quality of work produced in relation to specific agreed criteria

# MOCK TRIAL

The following assessment task was developed for HASS learning in Years 5, 6 and 7. The curriculum connections learners are working towards are:

- How does Australia's legal system aim to provide justice, including through the rule of law, presumption of innocence, burden of proof, right to a fair trial and right to legal representation?
- How are laws developed in Australia?
- How do laws affect the lives of citizens?
- What principles of justice help to protect the individual's rights to justice in Australia's system of law?

**mock trial** a simulated role play of trial legal proceedings undertaken by learners to develop understanding around the processes and procedures of court proceedings

Learners use a familiar children's story/fairy tale to develop and create a **mock trial** to explore the legal concepts they have learnt about throughout the unit of work. They use the knowledge gained from their research in courts to conduct a fair trial. The trial will involve every learner in the class and will be presented to parents and the community on 'Trial Day'.

Snippets of an example mock trial can be used to scaffold learners on how to conduct a fair trial. The story of 'Goldilocks and the Three Bears' could be used to develop a case against Goldilocks using the constraints of the legal system to seek justice.

Learners conduct their mock trial and present their evidence, walking through the process of a criminal trial. Guests from the community can be invited, as well as parents, staff and students from other classes. This summative assessment task has scope to be educator, peer and self-assessed through the development of rubrics outlining the key components of a successful trial.

For more discussion of these issues, see http://www.adelaidelawcourts.weebly.com.

**Reflection**

How could you, as an educator, develop a similar style of task for learners in a topic area you have explored previously?

How have you altered the previous task or the way in which it was delivered?

# CONCLUSION

Early in my career, I came to the intense realisation that there was a diversity of learner needs in my classroom. Tumbling after that thought came the realisation that there was a lot of knowledge I would need to gather quickly in order to meet those needs. Scaffolding learning and designing tasks that are rich and engaging is the key to developing powerful lifelong learners who have a passion for discovery and are inspired to tackle challenges. This cannot be achieved without clear information about the learners with whom we are working and in particular the knowledge they bring with them.

The most important gift educators can impart to learners is a belief in their ability to be successful. Beyond the constraints of their outside influences, we must hold high expectations for learners and always remain true to the fact that the educator's role is to help them to progress and succeed.

Highly effective educators maintain a commitment to continual development and critical reflection on their practice. As an early career educator, strive to be true to yourself and your beliefs about teaching and learning, and with a rich scope of skills and knowledge to share, have the confidence to do things differently. Aspire to open doors for learners – introduce them to the wonders of the past, present and future.

## REVIEW QUESTIONS

1. Describe a connection between the HASS concept, democratic decision making in Australia, and another learning area in the Year 5 curriculum.

2. Develop a list of field trip ideas related to HASS curriculum concepts that are accessible for you to attend with learners in your local area.

3. Imagine that your year-level team has decided that the focus area of your next HASS unit of work will be natural disasters. Explain how you might introduce this theme and engage learners in the learning experience. Include key questions you might ask as well as any resources or representations you might use.

4. Design a sequence of learning activities that could be used to develop understanding around timelines and the concepts of BCE and CE.

5. Design an activity to assess learners' understanding of the Year 3 inquiry question: What events do different people and groups celebrate and commemorate and what does this tell us about our communities?

## LEARNING EXTENSION

All of us want to know how the world works: why a piece of music is beautiful to one person and cacophonous to another, how engines are able to make cars move, why green leaves turn brown and helium balloons stay aloft, or how new languages develop. Living means perpetually searching for meaning. Schools need to be places that keep this search alive. (Brooks & Brooks 1999, p. 102)

Respond to this statement, reflecting in particular on the final sentence. Referring to the concepts discussed in the steps outlined in this chapter, provide some suggestions of ways educators can create the type of environment alluded to by Brooks and Brooks, supporting learners on their search for meaning in HASS.

## FURTHER READING

Fridley, D. (2011). Easier than it looks: Using web resources in the humanities. In *Teaching the Humanities Online: A practical guide to the virtual classroom*. New York: Armonk, pp. 112–24.

Green, B. (2003). An unfinished project?: Garth Boomer and the pedagogical imagination. *Opinion: Journal of the South Australian English Teachers' Association*, 47(2), 13–24.

Halat, E. (2008). A good teaching technique: WebQuests. *The Clearing House: A Journal of Educational Strategies, Issues and Ideas*, 81, 109–12.

Reynolds, R. (2014). Inquiry pedagogy. In *Teaching Humanities and Social Sciences in the Primary School*, 3rd edn (pp. 32–98). Melbourne: Oxford University Press.

Romero, T. & Carroll, M. (2011). Using a democratic classroom approach to teach humanities. *An Interactive Model, International Journal of Arts & Sciences*, 4(21), 169–74.

## REFERENCES

ACARA (Australian Curriculum, Assessment and Reporting Authority). (2018). *Australian Curriculum: F-10, v8.3*. Retrieved from: https://www.australiancurriculum.edu.au/f-10-curriculum.

Brooks, M.G. & Brooks, J.G. (1999). The courage to be constructivist. In J.G. Brooks & M.G. Brooks, *In Search of Understanding: The case for constructivist classrooms*. Alexandria, VA: ASCD.

Bruner, J. (1964). The course of cognitive growth. *American Psychologist*, 19(1), 1–15.

Cranage, T., Gurry, T., Lewis, R. & Neal, D. (2004). Australian History Mysteries: What was life like for female convicts at a female factory? National Museum of Australia, sourced from Mitchell Library Tasmanian Papers, No. 90, 8770 October 1847.

Erikson, E.H. (1950). *Childhood and Society*. New York: W.W. Norton.

Hoodless, P. (2008). Understanding and using teaching strategies in primary history. In P. Hoodless, *Teaching History in Primary Schools*. Exeter: Learning Matters.

McInerney, M. (2010). Implications of 21st century change and the geography curriculum. *Geographical Education*, 23, 23–31.

McTighe J. & Wiggins, G. (1999). *The Understanding by Design Handbook*. Alexandra, VA: ASCD.

Mills, K. (2013). *Teaching History in the Digital Age (Digital Humanities)*. Ann Arbor, MI: University of Michigan Press.

Murdoch, K. (2010). *The Power of Inquiry*. Melbourne: Seastar Education.

SA TfEL (2010). *South Australian Teaching for Effective Learning: Framework guide*. Adelaide: Government of South Australia. Retrieved from: https://www.education.sa.gov.au/sites/g/files/net691/f/tfel_framework_guide_complete.pdf.

Sigel, I.E. & Cocking, R.R. (1977). *Cognitive Development from Childhood to Adolescence: A constructivist perspective*. New York: Holt, Rinehart and Winston.

Touhill, L. (2012). Inquiry-based learning. *National Quality Standard Professional Learning Program e-newsletter*, no. 45, July, Australian Children's Education and Care Quality Authority (ACECQA). Sydney: ACECQA.

# Index

Aboriginal and Torres Strait Islander cross-curriculum priorities
    challenges and shortcomings, 309
    making curriculum work, 319–20
    moral imperative, 310
    and pedagogy, 310–11
    REFLECT framework, 312–15
    Sustainability, 344, 351–2
Aboriginal and Torres Strait Islander histories and cultures
    and Australian Curriculum, 308–11
    described, 21
    Economics and Business, 183–4
Aboriginal and Torres Strait Islander learners, 309, 315–19
Aboriginal and Torres Strait Islander peoples
    Indigenous agency, 308
    Indigenous cultural competence, 114–15
    Indigenous cultural protocols, 317
    Indigenous knowledges, 344–6
    Indigenous perspectives, 351–2
    meaningful discussions, 317–19
    terminology, 309
    working with Elders, 413
Aboriginal Education Consultative Group (AECG), 317
Aboriginal Interpreter Service (AIS), 317
achievement standards
    and capabilities, 302–4
    and concepts, 99
    definition, 20, 264
    Geography, 153
    Year 6, 405
    Year 7, 98–100
    year level, 31
acquisition learning, 459
acting, 506–7
active citizenship, 106
active learning, 111, 200–1
advertising, 191
affective skills, 202
aims, 166
analysis, 29, 130, 162, 188–9
Anglocentric traditions, 329
animation, 462
Anthropocene, 145, 344
ANZACs, 207
archives, 440
art forms, 183
artefacts, 440, 515
arts, sustainability, 355–6
artwork, 111
Asia, 22, 328, 476
Asia and Australia's engagement with Asia
    Australian Curriculum, 327, 333
    *Australian Curriculum: HASS*, 330–4, 338–9
    and capabilities, 334–7
    described, 22, 327

Economics and Business, 183–4
    in educational setting, 336–7
    key organising ideas, 333–4
    why study, 328–9
Asia literacy, 329–30
assessment
    Australian Curriculum, 48–53
    authentic, 269, 525
    characteristics of quality, 270–4
    and concepts, 97
    criteria, 265
    described, 263
    early childhood setting, 116
    Early Years Learning Framework (EYLF), 48–53
    effective, 265–9
    Geography, 153
    and integrated curriculum, 36
    methods, 267
    principles, 265
    purpose, 263–5
    *see also* evidence
assessment for learning (AfL), 131
assessment literacy, 267–9
assessment tasks
    authentic, 269
    definition, 264
    designing, 525
    quality, 270–2
augmentation of technology, 453
Australian Bureau of Statistics (ABS), 184, 251
Australian communities, 127
Australian Curriculum
    and Aboriginal and Torres Strait Islander histories and cultures, 308–11
    achievement standards, 264
    Asia and Australia's engagement with Asia, 327, 333
    assessment, 48–53
    capabilities, 22, 49, 169, 285–93, 334
    changes over time, 8
    components, 47, 123
    critical and creative thinking, 287
    cross-curriculum priorities, 21–3, 53
    definition, 3
    and Early Years Learning Framework (EYLF), 46–53
    ethical understanding, 292–3
    Foundation–Year 10, 282
    History in, 122–3
    history of, 6–8
    information and communication technology (ICT) capability, 287
    inquiry and skills strand, 518
    inquiry skills, 28–9
    intercultural understanding, 291, 334–5
    interdisciplinary concepts, 30
    learners living with a disability, 411
    learning areas, 8–9

Australian Curriculum (cont.)
   literacy, 248, 286
   and *Melbourne Declaration on Educational Goals for Young Australians*, 49
   navigating, 19–20
   numeracy, 287
   personal and social capability, 289–90
   resources, 125
   sequence of achievement, 125
   in states and territories, 9–10
Australian Curriculum, Assessment and Reporting Authority (ACARA), 8, 122, 285, 294, 307, 310–11
*Australian Curriculum: Civics and Citizenship*
   aims, 423
   connections, 167–71
   cross-curriculum priorities, 168–9
   inquiry and skills strand, 162–3
   knowledge and understanding strand, 161–3
   rationale, 161
   teaching/learning ethos, 164–7
*Australian Curriculum: Economics and Business*, knowledge and understanding strand, 176–85
*Australian Curriculum: Geography*
   community resources, 425
   concepts, 81–3, 137, 139, 143, 151
   F-10, 25
   teaching, 153–5
*Australian Curriculum: HASS*
   Asia and Australia's engagement with Asia, 330–4, 338–9
   background, 77
   and capabilities, 294–302
   concepts, 30–1, 78–80
   critical and creative thinking, 297–8
   definition, 3
   described, 10–11
   early learning context, 45
   ethical reasoning, 368–9
   ethical understanding, 300–2
   F-1, 49
   F-10 curriculum, 25, 27
   global emphases, 481
   inclusive, 404–5
   information and communication technology (ICT) capability, 296–7, 456–8
   inquiry and skills strand, 27–9
   intercultural understanding, 300
   investigation, 513–14
   key ideas, 11–14
   knowledge and understanding strand, 24–6
   and librarians, 469–75
   and libraries, 466–9
   literacy, 248, 295
   nature and purpose, 60–2
   numeracy, 295–6
   orientation, 45
   pedagogies for, 62–7
   personal and social capability, 298–9
   rationale, 3, 44, 465
   sequence of achievement, 125
   sequence of content, 125, 130
   strands, 54
   structure, 45
   subjects, 79–80
   sub-strands, 11
   and technology, 455–6
   value judgements, 368–9
   values, 12, 365–6
   years offered, 11, 24
*Australian Curriculum: History*
   background, 121
   F-10, 25
Australian Professional Standards for Teachers (APST), 267, 403, 411
Australian War Memorial, 427
authentic assessment, 269, 525
authentic learning, 206, 429–30

backward planning, 32–4
Bajau fisherman, 144
*Becoming, Belonging and Being: The Early Years Learning Framework for Australia. See* Early Years Learning Framework (EYLF)
belonging, sense of, 438
big questions, 216
biosphere, 143
books, 225, 252–5, 470–3
   *see also* picture books
*The Boy Who Cried Wolf*, 368
BRIDGE program, 336–7
Bruner, J., 206
budgets, 182
business, 175
Business. *See* Economics and Business
business environment, 182–3
business plans, 185

capabilities
   and achievement standards, 302–4
   and Asia and Australia's engagement with Asia, 334–7
   Australian Curriculum, 22, 49, 169, 285–93, 334
   and *Australian Curriculum: HASS*, 294–302
   described, 22
   and Early Years Learning Framework (EYLF), 293–4
   *see also* information and communication technology (ICT) capability; personal and social capability
capabilities perspective, 402
cause and effect, 82, 90–1, 99, 128
change, 82, 99, 148–9
   *see also* continuity and change
chat rooms, 460
child-centred learning, 202
child labour, 480
children's literature, 250, 252–5
China, 330–1
chocolate, 480
choice, 95, 99, 178
chronology, 70, 111
citations, 474
citizen capacity, 283–5

citizen science, 354–5
citizenry, 92
citizens, 161, 422–3
citizenship, 157, 159–60, 162, 380–6, 475
civics, 157
Civics and Citizenship
    achievement standards, 99
    concept wheels, 163
    concepts, 30, 92–3, 161–2
    definition, 78
    described, 160–1
    early childhood setting, 104–7, 111–16
    and Early Years Learning, 106
    eight ways to deliver, 165–6
    forms of learning, 111
    information and communication technology (ICT)
      capability, 457
    integrating education, 165–6
    key ideas, 13
    learning environments, 164–5
    learning sequences, 113–14
    and other subjects, 169
    and school types, 167
    teaching strategies, 111–12
    Year 3, 158–9
    Year 7, 99
    years offered, 11, 24
    *see also Australian Curriculum: Civics and*
      *Citizenship*
cloud-based services, 453
co-construction, 230, 241–2
co-design principles, 412–14
cognitive skills, 202
collaborative learning, 111, 460–1
collaborative moderation, 275–6
collaborative problem-solving, 272
collages, 93
collections, 440
common good, 66
communication, 29, 130, 162, 191–3, 202
communities, 170–1, 438–9
community engagement, 315–19, 515
community members, 413, 442–3, 445–8
community museums, 440, 445
community of ethical inquiry, 373–5
community of inquiry
    components, 216–19
    described, 215, 369–70
    discussion, 372–3
    ethical inquiry, 373–5
    preparation, 371–2
    prior-to-school settings, 221
    social justice, 371–2
    structure of sessions, 215–17
    units on, 23–4
    use of, 214–15
community organisations, 441
community resources
    advantages of using, 426–7
    contribution to learning, 428–31
    described, 424

    early childhood setting, 444–5
    examples, 434
    and inquiry learning, 431
    limitations, 427–8
    local, 439–43
    types of, 424–6
    using, 443–8
competitive advantage, 191
complex issues, 259
comprehension, 189
concept wheels, 82–3, 163
concepts
    and achievement standards, 99
    and assessment, 97
    Civics and Citizenship, 92–3, 161–2
    definition, 5, 59, 78–9, 81
    Economics and Business, 93–7
    first-order, 126
    Geography, 81–3, 137–51
    History, 83–92
    second-order, 126–7
    Year 7, 98–100
conceptual development, 206
conceptual exploration, 222
conceptual thinking, 79
conceptual understanding, 126–30
conflict resolution, 486
connected education, 249
consequences, 192
construction stage, 154
constructivism, 31
constructivist theorists, 205–9
consultation, 317
consumer literacy, 180–2
consumerism, 97, 99
consumers, 175, 178
containers, single-use, 356
content, 515–16
content descriptors, 20, 187–8, 190, 192
contention, 92
contestability, 88–9, 99, 129
continuity and change, 87–8, 99, 128
controversial issues, 259, 490–1
copyright, 475
cosmologies, 379
Council of Australian Governments (COAG), National
    Education Agreement (NEA), 19
creative body-based pedagogy, 407–9
Creative Commons, 475
creative thinking, 287, 297–8
creativity, 355–6
critical educators, 382
critical learning, 111
critical thinking, 206, 256–60, 287, 297–8
cross-curriculum priorities, 21–3, 49, 53, 168–9
cultural diversity, 251, 380–3, 386–7, 484–5
cultural globalisation, 482
cultural organisations, 439–40
culturally diverse classrooms, 312
culturally responsive education, 308
culturally responsive pedagogy, 312–15, 387–96, 406–7

curiosity, 44–5
curriculum
    definition, 3, 43, 404
    and educators, 112, 405, 513–14
    emergent, 34–6, 55
    integrated, 36–7
    planning, 34–6
    see also Australian Curriculum; Early Years Learning
        Framework (EYLF)
custodianship, 308
cycle of planning, 503–8

daily life, 410
data, 187, 269, 296, 457
death, 55
debate, 71–2
decision-making, 162, 189–90, 223
deconstruction stage, 154
democracy, 160–1, 257
democratic processes, 12
Design and Technologies, 180, 186
Dewey, J., 207
diagnostic assessment, 267
dialogic pedagogies, 214–15
dialogic spaces, 218
differentiation, 131, 411–12
digital artefacts, 425
digital citizenship, 475
digital technologies, 186, 457, 470
discernment, 510
disciplinary frameworks, 121
disciplinary knowledge, 64, 67–72
discussion, 372–3, 460
diverse learners, 400
diversity, 5, 92, 162, 220, 383–4
    see also cultural diversity; religious diversity
documentation, 34
documents, 441
drama-based pedagogy (DBP), 407–8
drama body-based learning (DBL), 407

early childhood education, 5
early childhood pedagogy, 500
early childhood setting
    assessment, 116
    Civics and Citizenship, 104–7, 111–16
    community resources, 444–5
    daily life, 410
    Economics and Business, 176
    History, 104–16
    inclusive principles, 414
    learning sequences, 113–14
early childhood teachers, 42
Early Years Learning Framework (EYLF)
    assessment, 48–53
    and Australian Curriculum, 46–53
    and Australian Curriculum: HASS, 11
    and capabilities, 293–4
    and Civics and Citizenship, 106
    and community resources, 444–5
    described, 4–6, 43

and History, 106
inclusive practice, 414
and learning, 460
learning outcomes, 46, 49, 116, 293–4, 455
and librarians, 469
and Melbourne Declaration on Educational Goals for
    Young Australians, 49, 422
and planning, 112–13
practices, 5–6, 46
principles, 5, 46
and technology, 454–5
ecojustice, 346–8
ecological footprints, 350
ecological sustainability, 12
economic decisions, 179–80
economic globalisation, 482
economic reasoning, 189–90
economic sustainability, 12
economics, 174
Economics and Business
    Aboriginal and Torres Strait Islander histories and
        cultures, 183–4
    achievement standards, 99
    Asia and Australia's engagement with Asia, 183–4
    concepts, 30, 93–7
    definition, 78
    described, 175
    and Design and Technologies, 180, 186
    and Digital Technologies, 186
    early childhood setting, 176
    and English, 186
    and Geography, 178, 183
    information and communication technology (ICT)
        capability, 457
    inquiry and skills strand, 185–93
    integration with other subjects, 180
    key ideas, 13
    and Mathematics, 180, 186
    and other learning areas, 186–7
    and Science, 180, 186
    Year 7, 99
    years offered, 11, 24
    see also Australian Curriculum: Economics and
        Business
educating for sustainability (EfS), 168, 343, 345, 347–56
educator-centred approach, 201
educator roles
    co-constructor, 241–2
    and different views, 72
    educator–learner roles within inquiry, 209
    facilitators, 217, 237–8, 371
    and inquiry approach, 209–11
    inquiry learning, 56
    observer, listener, reflector, 239–41
    planners, 238–9
    playful pedagogies, 237–42
    thinking environment, 241–2
educators
    assessment literacy, 267–9
    beliefs about Aboriginal and Torres Strait Islander
        learners, 316–17

and content, 515–16
controversial issues, 490–1
critical, 382
culturally responsive pedagogy, 388–9
and curriculum, 112, 405, 513–14
and immersion, 521–4
inclusive HASS pedagogy, 406–9
inclusive principles, 403–5
and judgements, 275–6
key skills, 516
lesson planning, 517–21
and reconciliation, 310
effect. *See* cause and effect
efficacy, 167
emergent curriculum, 55
emergent planning, 34–6
emotive stimulus, 224
empathic concerns, 218
empathy, 86, 99, 107, 110, 129
engagement, 34, 331, 401, 522–4
English, 186, 248
entrepreneurs, 175
entrepreneurship, 182–3
environment, 82, 99, 143–4, 289
environmental globalisation, 482
ephemera, 465
epistemology, 379, 385
e-portfolios, 462
equity, 5, 92
ESTEAM (entrepreneurship, science, technology,
    engineering, arts and mathematics), 175
ethical inquiry, 373–5
ethical reasoning, 366–9
ethical understanding, 169, 214–15, 219–25, 292–3,
    300–2
ethics, 370–1
ethics of hope, 251
evaluation, 29, 130, 189
evidence, 89–90, 99, 121, 128, 272–6
experimental learning, 430
explicit teaching, 201
exploration, 222, 331
exploratory talk, 218
expressive language skills, 256

facilitators, 217, 237–8, 371
fair use, 475
families, 492–3
family history, 68
family stories, 270
feedback, 264, 276
fiction, 111
financial literacy, 180–2
firefighting, 104
First Fleet, 236
first-order concepts, 126
fishing, 150
floor books, 218
food, 187
formative assessment, 165, 265
forums, 460

forward planning, 112
frameworks, 43
funds of knowledge, 381
future scenarios, 350
futures, 21, 184–5
futures-oriented images, 347

galleries, 440
gambling, 184
game theory, 194
games, 461
Gapminder (website), 148
gardening, 356
Geographical Information Systems (GIS), 140–2
geographical thinking, 71, 137–51, 153–5
Geography
    achievement standards, 99, 153
    assessment, 153
    concept wheels, 82
    concepts, 30, 81–3, 137–51
    core knowledge, 80
    definition, 68, 78
    and Economics and Business, 178, 183
    everyday, 68–70
    information and communication technology (ICT)
        capability, 457
    inquiry questions, 25
    key ideas, 13
    and numeracy, 296
    skills in, 70
    taking action phase, 520
    teaching personal, 67–8
    themes, 25
    Year 7, 99
    years offered, 11, 24
    *see also Australian Curriculum: Geography*
GeogSpace, 148
geo-literacy, 256
Gilbert, Eddie, 91–2
Gilbert River goldfield, 332–3
global citizenship, 65, 483, 485
global education
    building blocks, 485–8
    connecting with curriculum, 492, 494
    definition, 484
    described, 483–5
    names for, 484
    pedagogies for, 489–91
    understanding, 481–3
*Global Perspectives: A framework for global education in
    global schools*, 339, 485–6
Global Positioning System (GPS) technologies, 457
Global School Partners, 259
globalisation, 95, 99, 479, 482–3, 485
goals, 43, 509
governance, 92
government and democracy, 161
grades, 264, 275
grief, 56
guided discovery, 209

hands-on-learning, 207, 238
harvesting stage, 154
headlines, 256
heritage sites, 107, 111
higher-order thinking, 516
historical inquiry, 123, 125–6, 130–2
historical knowledge, 123–4
historical thinking, 68
History
    achievement standards, 99
    in Australian Curriculum, 122–3
    case studies, 91–2
    components, 123
    concept wheels, 83
    concepts, 30, 83–92
    conceptual understanding, 126–30
    definition, 78
    as discipline, 121–2
    early childhood setting, 104–16
    and Early Years Learning Framework (EYLF),
      106
    forms of learning, 111
    identifying our personal, 68
    information and communication technology (ICT)
      capability, 457
    inquiry questions, 25
    key ideas, 13
    learning sequences, 113–14
    and numeracy, 295
    skills in, 70
    teaching personal, 67–8
    teaching strategies, 111–12
    themes, 25
    year level descriptors, 106, 248
    years offered, 11, 24
    *see also Australian Curriculum: History*
Hobart Declaration, 309
homogenous 'Other', 330
hospitals, 113–14
human rights, 65, 484, 486
Humanities and Social Sciences (HASS). *See*
    *Australian Curriculum: HASS*

*I, Pencil* (video), 147
identity, 106–7, 110, 162, 394–5, 485
immersion, 521–4
inclusion discourse, limitations, 383–4
inclusive practice, 414
inclusive principles, 401–4
    early childhood setting, 414
income, 184
Indigenous agency, 308
Indigenous cultural competence, eight ways framework,
    114–15
Indigenous cultural protocols, 317
Indigenous knowledges, 344–6
Indigenous Literacy Foundation, 259
Indigenous perspectives, 351–2
indigenous plants, 349–50
indoctrination, 365

information and communication technology (ICT)
    capability, 407
      Australian Curriculum, 287
      *Australian Curriculum: HASS*, 296–7, 456–8
      and BRIDGE program, 336–7
      and Civics and Citizenship, 457
      definition, 287
      described, 455–6
      Economics and Business, 457
      and Geography, 457
      and History, 457
      middle years, 457–8
      primary school settings, 456–7
      *see also* technology
information literacy, 473–5
inquiry
    approach, 204, 209–11
    and constructivist theorists, 207–9
    definition, 215
    driving, 218–19
    educator–learner roles, 209
    ethical, 373–5
    historical, 123, 125–6, 130–2
    intent of, 199–200
    questions for, 520
    research underpins methodology, 206–7
    skills, 28–9
    theory that underpins, 205–6
inquiry and skills strand, 27–9, 130, 162–3, 185–93, 518
inquiry learning, 45
    and community resources, 431
    definition, 199, 298, 421
    described, 53, 63–4, 501
    educator role, 56
    examples, 64–6, 502
    planning with, 518–19
    stages, 54, 153–5
    *see also* community of inquiry
inquiry learning model, 518–19
inquiry planning cycle, 34
inquiry questions
    business environment, 182
    consumer and financial literacy, 180–2
    definition, 20, 63
    Geography, 25
    History, 25
    and planning, 132
    scarcity, 178
    subject, 63
    sub-strand, 63
    work and work futures, 184
inquisitive manner, 525
inside-outside circle, 257–9
integrated curriculum, 36–7
integrating socially inquiry model, 432
interactions, 249
interactive learning, 111
interconnection, 82, 99, 145–8
intercultural understanding, 169, 291, 300, 334–5, 386–7
interdependency, 144, 485
interdisciplinary concepts, 30

internet, 455, 462–3
interpretation, 188–9, 442
intersubjective space, 224
interviews, 446–8
intrinsic motivation, 228
investigation, 459–60, 514
iPad, 455
Islamophobia, 383
issue-based learning, 489

judgements, 275–6
justice, 92

Kangiqsujuaq people, 144
knowledge, 79, 101, 201, 380
knowledge and understanding strand, 24–6, 161–3,
 176–85

Lake Antobo, Mali, 150
language, 256–60, 268
law, 161
learner-centred learning, 56
learner-centred pedagogy, 56
learner-initiated learning, 232
learners
 Aboriginal and Torres Strait Islander, 309, 315–19
 as interviewers, 446–8
 living with a disability, 411
learning
 and communities, 438–9
 and community resources, 428–31
 connecting with prior, 14–15
 design, 520
 forms of, 111
 how done, 200
 intentions, 269
 lifelong, 199, 438, 473
 making relevant, 200
 ongoing, 5
 play-based, 53, 63
 sequences, 113–14
 and technology, 458–63
 through acquisition, 459
 through collaboration, 460–1
 through culture, 312–15
 through discussion, 460
 through investigation, 459–60
 through practice, 461
 through production, 462
learning environments, 164–5, 501
learning experiences, 412–14, 507–8
learning outcomes, 32, 49, 116, 273–4, 293–4, 455, 503–8
legal deposit, 468
lessons
 and content, 515 16
 and immersion, 521–4
 phases of planning, 133
 programming, 517–18
librarians
 and Australian Curriculum: HASS, 469–75
 as curators of curiosity, 470–1

described, 465, 469
 and Early Years Learning Framework (EYLF), 469
 and information literacy, 473–5
 and literature, 471–3
 using, 475–6
libraries, 441, 466–9
lifelong learning, 199, 438, 473
lifeworld pedagogies, 382
light pollution, 354
listening, 239–41
literacy
 Australian Curriculum, 248, 286
 Australian Curriculum: HASS, 248, 295
 challenges to achieving, 249
 definition, 247–8, 286
 skills, 249–50
 strategies to develop, 256–60
literate person, 247
literature, 250, 252–5, 471–3
living conditions in London, 124–5
location, 190
logistics, 190–1
London, living conditions in, 124–5

manipulative skills, 202
mapping, 140–2
maps, 70, 139
market research, 187
markets, 97, 99, 175
materials, 238
Mathematics, 180, 186
McDowell County, 139
meaning making, 80
Melbourne Declaration on Educational Goals for Young
 Australians, 19, 160, 328, 364, 438, 483
 and Australian Curriculum, 49
 described, 3, 6, 281–2
 and Early Years Learning Framework (EYLF), 49
 goals, 7, 43, 48, 61, 422
metacognitive strategies, 127
metacognitive thinking, 230
middle years, 457–8
MIDWAY: A message from the gyre, 289
migrant experiences, 443
Ministerial Council on Education, Employment, Training
 and Youth Affairs (MCEETYA), 7
missions, 166
mobile technology, 460
mock trials, 526
modelling, 111
models, 43
moderation, 275–6
modification of technology, 453
moral integrity, 366
multimedia resources, 459
Museum of Australian Democracy (MOAD), Canberra, 429
museums, 107, 111, 424–5, 427, 440, 445, 457
Muslim learners, 381–3, 387
mussel gathering, 144
My Two Blankets (Kobald and Blackwood), 251

narratives, 471
National Archives of Australia, 441
National Assessment Program sample testing
    of Civics and Citizenship (NAP-CC),
    283–5
*National Framework for Values Education in Australian
    Schools*, 363
National Library of Australia, 424, 468–9
National Trust, 441
needs, 174
networks, 471
New South Wales and Australian Curriculum, 10
non-fiction texts, 471, 473
note taking, 475
numeracy, 287, 295–6

observation, 239–41
open-ended questions, 512
Operation Magpie, 354–5
opportunity, 95, 99
opportunity cost, 179
Orange Sky Laundry, 259
outdoor environment, 63
Oxfam, 490
OzHarvest, 259

paintings, 111
parent–teacher nights, 19, 212
parents, 117
Parliament House, Canberra, 427–8, 430
participative learning, 111
participatory experience, 413
partnerships, 5, 317–19, 438–9
paying it forward, 349
peace, 12
peace building, 486
Pedagogical Content Knowledge (PCK), 79
pedagogical diversity, 385
pedagogical reasoning, 427
pedagogies
    and Aboriginal and Torres Strait Islander cross-
        curriculum priorities, 310–11
    *Australian Curriculum: HASS*, 62–7
    connecting, 53
    definition, 229
    for global education, 489–91
    inclusive, 406–9
    play-based, 48
pencils, 147
personal and social capability, 169, 289–90,
    298–9
perspective, 84–5, 99, 129
philosophy of engagement, 401
photographs, 111
Piaget, Jean, 105, 206–7
picture books, 250–5, 368, 472
place, 82, 99, 137–9, 142, 242, 273,
    349–50
place-based education, 349
plagiarising, 475
planners, 238–9

planning
    backward planning, 32–4
    cycle of, 503–8
    described, 505–6
    and Early Years Learning Framework (EYLF),
        112–13
    emergent, 34–6
    forward planning, 112
    historical inquiry process, 131–3
    playful pedagogies, 238–9
planning triangle, 37–8
plants, 349–50
play
    activities, 112
    benefits, 228–30
    characteristics of, 233–4
    complexity of, 230–1
    definitions, 231–3
    described, 500–1
    natural instinct, 228
    role of, 230
    types of, 235–6
    use of word, 232
play-based curriculum, 238–9
play-based learning, 53, 63
play-based pedagogy, 48, 62
playful pedagogies, 234–5
playfulness, 234
pledges, 351
PMI (plus, minus, interesting) inquiry strategy, 428
political globalisation, 482
portfolios, 274–5, 462
powerful knowledge, 79, 101
practice, 461
primary education, 11
primary school settings, 221–5, 410, 456–7
primary sources, 38, 128, 468
prior knowledge, 201
prior-to-school settings, 219–21
problem-based learning, 489
problem-solving, 162, 272
problems, 525
production, 462
professional development, 508–11
professional learning, 508–10
Progressive Curriculum Frameworks, 10
public issues, 162
public libraries, 424, 467–8
puppets, 111, 240

qualitative analysis, 188
quantitative analysis, 189
Queensland and Australian Curriculum, 10
questioning, 28, 34, 130, 162, 187–8, 505
questioning stage, 154
questions, 216, 372–3, 512, 520
    *see also* inquiry questions
Quick Response (QR) codes, 459

receptive language skills, 256
reciprocity, 383

reconciliation, 310
records, 440, 457
redefinition, 454
referencing, 469, 474
REFLECT framework, 312–15
reflection, 5, 29, 34, 130, 162, 191–3, 239–41, 331, 503–5, 516
Refugee Action Coalition, 259
Reggio Emilia approach, 113, 501
relationality, 383
relationships, 5, 219
religious diversity, 380–3, 386–7
reports, 332
representation, 332
research, 28, 130, 162, 187–8, 202
resources, 38–9, 125
     *see also* community resources
resources (concept), 97, 99, 174, 178
respect for diversity, 220
responsibilities, 224–5
rhetorical questions, 372–3
rights, 224–5
role play, 111
Ross Female Factory, Tasmania., 523
rubrics, 272–3, 525
rules, 158

SAMR model, 452–4
savings, 184
scaffolding, 209, 518
scale, 82, 151–3
scarcity, 178
school libraries, 467
schools, 438–9
Science, 180, 186
Scootle, 473
search engines, 473
second-order concepts, 126–7
secondary sources, 38, 128, 468
selecting materials, 473–4
sensitive issues, 259
service-learning, 170–1, 490
*Shanyi Goes to China* (Sungwan So), 331
*Shape of the Australian Curriculum: History*, 121
*Shape of the Curriculum: Version 4.0*, 53
significance, 87, 99, 107, 109–10, 128
significant sites, 108, 442
Sikh culture, 507
skills, 10, 28–9, 70, 201–4, 249–50, 516
     *see also* inquiry and skills strand
*Snapshots of Asia: China* (Commonwealth of Australia), 331
social capability, 169, 289–90, 298–9
social capital, 422
social emotional learning (SEL), 213
social history, 440
social inclusion, 384
social interaction, 207
social justice, 12, 257–9, 367–8, 371–2, 483, 486
social language, 206
social media, 456, 458
social order, 92

social play, 235
social skills, 202
sociodramatic play, 236
SOLO structure, 273–4
sources, 38, 121, 128, 468, 473–5
space, 82, 99, 139–42
spatial technologies, 457
state libraries, 468
stimulation activities, 111
stimulus materials, 215, 374–5
stories, 111, 226, 250, 471
stormwater drains, 44
substantive knowledge, 126
substitution of technology, 452
suitcases, 64
summative assessment, 165, 267
Sustainability
     Aboriginal and Torres Strait Islander cross-curriculum priorities, 344, 351–2
     achievement standards, 99
     as concept, 82
     definition, 149, 168
     described, 21, 149–50, 347
     illustration of understanding, 150
     in classroom, 348–56
     living, 343–5
     transdisciplinary examples, 352–4
     units on, 23–4
     *see also* educating for sustainability (EfS); ecojustice
sustainable futures, 486
sustained shared thinking, 241
systems, 21

Taroona Shot Tower, 108
tasks. *See* assessment tasks
teachable moments, 431
teaching, 31, 203
     *see also* educator roles
Teaching for Effective Learning Framework, 520
teaching strategies, 111–12
technology
     and *Australian Curriculum: HASS*, 455–6
     described, 451
     and Early Years Learning Framework (EYLF), 454–5
     SAMR model, 452–4
     types of, 458–63
     using, 425, 451
     *see also* Design and Technologies; information and communication technology (ICT) capability
telephones, 455
territory libraries, 468
*The Arrival* (Tan), 225
*The Lorax* (Dr Seuss), 23
thematic mapping, 320
thinking circles, 112
thinking environment, 241–2
tick-box curriculum, 285
time, 70, 128, 349–50
timing, 190

tours, 441
toys, 502
trails, 441
transdisciplinary curriculum, 343
transdisciplinary pedagogy, 345–6
transmission learning, 229
transmission teaching, 201
trials, mock, 526
Trove database, 424, 468
two-sector circular flow model, 178
two questions and one statement (2Q1S), 257

understanding by design (UbD), 431–2, 520
United Nations Convention of the Rights of the Child, 230
units of work. *See* lessons
universal design for learning (UDL), 409–11

value judgements, 366–9
values, 12, 166, 224–5, 363, 365–6, 370–1
        *see also* ethical inquiry
values education, 364–5
values inquiry, 364
Victoria and Australian Curriculum, 10
videos, 111
views, voicing different, 71–2

virtual visits, 425, 429, 457, 461
visitors to school, 111
visits
        preparation, 448
        to heritage sites, 107, 111
        to museums, 107, 111, 424–5, 427, 445
        virtual, 425, 429, 457, 461
        *see also* community resources
volunteer work, 349
Vygotsky, L., 206, 288

Walt Disney Company (Disney), 186
wants, 174
WebQuest, 524
Wikipedia, 474
wolves, 147
work, 95, 99, 184–5
world, making sense of, 66
world history approach, 425
world views, 21, 380

Yarning Circle – *Nga Tana Lui Dha* model, 390–6
year level descriptors, 19, 106
Yellowstone National Park, 147
YGAP, 356
*You and Me, Murrawee* (Hashmi), 23, 28